The Human Species

Other McGraw-Hill/Mayfield titles in Biological Anthropology

Angeloni, *Annual Editions: Physical Anthropology*
Omohundro, *Mystery Fossil*
Park, *Biological Anthropology*
Park, *Biological Anthropology: An Introductory Reader*
Stein/Rowe, *Physical Anthropology*
Stein/Rowe, *Physical Anthropology: The Core*

FIFTH EDITION

The Human Species

An Introduction to Biological Anthropology

JOHN H. RELETHFORD

State University of New York
College at Oneonta

Mc
Graw
Hill

Boston   Burr Ridge, IL   Dubuque, IA   Madison, WI   New York   San Francisco   St. Louis
Bangkok   Bogotá   Caracas   Kuala Lumpur   Lisbon   London   Madrid   Mexico City
Milan   Montreal   New Delhi   Santiago   Seoul   Singapore   Sydney   Taipei   Toronto

McGraw-Hill Higher Education

A Division of The McGraw-Hill Companies

2 3 4 5 6 7 8 9 0 WCK/WCK 0 9 8 7 6 5 4 3

Library of Congress Cataloging-in-Publication Data

Relethford, John.
    The human species : an introduction to biological anthropology / John H. Relethford.—5th ed.
      p.   cm.
    Includes bibliographical references and index.
    ISBN 0-7674-3022-0
    1. Physical anthropology.   I. Title.

    GN60 .R39 2002
    599.9—dc21   2002025084

Publisher, Phillip A. Butcher; sponsoring editor, Kevin M. Witt; production editor, Holly Paulsen; manuscript editor, Kay Mikel; design manager, Jean Mailander; art manager, Robin Mouat; text and cover designer, Susan Breitbard; illustrators, Patty Isaacs and John & Judy Waller; photo researcher, Brian J. Pecko; production supervisor, Pam Augspurger. The text was set in 10.5/12.5 Legacy Serif Book by Thompson Type and printed on acid-free 45# Publishers Matte by Quebecor World Versailles.

Cover images: photos (from left), © Spencer Grant/PhotoEdit, © Vic Bider/PhotoEdit, © Amy Etra/PhotoEdit, © Michael Newman/PhotoEdit; DNA, © Carolyn Iverson/Photo Researchers, Inc.

www.mhhe.com

Contents

May 22

May 22

PART II Human Biological Variation   117

May 27

5 *The Study of Human Variation   119*

May 29

6 *Microevolution in Human Populations   145*

May 29

PART III Our Place in Nature   199

*June 3
pg 280-285*

June 5

Preface

This text introduces the field of biological anthropology (also known as physical anthropology), the science concerned with human biological evolution and variation. The text addresses the major questions that concern biological anthropologists: "What are humans?" "How are we similar to and different from other animals?" "Where are our origins?" "How did we evolve?" "Are we still evolving?" "How are we different from one another?" and "What does the future hold for the human species?"

ORGANIZATION

This book is divided into four parts. Part I, "Evolutionary Background," provides basic background in genetics and evolutionary theory used throughout the remainder of the book. Chapter 1 provides a general introduction to the science of biological anthropology, the nature of science, and the history of evolutionary thought. Chapter 2 reviews molecular and Mendelian genetics as applied to humans, providing genetic background for later chapters and including a basic review of cell biology for those whose high school biology is a bit rusty. Chapter 3 focuses on the evolutionary forces, the mechanisms that produce evolutionary change within populations. Chapter 4 looks at evolution over longer periods of time, focusing on the origin of new species, and includes a brief review of the history of life on our planet.

Part II, "Human Biological Variation," examines biological variation in our species today from an evolutionary perspective. Chapter 5 focuses on the analysis of human variation, including a contrast between racial and evolutionary approaches to variation. Chapter 6 reviews a number of case studies of human microevolution, with particular emphasis on natural selection. Chapter 7 continues examining human variation from the broad perspective of human adaptation, both biological and cultural.

Part III, "Our Place in Nature," examines the biology, behavior, and evolution of the primates, the group of mammals to which humans belong. A main focus of this section are the questions "What are humans?" and "How are we related to other living creatures?" Chapter 8 examines issues in classification and looks at the basic biology and behavior of mammals in general, and primates in particular. Chapter 9 looks at the different types of primates in terms of classification, biology, and behavior, with particular attention given to our close relatives, the apes. Chapter 10 looks specifically at the human species and includes a comparison of human traits with those of apes. Chapter 11 provides some background on the analysis of the fossil record and summarizes the major events of primate origins and evolution, from the time of the disappearance of the dinosaurs 65 million years ago to the split of ape and human lines 6–5 million years ago.

Part IV deals with "Human Evolution" in both a biological and a cultural sense. Chapter 12 begins with a brief review of human evolutionary history and follows with a detailed summary of the earliest hominids and the origin of bipedalism. Chapter 13 examines the origin and biological and cultural evolution of the genus *Homo*. Chapter 14 looks at the fossil, archaeological, and genetic evidence for the origin of modern humans and includes a discussion of current controversies (Did modern humans evolve throughout the world, or are our recent ancestors exclusively from Africa?). Chapter 15 examines recent human evolution (over the past 12,000 years) and focuses on the biological impact of culture change, with particular emphasis on changing patterns of disease, mortality, fertility, and population growth.

The organization of this text reflects my own teaching preference for four units arranged in the same sequence. Not all instructors will use the same sequence of chapters. Some may prefer a different arrangement of topics. I have attempted to write chapters in such a way as to accommodate such changes whenever possible. Although I prefer to discuss human variation (Chapters 5–7) before the fossil record of human evolution (Chapters 12–14), others prefer the reverse, and the chapters have been written and revised so that this alternative organizational structure can be used.

FEATURES

Throughout the text, I have attempted to provide new material relevant to the field and fresh treatments of traditional material. Key features include the following:

- All areas of contemporary biological anthropology are covered. In addition to traditional coverage of areas such as genetics, evolutionary theory, primate behavior, and the fossil record, the text includes material often neglected in introductory texts, including human growth, epidemiology, and demography.
- The relationship between biology and culture is a major focus. The biocultural framework is introduced in the first chapter and integrated throughout the text.
- Behavior is discussed in an evolutionary context. The evolutionary nature of primate and human behavior is emphasized in a number of chap-

ters, including those on primate biology and behavior (Chapters 8–10) and the fossil record of human evolution (Chapters 12–14).

- Emphasis is on the human species in its context within the primate order. Discussions of mammals and nonhuman primates continually refer to their potential relevance for understanding the human species. In fact, Chapter 10 is devoted entirely to treating our species from a comparative perspective.

- Hypothesis testing is emphasized. From the first chapter, where students are introduced to the scientific method, I emphasize how various hypotheses are tested. Rather than provide a dogmatic approach with all the "right" answers, the text examines evidence in the context of hypothesis testing. With this emphasis, readers can see how new data can lead to changes in basic models and can better understand the "big picture" of biological anthropology.

NEW TO THIS EDITION

Every chapter has been revised in light of new findings in the field and comments from users of the fourth edition. In addition, certain parts of the text's structure have been changed based on the helpful feedback I received from colleagues. To make the text as clear, accessible, and up-to-date as possible, I've made the following specific changes:

- The chapter on macroevolution and the origin of species has been placed earlier in the book (Chapter 4) to better link the evolutionary forces with long-term patterns of evolutionary change.

- The chapters on disease and demography have been streamlined and combined into a single chapter (Chapter 15) organized around the biological impact of culture change.

- Discussion of the human fossil record has been substantially rewritten to include three new species (*Orrorin tugenensis, Kenyanthropus platyops,* and *Australopithecus garhi*) and new information, such as *Homo erectus* in Europe, Acheulian-like tools in Asia, and new studies of Neandertal DNA.

- A number of new topics have been added. Additions include the Human Genome Project, quantitative genetics and sexual orientation, the evolution of cystic fibrosis genes, an entire section on nutritional adaptation (Chapter 7), critiques of the "small but healthy" hypothesis, primate behavioral ecology, evolutionary significance of parent–child cosleeping, pollution and human biology, and the emergence and reemergence of infectious disease.

STUDY HELPS

To make the text more accessible and interesting, I have included frequent examples and illustrations of basic ideas as well as abundant maps to help orient students. I have kept the technical jargon to a minimum, yet every introductory text contains a number of specialized terms that students must learn. The first mention of these terms in the text appears in boldface type and accompanying short definitions appear in the text margins. A glossary is provided at the end of the book, often with more detailed definitions.

Each chapter ends with a summary and a list of supplemental readings. A short list of useful Internet resources has been added to each chapter. Several appendices provide additional reference material, including a primer on mathematical population genetics, a list of primate species, and a short review of comparative primate anatomy. A list of references appears at the end of the book, providing the complete reference for studies cited in the text.

ANCILLARIES

The Instructor's Manual includes a test bank of more than 700 questions, as well as chapter overviews and outlines, topics for class discussion, and sources for laboratory equipment. A Computerized Test Bank is available free of charge to qualifying adopters. Also available to qualifying adopters is a package of 80 color and black-and-white transparency acetates. In addition, an Online Learning Center is available to both instructors and students at www.mhhe.com/relethford5.

ACKNOWLEDGMENTS

My thanks go to the dedicated and hardworking people at McGraw-Hill, both those I have dealt with personally and the others behind the scenes. I give special thanks to Jan Beatty, my initial sponsoring editor, for continued encouragement and support throughout the history of this text. Thanks also to Phil Butcher, the publisher at McGraw-Hill, for providing a smooth transition to a new company. I also appreciate Kevin Witt, my new sponsoring editor, for his help and insight. Special thanks to Holly Paulsen, production editor, for her excellence and professionalism and her uncanny ability to read my scribbled notes. Thanks also to Marty Granahan, permissions editor; Kay Mikel, manuscript editor; Jean Mailander, design manager; Robin Mouat, art manager; and Brian Pecko, photo researcher.

I also thank my colleagues who served as reviewers:

David Begun, *University of Toronto*   Susan Pfieffer, *University of Toronto*
Richard Davis, *Bryn Mawr College*   Brian Richmond, *University of Illinois*
Greg Laden, *University of Minnesota*   Robert Shanafelt, *University of Florida*
William Leonard, *Northwestern University*   Richard Sherwood, *University of Wisconsin*
Debra Overdorff, *University of Texas*   Andrea Wiley, *James Madison University*

Having been a reviewer myself, I appreciate the extensive time and effort these individuals have taken. I also thank other colleagues who have offered many valuable suggestions regarding structure and/or content: Gary Heathcote, University of Guam; Lorena Madrigal, University of South Florida; Brandy O'Neill, University of Pennsylvania; and J. Kenneth Smail, Kenyon College. I only know one of you in person, but thank you all for your valuable suggestions.

Last, but not least, I dedicate this as always to my family. To my wonderful sons, David, Benjamin, and Zane—thanks for all the smiles and hugs, which make it all worthwhile. Thanks also for all those questions that really make me think (the ones I couldn't answer as well as those I could). Finally, to my wife, Hollie, love of my life and best friend—thanks for love, friendship, and support. I couldn't have done this without you.

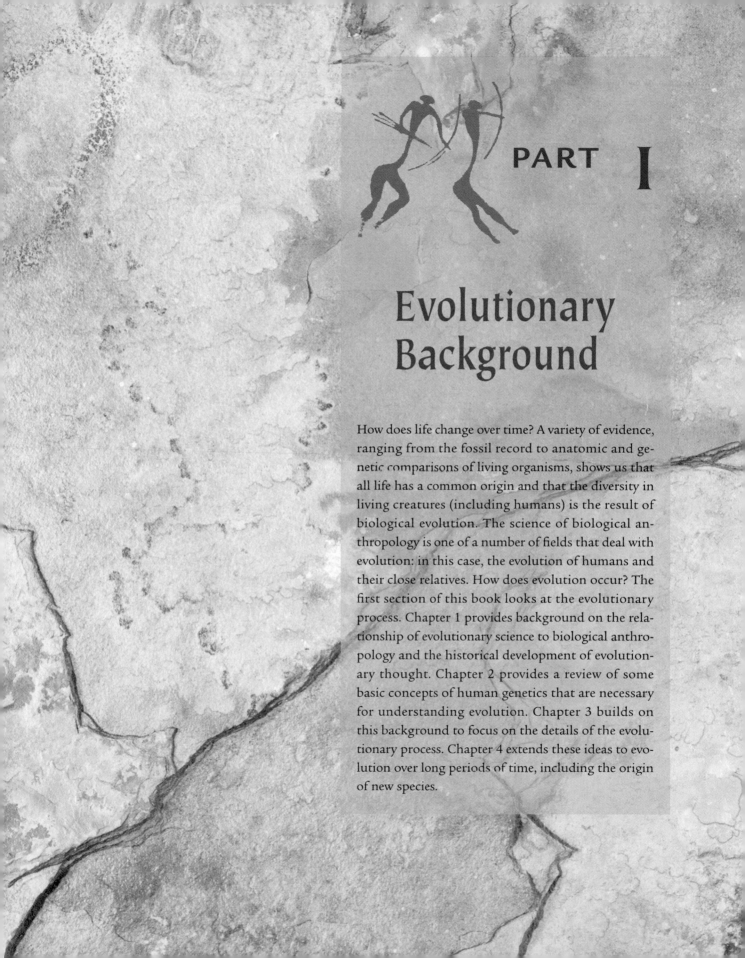

PART I

Evolutionary Background

How does life change over time? A variety of evidence, ranging from the fossil record to anatomic and genetic comparisons of living organisms, shows us that all life has a common origin and that the diversity in living creatures (including humans) is the result of biological evolution. The science of biological anthropology is one of a number of fields that deal with evolution: in this case, the evolution of humans and their close relatives. How does evolution occur? The first section of this book looks at the evolutionary process. Chapter 1 provides background on the relationship of evolutionary science to biological anthropology and the historical development of evolutionary thought. Chapter 2 provides a review of some basic concepts of human genetics that are necessary for understanding evolution. Chapter 3 builds on this background to focus on the details of the evolutionary process. Chapter 4 extends these ideas to evolution over long periods of time, including the origin of new species.

CHAPTER 1

May 13 pg 4 - 11
May 15 pg 12 - 29

Biological Anthropology and Evolution

What is anthropology? To many people, it is the study of the exotic extremes of human nature. To others, it is the study of ancient ruins and lost civilizations. The study of anthropology seems strange to many, and the practitioners of this field, the anthropologists, seem even stranger. The stereotype of an anthropologist is a pith-helmeted, pipe-smoking eccentric, tracking chimpanzees through the forest, digging up the bones of million-year-old ancestors, interviewing lost tribes about their sexual customs, and recording the words of the last speakers of a language. Another popular image presented in the media is Indiana Jones, the intrepid archaeologist of the film *Raiders of the Lost Ark*. Here is a man who is versed in the customs and languages of many societies past and present, feels at home anywhere in the world, and makes a living teaching, finding lost treasures, rescuing beautiful women in distress, and fighting Nazis (Figure 1.1).

Of course, Indiana Jones is a fictional character and more a treasure hunter than a scientific archaeologist. However, some real-life anthropologists are almost as well known: Jane Goodall, the late Margaret Mead, the late Louis Leakey, and the late Dian Fossey. These anthropologists have studied chimpanzees, Samoan culture, the fossils of human ancestors, and gorillas. Their research conjures up images of anthropology every bit as varied as the imaginary adventures of Indiana Jones. Anthropologists do study all these things and more. The sheer diversity of topics investigated by anthropologists seems almost to defy any sort of logic. The methods of data collection and analysis are almost as diverse. What pulls these different subjects together?

◀ *Paleoanthropologist Bill Kimble of the Institute of Human Origins examines a fossil of a human ancestor from Ethiopia. Biological anthropology is the study of the biological evolution and variation of the human species. The fossil record is one source of information on our evolution. (© Enrico Ferorelli)*

FIGURE 1.1

Indiana Jones, the fictional archaeologist who serves as many people's model for an anthropologist. (Everett Collection)

In one obvious sense, they all share an interest in the same subject—human beings. In fact, the traditional textbook definition of anthropology is the "study of humans." Though this definition is easy to remember, it is not terribly useful. After all, scientists in other fields, such as researchers in anatomy and biochemistry, also study humans. And there are many fields within the social sciences whose sole interest is humans. History, geography, political science, economics, sociology, and psychology are all devoted to the study of human beings, and no one would argue that these fields are merely branches of anthropology.

WHAT IS ANTHROPOLOGY?

What, then, is a suitable definition of anthropology? **Anthropology** could be described as the science of human cultural and biological variation and evolution. The first part of this definition includes both human culture and biology. **Culture** is shared learned behavior. Culture includes social and economic systems, marriage customs, religion, philosophy, and all other behaviors that are acquired through the process of learning rather than through instinct. The joint emphasis on culture and biology is an important feature of anthropology, and one that sets it apart from many other fields. A biochemist may be interested in specific aspects of human biology and may consider the study of human cultural behaviors less important. To a sociologist, cultural behaviors and not human biology are the main focus of attention. Anthropology, however, is characterized by a concern with *both* culture and biology as vital in understanding the human condition.

anthropology The science that investigates human biological and cultural variation and evolution.

culture Behavior that is shared, learned, and socially transmitted.

Biology and Culture

To the anthropologist, humans must be understood in terms of shared learned behavior as well as biology. We rely extensively on learned behaviors in virtually all aspects of our lives. Even the expression of our sexual drives must be understood in light of human cultural systems. Although the actual basis of our sex drive is biological, the ways in which we express it are shaped by behaviors we have learned. The very inventiveness of humans, with our vast technology, is testimony to the powerful effect of learning. However, we are not purely cultural creatures. We are also biological organisms. We need to eat and breathe, and we are affected by our external environment. In addition, our biology sets certain limits on our potential behaviors. For example, all human cultures have some type of social structure that provides for the care of children until they are old enough to fend for themselves. This is not simply kindness to children; our biological position as mammals requires such attentiveness to children for survival. In contrast with other animal species, whose infants need little or no care, human infants are physically incapable of taking care of themselves.

Anthropology is concerned not only with culture and biology but also with their interaction. Just as humans are not solely cultural or solely biological, we are not simply the sum of these two either. Humans are biocultural organisms, which means that our culture and biology influence each other. The **biocultural approach** to studying human beings is a main theme of this book, and you will examine many examples of biocultural interaction. For now, however, consider one—population growth (which will be covered in greater detail in Chapter 15). The growth of a population depends, in part, on how many people are born relative to how many die. If more people are born than die in a given period of time, then the population will grow. Obviously, population growth is in part caused by biological factors affecting the birth and death rates. A variety of cultural factors, such as economic system and marriage patterns, also affect population growth. Many factors, including technological changes and ideological outlooks, affect the birth rate. Developments in medicine and medical care change the death rate. The entire process of population growth and its biological and cultural implications is considerably more complicated than described here. The basic point, however, should be clear: By studying the process of population growth, we can see how cultural factors affect biological factors and vice versa.

The biocultural perspective of anthropology points to one of the unique strengths of anthropology as a science: It is **holistic,** meaning that it takes into consideration all aspects of human existence. Population growth again provides an example. Where the sociologist may be concerned with effects of population growth on social structure and the psychologist may be concerned with effects of population growth on psychological stress, the anthropologist is interested potentially in all aspects of population growth. In a given study, this analysis may include the relationship among diet, fertility, religion, disease, social systems, and political systems, to name but a few factors.

biocultural approach Studying humans in terms of the interaction between biology and culture in evolutionary adaptation.

holistic Integrating all aspects of existence in understanding human variation and evolution.

The biocultural nature of anthropology makes it a difficult subject to classify in college catalogs. By now you are aware that different academic departments are grouped under the arts, humanities, natural sciences, mathematics, and social sciences. Where does anthropology, with its interest in both human culture and biology, fit in? Is it a natural science or a social science? Most colleges and universities place departments of anthropology with the social sciences, primarily because historically most anthropologists have been concerned with cultural anthropology. Many schools, however, allow completion of a biological anthropology course to fulfill a natural science requirement. The distinctions drawn between different branches of learning should not prevent you from seeing that anthropology has strong ties with both the natural and social sciences.

Variation

A major characteristic of anthropology is its concern with **variation.** In a general sense, variation refers to differences among individuals or populations. The anthropologist is interested in differences and similarities among human groups in terms of both biology and culture. Anthropologists use the **comparative approach** to attempt to generalize about those aspects of human behavior and biology that are similar in all populations and those that are unique to specific environments and cultures. *How* do groups of people differ from one another? *Why* do they differ? These are questions about variation, and they apply equally to cultural and biological traits (Figure 1.2). For example, do all human cultures practice the same marriage customs? (They don't.) Are there discernible reasons one group has a certain type of marriage system? An example of a biological trait that raises questions about variation is skin color. Can groups be characterized by a certain skin color, or does skin color vary within groups? Is there any pattern in the distribution of skin color that makes sense in terms of environmental differences?

Evolution

Evolution is change in living organisms over time. Both cultural and biological evolution interest anthropologists. How and why do human culture and biology change? For example, anthropologists may be interested in the origin of marriage systems. When, how, and why did certain marriage systems evolve? For that matter, when did the custom of marriage first originate, and why? As for skin color, an anthropologist would be interested in what skin color the first humans may have had and where, when, how, and why other skin colors may have evolved.

Adaptation

In addition to the concepts of variation and evolution, the anthropologist is interested in the process of **adaptation.** At the broadest level, adaptations

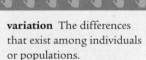

variation The differences that exist among individuals or populations.

comparative approach Comparing human populations to determine common and unique behaviors or biological traits.

evolution Change in populations of organisms from one generation to the next.

adaptation The process of successful interaction between a population and an environment.

FIGURE 1.2

Biological variation in a group of children. (© Jeffry Myers/Stock Boston)

are advantageous changes. Any aspect of biology or behavior that confers some advantage on an individual or population can be considered an adaptation. Cultural adaptations include technological devices such as clothing, shelter, and methods of food production. Such technologies can improve the well-being of humans. Cultural adaptations also include social systems and rules for behaviors. For example, the belief in certain societies that sexual relations with a woman must be avoided for some time after she gives birth can be adaptive in the sense that these behaviors influence the rate of population growth.

Cultural adaptations may vary in their effect on different members of a population. What is adaptive for some people may not be adaptive for others. For example, changes in certain tax laws may be advantageous for certain income groups and disadvantageous for others. Beliefs that reduce population growth can be adaptive in certain environments but nonadaptive in others.

Adaptations can also be biological. Some biological adaptations are physiological in nature and involve metabolic changes. For example, when you are too hot, you will sweat. Sweating is a short-term physiological response that removes excess heat through the process of evaporation. Within limits, it aids in maintaining a constant body temperature. Likewise, shivering is an adaptive response to cold. The act of shivering increases metabolic rate and provides more heat.

Biological adaptations can also be genetic in nature. Here, changes in genes over many generations produce variation in biological traits. The darker skin color of many humans native to regions near the equator is one example of a long-term genetic adaptation. The darker skin provides protection from the harmful effects of ultraviolet radiation (see Chapter 6 for more information on skin color and variation).

Anthropologists look at patterns of human variation and evolution in order to understand the nature of cultural and biological adaptations. In some cases, explanations are relatively clear, whereas in others we still seek explanations for the adaptive value of any given behavior or trait. In such a quest, we must always remember two important rules about adaptation. First, adaptations are often specific to a particular environment. What is adaptive in one environment may not be in another environment. Second, we must keep in mind that not all aspects of behavior or biology are adaptive. Some people have earlobes that are attached to the skin of their skulls, whereas others have earlobes that hang free. There is no adaptive significance to either trait.

The Subfields of Anthropology

In a general sense, anthropology is concerned with determining what humans are, how they evolved, and how they differ from one another. Where other disciplines focus on specific issues of humanity, anthropology is unique in dealing simultaneously with questions of origins, evolution, variation, and adaptation.

Even though anthropology has a wide scope and appears to encompass anything and everything pertaining to humans, the study of anthropology in North America is often characterized by four separate subfields, each with a specific focus. These four subfields are cultural anthropology, archaeology, linguistic anthropology, and biological anthropology. Some anthropologists add a fifth subfield—applied anthropology, which is concerned with the application of anthropological findings to contemporary matters and issues. Whether one characterizes applied anthropology as a separate subfield or as the practical extension of research in the four subfields, there is growing interest (and employment) in areas in which anthropological ideas and methods can add value. Some examples include public health, economic policy, agricultural and industrial development, and population control, to name a few.

Cultural Anthropology   **Cultural anthropology** deals primarily with variation in the cultures of populations in the present or recent past. Its subjects include social, political, economic, and ideological aspects of human cultures. Cultural anthropologists look at all aspects of behavior within a society. Even when they are interested in a specific aspect of a culture, such as marriage systems, they look at how these behaviors relate to all other aspects of culture. Marriage systems, for example, may have an effect on the system of inheritance and may also be closely related to religious views. Comparison of cultures is used to determine common and unique features among different cultures. Information from this subfield will be presented later in the book to aid in the interpretation of the relationship between human culture and biology.

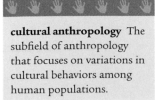

cultural anthropology The subfield of anthropology that focuses on variations in cultural behaviors among human populations.

Archaeology   **Archaeology** is the study of cultural behaviors in the historic and prehistoric past. The archaeologist deals with such remains of past societies as tools, shelters, remains of animals eaten for food, and other objects that have survived. These remains, termed *artifacts,* are used to reconstruct past behavior. To help fill in the gaps, the archaeologist makes use of the findings of cultural anthropologists who have studied similar societies. Archaeological findings are critical in understanding the behavior of early humans and their evolution. Some of these findings for the earliest humans are presented later in this text.

Linguistic Anthropology   **Linguistic anthropology** is the study of language. Spoken language is a behavior that appears to be uniquely human. This subfield of anthropology deals with the analysis of languages usually in nonliterate societies and with general trends in the evolution of languages. A major question raised by linguistic anthropology concerns the extent to which language shapes culture. Is language necessary for the transmission of culture? Does a language provide information about the beliefs and practices of a human culture?

Biological anthropology must consider many of the findings of linguistic anthropology in the analysis of human variation and evolution. When comparing humans and apes, we must ask whether language is a unique human characteristic. If it is, then what biological and behavioral differences exist between apes and humans that lead to the fact that one species has language and the other lacks it? Linguistics is also important in considering human evolution. When did language begin? Why?

Biological Anthropology   The subject of this book is the subfield of **biological anthropology,** which is concerned with the biological evolution and variation of the human species, past and present. Biological anthropology is often referred to by another name—*physical anthropology.* The course you are currently enrolled in might be known by either name. Actually, the two names refer to the same field. Early in the twentieth century the field was first known as physical anthropology, reflecting its then primary interest in the *physical* variation of past and present humans and our primate relatives. Much of the research in the field focused on descriptive studies of physical variations, with little theoretical background. Starting in the 1950s, physical anthropologists became more familiar with the rapidly growing fields of genetics and evolutionary science. As a result, the field of physical anthropology became more concerned with biological processes, particularly with genetics. After a while, many in the field began using the term *biological anthropology* to emphasize the new focus on biological processes. In most circles today, the two terms are used more or less interchangeably.

It is useful to consider the field of biological anthropology in terms of four major questions it seeks to answer. First, *What are humans?* That is, how are we related to other living creatures? Who are our closest living relatives? What makes us similar to other living creatures? How are we unique? A second major question concerns our past. *What is the fossil record for human evolution?*

archaeology The subfield of anthropology that focuses on cultural variation in prehistoric (and some historic) populations by analyzing the culture's remains.

linguistic anthropology The subfield of anthropology that focuses on the nature of human language, the relationship of language to culture, and the languages of nonliterate peoples.

biological anthropology The subfield of anthropology that focuses on the biological evolution of humans and human ancestors, the relationship of humans to other organisms, and patterns of biological variation within and among human populations. Also referred to as physical anthropology.

SPECIAL TOPIC

Biological Anthropologists at Work

The research interests of biological anthropologists are quite varied. This photo essay provides some examples.

Dr. Barry Bogin is a professor of anthropology in the Department of Behavioral Sciences at the University of Michigan at Dearborn. His area of specialization is the study of human growth, including studies of seasonal variation in growth rates, the evolution of human growth patterns, and the relationship between social and cultural factors and child growth. Much of his recent research has focused on an analysis of the cultural correlates of differences in growth patterns of Ladinos and Mayans in Guatemala and the United States. He is shown here measuring the height of a Mayan woman who has immigrated to the United States.

Dr. Michael Crawford is a professor of anthropology at the University of Kansas. He specializes in anthropological genetics, the study of the forces affecting genetic variation between and within human populations. Dr. Crawford's research includes studies of genetic markers, DNA, body and cranial measures, fingerprints, and dental measurements from human populations across the globe. His research has taken him to Mexico, Belize, Ireland, Italy, Alaska, and Siberia. He is shown here with the Altai reindeer herders of Siberia as he investigates their genetic relationship to the first inhabitants of the New World and their adaptation to extremely cold climates.

Dr. Katherine Dettwyler is an associate professor of anthropology at Texas A&M University. Her research interests include child growth and health and biocultural studies of breast feeding. Her book *Dancing Skeletons* (1994) describes her research on infant and child growth as it relates to health and nutrition in Mali, West Africa. Dr. Dettwyler is actively involved in a number of organizations to promote improved nutrition in Mali.

Dr. Dean Falk is a professor of anthropology at Florida State University. Her primary research interest is the evolution and comparative anatomy of primate brains, including the human brain. Dr. Falk is an expert in the field of paleoneurology, which involves the reconstruction of brain anatomy from fossil evidence. Her recent research deals with how the brain cools itself, including implications for human evolution and the origin of an

Barry Bogin (© Barry Bogin)

Michael Crawford (Courtesy Michael Crawford)

Katherine Dettwyler (Courtesy Dr. Katherine Dettwyler)

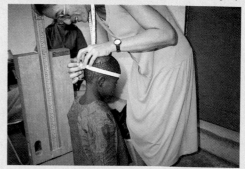

Dean Falk
(Courtesy Dr. Dean Falk)

enlarged brain in our early ancestors. Her model of brain evolution is described in *Braindance* (1992).

Dr. Lyle Konigsberg, a professor of anthropology at the University of Tennessee, is particularly interested in integrating the study of prehistoric human skeletal remains with genetic and demographic theory. Dr. Konigsberg investigates patterns of prehistoric biological variation across space and time. His current work involves an analysis of prehistoric Native American populations, dating between 500 and 6,000 years ago.

Dr. Rachel Caspari is an adjunct assistant professor at the University of Michigan. Her primary research interest is the anatomy of recent humans and their evolutionary relationship with earlier humans. Her most recent research has focused on the skeletal morphology of the neck region in central European human fossils. She is also interested in the history of biological anthropology and is coauthor of the recent book *Race and Human Evolution* (Wolpoff and Caspari 1997).

Dr. Lorena Madrigal, an associate professor of anthropology at the University of South Florida, studies the

biology and microevolution of human populations in Costa Rica, particularly demography and genetics. Her earlier work focused on the relationship among fertility, genetic change, and the sickle cell gene. Recently, her work has expanded to include aspects of maturation, miscarriage, frequency of twinning, and seasonal variation in demographic rates, among other topics. Most recently, Dr. Madrigal has been involved in the historical demography of Escazú, a small rural population in Costa Rica.

Dr. Karen Strier is a professor of anthropology at the University of Wisconsin at Madison. Her primary research interests are in comparative primate behavioral ecology and its links to conservation biology. Since 1982, Dr. Strier has studied the endangered muriqui monkeys of Brazil's Atlantic forest. Her research has demonstrated that muriquis differ from most other primates in their nonaggressive, egalitarian societies. More recently, she has expanded her behavioral studies to include investigations into muriqui reproductive and life history strategies.

Lyle Konigsberg (Courtesy Dr. Lyle Konigsberg) *Rachel Caspari (Courtesy Dr. Rachel Caspari)*

Lorena Madrigal
(Courtesy Dr. Lorena Madrigal)

Karen Strier (Photo by Toni E. Ziegler)

Where have we come from? What does the history of our species look like? A third question concerns variation among modern humans. *How are humans around the world like, or unlike, each other?* What causes the patterns of human variation that we see? The fourth question relates back to the biocultural nature of human beings: *How does culture affect biology, and vice versa?* What impact have the rapid and amazing cultural changes in our species' recent past had on our biology? Are our biological and cultural adaptations out of synch?

There are several traditionally defined areas within biological anthropology, such as primate studies, paleoanthropology, and human variation. Primate studies are concerned with defining humans in the natural world, specifically in terms of the primates (a group of mammals that includes monkeys, apes, and humans). Primate studies look at the anatomy, behavior, and evolution of the other primates as a standard of comparison with those aspects of humans. In this way, we can learn something about what it is to be human.

Paleoanthropology is the study of the fossil remains of human evolution. Researchers in this field are interested in determining who our ancestors were and when, how, and why they evolved. Paleoanthropologists work closely with archaeologists to reconstruct the behaviors of our ancestors.

The study of human variation is concerned with how and why humans differ from each other in their biological makeup. This subfield considers the ways in which culture and biology interact in the modern world, including such topics as the genetics of populations, demography (the study of population size and composition), physical growth and development, and human health and disease. Several decades ago, human variation was the concern of only a few biological anthropologists. Today it is perhaps the largest research area within biological anthropology.

SCIENCE AND EVOLUTION

Biological anthropology is an evolutionary science. All the major questions just presented may be addressed using modern evolutionary theory. Biological evolution simply refers to change in the genetic makeup of populations over time.

Characteristics of Science

Before we consider how evolution works, it is important to understand exactly what a science is.

Facts   At one time or another, you have probably heard someone make the statement that evolution is a theory, not a fact. Or you might have heard that it is a fact, not a theory. Which is it, theory or fact? The truth of the matter is that someone who makes either of these statements does not understand what a theory or a fact is. Evolution is both fact and theory. A fact is simply a verifiable truth. It is a scientific fact that the earth is round. It is a fact that

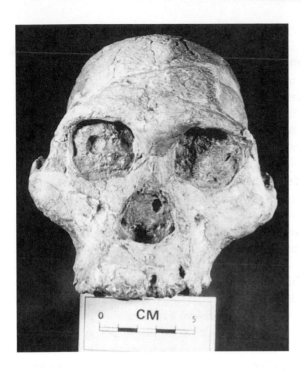

FIGURE 1.3

A skull of Australopithecus africanus, *a human ancestor that lived 2 to 3 million years ago.* (© K. Cannon-Bonventure/ Anthro-Photo)

when you drop something, it falls to the ground (assuming you are in the presence of a gravitational field and you are not dropping something that floats or flies away!). Evolution is a fact. Living organisms have changed in the past and they continue to change today. There are forms of life living today that did not exist millions of years ago. There are also forms of life that did live in the past but are not around today, such as our ancestors (Figure 1.3). Certain organisms have shown definite changes in their biological makeup. Horses, for example, used to have five toes, then three, and today they have one. Human beings have larger brains and smaller teeth today than they did a million years ago. Some changes are even apparent over shorter intervals of time. For example, human teeth are on average smaller today than they were only 10,000 years ago. All of these statements and many others are verifiable truths. They are facts.

Hypotheses   What is a hypothesis? A **hypothesis** is simply an explanation of observed facts. For example, consider gravity. Gravity is a fact. It is observable. Many hypotheses could be generated to explain gravity. You could hypothesize that gravity is caused by a giant living in the core of our planet drawing in air, thus causing a pull on all objects on the earth's surface. Bizarre as it sounds, this is a scientific hypothesis because it can be tested. It is, however, easily shown to be incorrect (air movement can be measured and it does not flow in the postulated direction).

Testability   To be scientific, a hypothesis must be testable. The potential must exist for a hypothesis to be rejected. Just as the presence of the hypothetical

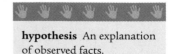

hypothesis An explanation of observed facts.

giant in the earth can be tested (it doesn't exist!), predictions made about gravitational strength can also be tested. Not all hypotheses can be tested, however, and for this reason they are not scientific hypotheses. That doesn't necessarily mean they are true or false but only that they cannot be tested. For example, you might come up with a hypothesis that all the fossils we have ever found were put in the ground by God to confuse us. This is not a scientific hypothesis because we have no objective way of testing the statement.

Many evolutionary hypotheses, however, are testable. For example, specific predictions about the fossil record can be made based on our knowledge of evolution. One such prediction is that humans evolved after the extinction of the dinosaurs. The potential exists for this statement to be rejected; all we need is evidence that humans existed before, or at the same time as, the dinosaurs. Because we have found no such evidence, we cannot reject the hypothesis. We can, however, imagine a situation in which the hypothesis could be rejected. If we cannot imagine such a situation, then the hypothesis cannot be tested. For example, imagine that someone tells you that all the people on the earth were created 5 minutes ago, complete with memories! Any evidence you muster against this idea could be explained away. Therefore, this hypothesis is not scientific because there is no possible way to reject it.

Theories   What is the difference between a theory and a hypothesis? In some disciplines, the two terms are sometimes used to mean the same thing. In the natural and physical sciences, however, theory means something different from hypothesis. A **theory** is a set of hypotheses that have been tested repeatedly and that have not been rejected. Evolution falls into this category. Evidence from many sources has confirmed the basic hypotheses making up evolutionary theory (discussed later in the chapter).

The Development of Evolutionary Theory

As with all general theories, modern evolutionary theory is not static. Scientific research is a dynamic process, with new evidence being used to support, clarify, and, most important, reject previous ideas. There will always be continual refinements in specific aspects of the theory and its applications. Because science is a dynamic process, evolutionary theory did not come about overnight. Charles Darwin (1809–1882) is most often credited as the "father of evolutionary thought" (Figure 1.4). It is true that Darwin provided a powerful idea that forms the center of modern evolutionary thought. He did not work in an intellectual vacuum, however, but rather built on the ideas of earlier scholars. Darwin's model was not the first evolutionary theory; it forms, rather, the basis of the one that has stood the test of time.

Pre-Darwinian Thought   To understand Darwin's contribution and evolution in general, it is necessary to take a look at earlier ideas. For many centuries the concept of change, biological or otherwise, was rather unusual in

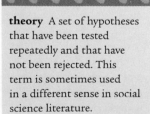

theory A set of hypotheses that have been tested repeatedly and that have not been rejected. This term is sometimes used in a different sense in social science literature.

Western thought. Much of Greek philosophy, for example, posits a static, unchanging view of the world. In later Western thought, the universe, earth, and all living creatures were regarded as having been created by God in their present form, showing little if any change over many generations. Many biologists (then called natural historians) shared this view, and their science consisted mainly of description and categorization. A good example is Carolus Linnaeus (1707–1778), a Swedish naturalist who compiled one of the first formal classifications of all known living creatures. **Taxonomy** is the science of describing and classifying organisms. Linnaeus's taxonomic research produced a classification of all known living creatures into meaningful groups. For example, humans, dogs, cats, and many other animals are mammals, characterized primarily by the presence of mammary glands to feed offspring. Linnaeus used a variety of traits to place all then-known creatures into various categories. Such a classification helps clarify relationships between different organisms. For example, bats are classified as mammals because they possess mammary glands—and not as birds simply because they have wings.

Linnaeus also gave organisms a name reflecting their genus and species. A **species** is a group of populations whose members can interbreed and produce fertile offspring. A **genus** is a group of similar species, often sharing certain common forms of adaptation. Modern humans, for example, are known by the name *Homo sapiens*. The first word is the genus and the second word is the species (more detail on genus and species is given in Chapters 4 and 8).

The reason for the relationships among organisms, however, was not often addressed by early natural historians. The living world was felt to be the product of God's work, and the task of the natural historian was description and classification. This static view of the world began to change in the eighteenth and nineteenth centuries. One important reason for this change was that excavations began to produce many fossils that did not fit neatly into the classification system. For example, imagine that you found the remains of a modern horse. This would pose no problem in interpretation; the bones are those of a dead horse, perhaps belonging to a farmer several years ago. Now suppose you found what at first glance appeared to be a horse but was somewhat smaller and had five toes instead of the single hoof of a modern horse. If you found more and more of these five-toed horses, you would ask what creature the toes belonged to. Because horses do not have five toes today, your only conclusion would be that there once existed horses with five toes and that they do not exist anymore. This conclusion, though hardly startling now, was a real thunderbolt to those who believed the world was created as it is today, with no change.

Apart from finding fossil remains of creatures that were somewhat similar to modern-day forms, excavations also uncovered fossil remnants of truly unusual creatures, such as the dinosaurs. Discovery of the fossil record began to chip away at the view that the world is as it always had been, and the concept of change began to be incorporated into explanations of the origin of life. Not all scholars, however, came up with the same hypotheses.

FIGURE 1.4

Charles Darwin. (© Stapleton Collection/Corbis)

taxonomy The science of describing and classifying organisms.

species A group of populations whose members can interbreed naturally and produce fertile offspring.

genus Groups of species with similar adaptations.

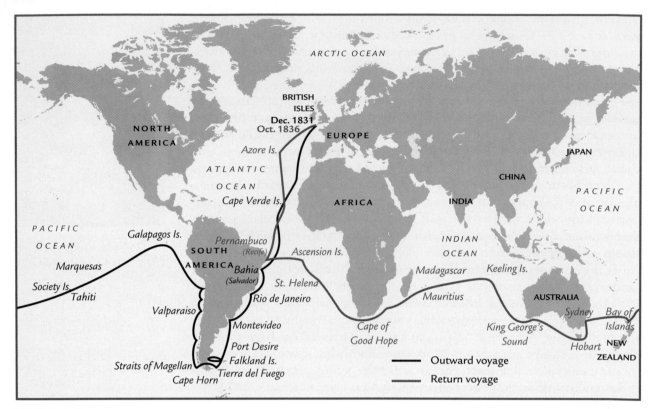

FIGURE 1.5

Darwin's observations of variation in the different regions he visited aboard the H.M.S. Beagle shaped his theory of natural selection.

One French anatomist, Georges Cuvier (1769–1832), analyzed many of the fossil remains found in quarries. He showed that many of these belonged to animals that no longer existed; that is, they had become extinct. Cuvier used a hypothesis called catastrophism to explain these extinctions. The hypothesis posited a series of catastrophes in the planet's past, during which many living creatures were destroyed. Following these catastrophes, organisms from unaffected areas moved in. The changes over time observed in the fossil record could therefore be explained as a continual process of catastrophes followed by repopulation from other regions (Mayr 1982).

The work of the French scientist Jean-Baptiste Lamarck (1744–1829) more explicitly attempted an explanation of evolution. He believed that the environment would affect the future shape and organization of animals (Mayr 1982). His specific mechanism stressed the use and disuse of body parts. For example, a jungle cat that developed stronger legs through constant running and jumping would pass these changes on to its offspring. Although we now know that Lamarck's ideas are not genetically correct, it is important to note that he was quite astute in noticing the relationship between organisms, their environment, and evolution.

Charles Darwin and Natural Selection   Cuvier and Lamarck are perhaps the best-known examples of what many have called "pre-Darwinian" theorists. Evolution was well accepted, and various models were being developed to explain this fact, before Darwin. Charles Darwin developed the theory of natural selection that has since been supported by testing. His major contribution was to combine information from a variety of different fields, such as geology and economics, to form his theory.

With this background in mind, let us look at Darwin and his accomplishment. Charles Darwin had been interested in biology and geology since he was a small child. Born to well-to-do parents, Darwin attended college and had planned to enter the ministry, although he was not as enthusiastic about this career as he was about his studies of natural history. Because of his scientific and social connections, Darwin was able to accompany the scientific survey ship *Beagle* as an unpaid naturalist. The *Beagle* conducted a 5-year journey around the world collecting plant and animal specimens in South America and the Galapagos Islands (in the Pacific Ocean near Ecuador), among other places (Figure 1.5).

During these travels, Darwin came to several basic conclusions about variation in living organisms. First, he found a tremendous amount of observable variation in most living species. Instead of looking at the world in terms of fixed, rigid categories (as did mainstream biology in his time), Darwin saw that individuals within species varied considerably from place to place. With careful attention, you can see the world in much the same way that Darwin did. You will see, for example, that people around you vary to an incredible degree. Some are tall, some are short, some are dark, and some are light. Facial features, musculature, hair color, and many other characteristics come in many different forms, even in a single classroom. Remember, too, that what you see are only those visible characteristics. With the right type of equipment, you could look at genetic and biochemical variation within your classroom and find even more evidence of tremendous diversity.

Darwin also noted that the variations he saw made sense in terms of the environment (Figure 1.6). Creatures in cold climates often have fur for protection. Birds in areas where insects live deep inside tree branches have long beaks to enable them to extract these insects and eat them. In other words, organisms appear well adapted to specific environments. Darwin believed that the environment acted to change organisms over time. But how?

To help answer this question, Darwin turned to the writings of the economist Thomas Malthus (1766–1834), who had noted that more individuals are born in most species than can possibly survive. In other words, many organisms die before reaching maturity and reproducing. If it were not for this mortality, populations would grow too large for their environments to support them. Certain fish, for example, can produce as many as 8,000 eggs in a single year. Assume for the moment that half of these eggs are female. Now assume that each of these females then also lays 8,000 eggs in a single year. To make things simple, let us further assume that a female fish breeds only once in her life. If you start with two fish (one male and one female), in the next generation you have 8,000 fish. Half of these are females, and each produces 8,000 more fish, for a total of 32 million fish. If the fish continue

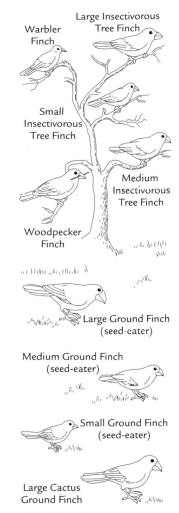

FIGURE 1.6

The sizes, beak shapes, and diets of this sample of Darwin's finches show differences in adaptation among closely related species. (From E. Peter Volpe, Understanding Evolution, *5th ed. © 1985 Wm. C. Brown Communication, Inc., Dubuque, Iowa. All rights reserved. Reprinted by permission of the McGraw-Hill Companies)*

reproducing in this way, there will be roughly 2.1×10^{36} fish (that is, 2.1 followed by 36 zeroes) after only 10 generations! Suppose these are relatively small fish, each one weighing only 100 grams (a little less than a quarter of a pound). The total weight of all fish after 10 generations would be roughly 2.1×10^{38} grams (or roughly 2.3×10^{32} tons).

To give you an idea of exactly how large these numbers are, consider the fact that the total weight of our sun is 1.99×10^{33} grams (Pasachoff 1979). If the cycle begins with two fish, after 10 generations the total weight of the fish will be greater than the weight of the sun. Because we are not all currently smothered in fish, something is wrong with this simple model.

Malthus provided the answer. Most of the fish will die before they reproduce. Some eggs will become diseased and die, and others will be eaten by predators. Only a small number of the eggs will actually survive long enough to reproduce. Malthus is best known for extrapolating the principle of population growth into human terms; his lesson is that unless we control our growth, there will soon be too many of us to feed.

To Charles Darwin, the ideas of Malthus provided the needed information to solve the problem of adaptation and evolution. Not all individuals in a species survive and reproduce. Some failure to reproduce may be random, but some is related to specific characteristics of an individual. If there are two birds, one with a short beak and one with a long beak, in an environment that requires reaching inside branches to feed, it stands to reason that the bird with the longer beak is more likely to feed itself, survive, and reproduce. In certain environments, some individuals possess traits that enhance their probability of survival and reproduction. If these traits are due, in part or whole, to inherited characteristics, then they will be passed on to the next generation.

In some ways, Darwin's idea was not new. Animal and plant breeders had used this principle for centuries. Controlled breeding and artificial selection had resulted in many traits in domesticated plants and animals, such as livestock size, milk production in cows, and a variety of other traits. The same principle is used in producing pedigreed dogs and many forms of tropical fish. The difference is that Darwin saw that nature (the environment) could select those individuals that survived and reproduced. Hence, he called his concept **natural selection.**

Although the theory of evolution by natural selection is most often associated with Charles Darwin, another English natural historian, Alfred Russel Wallace (1823–1913), came up with essentially the same idea. In fact, Darwin and Wallace communicated their ideas to each other and first presented the theory of natural selection in a joint paper in 1858. Many scholars feel that Wallace's independent work urged Darwin finally to put forward the ideas he had developed years earlier but had not published. To ensure timely publication, Darwin condensed his many years of work into a book titled *On the Origin of Species by Means of Natural Selection,* published in 1859.

Examples of Natural Selection   One excellent example of how natural selection works is the story of populations of the peppered moth in England

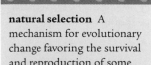

natural selection A mechanism for evolutionary change favoring the survival and reproduction of some organisms over others because of their biological characteristics.

FIGURE 1.7

Adaptation in the peppered moth. The dark-colored moth is more visible on light-colored tree trunks and therefore at greater risk of being seen and eaten by a bird (left). The light-colored moth is at greater risk of being eaten on dark-colored tree trunks (right).
(© Michael Tweedie/Photo Researchers, Inc.)

over the last few centuries (Figure 1.7). These moths come in two distinct colors, dark and light. Early observations found that most of these moths were light-colored, thus allowing them to camouflage themselves on tree trunks covered by light-colored lichen. By blending in, they had a better chance of avoiding the birds that tried to eat them. Roughly 1 percent of the moths, however, were dark-colored and thus at an obvious disadvantage. In the century following the beginning of the Industrial Revolution in England, naturalists noted that the frequency of dark-colored moths increased to almost 90 percent (Grant 1985). This change was due to the massive pollution in the surrounding countryside that industrialization brought about. The pollution killed the lichen, exposing the dark tree trunks. The light moths were at a disadvantage, and the dark moths, now better camouflaged, were better off. Proportionately, more dark moths survived and passed their dark color to the next generation. In evolutionary terminology, the dark moths were *selected for* and the light moths were *selected against*. After antipollution laws were passed and the environment began to recover, the situation was reversed: once again light moths survived better, and were selected for, whereas dark moths were selected against.

This well-known study shows us more than just the workings of natural selection. It also illustrates several important principles of evolution. First, we cannot always state with absolute certainty which traits are "good" and which are "bad." It depends on the specific environment. When the trees were light in color, the light-colored moths were at an advantage, but when the situation changed, the dark-colored moths gained the advantage. Second, evolution does not proceed unopposed in one direction. Under certain situations, biological traits can change in a different direction. In the case of the moths, evolution produced a change from light to dark to light again. Third, evolution does not occur in a vacuum. It is affected by changes in the environment and by changes in other species. In this example, changes in the cultural evolution of humans led to a change in the environment, which further affected the evolution of the moths. Finally, the moth study shows us the critical importance of variation to the evolutionary process. If the original population of moths did not possess the dark-colored variation, they might have been wiped out after the trees turned darker in color. Variation must exist for natural selection to operate effectively.

Another example of natural selection is found in P. R. Grant's continuing work on the variation and evolution of Galapagos finches. Grant found that average beak size changed over time in direct response to changes in the environment. In drought years, the average beak is larger. Why? The simplest explanation is that drought conditions make those finches with larger beaks better able to crack the larger seeds that are more common under drought conditions. Grant has observed these changes over several decades. The changes in beak size over time shows that the changing environment affects the probability of survival and reproduction (Grant 1991, Weiner 1994).

Modern Evolutionary Thought   Darwin provided part of the answer of how evolution worked, but he did not have all the answers. Many early critics of Darwin's work focused on certain questions that Darwin could not answer. One important question concerns the origins of variation: Given that natural selection operates on existing variation, then where do those variations come from? Why, at the outset, were some moths light and others dark? Natural selection can act only on preexisting variation; it cannot create new variations. Another question is, How are traits inherited? The theory of natural selection states that certain traits are selected for and passed on to future generations. How are these traits passed on? Darwin knew that traits were inherited, but he did not know the mechanism. Still another question involves how new forms and structures come into being.

Darwin is to be remembered and praised for his work in providing the critical base from which evolutionary science developed. He did not, however, have all the answers, as no scientist does. Even today people tend to equate evolutionary science with Darwin to the exclusion of all work since that time. Some critics of evolutionary theory point to a single aspect of Darwin's work, show it to be in error, and then proceed to claim all of evolutionary thought suspect. In reality, a scientific theory will continue to change as new evidence is gathered and as further tests are constructed.

Modern evolutionary theory relies not only on the work of Darwin and Wallace but also on developments in genetics, zoology, embryology, physiology, and mathematics, to name but a few fields. The basic concept of natural selection as stated by Darwin has been tested and found to be valid. Refinements have been added, and some aspects of the original idea have been changed. We now have answers to many of Darwin's questions.

Biological evolution consists of changes in the genetic composition of populations. As shown in Chapter 3, the relative frequencies of genes change over time because of four mechanisms, or evolutionary forces. Natural selection is one of these mechanisms. Those individuals with genetic characteristics that improve their relative survival or reproduction pass their genetic material on to the next generation. In the peppered moth example discussed earlier, the dark moths were more likely to survive in an environment where pollution made the trunks of trees darker in color. Thus, the relative frequency of genes for dark moth color increased over time (at least until the environment changed again).

Evolutionary change from one generation to the next, or over many generations, is the product of the joint effect of the four evolutionary forces. Our discussion here simplifies a complex idea, but it does suggest that evolution is more than simply natural selection. Modern evolutionary theory encompasses all four evolutionary forces and will be discussed in greater detail in the next three chapters.

Evidence for Evolution

Because this book is concerned with human variation and evolution, you will be provided with numerous examples of how evolution works in human populations, past and present. It is important to understand from the start that biological evolution is a documented fact and that the modern theory of evolution has stood up under many scientific tests.

The fossil record provides evidence of evolution. The story the fossils tell is one of change. Creatures existed in the past that are no longer with us. Sequential changes are found in many fossils showing the change of certain features over time from a common ancestor, as in the case of the horse. Apart from demonstrating that evolution did occur, the fossil record also provides tests of the predictions made from evolutionary theory. For example, the theory predicts that single-celled organisms evolved before multicelled organisms. The fossil record supports this prediction—multicelled organisms are found in layers of earth millions of years after the first appearance of single-celled organisms. Note that the possibility always remains that the opposite could be found. If multicelled organisms were indeed found to have evolved before single-celled organisms, then the theory of evolution would be rejected. A good scientific theory always allows for the possibility of rejection. The fact that we have not found such a case in countless examinations of the fossil record strengthens the case for evolutionary theory. Remember, in science you do not prove a theory; rather, you fail to reject it.

The fossil record is not the only evidence we have that evolution has occurred. Comparison of living organisms provides further confirmation. For example, the African apes are the closest living relatives of humans. We see this in a number of characteristics. African apes and humans share the same type of dental pattern, have a similar shoulder structure, and have DNA (the genetic code) that is over 98 percent identical. Even though any one of these traits, or others, could be explained as coincidental, why do so many independent traits show the same pattern? One possibility, of course, is that they were designed that way by an ultimate Creator. The problem with this idea is that it cannot be tested. It is a matter of faith and not of science. Another

FIGURE 1.8

The percentage of genetic difference between humans and the great apes (chimpanzee, gorilla, and orangutan). Combined with other biological evidence, genetic data show us how closely related we are to the apes, especially the chimpanzee. (From Human Evolution: An Illustrated Introduction *by Roger Lewin, © 1984 by Blackwell Scientific Publications. Reprinted by permission by W. H. Freeman and Company)*

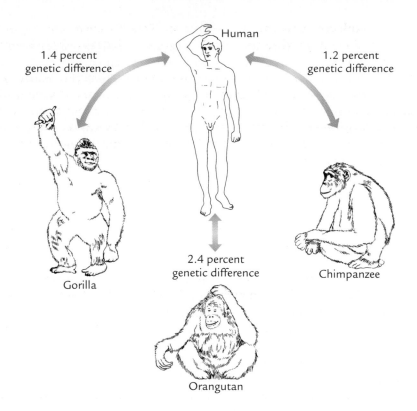

problem is that we must then ask ourselves why a Creator would use the same basic pattern for so many traits in different creatures. Evolution, on the other hand, offers an explanation. Apes and humans share many characteristics because they evolved from a common ancestor (Figure 1.8).

Another example of shared characteristics is the python, a large snake. Like many vertebrates, the python has a pelvis, the skeletal structure that connects the lower legs to the upper body (Futuyma 1983). From a structural standpoint, of what possible use is a pelvis to a creature that has no legs? If the python was created, then what purpose would there have been to give it a pelvis? We can of course argue that no one can understand the motivations of a Creator, but that is hardly a scientific explanation. Evolutionary reasoning provides an answer: The python has retained the pelvis from an earlier ancestor that did have legs. In fact, new fossil discoveries dating back 95 million years provide evidence of early snakes that actually had limbs (Tchernov et al. 2000).

Further, fascinating evidence of shared characteristics is the discovery of fossils of early whales with reduced hind limbs (Gingerich et al. 1990). Whales are aquatic mammals that have lost hind limbs and pelvic bones since their evolutionary separation from other mammals more than 50 million years ago. The discovery of fossil whales with small, and perhaps somewhat functional, hind limbs provides another example of shared characteristics that can be explained only through evolution. This discovery also provides an excellent illustration of a transitional form—a fossil that links both early and modern forms.

Another line of evidence supporting evolution is the laboratory and field studies of living organisms. Ongoing evolutionary change has been documented in many organisms, including humans. Specific predictions of the effect of evolutionary mechanisms have been tested and verified in controlled experiments and observational studies. The study of moth color is but one of many examples of this kind of analysis.

Science and Religion

The subject of evolution has always been controversial, and the implications of evolution have sometimes frightened people. For example, the fact that humans and apes evolved from a common ancestor has always upset some people who feel that their humanity is somehow degraded by having ancestors supposedly less worthy than ourselves. Another conflict lies in the implications evolution has for religious views. In the United States, a number of laws prohibited teaching evolution in public schools. Many of these laws stayed on the books until the late 1960s.

Numerous legal battles have been fought over these anti-evolution laws. Perhaps the most famous of these was the "Scopes Monkey Trial" in 1925. John Scopes, a high school teacher in Dayton, Tennessee, was arrested for violating the state law prohibiting the teaching of evolution. The town and trial quickly became the center of national attention, primarily because of the two celebrities in the case—William Jennings Bryan, a former U.S. Secretary of State, who represented the state of Tennessee, and Clarence Darrow, one of the most famous American trial lawyers ever, who represented Scopes. The battle between these two eloquent speakers captured the attention of the country (Figure 1.9). In the end, Scopes was found guilty of violating the law, and he was fined $100. The fine was later suspended on a legal technicality. The story of this trial, which has been dramatized in play and movie versions as *Inherit the Wind,* is a powerful story portraying the fight of those who feel strongly about academic freedom and freedom of speech against ignorance and oppression. In reality, the original arrest of Scopes was planned by several local people to gain publicity for the town (Larson 1997).

Creation Science   In retrospect, the Scopes trial may seem amusing. We laugh at early attempts to control subject matter in classrooms and often feel that we have gone beyond such battles. Nothing could be further from the truth, however. For many people, evolution represents a threat to their beliefs in the sudden creation of all life by a creator. Attempts to legislate the teaching of the Biblical view of creation in science classes, however, violate the First Amendment of the Constitution as an establishment of religion. To circumvent this problem, opponents of evolution have devised the strategy of calling their teachings "creation science," supposedly the scientific study

FIGURE 1.9

The Scopes trial. William Jennings Bryan (right) represented the state of Tennessee, and Clarence Darrow (left) represented John Scopes. (© AP/Wide World Photos)

of special creation. The word *God* does not always appear in definitions of creation science, but the word *creator* often does.

In March 1981, the Arkansas state legislature passed a law (Act 590) requiring that creation science be taught in public schools for equal amounts of time as evolution. The American Civil Liberties Union challenged this law, and it was overturned in a federal district court in 1982. A similar law passed in Louisiana in 1981 was later overturned. The Louisiana case has since been appealed and brought to the U.S. Supreme Court, which upheld the ruling of the lower court in 1987. Among other legal problems they raise, both the Arkansas and Louisiana laws have been found to be unconstitutional under the First Amendment.

What is "creation science"? Why shouldn't it be taught in science classes? Shouldn't science be open to new ideas? These questions all center on the issue of whether creation science is a science or not. As typically applied, creation science is not a science; at best, it is a grab bag of ideas spruced up with scientific jargon. One of the original definitions is found in Act 590 of the Arkansas law, which defines creation science as

> the scientific evidence for creation and inferences from these scientific evidences. Creation-science includes the scientific evidences and related inferences that indicate: (1) Sudden creation of the universe, energy, and life from nothing; (2) The insufficiency of mutation and natural selection in bringing about development of all living kinds from a single organism; (3) Changes only within fixed limits of originally created kinds of plants and animals; (4) Separate ancestry for man and apes; (5) Explanation of the earth's geology by catastrophism, including the occurrence of a worldwide flood; and (6) A relatively recent inception of the earth and living kinds. (Montagu 1984: 376–377)

None of these statements is supported by scientific evidence, and creationist writers generally use very little actual evidence to support their views. Some have written that the Biblical Flood can be supported by the fossil record. Earth's past is essentially recorded by the order in which different levels of earth and fossils are found. In general, that is, the deeper a fossil is found, the older it is. Creationists explain this order as being caused by the flight of animals from the Flood. As the waters rose, they say, birds flew and small mammals ran up mountains to escape drowning; these creatures were therefore drowned at higher elevations.

According to creationists, then, you will find fish at lower levels and birds and mammals at higher levels. The fossil record does show this phenomenon. Isn't this proof for "creation science"? No. Think about the Flood scenario for a moment and you will see that it just doesn't make sense. Why didn't the winged reptiles fly away like the birds did? Why are single-celled organisms found earlier than multicelled organisms of similar size and overall shape? Why did large, heavy creatures such as giant tortoises and hippopotami survive instead of sinking? Why didn't the small, fast dinosaurs survive? Why did certain fish die before others, when they were just as swift and just as good at swimming? Many challenges can be raised to the idea of a single gigantic flood causing the order found in the fossil record (Kitcher 1982; Futuyma 1983). The fossil record, in short, provides ample evidence to reject the Flood hypothesis.

Another example cited by creationists as "proof" of special creation is the "fact" that dinosaur and human footprints have been found at the same geological level along the Paluxy River in Texas. Closer examination has shown that the human footprints were actually eroded dinosaur tracks as well as human-made carvings.

The main "scientific" work of the creationists consists of attempting to find fault with evolutionary theory. The reasoning is that if evolution can be rejected, then special creation must be true. This strategy actually uses an important feature of scientific research by attempting to reject a given hypothesis. The problem is that none of the creationists' attacks on evolution has been supported by scientific evidence. Certainly some predictions of evolutionary theory have been proven incorrect, but that is to be expected because science is a dynamic process. The basic finds of evolution, however, have been supported time and time again.

Another problem is that this method works only when the hypothesis and its alternative cover all possible cases. Are evolution and special creation by a single creator the only possible explanations? Perhaps the universe was created by several creators. Perhaps the universe and natural law were created by a creator, but life evolved from natural law. You might try to think up other alternatives. Remember, however, that to be scientific a hypothesis must be testable.

On an emotional level, the doctrines of "creation science" attract many people. Given the concept of free speech, why shouldn't creation science be given equal time? The problem with equal time is that it assumes that both ideas have equal merit. Consider that some people still believe the earth is

TABLE 1.1	Some Religious Organizations Opposed to Creation Science

American Jewish Congress
Central Conference of American Rabbis
General Convention of the Episcopal Church
Lutheran World Federation
Roman Catholic Church
Unitarian Universalist Association
United Methodist Church
United Presbyterian Church

Source: National Center for Science Education Web page (www.ncseweb.org)

flat. They are certainly entitled to their opinion, but it would be absurd to mandate "equal time" in geography and geology classes for this idea. Also, the concept of equal time is not really that fair-minded after all. The specific story many creationists refer to is the Biblical story of Genesis. Many other cultures have their own creation stories. Shouldn't they receive equal time as well? In one sense, they should, though the proper forum for such discussions is probably a course in comparative religions, not a science class.

Perhaps the biggest problem advocates of "creation science" have introduced is that they appear to place religion and science at odds with each other. Religion and science both represent ways of looking at the world, and though they work on different levels, they are not contradictory. You can be religious and believe in God and still accept the fact of evolution and evolutionary theory. Only if you take the story of Genesis as a literal, historical account does a conflict exist. Most major religions in the world accept the findings of evolution. Many people, including some scientists, look to the evolutionary process as evidence of God's work, an idea known as **theistic evolution.** As such, many religions support the teaching of evolution in science education rather than creation science (Table 1.1). As further evidence that there is no necessary conflict between religion and evolution, Pope John Paul II stated in his October 22, 1996, message to the Pontifical Academy of Sciences that "knowledge has led to the recognition of the theory of evolution as more than a hypothesis" (Gould 1999: 81).

Intelligent Design   In recent years, another approach to creationism has become popular within the United States. Known as **intelligent design creationism,** this approach stresses the idea that the biological world was created by an intelligent Creator. Supporters of this view claim that many of the characteristics of biological organisms, such as the structure of DNA or the anatomy of the eye, are too complex to have occurred through natural processes and that, therefore, life *must* have been created. The basic idea of intelligent design creationism is often expressed by the "watchmaker anal-

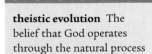

theistic evolution The belief that God operates through the natural process of evolution.

intelligent design creationism The idea that the biological world was created by an intelligent entity and did not arise from natural processes.

ogy" of eighteenth-century theologian William Paley, who argued that a complex mechanical object such as a watch, with all of its intricate mechanisms, could not arise naturally and therefore automatically implied the existence of a watchmaker (Dawkins 1987).

Much of the substance of intelligent design creationism is similar to that of biblical creation science. The basic methodology is to attack the claims and findings of evolutionary science with this goal: If evolution is rejected, then there must be a designer. As such, intelligent design creationism uses the same either-or dichotomy employed by biblical creation science. Anything that is not explained by evolutionary theory must therefore be proof of a creation, even though science never claims to have all of the answers at any given point in time.

From a scientific perspective, there are no testable hypotheses regarding the specific actions of a creator, or any way to check on the proposed hypothesis. The bottom line is that anything and everything is explained simply as the result of the actions of a creator (Pennock 1999). The reliance on supposed disproof of evolution further weakens the case, as a number of researchers have shown that complex structures can indeed arise through natural processes (Dawkins 1987; Pennock 1999). It is important to note again that science deals with testable hypotheses about natural processes. Supernatural actions or entities do not fall within the realm of science. Science does not *require* a creator or creation, but it does not rule them out; creationism, on the other hand, requires both.

Science and Society   Despite scientific, legal, and theological objections, creationism has not gone away. There remains considerable support within the United States for the inclusion of some form of creationism in the public school curriculum. Some local communities and states continue to insist on a "balanced" treatment, including modification of school curriculum, changes in existing textbooks, and adoption of more creationism-oriented texts. Perhaps one of the more noticeable casualties of this debate has been the erosion in science education. Due to continued and often very vocal opposition to the teaching of evolution, educational standards have been altered to avoid confrontation. In a recent analysis of state science standards, Lerner (2000) found that 19 out of 50 states do a poor job in dealing with evolution in their published standards, including 12 that avoid using the word *evolution* and 4 that do not teach evolution at all.

The arguments about creationism and evolution also play a role in individuals' views on ethics, morality, and social philosophy. Many creationists fear that science has eroded our faith in God and has therefore led to a decline in morals and values. They imply that science (and evolution in particular) makes statements about human morality. It does not. Science has nothing to say about right and wrong; that is the function of social ethics, philosophies, and religion. Religion and science are important to many people. To put them at odds with each other does both a disservice. It is no surprise that many ministers, priests, and rabbis have joined in the fight against creationism.

SUMMARY

Anthropology is the study of human biological and cultural variation and evolution. Anthropology asks questions that focus on what humans are and the origins, evolution, and variation of our biology and behaviors, because humans are both biological and cultural organisms. In the United States, anthropology is characterized by four subfields with specific concerns: cultural anthropology (the study of cultural behavior), anthropological archaeology (the study of past cultures), linguistic anthropology (the study of language as a human characteristic), and biological anthropology (the study of human biological evolution and variation).

As a science, anthropology has certain requirements and characteristics. Hypotheses must be testable and verifiable. The main theoretical base of biological anthropology is the theory of evolution. A major feature of evolutionary theory is Darwin's idea of natural selection. In any environment in which resources are necessarily limited, some organisms are more likely to survive and reproduce than others because of their biological characteristics. Those who survive pass these traits on to the next generation.

A current controversy involves the efforts of people who advocate that creationism be taught in public schools. Examination of this field shows that it is not a science at all. Apart from these debates, it should be noted that today there is little conflict between religion and science in the United States. Each perspective addresses different questions in different ways.

SUPPLEMENTAL READINGS

Futuyma, D. J. 1995. *Science on Trial: The Case for Evolution,* rev. ed. Sunderland, Mass.: Sinauer Associates. An excellent review and critique of creationism that is particularly strong in its discussion of scientific method and evidence for evolution. Originally published in 1983, this revised edition includes a postscript with updated information on evolution and creationism.

Larson, E. J. 1997. *Summer for the Gods: The Scopes Trial and America's Continuing Debate over Science and Religion.* Cambridge, Mass.: Harvard University Press. Winner of the Pulitzer Prize in History, an excellent book that provides a comprehensive description and analysis of the Scopes trial and creationism in the United States.

Pennock, R. T. 1999. *Tower of Babel: The Evidence against the New Creationism.* Cambridge, Mass.: MIT Press. A detailed description and critique of intelligent design creationism.

Weiner, J. 1994. *The Beak of the Finch.* New York: Vintage Books. A highly readable account of the work of Peter and Rosemary Grant on natural selection and evolution among finch populations.

INTERNET RESOURCES

http://physanth.org
Web page for the American Association of Physical Anthropologists, the world's leading professional organization for biological anthropologists. This site contains news about publications, meetings, and careers.

http://www.talkorigins.org
The Talk.Origins Archive, a Web page that includes much information about evolutionary theory as well as critiques of scientific creationism and intelligent design creationism.

http://www.ncseweb.org
Web page for the National Center for Science Education, an organization that defends teaching evolution in public schools. This site includes information on evolution, critiques of creationism, and current events.

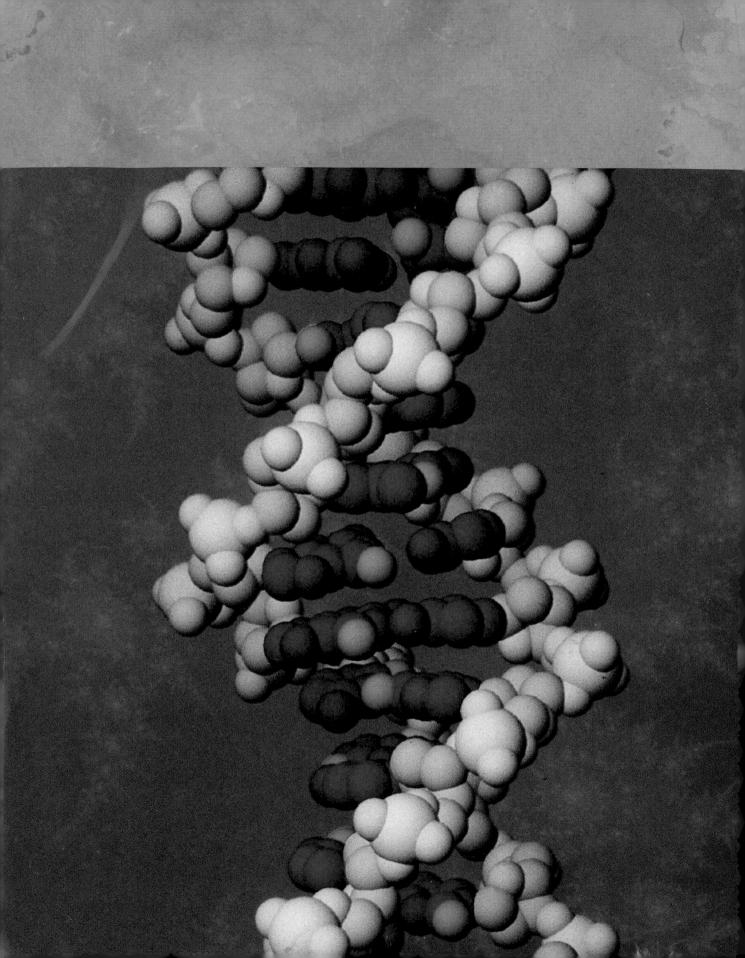

CHAPTER 2

May 20

Human Genetics

Is human behavior the result of biology *or* culture? This question has been asked countless times in human history, often with serious cultural and political consequences. To anthropologists, the question is somewhat meaningless; we recognize *both* biological and cultural factors as important and look at the relative potential contributions of both. It is hard to untangle these effects.

To understand human biological variation and evolution, we must consider the science of genetics. The study of genetics actually encompasses a number of different areas, depending on the level of analysis. Genetics can be studied on the molecular level, with the focus on what genes are and how they act to produce biological structures.

Genetics also involves the process of inheritance. To what extent are we a reflection of our parents? How are traits inherited? This branch of the field is called **Mendelian genetics,** after the scientist Gregor Mendel, who first worked out many of the principles of inheritance.

Finally, genetics can be studied at the level of a population. Here we are interested in describing the patterns of genetic variation within and among different populations and their relationship with biological evolution. The changes that take place in the frequency of genes within a population constitute the process of **microevolution.** At the level of the population, we seek the reasons for evolutionary change from one generation to the next. Projection of these findings allows us to better understand the long-term pattern

◀ *Computer-generated model of DNA, the molecule that provides the genetic code. The study of human genetics includes the biochemical makeup of DNA and the transmission of genes from one generation to the next. (© Ken Edward/ Photo Researchers, Inc.)*

Mendelian genetics The branch of genetics concerned with patterns and processes of inheritance. This field was named after Gregor Mendel, the first scientist to work out these principles.

microevolution Short-term evolutionary change.

FIGURE 2.1

Computer representation of the DNA molecule (left) and the structure of the DNA molecule (right). DNA consists of two strands arranged in a helix joined together by chemical bases. (Photo © Will & Deni McIntyre/Photo Researchers, Inc.)

of evolution over thousands and millions of years and the origin of new species (**macroevolution**).

MOLECULAR GENETICS
DNA: The Genetic Code

The study of genetics at the molecular level concerns the amazing properties of a molecule known as deoxyribonucleic acid, or **DNA** for short. The DNA molecule provides the codes for biological structures and the means to translate this code. It is perhaps best to think of DNA as a set of instructions for determining the makeup of biological organisms. Quite simply, DNA provides information for building, operating, and repairing organisms. In this context, the process of genetic inheritance is seen as the transmission of this information or the passing on of the instructions needed for biological structures. Evolution can be viewed in this context as the transfer of information from one generation to the next, along with the possibility that this information will change.

An understanding of both the structure and function of DNA is necessary to understand the processes of genetic inheritance and evolution. The exact biochemistry of DNA is beyond the scope of this text, but its basic nature can be discussed in the context of information transfer.

The Structure of DNA   The physical appearance of the DNA molecule resembles a ladder that has been twisted into the shape of a helix (Figure 2.1). In biochemical terms, the rungs of the ladder are of major importance. These rungs are made up of chemical units called **bases.** There are four possible types of bases, identified by the first letter of their longer chemical names: A (adenine), T (thymine), G (guanine), and C (cytosine). These bases form the "alphabet" used in specifying and carrying out genetic instructions.

macroevolution Long-term evolutionary change.

DNA The molecule that provides the genetic code for biological structures and the means to translate this code.

base Chemical units (adenine, thymine, guanine, cytosine) that make up part of the DNA molecule and specify genetic instructions.

TABLE 2.1   DNA Base Sequences for Amino Acids

First Base	Second Base			
	A	T	C	G
A	AAA Phenylalanine	ATA Tyrosine	ACA Cysteine	AGA Serine
	AAT Leucine	ATT Stop	ACT Stop	AGT Serine
	AAC Leucine	ATC Stop	ACC Tryptophan	AGC Serine
	AAG Phenylalanine	ATG Tyrosine	ACG Cysteine	AGG Serine
T	TAA Isoleucine	TTA Asparagine	TCA Serine	TGA Threonine
	TAT Isoleucine	TTT Lysine	TCT Arginine	TGT Threonine
	TAC Methionine	TTC Lysine	TCC Arginine	TGC Threonine
	TAG Isoleucine	TTG Asparagine	TCG Serine	TGG Threonine
C	CAA Valine	CTA Aspartic acid	CCA Glycine	CGA Alanine
	CAT Valine	CTT Glutamic acid	CCT Glycine	CGT Alanine
	CAC Valine	CTC Glutamic acid	CCC Glycine	CGC Alanine
	CAG Valine	CTG Aspartic acid	CCG Glycine	CGG Alanine
G	GAA Leucine	GTA Histidine	GCA Arginine	GGA Proline
	GAT Leucine	GTT Glutamine	GCT Arginine	GGT Proline
	GAC Leucine	GTC Glutamine	GCC Arginine	GGC Proline
	GAG Leucine	GTG Histidine	GCG Arginine	GGG Proline

Rows refer to the first of the three bases, and columns refer to the second of the three bases. These base sequences are for the DNA molecule. The 64 different combinations code for 20 amino acids and one termination sequence ("Stop"). To convert to messenger RNA, substitute U for A, A for T, G for C, and C for G. To convert to transfer RNA, substitute U for A.

All biological structures, from nerve cells to blood cells to bone cells, are made up predominantly of proteins. Proteins in turn are made up of amino acids, whose chemical properties allow them to bond together to form proteins. Each amino acid is coded for by three of the four chemical bases just discussed. For example, the base sequence CGA provides the code for the amino acid alanine, and the base sequence TTT codes for the amino acid lysine. There are 64 (4^3) possible codes that can be specified, using some combination of three bases. This might not seem like a lot, but in fact there are only 20 amino acids that need to be specified by the genetic code. The three-base code provides more than enough possibilities to code for these amino acids. In fact, some amino acids have several different codes; alanine, for example, can be specified by the base sequences CGA, CGT, CGC, and CGG. Some of the base sequences, such as ATT, act to form "punctuation" for the genetic instructions; that is, they provide the code to start or stop "messages." A list of the different DNA sequences is shown in Table 2.1.

The ability of four different bases, taken three at a time, to specify all the information needed for the synthesis of proteins is astounding. It boggles the mind that the diverse structure of complex protein molecules can be specified with only a four-letter "alphabet." As an analogy, consider the way in which computers work. All computer operations, from word processing to complex mathematical simulations, ultimately are translated to a set of computer instructions that use only a simple two-letter alphabet—on or off! These two instructions make up a larger set of codes that provide information on computer operations. These operations are combined to generate computer languages that can be used to write a variety of programs.

The ability of the DNA molecule to use the different amino acid codes lies in a simple property of the chemical bases. The base A bonds with the base T, and the base G bonds with the base C. This chemical property enables the DNA molecule to carry out a number of functions, including the ability to make copies of itself and to direct the synthesis of proteins.

Functions of DNA   The DNA molecule can make copies of itself. Remember that the DNA molecule is made up of two strands that form the long arms of the ladder. Each rung of the ladder consists of two bases. If one part of the rung contains the base A, then the other part of the rung will contain the base T because A and T bond together.

To understand how DNA can make copies of itself, consider the following sequence of bases on one strand of the DNA molecule—GGTCTC. Because A and T bond together and G and C bond together, the corresponding sequence of bases on the other strand of the DNA molecule is CCAGAG. The DNA molecule can separate into two distinct strands. Once separate, each strand attracts free-floating bases. The strand GGTCTC attracts the bases CCAGAG, and the strand CCAGAG attracts the bases GGTCTC. When the new bases have attached themselves to the original strands, the result is two identical DNA molecules. This process is diagrammed in Figure 2.2. Keep in mind that this description is somewhat oversimplified—in reality, the process is biochemically much more complex.

The ability of the DNA molecule to control protein synthesis also involves the attraction of complementary bases but with the help of another molecule—ribonucleic acid, or **RNA** for short. In simple terms, RNA serves as the messenger for the information coded by the DNA molecule. One major difference between DNA and RNA is that in RNA the base A attracts a base called U (uracil) instead of T.

Consider the DNA base sequence GGT. In protein synthesis, the DNA molecule separates into two strands and one strand (containing CCA) becomes inactive. The active strand, GGT, attracts free-floating bases to form a strand of **messenger RNA.** Because A bonds with T and G bonds with C, this strand consists of the sequence CCA. The strand then travels to the site of protein synthesis. Once there, the strand of messenger RNA transfers its information via **transfer RNA,** which is a free-floating molecule. The sequence of messenger RNA containing the sequence CCA attracts a transfer RNA molecule with a complementary sequence—GGU. The result is that the amino acid proline (specified by the RNA sequence GGU or the DNA sequence GGT) is included in the chain of amino acids making up a particular protein. To summarize, one strand of the DNA molecule produces the complementary strand of messenger RNA, which attracts a complementary strand of transfer RNA, which carries the specified amino acid. This process is illustrated for the DNA sequence GGT in Figure 2.3.

RNA The molecule that functions to carry out the instructions for protein synthesis specified by the DNA molecule.

messenger RNA The form of RNA that transports the genetic instructions from the DNA molecule to the site of protein synthesis.

transfer RNA A free-floating molecule that is attracted to a strand of messenger RNA, resulting in the synthesis of a protein chain.

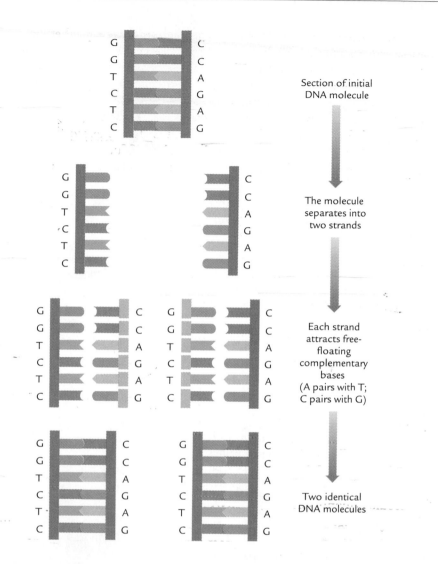

FIGURE 2.2

Replication of the DNA molecule.

This simplified discussion shows the basic nature of the structure and functions of the DNA molecule. More advanced discussion can be found in most genetics textbooks. For our purposes, however, the broad view will suffice. If we consider DNA as a "code," we can then look at the processes of transmission and change of information without actually having to consider the exact biochemical mechanisms.

Chromosomes and Genes

In many organisms (including humans), most of the DNA is contained in a separate part of the cell (the nucleus). Another form of DNA, contained in a part of the cell called the mitochondrion, is discussed later in Chapter 5. The DNA sequences are bound together by proteins in long strands called **chromosomes** that are found within the nucleus of each cell. With the

chromosome A long strand of DNA sequences.

1. Section of initial DNA molecule

2. DNA molecule temporarily separates and one strand becomes active. Free-floating complementary bases (with U replacing T) are attracted to form messenger RNA.

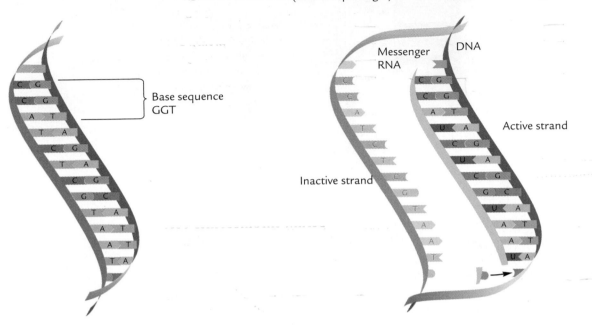

Base sequence GGT

Messenger RNA

DNA

Active strand

Inactive strand

3. Messenger RNA travels to the ribosomes, the site of protein synthesis. As ribosomes move along messenger RNA, transfer RNA picks up amino acids and lines up according to the base complements. Each transfer RNA molecule transfers its amino acid to the next active transfer RNA as it leaves, resulting in a chain of amino acids.

4. This chain of amino acids forms a protein.

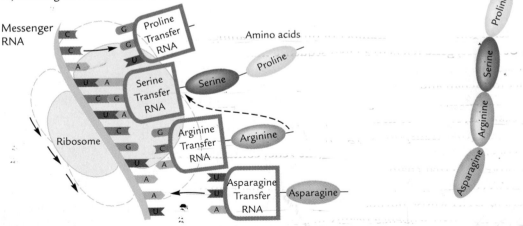

Messenger RNA

Proline Transfer RNA

Amino acids

Proline

Serine Transfer RNA

Serine

Ribosome

Arginine Transfer RNA

Arginine

Asparagine Transfer RNA

Asparagine

Proline

Serine

Arginine

Asparagine

FIGURE 2.3

Protein synthesis.

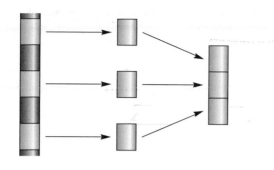

FIGURE 2.4

Diagram of messenger RNA (mRNA) showing regions of coding (exons) and noncoding (introns). The introns are removed from the pre-mRNA, and the exons then splice together to form the mature mRNA.

Pre-mRNA consists of exons (green) and introns (red).

Introns are removed.

Exons are spliced together to form mature mRNA.

exception of those in the sex cells (egg and sperm), chromosomes occur in pairs. Most body cells contain both members of these pairs. Different species have different numbers of chromosomes. For example, humans have 23 pairs, chimpanzees have 24 pairs, fruit flies have 4 pairs, and certain plant species have thousands of pairs. There is no relationship between the number of chromosome pairs a species has and its intelligence or biological complexity.

With certain exceptions, each cell in the human body contains a complete set of chromosomes and DNA. Nerve cells contain the same DNA as bone cells, for example, and vice versa. Some type of regulation takes place within different cells to ensure that only certain genes are expressed in the right places, but the exact nature of this regulation is not known completely at present.

polypeptide – compound containing many amino acids

Genes   The term *gene* can have a number of different meanings depending on context. Used here, **gene** refers to a DNA sequence that includes the code for a functional polypeptide (a compound containing many amino acids) or RNA product (Strachan and Read 1996), that is, a section of DNA that has an identifiable function, such as the gene that determines a particular blood group. One example, referred to in later chapters, is the **hemoglobin** molecule in your blood (that transports oxygen), which is made up of four protein chains. For each chain, a section of DNA (the gene) contains the genetic code for the proteins in that chain.

Not all DNA contains genes; much of our DNA is made up of noncoding sequences of DNA whose purpose (if any) is not known. Even within genes, not all of the DNA sequence results in a polypeptide product. The DNA sequence of a gene can contain both sections that code for amino acids that make up proteins (called **exons**) and sections that do not code for amino acids that make up proteins (called **introns**). The formation of mature RNA involves removal of the noncoding sections and splicing together of the coding sections (Figure 2.4).

gene A DNA sequence that codes for a functional polypeptide or RNA product.

hemoglobin The molecule in blood cells that transports oxygen.

exon A section of DNA that codes for the amino acids that make up proteins. It is contrasted with an intron.

intron A section of DNA that does not code for the amino acids that make up proteins. It is contrasted with an exon.

Aside from the manufacture of proteins, another function of genes is the regulation of biological processes. For example, in many humans the enzyme needed to digest milk sugar stops being produced several years after birth. Or consider the fact that sexual maturation in humans occurs during adolescence and not in infancy. The expression of many biological characteristics is regulated to take effect at particular times. Genes that are responsible for this regulation are known as **regulatory genes,** and they act by turning other genes on or off at the appropriate time.

Regulatory genes may have great evolutionary significance. For example, regulatory genes may help explain the great physical differences between chimpanzees and humans even though more than 98 percent of our structural genes are identical. The major genetic difference between humans and chimpanzees may be caused by regulatory genes, which act on the timing of growth and development and could lead to differences in brain size, facial structures, and other physical features.

A possible example of regulatory genes is the absence of teeth in birds. Evolutionary analysis has concluded that modern birds evolved from primitive reptiles. One major change in this evolution is that birds have no teeth (other than the egg tooth they use in hatching). In 1980, however, scientists were able to induce the tissue of a hen to grow teeth! Teeth are produced by certain outer embryonic tissues that form the enamel and other inner tissues that form the dentin underneath. In what appears at first to be a bizarre experiment, Kollar and Fisher (1980) combined the outer tissues of a hen with the inner tissues of a mouse. These grafts produced dentin and teeth. Modern birds lack the necessary type of tissue to form dentin but still have the capacity to form it when we combine their tissue in the laboratory with the appropriate tissue from another animal (the mouse, in this case). This experiment shows that the genetic code for teeth still exists in birds, but it is turned off, most likely by some combination of regulatory genes.

Another example suggesting the action of regulatory genes is the number of toes in horses. Modern horses have one single toe, although occasionally horses are born with two or three toes (Gould 1983). It appears that horses still have the genetic code for additional toes but that these instructions are turned off.

During the 1980s, a group of regulatory genes known as **homeobox genes** was discovered. These genes encode a sequence of 60 amino acids that regulate embryonic development. Specifically, they subdivide a developing embryo into different regions from head to tail that then form limbs and other structures. One fascinating aspect of this discovery is that these genes are similar in many organisms, such as insects, mice, and humans. Preliminary research suggests that the process of embryonic development into head, trunk, and tail may have occurred only once in evolution (De Robertis et al. 1990). Another example of homeobox genes was found in a study of the development of wings in insects. Some insects have wings and some do not. Recent analyses suggest that wings developed *once* in the common ancestor of all insects, but in some later forms homeobox genes repressed their develop-

regulatory gene Gene that codes for the regulation of biological processes such as growth and development.

homeobox genes A group of regulatory genes that encode a sequence of 60 amino acids regulating embryonic development.

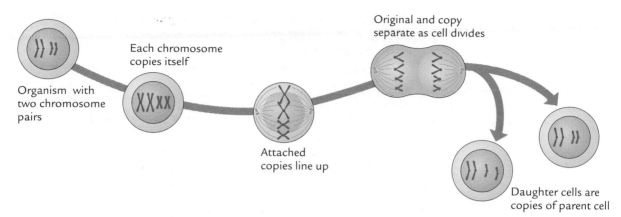

Organism with
two chromosome
pairs

Each chromosome
copies itself

Attached
copies line up

Original and copy
separate as cell divides

Daughter cells are
copies of parent cell

FIGURE 2.5

*The process of mitosis, the
formation of body cells. Each
chromosome copies itself, the
attached copies line up in the
cell, and the original and copy
split when the cell divides. The
result is two identical cells.*
(From Human Antiquity:
An Introduction to Physical
Anthropology and Archaeology,
4th ed., by Kenneth Feder and
Michael Park, Fig 4.4. Copyright
© 2001 by Mayfield Publishing
Company. Reprinted with
permission from The McGraw-Hill
Companies)

ment (Carroll et al. 1995). In other words, even wingless insects may carry the genetic code for wings—it has simply been "switched off."

Mitosis and Meiosis   The DNA molecule provides for the transmission of genetic information. Production of proteins and regulation are only two aspects of information transfer. Because organisms start life as a single cell that subsequently multiplies, it is essential that the genetic information within the initial cell be transferred to all future cells. The ability of DNA to replicate itself is involved in the process of cell replication, known as **mitosis** (Figure 2.5). When a cell divides, each chromosome duplicates and then splits. Each chromosome has replicated itself so that when the cell finishes dividing, the result is two cells with the full set of chromosomes.

The process is different when information is passed on from one generation to the next. The genetic code is passed on from parents to offspring through the sex cells—the sperm in males and the egg in females. The sex cells, however, do not contain the full set of chromosomes but only one chromosome from each pair (i.e., only one-half of the set). Whereas your other body cells have a total of 46 chromosomes (2 each for 23 pairs), your sex cells contain only 23 chromosomes (1 from each pair). When you have a child, you contribute 23 chromosomes and your mate contributes 23 chromosomes. Your child then has the normal complement of 46 chromosomes in 23 pairs. If both chromosomes in each pair were passed on, your children would have 23 pairs from both you and your mate, for a total of 46 pairs. Your children's children would receive 46 pairs from each parent, for a total of 92 pairs. If this process continued, there would soon not be enough room in a cell for all of the chromosome pairs.

Sex cells are created through the process of **meiosis** (Figure 2.6). In this process, chromosomes first replicate themselves, then the cell divides and then divides again without replicating. For sperm cells, four sex cells are produced from the initial set of 23 pairs of chromosomes. The process is similar in egg cells, except that only one of the four cells is functional.

The process of meiosis is extremely important in understanding genetic inheritance. Because only 1 of each pair of chromosomes is found in a

mitosis The process of replication of chromosomes in body cells.

meiosis The creation of sex cells by replication of chromosomes followed by cell division.

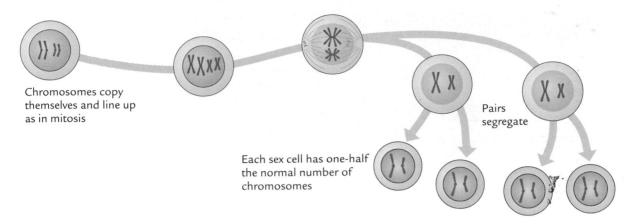

Chromosomes copy themselves and line up as in mitosis

Pairs segregate

Each sex cell has one-half the normal number of chromosomes

FIGURE 2.6

The process of meiosis, the formation of sex cells. Meiosis begins in the same way as mitosis: each chromosome makes a copy of itself. The pairs of chromosomes then segregate, forming four sex cells, each with one chromosome rather than a pair of chromosomes. (*Adapted from* Human Antiquity: An Introduction to Physical Anthropology and Archaeology, *4th ed., by Kenneth Feder and Michael Park, Fig. 4.4. Copyright © 2001 by Mayfield Publishing Company. Reprinted with permission from The McGraw-Hill Companies*)

functional sex cell, this means that a person contributes half of his or her genes to his or her offspring. The other half of their offspring's genes comes from the other parent. Usually, each human child has a full set of 23 chromosome pairs, 1 of each pair from each parent (Figure 2.7).

The Human Genome Project

The total DNA sequence of an organism is known as its **genome.** In humans, the genome is approximately 3 billion base pairs in length. Here is one way to appreciate the total length of the human genome. If you were to read the sequence aloud (A, T, T, etc.) at the rate of one base per second, it would take you close to 100 years to finish, assuming you never slept or did anything else. The past 15 years has seen the growth of new technologies that enabled researchers to completely sequence the genomes for a number of organisms, one of which being fruit flies.

The Human Genome Project (HGP) began in 1990 as an international effort to sequence the human genome. By the end of 2000, this sequencing was more than 95 percent complete. Preliminary reports were published in early 2001 by two different groups, the International Human Genome Sequencing Consortium (2001) and another group led by Celera Genomics (Venter et al. 2001). Although this is an incredible achievement, the sequencing of the human genome is just the start of a new era in genetics research. We now have most of the actual genetic code sequenced, but we are far from understanding how all of it operates, or the relationship of different genes to actual biological structures.

Preliminary analyses of the human genome have yielded some interesting results. Only a small fraction of our genome, roughly 1.1 percent to 1.5 percent, actually codes for proteins (Pennisi 2001). The remaining DNA does not contain coding DNA sequences and has often been referred to as "junk DNA." This label may simply be a reflection of our uncertainty, however, as it is suggested that some of this noncoding DNA may serve some purpose, such as the sequences that determine whether certain genes are turned on or off (Vogel 2001).

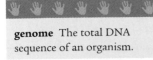

genome The total DNA sequence of an organism.

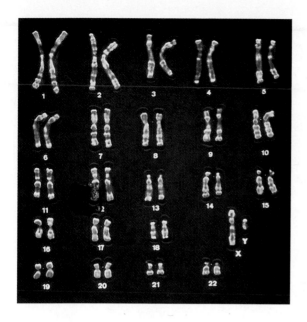

FIGURE 2.7

All 23 pairs of chromosomes typically found in a human being. This set of chromosomes came from a man—note that the 23rd pair has an X chromosome and a Y chromosome. (© CNRI/ Science Photo Library/Photo Researchers, Inc.)

One of the most unexpected results to date is the estimated number of genes in the human genome. Previous work had suggested a total of roughly 100,000 genes, but the Human Genome Project has yielded estimates of only 30,000 to 40,000 genes, which is only twice the number of genes found in worms or flies (International Human Genome Sequencing Consortium 2001). However, human genes are more complex and are able to serve multiple functions. Rather than the older view that a single gene codes for a single protein, it appears that human genes can code for three proteins on average by using different combinations of exons in a given gene (Pennisi 2001). The estimated number of genes is still tentative, and Wright et al. (2001) have suggested that the actual number might be higher, perhaps around 70,000.

Although the news media have focused attention of the results of the Human Genome Project on possible biomedical applications, such as genetic therapies for disease, we must keep in mind that we are still far from understanding the complexity of our genetic code. In addition, the genetic sequence tells us only a portion of the story; we also need to understand how genetic information is expressed in different environments. It would be overly simplistic to view genetics, and genetics alone, as determining our biology or behavior. Still, it is likely that continuing work on the human genome will contribute to our understanding of such complex issues and provide us with a clearer understanding of genetics in relationship to morphology, disease, behavior, population history, and other aspects of humanity.

MENDELIAN GENETICS

Many of the facts about genetic inheritance were discovered over a century before the structure of DNA was known. Although people knew where babies

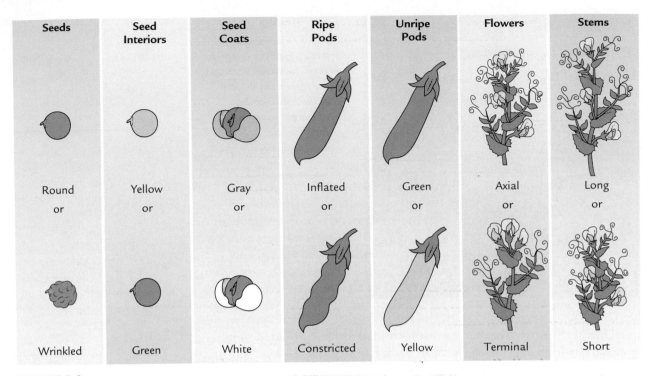

Seeds	Seed Interiors	Seed Coats	Ripe Pods	Unripe Pods	Flowers	Stems
Round	Yellow	Gray	Inflated	Green	Axial	Long
or	or	or	or	or	or	or
Wrinkled	Green	White	Constricted	Yellow	Terminal	Short

FIGURE 2.8

The seven phenotypic characteristics investigated by Gregor Mendel in his experiments on breeding in pea plants. Each of the seven traits has two distinct phenotypes.

came from and noted the close resemblance of parents and children, the mechanisms of inheritance were unknown until the nineteenth century. An Austrian priest, Gregor Mendel (1822–1884), carried out an extensive series of experiments in plant breeding. His carefully tabulated results provided the basis of what we know about the mechanisms of genetic inheritance.

Before Mendel's research, it was commonly assumed that inheritance involved the blending together of genetic information in the egg and sperm. The genetic material was thought to mix together in the same way that different color paints mix together. Mendel's experiments showed a different pattern of inheritance—that the genetic information is inherited in discrete units (genes). These genes do not blend together in an offspring.

In one experiment, Mendel crossed pea plants whose seeds were yellow with pea plants whose seeds were green (Figure 2.8). Under the idea of blending, one might expect all offspring to have mustard-colored seeds—a mixture of the yellow and green. In reality, Mendel found that all the offspring plants had yellow seeds. This discovery suggested that somehow one trait (yellow seed color) dominated in its effects.

When Mendel crossed the plants in this new generation together, he found that some of their offspring had yellow seeds and some had green seeds. Somehow the genetic information for green seeds had been hidden for a generation and then appeared again. Mendel counted how many there were of each color. The ratio of plants with yellow seeds to those with green seeds was very close to 3:1. This finding suggested to Mendel that a regular process occurred during inheritance that could be explained in terms of simple mathematical principles. With these and other results, Mendel formulated several principles of inheritance. Though Mendel's work remained virtually unknown during his lifetime, his work was rediscovered in 1900. In recognition of his accomplishments, the science of genetic inheritance is called Mendelian genetics.

Genotypes and Phenotypes

The specific position of a gene or DNA sequence on a chromosome is called a **locus** (plural loci). The alternative forms of a gene or DNA sequence at a locus are called **alleles.** For example, a number of different genetic systems control the types of molecules present on the surface of red blood cells. One of these blood groups, known as the MN system, determines whether or not you have M molecules, N molecules, or both on the surface of your red blood cells. The MN system has two forms, or alleles—*M* and *N*. Another blood group system, the ABO system, has three alleles—*A, B,* and *O*. Even though three different forms of this gene are found in the human species, each individual has only two genes at the ABO locus. Some genetic loci have only one allele, some have two, and some have three or more.

Mendel's Law of Segregation   The genetic basis of any trait is determined by an allele from each parent. At any given locus there are two alleles, one on each member of the chromosome pair. One allele came from the mother, and one allele came from the father. Within body cells, alleles occur in pairs, and when sex cells are formed, only one of each pair is passed on (**Mendel's Law of Segregation**).

The two alleles at a locus in an individual specify the **genotype,** the genetic endowment of an individual. The two alleles might be the same form or might be different. If the alleles from both parents are the same, the genotype is **homozygous.** If the alleles from the parents are different, the genotype is **heterozygous.**

The actual observable trait is known as the **phenotype.** The relationship between genotype and phenotype is affected by the relationship between the two alleles present at any locus. If the genotype is homozygous, both alleles contain the same genetic information. What happens in heterozygotes, where the two alleles are different?

Dominant and Recessive Alleles   In a heterozygote, an allele is **dominant** when it masks the effect of the other allele at a given locus. The opposite of a dominant allele is a **recessive** allele, whose effect may be masked. A simple example helps make these concepts clearer. One genetic trait in human beings is the ability to taste certain substances, including a chemical known as PTC. The ability to taste PTC appears to be controlled by a single locus and is also affected to some extent by environmental factors such as diet. There are two alleles for the PTC-tasting trait: the allele *T,* which is also called the "taster" allele, and the allele *t,* which is also called the "nontaster" allele. Given these two alleles, three combinations of alleles can be present in an

locus The specific location of a gene or DNA sequence on a chromosome.

allele The alternative form of a gene or DNA sequence that occurs at a given locus. Some loci have only one allele, some have two, and some have many alternative forms. Alleles occur in pairs, one on each chromosome.

Mendel's Law of Segregation Sex cells contain one of each pair of alleles.

genotype The genetic endowment of an individual from the two alleles present at a given locus.

homozygous Both alleles at a given locus are identical.

heterozygous The two alleles at a given locus are different.

phenotype The observable appearance of a given genotype in the organism.

dominant allele An allele that masks the effect of the other allele (which is recessive) in a heterozygous genotype.

recessive allele An allele whose effect is masked by the other allele (which is dominant) in a heterozygous genotype.

TABLE 2.2   Genotypes and Phenotypes for PTC Tasting

Genotype	Phenotype
TT	Taster
Tt	Taster
tt	Nontaster

Because *T* is dominant, the genotypes *TT* and *Tt* both produce the taster phenotype. This example is somewhat oversimplified because in reality the phenotype can also be affected by diet.

individual. A person could have the *T* allele from both parents, which would give the genotype *TT*. A person could have a *t* allele from both parents, giving the genotype *tt*. Both *TT* and *tt* are homozygous genotypes because both alleles are the same. The third possible genotype occurs when the allele from one parent is *T* and the allele from the other parent is *t*. This gives the heterozygous genotype of *Tt*. It does not matter which parent provided the *T* allele and which provided the *t* allele; the genotype is the same in both cases.

What phenotype is associated with each genotype? The phenotype is affected both by the relationship of the two alleles and by the environment. For the moment, let us ignore possible environmental effects. Consider the *T* allele as providing instructions that allow tasting and the *t* allele as providing instructions for nontasting. If the genotype is *TT*, then both alleles code for tasting and the phenotype is obviously "taster." Likewise, if the genotype is *tt*, then both alleles code for nontasting and the phenotype is "nontaster." What of the heterozygote *Tt*? One allele codes for tasting and one codes for nontasting. Does this mean that both will be expressed and that a person will have the tasting ability but not to as great a degree as a person with genotype *TT*? Or does it mean that only one of the alleles is expressed? If so, which one?

There is no way you can answer this question using only the data provided so far. You must know if either the *T* or *t* allele is dominant, and this can be determined only through experimentation. For this trait, it turns out that the *T* allele is dominant and the *t* allele is recessive. When both alleles are present in a genotype, the *T* allele masks the effect of the *t* allele. Therefore, a person with the genotype *Tt* has the "taster" phenotype (Table 2.2). The relationship between genotype and phenotype does not take into consideration known environmental effects on PTC tasting. Under certain types of diet, some "tasters" will show less ability to taste weaker concentrations of the PTC chemical.

The action of dominant and recessive alleles explains why Mendel's second-generation pea plants all had yellow seeds. The allele for yellow seed color is dominant, and the allele for green seed color is recessive.

Dominance and recessiveness refer only to the effect an allele has in producing a phenotype. These terms say nothing about the frequency or value of an allele. Dominant alleles can be common or rare, harmful or helpful.

TABLE 2.3	Genotypes and Phenotypes of the MN Blood Group System
Genotype	Phenotype
MM	M molecules
MN	M and N molecules
NN	N molecules

The M and N alleles are codominant, so they are both expressed in the heterozygote.

TABLE 2.4   Genotypes and Phenotypes of the ABO System

The ABO system has three alleles (A, B, O) that code for the type of molecule on the surface of the red blood cells (A, B, and O molecules). The A and B alleles are codominant, and the O allele is recessive to both A and B.

Genotype	Phenotype
AA	A
AO	A
BB	B
BO	B
AB	AB
OO	O

Note: There are also different forms of the A allele not shown here (A_1, A_2).

Codominant Alleles   Some alleles are **codominant**, meaning that when two different alleles are present in a genotype, then both are expressed. That is, neither allele is dominant or recessive. One example of a codominant genetic system in humans is the MN blood group, mentioned previously. There are two alleles—M, which codes for the production of M molecules, and N, which codes for the production of N molecules. Therefore, there are three possible genotypes: MM, MN, and NN.

The phenotypes for the homozygous genotypes are easy to determine. Individuals with genotype MM have two alleles coding for the production of M molecules and will have the M molecule phenotype. Likewise, individuals with the genotype NN will have two N alleles and will have the N molecule phenotype. But what of the heterozygote genotype MN? Again, there is no way to answer this question without knowing the pattern of dominance. Experimentation has shown that the M and N alleles are codominant. When both are present (genotype MN), then both are expressed. Therefore, an individual with genotype MN will produce both M and N molecules. Their phenotype is MN, indicating the presence of both molecules (Table 2.3).

In complex genetic systems with more than two alleles, some alleles may be dominant and some may be codominant. A good example of dominance and codominance in the same system is the ABO blood group. The alleles, genotypes, and phenotypes of this system are described in Table 2.4.

Predicting Offspring Distributions

When parents each contribute a sex cell, they are passing on to their offspring only one allele at each locus. The possible genotypes and phenotypes of the offspring reflect a 50 percent chance of transmittal for any given allele of a parent. This simple statement of probability allows prediction of the likely distribution of genotypes and phenotypes among the offspring.

codominant Both alleles affect the phenotype of a heterozygous genotype, and neither is dominant over the other.

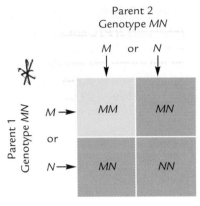
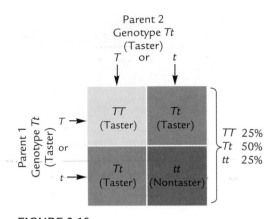

FIGURE 2.9

Inheritance of MN blood group genotypes for two parents, both with MN genotype.

FIGURE 2.10

Inheritance of PTC-tasting genotypes and phenotypes for two parents, both with the Tt *genotype. Phenotypes are shown in parentheses.*

Figure 2.9 illustrates this method using the MN blood group system for two hypothetical parents, each with the genotype *MN.* Each parent has a 50 percent chance of passing on an *M* allele and a 50 percent chance of passing on an *N* allele. Given these probabilities, we expect one out of four offspring (25 percent) to have genotype *MM,* and therefore phenotype M. In two out of four cases (50 percent), we expect the offspring to have genotype *MN,* and therefore phenotype MN. Finally, in one out of four cases (25 percent), we expect the offspring to have genotype *NN,* and therefore phenotype N. Of course, different parental genotypes will give a different set of offspring probabilities.

Remember that these distributions give the expected probabilities. The exact distributions will not always occur because each offspring is an independent event. If the hypothetical couple first has a child with the genotype *MN,* this will not influence the genotype of their next child. The distributions give the proportions expected for a very large number of offspring.

To help understand the difference between expected and actual distribution, consider coin flipping. If you flip a coin, you expect to get heads 50 percent of the time and tails 50 percent of the time. If you flip 10 coins one after another, you expect to get five heads and five tails. You may, however, get four heads and six tails.

Analysis of possible offspring shows that recessive alleles can produce an interesting effect; it is possible for children to have a different phenotype from either of the parents. For example, consider two parents, both with the genotype *Tt* for the PTC-tasting locus. Both parents have the "taster" phenotype. What genotypes and phenotypes will their children be likely to have? The expected genotype distribution is 25 percent *TT,* 50 percent *Tt,* and 25 percent *tt* (Figure 2.10).

Given this distribution of genotypes, what is the probable distribution of phenotypes? Genotypes *TT* and *Tt* are both "tasters," and therefore 75 percent of the children are expected to also be "tasters." Twenty-five percent of

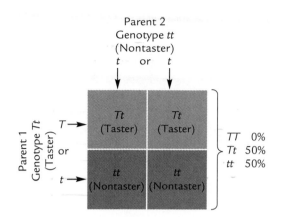

Parent 2
Genotype *tt*
(Nontaster)
t   or   *t*

Parent 1
Genotype *Tt*
(Taster)

| | *Tt* (Taster) | *Tt* (Taster) |
| | *tt* (Nontaster) | *tt* (Nontaster) |

TT 0%
Tt 50%
tt 50%

the children, however, are expected to have the genotype *tt* and will therefore have the "nontaster" phenotype. These children would have a different phenotype from either parent. An additional example, also using the PTC-tasting locus, is shown in Figure 2.11, which looks at the genotype and phenotype offspring distributions in the case where one parent has the *Tt* genotype and the other has the *tt* genotype.

A recessive trait, then, can remain hidden in one generation. This fact has great implications for genetic disease. For example, the disease cystic fibrosis occurs when a person is homozygous for a recessive allele. Therefore, two parents who have the heterozygous genotype do not manifest the disease, but they have a 25 percent chance of giving birth to a child who has the recessive homozygous condition and therefore the disease.

Chromosomes and Inheritance

Alleles occur in pairs. Mendel showed that when alleles are passed on from parents to offspring, only one of each pair is contributed by each parent. The specific chromosome at any pair that is passed on is random. There is a 50 percent chance of either chromosome being passed on each time a sex cell is created.

Mendel's Law of Independent Assortment   Mendel's experiments revealed another aspect of probability in inheritance and the creation of sex cells. **Mendel's Law of Independent Assortment** states that the segregation of any pair of chromosomes does not influence the segregation of any other pair of chromosomes. In other words, chromosomes from separate pairs are inherited independently.

For example, imagine an organism with three chromosome pairs that we will label 1, 2, and 3. To keep the members of each pair straight in our minds, we label each chromosome of each pair as A or B. This hypothetical organism has six chromosomes: 1A, 1B, 2A, 2B, 3A, and 3B. During the creation of a sex cell, the 1A chromosome has a 50 percent chance of occurring, and so does the 1B chromosome. This same logic applies to chromosome pairs 2

Mendel's Law of Independent Assortment
The segregation of any pair of chromosomes does not affect the probability of segregation for other pairs of chromosomes.

FIGURE 2.12

Schematic diagram illustrating Mendel's Law of Independent Assortment. This hypothetical organism has three pairs of chromosomes (1, 2, and 3), each of which has two chromosomes indicated by the letters A and B. For example, the chromosomes for chromosome pair 1 are 1A and 1B. During meiosis, only one of each pair is passed on to a sex cell, that is, 1A or 1B, 2A or 2B, and 3A or 3B. The probability of a particular chromosome being passed on from any pair is independent of the other pairs so that there are eight possible combinations.

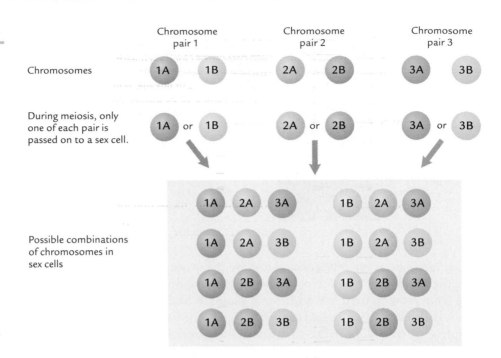

and 3. Mendel's Law of Independent Assortment states that the segregation of one pair of chromosomes does not affect the segregation of any other pair of chromosomes. It is just as likely to have a sex cell containing chromosomes 1A, 2A, and 3A as it is to have a sex cell containing chromosomes 1A, 2A, and 3B. There are eight possible and equally likely outcomes for the sex cells: 1A-2A-3A, 1A-2A-3B, 1A-2B-3A, 1A-2B-3B, 1B-2A-3A, 1B-2A-3B, 1B-2B-3A, and 1B-2B-3B (Figure 2.12). Given that any individual could have any one of the eight possible sex cells from *both* parents, the total number of combinations of offspring in this hypothetical organism is $8 \times 8 = 64$.

Independent assortment provides a powerful mechanism for shuffling different combinations of chromosomes and thus introduces great potential for genetic diversity. In humans, who have 23 chromosome pairs, the numbers are even more impressive. From any given individual, there are $2^{23} = 8,388,608$ possible combinations of chromosomes in sex cells. This means that two parents could produce a maximum of 70,368,744,177,664 genetically unique offspring!

Linkage   A major implication of Mendel's Law of Independent Assortment is that genes are inherited independently. This is true only to the extent that genes are on different chromosomes. Remember, it is the pairs of chromosomes that separate during meiosis, not each individual pair of alleles. When alleles are on the same chromosome, they are inherited together. This is called **linkage.** Linked alleles are not inherited independently because they are, by definition, on the same chromosome.

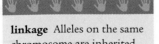

linkage Alleles on the same chromosome are inherited together.

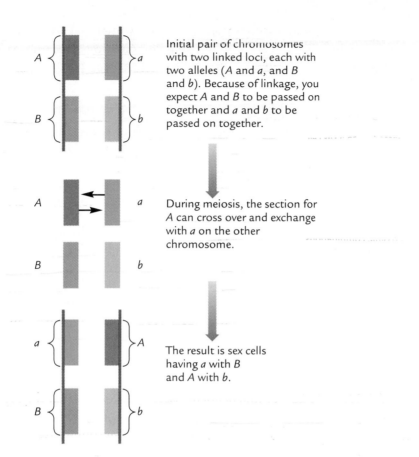

Initial pair of chromosomes with two linked loci, each with two alleles (*A* and *a*, and *B* and *b*). Because of linkage, you expect *A* and *B* to be passed on together and *a* and *b* to be passed on together.

During meiosis, the section for *A* can cross over and exchange with *a* on the other chromosome.

The result is sex cells having *a* with *B* and *A* with *b*.

FIGURE 2.13

Crossing over in chromosomes.

Recombination   When loci are linked, they will tend to be inherited as a unit. As an example, imagine that two loci, each with two alleles (*A* and *a* for the first locus and *B* and *b* for the second locus), are located on the same chromosome. Further, imagine that one of the chromosomes contains the *A* allele for the first locus and the *B* allele for the second locus and that the other chromosome contains the alleles *a* and *b* (Figure 2.13). Under linkage, we expect the two loci to be inherited as a unit. That is, your possible sex cells could have *A* and *B* or *a* and *b*. Any offspring inheriting the *A* allele would also inherit the *B* allele, and any offspring inheriting the *a* allele would also inherit the *b* allele.

This does not always happen. During meiosis, chromosome pairs sometimes exchange pieces, a process known as **crossing over.** For example, the segment of DNA containing the *a* allele could switch with the segment of DNA containing the *A* allele on the other chromosome. Therefore, you could have a sex cell with *a* and *B* or a sex cell with *A* and *b* (see Figure 12.13). The result of crossing over is known as **recombination,** the production of new combinations of genes and DNA sequences. (Recombination describes the result, and crossing over describes the process.)

crossing over The exchange of DNA between chromosomes during meiosis.

recombination The production of new combinations of DNA sequences caused by exchanges of DNA during meiosis.

Recombination does not change the genetic material. The alleles are still the same, but they can occur in different combinations. Recombination provides yet another mechanism for increasing genetic variation by providing new combinations of alleles.

Sex Chromosomes and Sex Determination   One of the 23 pairs of human chromosomes is called the sex chromosome pair because these chromosomes contain the genetic information determining the individual's sex. There are two forms of sex chromosomes, X and Y. Females have two X chromosomes (XX), and males have one X and one Y chromosome (XY).

The Y chromosome is much smaller than the X chromosome. Therefore, almost all genes found on X are not found on Y. This means that males possess only one allele for certain traits because their Y chromosome lacks the corresponding section of DNA. Therefore, males will manifest a trait for which they have only one allele, whereas females require the same allele from both parents to show the trait. An example of this sex difference is hemophilia, a genetic disorder that interferes with the normal process of blood clotting. The allele for hemophilia is recessive and is found on the segment of the X chromosome that has no corresponding portion on the Y chromosome. For females to be hemophiliac, they must inherit two copies of this allele, one from each parent. This is unlikely because the hemophilia allele is rare. Males, however, need to inherit only one copy of the X chromosome from the mother. As a result, hemophilia is more common in males than females.

[handwritten margin note: does this mean inheritance of disease from Mother's is higher?]

The Genetics of Complex Physical Traits

The discussion of genetics thus far has focused on simple discrete genetic traits. Traits such as the MN blood group are genetically "simple" because they result from the action of a single locus with a clear-cut mode of inheritance. These traits are also discrete, meaning that they produce a finite number of phenotypes. For example, you have the M or the N or the MN phenotype for the MN blood group system; you cannot have an intermediate phenotype. Your MN phenotype is also produced entirely from genetic factors. It is not influenced by the environment. Except for a complete blood transfusion, your MN blood group phenotype is the same all of your life.

These simple discrete traits are very useful for demonstrating the basic principles of Mendelian inheritance. It is not wise, however, to think of all biological traits as resulting from a single locus, exhibiting a finite number of phenotypes, or not being affected by the environment. Many of the characteristics of interest in human evolution, such as skin color, body size, brain size, and intelligence, do not fall into this simple category. Such traits have a complex mode of inheritance in that one or more genes may contribute to the phenotype and they may be affected by the environment. The combined action of genetics and environment produces traits with a continuous distribution. An example is human height. People do not come in three different

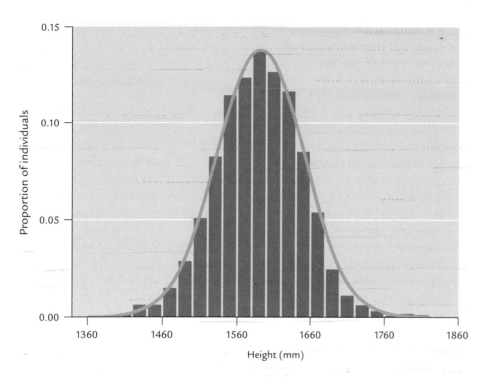

FIGURE 2.14

The distribution of a normally distributed continuous trait. This figure is based on the actual distribution of height (mm) of 1,986 Irish women (author's unpublished data). The height of the curve represents the proportion of women with any given height. Most individuals have a value close to the average for the population (the highest point on the curve, which corresponds to a height of 1,589 mm). The solid line is the fit of the normal distribution.

heights (short, medium, and tall), nor five, nor twenty. Height can take on an infinite number of phenotypes. People can be 1,700 mm tall, 1,701 mm tall, and any value in between, such as 1,700.3 mm or 1,700.65 mm.

Complex traits tend to produce more individuals with average values than extreme values. It is not uncommon to find human males between 1,676 and 1,981 mm (5.5 and 6.5 feet) tall. It is much rarer to find someone taller than 2,134 mm (7 feet). A typical distribution of a complex trait, human height, is shown in Figure 2.14.

Polygenic Traits and Pleiotropy Many complex traits are **polygenic,** the result of two or more loci. When several loci act to control a trait, many different genotypes and phenotypes can result. A number of physical characteristics, such as human skin color and height, may be polygenic. A single allele can also have multiple effects on an organism. When an allele has effects on multiple traits, this is referred to as **pleiotropy.** In chickens, one of the alleles that causes white feather color also acts to slow down overall body growth (Lerner and Libby 1976). In humans, the sickle cell allele affects the structure of the blood's hemoglobin and also leads to changes in overall body growth and health.

The concepts of polygenic traits and pleiotropy are important in considering the interrelated nature of biological systems. Analysis of simple discrete traits on a gene-by-gene basis is useful in understanding genetics, but it should not lead you to think that any organism is simply a collection of single, independent loci.

polygenic A complex genetic trait affected by two or more loci.

pleiotropy A single allele that has multiple effects on an organism.

a. Each gene has a distinct biological effect.

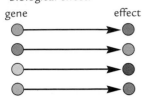

b. Polygenic trait: many genes contribute to a single effect.

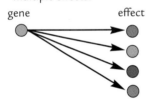

c. Pleiotropy: a gene has multiple effects.

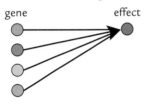

d. Polygenic traits and pleiotropy.

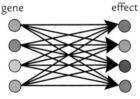

FIGURE 2.15

The relationship between a gene and a biological effect. (a) Single gene, single effect. (b) Polygenic trait. (c) Pleiotropy. (d) A polygenic trait and pleiotropy.

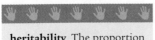

heritability The proportion of total variation of a trait due to genetic variation.

Figure 2.15 shows several different models of genetic interaction. Figure 2.15a represents the nature of some simple genetic traits, whereby each cause has a single effect. Figure 2.15b represents a polygenic trait, whereby many loci contribute to a single effect. Pleiotropic effects are shown in Figure 2.15c, whereby a single allele has multiple effects. Figure 2.15d is the most realistic model for many complex traits; each allele has multiple effects, and each effect has multiple causes. In this case, the trait is caused by polygenic and pleiotropic effects. To complicate matters, consider variations of this model in which not all alleles have the same effect, some alleles are dominant and some are not, and environmental factors act to obscure what we actually observe. It is no wonder that the study of the genetics of complex traits is extremely difficult, requiring sophisticated mathematical methods.

Heritability   Complex traits reflect the joint effect of genetics and the environment. A common measure in studies of complex traits is **heritability**, which is the proportion of total variance in a trait that is attributable to genetic variation in a specific population (the value can be different in different populations). Complex traits show variation; for example, some people are taller than others, and some people have longer heads than others. The variation that we see is the total phenotypic variation. Some of this variation is due to genetic factors; some people may have a genetic potential for being taller, for example. The variation caused by genetic factors is called the *genetic variation*. Some of the total variation is also due to differences in environmental factors. For example, some people may have different diets, which would affect their height. We call this the *environmental variation*. Thus, total variation is made up of two components: genetic variation and environmental variation (or, in mathematical terms, total variation = genetic variation + environmental variation). Heritability is simply the *proportion* of total variation that is due to genetic variation. That is,

$$\text{Heritability} = \frac{\text{Genetic variation}}{\text{Total variation}} = \frac{\text{Genetic variation}}{\text{Genetic} + \text{Environmental}}$$
$$\text{variation} \qquad \text{variation}$$

Heritability is computed with this formula using complex methods of comparing relatives and environmental factors to estimate the genetic and environmental components. Heritability can range from 0 (no genetic variation) to 1 (no environmental variation). A high heritability, say greater than 0.5, indicates that the majority of variation is caused by genetic variation.

Although useful, the concept of heritability can be misleading. When we hear of a trait that has a high heritability, we are tempted to conclude that the trait is controlled almost exclusively by genetic factors and that environmental factors have little effect. The problem with reading too much into the concept of heritability is that it is a *relative* measure of the degree of genetic variation in a *specific* environment. Consider, for example, an estimate of heritability for human height. If the specific population we are looking at has little variation in diet, disease, and other environmental factors that can affect height, then the environmental variation will be low. As a result, the heritability will be high. If, however, the environmental variation changes, resulting in greater differences within the population in terms of diet and other factors, then the environmental variation increases and heritability will be lower. Heritability, then, is a relative measure that can vary from one population to the next. It is not a measure of the extent to which genetics controls a trait; it is only a relative measure of variation.

Major Genes   Recently, more attention has been given to **major genes.** In a major gene model, a discernible portion of genetic variation is due to a single locus. The continuous distribution of the trait is the result of environmental effects and can be enhanced by the smaller effect of other loci. In contrast to certain polygenic models whereby all loci contribute equally, a major gene model postulates that a single locus has the greatest effect. A trait controlled by a major gene often shows the same type of distribution as a polygenic trait (see Figure 2.14). Developments in statistical analysis have allowed tests for major genes. Examples of major genes that have been discovered in humans include oxygen saturation of arterial hemoglobin (Beall et al. 1994) and obesity (Comuzzie et al. 1997). In each case, however, there was evidence that phenotypic variation was not due solely to a single gene and that other genes had a residual effect.

MUTATIONS

As shown earlier, the process of genetic inheritance produces genetic variation in offspring. The independent assortment of chromosomes during meiosis and the action of crossing over both act to create new genetic combinations. They do not act to create any new genetic material, however. To explain past evolution, we need a mechanism for introducing new alleles and variation. The origin of new genetic variation was a problem to Darwin, but we now know new alleles are brought about through the process of mutation.

Evolutionary Significance of Mutations

A **mutation** is a change in the genetic code. Mutations are the ultimate source of all genetic variation. Mutations are caused by a number of environmental factors such as background radiation, which includes radiation from the earth's crust and cosmic rays. Such background radiation is all around us, in the air we breathe and the food we eat. Mutations may also be caused by heat and ingested substances such as caffeine.

    A growing concern is the effect of environmental changes on mutation rates. Human-made radiation, as from certain industries, not only might be dangerous to exposed individuals but also might affect their future offspring by creating mutational effects in sex cells. Numerous studies of laboratory animals, such as fruit flies, have shown clearly that the mutation rate increases with exposure to radiation. Less is known about the effect of increased

major genes Genes that have the primary effect on the phenotypic distribution of a complex trait.

mutation A mechanism for evolutionary change resulting from a random change in the genetic code; the ultimate source of all genetic variation.

radiation on mutations in humans and other mammals. Studies of the children of survivors of the atomic bomb attacks in Japan at the end of World War II have so far failed to show definite evidence of any increase in the rate of mutations in sex cells (although mutations in body cells in the exposed parents were frequent). Given the definite evidence of radiation effects from experimental animals, this failure may reflect an inadequate sample size or other methodological difficulties in the human studies. Another possibility is that mammalian cells have a high capacity for DNA repair.

Mutations can take place in any cell of the body. To have evolutionary importance, however, the mutation must occur in a sex cell. A mutation in a skin cell on the end of your finger has no evolutionary significance because it will not be passed on to your offspring.

Mutations are random. That is, there is no way of predicting when a specific mutation will take place or what, if any, phenotypic effect it will have. All we can do is estimate the probability of a mutation occurring at a given locus over a given amount of time. The randomness of mutations also means that mutations do not appear when they might be needed. Many mosquitoes have adapted to insecticides because a mutation was present in the population that acted to confer some resistance to the insecticide. If that mutation had not been present, the mosquitoes would have died. The mosquitoes' need for a certain genetic variant had no effect on whether or not the mutation appeared.

Mutations can have different effects depending on the specific type of mutation and the environment. The conventional view of mutations has long been that they are mostly harmful. A classic analogy is the comparison of the genetic code with the engine of an automobile. If an engine part is changed at random, the most likely result is that the car will not operate, or at least not as well as it did before the change.

Some mutations, however, are advantageous. They lead to change that improves the survival and reproduction of organisms. In recent decades, we have also discovered that some mutations are neutral; that is, the genetic change has no detectable effect on survival or reproduction. There is continued controversy among geneticists about the relative frequency of neutral mutations. Some claim that many mutations are neutral in their effect. Others note the difficulties in detecting the effects of many mutations.

Whether or not a mutation is neutral, advantageous, or disadvantageous depends in large part on the environment. Genetic variants that are harmful in certain environments might actually be helpful in other environments.

Types of Mutations

We now recognize that there are a variety of ways in which mutations occur. Mutations can involve changes in a single DNA base, in larger sections of DNA, and in entire chromosomes. One example is the substitution of one DNA base for another, such as the widely studied **sickle cell allele.** The red blood cells produced in individuals with two copies of this allele (one from

sickle cell allele An allele of the hemoglobin locus. Individuals homozygous for this allele have sickle cell anemia.

FIGURE 2.16

Facial appearance of a child with Down syndrome. (Courtesy March of Dimes)

each parent) are misshapen and do not transport oxygen efficiently. The result is a severe form of anemia (sickle cell anemia) that leads to sickness and death. The specific cause of this allele is a mutation in the sixth amino acid (out of 146 amino acids) of the beta chain of hemoglobin. The DNA for the normal beta hemoglobin allele contains instructions for the amino acid, glutamic acid, at this position (CTC). The sickle cell mutation occurs when the base T is changed to an A, which specifies the amino acid valine (CAC). This small change affects the entire structure of the red blood cells and, in turn, the well-being of the individual.

Substitution of one base for another is only one type of mutation. Mutations can also involve the addition or deletion of a base or of large sections of DNA. In these cases, the genetic message is changed. Also, sections of DNA can be duplicated or moved from one place to another, and sections of DNA can be added or lost when crossing over is not equal.

The genetic information contained in the chromosomes can also be altered by the deletion or duplication of part or all of the chromosome. For example, an entire chromosome from a pair can be lost (**monosomy** = one chromosome) or can occur in duplicate, giving three chromosomes (**trisomy**). One result of the latter is Down syndrome, a condition characterized by certain cranial features (Figure 2.16), poor physical growth, and mental retardation (usually mild). Down syndrome is caused by the duplication of one of the 21st chromosome pair. Affected individuals have a total of 47 chromosomes, one more than the normal 46. Down syndrome can also be caused by mutations of the 21st chromosome. In some individuals, the change involves the exchange of parts of the 21st chromosome with other chromosomes.

monosomy A condition in which one chromosome rather than a pair is present in body cells.

trisomy A condition in which three chromosomes rather than a pair occur in body cells.

Several chromosomal mutations involve the sex chromosomes. One, known as Turner's syndrome, occurs when an individual has only one X chromosome instead of two. These individuals thus have only 45 chromosomes and develop as females. Those with Turner's syndrome are generally short, have undeveloped ovaries, and are sterile. Another condition, known as Klinefelter's syndrome, occurs in males with an extra X chromosome. Instead of the normal XY combination, these males have an XXY combination for a total of 47 chromosomes. They are characterized by small testes and reduced fertility.

Rates of Mutations

Specific mutations are relatively rare events, although the *exact* rate of mutations is difficult to determine in many cases. Part of the problem in determining the rate of mutations is the fact that several different base sequences can specify the same amino acid. For example, the amino acid glycine is specified by the sequence CCA. If a mutation occurs in which the third base changes from an A to a G, the net result is the sequence CCG, which also specifies glycine. This hypothetical mutation leads to no biochemical change and is considered neutral. If there is no observable change, then the mutation will usually go unnoticed.

A mutation is also more apparent if it involves a dominant allele, because a heterozygote receiving one copy of the mutant allele will show the mutant phenotype. If a mutant allele is recessive, then phenotypic expression will require two copies of the mutant allele, which is a less common event. Recessive mutant alleles go unnoticed under these circumstances.

Another problem in identifying mutations is that harmful mutations may result in spontaneous abortion (miscarriage) before pregnancy has been detected. Roughly 15 percent of all recognized conceptions result in spontaneous abortion, of which 50 percent can be traced to specific chromosomal mutations (Sutton and Wagner 1985). For such an event to be recorded, however, a woman must be aware that she is pregnant, which she usually doesn't know until a month or more after conception. Some researchers feel that a large number of unrecognized conceptions are expelled spontaneously during the first few weeks after conception. If so, any prediction of mutation rates based on recognized conceptions will be an underestimate.

Despite these problems, research has provided estimates of a range in the rates of mutation. For single-base mutations in humans, this range is from 1 to 100 mutations per million sex cells (Lerner and Libby 1976). This translates to a probability between 0.000001 and 0.0001 of a mutation occurring at a given locus for a given sex cell. Certain types of DNA sequences, such as repeated units, have higher rates.

Regardless of the specific mutation rates for a given gene or chromosome, one thing is clear—mutation rates are generally low. Given these low probabilities, it may be tempting to regard mutation as so rare that it has no special evolutionary significance. The problem with this reasoning is that the estimated rates refer to a *single* specific locus. Human chromosomes have many loci. The probability that a specific locus will show a mutation in any

PCR and Ancient DNA

In the summer of 1994, filmgoers were thrilled by the movie *Jurassic Park,* based on the novel of the same name by Michael Crichton (who studied anthropology as an undergraduate). The plot revolves around the construction of a dinosaur theme park—with live dinosaurs! In *Jurassic Park,* scientists recover amber dating back to the time of the dinosaurs. Trapped in the amber are mosquitoes who, prior to being encased in the tree sap that becomes amber, had drunk the blood of dinosaurs. Using this blood, the fictional scientists reconstruct the DNA of the original dinosaurs and bring a number of extinct species back to life.

A fascinating story, but how accurate is it? Could we reconstruct sufficient DNA sequences of ancient creatures to bring them back to life? At present, we lack the technology to do so. However, we *can* reconstruct some ancient DNA sequences (although not well enough to recreate a dinosaur). Fragments of ancient DNA *have been* reconstructed, including some from amber many millions of years old. We also have been able to obtain DNA fragments from human populations many thousands of years old (Stone and Stoneking 1993; Hagelberg 1994).

The heart of these achievements is a relatively new technique called the *polymerase chain reaction* (PCR). This technique involves the laboratory synthesis of millions of copies of DNA fragments from very small initial amounts (Erlich et al. 1991). The process is essentially cyclical—the DNA strands are separated and form the template for new strands, thus resulting in a doubling of the DNA each time through the cycle (see adjoining figure). This method is very efficient in extracting DNA sequences from very small samples. In fact, it is so efficient that one of the technical problems is that it often picks up DNA from people's cells floating around the lab as dust (Hagelberg 1994). The PCR method is also useful to anthropologists working on living human populations. Samples can be collected and transported easily—such as single plucked hairs.

The PCR method has also proven valuable in the field of forensics. Very small samples can yield sufficient DNA to help identify skeletal remains of murder victims. One notorious case involved the skeletal remains that were attributed to the infamous Nazi doctor Joseph Mengele. Extracts of bone were taken, and the DNA was amplified using PCR and then compared to the known surviving relatives of Mengele. Based on this comparison, the skeletal remains were definitely identified as having been Mengele (Hagelberg 1994). DNA analysis also has been used to look at the genetics of ancient humans dating back many tens of thousands of years. These studies are described in more detail in Chapter 13.

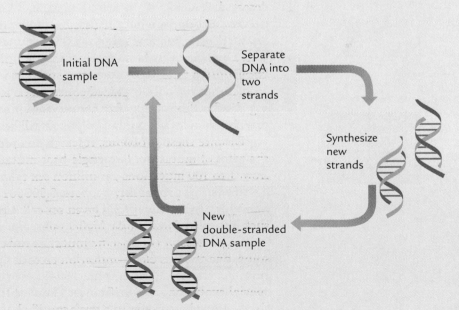

Simplified diagram of the polymerase chain reaction (PCR) used to amplify small amounts of DNA. Each time through the cycle the amount of DNA doubles.

Initial DNA sample

Separate DNA into two strands

Synthesize new strands

New double-stranded DNA sample

individual is low, but the probability of *any* locus showing a mutation is much higher.

Even though mutation is a rare event for any given locus, there is a high probability of at least one new mutation in each individual. When we consider the genetics of an entire population or species, the net result is that mutation is common within a single generation. In fact, many studies estimate that all of us carry at least one lethal recessive mutant allele.

GENETICS AND BEHAVIOR

Perhaps the most controversial topic in genetics is the question of the extent to which behavior is governed by genetic factors. The controversy arises not so much from academic debate but from the social implications, real and imagined, of this question. Problems arise out of a misunderstanding of the basic concepts of genetics or are produced by those seeking any "scientific" fact, regardless of truth, to support and further their own social or political agenda. Much of this controversy revolves around the concept of race, which is discussed in Chapter 5. The present section focuses on basic strategies involved in relating genes and behavior.

Is a behavior, such as intelligence or shyness, caused by genes ("nature") or by the physical and cultural environment ("nurture")? The debate over nature versus nurture has a long history in Western civilization. The prevalent view among scientists reflects not only current research but also the social and cultural climate of the times. Scientists are people too, as susceptible to biases and prejudices as everyone else. A major lesson of the history of science is that cultural beliefs influence the methodology and interpretation of scientific results.

At the beginning of the twentieth century, the prevalent view was that "nature" was the more important determinant of many behaviors, particularly intelligence. This emphasis shifted to "nurture" during the period from the 1930s to the 1960s, when environmental factors were seen as being the most, if not the only, important factor.

Much of the debate over nature versus nurture is nonsense, however. Any attempt to relegate human behaviors to either genetics *or* environment is fruitless. Genes and environment are both important in their effect on human behaviors. The proper question is not which is more important but rather how they interact.

Evidence of *some* genetic influence has been found for a variety of human behaviors, including intelligence test scores, autism, reading and language disabilities, eating disorders, schizophrenia, and sexual orientation, among others. These studies do not support a view that behavior is *caused* by genes but rather that genes can *influence* behavior. In a review of genetic studies of human behavior, Plomin et al. (1994) note that these analyses have consistently shown that there is at least as much environmental variation related to phenotypic variation as there is genetic variation. In other words, *both* genetic and environmental variation have been related to behavioral variation. Further, because environmental effects can be different in different populations, the relative influence of genetic and environmental variation will also differ from one population to the next.

What are the implications of the joint interaction between genetics and environment? If a behavior is affected to some extent by genetics, then is there an innate difference between people with different alleles? Not necessarily. Even if genetic differences in a behavior exist, this does not mean that those differences will override environmental factors. Studies of male sexual orientation, for example, have suggested a moderate heritability for homosexual orientation (Pillard and Bailey 1998), and some have suggested genetic susceptibility for male homosexuality is linked to a gene (or genes) on the X chromosome (Hamer et al. 1993; Hu et al. 1995). These results do not mean that there is a "gay gene" but rather that genetic factors can *influence* male sexual orientation in certain cases. Such studies also show that environmental factors play a large role in sexual orientation. As Pattatucci (1998) notes, sexual orientation is related to many factors, and "it is highly improbable that any single genetic variation or allele will be present in all homosexual individuals and absent from all heterosexual individuals" (p. 368). As is the case with many behavioral traits, the phenotype reflects a complex interaction of genetic and environmental factors.

Anne Fausto-Sterling 'How to Build a Man'

SUMMARY

The DNA molecule specifies the genetic code or set of instructions needed to produce biological structures. DNA acts along with a related molecule, RNA, to translate these instructions into proteins. The DNA is contained along structures within the cell called chromosomes. Chromosomes come in pairs. A segment of DNA that codes for a certain product is called a gene. The different forms of genes present at a locus are called alleles. The DNA molecule has the ability to make copies of itself, allowing transmission of genetic information from cell to cell and from generation to generation.

Meiosis is the process of sex cell formation that results in one of each chromosome pair being transmitted from parent to offspring. Each individual receives half of his or her alleles from each parent. The two alleles together specify the genetic constitution of an individual—the genotype. The physical manifestation of the genotype is known as the phenotype. The relationship between genotype and phenotype depends on whether an allele is dominant, recessive, or codominant. In complex physical traits, the phenotype is the result of the combined effect of genetics and environment.

The ultimate source of all genetic variation is mutation—a random change in the genetic code. Some mutations are neutral in effect; others are helpful or harmful. The effect of any mutation often depends on the specific environmental conditions. Mutations for any given allele are relatively rare events, but given the large number of loci in many organisms, it is highly probable that each individual has at least one mutant allele.

Genetic factors have been linked to human behaviors. Such behaviors appear to be influenced by both genetics and environment. Given the biocultural nature of human beings, it should be no surprise that both genes and environment have an effect on both biology and behavior.

SUPPLEMENTAL READINGS

Jones, S. 1993. *The Language of Genes: Solving the Mysteries of Our Genetic Past, Present and Future.* New York: Doubleday. A well-written general introduction to human genetics.

Marks, J. 1995. *Human Biodiversity: Genes, Race, and History.* New York: Aldine de Gruyter. A historically oriented review of different approaches to human biological variation, with many discussions of the nature of genes and the mechanisms of human genetics.

Nature, vol. 409, no. 6822 (February 15, 2001); *Science,* vol. 291, no. 5507 (February 16, 2001). These two specific issues of leading science journals both contain preliminary analyses of the human genome and include many commentaries regarding the history, current status, and possible use of data obtained from the Human Genome Project.

INTERNET RESOURCES

http://anthro.palomar.edu/biobasis/default.htm
Biological Basis of Heredity, an online tutorial about basic cell biology for anthropology students.

http://vector.cshl.org/dnaftb
DNA from the Beginning, an online tutorial of DNA.

http://www.nhgri.nih.gov/educationkit
The Human Genome Project: Exploring Our Molecular Selves, an educational Web site dealing with the Human Genome Project.

http://anthro.palomar.edu/mendel/default.htm
The Basic Principles of Genetics: An Introduction to Mendelian Genetics.

http://www3.ncbi.nlm.nih.gov/Omim
OMIM—Online Mendelian Inheritance in Man. This Web page provides a comprehensive catalog of human genes and genetic disorders.

This section, which focuses on the structure of the cell and on the processes of mitosis and meiosis, can be used as a supplement for students wishing to review the basic biology necessary for an understanding of the fundamental principles of Mendelian genetics.

THE CELL

All living creatures are made up of cells. Humans, like many organisms, are multicelled. Figure 2.17 shows some of the components of a typical cell. Two major structures are the *nucleus* and the *cytoplasm;* the latter contains a number of other structures. The entire body of the cell is enclosed by a *cell membrane.*

Within the cytoplasm, *mito-chondria* convert some cellular material into energy that is then used for cellular activity (see Chapter 5 for further discussion). *Ribosomes* are small particles that are frequently attached to a larger structure known as the *endoplasmic reticulum.* Composed of RNA and proteins, ribosomes serve as sites for the manufacture of proteins.

As discussed in Chapter 2, the DNA sequences that make up the genetic code are bound together by proteins in long strands known as *chromosomes.* In body cells, chromosomes come in pairs; humans have 23 pairs of chromosomes. The chromosomes within the nucleus of the cell contain all of the DNA, with the exception of something called mitochondrial DNA (see Chapter 5).

MITOSIS

DNA has the ability to make copies of itself. This ability is vital for transmitting genetic information from cell to cell and for transmitting genetic information from generation to generation. The replication of DNA is part of the process of cell replication. We will examine two basic processes: mitosis, the replication of body cells, and meiosis, the replication of sex cells.

Mitosis produces two identical body cells from one original. Between cell divisions, each chromosome produces an exact copy of itself, resulting in two pairs with two chromosomes

FIGURE 2.17

Schematic diagram of a cell.

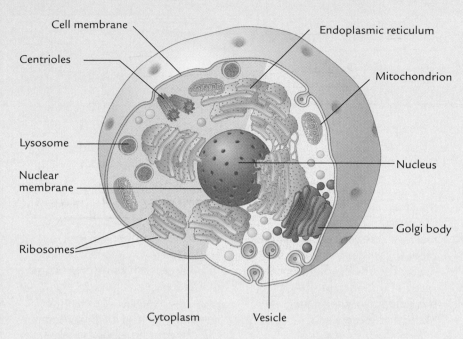

Cell membrane
Centrioles
Endoplasmic reticulum
Mitochondrion
Lysosome
Nucleus
Nuclear membrane
Ribosomes
Golgi body
Cytoplasm
Vesicle

each. When a cell divides, each part contains one of each of the pairs of chromosomes. Thus, two identical body cells, each with the full number of chromosome pairs, is produced. As outlined in Figure 2.18, five stages compose the process of mitosis: interphase, prophase, metaphase, anaphase, and telophase. (Some people do not refer to interphase as a stage.)

During *interphase,* the chromosomes that are dispersed throughout the nucleus duplicate. During *prophase,* the chromosomes, each of which is attached to its copy, become tightly coiled and move toward one another in the nucleus. Each of the two copies is called a *chromatid,* and their point of attachment is called the *centromere.* Small structures located outside the nuclear membrane, known as *centrioles* (see Figure 2.17), move toward opposite ends of the cell, and *spindle fibers* form between the centrioles. The nuclear membrane then dissolves.

During *metaphase,* the duplicated chromosomes line up along the middle of the cell and the spindle fibers attach to the centromeres. During *anaphase,*

the centromere divides and the two strands of chromatids (original and duplicate) split and move toward opposite ends of the cell. During *telophase,* new nuclear membranes form around each of the two clusters of chromosomes. Finally, the cell membrane pinches in the middle, creating two identical cells.

MEIOSIS

Meiosis, the production of sex cells (gametes), differs from mitosis in several ways. The main difference is that sex cells contain only half of an organism's DNA—one chromosome from each pair. Thus, when a new zygote, or fertilized egg, is formed from the joining of egg and sperm, the offspring will have 23 chromosome pairs. One

of each pair comes from the mother, and one of each pair comes from the father.

Meiosis involves two cycles of cell division (Figure 2.19). The total sequence of events following the initial duplication of chromosomes (interphase) involves eight stages: prophase I, metaphase I, anaphase I, telophase I, prophase II, metaphase II, anaphase II, and telophase II. Figure 2.19 presents a diagram of this process for the production of sperm cells, for a hypothetical organism with two chromosome pairs. Each of the two pairs of chromosomes has replicated itself by the start of prophase I, leading to eight chromatids: the two chromosomes of each pair duplicate, giving a total of $2 \times 2 \times 2 = 8$ chromatids, each pair of which attaches to one of the centromeres

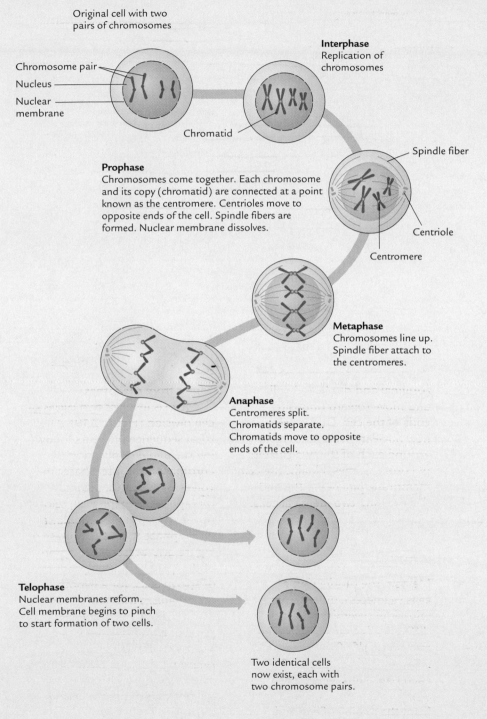

Original cell with two pairs of chromosomes

Chromosome pair
Nucleus
Nuclear membrane

Chromatid

Interphase
Replication of chromosomes

Prophase
Chromosomes come together. Each chromosome and its copy (chromatid) are connected at a point known as the centromere. Centrioles move to opposite ends of the cell. Spindle fibers are formed. Nuclear membrane dissolves.

Spindle fiber

Centriole

Centromere

Metaphase
Chromosomes line up. Spindle fiber attach to the centromeres.

Anaphase
Centromeres split. Chromatids separate. Chromatids move to opposite ends of the cell.

Telophase
Nuclear membranes reform. Cell membrane begins to pinch to start formation of two cells.

Two identical cells now exist, each with two chromosome pairs.

FIGURE 2.18

The five phases of mitosis. In this example, the original body cell contains two pairs of chromosomes. Mitosis produces two identical body cells, each containing two chromosome pairs (a total of four chromosomes each).

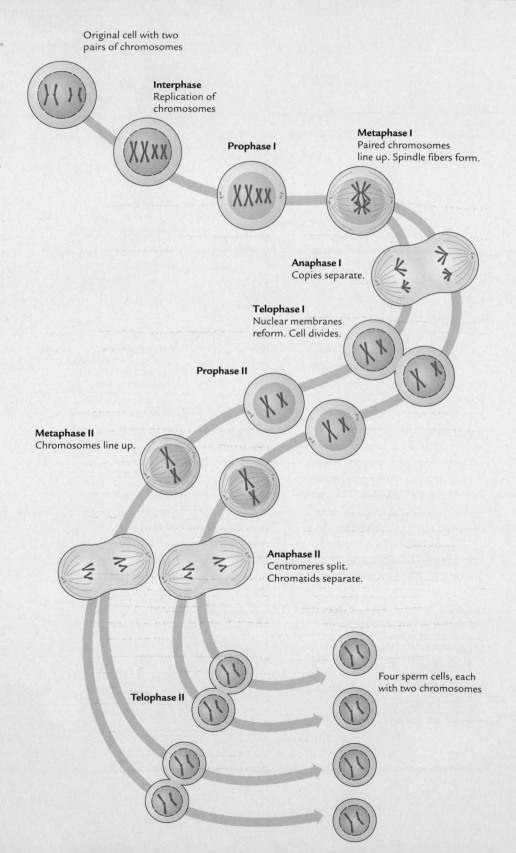

FIGURE 2.19

The phases of meiosis for a sperm cell. In this example, the original cell contained two chromosome pairs. As a result of meiosis, four sperm cells were produced, each with two chromosomes. The process is similar for egg cells, except that one egg cell and three polar bodies are produced.

Original cell with two pairs of chromosomes

Interphase
Replication of chromosomes

Prophase I

Metaphase I
Paired chromosomes line up. Spindle fibers form.

Anaphase I
Copies separate.

Telophase I
Nuclear membranes reform. Cell divides.

Prophase II

Metaphase II
Chromosomes line up.

Anaphase II
Centromeres split. Chromatids separate.

Telophase II

Four sperm cells, each with two chromosomes

through a process known as *synapsis*. At the end of prophase I the nuclear membrane dissolves. Then, during metaphase I, the paired chromosomes line up and spindle fibers form. The copies separate during anaphase I. During telophase I, the nuclear membranes reform and the cell divides. The realization of two cells, each containing eight chromatids, constitutes prophase II. During metaphase II, the chromosomes line up, after which the centromeres split and the chromatids separate, completing anaphase II. The nuclear membranes reform during telophase II, and the cell divides. The net result of this sequence of two cell divisions is four sperm cells, each with two chromosomes—half of the genetic material of the father. The process is similar for the production of egg cells from the female, except that the net result is one egg cell and three structures known as *polar bodies* that do not function as sex cells.

Meiosis thus allows half of a parent's genetic material to be passed on to the next generation. When a sperm cell fertilizes an egg cell, the total number of chromosomes is restored. For humans, the resulting zygote contains 23 + 23 = 46 chromosomes, or 23 chromosome pairs.

Sex cells may also contain genetic combinations not present in the parent. When synapsis occurs during prophase I and the chromosomes pair with their copies, becoming attached to one another at several places, the potential exists for genetic material to be exchanged, a process known as *crossing over*. The resulting genetic combinations allow for variation in each sex cell from its source.

Independent assortment also enhances genetic variability. As discussed in Chapter 2, according to this principle, the segregation of any pair of chromosomes does not affect the probability of segregation of any other pair of chromosomes. If you had two chromosome pairs, A and B, with two chromosomes each (A1 and A2, and B1 and B2), only one of each pair will be found in any sex cell. However, you might have one sex cell with A1 and B1 and another sex cell with A1 and B2. Whichever member of the first pair of chromosomes is found in any given sex cell has no bearing on whichever member of the second pair is also found in that sex cell. Independent assortment results from processes occurring during metaphase I. When the paired chromosomes line up, they do so at random and are not influenced by whether they originally came from the person's mother or father. This process allows for tremendous genetic variability in potential offspring.

CHAPTER 3

May 22

Evolutionary Forces

Biological evolution is genetic change through time and can be studied at two different levels. Microevolution consists of changes in the frequency of alleles in a population from one generation to the next. Macroevolution comprises long-term patterns of genetic change over thousands and millions of generations, as well as the process of species formation. This chapter deals with the general principles of microevolution. Macroevolution is discussed in Chapter 4.

[handwritten note: microevolution = changes in the frequency of alleles in a pop'n from one generation to the next]

POPULATION GENETICS

Microevolution takes into account changes in the frequency of alleles from one generation to the next. The focus is generally not on the specific genotypes or phenotypes of individuals but rather on the total pattern of an entire biological population. We are interested in defining the relative frequencies of different alleles, genotypes, and phenotypes for the entire population being studied. We then seek to determine if any apparent change in these frequencies has occurred over time. If changes have occurred, we try to explain them.

◄ *Two closely related species, a wolf and a dog. Similarities and differences between species, and between populations within a species, are the focus of evolutionary investigation. Changes over time reflect the action of several evolutionary forces: mutation, natural selection, genetic drift, and gene flow.*
(© Robert Clark)

What Is a Population?

The term **breeding population** is used frequently in evolutionary theory. In an abstract sense, a breeding population is a group of organisms that tend to choose mates from within the group. This definition is a bit tricky because it is not clear what proportion of mating within a group defines a breeding population.

For example, suppose you travel to a village in a remote mountain region. You find that 99 percent of all the people in the village are married to others who were born in the same village. In this case, the village would appear to fit our ideal definition. But what if only 80 percent of the people choose their mates from within the village? What if the number were 50 percent? At what point do you stop referring to the population as a "breeding population"? There is no quick and ready answer to this question.

On a practical level, human populations are initially most often defined on the basis of geographic and political boundaries. A small isolated island, for example, easily fits the requirements of a defined population. In most cases, the local geographic unit (such as town or village) is used. Because many human populations have distinct geographic boundaries, this solution often provides the best approach. We must take care, however, to ensure that a local geographic unit, such as a town, is not composed of distinct subpopulations, such as groups belonging to different religious sects. A rural Irish village fits this criterion because most of its residents belong to the same religion, social class, and occupational group. New York City, on the other hand, clearly contains a number of subpopulations defined in terms of ethnicity, religion, social class, and other factors. In this case, subpopulations defined on the basis of these factors would serve as our units of analysis.

In many cases, the definition of a population depends on the specific research question asked. For example, if the goal of a study is to look at spatial variation of biological variation, populations defined on the basis of geography are most suitable. If, however, the goal of a study is to look at genetic variation among ethnic groups, then ethnicity should be used to define the populations.

Another potential problem in defining populations is determining the difference between the total census population and the breeding population. Microevolutionary theory specifically concerns those individuals who contribute to the next generation. The total population refers to everybody, whether or not they are likely to breed. The breeding population is smaller than the total population because of a number of factors. First, some individuals in the total population will be too young or too old to mate. Second, cultural factors and geographic distribution may act to limit an individual's choice of mate, and as a consequence some individuals will not breed. If, for example, you live in an isolated area, there may not be enough individuals of the opposite sex from which to choose a mate. Such factors must be taken into consideration in defining a breeding population.

Once a population has been defined, the next step in microevolutionary analysis is to determine the frequencies of genotypes and alleles within the population.

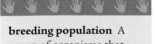

breeding population A group of organisms that tend to choose mates from within the group.

Genotype Frequencies and Allele Frequencies

The genotype frequency is a measure of the relative proportions of different genotypes within a population. Likewise, an allele frequency is simply a measure of the relative proportion of alleles within a population. Genotype frequencies are obtained by dividing the number of individuals with each genotype by the total number of individuals. For example, consider a hypothetical population of 200 people for the MN blood group system in which there are 98 people with genotype *MM*, 84 people with genotype *MN*, and 18 people with genotype *NN*. The genotype frequencies are therefore:

Frequency of *MM* = 98/200 = 0.49

Frequency of *MN* = 84/200 = 0.42

Frequency of *NN* = 18/200 = 0.09

Note that the total frequency of all genotypes adds up to 1 (0.49 + 0.42 + 0.09 = 1).

Allele frequencies are computed by counting the number of each allele and dividing that number by the total number of alleles. In the example here, the total number of alleles is 400 because there are 200 people, each with two alleles. To find out the number of *M* alleles for each genotype, count up the number of alleles for each genotype and multiply that number by the number of people with that genotype. Finally, add up the number for all genotypes. In the example, 98 people have the *MM* genotype, and therefore 98 people each have two *M* alleles. The total number of *M* alleles for people with the *MM* genotype is 98 × 2 = 196. For the *MN* genotype, 84 people have one *M* allele, giving a total of 84 × 1 = 84 *M* alleles. For the *NN* genotype, 18 people have no *M* alleles, for a total of 18 × 0 = 0 *M* alleles. Adding the number of *M* alleles for all genotypes gives a total of 196 + 84 + 0 = 280 *M* alleles. The frequency of the *M* allele is therefore 280/400 = 0.7. The frequency of the *N* allele can be computed in the same way, giving an allele frequency of 0.3. Note that the frequencies of all alleles must add up to 1. Another example of allele frequency computation is given in Table 3.1.

The method of counting alleles to determine allele frequencies can be used only when the number of individuals with each genotype can be determined. If one of the alleles is dominant, this will not be possible and we must use other methods. We may also need to use special methods to compute allele frequencies when more than two alleles are present at a given locus. Such methods are beyond the scope of this text but may be found in any comprehensive text on population genetics (e.g., Cavalli-Sforza and Bodmer 1971).

Hardy-Weinberg Equilibrium

At the beginning of the twentieth century, geneticists were faced with the problem of explaining why dominant alleles were not necessarily the most common. Some argued that, over time, recessive alleles would become less frequent while dominant alleles would increase in frequency. One case of particular

TABLE 3.1   Example of Allele Frequency Computation

Imagine you have just collected information on *MN* blood group genotypes for 250 humans in a given population. Your data are:

Number of *MM* genotype = 40
Number of *MN* genotype = 120
Number of *NN* genotype = 90

The allele frequencies are computed as follows:

Genotype	Number of People	Total Number of Alleles	Number of M Alleles	Number of N Alleles
MM	40	80	80	0
MN	120	240	120	120
NN	90	180	0	180
Total	250	500	200	300

The relative frequency of the *M* allele is computed as the number of *M* alleles divided by the total number of alleles: 200/500 = 0.4.

The relative frequency of the *N* allele is computed as the number of *N* alleles divided by the total number of alleles: 300/500 = 0.6.

As a check, note that the relative frequencies of the alleles must add up to 1.0 (0.4 + 0.6 = 1.0).

interest was a genetic condition known as brachydactyly (abnormally short fingers), which is due to a dominant allele. If someone inherits at least one of the dominant alleles, that person will show this condition. Some scientists argued that this dominant allele should therefore increase in frequency over time such that the majority of humans would have this condition, which is not the case. Two scientists, G. H. Hardy and W. Weinberg, showed independently that this is not the case, and there is no *inherent* tendency for a dominant allele to become more frequent or a recessive allele to be come less frequent (Hardy 1908). Given certain assumptions, the frequencies of these alleles will remain constant over time. Their solution, now known as the **Hardy-Weinberg equilibrium,** shows that, *given certain assumptions,* genotype and allele frequencies will remain constant from one generation to the next.

The Hardy-Weinberg equilibrium model is a mathematical statement relating allele frequencies to the expected genotype frequencies in the next generation. It is best explained using a simple model of a single locus with two alleles, *A* and *a*. By convention, the symbol p is used to represent the frequency of the *A* allele and the symbol q is used to represent the frequency of the *a* allele. These symbols are a form of shorthand; it is easier to use the symbol p than to say "the frequency of the *A* allele."

The Hardy-Weinberg equilibrium model states that, given allele frequencies of p and q, the expected genotype frequencies in the next generation are:

Frequency of the *AA* genotype = p^2
Frequency of the *Aa* genotype = $2pq$
Frequency of the *aa* genotype = q^2

Hardy-Weinberg equilibrium In the absence of nonrandom mating and evolutionary forces, genotype and allele frequencies will remain the same from one generation to the next.

The mathematical proof of this relationship is given in Appendix 1. As an example, assume a population with two alleles (A and a) with allele frequencies of $p = 0.6$ and $q = 0.4$. Using the Hardy-Weinberg equilibrium model, the expected genotype frequencies in the next generation are:

$AA = (0.6)^2 = 0.36$
$Aa = 2(0.6)(0.4) = 0.48$
$aa = (0.4)^2 = 0.16$

Further, application of the Hardy-Weinberg model to future generations (see Appendix 1) shows that, *given certain assumptions,* the genotype and allele frequencies will remain the same from one generation to the next. In the previous example, a population at Hardy-Weinberg equilibrium will have the same allele frequencies ($p = 0.6$, $q = 0.4$) in the next generation, in the generation after that, and so on into the future. The genotype frequencies will be $AA = 0.36$, $Aa = 0.48$, and $aa = 0.16$, and these, too, will remain the same over time.

This may not appear to make a lot of sense because the model appears to predict *no* evolution! After all, if we define microevolution as a change in allele frequencies over time, and if Hardy-Weinberg predicts *no* change, then what relevance does this have? The relevance becomes clear when we go back and examine that critical phrase—*given certain assumptions.*

When Hardy and Weinberg showed that there was no inherent tendency of the frequencies of dominant and recessive alleles to change over time, they used a simple model that had a number of assumptions. Simply put, the model makes a prediction—no change in allele frequency over time. In the real world, however, we have countless examples of allele frequencies changing over time in many species. When observed reality does not match the predictions of the model, this means that one or more of the assumptions of the model is incorrect. By framing the process of evolution in terms of the equilibrium model, population geneticists were able to discover exactly what *does* cause evolutionary changes.

What are the assumptions that Hardy-Weinberg makes? First, the model assumes random mating with respect to the locus of study. That is, every individual has an equal chance of mating with any individual of the opposite sex (both sexes are assumed to have equal allele frequencies). The Hardy-Weinberg equilibrium model also assumes that no new alleles are introduced by mutation; that there is no difference in fertility or survival of the different genotypes (no natural selection); that there are no changes caused by movement into or out of the population (no gene flow); and that there is no variation caused by random sampling (no genetic drift). Given all of these assumptions, there will be no change in the genotype frequencies or allele frequencies over time. If there *is* an observed change, then that means that one or more of these assumptions is incorrect. By extending the Hardy-Weinberg model mathematically, population geneticists have determined how these changes could take place and provided us with an understanding of the real world.

FIGURE 3.1

Inbreeding is used with many domesticated animals to produce certain types of characteristics. (© C. Seghers/ Photo Researchers, Inc.)

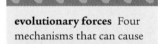

evolutionary forces Four mechanisms that can cause changes in allele frequencies from one generation to the next: mutation, natural selection, genetic drift, and gene flow.

nonrandom mating Patterns of mate choice that influence the distributions of genotype and phenotype frequencies.

inbreeding Mating between biologically related individuals.

assortative mating Mating between phenotypically similar or dissimilar individuals.

A population might not be in Hardy-Weinberg equilibrium for two basic reasons. Observed and expected genotype frequencies may differ because of the effects of evolutionary forces and/or nonrandom mating. **Evolutionary forces** are those mechanisms that can actually lead to a change in allele frequency over time. There are four evolutionary forces: mutation, natural selection, genetic drift, and gene flow (each is described in detail in the following section). These four forces are the only mechanisms that can cause the frequency of an allele to change over time. For example, if you observed a population with an allele frequency of 0.5 in a given population and returned a generation later to find that the allele frequency is 0.4, then you have observed evolution. This change could be due to mutation, natural selection, genetic drift, and/or gene flow. Given the large amount of change in a single generation, it is unlikely that mutation would be responsible because mutation usually causes much lower amounts of change in a single generation. In that case, you could conclude that the observed change was due to natural selection, genetic drift, and/or gene flow. You would need to examine more information, such as migration rates, population size, and environmental variation, to determine which factors were responsible for the change.

When allele frequencies change, so do genotype frequencies, but genotype frequencies can change without altering the underlying allele frequencies. This happens when there is significant **nonrandom mating,** which refers to the patterns of mate choice within a population and its genetic effects. One form of nonrandom mating is **inbreeding,** which occurs when there is mating between biologically related individuals (Figure 3.1). Another form of nonrandom mating is **assortative mating,** which is mating based on phenotypic similarity or dissimilarity (such as blondes having a preference to mate only with other blondes or tall people preferring to mate only with other tall people). In both inbreeding and assortative mating, there is no change in the actual allele frequency, but there is a change in the genotype frequencies. Thus, nonrandom mating does not cause evolution (because the allele frequencies do not change), but it can affect the *rate* of evolutionary change, as discussed later in this chapter.

EVOLUTIONARY FORCES

Mutation

Mutation introduces new alleles into a population. Therefore, the frequency of different alleles will change over time. For example, consider a genetic locus with a single allele, *A*, for a population of 100 people (and therefore 200 alleles, because each person has two alleles). Everyone in the population will have genotype *AA*, and the frequency of the *A* allele is 1.0 (100 percent). Now, assume that one of the *A* alleles being passed on to the next generation changes into a new form, *a*. Assuming the population stays the same size (to make the mathematics a bit easier), there will be 199 *A* alleles and 1 *a* allele in the next generation. The frequency of *A* will have changed from 1.0 to 0.995 (199/200), and the frequency of *a* will have changed from 0.0 to 0.005 (1/200).

If there is no further evolutionary change, the allele frequencies will remain the same in future generations. If this mutation continues to recur, the frequency of the *a* allele will slowly increase, assuming no other evolutionary forces are operating. For typical mutation rates, such a process would take a very long time.

Mutations can also occur in the reverse direction; that is, an *a* allele could mutate back to the original form *A*. Not much information is available on back mutation rates in human populations, but they do appear to be much rarer than the usual mutation rate.

Although mutations are vital to evolution because they provide new variations, mutation rates are low and do not lead, by themselves, to major changes in allele frequency. The other evolutionary forces increase or decrease the frequencies of mutant alleles. If you visited a population over two generations and noted that the frequency of a given allele changed from 0.30 to 0.40, it would be extremely unlikely that this magnitude of change would be due solely to mutation. The other evolutionary forces would be responsible for such large changes.

Many discrete genetic traits are **polymorphisms** (many forms). A genetic polymorphism is a locus with two or more alleles having frequencies too large to be a result of mutation alone. The usual, somewhat arbitrary, cutoff point for these allele frequencies is 0.01. If an allele has a frequency greater than 0.01, we can safely assume this relatively high frequency is caused by factors other than mutation. For example, a locus with allele frequencies of *A* = 1.0 and *a* = 0.0 would not be polymorphic because only one allele (*A*) is present in the population. Likewise, a locus with frequencies of *A* = 0.999 and *a* = 0.001 would also not be a genetic polymorphism because only one allele has a frequency greater than 0.01. If the allele frequencies were *A* = 0.2

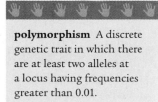

polymorphism A discrete genetic trait in which there are at least two alleles at a locus having frequencies greater than 0.01.

and $a = 0.8$, this would be evidence of genetic polymorphism. Both alleles have frequencies greater than 0.01. Such frequencies are explained by natural selection, genetic drift, and/or gene flow.

Natural Selection

As discussed in Chapter 1, natural selection filters genetic variation. Individuals with certain biological characteristics that allow them to survive to reproduce pass on the alleles for such characteristics to the next generation. Natural selection does not create new genetic variation (only mutation can do that), but it can change the relative frequencies of different alleles.

The analysis of natural selection focuses on **fitness,** the probability of survival and reproduction of an organism. For any locus, fitness is measured as the relative genetic contribution of a genotype to the next generation. Imagine a locus with two alleles, A and a, and the genotypes AA, Aa, and aa. If all individuals with genotypes AA and Aa survive and reproduce but only half of those with genotypes aa do, then the fitness of genotype aa is half of that of genotypes AA and Aa. Fitness refers to the proportion of individuals with a given genotype who survive and reproduce.

Depending on the fitness of each genotype, natural selection can have different effects. Some of the more common forms of natural selection are discussed here, along with a few examples from human populations. Additional examples will be presented in Chapter 6.

Selection against Recessive Homozygotes   Even simple genetic traits with only two alleles have a number of different models of natural selection to investigate. The result of natural selection depends on the initial allele frequencies, whether one allele is dominant or not, and the exact fitness values for each genotype.

Consider what happens when one allele is dominant and one is recessive. Let A be the dominant allele and a be the recessive allele. As you learned in Chapter 2, the genotypes AA and Aa will both give rise to the same phenotype because A is dominant. Because AA and Aa specify the same phenotype, they have the same fitness. For this hypothetical example, let us assume that the fitness of AA and Aa is 100 percent. That is, all individuals with these genotypes survive and reproduce in equal numbers. Now, let us further assume that the fitness of people with the recessive phenotype (those with the genotype aa) have a fitness of 0 percent; that is, no one with this genotype will survive and reproduce. This hypothetical example corresponds to a situation in which a recessive allele (a) is fatal for those who have two copies (aa). Now, assume a population of 200 people before selection with the following distribution of genotypes: $AA = 50$, $Aa = 100$, $aa = 50$. Using the methods discussed earlier, the allele frequencies can be found: the frequency of A is 0.5, and the frequency of a is 0.5.

Table 3.2 shows the process of natural selection using these hypothetical numbers. After selection, the number of individuals in each genotype is $AA = 50$, $Aa = 100$, $aa = 0$. All individuals with genotypes AA and Aa survive, and none of those with genotype aa survive. After selection, there are 150 individuals and the allele frequencies are $A = 0.6667$ and $a = 0.3333$.

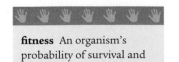

fitness An organism's probability of survival and reproduction.

TABLE 3.2   Example of Natural Selection against a Recessive Homozygote

This example uses an initial population size before selection of 200 people. The locus has two alleles, *A* and *a*. Initially there are 50 people with genotype *AA*, 100 people with genotype *Aa*, and 50 people with genotype *aa*. The allele frequencies before selection are therefore 0.5 for *A* and 0.5 for *a*. The fitness values have been chosen to illustrate total selection against the recessive homozygote.

	Genotype			
	AA	Aa	aa	*Total*
Number of people before selection	50	100	50	200
Fitness (percentage that survives)	100%	100%	0%	
Number of people after selection	50	100	0	150

There are 150 people after selection. Using the method of allele frequency computation shown in Table 3.1 and in the text, the allele frequencies after selection are 200/300 = 0.667 for the *A* allele and 100/300 = 0.333 for the *a* allele.

This example shows the effect of selection against the recessive homozygote. The frequency of the *a* allele drops from 0.5 to 0.3333. Because *a* is a harmful allele, however, you might expect that the *a* allele would be totally eliminated. This does not occur. Because the heterozygote (*Aa*) is not eliminated through selection, these individuals continue to pass the *a* allele on to the next generation. The recessive allele *a* cannot be eliminated in a single generation.

This simple example illustrates another feature of natural selection. Figure 3.2 shows the frequency of the *a* allele for 100 generations of natural selection. The allele frequencies in subsequent generations can be determined by finding out the expected genotype frequencies after selection (using the Hardy-Weinberg model) and examining the expected effects of another generation of selection. Note that the frequency of *a* does not decrease at the same rate over time. The amount of reduction in *a* actually slows down over time. As the frequency of *a* slowly approaches zero, an increasingly lower percentage of the population will be recessive homozygotes; consequently, fewer will be eliminated every generation. Ultimately, a balance will be reached as the reduction in the *a* allele due to selection is offset by new mutations from *A* to *a*. Because mutation rates are very low, this frequency of the *a* allele will be only slightly greater than zero.

Tay-Sachs disease is one case of selection against recessive homozygotes in humans. This affliction is caused by a metabolic disorder that results in blindness, mental retardation, and the destruction of the central nervous system. Children with Tay-Sachs disease generally die within the first few years of life. The disease is caused by a recessive allele and occurs in those individuals who are homozygous. Heterozygotes carry the allele but do not show any major biological impairments.

FIGURE 3.2

Change over time in the frequency of a recessive allele when there is complete selection against the recessive homozygote and the initial allele frequency is 0.5.

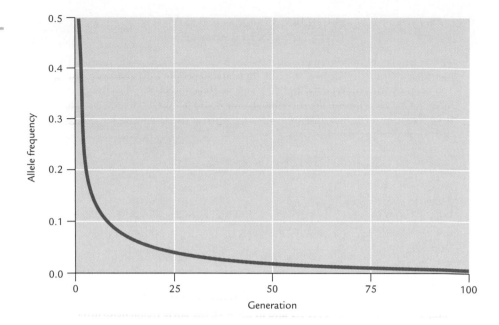

When deleterious alleles are recessive, such as with Tay-Sachs disease, the frequency is generally not zero, because heterozygotes continue to pass the allele on from generation to generation. Nonetheless, the frequency of a harmful recessive allele will still be very low. This low frequency is maintained by mutation but is kept from increasing by natural selection.

Selection for Recessive Homozygotes   What if a dominant allele is selected against? As an example, consider the same starting point as in the previous example: *AA* = 50, *Aa* = 100, and *aa* = 50, giving initial allele frequencies of *A* = 0.5 and *a* = 0.5. Complete selection against the dominant allele (*A*) will mean a fitness of 0 percent for genotypes *AA* and *Aa* and a fitness of 100 percent for the genotype *aa*. After selection, there are no *AA* individuals, no *Aa* individuals, and 50 *aa* individuals (Table 3.3). The allele frequencies after selection are *A* = 0.0 and *a* = 1.0. The dominant allele has been completely eliminated after one generation of selection. There will be no further change unless the allele is reintroduced into the population by mutation or migration from an area where fitness is not zero. If the fitness values of *AA* and *Aa* were greater than zero but less than 100 percent, then the *A* allele would not be eliminated, because some individuals with this allele would survive.

Achondroplastic dwarfism is an example of a dominant allele in human beings. This type of dwarfism (small body size and abnormal body proportions) is caused by a dominant allele found in very low frequencies in human populations—roughly 0.00005 (Figure 3.3). Because the achondroplastic allele is dominant, individuals with one or two of the alleles will show the disease. Virtually all achondroplastic dwarfs are heterozygotes. The condition is usually caused by a mutation occurring in the sex cells of one parent. We know that a mutation is involved in a majority of these cases because roughly 80 percent of dwarfs have two normal parents. Because the condition is caused

TABLE 3.3   Example of Natural Selection for the Recessive Homozygote

This example uses an initial population size before selection of 200 people. The locus has two alleles, *A* and *a*. Initially there are 50 people with genotype *AA*, 100 people with genotype *Aa*, and 50 people with genotype *aa*. The allele frequencies before selection are therefore 0.5 for *A* and 0.5 for *a*. The fitness values have been chosen to illustrate total selection against the dominant homozygote and the heterozygote.

	Genotype			
	AA	Aa	aa	*Total*
Number of people before selection	50	100	50	200
Fitness (percentage that survives)	0%	0%	100%	
Number of people after selection	0	0	50	50

There are 50 people after selection. Based on the method of allele frequency computation shown in Table 3.1 and in the text, the allele frequencies after selection are 0/100 = 0.0 for the *A* allele and 100/100 = 1.0 for the *a* allele. The dominant allele *A* has been eliminated in one generation of natural selection.

by a dominant allele, the only way a child could receive the allele would be from a parent or through mutation. If the parent had the allele, he or she would also be a dwarf. Therefore, when both parents of a dwarf are not dwarfs, we know the offspring's dwarfism is the result of a mutation. In cases where two dwarfs mate, the offspring can be homozygous for the disease, and such offspring generally die before, or shortly after, birth.

The low frequency of achondroplastic dwarfs is the result of natural selection acting to remove the harmful allele from the population. Although there is no major risk of mortality for a heterozygous achondroplastic dwarf, selection acts on differential reproduction. Given their physical appearance, these dwarfs have few opportunities to mate. The most likely mating is between two dwarfs. In these cases, there is additional selection because they have an increased risk of having children with two copies of the achondroplastic allele; these children generally die early in life. Thus, both differences in mortality and fertility can affect the degree of selection against an allele.

Selection for the Heterozygote   The previous examples discussed selection against recessive and dominant homozygotes, which acts to increase the frequency of one allele and decrease the frequency of another. Selection could also occur *for* recessive or dominant homozygotes, which would act to increase the frequency of an allele. With time, the allele frequencies will approach 0 or 1, depending on which allele is selected against.

These models might lead us to expect patterns of genetic variation whereby most populations have allele frequencies close to either 0 or 1 and few populations have intermediate values. However, studies of human genetic variation

FIGURE 3.3

Achondroplastic dwarfism is a genetic disorder caused by a dominant allele. This toddler has very short arms and legs. (*Courtesy March of Dimes*)

TABLE 3.4   Example of Natural Selection for the Heterozygote

This example uses an initial population size before selection of 200 people. The locus has two alleles, *A* and *a*. Initially there are 50 people with genotype *AA*, 100 people with genotype *Aa*, and 50 people with genotype *aa*. The allele frequencies before selection are therefore 0.5 for *A* and 0.5 for *a*. The fitness values have been chosen to illustrate selection for the heterozygote and partial selection against both homozygotes. Note that because this is a codominant system, each genotype specifies a different phenotype.

	Genotype			
	AA	Aa	aa	*Total*
Number of people before selection	50	100	50	200
Fitness (percentage that survives)	70%	100%	20%	
Number of people after selection	35	100	10	145

There are 145 people after selection. Using the method of allele frequency computation shown in Table 3.1 and in the text, the allele frequencies after selection are $170/290 = 0.586$ for the *A* allele and $120/290 = 0.414$ for the *a* allele.

have found that for many loci the allele frequencies are intermediate, with values such as 0.3, 0.5, or 0.8. We could argue that selection is not yet complete and that given enough time all allele frequencies would be close to 0 or 1, but the wealth of information regarding allele frequencies in human groups makes this very unlikely. Why, then, do many loci show intermediate frequencies? Is there a way that natural selection can produce such values?

A classic example of an intermediate allele frequency in human populations is the sickle cell allele, discussed briefly in the previous chapter. Because people homozygous for this allele have sickle cell anemia and are likely to die early in life, this appears to be a classic situation of selection against a homozygote. If this were the case, we might expect most human populations to have frequencies of the sickle cell allele close to 0, and, in fact, many do. However, a number of populations in parts of Africa, India, and the Mediterranean show higher frequencies. In some African groups, the frequency of the sickle cell allele is greater than 20 percent (Roychoudhury and Nei 1988). How can a harmful allele exist at such a high frequency?

The answer is a form of selection known as selection for the heterozygote (and therefore against the homozygotes). Consider fitness values of *AA* = 70 percent, *Aa* = 100 percent, and *aa* = 20 percent. Here, only 70 percent of those with genotype *AA* and 20 percent of those with genotype *aa* survive for every 100 people with genotype *Aa* (the heterozygote). Selection is for the heterozygote and against the homozygotes. Let the frequency of both the *A* and *a* alleles equal 0.5. In a population of 200 people, this means we start with 50 *AA* people, 100 *Aa* people, and 50 *aa* people before selection. Given these fitness values, there will be 35 people with *AA*, 100 with *Aa*, and 10 with *aa*

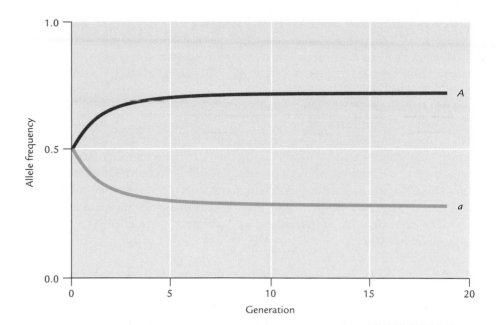

FIGURE 3.4

Change over time in allele frequencies when there is selection for the heterozygote (Aa). The initial allele frequencies are both 0.5. The fitness of each genotype (the relative frequency of survival) is: AA = 70%, Aa = 100%, *and* aa = 20%.

after selection. The allele frequencies after selection are $A = 0.586$ and $a = 0.414$ (Table 3.4).

Why would the frequency of the A allele increase and the frequency of the a allele decrease? In selection for the heterozygote, both alleles are being selected for, because every Aa person can contribute both alleles to the next generation. Also, both alleles are being selected against. When AA people die or fail to reproduce, two A alleles are lost from the population. When aa people die or fail to reproduce, two a alleles are lost from the population. Selection for the heterozygote involves selection for and against both alleles. Because the fitness of AA is greater in this example than the fitness of aa (70 percent versus 20 percent), proportionately more individuals with genotype AA will survive and reproduce. Hence, proportionately more A alleles will appear in the next generation.

Figure 3.4 shows the pattern of allele frequency change over 20 generations using the initial values and fitness values in this example. Note that the frequency of A continues to increase for the first few generations but soon levels off. There is no change in the allele frequency after approximately eight generations. This is the expected pattern when there is selection for the heterozygote. A balance is reached between selection for and against the two alleles A and a. The exact value of this balancing point will depend on the fitness values of the homozygous genotypes. Selection for the heterozygote is also called **balancing selection.**

Given this model, the distribution of sickle cell allele frequencies in humans makes sense. In many environments, there is selection against the sickle cell homozygote and the frequency is low. In environments in which malaria is common, the heterozygotes have an advantage because they are less susceptible to malaria. People homozygous for the sickle cell allele are likely to

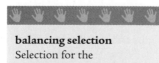

balancing selection
Selection for the heterozygote and against the homozygotes (the heterozygote is most fit).

suffer from sickle cell anemia and die. People homozygous for the normal allele are more likely to suffer from malaria. Thus, there is selection against both homozygotes (although more selection against those with sickle cell anemia) and selection for the heterozygote. A balance of allele frequencies is predicted and has been found in many human populations. A more complete discussion of the sickle cell example is given in Chapter 6.

Another possible example of balancing selection in humans concerns cystic fibrosis, a genetic disease caused by a recessive allele. Studies have shown that individuals heterozygous for the cystic fibrosis allele are resistant to other diseases, such as cholera (Rodman and Zamudio 1991) and typhoid fever (Pier et al. 1998). If so, then heterozygotes would have the greatest fitness and the optimal frequency of the cystic fibrosis allele would be determined by the balance between selection relating to cystic fibrosis and these other diseases.

Selection and Complex Traits   The previous examples used simple genetic traits to illustrate basic principles of natural selection. Selection also affects complex traits, however, such as those discussed in Chapter 2. For complex traits, we focus on measures of the average value and variation around this average. Because complex traits are continuous, we look at the effects of selection on the average value of a trait and on the lower and higher extremes.

There are several forms of selection on complex traits. **Stabilizing selection** refers to selection against both extremes of a trait's range in values. Individuals with extreme high or low values of a trait are less likely to survive and reproduce, and those with values closer to the average are more likely to survive and reproduce. The effect of stabilizing selection is to maintain the population at the same average value over time. Extreme values are selected against each generation, but the average value in the population does not change.

Human birth weight is a good example of stabilizing selection. The weight of a newborn child is the result of a number of environmental factors, such as mother's age, weight, and history of smoking, among many others. There is also a genetic component to birth weight. Newborns who are very small (less than 2.5 kg) are less likely to survive than newborns who are heavier. Very small babies are more prone to disease and have weaker systems, making their survival more difficult. Newborns who are too large are also likely to be selected against, because a very large child may create complications during childbirth and both mother and child may die. Thus, there is selection against both extremes, small and large.

Stabilizing selection on birth weight has been documented for a number of human populations. These studies show a definite relationship between birth weight and mortality. The results of one study based on 13,730 newborns (Karn and Penrose 1951) are shown in Figure 3.5. Mortality rates are highest for those newborns with low (less than 2.7 kg) and high (greater than 4.5 kg) birth weights.

Another type of selection for complex traits is known as **directional selection,** selection against one extreme and/or for the other extreme. In other

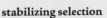

stabilizing selection
Selection against extreme values, large or small, in a continuous trait.

directional selection
Selection against one extreme in a continuous trait and/or selection for the other extreme.

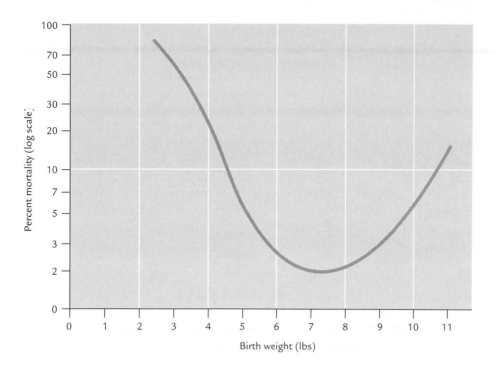

FIGURE 3.5

Stabilizing selection for human birth weight based on data from Karn and Penrose (1951). Babies born smaller or larger than the optimum birth weight have increased mortality. (From E. Peter Volpe, Understanding Evolution, *5th ed. Copyright © 1985 Wm. C. Brown Communications, Inc., Dubuque, Iowa. All Rights Reserved. Reprinted by permission of the McGraw-Hill Companies)*

words, a direct relationship exists between survival and reproduction on one hand and the value of a trait on the other. The result is a change over time in one direction. The average value for a trait moves in one direction or the other. Perhaps the most dramatic example of directional selection in human evolution has been the threefold increase in brain size over the last 4 million years. Another example is the lighter skin that probably evolved in prehistoric humans as they moved north out of Africa (see Chapter 6).

Genetic Drift

Genetic drift is the random change in allele frequency from one generation to the next. These random changes are the result of the nature of probability. Think for a moment about flipping a coin in the air. What is the probability of its landing with the head facing up? It is 50 percent. The coin has two possible values, heads and tails, and when you flip it you will get one or the other. Suppose you flip a coin 10 times. How many heads and how many tails do you expect to get? Because the probability of getting a head or a tail is 50 percent, you expect to get five heads and five tails. Try this experiment several times. Did you always get five tails and five heads? Sometimes you get five heads and five tails, but sometimes you get different numbers. You may get six heads and four tails, or three heads and seven tails, or, much less likely, all heads.

The probability for different combinations of heads and tails from flipping a coin 10 times is shown in Table 3.5. The probability of getting all heads (or all tails) is rather low—0.001. Note, however, that the probability of

genetic drift A mechanism for evolutionary change resulting from the random fluctuations of gene frequencies from one generation to the next.

TABLE 3.5	Probability of Getting Different Numbers of Heads and Tails from 10 Coin Flips	
Number of Heads	Number of Tails	Probability
0	10	0.001
1	9	0.010
2	8	0.044
3	7	0.117
4	6	0.205
5	5	0.246
6	4	0.205
7	3	0.117
8	2	0.044
9	1	0.010
10	0	0.001

These probabilities refer only to the case in which a coin is flipped 10 times. Other numbers of coins will give different probabilities.

getting four heads and six tails (or six heads and four tails) is much higher—0.205. Also note that the probability of getting exactly five heads and five tails is 0.246. This means that there is roughly a 75 percent chance of *not* getting exactly five heads and five tails.

The probability of 50 percent heads and 50 percent tails is the expected distribution. If you flip 10 coins enough times, you will find that the number of heads and tails grows closer to a 50:50 ratio. Often we hear about the "law of averages." The idea here is that if you flip a coin and get heads several times in a row, then you are very likely to get a tail the next time. This is wrong, and using this "law" is an easy way to lose money if you gamble. *Each* flip of the coin is an independent event. Whatever happened the time before cannot affect the next flip. *Each* time you flip the coin you have a 50 percent chance of getting a head and a 50 percent chance of getting a tail.

What does this have to do with genetics? The reproductive process in this way is like a coin toss. During the process of sex cell replication (meiosis), only one allele out of two at a given locus is used. The probability of either allele being passed on is 50 percent, just like a coin toss. Imagine a locus with two alleles, *A* and *a*. Now imagine a man and a woman, each with genotype *Aa*, who have a child. The man can pass on either an *A* allele or an *a* allele. Likewise, a woman can pass on either an *A* allele or an *a* allele. As we saw in the previous chapter, the probable distribution of genotypes among the children is 25 percent *AA*, 50 percent *Aa*, and 25 percent *aa*. If the couple has four children, you would expect one with *AA*, two with *Aa*, and one with *aa*. Thanks to random chance, however, the couple may get a different distribution of genotypes. You can model such a simple example by flipping a coin to

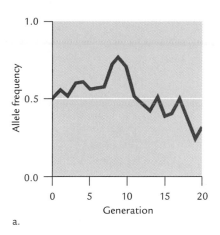
a.

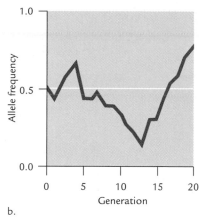
b.

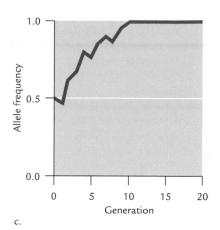
c.

FIGURE 3.6

Three computer simulations of 20 generations of genetic drift for populations of 10 individuals. Each simulation started with an initial allele frequency of 0.5.

simulate a child receiving an *A* allele or an *a* allele from either parent. Let "heads" represent the *A* allele and "tails" represent the *a* allele.

I performed this experiment four times to simulate four children born to these parents. Two of the children had genotype *AA,* and two had genotype *Aa.* Note that the allele frequencies have changed from the parent's generation to the children's generation. The allele frequencies of the parents were *A* = 0.5 and *a* = 0.5. The four children have a total of eight alleles, of which six are *A* and two are *a.* The frequency of *A* in the children is 6/8 = 0.75, and the frequency of *a* is 2/8 = 0.25. You might want to try this experiment several times to see the range of allele frequencies that can result.

When genetic drift occurs in populations, the same principle applies. Allele frequencies can change because of random chance. Sometimes the allele frequency will increase, and sometimes it will decrease. The direction of allele frequency change caused by genetic drift is random. The only time drift will not produce a change in allele frequency is when only one allele is present at a given locus. For example, if each parent passed on an *A* allele to each of the four children, the frequency of the *A* allele would be 1.0 among the children. The *a* allele would have been lost.

Genetic drift occurs in each generation. Such a process is too complicated to simulate by using coins, but computers or random number tables can be used to model the effects of drift over time (see Cavalli-Sforza and Bodmer 1971:389). Figure 3.6 shows the results of three computer simulations of drift. In each case, the initial allele frequency was 0.5 and the population size was equal to 10 individuals (20 alleles) in each generation. The simulation was allowed to continue in each case for 20 generations. The graphs show the changes in allele frequency over time. Note that each of the three simulations shows a different pattern. This is expected because genetic drift is a random process. Each simulation is an independent event.

In each of these three graphs, the allele frequency fluctuates up and down. In Figure 3.6a, the allele frequency after 20 generations is 0.3. In Figure 3.6b, the allele frequency after 20 generations is 0.75. In Figure 3.6c, the allele frequency is equal to 1.0 after 10 generations and it does not change any further. Given enough time, and assuming no other evolutionary forces affect

FIGURE 3.7

Allele frequency distributions for 1,000 computer simulations of 20 generations of genetic drift. The distributions show the number of times a given allele frequency was reached after 20 generations of drift. In all cases, the initial allele frequency was 0.5. Each graph represents a different value of population size: (a) = 10, (b) = 50, (c) = 100, (d) = 1,000.

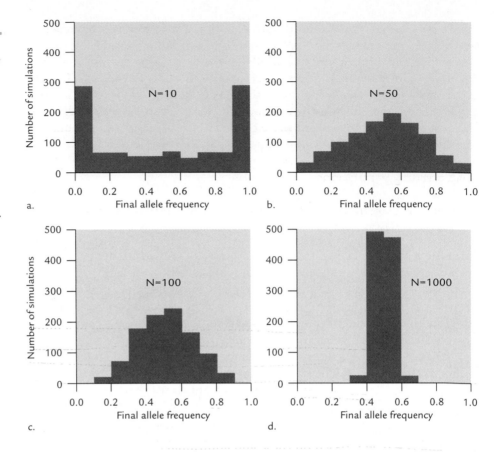

allele frequencies, genetic drift will ultimately lead to an allele's becoming fixed at a value of 0.0 or 1.0. Thus, genetic drift leads to the reduction of variation within a population, given enough time.

Population Size and Genetic Drift   The effect of genetic drift depends on the size of the breeding population. The larger the population size, the less change will occur from one generation to the next. Thinking back to the coin toss analogy will show you that this makes sense. If you flip a coin 10 times and get three heads and seven tails, it is not that unusual. If you flip a coin 1 million times, however, it would be much less likely that you would get the same proportions—300,000 heads and 700,000 tails. This is because of a basic principle of probability: the greater the number of events, the fewer deviations from the expected frequencies (50 percent heads and 50 percent tails).

The effect of population size on genetic drift is shown in Figure 3.7. These graphs show the results of 1,000 simulations of genetic drift for four different values of breeding population size: *N* = 10, 50, 100, 1,000. In each computer run, the initial allele frequency was set to 0.5 and the simulation was allowed to continue for 20 generations. The four graphs show the distribution of allele frequency values after 20 generations of genetic drift. Figure 3.7a shows this distribution for a population size of *N* = 10. Note that the majority of the 1,000 simulations resulted in final allele frequencies of less than 0.1 or greater than 0.9. In small populations, genetic drift more often results in a quick loss of one allele or another. Figure 3.7b shows the distribution of final allele frequencies for a population size of $N = 50$. Here there are fewer extreme values and more values falling between 0.3 and 0.7. Figures 3.7c and 3.7d show the distributions for population sizes of $N = 100$ and $N = 1,000$. It is clear from these graphs that the larger the population size, the fewer deviations in allele frequency caused by genetic drift. The main point here is that genetic drift has the greatest evolutionary effect in relatively small breeding populations.

Examples of Genetic Drift   Genetic drift in human populations is shown in a case study of a group known as the Dunkers, a religious sect that emigrated from Germany to the United States in the early 1700s. Approximately 50 families composed the initial group. Glass (1953) studied the genetic characteristics of the descendants of the original founding group living in Pennsylvania. These populations have never been greater than several hundred people and thus provide a unique opportunity to study genetic drift in a small human group. Glass found that the Dunker population differed in a number of genetic traits from both the modern German and U.S. populations. Furthermore, the allele frequencies of Germany and the United States were almost identical, suggesting that other factors such as natural selection were unlikely. For example, the allele frequencies for the MN blood group were roughly $M = 0.55$ and $N = 0.45$ for both the United States and German samples. In the Dunker population, however, the allele frequencies were $M = 0.655$ and $N = 0.345$. Based on these and additional data, Glass concluded that the genetics of the Dunker population were shaped to a large extent by genetic drift over two centuries. Although 200 years seems like a long time to you and me, it is a fraction of an instant in evolutionary time. Genetic drift can clearly produce rapid changes under the proper circumstances.

Genetic drift in human populations has also been found on Tristan da Cunha, a small island in the south Atlantic Ocean. In 1816, the English established a small garrison on the island. When they left, one man and his wife remained, to be joined later by a handful of other settlers. Given such a small number of original settlers, what do you suppose is the probability that the families represented all the genetic variation present in the population they came from? The probability would be very low. Genetic drift is often caused when a small number of founders form a new population: this type of genetic drift is known as **founder effect.** An analogy would be a barrel containing thousands of red and blue beads, mixed in equal proportions. If you reached into the barrel and randomly pulled out a handful of beads, you might not get 50 percent red and 50 percent blue. Because of random chance, founders are not likely to be an exact genetic representation of the original population. The smaller the number of founders, the greater the deviation will be.

Over time, the population of Tristan da Cunha remained small. The population size was further reduced twice because of emigration and disaster.

founder effect A type of genetic drift caused by the formation of a new population by a small number of individuals.

Given its initial small population, combined with two further reductions and a maximum population size less than 300, the island had the opportunity to experience considerable genetic drift. This effect is seen dramatically through analysis of historical records for the island; for example, it was found that two of the original founders contributed genetically to more than 29 percent of the 1961 population (Roberts 1968; Underwood 1979).

Gene Flow

The fourth evolutionary force is **gene flow,** the movement of alleles from one population to another. The term *migration* is often used to mean the same thing as gene flow. From a conservative standpoint, however, this is not completely accurate. Migration refers to the more or less permanent movement of individuals from one place to another. Why the confusion? After all, excepting artificial insemination, your alleles do not move unless you do. You can migrate, though, without passing on any alleles. You can also be involved in gene flow without actually making a permanent move to a new place. In many texts on microevolution, the terms *gene flow* and *migration* are used interchangeably. Keep in mind, however, that there are certain distinctions in the real world.

Genetic Effects of Gene Flow   Gene flow involves the movement of alleles between at least two populations. When gene flow occurs, the two populations mix genetically and tend to become more similar. Under most conditions, the more the two populations mix, the more similar they will become genetically (assuming that the two environments are not different enough to produce different effects of natural selection).

Consider a genetic locus with two alleles, *A* and *a*. Assume two populations, 1 and 2. Now assume that all the alleles in population 1 are *A* and all the alleles in population 2 are *a*. The allele frequencies of these two imaginary populations are:

Population 1	Population 2
Frequency of $A = 1.0$	Frequency of $A = 0.0$
Frequency of $a = 0.0$	Frequency of $a = 1.0$

Now imagine a situation in which 10 percent of the people in population 1 move to population 2, and vice versa. This movement constitutes gene flow. What effect will the gene flow have? After gene flow has taken place, population 1 is made up of 90 percent *A* alleles and 10 percent *a* alleles. Population 2 is made up of 10 percent *A* alleles and 90 percent *a* alleles. The allele frequencies of the two populations, though still different, have become more similar as the consequence of gene flow. If the same rate of gene flow (10 percent) continues generation after generation, the two populations will become more and more similar genetically. After 20 generations of gene flow, the two populations will be almost identical. The accumulated effects of gene flow over time are shown for this hypothetical example in Figure 3.8.

gene flow A mechanism for evolutionary change resulting from the movement of genes from one population to another.

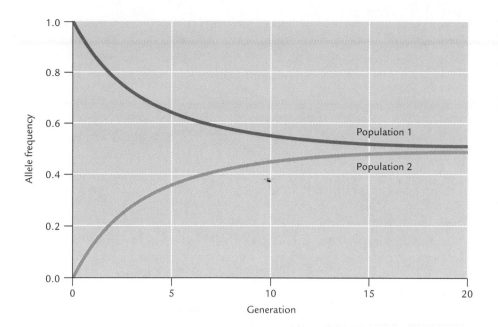

FIGURE 3.8

Effects of gene flow over time. Population 1 started with an allele frequency of 1.0, and population 2 started with an allele frequency of 0.0. The two populations exchange 10 percent of their genes with each generation. Over time, the continued gene flow acts to make the two populations more similar genetically.

Apart from making populations more similar, gene flow can also introduce new variation within a population. In the example, a new allele (*a*) was introduced into population 1 as the result of gene flow. A new mutation arising in one population can be spread throughout the rest of a species by gene flow.

Compared to many other organisms, humans are relatively mobile creatures. Human populations show a great deal of variation in degree of migration. Even today, many humans live and work within a small area and choose mates from nearby. Some people are more mobile than others, the extent of their mobility depending on a number of factors such as available technology, occupation, income, and other social factors.

In spite of local and regional differences, humans today all belong to the same species. Even though genetic variation exists among populations, they are in fact characterized more by their similarity. A critical factor in the cohesiveness of the human species, gene flow acts to reduce differences among groups.

Determinants of Gene Flow   The amount of gene flow between human populations depends on a variety of environmental and cultural factors. Geographic distance is a major determinant of migration and gene flow. The farther two populations are apart geographically, the less likely they are to exchange mates. Even in today's modern world, with access to jet airplanes and other devices, you are still more likely to choose a spouse from nearby than from across the country. Exceptions to the rule do occur, of course, but the influence of geographic distance is still very strong.

Studies of migration and gene flow often look at distance between birthplaces or premarital residences of married couples. If you had been born in New York City and your spouse had been born in Chicago, the distance

FIGURE 3.9

Percentage of marriages taking place at various marital distances (the distance between the premarital residences of bride and groom) for the town of Leominster, Massachusetts, 1800–1849. (Source: author's unpublished data)

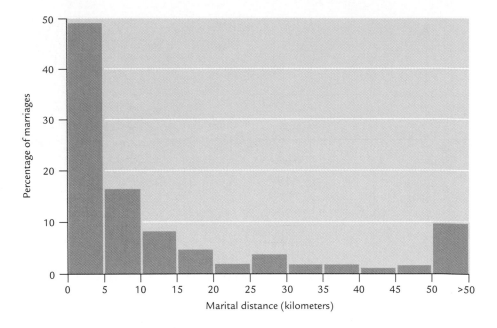

between your birthplaces would be approximately 1,300 km (roughly 800 miles). If both you and your spouse had come from the same neighborhood in the same city, your marital distance would be close to zero. The relationship between migration and geographic distance is similar in most human populations (Relethford 1992). Most marriages take place within a few kilometers, and the number of marriages quickly decreases as the distance between populations increases. This indicates that the majority of genes flowing into human populations come from a local area and a small proportion from farther distances.

The relationship between the frequency of marriages and geographic distance is shown in Figure 3.9. This graph presents the results of a historical study of migration into the town of Leominster, Massachusetts, using marriage records from the year 1800 through 1849. A total of 1,602 marriages took place in the population over the 50-year period. Of these, almost half (49.2 percent) were between a bride and groom who were both native to Leominster. An additional 16.5 percent of the marriages took place between couples whose premarital residences were between 5 and 10 km (roughly from 8 to 16 miles) apart. Note that the percentage of marriages diminishes quickly after a distance of 5 km. Also note that almost 10 percent of the couples come from distances greater than 50 km. This type of long-range migration (and gene flow) acts to keep populations from diverging too much from the rest of the species.

Geographic distance is a major determinant of human migration and gene flow, but it is not the only one. Ethnic differences also act to limit them. Most large cities have distinct neighborhoods that correspond to different ethnic communities. A large proportion of marriages takes place within these groups because of the common human preference for marrying within one's

TABLE 3.6	Rates of Marriage within Language Groups on Bougainville Island
Language Group	Percentage of Marriages Occurring within Language Group
Aita	95
Eivo	85
Nasioi	95
Rotokas	98
Simeku	90
Siwai	94
Torau	96
Uruava	70

Source: Friedlaender (1975:76).

own social and cultural group. Likewise, religious differences also act as barriers to gene flow because many, though not all, people prefer to marry within the same religion. Further, social class and educational differences can also limit gene flow.

In other parts of the world, we see other cultural differences that restrict gene flow. In many Pacific islands, for example, several different language groups coexist within a small geographic area. Differences in language enhance the cultural distances among populations and act to limit the number of marriages across language groups. Friedlaender's (1975) study of migration on Bougainville Island in Melanesia shows the effect of language differences on marriage frequency. He looked at marriages within and among small villages belonging to eight different language groups within roughly a 100-km range. The percentage of marriages within each language group are listed in Table 3.6. For the entire island, 90 percent of all marriages took place within the same language group (the percentage varies from 70 percent to 98 percent for the eight groups).

Interaction of the Evolutionary Forces

It is convenient to discuss each of the four evolutionary forces separately, but in reality they act together to produce allele frequency change. Mutation acts to introduce new genetic variants; natural selection, genetic drift, and gene flow act to change the frequency of the mutant allele. Sometimes the evolutionary forces act together, and sometimes they act in opposition. Their exact interaction depends on a wide variety of factors, such as the biochemical and physical effects of different alleles, presence or absence of dominance, population size, population distribution, and the environment, to name but a few.

Many biological anthropologists attempt to unravel some of these factors in human population studies.

In general, we look at how natural selection, genetic drift, and gene flow act to increase or decrease genetic variation within and between groups. (Mutation gets less attention because, even though it introduces new genetic variants, the change in allele frequency in one generation is low.) An increase in variation within a population means that individuals within the population will be more genetically different from one another. A decrease in variation within a population means the reverse; individuals will become more similar to one another genetically. An increase in variation among populations means that two or more populations will become more different from one another genetically, and a decrease in variation within populations means the reverse.

Let us first consider the effects of genetic drift, gene flow, and natural selection on allele frequency variation. Genetic drift tends to remove alleles from a population and therefore acts to reduce variation within a population. On the other hand, because genetic drift is a random event and occurs independently in different populations, the pattern of genetic drift will tend to be different on average in different populations. On average, then, genetic drift will act to increase variation between populations. Gene flow acts to introduce new alleles into a population and can have the effect of increasing variation within a population. Gene flow also acts to reduce variation between populations in most cases.

Natural selection can either increase or decrease variation within a population, depending on the specific type of selection and the initial allele frequencies. Selection against recessive homozygotes, for example, will lead to the gradual decrease of one allele and consequently reduce variation. Selection for an advantageous mutation, however, will result in an increase in the frequency of the mutant and act to increase variation within the population. Selection can also either increase or decrease variation between populations, depending on environmental variation. If two populations have similar environments, then natural selection will take place in the same way in both groups and therefore will act to reduce genetic differences between them. On the other hand, if the two populations are in different enough environments that natural selection operates in different ways, then variation between the populations may be increased. Table 3.7 summarizes the effects of different evolutionary forces on variation within and among populations.

Different evolutionary forces can produce the same, or opposite, effects. Different forces can also act in opposition to one another. Genetic drift and gene flow, for example, have opposite effects on variation within and between populations. If both of these forces operate at the same time, they can counteract each other.

Several examples help illustrate the ways in which different evolutionary forces can interact. Consider the forces of mutation and genetic drift. How might these two forces interact? Mutation acts to change allele frequency by the introduction of a new allele, whereas genetic drift causes random fluctuations in allele frequency from one generation to the next. If both operate at

TABLE 3.7	Summary of the Effects of Selection, Drift, and Gene Flow on Variation within and among Populations	
Evolutionary Force	Variation within Populations	Variation between Populations
Selection	Increase or decrease	Increase or decrease
Genetic drift	Decrease	Increase
Gene flow	Increase	Decrease

A decrease in variation within a population makes individuals more similar to one another, whereas an increase in variation within a population makes individuals less similar to one another. A decrease in variation among populations makes the populations more similar to one another, whereas an increase in variation among populations makes the populations less similar to one another. Note that natural selection can either increase or decrease variation; the exact effect depends on the type of selection and differences in environment (see text).

the same time, drift may act to increase or decrease the frequency of the new mutation. Consider what happens where everyone in a population has two *A* alleles and there is then a mutation from *A* to *a* in one individual. The person with the mutation can either pass on the *A* allele or the *a* allele, each with a 50 percent probability. It is possible that the new mutant allele will be lost from the population because of random chance. It is also possible that the frequency of the mutant allele will increase because of random chance. The person with the mutation may pass the mutant form on to all of his or her children, and each of them might continue to pass it on to their children.

To give you an idea of how mutation and genetic drift can interact, I performed a simple computer simulation that allowed for a single mutation followed by genetic drift. In this simulation, a population size of 10 was used in which all individuals initially had the same allele. A single mutation event was then allowed, which meant that the frequency of the mutant allele was $1/20 = 0.05$ (1 mutant allele out of all 20 alleles in the population). Genetic drift was then simulated for 20 generations. This entire simulation experiment was repeated 1,000 times, and the results are shown in Table 3.8.

As expected, genetic drift leads to the loss of the mutant allele most of the time (in this case, 889 out of 1,000 times). In most of the remaining cases, however, the frequency of the mutant allele actually increased. In 45 cases, the frequency of the mutant allele was greater than 0.5 after 20 generations. In five cases, the mutant allele had become fixed (a frequency of 100 percent) within the population! Such computer simulations are a bit simplistic and somewhat unrealistic, but they do show how two evolutionary forces can interact.

Many other possibilities for interaction also exist. For example, natural selection reduces the frequency of a harmful recessive mutant allele. Gene flow tends to counter the effects of genetic drift on variation among populations. Genetic drift can increase the frequency of a harmful allele even if it is being selected against.

TABLE 3.8	Results of Computer Simulation of Mutation and Genetic Drift

A total of 1,000 independent computer simulations were performed using a population size of 10 individuals with a single initial mutation (1 mutant allele out of 20 in the population, giving an initial allele frequency of $1/20 = 0.05$). Following mutation, the computer simulated genetic drift for 20 generations. The following shows the distribution of the frequencies of the mutant allele after 20 generations (see text).

Final Frequency of the Mutant Allele	Number of Cases
0.0	889
0.01–0.09	2
0.10–0.19	22
0.20–0.29	11
0.30–0.39	16
0.40–0.49	15
0.50–0.59	9
0.60–0.69	11
0.70–0.79	9
0.80–0.89	9
0.90–0.99	2
1.0	5

Much of microevolutionary theory deals with the mathematics describing such interactions. Studies of actual populations must take these interactions into account and try to control for them in analysis. There are some basic rules for interpreting genetic variation. If populations are large, then drift is unlikely to have much of an effect. Gene flow can be measured to some extent by looking at migration rates to determine how powerful an effect it would have. Natural selection can be investigated by looking at patterns of fertility and mortality among different classes of genotypes.

Imagine that you have visited a population over two generations. You note that the frequency of a certain allele has changed from 0.4 to 0.5. Furthermore, assume that the population has been totally isolated during the last generation and that the size of the breeding population has stayed at roughly 50 people. What could have caused the allele frequency change? Because mutation occurs at much lower rates, it could not be responsible. Given that the population was totally isolated, gene flow could not be responsible. Drift may have caused the change in allele frequency, for the size of the breeding population is rather low. Natural selection could also have produced the change. You would have to know more about the specific alleles and genotypes involved, environmental factors, and patterns of mortality and fertility to de-

Tay-Sachs Disease: Genetic Drift or Natural Selection?

Tay-Sachs disease is an example of a lethal recessive allele—people with two Tay-Sachs alleles generally die very early in life. As expected, the frequency of this disease tends to be rather low around the world, affecting roughly 1 in every 500,000 births. What is unusual about Tay-Sachs disease is the fact that among Jews of Eastern European ancestry (Ashkenazi Jews) the rate is much higher: Tay-Sachs affects roughly 1 in every 2,500 births in these populations (Molnar 1998). The occurrence of Tay-Sachs is also high in some other human populations.

What would be responsible for higher frequencies of a lethal allele in certain populations? Is it something related to their history, their environment, or some complex set of factors? One suggestion is genetic drift. Jewish populations have tended to be rather small and isolated, factors that increase the likelihood of genetic drift. Although selection acts to reduce the frequency of the allele, the random nature of genetic drift might have caused an increase relative to larger populations, which experienced less genetic drift.

Closer examination, however, argues against the genetic drift hypothesis. The Tay-Sachs disease is not due to a specific mutant allele but actually can arise from several different mutations. All of these mutant alleles have elevated frequencies in Ashkenazi populations. It seems unlikely that all of these mutant forms would drift to higher frequencies (Marks 1995).

What else could be responsible for the elevated frequency of Tay-Sachs disease? There is some evidence suggesting that people who carry one Tay-Sachs allele (heterozygotes) have increased resistance to tuberculosis. If so, then the heterozygotes would have greater fitness than either the normal homozygote (who would be more susceptible to tuberculosis) or those homozygous for the Tay-Sachs allele (who have zero fitness). This is a case of balancing selection and, as discussed in the text, would lead to a balance in allele frequencies.

However, why would this type of selection take place only among the Ashkenazi? Cultural and historical data provide a possible answer. Due to discrimination, the Jewish populations of Eastern Europe were frequently isolated into overcrowded ghettos under conditions that would increase the threat of tuberculosis (Marks 1995).

The tuberculosis hypothesis is just that—a possible explanation that remains to be fully tested. If correct, it provides us with yet another example of the compromises that occur during evolution. There is no "perfect" genotype. Everything has a price in terms of fitness, and natural selection often reflects this balance between cost and benefit.

termine whether selection had an effect. Even given this rather limited information, you can rule out mutation and gene flow and proceed to develop tests to determine the relative influence of drift and selection.

The study of any natural population is much more complex. With laboratory animals, you can control for a variety of factors to help your analysis. In dealing with human populations, however, you must rely on observations as they occur in nature.

Nonrandom Mating

Recall that one of the assumptions of the Hardy-Weinberg equilibrium model is random mating. Populations often show deviations from random mating, such as inbreeding, where mates are closely related. Actually, we are all inbred to some extent, but we generally reserve the term for "close" biological relatedness, such as between first cousins or closer. What is the genetic effect of inbreeding? Closely related individuals are more likely to have similar alleles inherited from a common ancestor. Thus, inbreeding increases the probability of having a homozygous genotype. For example, if two first cousins mate, the probability that their offspring will have a homozygous genotype is 6.25 percent greater than that for a noninbred mating (this number is called the inbreeding coefficient and is discussed further in Appendix 1).

The genetic effects of inbreeding are often harmful. Studies have shown that the incidence of congenital birth defects and mortality during the first year of life is higher among inbred offspring than among the offspring of others (Bittles et al. 1991). Some studies have suggested higher rates of mental retardation among inbred children, but others have not confirmed this. For the most part, overall rates of inbreeding in human populations tend to be low compared to rates among other organisms. These lower rates appear in part due to the high mobility of the human species (more gene flow) and in part reflect the fact that most societies have cultural rules discouraging, or prohibiting, mating with close relatives.

At a broader level, the evolutionary effect of inbreeding is to change *genotype* frequencies, but not *allele* frequencies. Inbreeding results in more homozygotes and fewer heterozygotes but does not change the frequency of the alleles (only their distribution into genotypes). As such, inbreeding does not change allele frequencies over time. Inbreeding can, however, affect the *rate* of allele frequency change. If, for example, there is selection against a homozygote, then inbreeding will produce more homozygotes to be selected against and the rate of selection will change.

Assortative mating is another form of nonrandom mating. With this type of mating, individuals choose mates who are biologically similar to themselves. Humans typically choose mates similar to themselves for a variety of social and biological traits (Buss 1985). A typical example is assortative mating for skin color; on average, people tend to choose mates with similar skin color. Evolutionarily, the effect is the same as for inbreeding—genotype frequencies are changed, but not allele frequencies.

SUMMARY

The study of microevolution looks at changes in the frequencies of alleles from one generation to the next. Such analyses allow detailed examination of the factors that can alter allele frequencies in the short term and also provide us with inferences about long-term patterns of evolution. Changes in allele frequencies stem from four evolutionary forces: mutation, natural selection, genetic drift, and gene flow.

Mutation is the ultimate source of all genetic variation but occurs at low enough rates that additional factors are needed to explain polymorphic frequencies (whereby two or more alleles have frequencies greater than 0.01). The other three evolutionary forces are responsible for increasing or decreasing the frequency of a mutant allele. Natural selection changes allele frequencies through the process of differential survival and reproduction of individuals having certain genotypes. Genetic drift is the random change in allele frequencies from one generation to the next and has the greatest effect in small populations. Gene flow, the movement of alleles between populations, acts to reduce genetic differences between different groups.

The rate of allele frequency change is affected by nonrandom mating patterns such as inbreeding and assortative mating. The allele frequencies do not change, but the genotype frequencies are affected. More homozygotes occur than expected from random mating, which can result in more rapid change in allele frequencies because of natural selection.

SUPPLEMENTAL READINGS

Gillespie, J. H. 1998. *Population Genetics: A Concise Guide.* Baltimore: Johns Hopkins University Press.

Hartl, D. L. 2000. *A Primer of Population Genetics,* 2d ed. Sunderland, Mass.: Sinauer Associates. These two books are good short introductions to population genetics with a minimum of mathematical background needed (basic algebra).

Hartl, D. L., and A. G. Clark. 1997. *Principles of Population Genetics,* 3d ed. Sunderland, Mass.: Sinauer Associates.

Hedrick, P. W. 2000. *Genetics of Populations,* 2d ed. Sudbury, Mass.: Jones and Bartlett. These two books are more comprehensive and advanced treatments of population genetics.

INTERNET RESOURCES

http://anthro.palomar.edu/synthetic/Default.htm ✳
Synthetic Theory of Evolution, a tutorial covering Hardy-Weinberg equilibrium and the evolutionary forces.

http://www.utm.edu/~rirwin/NaturalSelection.htm
The Natural Selection Model, an interactive simulation of natural selection.

http://www.utm.edu/~rirwin/Drift.htm
The Genetic Drift Model, an interactive simulation of genetic drift.

http://www.mhhe.com/mayfieldpub/relethford/student_resources/micro/index.htm
Download MICRO, a microevolution simulation program for Windows 9x.

CHAPTER 4

May 2 2

The Origin and Evolution of Species

When so-called creation scientists dispute evolution, they generally mean macroevolution. Few doubt the existence of short-term, microevolutionary changes when we can see such changes in our daily lives, from changing patterns of disease to the kinds of alterations brought about by animal and plant breeding. The long-term pattern of evolution, however, is generally more difficult to grasp. Creationism argues that we cannot directly observe changes over millions of years and therefore cannot make scientific tests. It is true that we cannot undertake laboratory tests lasting for millions of years, but we can still make scientific predictions. Many sciences, including geology and astronomy, are historical in nature. That is, we rely on some record (geologic strata or stellar configurations, for example) to note what has happened. We can establish the facts of change. The same is true of macroevolution. The fossil record provides us with information about what *has* happened. We must then utilize other information available to us to determine *why* such change has occurred. A geologist makes use of the fact that geologic processes occur in a regular manner and therefore occurred in the same way in ancient times. Geologists use available information about current geologic processes to explain patterns of change in the past. In much the same way, evolutionary science takes what we know about microevolution and extends it to explain the long-term pattern of macroevolution.

◀ *The fossil remains of* Confuciusornis sanctus, *the earliest known bird, found in China and dating to 130 million years ago. The study of long-term evolution, or macroevolution, is centered on the origin and evolution of new species. (© O. Louis Mazzatenta/National Geographic Society Image Collection)*

THE BIRTH AND DEATH OF SPECIES

The origin of new species has been observed in historical times and in the present. Some new species have been brought about by human intervention and controlled breeding; examples include many species of tropical fish. New species have also arisen naturally in the recent past, such as certain types of fruit flies. In addition, we have information on populations in the process of forming new species, such as certain groups of snails. We also have seen (and contributed to) many examples of extinction—the death of a species.

How do new species come into being? Why do some species die out? Even though the title of Darwin's book is *On the Origin of Species,* it is ironic that Darwin did not focus much on this question. Instead, Darwin sought to explain the basic nature of evolutionary change, believing that extension of these principles could explain the formation of new species.

What Is a Species?

The term *species* is used in a number of different ways in evolutionary biology (Ereshefsky 1992). In this chapter, the emphasis is on the **biological species concept,** which defines species in terms of reproductive capability. If organisms from two populations are capable of breeding naturally and can produce fertile offspring, then they are classified in the same species. Note that this definition has several parts. First, organisms from different populations must be capable of interbreeding. Second, these matings must occur in nature. Recent advances in biology have allowed individuals usually considered to belong to separate species to produce offspring under laboratory conditions. In understanding evolutionary history, we are interested in breeding that takes place naturally. Third, the offspring must be *fertile*—that is, capable of producing further offspring.

Perhaps the best-known example of an application of the biological species concept is the mule. Mules are farm animals produced as the offspring of a horse bred with a donkey. The horse and donkey interbreed naturally, which satisfies the first and second parts of the species definition. However, the offspring (mules) are sterile and cannot produce further offspring. The only way to get a mule is to mate a horse and a donkey. Because the offspring are not fertile, the horse and the donkey are considered separate species (Figure 4.1). All human populations around the world belong to the same species (*Homo sapiens*) because members can interbreed and produce fertile offspring.

The biological species concept assumes that two organisms either belong or do not belong to the same species. It does not allow for any kind of intermediate state. Why should this be a problem? Consider as an example two modern species that had a common ancestor at some point in the past. We usually draw an evolutionary "tree," showing the point at which a new "branch," or species, comes into being. If some populations of species A evolved into species B, then at what point did those populations stop being species A and start being species B? The species concept suggests that this change was instantaneous, because a creature either belongs to one species

biological species concept
A definition of species that focuses on reproductive capabilities, where organisms from different populations are considered to be in the same species if they naturally interbreed and produce fertile offspring.

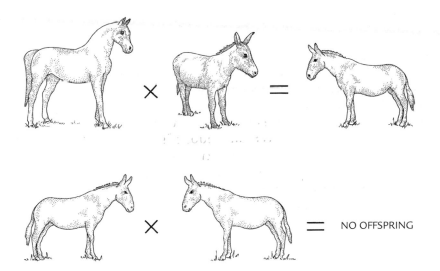

FIGURE 4.1

The horse and donkey can mate and produce offspring (a mule), but two mules cannot produce offspring. Therefore, the horse and donkey belong to two separate species although they are closely related.

NO OFFSPRING

or the other. Any system of classification tends to ignore variation within groups. In the real world, however, evolution and variation work to break down rigid systems of classification. Organisms become difficult to classify when they are constantly changing.

As an example of this problem, consider the populations of gypsy moths in Asia. When moths from the populations farthest apart are bred, their offspring are sterile. According to the biological species concept, these populations of moths belong to separate species. Populations that are closer together, however, are capable of producing fertile offspring, which suggests that they belong to the same species (Futuyma 1986).

The biological species concept is useful when comparing two or more populations living at a single point in time. How can the biological species concept be applied when comparing groups of organisms over a period of time? This question requires looking at two different modes of the evolutionary change of species.

First, a species can change over time. According to this mode of evolutionary change, a single species exists at any given point in time but evolves over a period of time. This mode of species change is known as **anagenesis,** or straight-line evolution. It is illustrated as a straight line, as shown in Figure 4.2, where form A evolves into form B and then into form C. Although this mode of evolutionary change is fairly straightforward, complications arise when considering the naming of species. Should form A be called a different species from form B? The problem is that the traditional biological species concept doesn't really apply. Form A and form B are by necessity isolated from each other reproductively because they lived at different times. There is no way they could interbreed any more than you could mate with an early human who lived 2 million years ago (we'll leave out science fiction and time machines here).

Many researchers modify the species concept to deal with this type of situation. Different physical forms along a single lineage (an evolutionary

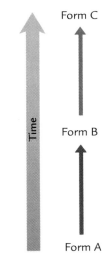

Form C

Form B

Form A

Time

FIGURE 4.2

Anagenesis, the linear evolution of a species over time. Form A changes over time into form B and then further changes into form C.

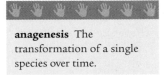

anagenesis The transformation of a single species over time.

FIGURE 4.3

Cladogenesis, the origin of new species. Species A splits and forms a new species B, which later splits to form species C. The process begins with a single species (A) and ends with three species (A, B, C).

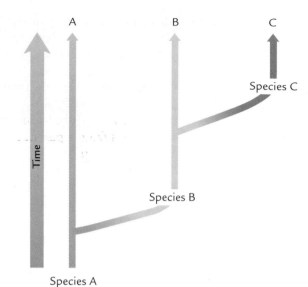

line such as that shown in Figure 4.2) are given different species names out of convenience and as a label to represent the types of physical change shown over time. Such forms are referred to as **paleospecies** and are used more as labels than as units representing the species concept. In recent years, there has been a tendency to move away from the use of paleospecies, at least among some evolutionary biologists.

Anagenesis is not the only mode of species change. If you think about it, anagenesis is not completely sufficient as an explanation of macroevolution. Where do new species come from? The other mode of species change is **cladogenesis,** or branching evolution. Cladogenesis involves the formation of new species (speciation) whereby one or more new species branch off from an original species. In Figure 4.3, a portion of species A first branches off to produce species B (living at the same time), then a portion of species B branches to produce species C. This example starts with one species and ends up with three. The factors responsible for speciation will be discussed later in this chapter.

The problem of species naming is complicated by the fact that evolutionary relationships among fossil forms are not always clear. Some of these problems will be addressed later. For now, keep in mind that species names often mean different things to different people. The naming of species might adhere to an evolutionary model or might serve only as convenient labels of physical variation.

Speciation

The fossil record shows many examples of new species arising. How? You know that genetic differences between populations come about as a result of evolutionary forces. For a population to become a new species, these genetic

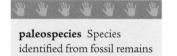

paleospecies Species identified from fossil remains based on their physical similarities and differences relative to other species.

cladogenesis The formation of one or more new species from another over time.

differences must be great enough to prevent successful interbreeding with the original parent species. For this to occur, the population must become reproductively isolated from the original parent species.

Reproductive Isolation   **Reproductive isolation** is genetic change that can lead to an inability to produce fertile offspring. How does this happen? Evolutionary forces can produce such a situation. The first step in **speciation** (the formation of a new species from a parent species) is the elimination or reduction of gene flow between populations. Because gene flow acts to reduce differences between populations, its continued action tends to keep all populations in the same species. Gene flow does not need to be eliminated altogether, but it must be reduced sufficiently to allow the other evolutionary forces to make the populations genetically different. Populations must become genetically isolated from one another for speciation to occur.

The most common form of isolation in animal species is geographic isolation. When two populations are separated by a physical barrier, such as a river or mountain range, or by great distances, gene flow is cut off between the populations. As long as the populations remain isolated, genetic changes occurring in one group will not spread to other groups. As we saw in Chapter 3, geographic distance limits gene flow even in our own highly mobile species. The effects of geographic distance in causing reproductive isolation are even more dramatic in other species.

Geographic separation is the most common means of producing reproductive isolation among animal populations, but other mechanisms may also cause isolation. Some of these can operate within a single geographic region. Populations may be isolated by behavioral differences such as feeding habits. Some groups may eat during the day and others at dusk. Because the groups are not in frequent contact with one another, there is opportunity for isolation to develop. Although geographic isolation is in theory not required, the actual probability of speciation occurring in geographically adjacent groups remains highly controversial. One reviewer notes that there is little evidence to date of speciation occurring without geographic isolation (Coyne 1992).

Genetic Divergence   Isolation is the first step in the speciation process. By itself, this isolation does not guarantee speciation. Elimination of gene flow provides the opportunity for speciation. Other evolutionary forces must then act upon this isolation to produce a situation in which the isolated groups have changed sufficiently to make fertile interbreeding no longer possible. Isolation, however, does not always lead to speciation.

How can the evolutionary forces lead to speciation? Mutation might act to increase variation among populations because it occurs independently in the genetic composition of separate groups. Without gene flow to spread them, individual mutations will accumulate in each group, making isolated populations genetically divergent. Genetic drift also contributes to differences in allele frequencies among small populations. In addition, if the two

reproductive isolation
The genetic isolation of populations that may render them incapable of producing offspring.

speciation The origin of a new species.

populations are in separate environments, then natural selection will lead to genetic differences. Once gene flow has been eliminated, the other evolutionary forces will act to make the populations genetically divergent. When this process continues to the point where the two populations can no longer interbreed and produce fertile offspring, they have become separate species.

There is continued debate over the role of the various evolutionary forces in producing genetic divergence. For many years, speciation was felt to be solely the by-product of natural selection. That is, as two populations came to occupy separate environments, the action of natural selection would cause these groups to become different. Speciation has been viewed as a consequence of this differential adaptation. In recent years, however, more attention has been given to the contributions to speciation of mutation and genetic drift in small populations. In the former view, the old species gradually formed two or more species, with natural selection operating on large populations. The more recent view is that new species often form from small populations and, as such, are affected extensively by mutation and genetic drift.

Adaptive Radiation

The process of speciation minimally results in two species: the original parent species and the new offspring species. Under certain circumstances, many new species can come into being in a short period of time. This rapid diversification of species is associated with changing environmental conditions. When new environments open up, or when new adaptations to a specific environment develop, many new species can form—a process known as **adaptive radiation.**

The Tempo and Mode of Macroevolution

During the past 30 years, considerable attention has been given to the tempo (how fast?) and mode (the mechanism) of macroevolutionary change. How quickly do new species form? Does speciation occur in large or small populations? What are the effects of natural selection and the other evolutionary forces in producing new species? These are all questions about the tempo and mode of macroevolution.

Gradualism   Charles Darwin saw speciation as a slow and gradual process, taking thousands or millions of years. To Darwin, natural selection acted on populations ultimately to produce new species. The view that macroevolution is a slow and gradual process is called **gradualism.** According to this view, small changes in each generation over time result in major biological changes.

Gradualism, then, regards speciation as a slow process that takes a long time to occur. New species form from large portions of an original species. In such large populations, genetic drift and mutation have little impact in

adaptive radiation
The formation of many new species following the availability of new environments or the development of a new adaptation.

gradualism A model of macroevolutionary change whereby evolutionary changes occur at a slow, steady rate over time.

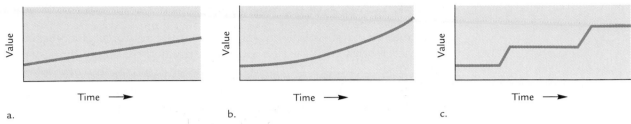

a.   b.   c.

FIGURE 4.4

The tempo of macroevolution: gradualism and punctuated equilibrium. Each portion of this figure has a line showing the change in value of a physical trait over time. (a) Gradualism: the change over time is linear and constant. (b) A geometric, gradual pattern. The rate of change increases with time, but the curve is still smooth; there are no discontinuities. (c) Punctuated equilibrium: there are periods of no change (stasis) punctuated by periods of rapid change; the net result is a "staircase" pattern.

each generation. Natural selection, slowly operating on some initial mutation(s), is primarily responsible for speciation.

The gradualistic model predicts that, given a suitable fossil record, we will see a smooth and gradual transition from one species into another. Although there are examples of such change in the fossil record, it is not always apparent. In some cases, we lack transitional forms. Does this lack of evidence indicate problems in the fossil record or in the theory of gradualism itself?

Punctuated Equilibrium   An alternative hypothesis has been suggested by Niles Eldredge and Stephen Jay Gould in the form of a model known as **punctuated equilibrium** (Eldredge and Gould 1972; Gould and Eldredge 1977). This hypothesis suggests that the pattern of macroevolution consists of long periods of time when little evolutionary change occurs (stasis) and short periods of time when rapid evolutionary change occurs. To Eldredge and Gould, the tempo of macroevolution is not gradual; rather, it is static at times and rapid at other times. Long periods of stasis are punctuated by short periods of rapid evolutionary change. Examples of gradualism and punctuated equilibrium are given in Figure 4.4.

Eldredge and Gould also view speciation as a rapid event occurring within small isolated populations on the periphery of a species range. Mutations can spread quickly in small populations as a consequence of inbreeding and genetic drift. If such genetic changes are adaptive and if the newly formed species gains access to the parental species' range, it may then spread throughout an area, replacing the original parent species. According to this model, most biological change occurs during speciation. Once a species has been established, it changes little throughout time. Eldredge and Gould argue that stabilizing selection and other factors act to keep a species the same over time. This view contrasts with the gradualistic model, which sees biological change occurring at a slow rate, ultimately leading to separate species.

Punctuated equilibrium makes a prediction about how the fossil record should look. Given stasis, we should see long periods of time when little evolutionary change takes place. Certain organisms, such as the cockroach and coelacanth, seem to follow this pattern—they have not changed much over many millions of years. The punctuated equilibrium model also predicts that new species will appear rather quickly, often without any evidence of a transitional state. Because the model predicts that speciation occurs within small isolated populations, there is little chance that we will have fossil evidence actually documenting the initial stages of the origin of a new species.

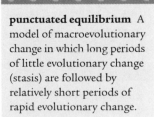

punctuated equilibrium A model of macroevolutionary change in which long periods of little evolutionary change (stasis) are followed by relatively short periods of rapid evolutionary change.

Extinctions and Mass Extinctions

In considering macroevolutionary trends, we must not forget the most common pattern of them all—extinction. It is estimated that more than 99 percent of all species that ever existed have become extinct (Futuyma 1986). In historic times, humans have witnessed (and helped cause) the extinction of a number of organisms, such as the passenger pigeon.

What causes extinction? When a species is no longer adapted to a changed environment, it may die. The exact causes of a species' death vary from situation to situation. Rapid ecological change may render an environment hostile to a species. For example, temperatures may change and a species may not be able to adapt. Food resources may be affected by environmental changes, which will then cause problems for a species requiring these resources. Other species may become better adapted to an environment, resulting in competition and ultimately the death of a species.

Extinction seems, in fact, to be the ultimate fate of all species. Natural selection is a remarkable mechanism for providing a species with the ability to adapt to change, but it does not always work. When the environment changes too rapidly or when the appropriate genetic variations do not exist, a species can become extinct.

The fossil record shows that extinction has occurred throughout the history of the planet. Recent analysis has also revealed that on some occasions a large number of species became extinct at the same time—a **mass extinction.** One of the best-known examples of mass extinction occurred 65 million years ago with the demise of dinosaurs and many other forms of life. Perhaps the most severe mass extinction occurred roughly 250 million years ago when more than 90 percent of marine species, about 70 percent of terrestrial vertebrates, and most land plants became extinct (Becker et al. 2001). Mass extinctions can be caused by a relatively rapid change in the environment, compounded by the close interrelationship of many species. If, for example, something were to happen to destroy much of the plankton in the oceans, then the oxygen content of our planet would drop, affecting even organisms not living in the oceans. Such a change would probably lead to a mass extinction.

MISCONCEPTIONS ABOUT EVOLUTION

Evolution is a frequently misunderstood subject. Many of our basic ideas regarding evolution are misconceptions that have become part of the general culture. The often used phrase "survival of the fittest" conjures up images that are sometimes at odds with the actual findings of evolutionary science. It is common for such misconceptions to continue even after initial exposure to evolutionary theory.

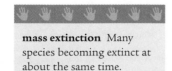

mass extinction Many species becoming extinct at about the same time.

The Nature of Selection

Many people have a basic understanding of the general principles of natural selection. The problem lies in our misinterpretation of the nature of natural selection.

SPECIAL TOPIC

Science Fiction and Orthogenesis

Evolution, especially human evolution, is a common theme in science fiction. Although a good many science fiction stories have a strong scientific base, others—most likely due to plot needs—do not. Even these stories, though, are valuable in terms of what they tell us about misconceptions about evolution, one of the themes of this chapter.

A personal favorite of mine is an episode of the 1960s science fiction television show *The Outer Limits*. The episode, entitled "The Sixth Finger," is an entertaining treatment of a popular science fiction question: What will humans evolve into? The story, aired in 1963, begins with a young coal miner, Gwyllm Griffiths, who yearns for something more than a life of manual labor. Through his girlfriend, Cathy, he meets a local scientist, Professor Mathers, who had once worked on an atomic bomb project. Because of guilt, the scientist is seeking an end to violence and war—through evolution. Reasoning that humans will someday evolve beyond the need for violence, and tormented by the "slow pace of evolution," Mathers invents a machine that will move an organism into its own predestined evolutionary future.

Gwyllm volunteers as a human subject, and the results are predictable. With each exposure to the machine, his head and brain increase in size, as does his intelligence. Additionally, he "evolves" a sixth finger (for "increased dexterity") and assorted mental powers (the sixth finger is particularly interesting because some people today are born with a sixth finger, and there does not appear to be any evolutionary advantage). Gwyllm also develops a dislike for the people around him and eventu-

ally decides to destroy them. On his way to demolish the town with his mental powers, he suddenly "evolves beyond the need for violence." He returns to the professor's laboratory and enlists the help of Cathy to operate the machinery while he evolves into "the man of the future." Once Gwyllm is in the machine's chamber, Cathy cannot bear to lose him forever and pushes the machine's lever to "Backward" rather than "Forward." For a brief moment she pushes too much and the viewer sees Gwyllm evolve back to some sort of subhuman ape, but she quickly corrects the lever and they live happily ever after (in one alternate ending, the script called for Gwyllm to continue evolving back to protoplasm) (Schow and Frentzen 1986).

This episode is quite entertaining and also provides some good examples of evolutionary misconceptions. For example, the doctrine of orthogenesis, the notion that evolution follows a particular path, is central to the entire plot. This message is not subtle—at one point, Gwyllm speaks about "the goal of evolution." The professor's machine embodies the idea of orthogenesis, with its lever marked "Forward" and "Backward," implying that all of life evolves along a fixed path from past to present. Orthogenesis is also apparent in the continued expansion of the brain and mental powers as Gwyllm evolves "forward," enabling him to read massive volumes at a glance and become a concert pianist overnight.

Despite the scientific inaccuracies, "The Sixth Finger" remains a captivating story. It was also somewhat controversial in that it dealt, on television, with evolution, a theme that had drawn criticism from the network's censor.

Misconception: Bigger Is Better　A common misconception is that natural selection will *always* lead to larger structures. According to this idea, the bigger the brain, the better, and the bigger the body, the better. At first, this idea seems reasonable. After all, larger individuals may be more likely to survive because they can compete more successfully for food and sexual partners. Therefore, larger individuals are more likely to survive and pass their genes on to the next generation. Natural selection is expected to lead to an increase in the size of the body, brain, and other structures. However, this isn't always true. There are numerous examples of species in which *smaller* body size or structures were more adaptive and selected for. Keep in mind that in evolution nothing is free. A larger body may be more adaptive because of sheer size, but a larger body also has greater energy needs. Any advantage gained by a larger body may be offset by the disadvantage of needing more food. What we have to focus on is a *balance* between the adaptive and nonadaptive aspects of any biological characteristic. By walking upright, humans have their hands free, which is rather advantageous. However, we pay the price with varicose veins, back pain, fallen arches, and other nonadaptive consequences of walking on two legs. Again, we need to focus on the relative costs and benefits of any evolutionary change. Of course, this balance will vary in different environments.

Misconception: Newer Is Better   There is a tendency to believe that traits more recent in origin are superior because they are newer. Humans walk on two legs, a trait that appeared close to 6 million years ago. We also have five digits (fingers and toes) that date back many hundreds of millions of years. Is upright walking better because it is newer? Of course not. Both features are essential to our toolmaking way of life. The age of a structure has no bearing on its usefulness.

Misconception: Natural Selection Always Works   The idea that natural selection will always provide an opportunity for some members of a species to survive is not accurate. Occasionally I have heard statements such as "we will evolve to tolerate air pollution." Such statements are absurdities. Natural selection only operates on variations that are present. If no genetic variation occurs to aid in breathing polluted air, natural selection will not help us. Even in cases where genetic variation is present, the environment may change too quickly for us to respond through natural selection. All we have to do is to examine the fossil record to see how inaccurate this misconception is—that 99 percent of all past species are extinct shows us that natural selection obviously doesn't always work!

Misconception: There Is an Inevitable Direction in Evolution   An idea popular in the nineteenth century was **orthogenesis,** the notion that evolution would continue in a given direction because of a vaguely defined nonphysical "force" (Mayr 1982). As an alternative to the theory of natural selection, orthogenesis suggested that evolutionary change would continue in the same direction until either a perfect structure was attained or a species became extinct. Apart from the problems of dealing with metaphysical "forces," orthogenesis has long been rejected by analysis of the fossil record and the triumph of natural selection as an explanatory mechanism for evolutionary change. Some of its basic notions, however, are still perpetuated. A common belief is that humans will evolve larger and larger brains, as a continuation of earlier trends (Figure 4.5). The view of orthogenesis is tied in with notions of "progress" and with the misconception that bigger is better. There are many examples from the fossil record of nonlinear change and many examples of reversals in sizes of structures. In the case of human evolution, brains actually stopped getting larger 50,000 years ago. In fact, the average brain size of humans since that time has decreased slightly as a consequence of a general decrease in skeletal size and ruggedness (Henneberg 1988).

Is it possible for a trend to continue to change in a given direction under the right circumstances? Of course, but change comes through the action of

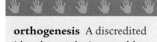

orthogenesis A discredited idea that evolution would continue in a given direction because of some vaguely defined "force."

natural selection, not some mysterious internal force. Continuation of any trend depends on the environment, present genetic variation, and basic biological limits. (A 50-foot spider can't exist because it wouldn't be able to absorb enough oxygen for its volume.) Such change also depends on the relative cost and benefits of change. Suppose that an increase in human brain size was combined somehow with an increase in pelvic size (assuming genetic variation was present for both features). A larger pelvis would make walking difficult or even impossible. Evolution works on the entire organism and not one trait at a time. Any change can have both positive and negative effects, but it is the net balance that is critical to the operation of natural selection.

Structure, Function, and Evolution

A number of misconceptions about evolution focus on the relationship between biological structures and their adaptive (or nonadaptive) functions.

Misconception: Natural Selection Always Produces Perfect Structures
There is a tendency to view nature as the product of perfect natural engineering. Granted, there are many marvelous and wondrous phenomena in the natural world, but a closer examination shows that biological structures are often far from perfect. Consider human beings. Is the human body perfect? Hardly. Just to note one aspect, consider your skeleton when you stand upright. What is holding in your internal organs? Skin and muscles. Your rib cage provides little support for lower internal organs because it reflects ancestry from a four-legged form. When humans stood up (adaptive), the rib cage offered less support. The result—a variety of complaints and complications, such as hernias. The human skeleton is not perfect but rather is the result of natural selection operating on the variation that was present.

Misconception: All Structures Are Adaptive   Natural selection is such a powerful model that it is tempting to apply it to all biological structures. Indeed, many anthropologists and biologists have done so. They examine a structure and explain its function in terms of natural selection. Are all structures adaptive? Many structures simply reflect a by-product of other biological changes and have no adaptive value of their own (Gould and Lewontin 1979). Other structures, such as the human appendix, may have served a function in the past but appear to have no present function.

A classic example of a presumably nonadaptive trait is the chin of modern human beings. The jutting chin is relatively modern (see Chapter 14). Earlier forms of *Homo sapiens* lacked the jutting chin in most cases. According to a strict adaptationist perspective, we would become concerned with the function of the jutting chin and attempt to explain it in terms of natural selection. Actually, the jutting chin is simply a by-product of different growth patterns in the human face and jaw. When the face receded, the lower jaw, under a different pattern of growth, stayed at its previous size. The result—a jutting chin that has nothing to do with adaptive value, except as a by-product of adaptive changes in the rest of the face.

FIGURE 4.5

The theory of orthogenesis predicts continued change in a given direction. Illustrated here is the popular but incorrect notion that humans in the future will have progressively larger brains.

Another example deals with an old question: "Why do human men have nipples?" Earlier explanations suggesting that in ancient times men could assist women in breast feeding are ludicrous. The true explanation is simple. Both male and female develop from the same basic body plan during the embryonic stage of prenatal life. Under the influence of sex hormones, various structures develop in different ways (just as the same structure develops into a penis in men and a clitoris in women). The basic body plan for nipples is present in both sexes; for women, these structures develop into breasts capable of lactation. In men, nipples serve no functional purpose. Thus, male nipples are a by-product of the fact that males and females share a similar developmental path and not the result of some adaptive value (Gould 1991).

Misconception: Current Structures Always Reflect Initial Adaptations
The idea here is that any given structure, with an associated function, originally evolved specifically for that function. Human beings, for example, walk on two legs; this allows them to hold tools and other objects that are constructed with the aid of an enlarged brain. Although it is tempting to say that both upright walking and a larger brain evolved at the same time because of the adaptive value of having both structures, this is not what happened. Upright walking evolved roughly 3.5 million years before the use of stone tools and the expansion of the brain (Chapter 12).

As another example, consider your fingers. You have five of these digits on each hand, which enable you to perform a variety of manipulative tasks. Humans use their hands to manipulate both natural and human-made objects. Manipulative digits are essential to our nature as tool-using creatures. We might therefore suggest that our grasping hands *first* evolved to meet this need; this is not the case. Grasping hands *first* developed in early primate ancestors to meet the needs of living in the trees (Chapter 11). Even though we don't live in trees, we have retained this trait and use it *for a different purpose*. Natural selection operates on the variation that is present. Structures are frequently modified for different uses.

A BRIEF HISTORY OF LIFE

The remainder of this book will deal with the biological variation and evolution of humans and their close relatives. This section provides some brief background on the history of life on our planet.

Perspectives on Geologic Time

We lose sight of the immense age of the universe (roughly 15 billion years) and earth (4.6 billion years) because we are not used to dealing with such large numbers. To many people, the difference between a million and a billion does not seem great because both numbers are so extremely large. The astronomer Carl Sagan (1977) used an analogy he called the "Cosmic Calendar" to help put these dates into perspective. Imagine the entire history of the universe, from its beginning to the present, as taking a single year. That is, the universe came into being at midnight on January 1 of the year, and the present time is midnight on January 1 a year later. Our own galaxy, the Milky Way, comes into being on March 20, the solar system on September 2, and the earth on September 14. Life on earth begins approximately on October 6. Eukaryotes (cells with nuclei) begin on November 14. Almost 11 complete months pass and nothing resembling a human being has yet evolved!

By December 1, a significant oxygen atmosphere has developed on earth. By December 17, the invertebrates have come into being. The first fish and vertebrates appear on December 19, and colonization of land by early insects and amphibians takes place on December 21. Reptiles appear on the 23rd, dinosaurs and the first mammals on the 26th. By December 30, the dinosaurs have become extinct, and the first primates appear the next day. It is not until the final day of the year, December 31, that apes and humans appear!

The first humans appear at 9:00 P.M. on the final day. Fire is used by 11:22 P.M., and it is not until 11:59:35 that agriculture is invented. The Roman Empire occurs around 11:59:56. The European Renaissance takes place at one second before midnight. Everything that has occurred since then takes place in the final second (Figure 4.6).

The Origin of Life

Geologists and paleontologists divide the history of the earth into two **eons,** each of which is broken into **eras,** which are further broken into **periods.** The **Precambrian eon** dates from the beginning of the planet 4.6 billion years ago until 545 million years ago (thus covering almost 90 percent of earth's history). Major events of the Precambrian eon are the origin of life (obviously a major event), the development of single-celled organisms, and the first appearance of multicelled organisms. Although the fossil record preserves some of the earliest life, we lack direct fossil evidence for the first signs of life, microscopic cells dating back more than 3.5 billion years. We must rely instead on a knowledge of the early conditions of the planet and combine these observations with laboratory evidence suggesting possible origins of life. The different hypotheses for the initial origin of life are too detailed to cover here but are reviewed by Cowen (1995) and Schopf (1999).

The last 545 million years of earth's history lies in the **Phanerozoic eon,** which is broken down into three geological eras: Paleozoic, Mesozoic, and Cenozoic. Table 4.1 on page 112 lists the eras and periods of the Phanerozoic eon and the major evolutionary events that occurred during each.

The Paleozoic Era

The **Paleozoic era** is the term given for the time period between 545 million and 245 million years ago. At the beginning of the Paleozoic era, there was a rapid diversification of many organisms. Of particular interest here is the origin of the first vertebrates, the jawless fish. Over time, some of these early vertebrates adapted to living partially on land—the first primitive amphibians.

eon The major subdivision of geologic time.

era Subdivision of a geologic eon.

period Subdivision of a geologic era.

Precambrian eon The eon from the earth's beginning (4.6 billion years ago) until 545 million years ago. During this eon, single-celled and simple multicelled organisms first evolved.

Phanerozoic eon The past 545 million years.

Paleozoic era The first geologic era of the Phanerozoic eon, dating roughly between 545 and 245 million years ago, when the first vertebrates appeared.

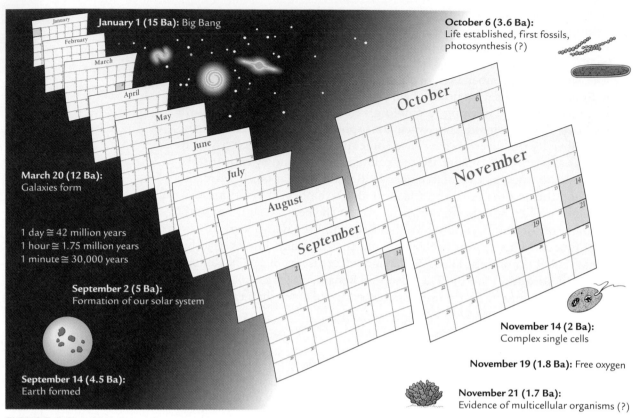

January 1 (15 Ba): Big Bang

October 6 (3.6 Ba):
Life established, first fossils, photosynthesis (?)

March 20 (12 Ba):
Galaxies form

1 day ≅ 42 million years
1 hour ≅ 1.75 million years
1 minute ≅ 30,000 years

September 2 (5 Ba):
Formation of our solar system

September 14 (4.5 Ba):
Earth formed

November 14 (2 Ba):
Complex single cells

November 19 (1.8 Ba): Free oxygen

November 21 (1.7 Ba):
Evidence of multicellular organisms (?)

FIGURE 4.6

Carl Sagan's "Cosmic Calendar." The history of the universe is compressed into a single year, with the origin of the universe happening on January 1 and the present day occurring at midnight on the following January 1. See the text for additional dates. The following abbreviations are used: ya = years ago, Ma = millions of years ago, and Ba = billions of years ago. (Source: Sagan [1977], with recent updates)

therapsid An early group of mammal-like reptiles; therapsids were the ancestors of later mammals.

Later in the Paleozoic era, complete adaptation to living on land occurred in the first primitive reptiles. The evolutionary changes that allowed colonization of the land are too detailed to discuss here but can be found in any current treatment of the fossil record (e.g., Cowen 1995).

Mammals (and birds) eventually evolved from reptiles. The evolution of mammals from reptiles suggests an intermediate form of animal. To many, an intermediate form implies some sort of "missing link," or a creature with a mixture of *modern* reptilian and mammalian features. This is an incorrect view of evolution. Modern reptiles and mammals represent millions of years of evolution from a common ancestor. The first reptiles did not look exactly like modern-day reptiles. In fact, some of the earliest primitive reptiles included a group referred to as the **therapsids,** or mammal-like reptiles. By the end of the Paleozoic era, reptiles had begun evolution in two different directions. One group ultimately led to modern-day reptiles, as well as dinosaurs and birds. The other group was the mammal-like reptiles.

The therapsids are classified as reptiles because they have more features that we would call reptilian. However, they also possessed certain mammalian features, such as different types of teeth (see Chapter 8). We therefore call them, for lack of a better term, mammal-like reptiles. Therapsids underwent an adaptive radiation during the Permian period of the Paleozoic era, with a wide variety of shapes and sizes emerging.

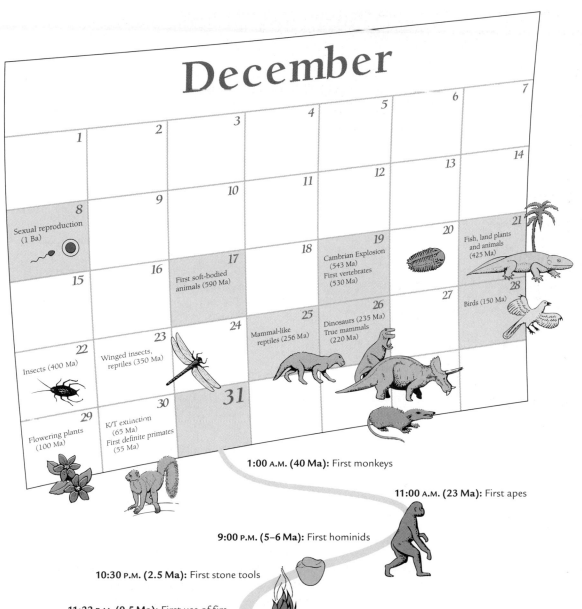

December

1

2

3

4

5

6

7

8 Sexual reproduction (1 Ba)

9

10

11

12

13

14

15

16

17 First soft-bodied animals (590 Ma)

18

19 Cambrian Explosion (543 Ma) First vertebrates (530 Ma)

20

21 Fish, land plants and animals (425 Ma)

22 Insects (400 Ma)

23 Winged insects, reptiles (350 Ma)

24

25 Mammal-like reptiles (256 Ma)

26 Dinosaurs (235 Ma) True mammals (220 Ma)

27

28 Birds (150 Ma)

29 Flowering plants (100 Ma)

30 K/T extinction (65 Ma) First definite primates (55 Ma)

31

1:00 A.M. (40 Ma): First monkeys

11:00 A.M. (23 Ma): First apes

9:00 P.M. (5–6 Ma): First hominids

10:30 P.M. (2.5 Ma): First stone tools

11:22 P.M. (0.5 Ma): First use of fire

11:59 P.M. (30,000 ya): Cave paintings

11:59:35 P.M. (12,000 ya): Farming

11:59:55 P.M. (2,000 ya): Common Era begins

11:59:59 P.M. (500 ya): Renaissance

		Millions of	
Era	*Period*	*Years Ago*	*Some Major Evolutionary Events*
Cenozoic	Quaternary	1.7 today	Evolution of the genus *Homo*
	Tertiary	65–1.8	Origin and evolution of the primates; origin of hominids
Mesozoic	Cretaceous	145–65	Extinction of the dinosaurs; first birds and placental mammals
	Jurassic	210–145	Dinosaurs dominate; first birdlike reptiles
	Triassic	245–210	First dinosaurs; egg-laying mammals
Paleozoic	Permian	290–245	Radiation of reptiles; mammal-like reptiles
	Carboniferous	360–290	Radiation of amphibians; first reptiles and insects
	Devonian	410–360	Many fish; first amphibians; first forests
	Silurian	440–410	First fish with jaws; land plants
	Ordovician	505–440	Early vertebrates, including jawless fish; trilobites and many other invertebrates
	Cambrian	545–505	"Explosion" of life; marine invertebrates

TABLE 4.1   Geological Eras and Periods of the Phanerozoic Eon

Sources: Cowen (1995), Fleagle (1999), Schopf (1992)

The dental adaptations of the therapsids were well suited to life on land, allowing them to forage and hunt. Although this group was highly successful, they ultimately declined following an adaptive radiation of dinosaurs during the Mesozoic era.

The Mesozoic Era

The **Mesozoic era,** lasting from 245 million to 65 million years ago, is often called the "Age of Reptiles" because it was the time when reptiles became the dominant form of life on the earth's surface. One of the most successful groups of reptiles was the dinosaurs (Figure 4.7). The major characteristic of the dinosaurs was the modification of the leg and pelvic structures. Many dinosaurs were bipedal, and some appear to have been extremely quick movers and efficient walkers and runners (Wilford 1985). The therapsids, on the other hand, did not change much beyond the earliest land vertebrates except for modifications in their teeth. Therapsids were not fast movers and had few defensive or offensive abilities. In the Permian period, they did not need such adaptations. The world lay open for them to colonize.

Unfortunately for the therapsids, the ancestors of the dinosaurs developed quicker and more efficient locomotion, and many species further developed powerful hands and teeth to capture prey. Ultimately, the dinosaurs emerged as the dominant form of animal life on land, and the therapsids de-

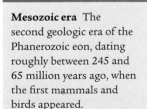

Mesozoic era The second geologic era of the Phanerozoic eon, dating roughly between 245 and 65 million years ago, when the first mammals and birds appeared.

clined in number. Eventually the therapsids became extinct, but before this happened some of the therapsids evolved into what we call "true mammals."

During the Triassic period, the monotremes, or egg-laying mammals, evolved. Some, such as the platypus, have survived until the present day. The first placental mammals evolved during the Jurassic period, which was the heyday of the dinosaurs. Birdlike reptiles also evolved during this time period. At the end of the Cretaceous period, the dinosaurs became extinct and mammals became the dominant animal life.

Why did the dinosaurs (and many other organisms) become extinct? Some of the more fanciful suggestions include excessive constipation because of changes in plant life. Most theories of dinosaur extinction rely on environmental change, such as the cooling of the earth. If the temperature dropped, then the warm-blooded mammals would seem to be better adapted than the cold-blooded reptiles. A problem with this idea is that there is evidence that at least some of the dinosaurs were warm-blooded. Recent explanations of dinosaur extinction have relied on the idea that an asteroid or comet hit the earth with tremendous force, kicking up clouds of dust and blocking the sun. Temperatures dropped, and many plant forms became extinct. As plants died, so did the plant eaters and those who ate the plant eaters. In other words, the entire ecology of the planet was altered. There is considerable geologic evidence for such a catastrophic event (e.g., Sheehan et al. 1991).

The Cenozoic Era

When the dinosaurs died out, a variety of new opportunities opened up for the mammals, and they began a series of adaptive radiations that filled vacant environmental niches. The last 65 million years of earth's history is the

Cenozoic era, often called the "Age of Mammals." It is during this time that all modern groups of mammals evolved, including the primates, the group of mammals to which humans belong. The earliest primates appear by 50 million years ago. Early apelike primates evolve by about 20 million to 25 million years ago, and the first bipeds (early human ancestors) appear about 6 million years ago. Other changes in human evolution, such as the increase in brain size and the manufacture of stone tools, have taken place only within the past 2.5 million years. The history of primate and human evolution is described in later chapters. For the moment, it is sufficient to simply understand the long span of time of earth's history and to remember that humans are a recent evolutionary development.

SUMMARY

Macroevolution, the process of long-term evolution, can occur in two ways: anagenesis, the evolution of a single species over time, or cladogenesis, the splitting off of one or more new species from the original parent species. In cladogenesis, new species form through the process of reproductive isolation followed by genetic divergence. Both steps are understood in terms of evolutionary forces. Reduction or elimination of gene flow provides for the beginning of reproductive isolation. Mutation, genetic drift, and selection can then act on this isolation to produce a new species. The relative importance of the evolutionary forces in speciation is still debated.

Two models of macroevolutionary change can be applied to the fossil record. Gradualism states that most evolutionary change is the result of slow but constant change over many generations. New species are believed to form as a by-product of natural selection operating over time. Punctuated equilibrium states that there are long periods of time with little evolutionary change (stasis), punctuated by rapid evolutionary events. New species are seen as forming in small, isolated populations.

The most common evolutionary pattern is extinction. Some scientists have argued that the evolutionary record is best understood as the process of new species forming from old, with many species becoming extinct. The evolutionary trends we observe in the fossil record may reflect the differential survival of species with certain adaptations.

There are many misconceptions regarding natural selection and evolution. Some of the more common of these are that bigger is better, that newer is better, that natural selection always works, and that there is an inevitable direction to natural selection. There are also misconceptions regarding the relationship of biological structures, their functions, and their evolutionary origin.

Life on earth began following a period of chemical evolution. The earliest life forms evolved in ancient oceans. The first vertebrates were the jawless fish, which evolved into fish with jaws. One group of jawed fish, the lobe-fins, were the ancestors of all later land vertebrates. After the amphibians conquered the land, an adaptive radiation of reptiles fully adapted to land conditions began. One of the first sort of reptiles was the therapsids, or mammal-

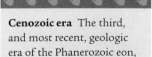

Cenozoic era The third, and most recent, geologic era of the Phanerozoic eon, dating roughly to the last 65 million years. The first primates appeared during the Cenozoic era.

like reptiles. These forms possessed certain dental traits that allowed them to exploit new types of food. The later adaptive radiation of the dinosaurs ultimately led to the extinction of the therapsids. Before they disappeared, however, some therapsids evolved into the first true mammals. For millions of years, the dinosaurs were the dominant land animals and the mammals existed in the fringe environmental niche of arboreal nocturnal life. When the dinosaurs disappeared during the mass extinction at the end of the Mesozoic era, the mammals had the opportunity to expand into newly available niches.

SUPPLEMENTAL READINGS

Cowen, R. 1995. *History of Life*. 2d ed. Boston: Blackwell Scientific Publications. An up-to-date and very thorough review of the fossil record from the origins of life to the present.

Futuyma, D. J. 1997. *Evolutionary Biology*. 3d ed. Sunderland, Mass.: Sinauer Associates. A comprehensive treatment of evolutionary theory and the history of life.

Schopf, J. W. 1999. *Cradle of Life: The Discovery of Earth's Earliest Fossils*. Princeton: Princeton University Press. A highly readable summary of the fossil evidence for the earliest life on our planet and a discussion of different models of the origin of life.

INTERNET RESOURCES

http://www.talkorigins.org/faqs/faq-intro-to-biology.html
Introduction to Evolutionary Biology, a review of microevolution and macroevolution.

http://anthro.palomar.edu/synthetic/synth_9.htm
Micro and Macro Evolution, a tutorial on evolutionary theory with an emphasis on speciation.

http://www.talkorigins.org/faqs/punc-eq.html
Punctuated Equilibria, a summary of the model, including discussion of some common misinterpretations.

http://seaborg.nmu.edu/earth/Life.html
A Pictorial History of Life on Earth, a Web page with many links organized around geologic eras and periods.

PART II

Human Biological Variation

How and why are human beings different from one another? We all encounter biological variation (diversity) every day of our lives. Some people are taller than others or have rounder heads or lighter skin color. Additional diversity exists in many genetic traits that are not visible to the naked eye, such as blood groups and DNA sequences. Biological anthropologists are interested in describing and explaining such variation. After reading the previous four chapters, it should come as no surprise to you that biological anthropologists examine diversity from an evolutionary perspective. The variation that we see in living humans is a reflection of past evolutionary events. Furthermore, the study of biological variation provides us with a context within which to judge variation in the past (see Parts III and IV). Chapter 5 describes the different data and methods used by biological anthropologists to study human diversity. Chapter 6 provides a number of case studies of human microevolution that illustrate how we draw evolutionary conclusions from data from living peoples. Finally, Chapter 7 examines biological diversity from the perspective of biocultural adaptation.

May 27

The Study
of Human Variation

Every day we encounter human biological diversity (Figure 5.1), but we seldom speak of what we see in evolutionary terms. On a day-to-day basis,
most people think about variation in terms of the widely used but imprecise
word *race*. People are often surprised to learn that anthropologists today
look at variation in terms of evolutionary forces and are not concerned (except in a historical sense) with race or racial classifications. Race is a descriptive concept and not an analytic tool. At best, it provides a crude and often
misleading label for variation and explains nothing.

However, because the concept of race is so ingrained in society and structures many of our ideas on variation, we need to review exactly what race is
and is not. Throughout much of this chapter, then, we review the concept of
race and then examine the evolutionary alternative. As we shall see, the evolutionary forces discussed in Chapter 3 form the basis for our understanding
of the patterns and causes of human biological variation.

MEASURING HUMAN VARIATION

Exactly *what* are we talking about? Whether we approach human variation
from a racial perspective or an evolutionary perspective, we need to know what
we mean by "human variation." Variation, of course, means the differences

◄ *Lapp people of northern Europe during the spring migration of their reindeer
herd. The Lapps are genetically similar to populations in both Europe and
Asia. Human variation and the biological relationship between different
groups of humans and their origin has long been a focus of biological
anthropology. (© George F. Mobley/National Geographic Society Image Collection)*

FIGURE 5.1

*Human biological diversity in external physical traits. (*Top left, © Bill Bachmann/The Image Works; top center, © Alan Carey/ The Image Works; top right, © John Moss/Photo Researchers, Inc.; bottom left, © Renee Lynn/Photo Researchers, Inc.; bottom center, © Bachmann/Photo Researchers, Inc.; bottom right, © David Young-Wolff/PhotoEdit)

that exist among people and populations. We are all aware of biological variation—some people are taller, or darker, or have differently shaped skulls. We also know from Chapters 2 and 3 that people frequently have different blood groups or other varying aspects of their biochemical makeup. Is the measure of human variation simply a matter of examining how different people look? Although we frequently do just that in our daily lives, simple observation is not adequate for scientific analysis. First of all, it is too subjective. Looking at people and rating them as "tall" versus "short" or "dark" versus "light" is too fraught with problems of observer bias to be much use. Second, our mental categories of variation (e.g., "light" versus "dark") do not acknowledge that traits such as human skin color do not come in three or four groups but are

TABLE 5.1   Determining a Person's ABO Blood Type

		Reaction with Antibody	
Blood Type	Antigen(s) Present in Blood	anti-A	anti-B
A	A	Yes	No
B	B	No	Yes
AB	A and B	Yes	Yes
O	None	No	No

instead continuous. Third, much of the genetic variation that exists is invisible to our eyes—you cannot tell a person's blood group by looking at him or her.

Many different measures and methods have been devised to assess biological variation, and new methods are being developed all the time. A few of these methods are reviewed here briefly.

Biochemical Variation

First we examine "simple" genetic traits—those that are not affected by the environment during a person's life and that reflect a simple relationship between genotype and phenotype. These traits reflect differences in biochemistry, such as blood types and DNA sequences.

Blood Types and Other Genetic Markers   One of the most common genetic measures used in studies of human variation is a person's blood type, such as the ABO blood type and the MN blood type discussed in Chapter 2. These are only a couple of the blood type systems that have been discovered; others include the Rhesus, Diego, Duffy, and Kell blood group systems, to name only a few. Different blood group systems are identified by the types of molecules present on the surface of the red blood cells. Each blood group system has a particular antibody–antigen reaction that can be used to identify the different blood groups. **Antibodies** are substances that react to foreign substances (**antigens**) invading the blood stream. This antibody–antigen reaction (clumping of red blood cells) allows us to classify different blood groups.

As an example, consider the ABO blood group discussed in Chapter 2. Remember that this system has three alleles (*A, B,* and *O*), where *A* and *B* are codominant and *O* is recessive. There are four different phenotypes: type A (genotypes *AA* and *AO*), type B (genotypes *BB* and *BO*), type O (genotype *OO*), and type AB (genotype *AB*). Two antibodies react to specific antigens. One of these, anti-A, reacts to A-type molecules (in people with blood type A or AB). The other, anti-B, reacts to B-type molecules (in people with blood type B or AB). Because each blood type has a different combination of A and B antigens (Table 5.1), these reactions allow us to find out which of the four ABO blood types a person has. For example, people with type A blood have the A antigen but not the B. Suppose we take a sample of a person's blood and

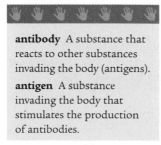

antibody A substance that reacts to other substances invading the body (antigens).

antigen A substance invading the body that stimulates the production of antibodies.

FIGURE 5.2

*Dr. Michael Crawford
collecting hair samples from
the Evenki, a group of reindeer
herders in Siberia. DNA can
be extracted from hair samples.*
(Courtesy of Michael Crawford)

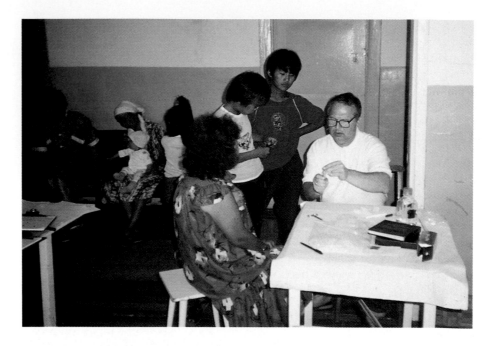

FIGURE 5.2

*Dr. Michael Crawford
collecting hair samples from
the Evenki, a group of reindeer
herders in Siberia. DNA can
be extracted from hair samples.*
(Courtesy of Michael Crawford)

find that the blood clumps when exposed to anti-A antibodies but not when exposed to anti-B antibodies. This means the person has A antigens but not B antigens and therefore has type A blood. The same basic method (although sometimes more complex) is used for determining the phenotypes of other blood group systems.

In addition to red blood cell groups, genetic analyses have been done on many populations for red blood cell enzymes and proteins and for proteins in blood serum (the fluid part of the blood). One method used for detecting variants of such traits is **electrophoresis.** With this method, blood samples are placed on a gel that is electrically charged. Proteins move along the flow of electrons from negative to positive, and some proteins move at faster rates. This difference in movement allows us to determine a person's genotype.

DNA Analysis   Many new methods focus on the direct examination of sequences of DNA that can be extracted from body tissues (Figure 5.2). One method of DNA analysis focuses on **restriction fragment length polymorphisms (RFLPs).** Certain enzymes produced by different species of bacteria, known as *restriction enzymes,* bind to sections of DNA and cut the DNA sequence at a given point. A difference in a person's DNA sequence will change the location where it is cut, and hence change the length of the DNA fragment (White and Lalouel 1988). Differences in the *length* of DNA sequences provide us with yet another measure of human variation.

A recent development in genetics is the analysis of noncoding DNA sequences that are repeated. One example is **microsatellite DNA,** which consists of repeated short sections of DNA (2–5 bases). One type of analysis counts the number of repeats. For example, the DNA sequence CACACACACA contains five repeats of the CA sequence, and the DNA sequence CACACA con-

electrophoresis A laboratory method that uses electric current to separate proteins, allowing genotype to be determined.

restriction fragment length polymorphism (RFLP) A genetic trait defined in terms of the length of DNA fragments produced when certain enzymes cut the DNA sequence.

microsatellite DNA Repeated short sequences of DNA; the number of repeats is highly variable.

tains three repeats. The number of such repeats is highly variable and of use in detecting population relationships (e.g., Jorde et al. 1997).

Another interesting method of analysis focuses on ***Alu*** **insertions,** which are short DNA sequences that have replicated and moved to different locations on different chromosomes. It is estimated that roughly 5 percent of human DNA consists of these repeated elements (Stoneking et al. 1997). Polymorphisms are identified by noting the presence or absence of an *Alu* insertion at a given chromosome location. This trait has proven useful in analyses of human population history.

Recent investigations in genetics have focused on **single-nucleotide polymorphisms (SNPs),** loci where DNA sequences differ by one base. For example, consider the following two DNA sequences:

Sequence 1: GAACCTTTA

Sequence 2: GAATCTTTA

These two sequences differ in the fourth position, where sequence 1 has a C and sequence 2 has a T. Preliminary results from the Human Genome Project estimate that there are between 1.4 million and 2.1 million SNPs in the human genome, much within noncoding DNA (International Human Genome Sequencing Consortium 2001; Venter et al. 2001). The existence of so many SNPs provides geneticists with the ability to map the genome and look for linkages with a number of traits, including genes that might influence disease susceptibility.

Geneticists and anthropologists also compare entire DNA sequences across individuals and populations. One method of analysis consists of examining the "mismatch," the number of differences between sequences. Consider, for example, the following DNA sequences from three different individuals:

Individual 1   GGTGGTGAATCC

Individual 2   GGTCGTGAATCC

Individual 3   GGTGGTGTTTCC

If you look closely at each sequence, you will see that individual 1 and individual 2 differ at one position. Further, individual 1 and 3 differ by two positions, and individuals 2 and 3 differ by three positions. From such comparisons (performed on *much* longer sequences), we can make inferences regarding genetic similarity and the evolutionary history of DNA sequences.

One genetic locus that has been important in the debate over modern human origins (which will be covered in Chapter 14) is **mitochondrial DNA.** As discussed in Chapter 2, almost all of our DNA is contained in the chromosomes within the nuclei of our cells. Mitochondrial DNA (mtDNA) is an exception—it is a small section of DNA that exists within the mitochondrion, a part of the cell outside of the nucleus that is involved in energy production. Mitochondrial DNA is particularly interesting because of its mode of inheritance. For most traits *both* parents contribute genetically to the child. For mtDNA, however, *only* the female contributes genetically (Stoneking 1993). This happens because female sex cells contain mitochondria, whereas male

***Alu* insertion** A sequence of DNA repeated at different locations on different chromosomes.

single-nucleotide polymorphisms (SNPs) Specific positions in a DNA sequence that differ at one base. For example, the DNA sequences CCTGAA and CCCGAA differ in the third position—one sequence has the base T and the other the base C.

mitochondrial DNA A small amount of DNA that is located in the mitochondria of cells. Mitochondrial DNA is inherited only through the mother.

FIGURE 5.3

The author measures his son's stature. Stature and weight are two of the most common anthropometric measures.
(Photograph by Hollie Jaffe)

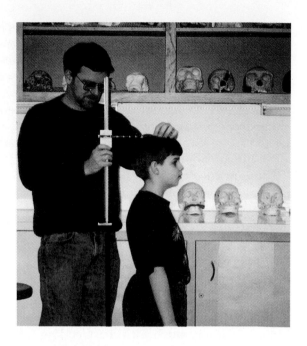

sex cells contain only the nucleus. In other words, mtDNA is inherited only from the mother. Your mtDNA came only from your mother, who obtained it from her mother, and so on. You inherit the rest of your DNA from both parents, who each inherited from two parents, and so forth. For most traits, the number of ancestors doubles every generation you go back: two parents, four grandparents, eight great-grandparents, and so forth. For mtDNA, you have only one ancestor in any given generation. This property allows patterns of genetic relationship to be reconstructed without the complication of the gene shuffling that occurs every generation for the rest of your DNA. Similar analyses are done with Y-chromosomes, which are inherited through the father's line (Hammer and Zegura 1996).

Complex Traits

Many of the traits of interest in studying human variation are complex traits—those that are frequently affected by growth and the environment and that reflect a much more complicated relationship between genotype and phenotype.

Anthropometrics   Measurements of the human body, including the head and the face, are known as **anthropometrics.** Two of the most commonly used anthropometric measures are height and weight (Figure 5.3). Other measurements of the body include the length of limbs and limb segments and the width of the body at different places, such as the shoulders and the hips. There are many measurements of the skull, such as the length, width, and height of the head, the relative width of the head at different points, and the size of the nose. Anthropometrics are applied to skeletal data as well as to living people.

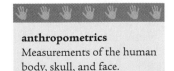

anthropometrics
Measurements of the human body, skull, and face.

Skin Color   In the past, skin color was often measured by comparing a person's skin to a set of standardized tiles. This method is too subjective and inaccurate, and the more common method today involves the use of a reflectance spectrophotometer—a device that measures the percentage of light reflected back from a given source at different wavelengths. To minimize the effects of tanning, we measure skin color on the inside of the upper arm, which is generally not as exposed to the sun as other parts of the body. The more light that is bounced back off the skin, the lighter the person is. Instead of trying to shove people into categories such as "light" or "dark," we can measure skin color precisely.

Other Measures   Measures of the size of the teeth are known as **odontometrics.** From a cast made of a person's upper and lower jaws, researchers can measure the length and width of each tooth. Finger and palm prints are also useful in studying human variation; these measures are called **dermatoglyphics.** They include classification of different types of prints, as well as counts of the number of ridge lines on each digit. In addition to all these measures (and others), anthropologists often measure a variety of physiologic traits, such as blood pressure, heart rate, and aerobic functioning.

THE RACIAL APPROACH TO VARIATION

Given all these different measures, how do we make sense of it all? Although we focus today on evolutionary forces, the dominant perspective in the past, as noted earlier, was one of race and racial classification. This approach is also used by most people today in their daily exposure to human variation. A problem here is that we use such words as *race* without defining them. What do phrases like the "white race," the "Japanese race," and the "Jewish race" mean to you? They are extremely confusing because the term *race* is used to stand for a variety of factors, such as skin color, national origin, and religion. Sometimes we use the term in a biological sense, sometimes in a social sense.

The definition of race is no mere academic issue. Race is discussed daily in the newspapers and other media. Race has been used to justify discrimination and persecution of people, as well as to grant favored status. Statistics on race are gathered by local, state, federal, and international organizations. Economic and political decisions are often based on race.

Obviously, race is an important concept in our lives. But what exactly is it? How many races are there? What are the differences between races?

The Biological Concept of Race

From a biological standpoint, a **race** is generally defined as "a division of a species that differs from other divisions by the frequency with which certain hereditary traits appear among its members" (Brues 1977:1). Race in this definition has two characteristics. First, it is a group of populations that share

odontometrics
Measurements of the size of teeth.

dermatoglyphics
Measurements of finger and palm prints, including type classification and ridge counts.

race A group of populations sharing certain biological traits that make them distinct from other groups of populations. In practice, the concept of race is very difficult to apply to patterns of human variation.

some biological characteristics. Second, these populations differ from other groups of populations according to these characteristics. The concept of race seeks to fill the void between the single "human race" and the thousands of local human populations. Race is meant to provide a classification of biologically similar populations.

The race concept works better biologically with some organisms than with others. For organisms that are isolated from one another in different environments, the race concept often provides a usable, though rough, means of summarizing biological variation. For other organisms, such as humans, the concept has less utility. Humans inhabit a wide number of environments and move between them frequently. The high degree of gene flow among human populations, compared to that of many other organisms, means that clear-cut boundaries among groups of populations are difficult to establish.

The race concept presents a number of problems that are outlined in the next section. Given these problems, race and racial classifications provide only a crude tool for description, one with little utility for today's biologist or anthropologist, when sophisticated statistical methods and computers allow us to analyze patterns of biological variation more precisely than ever before. Indeed, some authors have suggested that we drop the entire concept, for it has little use biologically (Livingstone 1964).

Problems with the Concept of Race

What is wrong with classifying people into races? After all, we can do it accurately. Or can we?

The Number of Human Races   A major problem with the race concept is that scientists have never agreed on the number of human races. How many can you name, or see? Some have suggested that there are three human races: Europeans, Africans, and Asians (often referred to by the archaic terms "Caucasoid," "Negroid," and "Mongoloid," which are almost never used in scientific research today). But many populations do not fit neatly into these three basic categories. What about native Australians (aborigines)? As shown in Figure 5.4, these are dark-skinned people who frequently have curly or wavy (and, in some cases, blond) hair. On the basis of skin color, we might be tempted to label these people as African, but on the basis of hair and facial shape they might be classified as European. One approach has been to create a fourth category, the "Australoid" race.

As we travel around the world, however, we find more and more populations that do not fit a three- or four-race system. As a result, some authors have added races to their list. There has never been clear consensus on the actual number, though. In 1758, for example, Linnaeus described four major human races in his classification of humans. Since that time, different authors have suggested four, five, and nine major races, among other numbers. During the twentieth century, hierarchies of races were suggested. That is, a varying number of major races can be subdivided into minor races, which

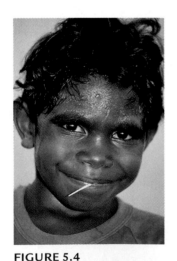

FIGURE 5.4

An Australian aborigine with dark skin and curly hair.
(© *Belinda Wright/National Geographic Society Image Collection*)

are further subdivided into even smaller races. Some anthropologists have divided "primary races" into "primary subraces" (Hooton 1946). Others have suggested subdividing major "geographic races" into "local races," which are further subdivided into "microraces" (Garn 1965). Additional populations that are the result of admixture, such as African Americans, are often referred to as "composite races." In each case there has been little agreement on the number of races or subraces.

Two points emerge from a study of the history of attempts to classify and apply the race concept to human populations. First, the lack of agreement among different researchers indicates that the entire concept of race is arbitrary as it applies to humans. If clearly discernible races existed, their number should have long since been determined without argument. How useful is a classification system when there is so much disagreement about the number of units? Second, something is being described here, although in a crude manner. All racial classifications, for example, note the wide range in skin color among human populations and further note an association with geography. The native peoples of Africa tend to have darker skin than those of northern Europe. The geographic distribution of many traits, such as skin color, is well known. Then why doesn't the race concept work well when describing biological variation?

The Nature of Continuous Variation   Biological variation is real; the order we impose on this variation by using the concept of race is not. One reason race fails to describe variation accurately is that much variation is continuous, whereas race is a discrete unit. In other words, we must reduce variation into a few small categories.

Consider human height as an example. Most of us cannot describe a person's height to the nearest centimeter without actually measuring that person. When we look at someone, we are unlikely to know *exactly* how tall that person is. We would not, however, describe everyone as the same height simply because we do not know the exact values. Instead, we use relative terms such as "short," "medium," and "tall." Often our definitions of these categories do not agree with other people's (many people call anyone shorter than themselves "short" regardless of their actual height). Also, some people might add categories, such as "medium tall" or "very short." In any case, these categories have some limited use. When we say that a basketball player is "tall," most people know roughly how tall we mean. But are these categories real? When we forget that these are only convenient crude levels for classification, we can fall into the trap of thinking that they have a reality of their own. Do you actually think all people fall into one of three categories— "short," "medium," or "tall"? Height is a continuous trait that can have an infinite number of values within a certain range.

The same problem applies to races. Many racial classifications in Western societies use skin color as a major distinguishing feature. The races correspond to different measures of skin color—"white," "yellow," "red," "brown," and "black," for example. We know, however, that skin color does not fall

FIGURE 5.5

Variation in skin color in three selected human populations (males). Dots indicate the mean skin reflectance measured at a wavelength of 685 nanometers; lines indicate 1 standard deviation on each side of the mean. Compare this with Figure 5.6, which shows more populations. The discontinuity in skin color shown here disappears when more of humanity is sampled. (All data from published literature. Original references listed in Relethford 1997)

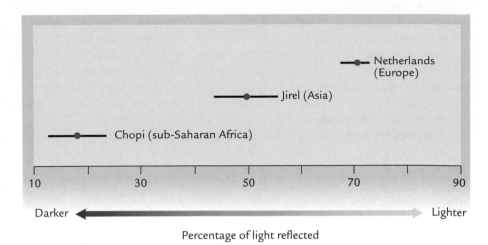

Percentage of light reflected

into 5, or even 50, different categories. Skin color is a continuous variable. This means that any attempt to divide the continuous range into discrete units (races) is going to be arbitrary.

Figure 5.5 shows the average skin reflectance for three samples of males— one from sub-Saharan Africa (Chopi), one from Asia (Jirels), and one from Europe (the Netherlands). For each sample, the dot represents the average value and the lines represent 1 standard deviation below and above the average. (A standard deviation is a statistical measure of variation. Roughly 68 percent of the cases in each sample lie between the ends of the lines drawn in the figure. Each sample contains some individuals who are lighter or darker.) These three samples are quite distinct from one another. There is no overlap in skin color, and it would be very easy to classify a given person into one of the three groups based on his skin color. Isn't this an accurate reflection of three distinct races?

No. The appearance of three distinct races is a biased reflection because humanity is made up of more than simply these three populations. When we add more populations to the picture, the interpretation changes. Figure 5.6 shows the average skin reflectance and standard deviations for 22 male samples from Africa, Asia, and Europe. Note that there are no longer discrete boundaries that can be used to identify different races. The ranges in skin reflectance overlap one another. In other words, on the basis of skin color, it is not possible to tell where one "race" ends and another starts. We can identify the extremes, but there are no discrete clusters.

Despite these arguments, many people are still convinced that human races are easily identifiable. After all, they say, you can walk down any city street in the United States and point out who is "white" and who is "black" (ignoring for the moment those people who are difficult to classify). Under such circumstances, race is easily identifiable (or is it?). This may be true in a limited area, such as a street in a medium-sized American city, but it does not hold true when we look at the world in general. Races seem distinct in certain situations because disproportionate numbers of peoples from different geo-

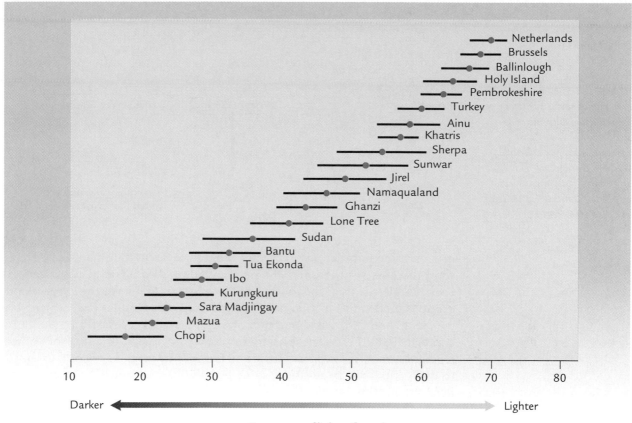

Darker ← Lighter

Percentage of light reflected

FIGURE 5.6

Variation in skin color in 22 human populations (males). Dots indicate the mean skin reflectance measured at a wavelength of 685 nanometers; lines indicate 1 standard deviation on each side of the mean. (All data from published literature. Original references listed in Relethford 1997)

graphic regions are present. We do not find equal representation of all human populations on most U.S. city streets. For example, we tend to see far fewer Australian aborigines than we see people of predominantly European or African ancestry.

In short, the overall composition of the U.S. population tends to give us a distorted view of the total variation in the world. The majority of early settlers in the United States came from Western Europe, one of the regions in the world whose human populations show the lightest skin color. During the next few centuries, many enslaved people were brought from West Africa, one of the regions where human skin color is darkest. The result has been a disproportionate representation of the range of skin color. More people in the United States have either very light or very dark skin than any shade in between (Figure 5.7). On the other hand, a tour through other parts of the world will soon give you a different picture. Many of the people in the world are neither so dark nor so light.

Not all biological traits show continuous variation. Blood group phenotypes, for example, are discrete traits. We do not, however, often find situations in which all members of one race have one phenotype and all members of another race have a different phenotype. Some genetic markers are useful

FIGURE 5.7

Original settlement of the United States from the perspective of skin color. From the continuous range of skin color in the human species, the majority of earliest settlers were from the two extreme ends— dark-colored West Coast Africans and light-colored Western Europeans. This differential settlement gives rise to the seeming existence of two distinct races in the United States based on skin color.

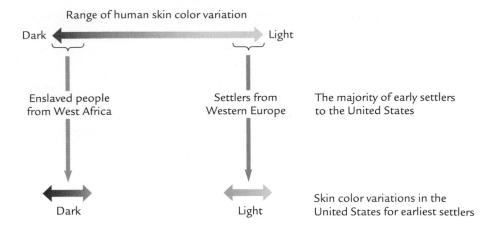

in separating populations in certain geographic areas, but many such traits show patterns of variation that are not well described by racial classification. For example, the frequency of the *a* allele for a trait known as the Diego blood group is moderately high in native South American populations, ranging up to 0.32. In both Africa and Europe, however, the frequency is 0 (Roychoudhury and Nei 1988). This allele is useful in separating South America from other regions but does not separate Africa and Europe—two regions typically assigned to different races. In addition, some populations in South America have a near-zero allele frequency. If we used the Diego blood group, we would have to assign these South American populations to a mixed European/African race!

Another example of a discrete trait is eye form. The so-called slanted eyes of Asians are caused in part by a fold of skin at the inner corner of the eye. (This shape is also related to the size and projection of the root of the nose.) This eye shape is found in many Asian populations and to a lesser extent in other groups as well. At first this trait might seem like a good "racial" trait because its presence allows us to separate populations of Asian ancestry from other groups. It does not, however, separate other groups, such as those of African or European ancestry.

Correspondence of Different Traits   If race were to be a useful biological concept, the classifications would have to work for a number of independent traits. A classification developed from skin color would also need to show the same racial pattern in other traits, such as head shape, nasal shape, and hair color. If each trait produces a different set of races, then the race concept is not very useful as a description of overall biological similarity. In fact, racial classifications vary according to the biological trait used.

High frequencies of the sickle cell allele are found not only in populations belonging to "African races" but also in parts of Europe and India. Any racial classification based on high or low frequencies of the sickle cell allele in a population would not produce the same distribution as skin color. Another example is the frequency of lactase persistence, which refers to the ability to produce the lactase enzyme into adulthood. Although lactase persistence is found in *some* European populations, it is not found in all of them. Further, it is also found in some African populations. Lactase persistence is not a "racial" trait but instead is found in populations that have a long history of dairy farming (as discussed in Chapter 6).

Using different traits often results in different groupings of populations. For examples such as sickle cell and lactase persistence, we expect this to be the case because the variation in a trait is related to natural selection, which will operate differently in diverse environments. In using racial classifications, however, we often find that as we add more traits the situation becomes even more complex. The fact that traits show different distributions argues against the utility of the race concept for describing human variation.

With the proper choice of variables, however, we can find combinations that are useful in looking at the relationships between populations on a worldwide basis. By examining a number of traits presumed neutral in terms of natural selection, we try to come up with an average pattern that reflects the tendency of gene flow and genetic drift to affect all loci to the same extent. Often we find clusters of populations that agree in a limited sense with geography. That is, we can identify some separation between sub-Saharan African populations, European populations, Middle Eastern populations, and so on. This is expected, given the close relationship of geographic distance and gene flow in human populations. Sub-Saharan African populations should be more similar to each other, on average, than they are to European populations. We can identify large geographic regions that have a *rough* correspondence with the usual definitions of race. But how useful are these labels for describing variation? To answer that, we must look closely at the difference between variation *within* a population and variation *between* populations.

Variation between and within Groups Racial classifications focus on differences between groups. This is apparent in the use of group stereotypes (e.g., "they are short," or "they have broad heads"). Such statements provide information about the *average* in a group but say nothing about variation *within* the group. For example, consider the statement that adult males in the United States tend to be taller than adult females in the United States. No one can argue with this basic fact regarding the average height of adult men and women. However, does it imply that *all* males are taller than *all* females? Of course not. There is variation within both sexes and a great deal of overlap.

The problem with the biological race concept is that it does not represent this overlap in genetic characteristics; the focus is on differences *between* populations and not *within* populations. This focus would be permissible to some extent if the majority of genetic variation actually existed between populations, and much less within populations. In fact, however, the opposite pattern applies to most genetic characteristics—there is much more genetic variation within populations than between them.

A number of studies have quantified the relative amount of genetic variation between and within different groupings of humanity. We start by acknowledging that genetic variation exists within our species. Our question here is how this variation is partitioned. If everyone is genetically the same within a race and the races are genetically different, then the percentage of variation *between* the races will equal 100 percent and the percentage of variation *within* the races will equal 0 percent. On the other hand, if there are genetic differences between individuals within each race but the allele frequencies are the same across races, then the percentage of variation between races will be 0 percent and the percentage of variation within races will be 100 percent (Figure 5.8). The main point here is that the race concept works best when most of the variation exists between groups (thus conforming to the stereotypic statement that "they all look alike").

Anthropologists and geneticists have computed these percentages based on data on indigenous populations from various large geographic regions of the world (e.g., sub-Saharan Africa, Europe, eastern Asia, and North America) that have often been suggested by proponents of the race concept as representing different major "racial" groupings. Studies of blood groups and other genetic polymorphisms show that roughly 10 percent to 12 percent of the total variation in our species exists *between* these regions, with the remaining 88 percent to 90 percent existing *within* regions (Brown and Armelagos 2001; Relethford 2001c). Analysis of DNA polymorphisms shows the same basic pattern (Barbujani et al. 1997). The same pattern also applies to cranial and facial measurements (Relethford 1994). The bottom line is that geographic race explains only 10 percent to 12 percent of the total variation in the human species. This fact, combined with the arbitrary nature of geographic classifications, shows that the race concept is not very useful in describing human biological diversity.

What Use Is the Race Concept?   In view of the many problems associated with using race to explain human variation, does the concept have any use? In the scientific study of human variation, the answer is little, if any. It is a descriptive tool, not an analytic one. If we examine the biological characteristics of a population and then assign the population to a given race, all we have accomplished is to label some observed phenomenon. We have not explained the causes of variation nor why some groups are similar to or different from others. The name explains nothing. The race concept does not ask or answer any interesting questions.

Until the 1950s, much of biological anthropology was devoted to racial description and classification. Most sciences go through a descriptive phase, followed later by an explanatory phase in which hypotheses are proposed and tested. Indeed, at least until the work of Charles Darwin, much of biology was basically a descriptive science. Today biological anthropologists rarely treat race as a concept. It has no utility for explanation, and its value for description is limited.

In contemporary society, however, race is still a common category. In this context the term has a social connotation more than a biological one. In state and federal government reports, "race" identifies some aspect of geographic origin and ethnic identity. For example, "black" refers to African or African American descent. "Hispanic" refers to Spanish speakers but actually

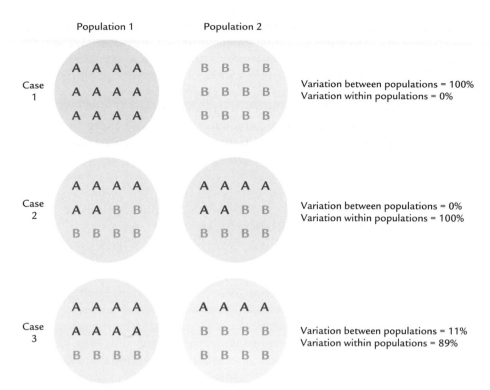

FIGURE 5.8

Three different examples showing how variation is partitioned between and within populations. The circles each enclose a population with a specific number of two alleles, A and B. In case 1, population 1 consists entirely of A alleles and population 2 consists entirely of B alleles. There is no variation within *either population, but the two populations are completely different in terms of the frequencies of the A and B alleles. As such, 100 percent of the variation is* between *the populations and 0 percent is* within *populations. Case 2 shows the opposite pattern. The genetic composition of both populations is the same—50 percent A alleles and 50 percent B alleles. There is therefore no variation* between *the populations, and all of the variation occurs* within *populations. Case 3 shows a less extreme condition, where the frequency of the A allele is 8/12 = 0.67 in population 1 and 4/12 = 0.33 in population 2. There is variation* within *each population, and there is some variation* between *the populations. The actual partitioning of variation (11 percent between populations and 89 percent within populations) is of the magnitude seen among major geographic regions of humans (see text)—most genetic variation exists* within *populations. Both populations have A and B alleles but differ in their relative frequency. Note: the percentage of variation within and between populations was computed using a measure known as F_{ST}, which relates allele frequencies to the proportion of variation between populations (Harpending and Jenkins 1973).*

encompasses a wide variety of peoples from Mexicans to Bolivians. Such classifications have their use, particularly in defining groups of people who have suffered social inequities, but they are not without their own problems. Classification into discrete groups always means that we obscure the subtle gradations of human variation.

Human variation is best analyzed using an approach that focuses on microevolutionary forces and uses individuals or local populations as the unit of analysis. This approach, aided by modern statistical and computer methods, allows better description than the race concept, avoids the problems of classification, and provides a focus for *explanation*.

In any case, we should not confuse social and biological categories, nor draw biological inferences from social identity. Race as a concept has little utility for analyzing human biological variation. Although we still distinguish "social" races, the term tends to generate misunderstanding even when used in this sense.

THE EVOLUTIONARY APPROACH TO VARIATION

When dealing with human biological variation, we need methods to describe and analyze patterns that we observe. As noted in the last section, the race concept is at best a crude description of variation, and it provides nothing in terms of explanation. The alternative approach stressed by biological anthropologists for the past 30–40 years or so is an evolutionary one. Here we look at the pattern of biological variation in terms of the evolutionary forces: mutation, selection, gene flow, and genetic drift.

Different methods are used to analyze human variation depending on the specific questions being asked. Are we interested in the history of a set of populations? If so, we want to consider factors such as gene flow, which in turn might be related to patterns of marriage, migration, and changes in population size. In such cases, we would want as much information from as many different traits as possible in order to obtain some measure of overall genetic similarity. Or are we interested in the patterns of variation of a specific trait, such as the ABO blood group or skin color? In that case, we would focus on that specific trait.

Given this contrast, we can draw a distinction between **univariate analysis** (one trait at a time) and **multivariate analysis** (many traits at one time). The differences in these approaches relate to the goals of a given study and whether the focus is on the forces of gene flow and genetic drift on one hand or on natural selection on the other.

The basic starting point is that gene flow and genetic drift are expected to affect *all* loci to the same degree, whereas natural selection is expected to affect each locus differently. For example, if you move from one population to another and have offspring in your new population, all of your genetic material moves with you: gene flow should affect all loci the same. Likewise, the *average* effect of genetic drift is expected to be the same for all loci. (Numerous loci or traits must be used for this to work. Genetic drift will lead to deviations for each individual locus or trait, and many of them need to be sampled to obtain an average.) Natural selection, however, should affect each locus differently—unless, of course, the loci are both related to the same selective force.

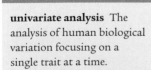

univariate analysis The analysis of human biological variation focusing on a single trait at a time.

multivariate analysis The analysis of human biological variation that considers the interrelationships of several traits at a time.

TABLE 5.2	Allele Frequencies of African American and European American Populations in Claxton, Georgia			
Locus	Allele	West Coast African	Claxton African Americans	Claxton European Americans
Rhesus	d	0.211	0.230	0.358
ABO	A	0.148	0.158	0.246
ABO	B	0.151	0.129	0.050
MN	M	0.476	0.485	0.508
Duffy	Fy^a	0.000	0.046	0.422
P	P	0.780	0.757	0.526
Hemoglobin	S	0.110	0.043	0.000

Source: Workman et al. (1963:451)

As a result, we tend to study natural selection one locus or trait at a time, unless we are looking at related traits. If we wish to study the effects of genetic drift and gene flow, we try to sample as many loci or traits as possible with the goal of getting the best estimate of overall effect. Of course, any study must consider *all* of the evolutionary forces. The univariate and multivariate approaches together often provide us with information regarding a number of these evolutionary forces.

An example of the multivariate approach is Workman and colleagues' (1963) study of allele frequencies of African Americans in Claxton, Georgia. Table 5.2 lists the frequencies of seven alleles from six loci for the African American and European American populations of Claxton and those of the West Coast of Africa (a presumed source of many ancestors for the Claxton African Americans). In all cases, the allele frequencies for the Claxton African Americans lie between those of West Coast Africans and the Claxton European Americans. In most cases, the allele frequencies of the Claxton African Americans are more similar to those of West Coast Africans. This is expected, given the predominantly African ancestry of the Claxton African American population. European gene flow, however, has caused the Claxton African American allele frequencies to move further away from the West African frequencies. This example shows how admixture of Europeans has occurred in the African American population of Claxton.

Is gene flow the only factor operating on the Claxton African American allele frequencies? If so, then the relative position of the Claxton African Americans should be the same for all alleles because gene flow is expected to have the same effect on all loci. Figure 5.9 plots their relative positions for the seven alleles. Most of the Claxton African American allele frequencies plot in a similar location, as expected from gene flow. The allele frequency for the sickle cell allele (*S*) is quite different. It does not fit the pattern of the other alleles, which suggests that natural selection has been operating on this locus.

FIGURE 5.9

The relative genetic position of the African American population in Claxton, Georgia, as compared to the European American population of Claxton and to West Coast Africans. Seven alleles are shown here (see Table 5.2). Six of the alleles cluster together, suggesting the common effect of gene flow. The hemoglobin allele (S) shows a different relative position, suggesting the effect of natural selection (see text).

West
Coast
Africans

Claxton
European
Americans

The Analysis of Gene Flow and Genetic Drift

A number of methods are used to examine the joint effect of gene flow and genetic drift on patterns of human variation. Two of the more common approaches are discussed here.

Genetic Distance Analysis   When comparing a number of biological traits across populations, we frequently compute a summary measure known as a **genetic distance.** This is an average measure of relatedness between groups based on a number of traits (i.e., a multivariate approach). Quite simply, the larger the genetic distance, the *less* similar two populations are to each other. For example, imagine that you have investigated a number of traits for three groups, called A, B, and C. You compute one of a number of genetic distance measures and obtain the following distances (don't worry about the units of measure; most distance measures are relative):

Distance between A and B = 0.010

Distance between A and C = 0.067

Distance between B and C = 0.126

Interpretation of these results is fairly straightforward. Populations A and B have the smallest distance, so they are the *most* similar to each other. Population C is the most distant and so is the least similar genetically. Further analysis would require additional data on the history and location of these groups to determine *why* population C is the most different. If, for example, you also knew that population C was on the other side of a mountain from populations A and B, then it would seem reasonable to assume that the mountain acted as a barrier to gene flow and caused population C's genetic dissimilarity.

Interpretation is difficult when more than three populations are being considered. For that reason, we often take the genetic distance measures and use them to construct what is known as a **genetic distance map,** a picture showing the genetic relationships between groups. These maps are easy to interpret—the closer two populations are on the map, the closer they are genetically. An example of a genetic distance map is shown in Figure 5.10, which shows five hypothetical populations (A, B, C, D, E). It is clear that populations A, B, and C are all similar to one another genetically, as is population D to population E. The most striking feature is that populations D and E are quite distant genetically from the other three populations. Additional data

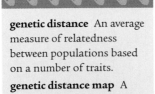

genetic distance An average measure of relatedness between populations based on a number of traits.

genetic distance map A picture showing the genetic relationships between populations, based on genetic distance measures.

FIGURE 5.10

Example of a genetic distance map for five hypothetical populations (A, B, C, D, E). The closer populations are genetically, the closer they plot near each other on the map.

would be needed to determine why. Are D and E separated geographically from the other three populations? This would be easy to check: simply compare the genetic distance map with a geographic distance map. Other hypotheses, such as differences in religion or other cultural variables, could also be tested using a comparative approach. Several examples of genetic distance maps from actual studies will be presented in Chapter 6.

Demographic Measures   Much information regarding the effect of genetic drift and gene flow can be extracted from analysis of demographic measures, especially population size and migration. These measures can be used to estimate the likely effect of genetic drift and gene flow by means of a variety of complex mathematical methods. If information is available for genetic traits, then these estimates can be compared with observed reality. This type of comparison allows us to test various assumptions of models and to determine the relative effect of gene flow and genetic drift. When genetic traits are not available, the analysis of demographic measures still provides us with an idea of the relative magnitude of genetic change *likely* under certain conditions.

The relationship between demographic measures and microevolution is relatively straightforward. Because the magnitude of genetic drift is related to population size (the smaller the population, the greater the effect of drift), a knowledge of population size can give us an estimate of the effects of genetic drift. Much gene flow is related to migration, so an analysis of marriage records and other vital statistical data can provide us with an idea of the relative magnitude of gene flow. Using appropriate models, scientists can consider the effects of gene flow and genetic drift simultaneously to predict genetic distances and then compare them with actual genetic distances. This approach also gives us an opportunity to study demographic shifts in historical populations—groups for which we have no genetic data but do have demographic information.

The Analysis of Natural Selection

The analysis of natural selection in human populations is complex. Rather than set up laboratory experiments, most of the time we must rely on comparisons of situations existing in nature. Consider the following hypothetical situation. You are interested in testing the hypothesis that mammalian body size is related to temperature. If you were dealing with laboratory animals such as mice, you would set up an experiment in which you would expose different groups of mice to different ambient temperatures and then determine what change, if any, takes place from one generation to the next. But what if you were interested in testing this hypothesis on elephants? It is unlikely you would be able to overcome the large number of practical difficulties involved in such a project. Where would you get enough space? How many elephants would you need? Could you obtain these elephants? Finally, you would also have to deal with the problem of a long generation length.

If you were interested in humans, the whole laboratory approach would be immoral and illegal, as well as impractical. Does this mean that the hypotheses cannot be tested? No, because you could examine a natural experiment. You would collect data on body size and temperature from human populations across the world to determine if a relationship in fact existed. Your study could be improved by trying to control for other effects. For example, you would not want to select an undernourished population from Africa and a well-nourished population from northern Europe because the differences in body size could be the result of both temperature and nutrition. Careful choice of samples in this type of natural experiment is critical. Though research on human populations is extremely difficult, the challenge is also part of the appeal for many biological anthropologists.

There are several approaches to measuring natural selection in human populations. The most direct method involves comparing measures of survival and reproduction (fitness) among individuals with different genotypes. Another method is to look at regional or worldwide variation in a trait to determine if it has any relationship with climate or other environmental factors. A third method is to look at the potential for natural selection by using measures of births and deaths from demographic data.

Genetic Associations   Because natural selection refers to the process by which individuals with certain genetic characteristics are more likely to survive or reproduce, we want to determine whether individuals with certain genotypes have a greater probability of surviving or reproducing. If you were interested in looking at the potential effects of natural selection on the MN blood group system, you would want to separate your sample into groups of individuals with the same genotype (*MM, MN,* or *NN*). You would then attempt to determine if there were any differences in mortality or fertility among these groups. For instance, do individuals with one genotype live longer than those with other genotypes? Is there any relationship between genotype and the individual's history of disease? Do individuals with certain genotypes have more surviving children than those with other genotypes? Are individuals with one genotype more likely to be sterile than others?

These questions and others can be answered in principle by looking at the associations among some measure of health, survival, or fertility and different genotypes. Suppose you were interested in whether or not different *MN* genotypes have different susceptibilities to diseases. You could select a group, determine its *MN* genotypes, and monitor its members for the rest of their lives to track their disease histories. Alternatively, you could select a group of individuals who have had a given disease and compare their *MN* genotypes with those of a random sample of people who have not had the disease.

Environmental Correspondence One way of looking for the effects of natural selection is to analyze patterns of variation over a large geographic region. Given that natural selection is related to environmental variation, differences among locations might reflect changes in environment and in genotype. The goal is to determine the level of correspondence between some aspect or aspects of the physical environment and a genotype. To test the idea that climate is related to body size, you would look at the distribution of body size and see how well it matches the distribution of climatic variables. Again, proper selection of your samples is necessary to ensure that you do not measure some other factor affecting biological variation. This method has other potential problems, such as the fact that migration can affect the level of correspondence. For example, if you were looking at the relationship of skin color and latitude, you would not want to include African Americans or European Americans in your analysis because they are relatively recent migrants to the United States.

Demographic Measures Natural selection operates on differences in mortality and fertility, both of which may be measured from demographic records. The death rate of a population is a measure of the proportion of deaths occurring within a given period of time. The birth rate measures fertility within a population. These measures can provide an idea of the overall potential for natural selection. They do not tell us what specific effect natural selection will have on a particular set of loci. These measures are also so highly dependent on cultural variation that we cannot always extrapolate to genetic factors. For example, two populations may show different disease rates. Even though it might be tempting to suggest that the difference in disease patterns is due to genetic differences, we must first control for other sources of this variation, cultural and environmental.

Nonetheless, demographic measures do provide us with some information about the potential for natural selection to operate (Crow 1958). With proper controls and research strategies, such measures can even be used to test biological hypotheses in the absence of any direct biological data. A good example of this approach is Meindl and Swedlund's (1977) study of mortality in the populations of Deerfield and Greenfield in historical Massachusetts. Historical data indicated that both populations experienced epidemics of childhood dysentery, a serious disease, between 1802 and 1803. Meindl and Swedlund used death records to determine the effect of these epidemics on the mortality of those who survived the disease. They found that the individuals who survived the disease actually lived longer than those who were not exposed to it. They concluded that the greater longevity of those individuals reflected, in part, genetic differences. One possible interpretation is that those who survived had genetic characteristics that gave them greater resistance to dysentery; this is natural selection in action.

Another possibility is that those exposed to the disease developed stronger immune systems as a response. Such augmented resistance is a physiological response, although there is most likely also a genetic component involved. Though such demographic analyses cannot provide any definite answers regarding natural selection, they do provide useful supplements to traditional genetic analysis.

Problems in Analysis   Some problems are common to any study of natural selection in human populations, regardless of the specific methods of study. The methods described here can demonstrate a relationship between some measure of fitness and some environmental factor. Correlation does not necessarily imply causation, however. We still need to document the link among genetics, environment, and the action of natural selection.

For example, a high degree of association between a specific blood group genotype and a given disease is suggestive but not conclusive. To complete the analysis, it is necessary to look at the specific biochemical nature of the blood group genotype. What changes in biological structure are related to this genotype, and how do these changes relate to the specific disease? A knowledge of the biochemical nature of the blood groups is required to answer these questions.

Another potential problem is that whatever association we detect may not have been present in the past. It is also possible that natural selection operated on a specific allele in the past but no longer does so. Certain blood group genotypes, for example, are associated with susceptibility to the disease smallpox. Today, smallpox has been eradicated as the result of intensive health care and immunization programs. In the past, however, smallpox was devastating. Thus, smallpox may have been a factor in the natural selection of certain blood types in the past, but it is not at present.

We have an unfortunate tendency to view natural selection in terms of *major* differences between different genotypes. Natural selection is often looked at as an all-or-none phenomenon—one individual survives and another does not. In reality, natural selection often operates on very small differences between different genotypes. One genotype may have only a slight advantage—1 percent, or 2 percent, or even lower—relative to another. If natural selection works with small differences, then how can substantial change result? The key to understanding this problem is to realize that small changes can have a large impact over a long period of time. Like compound interest in a bank account, the effects of even small levels of natural selection can add up over long periods. Of course, such low amounts of natural selection may be difficult to detect in a single generation. Imagine a population of organisms in which the average body weight is 10 kg (22 lb). Suppose there is a small amount of selection for those individuals with larger body sizes. Each generation, the average body size would increase in the population as a result of natural selection. Suppose the change is only one-tenth of 1 percent. The change in the first generation would be only from 10 kg to 10.001 kg, which is not noticeable. If this selection continues for 1,000 generations, however, the average body size would be over 27 kg (almost 60 lb). Also, remember that 1,000 generations is a very short time in evolution. Of course,

Genetics, Race, and IQ

Perhaps the most controversial topic in the study of human variation is the question of the relationship of genetics, race, and intelligence. What is intelligence? Are IQ tests an accurate measure of intelligence? Are IQ scores due to genetic inheritance or environmental factors or both? Are there "racial" differences in IQ scores? If so, do they reflect genetics or environment or both?

Over time, as observations were collected that showed "racial" differences in intelligence test scores, several researchers argued that this difference is at least partially due to genetic differences between the races. A common line of argument goes as follows:

1. IQ scores are a measure of intelligence.
2. Differences in IQ scores are partly due to genetic differences.
3. The races have different average IQ scores.
4. Because races are by definition genetically different, the racial differences in IQ scores are genetic.

It is worthwhile to examine briefly each of these claims.

What is IQ? It stands for "intelligence quotient" and is a measure derived by dividing a person's "mental age" by her or his chronological age; it is designed so that the average score for a reference population is 100. The IQ test was developed in France by Alfred Binet, who sought a means by which to identify children with learning disabilities. The purpose of the test was not to measure intelligence per se but rather to identify those children who would most likely require special education. The test was not meant to provide a ranking of intelligence among the rest of the students. That is, someone with an IQ score of 120 was not to be considered inherently "better" or "smarter" than someone with a score of 110.

Is intelligence a single "thing" that can be measured accurately by an IQ test? Although some argue that IQ is a fair measure of intelligence (Herrnstein and Murray 1994), others note that there are many different types of intelligence, some of which may not be assessed as well by conventional IQ tests (Bodmer and Cavalli-Sforza 1976; Hunt 1995). There is an unfortunate tendency to assume that intelligence is a single thing, measurable with a single test (Gould 1981).

These problems change the questions somewhat. Instead of looking at genetic and environmental factors affecting intelligence, what we are really doing is looking at genetic and environmental factors affecting IQ test scores, which might not be the same thing. In terms of IQ, there is evidence for a strong inherited component (Bouchard et al. 1990) and strong environmental components, including diet, education, social class, and health, among others (Gould 1981). The exact heritability of IQ has been widely debated. Some have suggested that up to 60–80 percent of the variation in IQ scores may be due to genetic variation. More recent work suggests that heritability might be closer to 34–48 percent (Devlin et al. 1997).

The third point in the list is that there are "racial" differences in IQ test scores. In the United States, for example, European Americans tend to score, on average, roughly 15 points higher than African Americans. Asian Americans tend to score, on average, several points higher than European Americans. However, is this what we mean by a "racial" difference? Categories such as "European American," "African American," and "Asian American" are broad groupings based on ethnicity and national origin, but they are not by any stretch of the imagination homogeneous populations. People within any of these broad ancestral groupings can come from a wide variety of countries and environments. Does it make sense to talk about a "European American race"? Problems arise when we take our labels as accurate reflections for the true nature of biological variation.

Putting aside for the moment the utility of even looking at IQ by "race," the largest problem is point 4 in the list. We assume that *any* group differences of a trait that has a genetic basis *must* be genetic in nature. However, we also know of genetic traits that do *not* vary across humanity. Some traits vary among groups, and some do not. We have no way of knowing beforehand which kind of trait IQ test performance will turn out to be. The answer requires testing. The other problem with analysis is that we also know that different groups have different environmental conditions (e.g., education, income, and others) that affect performance on IQ tests. To date, the bulk of the evidence supports an environmental explanation of "racial" difference in IQ test scores (Loehlin et al. 1975; Gould 1981; Mackintosh 1998). Direct tests have also been made of the hypothesis that group differences are genetic. If this were true, then IQ test scores among African Americans should vary proportionately according to the degree of European admixture; those with greater European ancestry should score higher. An analysis of this hypothesis, however, showed no relationship between amount of European component and IQ scores (Scarr and Weinberg 1978).

The entire debate over "race" and IQ is obviously influenced by political, economic, and social ideologies. From a scientific viewpoint, much of the debate is flawed because of overreliance on the biological race concept.

change is not likely to occur in a steady, uniform manner. This hypothetical example, which is very simple, does show the cumulative nature of natural selection over long periods of time.

Slight differences in survival and reproduction, then, can add up over time. Slow change over time, however, poses a problem for our analyses of natural selection. If differences are slight, we may not be able to detect them in a short period of time or we might require extremely large samples. Other evolutionary forces, such as drift and gene flow, would also alter the degree of change from one generation to the next. In many studies of human populations, we find that gene flow "swamps" the effect of natural selection. This does not mean that we cannot study natural selection; it merely shows us one of the potential problems we must take into account.

SUMMARY

The study of human variation looks at the patterns and causes of biological diversity among living human beings. Human variation has been studied using a racial approach and an evolutionary approach. The biological concept of race emphasizes differences between groups and deemphasizes variation within groups. In the past, race was used as a crude means by which to describe patterns of human variation. A major problem in using race as a concept is that distinct "races" take on a reality of their own in people's minds. The race concept has limited use in analyses of biological variation, however, particularly for widespread species such as human beings. The race concept uses arbitrary classifications of predominantly continuous variation, does not account for patterns of variation among different traits, and does not account for variation within groups. These problems aside, the race concept is further limited because it is purely descriptive and offers no explanation of variation.

The evolutionary approach looks at biological variation in terms of the evolutionary forces of mutation, natural selection, gene flow, and genetic drift. The focus of microevolutionary studies depends on the specific problem being analyzed. If the purpose is to look at average patterns reflecting gene flow and genetic drift, then many traits are analyzed at the same time (multivariate) because these two evolutionary forces affect all loci the same. If the purpose is to look at natural selection, then one trait is analyzed at a time (univariate) in order to find correlations with survival and/or reproduction. The microevolutionary approach is somewhat difficult to use for humans, as compared to laboratory animals, because there are no controls. Nonetheless, various methods have been developed to extract as much information as possible from patterns of human biological diversity.

SUPPLEMENTAL READINGS

Corcos, A. F. 1997. *The Myth of Human Races*. East Lansing: Michigan State University Press. A short introduction to the problems of using the biological race concept to describe patterns of human variation.

Gould, S. J. 1981. *The Mismeasure of Man*. New York: W. W. Norton. An excellent review of the historical controversies regarding intelligence tests, which also addresses problems with the race concept.

Mackintosh, N. J. 1998. *IQ and Human Intelligence*. Oxford: Oxford University Press. A comprehensive review of IQ testing, including discussions of genetic and environmental hypotheses regarding ethnic group differences in IQ.

INTERNET RESOURCES

http://anthro.palomar.edu/vary/vary_2.htm
Models of Classification, a tutorial comparing racial and evolutionary approaches to human variation.

http://www-sul.stanford.edu/depts/ssrg/misc/race.html
Race, Genes and Anthropology, a collection of links on a variety of topics, including race in anthropology, genetics and behavior, and racism.

http://webusers.anet-stl.com/~civil/bellcurveillustration2.html
The Bell Curve Workbook, a collection of links relating to the controversial book *The Bell Curve* by Herrnstein and Murray.

CHAPTER 6

May 29

Microevolution in Human Populations

In this chapter we examine several case studies of human microevolution in order to illustrate the different evolutionary approaches discussed in the previous chapter. The first part deals with studies that look primarily at the joint effects of gene flow and genetic drift. The remainder of the chapter looks at several studies focusing on natural selection.

CASE STUDIES OF GENE FLOW AND GENETIC DRIFT

Many studies of human microevolution are concerned with population history. How are different populations related? Did they have different histories in terms of settlement or contact with other groups? Did invaders leave traces of their genes behind? Were populations always the same size, or did some grow and expand, while others shrank or became isolated? These are but a few of the types of questions that we deal with when we use biological data to answer questions of human history.

When we look at the biological history of human populations, we are looking primarily at the joint effects of gene flow and genetic drift. Any past migrations, invasions, or contacts between peoples ultimately involves gene flow, so we can analyze gene flow in such a way as to reconstruct these past events. Because the history of human populations also involves changes in population size, we must also consider the effect of genetic drift. Looking at

◄ *A Yanamamo Indian hunting. The Yanamamo live in the rain forests of South America. Their social organization, with frequent splits and mergers of different groups, has a noticeable effect on their patterns of genetic variation.*
(© Michael Nichols/National Geographic Society Image Collection)

gene flow and genetic drift at the same time can be somewhat tricky. Imagine, for example, that you find two small, isolated populations that appear rather genetically distinct. Is this distinctiveness due to cultural or geographical isolation (low gene flow), or might it be due to the small size of the populations and the increased effect of genetic drift?

We must also remember that any attempt to reconstruct population history must involve as many traits as possible to have the best chance of seeing average patterns. In other words, we must use the multivariate approach discussed in the previous chapter. Again, the reason we do this is that gene flow and genetic drift are expected to have the same average effect on all traits.

Two case studies are presented here to illustrate how we can analyze past patterns of gene flow and genetic drift. The first focuses on variation on a local level—small tribes in South America. The second looks at patterns of variation on a regional level—Irish counties.

Social Organization and Genetics of South American Indians of the Rain Forest

A number of genetic studies have been carried out on the tribal populations living in the rain forests of South America. Studies of these populations have allowed investigation into the ways in which the social structure of small tribes contributes to genetic diversity. Of course, the small size of the populations and their general isolated nature act to increase the likelihood of genetic drift. What makes these studies so fascinating is the specific social and political structures that act in certain ways to increase drift and in other ways to counter it.

Many of these populations have a fission–fusion structure. As populations grow, the limits of the environment are soon reached. Political factions develop, creating unrest within the local villages resulting from too many people in one place. When populations become too large, they will often fission into separate groups. Some of these separate groups will be too small to remain viable villages, and smaller groups may then undergo fusion to form a large group (Figure 6.1).

The formation of new, smaller villages from old (fission) is expected to lead to increased opportunity for genetic drift. The merging of smaller villages to form large ones (fusion) acts to some extent to counter the effects of genetic drift. Adding to this complex situation is the fact that all villages practice **exogamy** (finding a mate in another group) to some extent. Exogamous marriage results in gene flow between villages, which also acts to counter the effects of genetic drift.

Village fissioning is a form of the founder effect and is expected to lead to group differences because of genetic drift. The amount of genetic drift can be predicted and then compared to observed allele frequencies to test the hypothesis that genetic variation is being affected by drift. Following up on pioneering work by James Neel, Peter Smouse (1982) and colleagues per-

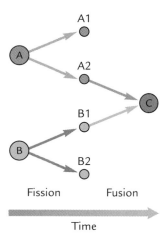

A1
A2
B1
B2
A
B
C
Fission   Fusion
Time

FIGURE 6.1

Fission–fusion social structure. Fissioning is the splitting of a population into two or more smaller populations. Fusioning is the merging of two or more populations into a larger population. Circles in this figure indicate the relative sizes of each population: populations A and B both split into two smaller populations; populations A2 and B1 then merge to form a larger population, C.

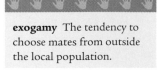

exogamy The tendency to choose mates from outside the local population.

FIGURE 6.2

The Yanomamo Indians of the South American rain forest. (© Michael K. Nichols/National Geographic Society Image Collection)

formed extensive analyses on a number of genetic systems for several tribal populations, such as the Yanomamo (Figure 6.2), and found that the observed level of genetic differences between groups exceeded the level expected under random genetic drift. Closer analysis has shown that the village fissions were not random. Rather, many fissions take place along kinship lines. Instead of a random group of individuals forming a new village, often a group of related individuals does so. This nonrandom splitting actually enhances the effects of genetic drift because new villages are less likely to have an equal representation of alleles from the original population. Thus, the individual pattern of village fissioning adds to the effect of genetic drift.

Complicating matters further, mating practices add to the process of genetic drift in these populations. Under the marriage system in these societies, the more politically powerful and wealthy men often have multiple wives. Differences in local political power mean that some men have more wives than others and therefore contribute in greater frequencies to the next generation. Though the entire analysis of Smouse and colleagues is too lengthy to discuss here, it should be clear that the complexity of human populations can affect genetic drift in many ways.

The Population History of Ireland

From the perspective of biological variation, the population history of Ireland is fascinating because of the numerous possibilities for gene flow in the island's past ("Ireland" refers here to the entire island, which is currently made up of two countries—the Republic of Ireland and Northern Ireland). In the past, Ireland has seen many different invasions and settlements from

FIGURE 6.3

Geographic map of Irish counties used in the genetic distance analysis. The labels correspond to six regions: W = west coast, SW = southwest, M = midlands, N = north, E = east, S = south. This map can be compared with the genetic distance map in Figure 6.4. One county in the east is not labeled because data were not available for that county.
(Relethford and Crawford 1995)

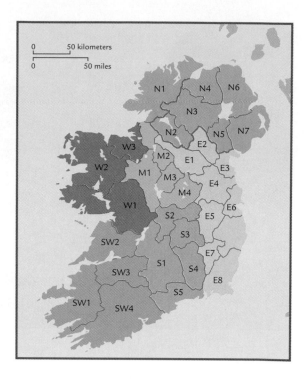

England, Scotland, Wales, and Scandinavia. What was the impact of these different sources of gene flow?

Relethford and Crawford (1995) investigated the patterns of biological variation among Irish populations using ten anthropometric measures of the head and face. With appropriate methods, anthropometric data can be used to derive genetic distances (Relethford and Blangero 1990). These data were originally collected during the 1930s on more than 7,000 adult Irish men. Relethford and Crawford used the data to look at genetic distances between 31 Irish counties (political units). Figure 6.3 shows the geographic location of the 31 counties, and Figure 6.4 shows the genetic distance map. For easy comparison of these two figures, counties have been grouped into six major geographic units (west coast, southwest, midlands, northern, eastern, and southern counties). As discussed in Chapter 5, genetic distance maps are interpreted based on the relative proximity of the populations to each other on the map. Populations plotting closer together on the map are genetically more similar to each other than populations that plot farther away from one another. The major pattern shown in Figure 6.4 is the distinctiveness of the four midland counties (M1–M4), which are dissimilar from the rest of Ireland. Looking at Figure 6.3, we see that these four counties are right in the middle of the island, posing an interesting question—if genetic variation is related to geography, we would expect the midland counties to be geographically and genetically similar to all other counties because they are right in the middle of all possible migration patterns from one part of Ireland to another. This is clearly not the case. What then accounts for the genetic distinctiveness of the midlands?

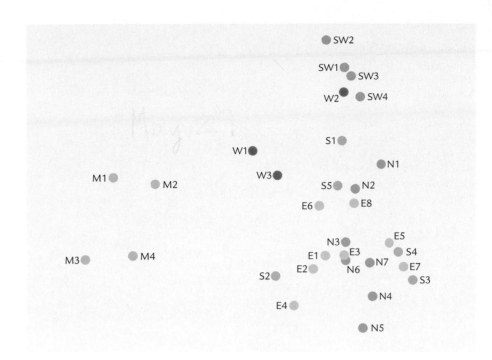

FIGURE 6.4

Genetic distance map of 31 Irish counties based on head and facial measurements of adult Irish males. The labels are the same as in Figure 6.3. The midland counties (M1–M4) are clearly the most distinct. There is also some correlation with longitude along the horizontal axis; counties in the western part of Ireland plot near the top, and those in the eastern part of Ireland plot near the bottom. (Relethford and Crawford 1995)

One possibility is gene flow from Viking invasion and settlement. Irish history reveals that the Vikings first came into contact with Ireland in A.D. 794 and that contact continued through the early thirteenth century. Although some Viking settlements were on the coast, there were a number of substantial Viking movements into the Irish midlands. At least one of these incursions involved as many as 12,000 men, which would be expected to have a noticeable genetic impact. Relethford and Crawford (1995) suggest that the distinctiveness of the Irish midlands reflects this Viking influence and that Viking settlements along the Irish coast had less impact because the genetic makeup of later migrants from England and Wales overrode any Viking influence.

Figure 6.4 also shows another interesting pattern. Separation along the vertical dimension of the plot corresponds strongly to longitude. Populations at the top of the figure are in the west and southwest of Ireland, whereas populations toward the bottom are in the north and east of Ireland. Thus, there is separation along a west to east gradient, a pattern also seen in a number of studies of Irish blood groups and other genetic polymorphisms (e.g., North et al. 2000; Tills et al. 1977). This gradient most likely reflects differences in immigration into Ireland in the past. Historically, we know that much immigration from England and Wales started in the early 1600s, and these immigrants settled predominantly in the north, east, and southeast of Ireland.

If these hypotheses are correct, then we can make two predictions regarding the similarity of the regions of Ireland with other European populations. First, if the Vikings had a disproportionate effect on the Irish midlands, then the midlands should be the most similar of all of Ireland to Norway and Denmark, the populations from which the Vikings came. Second, if the west–east

FIGURE 6.5

Genetic distance map comparing six regions of Ireland with data from Denmark, Norway, and England. The genetic distances were based on head and facial measurements. The Irish midlands are closest to Norway and Denmark, whose populations represent the source of Viking invaders to Ireland. This analysis supports the hypothesis of Viking gene flow. The closer proximity of the eastern, northern, and southern counties to England support the hypothesis that English immigration occurred primarily in these parts of Ireland, and less so in the west.
(Relethford and Crawford 1995)

gradient is due to immigrants from England and Wales, then the eastern counties of Ireland should be the most similar to those populations. Relethford and Crawford (1995) compared their data with those from several other European countries. The genetic distance map, shown in Figure 6.5, confirms their hypotheses. The midlands plot more closely to Norway and Denmark than any other Irish sample, whereas the eastern part of Ireland is the most similar to England.

CASE STUDIES OF NATURAL SELECTION

In this section we look at several examples of natural selection in human populations. Because natural selection operates differently on different loci, the focus will be on individual loci or traits rather than on specific populations.

Hemoglobin, Sickle Cell, and Malaria

Perhaps the best-known example of natural selection operating on a discrete genetic trait is the relationship of hemoglobin variants to malaria. One of the proteins in red blood cells is hemoglobin, which functions to transport oxygen to body tissues (see Chapter 2). The normal structure of the beta chain of hemoglobin is coded for by an allele usually called hemoglobin *A*. In

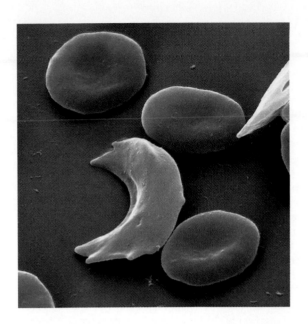

FIGURE 6.6

Sickle cell anemia. The blood cell to the left is twisted and deformed compared to the round, normal red blood cells. (© Meckes/Ottawa/Photo Researchers, Inc.)

many human populations, the *A* allele is the only one present, and as a result everyone has the *AA,* or normal adult hemoglobin, genotype.

Hemoglobin Variants   Many hemoglobin variants are produced by the mutation of an *A* allele to another form. The most widely studied mutations include hemoglobin *S, C,* and *E.* The *S* allele is also known as the sickle cell allele. A person who has two *S* alleles (genotype *SS*) has **sickle cell anemia,** a condition whereby the structure of the red blood cells is altered and oxygen transport is severely impaired (Figure 6.6). Untreated, few people with sickle cell anemia survive to adulthood.

If the *S* allele is harmful in homozygotes, we expect natural selection to eliminate *S* alleles from the population in such a way that the frequency of *S* should be relatively low. Mutation introduces the *S* allele, but natural selection eliminates it. Indeed, in many parts of the world the frequency of *S* is extremely low, fitting the model of mutation balanced by selection. In a number of populations, however, the frequency of *S* is much higher—often between 5 percent and 20 percent. Such high frequencies seem paradoxical, given the harmful effect of the *S* allele in the homozygous genotype. Why does *S* reach such high frequencies? Genetic drift might seem likely, except for the definite association of geography and higher frequencies of *S.* That is, higher frequencies of *S* occur only in certain environments. Genetic drift is random and influenced by population size, not environment. If genetic drift were responsible for the high frequencies of *S,* we would expect to see high frequencies in isolated groups in many different environments.

Distribution of the Sickle Cell Allele and Malaria   The distribution of the sickle cell allele is related to the prevalence of a certain form of malaria. Malaria

sickle cell anemia A genetic disease that occurs in a person homozygous for the sickle cell allele, which alters the structure of red blood cells.

The Biological History of the Ancient Egyptians

The ancient Egyptians have long been a source of fascination. Egyptian civilization dates back roughly 5,000 years and is best known because of its many pyramids. There have been many debates over the origin of the ancient Egyptians. Some argue that this population is distinctly related to Europeans, whereas others favor a sub-Saharan origin. Still others suggest that the ancient Egyptians did not come from any one specific group but rather represent an in-place evolution in northeastern Africa, with contact with other populations.

The origin of the ancient Egyptians has been argued on the basis of archaeology and other clues. Here, we examine what inferences can be made from patterns of biological variation. One example is given. Genetic distances were computed among 13 samples of ancient skulls—three populations each from sub-Saharan Africa, Europe, the Far East, and Australia, and a sample from the ancient Egyptians (26th–30th dynasties, dating between 2550 and 2150 years B.P.). The data consisted of 57 measurements of the skull and face, provided by Dr. W. W. Howells (Howells 1989). These data were used to estimate genetic distances (Relethford and Blangero 1990).

Different patterns of genetic distances would result depending on which historical hypothesis was correct. If, for example, the ancient Egyptians came primarily from Europe, then they should be most similar to European populations. If they came from sub-Saharan Africa, then they should be most similar to sub-Saharan African populations. If, however, the ancient Egyptians were not the result of primary movement from one region or another, then their biological relationships would be somewhere intermediate between other geographic regions.

The figure here shows the results very clearly. The ancient Egyptian sample does not cluster with either Europeans or sub-Saharan Africans. More extensive analyses have shown similar results (Brace et al. 1993)—the ancient Egyptians are Egyptian. Their biological affinities reflect their geographic position more than anything else. The fact that Egypt is part of the African continent does not mean that they are closer to other African populations than to non-African groups.

This analysis reveals an important feature of human variation. If we ignore Egypt for the moment, we can see four recognizable clusters—Europe, sub-Saharan Africa, the Far East, and Australia. The clear separation of these clusters seems to argue strongly for four distinct "races." Or does it? By adding Egypt to the analysis, we see the problem of inferring race from widespread geographic samples; other populations fall in between, thus forcing us to add a fifth "race." Of course, if we add still other groups, we have to continually increase our number of races. Our image of distinct races often results from not using a full sampling of humanity.

---

is an **infectious disease**—that is, a disease caused by the introduction into the body of an organic foreign substance, such as a virus or parasite (a disease that is not caused by an organic foreign substance is a **noninfectious disease**). Malaria is caused by a parasite that enters an organism's body, and four different species of the malarial parasite can affect humans. Malaria remains one of the major infectious diseases in the world today. The World Health Organization (1997) estimates that there are between 300 million and 500 million people in the world who have some form of malaria, of which an estimated 1.5 million to 2.7 million people die each year.

The Old World shows a striking correspondence between higher frequencies of the S allele (Figure 6.7) and the prevalence of malaria caused by the parasite *Plasmodium falciparum* (Figure 6.8). This parasite is spread through the bites of certain species of mosquitoes. Except through blood transfusions, humans cannot give malaria to one another directly. Those areas with frequent cases of malaria, such as Central Africa, also have the highest frequencies of the sickle cell allele. The falciparum form of malaria, the most serious of all forms of malaria, is often fatal.

infectious disease A disease caused by the introduction of an organic foreign substance into the body.

noninfectious disease A disease caused by factors other than the introduction of an organic foreign substance into the body.

Europe

Far East

Egypt

Australia

Sub-Saharan Africa

The strong geographic correspondence suggests that sickle cell anemia and malaria both related to the high frequencies of the *S* allele. Further experimental work has confirmed this hypothesis. Because the *S* allele affects the structure of the red blood cells, it makes the blood an inhospitable place for the malaria parasite.

In a malarial environment, people who are heterozygous (genotype *AS*) actually have an advantage. The presence of one *S* allele does not give the person sickle cell anemia, but it does change the blood cells sufficiently so that the malaria parasite does not have as serious an effect. Overall, the heterozygote has the greatest fitness in a malarial environment. As discussed in Chapter 3, this is a case of balancing selection, in which selection occurs for the heterozygote (*AS*) and against both homozygotes (*AA* from malaria and *SS* from sickle cell anemia).

In addition to greater survival of the heterozygote in malarial environments, it has also been suggested that women with genotype *AS* have greater fertility. If so, then is selection for the heterozygote in environments with malaria a function of differential mortality, differential fertility, or both?

FIGURE 6.7

Distribution of the sickle cell allele in the Old World. Compare high-frequency areas with the high-frequency areas of malaria in Figure 6.8.

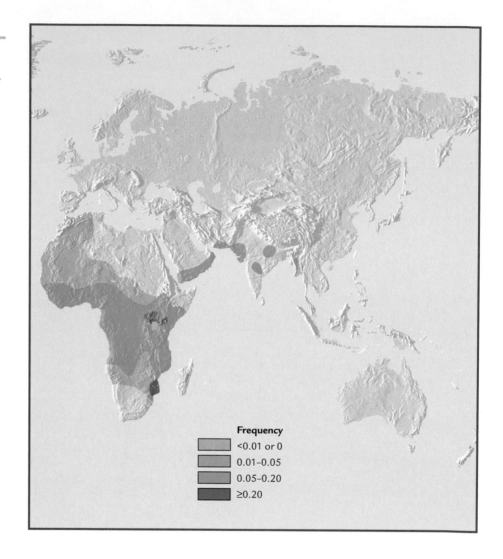

Frequency
<0.01 or 0
0.01–0.05
0.05–0.20
≥0.20

Madrigal (1989) studied this problem by examining the hemoglobin geno-type and reproductive histories of women in Limon, Costa Rica. She found that there was no difference between *AA* and *AS* women for a number of mea-sures of differential fertility (family size, number of pregnancies, number of live births, and number of spontaneous abortions). More recently, Hoff et al. (2001) conducted a study on almost 10,000 African American women in Mo-bile, Alabama, and found that women with the *AS* genotype had a higher number of live births, suggesting the possibility that fertility does influence selection for the *S* allele in some populations.

If the effects of sickle cell anemia and malaria were equal, then we would expect the frequencies of the normal allele (*A*) and the sickle cell allele (*S*) ul-timately to reach equal frequencies. The two diseases, however, are not equal in their effects. Sickle cell anemia is much worse. The balance between these two diseases is such that the maximum fitness of an entire population occurs

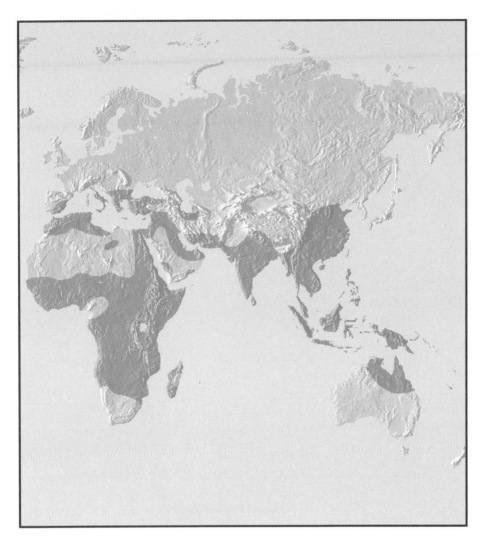

FIGURE 6.8

Regions where falciparum malaria is common (shown in green).

when the frequency of *S* is somewhere between 10 percent and 20 percent (Figure 6.9).

An analysis of one African population suggests that for every 100 people with *AS* who survive to adulthood, 88 people with *AA* and only 14 of those with *SS* survive (Bodmer and Cavalli-Sforza 1976). Clearly, the relationship among hemoglobin, sickle cell anemia, and malaria represents a very strong case of natural selection. Instead of a difference in survival between genotypes of only several percent, the differences are quite striking. Such differences can lead to major changes in allele frequencies in a very short period of time. To illustrate the rapidity of such change, Figure 6.10 shows a hypothetical example of changes in the frequency of the sickle cell allele. In this example, the initial frequency of *S* from mutation was set equal to a reasonable estimate of 0.00001. The fitness values mentioned earlier were used to examine the kind of change in the frequency of *S* that could take place. Because the

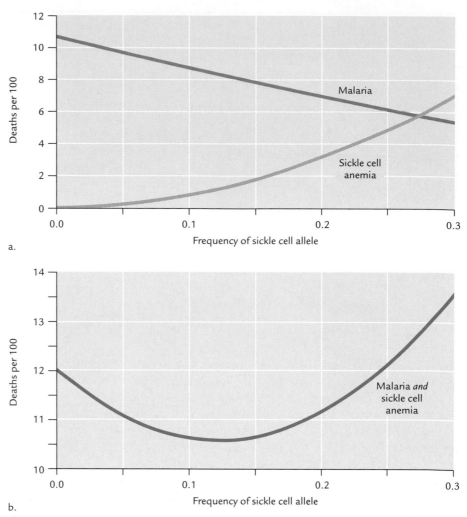

FIGURE 6.9

Illustration of balancing selection for the hemoglobin S allele. Selection was modeled using these estimates of fitness from Bodmer and Cavalli-Sforza (1976): 88 percent of individuals with the genotype AA survive, but 12 percent die due to malaria; 14 percent of individuals with the genotype SS survive, but 86 percent die due to sickle cell anemia; everyone with genotype AS survives. Figure 6.9a shows the expected number of deaths due to malaria and sickle cell anemia for every 100 people in the population. As the frequency of S increases, the number of deaths due to malaria declines because more people now have the genotype AS and fewer people have the genotype AA. At the same time, however, the number of deaths due to sickle cell anemia increases because there are more people with genotype SS in the population. The result is a trade-off. Figure 6.9b shows what happens when we consider the total *number of deaths due to malaria* and *sickle cell anemia. The total number of deaths declines at first because of increased resistance to malaria. The total number of deaths reaches a minimum point for a frequency of 0.122 for the S allele. If S were to increase further, the increased number of sickle cell anemia deaths would offset the decrease in malaria deaths. Natural selection will lead to an optimal balance corresponding to the minimum number of total deaths.*

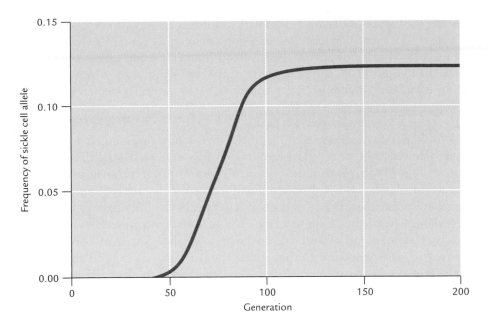

FIGURE 6.10

Reconstruction of past changes in sickle cell allele frequency in malarial Africa. This simulation assumes an initial allele frequency of 0.00001 caused by mutation. Relative fitness values are assumed constant over time: AA = 88%, AS = 100%, SS = 14%. The first 40 generations would show little change because the initial allele frequency was so low. After 40 generations, the allele frequency would increase rapidly, reaching an equilibrium after roughly 100 generations.

initial allele frequency is low, there is little change for the first 40 generations or so. (Of course, if the initial allele frequency were higher, the rate of change would be greater; a higher initial frequency could occur due to genetic drift or the initial occurrence of the mutation in a small population.) As the frequency of S increases, change takes place more rapidly because there are more people with the AS genotype to be selected for. After 100 generations, there is little change in the frequency of the S allele because it has reached an equilibrium based on the balance between the effects of sickle cell anemia and malaria. In this example, the sickle cell allele would reach an equilibrium frequency of 0.122. Of course, this simple illustration does not take other evolutionary forces into account, but it does show how quickly allele frequencies can change under strong natural selection.

The sickle cell example clearly shows the importance of the specific environment on the process of natural selection. In a nonmalarial environment, the AS genotype has no advantage in terms of differential survival and the AA genotype has the greatest evolutionary fitness. In such cases, the frequency of the S allele is very low, approaching zero. In a malarial environment, however, the situation is different and the heterozygote has the advantage. Clearly, we cannot label the S allele as intrinsically "good" or "bad"; it depends on circumstances.

The example of sickle cell also shows that evolution has a price. The equilibrium is one in which the fitness for the entire population is at a maximum. The cost of the adaptation, however, is an increased proportion of individuals with sickle cell anemia, because the frequency of S has increased. People with the heterozygous genotype AS have the greatest fitness, but they also carry the S allele. When two people with the AS genotype mate, they have a

25 percent chance of having a child with sickle cell anemia (in the previous example, 1.5 percent of all children in a population are expected to have the *SS* genotype). This is not advantageous from the perspective of the individual with the disease. From the perspective of the entire population, however, it is the most adaptive outcome. Every benefit in evolution is likely to carry a price.

Effects of Culture Change on Sickle Cell Frequency   Sickle cell anemia also provides an excellent example of the interaction of biology and culture. Livingstone (1958) and others have taken information on the distribution and ecology of the malaria parasite and the mosquito that transmits it, along with information on the prehistory and history of certain regions in Africa, and have presented a hypothesis about changes in the frequency of the sickle cell allele. Several thousand years ago, the African environment was not conducive to the spread of malaria. Large areas of the continent consisted of dense forests. The mosquito that spreads malaria thrives best in ample sunlight and pools of stagnant water. Neither condition then existed in the African forests. The extensive foliage prevented much sunlight from reaching the floor of the forest. In addition, the forest environment was very absorbent, so water did not tend to accumulate in pools. In other words, the environment was not conducive to large populations of mosquitoes. Consequently, the malaria parasite did not have a hospitable environment, either.

This situation changed several thousand years ago when prehistoric African populations brought horticulture into the area. **Horticulture** is a form of farming employing only hand tools and no animal labor or irrigation. As the land was cleared for crops, the entire ecology shifted. Without the many trees, it was easier for sunlight to reach the land surface. Continued use of the land changed the soil chemistry, allowing pools of water to accumulate. Both changes led to an environment ideal for the growth and spread of mosquito populations and therefore the spread of the malaria parasite. The growth of the human population also provided more hosts for the mosquitoes to feed on, thus increasing the spread of malaria.

Before the development of horticulture in Africa, the frequency of the sickle cell allele was probably low, as it is in nonmalarial environments today. When the incidence of malaria increased, it became evolutionarily advantageous to have the heterozygote *AS* genotype because those who had it would have greater resistance to malaria without suffering the effects of sickle cell anemia. As shown earlier, this change could have taken place in a short period of time, roughly 100 generations, because of the large differences in fitness among hemoglobin genotypes. The initial introduction of the sickle cell allele, through mutation or gene flow, was followed by a rapid change, reaching an equilibrium point in which the fitness of the entire human population was at a maximum.

This scenario shows that human cultural adaptations (horticulture) can affect the ecology of other organisms (the mosquito and malaria parasite), which can then cause genetic change in the human population (an increase in the frequency of the sickle cell allele). This sequence of events is summarized in Figure 6.11.

horticulture A form of farming in which only simple hand tools are used.

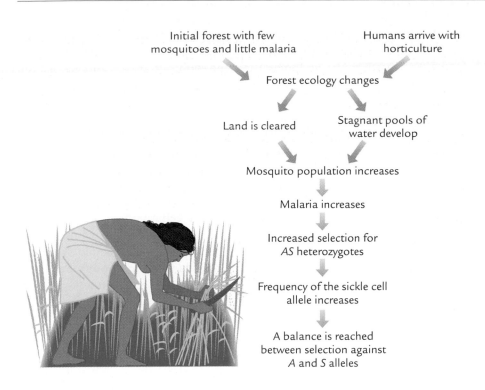

Initial forest with few
mosquitoes and little malaria

Humans arrive with
horticulture

Forest ecology changes

Land is cleared

Stagnant pools of
water develop

Mosquito population increases

Malaria increases

Increased selection for
AS heterozygotes

Frequency of the sickle cell
allele increases

A balance is reached
between selection against
A and *S* alleles

FIGURE 6.11

*Sequence of cultural and
environmental changes leading
to changes in the frequency of
the sickle cell allele in malarial
Africa.*

Of course, we cannot observe these events directly because they occurred in the past. Nonetheless, all available evidence supports this hypothesis. We know the physiological differences between different hemoglobin types. We also know that low frequencies of *S* occur in nonmalarial environments and higher frequencies occur where there is malaria. Archaeological evidence shows when and where the spread of horticulture took place in Africa. From studies of modern-day agriculture, we also know that malaria spreads quickly following the clearing of land. Taking all this information together, we find that the scenario for changes in the frequency of the sickle cell allele in Africa is most reasonable.

The study of human history also provides another example of the evolution of the sickle cell allele. In African American populations, the frequency of *S* ranges from 0.02 to 0.06, which is higher than the frequency in European Americans (essentially zero) but less than that in malarial regions of Africa (Workman et al. 1963). The biological history of African Americans explains part of this difference; some degree of European admixture has taken place. This admixture would have the effect of reducing the frequency of *S* in African Americans. Extensive calculations have shown, however, that admixture is not the only factor involved. Researchers found that if admixture alone were operating, then the frequency of *S* in African Americans should be higher than it actually is. Another reason that the frequencies of the sickle cell allele are lower in African Americans than in West Africans is that natural selection has been operating to remove the *S* allele from the population. In general, malaria has not been epidemic in the United States. The enslaved people brought into the United States came from areas in Africa with high frequencies of malaria and the sickle cell allele. When they arrived in the United States, there was no longer the same evolutionary advantage for high frequencies of *S* because there was less malaria. As a result, the frequency of *S* has been reduced through natural selection, along with European admixture. We might expect that the *S* allele will continue to decrease in frequency. However, Hoff et al. (2001) suggest that selection for the heterozygote may continue, even in the absence of selection due to malaria, because of higher fertility of women with the *AS* genotype.

Sickle cell anemia is a health problem among modern African Americans. During the 1960s there was a tendency to label sickle cell anemia as a "black disease." The reason for higher levels of sickle cell anemia among African Americans has nothing to do with skin color but is rather the result of their ancestors coming from a malarial environment with high frequencies of the *S* allele. Sickle cell anemia is not confined to dark-skinned populations in Africa. High frequencies of *S* are also found in malarial environments in parts of Europe, India, and South Asia.

Other Relationships with Malaria   A number of other genetic loci appear to have been affected by natural selection from malaria. Two different alleles of the hemoglobin locus, *C* and *E*, appear in high frequencies in certain malarial environments. Several inherited biochemical disorders, collectively known as thalassemia, are also related to malaria. These disorders do not directly affect the structure of the adult hemoglobin molecule but do interfere with its production. Another genetic trait, G6PD deficiency, leads to a deficiency of a certain enzyme and also appears to confer some resistance to malaria. It is not surprising to find a number of loci related to malaria because it is a severe disease, and any trait that alters the blood sufficiently to confer resistance to the parasite might be selected for over time.

Blood Groups and Natural Selection

The relationship between the sickle cell allele and malaria is the most well-studied example of natural selection for a discrete genetic trait in human populations. It is often frustrating that the situation is not as clear for other traits. The differences in fitness between different genotypes are often much less than those seen for the hemoglobin locus. Also, we often find evidence of multiple relationships between genetic traits and natural selection. It is often difficult to determine which factor is the most important or which was initially responsible for the evolution of a trait.

The human blood groups have been the subject of many investigations of natural selection. There are many different blood groups, defined on the basis of the type of molecules present on the surface of the red blood cells. Some blood groups are associated with different antibodies that react to various substances invading the blood stream (foreign antigens). Two blood groups—MN and ABO—have already been mentioned in previous chapters.

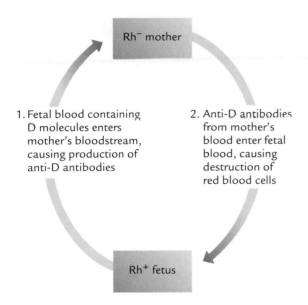

1. Fetal blood containing D molecules enters mother's bloodstream, causing production of anti-D antibodies

2. Anti-D antibodies from mother's blood enter fetal blood, causing destruction of red blood cells

FIGURE 6.12

Sequence of events in Rhesus incompatibility between an Rh⁻ mother and an Rh⁺ fetus. Because it normally takes time to produce anti-D antibodies, the first Rh⁺ fetus is not affected. Subsequent Rh⁺ fetuses, however, are affected.

Other red blood cell groups include Rhesus, Diego, Duffy, Lutheran, Lewis, and Xg, to name but a few. Some of these blood groups appear to be neutral in terms of natural selection, or perhaps we just have not been able to detect any effects. Also, some may have been selected for or against in the past, but not at present. Others are definitely related to natural selection but in ways that are difficult to discern.

Rhesus Blood Group   The Rhesus blood group (also called the Rh blood group) has a complicated mode of genetic inheritance involving three linked loci called C, D, and E. One locus, D, is particularly important in terms of natural selection. This locus has two alleles, *D* and *d*, where *D* is dominant. Individuals with genotypes *DD* or *Dd* are called *Rh positive,* and those with genotype *dd* are called *Rh negative.* Those with Rh positive blood have certain antigens in their red blood cells (D), and those with Rh negative blood can produce an opposing antibody (anti-D). In terms of blood chemistry, anti-D antibodies can destroy red blood cells with D molecules on their surface.

Selection occurs for the Rhesus blood group through **Rhesus incompatibility,** a condition in which a pregnant woman and her fetus have incompatible Rhesus blood groups. Rhesus incompatibility occurs when an Rh negative mother has an Rh positive fetus. Normally, the circulatory systems of mother and fetus are separate, but some fetal blood may enter the mother's bloodstream at the time of delivery. The fetus's blood carries D molecules. When these molecules enter the mother's bloodstream, the mother's immune system produces anti-D antibodies to destroy the red blood cells carrying these "invaders." Once produced, the antibodies can leak back to destroy blood cells of a fetus. The destruction of fetal blood cells leads to a form of anemia that can be fatal (Figure 6.12). Interestingly, Rhesus incompatibility

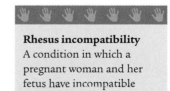

Rhesus incompatibility
A condition in which a pregnant woman and her fetus have incompatible Rhesus blood group phenotypes.

TABLE 6.1   Possible Rhesus-incompatible Matings

Mother		Father		Incompatible Mating
Genotype	Phenotype	Genotype	Phenotype	
DD	Rh⁺	DD	Rh⁺	No
DD	Rh⁺	Dd	Rh⁺	No
DD	Rh⁺	dd	Rh⁻	No
Dd	Rh⁺	DD	Rh⁺	No
Dd	Rh⁺	Dd	Rh⁺	No
Dd	Rh⁺	dd	Rh⁻	No
dd	Rh⁻	DD	Rh⁺	Yes, 100%
dd	Rh⁻	Dd	Rh⁺	Yes, 50%
dd	Rh⁻	dd	Rh⁻	No

is generally not a problem for the first Rh positive fetus born to the mother. The antibodies need time to be produced, and the first Rh positive infant's blood is rarely affected.

Today, Rhesus incompatibility is less of a problem than it once was because we can check blood types and use various techniques to control its effects. In the past, and even in many parts of the world today, this anemia often resulted in death. From an evolutionary standpoint, this is selection against the heterozygote. An Rh negative mother has genotype *dd,* which means that the fetus will receive a *d* allele from her. A fetus with a *d* allele from the mother requires a *D* allele from the father to be Rh positive. The fetus will then have the heterozygous genotype *Dd.* We also know that the father of a heterozygous fetus is Rh positive because that is the only way he could contribute a *D* allele to the fetus. Table 6.1 lists all possible matings between a man and woman according to their genotypes.

Selection against the heterozygote eliminates both alleles (*D* and *d*) from the population in equal amounts, since each heterozygote contains, by definition, one of each allele (*Dd*). Given enough time, this type of selection will result in the loss of the allele that was initially less common. Therefore, we should see the total elimination of one allele or the other. Although the *D* allele is more common in human populations today, the *d* allele has not been eliminated; in fact, it is relatively high in a number of human populations. This observation shows that selection against the heterozygote is not the *only* factor that has affected the evolution of the Rhesus blood group. It is possible that there might be some sort of balancing selection acting to keep the *d* allele from disappearing.

ABO Blood Group   The ABO blood group is the most widely studied simple genetic trait in human populations. As shown in Chapters 2 and 3, there are three different alleles (*A, B, O*) in this group: *A* and *B* are codominant and *O* is recessive. There are four possible phenotypes: type A (genotypes *AA* and

TABLE 6.2	ABO Blood Group Phenotypes and Antibodies		
Genotypes	Phenotypes	Antigens	Antibodies
AA	A	A	anti-B
AO			
BB	B	B	anti-A
BO			
AB	AB	A, B	none
OO	O	none	anti-A, anti-B

AO), type B (genotypes *BB* and *BO*), type O (genotype *OO*), and type AB (genotype *AB*).

Worldwide, the *O* allele is the most common in almost all human populations, followed by *A* and *B*. There is considerable variation in the ABO alleles among populations. The frequency of the *O* allele ranges from 0.46 to 1.0, the frequency of the *A* allele ranges from 0 to 0.5, and the frequency of the *B* allele ranges from 0 to 0.34 (Roychoudhury and Nei 1988). These allele frequencies cannot be explained solely by mutation. Although there are numerous examples of the influence of genetic drift and gene flow on the ABO frequencies, there is also strong evidence that natural selection has contributed significantly to the observed variation.

One possible clue to the effects of natural selection on the ABO blood groups is that certain antibodies are associated with different blood groups. Recall from Chapter 5 that there are two antibodies in the ABO system: anti-A and anti-B. Unlike the Rhesus system, the ABO antibodies are present throughout an individual's life. The anti-A antibody reacts to destroy A-type molecules, and the anti-B antibody reacts to destroy B-type molecules. There is no antibody for O. People with blood type A have the anti-B antibody, people with blood type B have the anti-A antibody, people with blood type O have both, and people with blood type AB have neither (Table 6.2).

The fact that different blood types have different antibodies also has implications for natural selection and susceptibility to different diseases. If you have blood type A, and hence anti-B antibodies, your immune system will tend to fight off any microorganisms that are biochemically similar to type B molecules. For example, the microorganism that causes venereal syphilis is biochemically similar to A molecules. Therefore, people with blood types B and O will have greater resistance to syphilis because they have the anti-A antibodies. People with blood types A and AB will not have this resistance because they lack the anti-A antibodies. It has been suggested that a link exists between various ABO blood types and a number of infectious diseases, such as smallpox, typhoid, influenza, bubonic plague, and others. Many of these diseases were indeed serious in the past, and differential resistance could be a possible factor in explaining the range of allele frequencies for the ABO system.

TABLE 6.3   ABO Blood Group Maternal-Fetal Incompatibilities

Mother's Genotype	Incompatible Fetal Genotypes
AA	AB
AO	AB, BO
BB	AB
BO	AB, AO
AB	none
OO	AO, BO

In any case, the action of natural selection is complex because of the wide variety of different disease microorganisms and their relationships to ABO blood types. It has been suggested that each blood type is more susceptible than others to certain diseases. For example, type A seems more susceptible to smallpox, type B seems more susceptible to infantile diarrhea, and type O seems more susceptible to bubonic plague. If these hypotheses are verified, it seems that the frequencies of the *ABO* alleles are subject to a variety of different types of selection. This makes analysis extremely difficult.

ABO blood types also appear to be related to noninfectious diseases. Some hospital studies have suggested that people with blood type O have a greater chance of getting duodenal and stomach ulcers (this might be related to antibodies because recent work has confirmed that some ulcers are actually infectious in nature, being caused by bacteria). People with blood type A have a greater chance of getting certain forms of cancer. The differences between the phenotypes appear strong, but we do not understand the reasons for these associations. In any case, it is unclear what evolutionary importance these associations have. Most of the noninfectious diseases have severe effects late in life and therefore should not be subject to natural selection because they usually occur after an individual's reproductive life is over. Some people, however, do acquire these diseases early enough in life so that at least the possibility exists that natural selection could be operating through differential survival to noninfectious diseases. We must demonstrate, however, that such selection did (or does) in fact take place, and not merely that it is possible.

Natural selection may also be operating on ABO blood groups because of incompatibility between mother and fetus, leading to destruction of red blood cells in the fetus. Incompatibility occurs when the fetus has an antigen not present in the mother, such as the mother having type A blood and the fetus having type B blood. Here, the fetus has an antigen (B) not present in the mother, and the mother has the antibody (anti-B) that destroys these fetal red blood cells. Often, ABO incompatibility will lead to spontaneous abortion of the fetus (miscarriage). All possible types of incompatibility are shown in Table 6.3. Note that in each case the fetal genotype is a heterozygote. Under selection against heterozygotes we would ultimately expect to see the less common alleles (*A, B*) disappear, and this has not happened.

However, there might be some selective advantage in some incompatible pregnancies. Bottini et al. (2001) looked at the blood types of infants born to women who had a history of recurrent spontaneous abortion and compared these with infants born to a sample of healthy pregnancies. They found that there were a greater number of infants born to mothers with the anti-B antibody than born to mothers with the anti-A antibody. Thus, ABO incompatible pregnancies, where the mother had anti-B, seem to be at an advantage. Bottini et al. suggest that there is some sort of protective effect in such pregnancies, although it is not yet clear how this works. Differential fitness might explain some of the variation in ABO allele frequencies seen in our species.

Duffy Blood Group   A striking association has been found between infectious disease and the Duffy blood group system. There are three alleles for the Duffy blood group: *Fy^a*, *Fy^b*, and *Fy*. The *Fy* allele is also referred to as the Duffy negative allele and is recessive. Individuals with two Duffy negative alleles (the genotype *FyFy*) are completely resistant to a form of malaria caused by the parasite *Plasmodium vivax* (the earlier example of sickle cell dealt with a different parasite—*Plasmodium falciparum*). It has been suggested that the vivax parasite enters the blood by clinging to *Fy^a* or *Fy^b* molecules. Individuals with the *FyFy* genotype lack both of these molecules and are therefore resistant to the vivax parasite.

The worldwide distribution of the Duffy negative allele, however, is somewhat confusing. The highest frequencies are found in West and Central Africa, often reaching 100 percent, but it is virtually absent in most of Europe and Asia. In areas where the frequency of the Duffy negative allele is high, vivax malaria is absent. At first glance, we might expect the opposite—given the resistance of the Duffy negative allele, we might expect higher frequencies in areas where vivax malaria was common. Livingstone (1984) has suggested that this negative correlation is a reflection of past evolution. By chance, some populations developed higher frequencies of the Duffy negative allele (perhaps because of genetic drift). The preexisting high frequency of the Duffy negative allele prevented the introduction and spread of vivax malaria in these populations. This is a good example of how chance variations may provide an evolutionary advantage in some environments.

Lactase Persistence and Lactose Intolerance

As mammals, human infants receive nourishment from mothers' milk. Infants produce an enzyme, lactase, which allows milk sugar to be digested. In most human populations, lactase production stops by around 5 years of age. Some individuals, however, possess a dominant allele that results in the ability to produce lactase throughout their adult life, a condition known as **lactase persistence.** Individuals with the recessive homozygote (who do not have the dominant allele) will not produce lactase later in life and have difficulty digesting milk, a condition known as **lactose intolerance,** which leads to diarrhea, cramps, and other intestinal problems (Beall and Steegmann 2000).

lactase persistence The ability to produce the enzyme lactase after 5 years of age.

lactose intolerance A condition characterized by diarrhea, cramps, and other intestinal problems resulting from the ingestion of milk.

TABLE 6.4   Frequencies of Lactose Intolerance in Some Human Populations

Population		Percentage of Lactose Intolerance
African ancestry	African Americans	70–77
	Ibos	99
	Bantus	90
	Fulani	22
	Yoruba	99
	Baganda	94
Asian ancestry	Asian Americans	95–100
	Thailand	97–100
	Eskimos	72–88
	Native Americans	58–67
European ancestry	European Americans	2–19
	Finland	18
	Switzerland	12
	Sweden	4

Sources: Lerner and Libby (1976:327); Molnar (1998:133)

Table 6.4 lists the frequency of lactose intolerance in a number of human populations. In general, the frequency of lactose intolerance is high in most African and Asian populations and tends to be low in European populations. A noticeable exception to this rule is the Fulani in Africa, who have a much lower prevalence (22 percent) of lactose intolerance. A number of analyses have found that the frequency of lactose intolerance is lowest in populations that have a history of dairy farming (Holden and Mace 1997; Leonard 2000).

According to this model, the original condition in our ancestors was the cessation of lactase production early in childhood. A dominant allele conferring lactase persistence arose and was selected for in human populations that relied extensively on dairy farming for survival. In situations where milk provided a critical addition to the diet, individuals who were lactase persistent had an evolutionary advantage because of increased dietary resources, and they passed the allele on to the next generation. The variation in allele frequencies thus corresponds to the specific cultural history of populations. This variation is clearest in Africa, where populations such as the Ibo and Bantus—known agricultural populations that did not practice dairy farming—have typically high rates of lactose intolerance. The Fulani, however, are nomadic cattle herders who rely extensively on milk in their diet. The rise of the lactase persistence allele in some human populations provides a good example of rapid natural selection. Dairy agriculture is less than 12,000 years old, and the observed differences between dairy- and nondairy-producing economies must have arisen since then.

There may be a relationship between lactase persistence, dairy farming, and latitude. Calcium is needed for proper bone growth, and vitamin D facilitates the absorption of calcium. Before the introduction of vitamin D into food products, the major source of vitamin D was the sun, as ultraviolet radiation is needed for the synthesis of vitamin D. Ultraviolet radiation is strongest at the equator and less strong further north or south of the equator. Populations living farther from the equator would thus be at increased risk for inadequate vitamin D production and would therefore have problems with calcium absorption and bone growth. In such environments, the ability to digest lactose throughout one's life would be an advantage because lactose increases calcium absorption (Allen and Cheer 1996; Beall and Steegmann 2000). Although the frequency of lactose intolerance does correlate to some extent with latitude, the relationship is far from perfect, as illustrated by the Fulani case. It may be the case that specific dietary requirements relating to calcium absorption influenced selection for lactase persistence in some populations, while the general need for improved nutrition was a factor in others.

Research by Allen and Cheer (1996) suggests that the evolution of lactase persistence may be evolutionarily related to rates of noninsulin-dependent diabetes mellitus (NIDDM, also sometimes referred to as adult-onset diabetes), a disease characterized by the inability to metabolize glucose, a simple sugar. NIDDM has often been viewed as due to a "thrifty genotype" that led to metabolic efficiency in earlier times when the diet was low on simple sugar. When human diet changed, this genotype was no longer beneficial and resulted in diabetes. Allen and Cheer argue that as human populations developed dairy farming, there was an increase in the amount of lactose in the diet, thus leading to an increased risk of diabetes. According to Allen and Cheer, diabetes became the "price" paid by the development of dairy farming; a good potential example of how human cultural change can rapidly affect our biology.

Studies of lactase persistence illustrate that we need to consider biological variation and evolutionary change when making policy decisions. In the United States, which has a large dairy economy, milk is regarded as an essential part of a "normal" diet. We think of milk as intrinsically good and in the past have sent milk to people in less developed nations in the belief that what is good for us must be good for them. It soon became clear, however, that many of these people were lactose intolerant and that milk was not good for them. Health and dietary policies must always consider biological and cultural diversity.

Skin Color

Human skin color is a complex trait. It has a strong genetic component (Williams-Blangero and Blangero 1992) and is also affected by the environment, particularly the amount of direct sunlight.

The Biology of Skin Color One pigment, *melanin,* is responsible for the majority of variation in lightness and darkness in skin color. Melanin is a

FIGURE 6.13

Geographic distribution of human skin color for 102 male Old World samples. Circles indicate the mean skin reflectance measured at a wavelength of 685 nanometers plotted against latitude. Negative values of latitude correspond to the Southern Hemisphere (below the equator), and positive values of latitude correspond to the Northern Hemisphere (above the equator). The solid line indicates the best-fitting curve relating skin color and latitude. Closer analysis shows that skin color is darker in the Southern Hemisphere than in the Northern Hemisphere at equivalent distance from the equator. (Adapted from Relethford 1997)

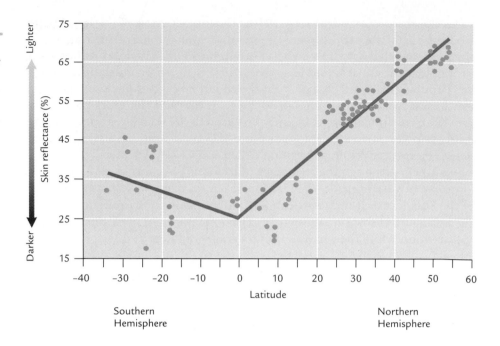

brown pigment secreted by cells in the bottom layer of the skin. Much of the variation in melanin may be due to variation in two major genes that affect the tyrosinase enzyme, which affects melanin production (Sturm et al. 1998).

Another pigment affecting skin color is *hemoglobin,* which gives oxygenated blood cells their red color. Light-skinned people have little melanin near the surface of the skin and so the red color shows through. Because of this effect, "white" people are actually "pink."

Skin color is also affected to a certain extent by sex and age. In general, males are darker than females, probably because of differential effects of sex hormones on melanin production. Age also produces variation. The skin darkens somewhat during adolescence, particularly in females.

The Distribution of Human Skin Color   As mentioned in the previous chapter, human skin color is measured by the percentage of light reflected off the skin at a given wavelength of light. Figure 6.13 shows the worldwide distribution of human skin color based on data from 102 male samples from the Old World. Skin color is darkest at the equator and tends to be lighter with the increasing distance from the equator, north or south. Closer investigation shows that there is also a hemispheric difference—skin color tends to be darker in the Southern Hemisphere (below the equator) than in the Northern Hemisphere, even at equivalent latitudes (Relethford 1997). The distribution of skin color and latitude corresponds to the amount of ultraviolet radiation received at the earth's surface. Because of the way sunlight strikes the earth, ultraviolet radiation is strongest at the equator and diminishes in strength away from the equator. Further, ultraviolet radiation tends to be greater in the Southern Hemisphere than in the Northern Hemisphere due to a number of astronomical and meteorological factors (McKenzie and Elwood 1990, Relethford 1997). Jablonski and Chaplin (2000) have confirmed that human skin color is correlated with ultraviolet radiation; populations living in areas with high levels of ultraviolet radiation tend to be darker than those living in areas with less ultraviolet radiation.

The distribution of human skin color in the world today suggests past evolutionary events relating to natural selection. Current thinking suggests that dark skin evolved among our early ancestors in Africa as a means of protecting against the damaging effects of ultraviolet radiation, most likely relating to the loss of hair and increase in sweat gland density that we suspect took place as our ancestors became increasingly adapted to the hot climate in Africa. Later, as some humans began moving out of Africa, lighter skin color evolved farther away from the equator. This scenario poses two questions: (1) What were the selective effects of ultraviolet radiation leading to dark skin near the equator? and (2) Why did light skin evolve in regions with less ultraviolet radiation?

The Evolution of Dark Skin   Ultraviolet radiation can have several harmful effects. Loomis (1967) suggested that dark skin protects from overproduction of vitamin D. As noted earlier, the major source of vitamin D throughout human history has been the sun, which stimulates vitamin D synthesis. Too much vitamin D, Loomis argued, would be harmful, and darker individuals would be at less risk for vitamin toxicity. However, Holick and colleagues (1981) have shown that vitamin D synthesis reaches a maximum level during continued exposure to ultraviolet radiation and does not reach toxic levels, thus rejecting Loomis's hypothesis.

Several hypotheses have focused on damage to the skin. In sufficient amounts, ultraviolet radiation can lead to skin cancer. The greater the intensity of ultraviolet radiation, the greater the risk for skin cancer at any given level of pigmentation. Among the European American populations of the United States, skin cancer rates are much higher in Texas than in Massachusetts (Damon 1977). Dark-skinned individuals have lower rates of skin cancer because the heavy concentration of melanin near the surface of the skin blocks some of the ultraviolet radiation. Some have suggested that dark skin evolved in human populations near the equator to protect against skin cancer (Robins 1991). Others have rejected skin cancer as a significant factor in the evolution of human skin color because it tends to affect primarily individuals past their reproductive years (Blum 1961; Jablonski and Chaplin 2000). If someone dies from skin cancer after reproducing, his or her death does not affect the process of natural selection.

Sunburn has also been suggested as a potential factor in natural selection. Severe sunburn can lead to infection and can interfere with the body's ability to sweat effectively. Dark skin could protect from these effects and thus be selected for in areas of high ultraviolet radiation (Robins 1991), although the exact magnitude of this selection is not clear.

Jablonski and Chaplin (2000) argue that the potential selective effects of skin cancer and sunburn are minimal and that the most significant factor leading to darker skin in equatorial populations was the damaging effect of ultraviolet radiation on folate levels in the body. Folic acid, a necessary nutrient, is converted into folate in the body. Ultraviolet radiation can destroy folate, leading to several serious consequences. Folate deficiency has been linked to disorders in developing fetuses, including an increase in neutral tube defects, which reduces survivability. Folate levels also affect reproductive capabilities; folate deficiency can disrupt the production of sperm and lead to male infertility. Jablonski and Chaplin suggest that photodestruction of folate has serious consequences for both mortality and fertility and that dark skin evolved for protection in areas with high levels of ultraviolet radiation. Although it remains possible that there were selective consequences resulting from skin cancer and sunburn, the evidence to date suggests that photodestruction of folate was the primary mechanism.

The Evolution of Light Skin   As some humans moved farther from equatorial regions, they lived in areas with lower levels of ultraviolet radiation and consequently the risks from ultraviolet radiation decreased. Lighter skinned individuals would be at less risk from folate deficiency (as well as sunburn and skin cancer if they are indeed selective factors). This does not explain *why* light skin evolved farther from the equator, however, only that it *could* evolve. To construct a complete model for the evolution of human skin color variation, we need to have one or more reasons *why* light skin would have been adaptive farther from the equator. In the absence of such reasons, we would not expect a strong correlation with latitude. Factors that explain the evolution of dark skin near the equator do not explain light skin farther from the equator.

The most widely accepted model for the evolution of light skin focuses on the synthesis of vitamin D. As noted earlier, the major source of vitamin D throughout human history and prehistory has been the sun because ultraviolet radiation stimulates vitamin D synthesis. Today we may receive vitamin D through vitamin supplements or through the injection of vitamin D into our milk. Both of these dietary modifications are recent human inventions, however. Formerly, humans had to obtain their vitamin D through diet or through stimulation of chemical compounds by ultraviolet radiation. Some foods, such as fish oils, are high in vitamin D but are not found in all environments. For most human populations in the past, the major source of vitamin D was the sun.

Vitamin D deficiency can cause a number of problems relating to poor bone development and maintenance, including diseases such as rickets, which leads to deformed bones. Such health hazards can affect fertility as well as mortality. One frequent consequence of childhood rickets is the deformation of a woman's pelvis, an effect which can hinder or prevent successful childbirth. In one U.S. study, only 2 percent of European American women had such pelvic deformities as compared to 15 percent of African

American women (Molnar 1998). This difference presumably relates to skin color; darker women are unable to absorb enough vitamin D for healthy bone growth.

Vitamin D deficiency can be linked to the evolution of light skin. As discussed previously, dark skin protects against the harmful effects of ultraviolet radiation in populations near the equator where ultraviolet radiation is the most intense. As human populations moved away from the equator, these risks declined and the risk for vitamin D deficiency increased because darker skin blocked too much ultraviolet radiation. Natural selection thus produced a change toward lighter skin color that would be adaptive in such environments.

Temperature has also been suggested as a factor in the evolution of light skin. Because temperature is roughly correlated with latitude, some have suggested that the correlation between human skin color and latitude is actually a reflection of a link between skin color and cold adaptation. Reviewing a wide range of data, Post and colleagues (1975) noted that, in cold climates, dark-skinned individuals are at greater risk for frostbite than light-skinned individuals. Data reporting this difference are available on soldiers during the first and second World Wars and the Korean War. During the Korean War, African American soldiers were more than four times as likely to get frostbite as European American soldiers. Closer analysis of the data shows that this difference persists even after controlling for other sociological and health factors. These observations suggest that in the colder northern climates darker skin is more prone to cold injury than lighter skin, a hypothesis supported by laboratory experiments on piebald guinea pigs (having both light and dark skin). Cold injury could be induced more frequently and more severely in the darker patches of skin. Beall and Steegmann (2000) question the cold-injury hypothesis, noting that the higher rates of frostbite among African and African American soldiers reflect differences in vascular responses to cold, and not skin color. They also note that the guinea pig data are not useful because the temperatures involved in the lab experiments are not typical of those experienced during human evolution and are therefore not relevant.

There has been considerable debate over causal factors in the evolution of human skin color and their relative importance. As noted by Jablonski and Chaplin (2000), current evidence suggests that the primary reason for the evolution of human skin color is the balance between the need for darker skin to protect against photodestruction of folate and the need for lighter skin to facilitate vitamin D synthesis. At any given latitude, the optimal skin color reflects the balance between these risks. Near the equator, the primary risk is folate deficiency, leading to darker skin for protection. As we go farther from the equator, this risk decreases and the risk for vitamin D deficiency increases, thus leading to lighter and lighter skin color farther and farther from the equator (Figure 6.14). It is possible that other factors, such as protection against sunburn near the equator, also contribute to the observed correspondence between skin color and latitude.

FIGURE 6.14

Schematic diagram of the relationship between latitude, ultraviolet radiation, and the relative risks of folate deficiency and vitamin D deficiency. Near the equator, dark skin is selected for to block the photodestruction of folate due to high levels of ultraviolet radiation. Farther away from the equator, this risk decreases and the risk for vitamin D deficiency increases, facilitating the evolution of lighter skin color to allow sufficient vitamin D synthesis.

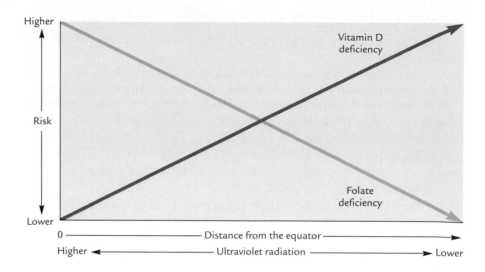

SUMMARY

Case studies of human microevolution presented in this chapter illustrate some of the methods and results of studies dealing with an evolutionary approach to contemporary human biological variation. The case studies of gene flow and genetic drift emphasize how factors such as social structure, population size, migration patterns, cultural barriers, and history all affect the genetic relationships among human populations.

Several examples of natural selection in human populations are reviewed. Perhaps the best-documented example is the relationship between hemoglobin alleles and two selective forces: sickle cell anemia and malaria. In environments where malaria is common, selection has led to an increase in the sickle cell allele because the heterozygotes are the most fit—they show greater resistance to malaria but do not suffer from the adverse effects of sickle cell anemia. Studies of blood groups and other genetic markers also suggest a role for natural selection in human variation. Skin color is another example of a trait that shows a strong environmental correlation, in this case with latitude. This distribution, combined with other evidence, suggests that dark skin is selected for near the equator primarily to protect against the harmful effects of excess ultraviolet radiation (photodestruction of folate). Light skin may have evolved farther from the equator to facilitate sufficient vitamin D synthesis.

SUPPLEMENTAL READINGS

Cavalli-Sforza, L. L., P. Menozzi, and A. Piazza. 1994. *The History and Geography of Human Genes.* Princeton: Princeton University Press.

Crawford, M. H., and J. H. Mielke, eds. 1982. *Current Developments in Anthropological Genetics.* Vol. 2. *Ecology and Population Structure.* New York: Plenum Press. This book and the preceding one by Cavalli-Sforza et al. (1994) are somewhat detailed but provide many examples of the use of genetic distance analysis to unravel the effects of gene flow and genetic drift on human biological variation.

Jablonski, N.G., and G. Chaplin. 2000. The evolution of human sk... *Human Evolution* 39: 57–106. This long article provides the best cu... thesis regarding the evolution of human skin color.

Stinson, S., B. Bogin, R. Huss-Ashmore, and D. O'Rourke. 2000. *Human Bi... tionary and Biocultural Perspective.* New York: John Wiley & Sons. A compre... ume consisting of review chapters on a variety of topics relating to human po... biology. Many chapters include valuable summaries of topics considered here, i... ing population history, genetic polymorphisms, lactase persistence, and skin color.

INTERNET RESOURCES

http://anthro.palomar.edu/blood/default.htm
Human Blood, a review of the genetics of ABO and Rh blood groups.

http://anthro.palomar.edu/vary/vary_3.htm
Distribution of Blood Types, including maps of the distribution of the ABO alleles.

http://jove.prohosting.com/~scarfex/blood/groups.html
Human Blood Group Systems, which provides information on the genetics of 26 different blood group systems.

CHAPTER 7

May 29

Human Adaptation

As discussed in Chapter 1, adaptation is the successful interaction of a population with its environment. Thus far, adaptation has been discussed in terms of genetic adaptation—that is, natural selection. In this chapter, we examine a broader perspective. Central to the study of adaptation is the concept of **stress,** broadly defined as any factor that interferes with the normal limits of operation of an organism. Organisms maintain these limits through an ability known as **homeostasis.** As ways of dealing with the stresses that alter your body's functioning, adaptations restore homeostasis. For example, within normal limits, your body maintains a relatively constant body temperature. When you stand outside in a cold wind, you may shiver. This is your body's way of adapting to cold stress. You might also choose to put on a heavy jacket.

As human beings, we can adapt both biologically and culturally. It is important to note, however, that our biocultural nature can work against us. In adapting to stresses culturally, we can introduce other stresses as a result of our behavior. Pollution, for example, is a consequence of cultural change that has had a negative impact on our physical environment in numerous ways.

Key to the interaction between human biology and culture, human adaptation operates on a number of levels—physiologic, developmental, genetic, and cultural—all of which are interrelated, for better or for worse. Thus, countering a biological stress such as disease by the cultural adaptation of medicine can lower the death rate for human populations but can also increase

◀ Sherpas in Nepal returning from a trip to Mount Everest. The Sherpa are an example of a population that has adapted, both biologically and culturally, to the stresses of living at high altitudes. (© Bobby Model/National Geographic Society Image Collection)

stress Any factor that interferes with the normal limits of operation of an organism.

homeostasis In a physiologic sense, the maintenance of normal limits of body functioning.

population size, which in turn can lead to further stresses, such as food shortages and environmental degradation.

TYPES OF ADAPTATION

How do humans adapt? What are the different ways we have to cope with the stresses of the physical and cultural environments?

Physiologic, Genetic, and Cultural Adaptation

Besides genetic and cultural adaptation, humans are capable of three other forms of adaptation that are physiologic in nature: acclimation, acclimatization, and developmental acclimatization. **Acclimation** refers to short-term changes that occur very quickly after exposure to a stress, such as sweating when you are hot. **Acclimatization** refers to physiologic changes that take longer, from days to months, such as an increase in red blood cell production after moving to a high-altitude environment. When a change occurs during the physical growth of any organism, it is known as **developmental acclimatization.** An example (covered later in the chapter) is the increase in chest size that occurs when a person grows up in high altitudes. The ability of organisms to respond physiologically or developmentally to environmental stresses is often referred to as **plasticity.**

Adaptation to Ultraviolet Radiation: An Example

A focus on ultraviolet radiation is a useful way of coming to grips with some of the basic concepts of adaptation. As mentioned in Chapter 6, excessive ultraviolet radiation can cause a number of problems. How have humans adapted, or attempted to adapt, to this stress?

Short-term exposure to ultraviolet radiation results in darkening of the skin, or tanning, which can take two different forms. *Immediate tanning* darkens the skin within 1 to 2 hours and fades away during the first 24 hours after exposure. *Delayed tanning* is a more gradual process caused by repeated exposure. Delayed tanning begins within 2 to 3 days of initial exposure and reaches a maximum after 19 days. The effects of delayed tanning can last as long as 9.5 months (Robins 1991). From a physiologic perspective, tanning is a response to skin cell damage. Delayed tanning is an adaptive response whereby darkening of the skin provides some protection against further damage. Immediate tanning does not appear to be effective in this respect.

Tanning is not the only form of adaptation to ultraviolet radiation. There is strong evidence that in equatorial regions dark skin evolved in response to the stress of excessive levels of ultraviolet radiation (Chapter 6). Individuals with darker skin were more likely to survive and therefore more likely to pass

acclimation Short-term physiologic responses to a stress, usually within minutes or hours.

acclimatization Long-term physiologic responses to a stress, usually taking from days to months.

developmental acclimatization Changes in organ or body structure that occur during the physical growth of any organism.

plasticity The ability of an organism to respond physiologically or developmentally to environmental stress.

on the genes for darker skin to the next generation. In other words, natural selection produced a genetic adaptation.

Cultural adaptations can also deal with exposure to ultraviolet radiation. If your occupation or leisure activity increases your risk of exposure, you can wear protective clothing, such as hats or long-sleeved garments, or apply chemical sunscreens. Changes in the hours you work or play outdoors can also help minimize exposure. With the growing concern about skin cancer in the United States, increasing numbers of people are turning to behaviors that provide protection from ultraviolet radiation, or at least minimize exposure.

CLIMATE AND HUMAN ADAPTATION

Though originally tropical primates, we humans have managed to expand into virtually every environment on our planet. Such expansion has been possible largely because of multiple adaptations to the range of temperatures around the world.

Physiologic Responses to Temperature Stress

As warm-blooded creatures, humans have the ability to maintain a constant body temperature. This homeostatic quality works well only under certain limits.

Cold Stress   When you are cold, your body is losing heat too rapidly. One response is to increase heat production temporarily through shivering, which also increases your metabolic rate. This response is not very efficient and is costly in terms of energy. A more efficient physiologic response to cold stress is minimization of heat loss through alternate constriction and dilation of blood vessels. **Vasoconstriction,** the narrowing of blood vessels, reduces blood flow and heat loss. **Vasodilation,** the opening of the blood vessels, serves to increase blood flow and heat loss. These responses are examples of acclimation to cold stress.

When a person is first subjected to cold stress, vasoconstriction acts to minimize the loss of heat from the body to the extremities (i.e., the hands, feet, and face). As a result, skin temperature drops. This response becomes dangerous, however, if it continues too long. Should this start to happen, vasodilation begins, causing blood and heat to flow from the interior of the body to the extremities. The increased blood flow prevents damage to the extremities, but now the body is losing heat again! Neither vasoconstriction nor vasodilation by itself provides an effective physiologic response to cold stress. *Both* must operate, back and forth, to maintain a balance between heat loss and damage to the extremities.

An interesting phenomenon occurs after initial exposure to cold stress. The cycles of alternating vasoconstriction and vasodilation, accompanied by

vasoconstriction The narrowing of blood vessels, which reduces blood flow and heat loss.

vasodilation The opening of the blood vessels, which increases blood flow and heat loss.

FIGURE 7.1

The Lewis hunting phenomenon. Initial exposure of a finger into ice water produces a decrease in skin temperature, caused by vasoconstriction. After a while, this response gives way to vasodilation, which causes skin temperature to increase. The cycles continue over time but become more frequent and less extreme, thus providing more efficient adaptation. (Modified after Frisancho [1993:85])

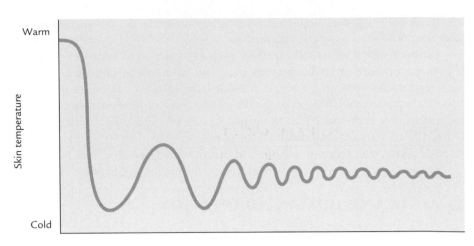

Time after exposure to ice water

alternating cycles of cold and warm skin temperatures, begin to level out, becoming more frequent and less extreme. Skin temperature changes more quickly, but the increases and decreases are not as great. This pattern, called the *Lewis hunting phenomenon,* demonstrates how effective the body's ability is to adapt. The smaller and more frequent cycles are more efficient (Figure 7.1).

Heat Stress　When experiencing heat stress, your body is not removing heat quickly enough. There are four ways in which heat is lost from the body, three of which can also increase heat (Frisancho 1993). *Radiation* is heat flow from objects in the form of electromagnetic radiation. The body removes heat through radiation but also picks up heat radiated by other objects. *Convection* refers to the removal or gain of heat through air molecules. Heat flows from a warm object to a cooler object. *Conduction* is heat exchange through physical contact with another object, such as the ground or clothes. Conduction generally accounts for a very small proportion of heat exchange. *Evaporation* is the loss of heat through the conversion of water to vapor. In the process of sweat evaporation, heat energy is consumed. Evaporation is the only one of these four mechanisms that results in heat loss without heat gain.

The amount of heat loss through these mechanisms varies according to both temperature and humidity. As the temperature increases, the only way your body can cope is to increase the amount of evaporation (your body can't amplify any of the other three mechanisms). As a result, evaporation is the most effective mechanism for heat removal in excessively hot temperatures. At comfortable temperatures, most heat is lost through radiation, and evaporation accounts for only 23 percent of the total lost. At hot temperatures (35° C = 95° F), evaporation accounts for 90 percent. Vasodilation is also important in heat loss. The opening of the blood vessels helps remove internal heat to the outside skin. The heat can then be transferred to the environment through radiation, convection, and evaporation.

Evaporation has its drawbacks. The removal of too much water from the body can be harmful or even fatal. The efficiency of evaporation is also affected by humidity. In humid environments, evaporation is less efficient, making heat loss more difficult under hot and humid conditions than under hot and dry conditions.

Climate and Morphological Variation

Differences in physiologic responses and certain morphological variations, most notably the size and shape of the body and head, affect people's ability to handle temperature stress. Nose size and shape are related to humidity.

The Bergmann and Allen Rules Human populations in colder climates tend to be heavier than those in hotter climates. This does not mean that all people in cold climates are heavy and all people in hot climates are light. Every human group contains a variety of small and large people. Some of this variation is caused by factors such as diet. However, a strong relationship of *average* body size and temperature does exist among indigenous human populations (Roberts 1978).

A nineteenth-century English zoologist, Carl Bergmann, noted the relationship between body size and temperature in a number of mammal species. Bergmann explained his findings in terms of mammalian physiology and principles of heat loss. **Bergmann's rule** states that if two mammals have similar shapes but different sizes, the smaller animal will lose heat more rapidly and will therefore be better adapted to warmer climates, where the ability to lose heat is advantageous. Larger mammals lose heat more slowly and are therefore better adapted to colder climates.

The reason for these relationships is that heat production is a function of the total volume of a mammal, whereas heat loss is a function of total surface area. Consider two hypothetical mammals whose body shape is that of a cube. Imagine that one cube is 2 cm long and the other is 4 cm long in each dimension (Figure 7.2). As a measure of heat production, we can compute the volume of each cube (volume = length × width × height). The volume of the 2-cm cube is 8 cm³; that of the 4-cm cube is 64 cm³. The larger cube can produce more heat because of its greater volume. The greater the volume of a mammal, the greater the heat produced.

As a measure of heat loss, we can compute the surface area of each cube. The surface area of each side is length times width. There are six sides to a cube, so we multiply our result by 6. The surface area of the 2-cm cube is 24 cm²; that of the 4-cm cube is 96 cm². With the greater surface area, the larger cube seems to produce more heat and to lose it at a greater rate. The relevant factor in heat loss in mammals, however, is the ratio of surface area to volume—that is, the rate of heat loss relative to the amount of surface area. The surface area/volume ratio is 24/8 = 3 for the smaller cube and 96/64 = 1.5 for the larger cube. Therefore, the larger cube loses heat at a slower rate relative to heat production. In cold climates, the larger cube would be at an advantage

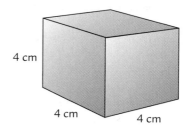

Surface area = 24 cm²
Volume = 8 cm³
Surface area/volume = 3

Surface area = 96 cm²
Volume = 64 cm³
Surface area/volume = 1.5

FIGURE 7.2

Geometric representation of Bergmann's rule relating body size and heat loss. The larger cube has a larger volume (heat production) and a larger surface area (heat loss). The larger cube also has a smaller surface area/volume ratio, however, indicating that it would lose heat less rapidly and therefore be adaptive in colder climates.

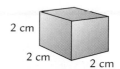

Bergmann's rule States that (1) among mammals of similar shape, the larger mammal loses heat less rapidly than the smaller mammal, and that (2) among mammals of similar size, the mammal with a linear shape will lose heat more rapidly than the mammal with a nonlinear shape.

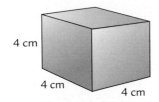

Surface area = 96 cm^2
Volume = 64 cm^3
Surface area/volume = 1.5

Surface area = 112 cm^2
Volume = 64 cm^3
Surface area/volume = 1.75

FIGURE 7.3

Geometric representation of Bergmann's rule relating body shape and heat loss. The cube has a lower surface area/volume ratio than the rectangular block and would therefore lose heat less rapidly.

Allen's rule States that mammals in cold climates tend to have short, bulky limbs, allowing less loss of body heat, whereas mammals in hot climates tend to have long, slender limbs, allowing greater loss of body heat.

because it loses heat less quickly. In hot climates, the reverse would be true; hot climates would favor the smaller cube, with its quicker rate of heat loss.

Another aspect of Bergmann's rule involves the shape of an object and its relationship to heat production and loss. Figure 7.3 shows two objects with the same volume but different shapes. The first object is a 4-cm cube with a volume of 64 cm^3, a surface area of 96 cm^2, and a surface area/volume ratio of 1.5. The second object is a rectangular block 2 cm wide, 4 cm deep, and 8 cm high. The volume of this block is also 64 cm^3. The surface area is 112 cm^2, and the surface area/volume ratio is 112/64 = 1.75. Even though both objects produce the same amount of heat as measured by their volumes, the rectangular block loses heat more quickly. Linear objects such as the block would be at an advantage in hot climates, whereas less linear objects such as the cube would be at an advantage in cold climates. Accordingly, Bergmann's rule predicts that mammals in hot climates will have linear body shapes and mammals in cold climates will have less linear body shapes. Another zoologist, J. Allen, applied these principles to body limbs and other appendages. **Allen's rule** predicts that mammals in cold climates should have shorter, bulkier limbs, whereas mammals in hot climates should have longer, narrower ones.

Body Size and Shape   Do the Bergmann and Allen rules hold for human body size and shape? Figure 7.4 shows a Masai cattle herder from Africa and an Inuit (Eskimo) man. Note the thinness and length of the Masai's body and limbs. Those of the Inuit are shorter and bulkier. These physiques do in fact conform to Bergmann's and Allen's predictions. Analysis of data from many human populations has found the rules to be accurate in describing the *average* trends among populations in the world today as well as in the past (Ruff 1994). Again, don't forget that extensive variation exists within populations. Also, some populations are exceptions to the general rule. African pygmies, for example, are short and have short limbs, yet they live in a hot climate. The pygmy's short size appears to be due to a hormonal deficiency (Shea and Gomez 1988).

The Bergmann and Allen rules apply to adult human body size and shape. Are these average patterns the result of natural selection (i.e., genetic adaptation) or changes in size and shape during the growth process (i.e., developmental acclimatization)? Do infants born elsewhere who move into an environment attain the same adult size and shape as native-born infants? If so, this suggests a direct influence of the environment on growth. If not, then the growth pattern leading to a certain adult size and shape may be genetic in nature and determined by natural selection. If the growth pattern is entirely genetic, then we may expect to see the same ultimate size and shape regardless of environment. That is, an infant born in a cold climate but raised in a hot climate would still show the characteristic size and shape of humans born in cold climates. Of course, if *both* environmental and genetic factors are responsible for adult size and shape, then the expected pattern is more complex. Unraveling the potential genetic and climatic effects is a difficult process because other contributing influences, such as nutrition, also vary with climate.

FIGURE 7.4

An Inuit (left) and a Masai cattle herder (right) illustrate the relationship between body size, body shape, and climate predicted by the Bergmann and Allen rules. (Left, Neg. #231604, Photo by D.B. MacMillan. Courtesy Department of Library Services, American Museum of Natural History; right, © Bruce Dale/ National Geographic Society Image Collection)

The evidence to date suggests that both genetic and environmental factors influence the relationship among climate, growth, body size, and body shape. When children grow up in a climate different from that of their ancestors, they tend to grow in ways the indigenous children do (Malina 1975; Roberts 1978). Changes in nutritional patterns also have an effect. Katz-marzyk and Leonard (1998) examined the relationship between body size and shape and average annual temperature using data collected over the past 40 years and compared their results with previous studies. They found that the effect of changing environmental conditions in the past 40 years still show the patterns expected from the Bergmann and Allen rules, but the strength of the relationship has declined. This change was attributed to the impact of modernization on nutrition and health care, which has reduced the climatic effect on morphology to some extent.

Cranial Size and Shape   The size and shape of the human head has long been of interest to anthropologists. In past times, the shape of the head was the focus of studies of racial classification. In the nineteenth century, the Swedish anatomist Anders Retzius developed a measure of cranial shape called the **cephalic index.** This index is derived from two measurements: the total length of the head and its maximum width. To compute the index, you simply divide the width of the head by the length of the head and multiply the result by 100. For example, if a person has a head length of 182 mm and a head width of 158 mm, the cephalic index is (158/182) × 100 = 86.8. That is, the person's

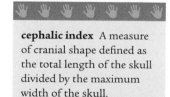

cephalic index A measure of cranial shape defined as the total length of the skull divided by the maximum width of the skull.

FIGURE 7.5

Relationship between cranial shape (cephalic index) and average annual temperature across the world. The solid line indicates the best-fitting linear equation. The cephalic index is greater (broader head) in colder climates because a round shape has a lower surface area/ volume ratio, which minimizes heat loss. (Source of data: Kenneth Beals, unpublished data)

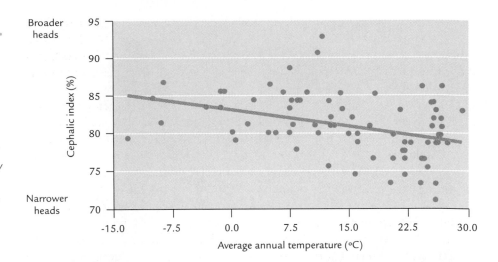

head width is almost 87 percent of head length. Among human populations today, the cephalic index ranges from roughly 70 percent to 90 percent.

At first, cranial shape was felt to be a measurement capable of determining racial groupings. For example, African skulls were found to have lower cephalic indices than European skulls. Further study showed *rough* agreement but also produced many examples of overlap and similar values in different populations. For example, both Germans and Koreans have average cephalic indices of about 83 percent. Likewise, both African pygmies and Greenland Eskimos have average cephalic indices of approximately 77 percent (Harrison et al. 1988). These values do not correspond to any racial classification; they represent *averages* for each population. There is also considerable variation *within* each population.

As more data were obtained and compared geographically, a different pattern emerged—a correspondence was found to exist between cranial shape and climate. Beals (1972) examined the cephalic index and climate around the world. He found a direct relationship: Populations in colder climates tend to have wider skulls relative to length than those in hot climates (Figure 7.5). In particular, he found the average cephalic index for populations that experienced winter frost to be higher than for those in tropical environments.

This correspondence makes sense in terms of the Bergmann and Allen rules. The shape of the upper part of the skull is related to heat loss. Rounded heads (those with a high cephalic index) lose heat slowly and therefore are at an advantage in cold climates. Narrow heads lose heat more quickly and are therefore at an advantage in hot climates. It appears that as human populations moved into colder climates, natural selection led to a change in the relative proportions of the skull. Beals and colleagues (1983) have extended this analysis to fossil human crania over the past 1.5 million years and found similar results.

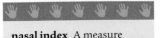

nasal index A measure of the shape of the nasal opening, defined as the width of the nasal opening divided by the height.

Nasal Size and Shape   The shape of the nasal opening in the skull is another morphological variation that has a strong relationship to climate. The **nasal index** is the width of the nasal opening divided by the height of the nasal opening, multiplied by 100. Typical values of the nasal index range from roughly 64 percent to 104 percent (Molnar 1998). Stereotypic racial views associate wide noses (large nasal indices) with African peoples. Although it is true that some African populations have very wide noses, others have long, narrow noses.

Numerous studies have found positive associations between the average nasal index of populations and average temperature. Populations in cold climates tend to have narrow noses; those in hot climates tend to have wide noses. Relationships have also been found between average nasal index and average humidity. Populations in dry climates tend to have narrow noses; those in humid climates tend to have wide noses (Franciscus and Long 1991). The mucous membranes of the nose serve to warm and moisten incoming air. High, narrow noses can warm air to a greater extent than low, wide noses and therefore may be more adaptive in cold climates. High, narrow noses also have a greater internal surface area with which to moisten air and are thus more adaptive in dry climates.

Cultural Adaptations

In Western societies, we tend to take cultural adaptations to temperature stress for granted. Housing, insulated clothing, heaters, air conditioners, and other technologies are all around us. How do people in other cultures adapt to excessive cold or heat?

Cold Stress   The Inuit, or Eskimo people, of the Arctic have realized effective cultural adaptations to cold stress, most notably in their clothing and shelter. It is not enough just to wear a lot of clothes to stay warm; if you work hard, you tend to overheat. The Inuit wear layered clothing, trapping air between layers to act as an insulator. Outer layers can be removed if a person overheats. Also, the Inuit design their clothing with multiple flaps that can be opened to prevent buildup of sweat while working.

While out hunting or fishing, the Inuit frequently construct temporary snow shelters, or igloos, that are quite efficient protection from the cold. The ice is an excellent insulator, and its reflective surface helps retain heat (Figure 7.6). More permanent shelters also provide ample protection from the cold. Inuit houses have an underground entry, which is curved to reduce incoming wind. Inside, the main living area lies at a higher level than the fireplace; this architectural feature serves to increase heat and minimize drafts (Moran 1982).

Not all cold-weather housing is as effective as the types constructed by the Inuit. Among the Quechua Indians of the Peruvian highlands, the temperature inside temporary houses is often not much warmer than it is outside. However, these shelters do provide protection against rain and to some extent the cold. The bedding used by the Quechua is their most effective protection against heat loss (Frisancho 1993).

Heat Stress   Human populations live in environments that are dry and hot (i.e., deserts) and that are humid and hot (i.e., tropical rain forests). Moran

FIGURE 7.6

Forms of human shelter such as this igloo (top) and this Pueblo house (bottom) reflect adaptation to a wide range of climatic conditions. (Top, © *Fred Bruemmer/Peter Arnold, Inc.;* bottom, © *Owen Franken/Corbis)*

(1982) has summarized some basic principles of clothing and shelter that are used in desert environments, where the objectives are fourfold: to reduce heat production, to reduce heat gain from radiation, to reduce heat gain from conduction, and to increase evaporation. Clothing is important because it protects from both solar radiation and hot winds. Typical desert clothing is light and loose, thus allowing circulation of air to increase evaporation. The air between the clothing and the body also provides excellent insulation.

Shelters are frequently built compactly to minimize the surface area exposed to the sun. Light colors on the outside help reflect heat. Doors and windows are kept closed during the day to keep the interior cool. Building materials are also adaptive. Adobe, for example, is efficient in absorbing heat during the day and radiating it at night (see Figure 7.6); nighttime temperatures may drop precipitously in desert environments.

Heat stress in tropical environments is often a problem because the extreme humidity greatly reduces the efficiency of evaporation through sweating. Cultural adaptations to tropical environments are similar throughout the world. Clothing is minimal, helping to increase the potential for evaporation. In some cultures, shelters are built in an open design, without walls, to augment cooling during the day; in others, shelters are built closed to increase warmth at night. The combination of high heat and humidity obviously affects daily routines. Generally, people start work early in the day, taking long midday breaks to keep from overheating.

In sum, humans have adapted to a number of environments that produce temperature stress. Humans have managed to adapt to extremes of hot and cold through physiologic changes, long-term genetic adaptations, and adaptive behaviors, particularly those manifested in clothing and shelter technology and in the pace of daily life.

HIGH-ALTITUDE ADAPTATION

Some human populations have lived for long periods of time at elevations of over 2,500 meters, or roughly 8,200 feet. An estimated 25 million people currently live between 2,500 and 5,000 meters (Harrison et al. 1988).

High-Altitude Stresses

High-altitude environments produce several stresses, including oxygen starvation, cold, and sometimes poor nutrition. Studies of high-altitude populations have provided insight into how humans cope with multiple stresses.

Hypoxia   Oxygen starvation, or **hypoxia,** is more common at high altitudes because of the relationship of barometric pressure and altitude. Although the percentage of oxygen in the atmosphere is relatively constant up to almost 70 miles above the earth, barometric pressure decreases quickly with altitude (Figure 7.7). Because air is less compressed at high altitudes, its oxygen content is less concentrated, and less oxygen is thus available to the hemoglobin in the blood. The percentage of arterial oxygen saturation decreases rapidly with altitude (Figure 7.8). For persons at rest, hypoxia generally occurs above 3,000 meters; for active persons, it can occur as low as 2,000 meters (Frisancho 1993).

Other Stresses   Because the air is thinner at high altitudes, the concentration of ultraviolet radiation is greater and the air itself offers less protection against it. The thinner air also causes considerable heat loss from the atmosphere, resulting in cold stress. In many high-altitude environments, conditions are also extremely dry because of mountain winds and low humidity. In addition, hypoxia affects plants and animals; for lack of oxygen, trees cannot

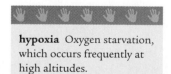

hypoxia Oxygen starvation, which occurs frequently at high altitudes.

FIGURE 7.7

The relationship between barometric pressure and altitude. Barometric pressure decreases as altitude increases, causing a decrease in the percentage of arterial oxygen saturation (see Figure 7.8). *(Source of data: Frisancho [1979:104])*

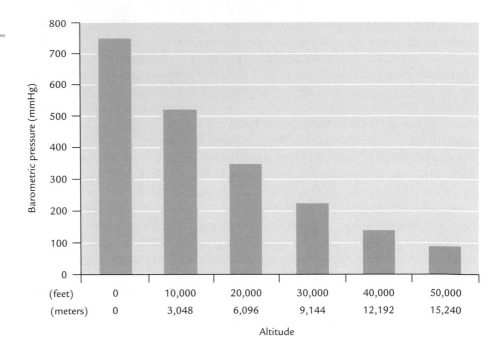

FIGURE 7.8

The relationship between arterial oxygen saturation and altitude. (Source of data: Frisancho [1979:104])

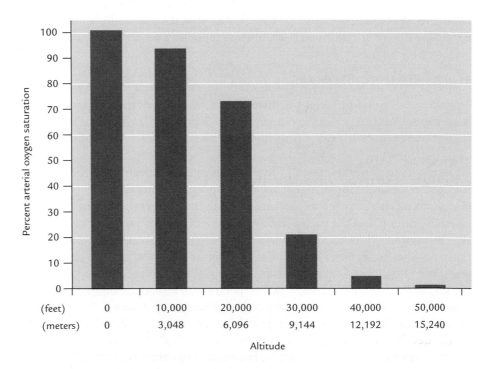

grow above 4,000 meters. The limited availability of plants and animals means that nutritional stress is likely in many high-altitude environments.

Numerous studies have compared the physiology and morphology of high-altitude and low-altitude populations. Early research tended to attribute any differences to the effects of hypoxia on the human body. More recent studies have shown that other stresses of high altitude are significant factors as well (Frisancho 1990). When dealing with human adaptation, we do best to consider the effect and interaction of *multiple* stresses.

Physiologic Responses to Hypoxia

People who live at low altitudes experience several physiologic changes when they enter a high-altitude environment. Some of these happen immediately; others occur over several months to a year. Such physiologic responses help to maintain sufficient oxygen levels. Respiration increases initially but returns to normal after a few days. Red blood cell production increases for roughly 3 months. The weight of the right ventricle of the heart is greater than the weight of the left ventricle in individuals who have grown up at high altitudes. Other changes include possible hyperventilation, higher hemoglobin concentration in the blood, loss of appetite, and weight loss. Memory and sensory abilities may be affected, and hypoxia may influence hormone levels. These changes are not all necessarily adaptive, and some (such as weight loss) can be harmful.

The physiologic differences between high-altitude and low-altitude natives are primarily acquired during the growth process. Studies of children who were born at low altitudes but moved into high altitudes during childhood clearly substantiate this phenomenon. In terms of aerobic capacity, for example, the younger the age of migration, the higher the aerobic capacity (Frisancho 1993). In other words, the longer a child lives in a high-altitude environment, the greater the developmental response to that environment. Age at migration has no effect on the aerobic capacity of adults, however, further indicating that most physiologic changes are the result of developmental acclimatization.

Physical Growth in High-Altitude Populations

Studies conducted by Paul Baker and his colleagues of high-altitude and low-altitude Indian populations in Peru found two peculiarities in growth. Chest dimensions and lung volume were greater at all ages in the high-altitude group (Figure 7.9), and high-altitude populations were also shorter at most ages than low-altitude populations (Figure 7.10) (Frisancho and Baker 1970). The shorter stature is related to delayed maturation, whereas the increase in chest size is due to growth acceleration during childhood.

Initially, the researchers interpreted both patterns of physical growth as direct developmental responses to hypoxia and cold stress at high altitude. Larger chests and larger lung volumes relative to body size would be better able to provide sufficient oxygen levels. More energy devoted to the growth of oxygen transport systems, however, would leave less energy available for growth in other organ systems, especially the skeletal and muscle systems. Compounded by cold stress at high altitudes, this energy deficit would lead to an increase in basal metabolic rates and further reduction in energy available for body growth. As discussed later, this view is now being questioned.

FIGURE 7.9

Distance curves for chest circumference for high-altitude and low-altitude Peruvian Indian populations. At all ages, the high-altitude population has the greatest chest circumference. (Courtesy A. R. Frisancho)

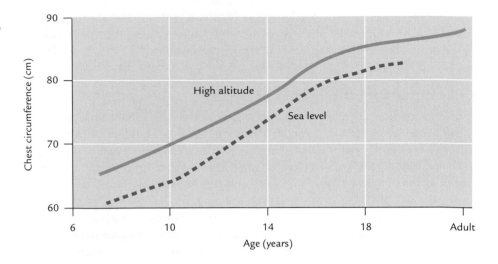

FIGURE 7.10

Distance curve for stature for high-altitude and low-altitude Peruvian Indian populations. At most ages, the low-altitude population is taller. (Courtesy A. R. Frisancho)

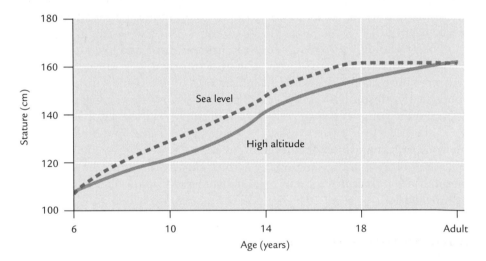

Studies in high-altitude environments around the world show a similar pattern of growth in chest dimensions, although the extent of growth varies. Migrants to high-altitude populations also show an increase in chest dimensions, particularly among those that migrate at an early age. Increased growth of oxygen transport systems appears to be a developmental response to hypoxia.

Are the developmental changes in chest and lung growth in high-altitude populations genetic in nature? Were they shaped by natural selection? Most research to date assigns a relatively minor role to genetic factors. One study examined high-altitude and low-altitude populations of European ancestry in Bolivia (Greksa 1990). Because these groups do not have a long history of residence at high altitude, they would not possess any genetic predisposition for high-altitude adaptations. The study showed there was an increased capacity of the oxygen transport system in these populations at high altitude even though they were not of high-altitude ancestry. The observed changes were instead direct effects of a chronic hypoxic stress. Weitz and colleagues

(2000) did not find any such effect in low-altitude Han Chinese who had migrated to a high-altitude environment, however, suggesting that there might be genetic differences between populations that underlie their differential response to hypoxia. It appears that chest dimensions and size of the lungs are affected by both developmental and genetic factors that interact differently in different human populations (Greksa 1996).

The delayed maturation and small stature of the Peruvians have not been found in all studies of growth in high-altitude populations. As a result, some researchers have questioned the initial premise that hypoxia and cold stress have necessarily led to these characteristics, suggesting instead that other causal factors might be at work. A study undertaken in Peru has in fact shown that nutrition has had a major influence on stature (Leonard et al. 1990). Though high altitude may play a role in nutritional stress in the Peruvian highlands, income levels and access to land are of greater consequence. Also, other high-altitude populations, such as those found in Ethiopia, have a higher standard of living and do not show the growth deficits observed in Peru. Thus, it appears that although increased chest growth is a functional adaptation to hypoxia, the smaller body size is not necessarily related to high altitude. These results amply illustrate the complexity in assessing the relative value of stresses in any given environment.

NUTRITIONAL ADAPTATION

The previous examples of human adaptation have focused on adaptive responses to the stresses imposed by the physical environment, specifically temperature and high-altitude stress. This section examines adaptation to nutritional needs and differences in the availability of food resources.

Basic Nutritional Needs

Proper nutrition is needed for body maintenance, growth, and the energy needs of daily activity. Ingested nutrients provide the energy for these. During infancy, childhood, and adolescence, a greater proportion of nutrient energy goes into physical growth. Too little energy can result in a reduction in overall size and speed of maturation. Too much nutrient energy can result in accumulation of fat and acceleration of maturation. Inadequate amounts of certain critical nutrients can also affect basic biological processes, such as insufficiency in vitamin A or C, both of which can increase susceptibility to certain diseases.

Ingested energy (measured in calories) comes from carbohydrates, proteins, and fats. Dietary proteins are also necessary for certain metabolic functions. Proteins provide amino acids, of which 20 are needed by the body for synthesis and repair of body tissues. Although the body synthesizes some amino acids, adult humans require 8 amino acids available only through diet (children need 9). Without adequate sources of protein in the diet, lack of these amino acids can lead to growth retardation, illness, and death. The major sources of proteins in Western human populations are animal products,

TABLE 7.1   Recommended Daily Allowances (RDA) of Calories and Proteins for Infants and Children in the United States

Age (years)	Energy (kilocalories)	Protein (grams)
0–0.5	650	13
0.5–1.0	850	14
1–3	1300	16
4–6	1800	24
7–10	2000	28

Source: National Academy of Sciences (1989)

TABLE 7.2   Recommended Daily Allowances (RDA) of Calories and Proteins for Adolescents and Adults in the United States

Age (years)	Energy (kilocalories)		Protein (grams)	
	Males	Females	Males	Females
11–14	2500	2200	45	46
15–18	3000	2200	59	44
19–24	2900	2200	58	46
25–50	2900	2200	63	50
51+	2300	1900	63	50

Note: For pregnant women, add 300 kilocalories per day of energy and increase protein intake to 60 grams per day. For women who are breast-feeding, add 500 kilocalories per day of energy and increase protein intake to 65 grams per day for the first 6 months (62 grams per day for the second 6 months).

Source: National Academy of Sciences (1989)

including meat, eggs, fish, and milk. Plants provide proteins, but they are lacking in one or more amino acids and must be eaten in combination with other plants to ensure adequate nutrition.

As an example, the recommended daily intake of calories and proteins for infants and children in the United States is shown in Table 7.1. Note that both energy and protein needs increase with age, corresponding to body growth. Table 7.2 reports the recommended daily intake of calories and proteins for adolescents and adults in the United States. Energy needs generally decline with age, whereas recommended protein intake increases somewhat with age. Recommended intake of both calories and proteins is considerably higher for women who are pregnant or breast-feeding, as both activities require additional nutrients. The recommended daily intake of calories increases

14 percent during pregnancy and 23 percent while breast-feeding, and the recommended daily intake of protein increases 20 percent during pregnancy and 30 percent during breast-feeding.

There is, of course, variation in these figures depending on specific conditions and individual needs; these figures represent *averages* for the U.S. population. In addition, keep in mind that other agencies and countries have somewhat different standards (Leonard 2000).

Our bodies also require other nutrients, such as fatty acids, vitamins, and minerals. A diet lacking in one or more of these nutrients can lead to medical problems. A lack of iodine, for example, can lead to thyroid problems, and a lack of vitamin C can lead to the disease scurvy.

Variation in Human Diet

Human nutritional needs have been shaped by evolution. In a general sense, the nutritional needs of humans are similar to other omnivorous primate species. Our physiology reflects the general primate adaptation to a diet comprised of large amounts of fruit and vegetation, such as our shared inability to synthesize vitamin C, forcing us to acquire it from our diet (Leonard 2000). Humans, however, have a considerably more diverse diet, reflecting the broad range of environments we have adapted to and the diversity in cultural adaptations developed to acquire food.

As is discussed in detail in later chapters, the primary means of acquiring food throughout most of human evolution has been hunting and gathering. This way of life began close to 2 million years ago and was the only way humans obtained food until about 12,000 years ago, when an increasing number of human populations became reliant on agriculture. As discussed further in Chapter 15, this shift in subsistence has had a noticeable biological impact on our health as we frequently eat a diet quite unlike that which we adapted to in the past.

Hunting and Gathering Hunting and gathering populations do not all have the same type of diet; their specific patterns of resource utilization are shaped by their specific environments (e.g., you can't fish if there are no fish around). Australian aborigines must cope with a very dry environment with little water. Migration of groups tends to be structured around the availability of water. Hunting provides only a portion of their caloric intake; most comes from tubers, seeds, and small fruits. Among the San of the Kalahari Desert in Africa, water resources also restrict migration. More hunting is available than in central Australia, but the bulk of the diet still comes from plants, especially nuts and seeds (Molnar and Molnar 2000). In general, hunting-gathering populations obtain a greater proportion of their calories from gathering, averaging about 70 percent to 80 percent, than from hunting. Among the San, for example, about two-thirds of the daily caloric intake came from nuts and other vegetable foods (Lee 1968). Across cultures, however, there is considerable variation. All hunting-gathering societies obtain *at least* 20 percent of their diet from hunting, but some, particularly those in arctic environments with fewer plant resources, derive most of their calories from hunting.

Agriculture   There is also variation among agricultural populations, dependent largely on available resources and the level of technology. Some populations practice simple horticulture, such as slash and burn agriculture; other populations rely on intensive agriculture. The specific food crop(s) exploited is dependent upon the environment; rice is a main crop in Southeast Asia, wheat in Europe, and corn in the Americas.

Different ways of processing food can improve its quality. Leonard (2000) discusses one example, corn among Native American populations. Corn (maize) has advantages and disadvantages; it is high in protein but lacks two amino acids (lysine and tyrptophan) and niacin. Many Native American populations use alkali substances, such as ash or lime, when cooking corn, which acts to increase amino acid and niacin concentrations. Comparative research has shown that the more a society relies on corn, the more they use such methods.

Malnutrition

We tend to equate the term **malnutrition** with a diet deficient in calories, proteins, or other nutrients, but it literally means "bad nutrition." Malnutrition often does refer to too little food (quantity and/or quality), but it can also refer to having too much. If you ingest more calories than are needed for growth, body maintenance, or physical activity, the excess is deposited as fat in your body. Obesity can lead to medical problems such as high blood pressure, heart disease, and diabetes. Obesity is a growing problem in industrialized nations such as the United States.

Throughout much of the world, however, the major nutritional problem is the lack of food, or at least the lack of a balanced diet. Poor nutrition acts to slow down the growth process, leading to small adult body size. In one sense, this change in growth is adaptive, because a smaller adult body size will require fewer nutrients. By focusing on this relationship, however, we ignore the problem that the slowing of growth is an indication of potential harm. Severe undernutrition, especially in infancy and childhood, can have severe effects. Not only is physical growth stunted but mental retardation also may result, and susceptibility to infectious disease increases. Severe undernutrition is common in much of the Third World, compounded by problems of poverty, overpopulation, inadequate sewage disposal, contaminated water, and economic and political conflicts.

A number of nutritional problems, collectively known as **protein-calorie malnutrition,** result from an inadequate amount of proteins and/or calories in the diet. Protein-calorie malnutrition is the most serious nutritional problem on the planet. Its various forms have different physical symptoms, but all stem from the basic problems of an inadequate diet and have the same ultimate effects, ranging from growth retardation to death.

The most severe types of protein-calorie malnutrition are **kwashiorkor** (a severe deficiency in proteins but not calories) and **marasmus** (severe defi-

malnutrition Poor nutrition, either from too much or too little food or the improper balance of nutrients.

protein-calorie malnutrition A group of nutritional diseases resulting from inadequate amounts of proteins and/or calories.

kwashiorkor An extreme form of protein-calorie malnutrition resulting from a severe deficiency in proteins but not calories.

marasmus An extreme form of protein-calorie malnutrition resulting from severe deficiencies in both proteins and calories.

The "Small But Healthy" Hypothesis and the Cost of Adaptation

A central focus of much current work in human adaptation is the study of nutritional adaptation, looking at the interrelationship between diet, human biology, culture, and the environment (Leonard 2000). One controversial topic is the "small but healthy" hypothesis, originally developed by economist David Seckler (1980), who suggested that roughly 90 percent of the world's population labeled as malnourished are actually "small but healthy" people. This hypothesis considers small body size as an adaptation to limited nutritional resources. In environments with limited nutrition, smaller individuals will be at an advantage because they can function on fewer calories than those with a larger body size. In this view, smaller body size results from a developmental adaptation due to nutritional stress.

Considering small body size only in terms of a potential advantage carries with it an assumption that reduced body size is without any biological cost. The small but healthy hypothesis ignores the fact that there are other biological consequences of reduced nutrition. Bogin (1995b) notes among the serious consequences of malnutrition are impairments in cognitive functioning, work capacity, and school performance. Further, the small but healthy hypothesis does not consider other causes of reduced body size that are harmful, such as infectious diseases.

The small but healthy hypothesis has policy implications far beyond the academic world. If small size is regarded as "normal," then no interventions, economic or otherwise, are needed for these populations (Bogin 1995b). Some anthropologists have argued that hypotheses about human adaptation, such as the small but healthy hypothesis, are not simply academic concerns but have a direct impact on the populations being studied. Some have further argued that the study of human adaptation needs to be informed by a political-economic perspective that takes such issues into account (Goodman and Leatherman 1998).

ciencies in *both* proteins and calories). Kwashiorkor occurs most often in infants and young children who are weaned from their mother's breast onto a diet lacking in proteins. The infant suffers growth retardation, muscle wasting, and lowered resistance to disease. One of the symptoms of kwashiorkor is the swelling of the body due to water retention (Figure 7.11). Marasmus is also most prevalent during infancy and similarly leads to growth retardation, muscle wasting, and death. A child suffering from marasmus typically looks emaciated (Figure 7.12).

Although the physical appearance of children with kwashiorkor and marasmus differs, both suffer from an inadequate diet. Population pressure and poverty certainly play a major role in much of protein-calorie malnutrition, but they are not the only factors. Some researchers, such as anthropologist Katherine Dettwyler, have argued that cultural beliefs regarding nutrition are at least as important. Such beliefs include stressing quantity over quality, postponing the age at which children eat solid foods, and other practices that compromise proper nutrition. Thus, the elimination of protein-calorie malnutrition will require more than an attack on population growth and the reduction of poverty and disease; it will also require nutritional education (Dettwyler 1994). Her work also shows us the folly of assuming that all cultural behaviors are necessarily adaptive.

The devastating impact of malnutrition should not be underestimated. More than 200 million children under the age of 5 in developing countries are undernourished. More than half of all deaths of children under the age of 5 in these countries are linked to poor nutrition (UNICEF 1998).

FIGURE 7.11

Child with kwashiorkor in Mali, West Africa. (Courtesy Katherine Dettwyler)

FIGURE 7.12

A child with marasmus, a severe protein and calorie deficiency. (World Health Organization photo by A. Isaza)

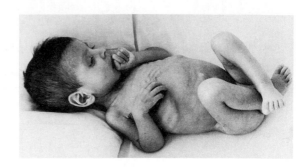

Biological Costs of Modernization and Dietary Change

Increasingly, formerly "traditional" societies have undergone economic and technological development. Compared to rates of change in historic and prehistoric times, modernization in many parts of the world today is occurring almost instantaneously. Such rapid modernization has produced many new biological stresses due to rapid population growth, economic and political change, increased use of natural resources, and increased levels of pollution, to name but a few. With these rapid changes, populations face new stresses. One of these changes is the impact of modernization on traditional diets.

Modernization and Obesity   There is a tendency for populations undergoing modernization to show increased height and weight. Weight gain, in particular, has often been quite dramatic in recently modernized populations, resulting in part from dietary changes and a more sedentary lifestyle. These populations show high rates of obesity, which in turn predisposes them to serious health problems (Figure 7.13).

A number of studies of the biological impact of modernization have been conducted in Samoa, a Polynesian island group in the southern Pacific Ocean. Samoa had been relatively homogeneous in both genetics and lifestyle until the beginning of the twentieth century, at which time dramatic differences in socioeconomic development took place. At present, Samoa is divided into two groups: Western Samoa, characterized by traditional diet and lifestyle, and American Samoa, characterized by a shift to modern employment patterns and diet. A study by James Bindon and Paul Baker (1985) found that adult males and females from modernized islands weighed more and had greater amounts of subcutaneous fat. They concluded that modernization has led to a rapid increase in the frequency of obesity. In the traditional sample, for example, 14 percent of adult males older than 45 years of age were obese, whereas 25 percent were obese on one modernized island and 41 percent on another. This study illustrates how quickly some aspects of human biology can change in response to a changing environment—and the dramatic cost of modernization in much of the world.

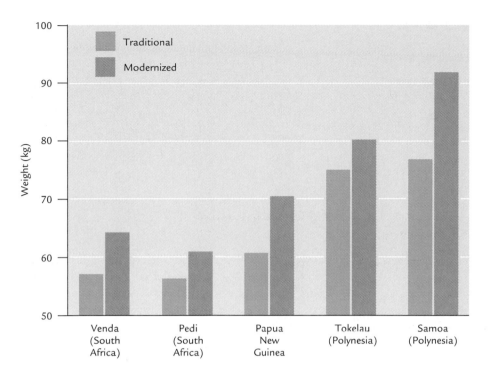

FIGURE 7.13

Comparison of average weight (in kilograms) for adult males in traditional and modernized groups within various populations. In each case, adult males in modernized groups weigh more. (Source of data: Harrison et al. [1988:536])

Modernization and Blood Pressure   Blood pressure provides a measure of health. Excessive blood pressure, or hypertension, is a serious condition, both in itself and as a risk factor for other diseases. Blood pressure is measured using two readings: *systolic* blood pressure is measured during ventricular contractions, and *diastolic* blood pressure is measured during ventricular relaxation. Blood pressure tends to be higher in modernized societies and increases with age in these populations (Little and Baker 1988). In traditional societies, blood pressure tends to be lower and does not increase with age. Changes in blood pressure patterns in modernized societies reflect a number of factors, including changes in diet, lifestyle, physical activity, and overall level of stress.

Figure 7.14 presents the results of a study of modernization and blood pressure conducted by Lewis (1990) in the Gilbert Islands of the Republic of Kiribati in the central Pacific Ocean. Measurements collected during two time periods were compared, the first from 1960, when the islands had a more traditional economy, and again in 1978, by which point the islands had undergone extensive modernization. There is a clear increase in blood pressure over time; blood pressure is higher in the 1978 sample than in the 1960 sample for all but one age group. There is also a noticeable increase in blood pressure with age in the 1978 sample, characteristic of a modernized population, but there is no apparent age-related pattern in the 1960 traditional sample. Culture change significantly affects human biology, and there is a biological cost to modernization.

FIGURE 7.14

Effects of modernization on adult male diastolic blood pressure (mm HG) in the Gilbert Islands. From 1960 to 1978, the area underwent modernization. Note that the average blood pressures in 1978 are higher than in 1960 and that they show an increase with age. These observations are common findings in studies of modernization and blood pressure. (Source of data: Lewis [1990:146])

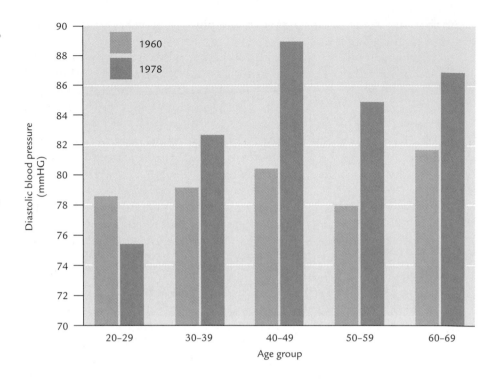

SUMMARY

Studies of adaptation focus on the many ways in which organisms respond to environmental stresses. Human adaptation is particularly interesting because humans not only adapt both biologically and culturally but also must deal with stresses from their physical and cultural environments. Biological adaptation includes physiologic responses and genetic adaptation (natural selection). Cultural adaptation includes aspects of technology, economics, and social structure. In any study of human adaptation, we must look at multiple stresses and multiple adaptive (or nonadaptive) mechanisms.

Many studies of human adaptation have focused on cold and heat stress. Though as mammals humans have the capacity for maintenance of body temperature, they must still cope with extremes in temperature. Physiologic responses of the human body to temperature stress include changes in peripheral blood flow and evaporation. Studies have shown that general relationships exist worldwide between body size and shape and temperature. These observed trends agree with the predictions of the Bergmann and Allen rules. In hot climates, small body size and linear body shape maximize heat loss. In cold climates, large body size and less linear body shape minimize heat loss. Cranial studies show that worldwide the shape of the skull also varies predictably, according to the principles of differential heat loss and the Bergmann and Allen rules. Although some of these biological features are the result of genetic adaptation, studies of children have revealed that response to temperature stress can affect growth. Cultural adaptations, especially those involving clothing, shelter, and physical activity, are also important in climatic adaptation.

More than 25 million people around the world live at high altitudes. The major stresses of a high-altitude population are hypoxia (oxygen shortage) and cold stress. Many physiologic changes have been documented in high-altitude peoples, including short-term responses and long-term increases in the size of the lungs and other components of the oxygen transport system. These changes are caused by hypoxic stress during the growth period, and their degree of change is related to the time spent living at high altitudes: the longer one has lived there as a child, the more adapted one is. Early studies of high-altitude populations also noted small body size that, along with delayed maturation, could be due to insufficient energy levels for body growth because of hypoxia and cold stress. More recent studies have shown that this is not always the case, because some high-altitude groups do not show this growth deficit. Instead, variation in diet appears to be the key factor.

Humans have adapted culturally to basic nutritional demands in a variety of ways. For millions of years, human ancestors utilized different methods of hunting and gathering to feed themselves, and about 12,000 years ago humans adopted agriculture as their primary means of subsistence. Although humans have a number of ways of adapting to their nutritional needs, there are some basic biological limits to adaptation, and an increasing number of children are malnourished. Modernization has altered traditional diets as well as other aspects of lifestyle, resulting in an increased biological cost in many cases.

SUPPLEMENTAL READINGS

Frisancho, A. R. 1993. *Human Adaptation and Accommodation.* Ann Arbor: University of Michigan Press. This text is a thorough review of adaptation studies, focusing on physiologic adaptation.

Moran, E. F. 1982. *Human Adaptability: An Introduction to Ecological Anthropology.* Boulder, Colo.: Westview Press. This general text provides another review of human adaptation but focuses more on cultural adaptations.

Stinson, S., B. Bogin, R. Huss-Ashmore, and D. O'Rourke. 2000. *Human Biology: An Evolutionary and Biocultural Perspective.* New York: John Wiley & Sons. A comprehensive volume consisting of review chapters on a variety of topics relating to human population biology. Several chapters deal with climatic, high-altitude, nutritional, and infectious disease adaptation.

INTERNET RESOURCES

http://anthro.palomar.edu/adapt/default.htm
Human Biological Adaptability, a tutorial including information on climatic, high-altitude, and nutritional adaptation.

http://www.princeton.edu/~oa/safety/altitude.html
Outdoor Action Guide to High Altitude, which provides information on high-altitude illness and acclimatization.

PART III

Our Place in Nature

What are humans? This question has been asked over and over again throughout human history by scientists, artists, philosophers, and others. Where do we fit into the animal world? In this section we look at human beings in a comparative framework, considering our species as part of the total diversity of life. The emphasis in this section is on the primates, a group of mammals to which humans belong. Chapter 8 starts by considering the nature of classification of living organisms and proceeds to a discussion of mammals and primates. Chapter 9 looks more closely at variation in the biology and behavior of living primates. In Chapter 10, I consider the human species, emphasizing the similarities and differences with our closest living relatives, the African apes. Chapter 11 reviews the fossil record of primate origins and evolution from their initial appearance to the split of ape and human lines roughly 6 million years ago.

CHAPTER 8

Primates in Nature

To understand the place of humans in nature, it is first necessary to understand the group of mammals to which humans belong—the **primates.** Humans are primates, as are other creatures such as the apes, the monkeys, and the primitive primates known as prosimians. The basic nature of primate biology and behavior is discussed in this chapter. However, because primates belong to a group known as mammals, who in turn belong to a larger group known as vertebrates, it is first necessary to understand the basic characteristics of these larger taxonomic groups. We begin, therefore, by first discussing vertebrates and then mammals and then go on to discuss the special characteristics of primates.

TAXONOMIC CLASSIFICATION

In Chapter 1, you read about Linnaeus's system of classification for all living creatures. Instead of simply making up a list of all known organisms, Linnaeus developed a scheme by which creatures could be grouped together according to certain shared characteristics. Even though we now make use of Linnaeus's scheme to describe patterns of evolution, Linnaeus himself did not have this objective in mind. Rather, he sought to understand the nature of God's design in living organisms.

We use systems of classification every day, often without being aware that we do so. We all have the tendency to label objects and people according

primates The order of mammals that has a complex of characteristics related to an initial adaptation to life in the trees.

◀ *A slow loris* (Nycticebus coucang), *one of the species of prosimian. The prosimians, along with monkeys, apes, and humans, make up the Order Primates, a group of mammals possessing grasping hands and depth perception.* (© OSF/David Haring/Animals Animals)

201

to certain characteristics. We often use terms such as "liberal" and "conservative" to describe people's political views and terms such as "white" and "black" to describe people's skin color. Movies are classified into different groups by a rating, such as G, PG, PG-13, and R.

If you think for a moment, you will realize that a great deal of your daily life revolves around your use and understanding of different systems of classification. In biology, we are interested in a system of classification that shows relationships between different groups of organisms. This may sound simple enough but can actually be rather difficult. For example, consider the following list of organisms: flounder, bat, shark, canary, lizard, horse, and whale. How would you classify these creatures? One way might be to put certain animals together according to size: the flounder, bat, canary, and lizard in a "small" category; the shark and horse in a "medium" category; and the whale in a "large" category. Another method would be to put the animals in groups according to where they live: the flounder, shark, and whale in the water; the bat and canary in the air; and the lizard and horse on the land. Still another method would be to put the shark in a separate category from all the others because the shark's skeleton is made of cartilage instead of bone.

The problem with this example is that none of these three ways of classification agrees with the other two. There is no consistency. Biologists actually classify these animals into the following groups: fish (flounder and shark), reptiles (lizard), birds (canary), and mammals (bat, horse, whale). These groups reflect certain common characteristics, such as mammary glands for the mammals. But what makes this system of classification any better than those based on size or habitat? For our purposes, we require classifications that reflect evolutionary patterns. As we will see, organisms can have similar traits because they inherited these traits from a common ancestor. Thus, the presence of mammary glands in the bat, horse, and whale represents a trait that has been inherited from a common ancestral species.

Classifications are useful in trying to understand evolutionary relationships. In order to reflect the evolutionary process, the classifications must reflect evolutionary changes. The groups of mammals, birds, reptiles, and fish are based on characteristics that reflect evolutionary relationships. The bat and the whale are placed in the same group because they have a more recent common ancestor than either does with the lizard, as reflected by certain shared characteristics such as mammary glands. Biological classification should reflect evolutionary processes, but only careful analysis of both living and extinct life forms allows us to discover what characteristics reflect evolutionary relationships.

Taxonomic Categories

The Linnaean system is a hierarchical classification. That is, each category contains a number of subcategories, which contain further subcategories, and so on. <u>Biological classification uses a number of categories</u>. The more commonly used categories are: <u>kingdom</u>, <u>phylum</u> (plural *phyla*), <u>class</u>, <u>order</u>, family, genus (plural *genera*), and species. In addition, we often add prefixes to distinguish further breakdowns within a particular category, such as subphylum or infraorder. The scientific name given to an organism consists of the genus and species names in Latin. The scientific name for the common house mouse is *Mus musculus.* Modern human beings are known as *Homo sapiens,* translated roughly as "wise humans."

Any given genus may contain a number of different species. The genus *Homo,* for example, contains modern humans (*Homo sapiens*) as well as extinct human species (*Homo erectus,* for example). These species are placed in the same genus because of certain common characteristics, such as large brain size.

The categories of classification are often vaguely defined. Genus, for example, refers to a group of species that shares similar environments, patterns of adaptation, and physical structures. An example is the horse and the zebra, different species that are placed in the genus *Equus* (there are several species of zebra). These species are four-legged, hoofed grazers. The basis for assigning a given species to one genus or another is often unclear. This uncertainty is even more problematic when fossil remains are assigned to different categories. The only category with a precise meaning is the species, and even that has certain problems in application.

Methods of Classification

Classification involves making statements regarding the similarity of traits between species. The process can be somewhat confusing because biological similarity can arise for different reasons.

Homology and Homoplasy   Two species may have the same trait for two different reasons. First, they may have inherited this trait from a common ancestor. Second, they may have evolved the same trait independently. **Homology** refers to similarity due to descent from a common ancestor. Humans and apes, for example, share certain features of their shoulder anatomy that enables them to hang by their arms. In this case, the similarity is because both humans and apes have inherited this anatomy from a common ancestor. Homology is often apparent by comparing the actual structure of different species. For example, Figure 8.1 shows the forelimb anatomy of three different animals—a human, a whale, and a bird. In each case, the basic anatomical structure is similar; all three have a limb made up of a single upper limb bone (humerus) and two lower limb bones (radius and ulna). Furthermore, note that the "hand" of each has five digits made up of carpal and metacarpal bones. These three animals use their limbs for different purposes, but the basic structure is the same; they are the same bones, but they differ in size, shape, and function. The reason for this similarity is descent from a common ancestor (an ancient vertebrate).

Homoplasy refers to similarity due to the independent evolution of the same trait(s) in both species. Birds and flies are both capable of flight, but this similarity is due to independent evolution of an anatomy capable of flight and not due to descent from a common ancestor. This is apparent

homology Similarity due to descent from a common ancestor.

homoplasy Similarity due to independent evolution.

FIGURE 8.1

An example of homology; the forelimbs of a human, whale, and bird. Note that the same bones are found in all three vertebrates. Even though the limbs are used differently by all three organisms, the bones show a structural correspondence, reflecting common ancestry. (Adapted with permission from T. Dobzhansky, F. J. Ayala, G. L. Stebbins, and U. W. Valentine, Evolution, 1977, page 264, publisher W. H. Freeman)

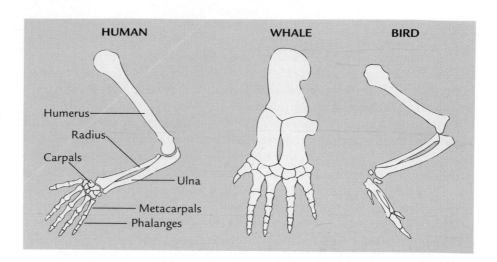

parallel evolution
Independent evolution of traits in closely related species.

convergent evolution
Independent evolution of similar traits in rather distinct evolutionary lines.

primitive trait A trait that has not changed from an ancestral state. The five digits of the human hand and foot are primitive traits inherited from earlier vertebrate ancestors.

when considering their anatomy (Figure 8.2); both creatures can fly, but their anatomy is quite different and reflects independent origins.

There are two different types of homoplasy. **Parallel evolution** is the independent evolution of similar traits in closely related species, such as the increase in dental size among a number of early human ancestors (see Chapter 12). **Convergent evolution** is the independent evolution of similar traits in more distantly related species, such as the evolution of flight in both birds and flies.

If we want our classification system to reflect evolutionary relationships, we need to focus on traits that exhibit homology. We would not want to include traits that reflect homoplasy, because those reflect independent evolutionary origins. For this reason, we classify birds and flies into different taxonomic categories because their similarity does not tell us anything about evolutionary relationships.

As an example, consider three of the organisms mentioned earlier in this chapter—a horse, a shark, and a whale. Which two are more similar to each other than to the third? Looking at overall similarity (including body shape, presence of fins rather than limbs, and where they live), you might conclude that the shark and the whale are more similar to each other than either is to the horse. The problem here is that these similarities all reflect homoplasy, specifically the independent evolution of characteristics related to living in the water in the shark and the whale. Focusing on homologous structures, such as the limb structure described previously, we would see that the horse and the whale are actually more closely related, and for that reason we classify them both as mammals, whereas the shark is classified as a fish.

Primitive and Derived Traits   Homologous biological traits can also be characterized as primitive or derived. When a trait has been inherited from an earlier form, we refer to that trait as **primitive.** Traits that have changed from an ancestral state are referred to as **derived.** As an example, consider the number of digits in humans and horses. Both humans and horses are

BIRD   **FLY**

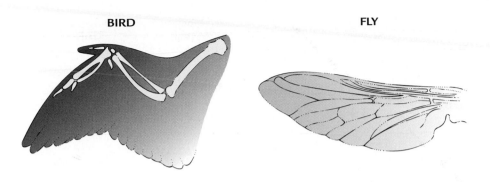

FIGURE 8.2

The wings of a bird and a fly. Even though both structures provide the same function (flight), they are structurally different, reflecting independent evolutionary origin. (Adapted with permission from T. Dobzhansky, F. J. Ayala, G. L. Stebbins, and U. W. Valentine, Evolution, 1977, page 264, publisher W. H. Freeman)

mammals. From fossil evidence we know that the first mammals had five digits on each hand and foot (as did other early land vertebrates). Humans have retained this condition, and we refer to the five digits of the human hand and foot as primitive traits. The horse's single digit (a toe), however, is a derived trait relative to the first mammals.

The concept of primitive and derived traits is relative. What is considered primitive at one level of comparison might be considered derived at another level. For example, neither modern apes nor modern humans have a tail. If apes are compared to humans, the absence of a tail is a primitive characteristic—they share this absence because they inherited this characteristic from a common ancestor. Monkeys, however, do have tails. If modern monkeys are compared to modern apes, the lack of a tail in the modern apes is a derived condition—it has changed since the common ancestor of monkeys and apes. The relative nature of primitive and derived traits must always be kept in mind.

To make any comparison, we must have information on modern and fossil forms so that we can determine whether a trait is primitive or derived. We cannot assume that any given organism will be primitive or derived for a given trait without knowing something about the ancestral condition. In other words, we cannot equate the terms *primitive* and *derived* with biased notions of "higher" or "lower" forms. In the past, there was a tendency to regard all traits of modern humans as derived relative to the apes. For some traits, such as increased brain size and upright walking, this holds true. For other traits, such as certain features of the teeth, the opposite is true.

Approaches to Classification

The problem of biological classification may be approached in many different ways. Though most agree that such classification should reflect evolutionary history, opinions differ about how this should be accomplished.

Phenetics   The classification of organisms on the basis of overall similarity is termed **phenetics.** According to this method, it doesn't matter whether such similarity is the result of common ancestry or parallel evolution. If parallel evolution is fairly common, phenetic classification may suggest a closer

derived trait A trait that has changed from an ancestral state.

phenetics A school of thought that stresses the overall physical similarities among organisms in forming biological classifications.

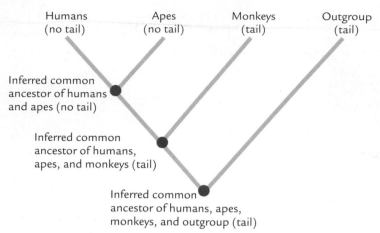

FIGURE 8.3

Illustration of the use of an outgroup in cladistic analysis. This diagram shows the relationship among humans, apes, and monkeys based on the presence or absence of a tail. Humans and apes lack a tail, which makes them different from monkeys. According to the principles of cladistics, lack of a tail can be considered a shared derived trait in humans and apes if the presence of a tail was indeed the primitive condition. Using an outgroup, such as other mammals, shows that the presence of a tail is very widespread apart from humans and apes, and it is the primitive condition. According to this model, monkeys have tails because they retained this primitive trait, whereas the inferred common ancestor of humans and apes lost the tail, a trait inherited in both from this common ancestor.

evolutionary relationship than actually exists. As a result, species that do not share a common ancestor may be grouped together in a taxonomic group. For example, a phenetic approach places crocodiles and lizards in the same taxonomic class—Reptilia (reptiles). Birds are usually placed in the Aves class. Although this classification fits traditional views of overall similarity, the problem is that birds and crocodiles are more closely related to each other than either is to lizards (Harvey and Pagel 1991).

Cladistics   An alternative approach, known as **cladistics,** attempts to focus on evolutionary relationships. A cladist would place birds and crocodiles in the same taxonomic group and lizards in another. The guiding principle of cladistics is that only shared derived traits should be used to construct classifications; shared primitive traits should not. The fact that both humans and monkeys have five digits would not be used to judge their relationship because comparative and fossil data have shown us that five digits are a primitive trait. Nor are all derived traits applicable. The large brain of humans cannot be used to determine an evolutionary relationship with monkeys or apes because it is *unique* to humans. In cladistics, only homologous traits that are both shared and derived can be used to evaluate the evolutionary relationship of two species. For example, both humans and apes share certain features of their shoulder anatomy (see Chapter 9) that are not shared with monkeys or other primates. Comparative anatomy and the fossil record show that both humans and apes have these traits in common because they inher-

cladistics A school of thought that stresses evolutionary relationships between organisms in forming biological classifications.

TABLE 8.1 Traditional Classification of Humans

Taxonomic Category	Taxonomic Name	Common Name
Kingdom	Animalia	Animals
Phylum	Chordata	Chordates
Subphylum	Vertebrata	Vertebrates
Class	Mammalia	Mammals
Subclass	Eutheria	Placental mammals
Order	Primates	Primates
Suborder	Anthropoidea	Anthropoids
Infraorder	Catarrhini	Old World anthropoids
Superfamily	Hominoidea	Hominoids
Family	Hominidae	Hominids
Genus/Species	*Homo sapiens*	Humans

Note: This "traditional" classification is found in many texts but is not without controversy, in particular with regard to the placement of humans as hominids. Some advocate that humans and the African apes should be classified as hominids and that humans should be considered a tribe (a subgroup of family) known as the hominins. This is discussed at greater length in Chapter 9.

ited them from a common ancestor that had changed from an ancestral state. That is, humans and apes are similar because of shared derived characteristics.

How do we tell if a given trait is primitive or derived? A commonly used method is to compare the groups of interest with an **outgroup,** a group that is more distantly related to the species being classified. For example, consider the presence or absence of a tail in three different related groups—humans, apes, and monkeys. Humans and apes do not have tails, but monkeys do. According to the cladistic method, we would place humans and apes in the same group if the absence of a tail were a shared derived trait—that is, one that was present in the common ancestor of humans and apes but not in the common ancestor of humans, apes, and monkeys. How do we know whether the common ancestor of all three groups had a tail or not? An appropriate outgroup for this example might be more distantly related primates or other mammals. Because the presence of a tail is found in most of these mammals, we would conclude that the primitive state was the presence of a tail and the absence of a tail in both humans and apes reflects their descent from a common ancestor not shared with monkeys (Figure 8.3).

The Vertebrates

As with all living creatures, human beings can be classified according to the different levels of Linnaean taxonomy—kingdom, phylum, class, and so on. A traditional taxonomic description of modern humans is given in Table 8.1.

The Animal Kingdom Kingdom is the most inclusive taxonomic category. All living organisms can be placed into one of five kingdoms: plants, animals, fungi, nucleated single-celled organisms, and bacteria. Major differences

outgroup A group used for comparison in cladistic analyses to determine whether the ancestral state of a trait is primitive or derived.

among these kingdoms are their source of food and their mobility. Whereas plants produce their own food through photosynthesis, animals must ingest food. Humans belong to the animal kingdom. Given that animals must ingest food, it is no surprise to see that most animals have well-developed nervous, sensory, and movement systems to enable them to sense and acquire food.

Vertebrate Characteristics   Humans belong to the phylum **Chordata** (the chordates, animals with a spinal cord). Perhaps the most important characteristic of chordates is that they possess at some point in their life a **notochord,** a flexible internal rod that runs along the back of the animal. This rod acts to strengthen and support the body. In humans, it is present early in gestation and is later reabsorbed.

Humans belong to the subphylum **Vertebrata** (the vertebrates, animals with backbones). One characteristic of vertebrates is that they have **bilateral symmetry,** which means that the left and right sides of their bodies are approximately mirror images. Imagine a line running down a human being from the top of the head to a spot between the feet. This line divides the body into two mirror images. This pattern contrasts with other phyla of animals such as starfish.

Another characteristic of vertebrates is an internal spinal cord covered by a series of bones known as vertebrae. The nerve tissue is surrounded by these bones and has an enlarged area of nerve tissue at the front end of the cord—the brain.

The general biological structure of human beings can be found in many other vertebrates. Figure 8.1 shows the limb bones of three vertebrates—human, whale, and bird. It is important to note the similarity among these three different organisms. Like most vertebrates, all have the same basic skeletal pattern: a single upper bone and two lower bones in each limb, and five digits. Some vertebrates have changed considerably from this basic pattern. For example, a modern horse has one digit (a toe) on the end of each limb. Humans may seem to be rather specialized and sophisticated creatures, but actually they have retained much of the earliest basic vertebrate skeletal structure.

The subphylum of vertebrates also includes several classes of fish along with the amphibians, reptiles, birds, and mammals. Humans belong to the class of mammals, and much of our biology and behavior can be understood in terms of what it is to be a mammal.

CHARACTERISTICS OF MAMMALS

The first primitive mammals evolved from early reptiles approximately 200 million years ago. The distinctive features of modern mammals and modern reptiles are the result of that long period of separate evolution in the two classes. It is important to realize that the further back in time we look, the more difficult it is to tell one form from another. Keep in mind that the definition

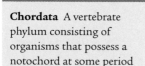

Chordata A vertebrate phylum consisting of organisms that possess a notochord at some period during their life.

notochord A flexible internal rod that runs along the back of an animal.

Vertebrata A subphylum of the phylum Chordata, defined by the presence of an internal, segmented spinal column and bilateral symmetry.

bilateral symmetry Symmetry in which the right and left sides of the body are approximately mirror images.

FIGURE 8.4

The spiny anteater, an egg-laying mammal. (© Gerard Lacz/Animals Animals)

and characteristics of any modern form reflect continued evolution from an earlier ancestor.

Because mammals and reptiles are related through evolution, it is logical and useful to compare these two classes to determine the unique features of each. Modern mammals differ from modern reptiles in reproduction, temperature regulation, diet, skeletal structure, and behavior. As we look at each of these factors separately, do not forget that they are interrelated.

Reproduction

Mammals are often identified as animals that give birth to live offspring, whereas other vertebrates lay eggs. This is not completely accurate. Some fish, such as guppies, give birth to live infants. Also, some mammals, such as the platypus, lay eggs. Others, such as kangaroos, give birth to an extremely immature fetus that completes development inside a pouch in the mother. The most common mammal found today belongs to the subclass of placental mammals, characterized by the development of the fetus inside of the mother's body. Humans are placental mammals.

Placental Mammals   The **placenta** is an organ that develops inside the female during pregnancy. It functions as a link between the circulatory systems of the mother and child, acting to transport food, oxygen, and antibodies, as well as to filter out waste products. The efficiency of the placenta means that the developing offspring of placental mammals have a much greater chance of survival than does a reptile developing in an egg or in a nonplacental mammal (both egg layers and marsupials, Figures 8.4 and 8.5). Development inside the mother provides warmth and protection along with proper nutrition.

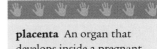

placenta An organ that develops inside a pregnant placental mammal that provides the fetus with oxygen and food and helps filter out harmful substances.

FIGURE 8.5

The wallaby, a marsupial mammal. (© Hans & Judy Beste/ Animals Animals)

Although placental mammals appear at first glance to be superior to egg-laying reptiles, the presence of a placenta has a cost as well as a benefit. Pregnant mammals consume a great deal of energy, making ample food resources vital to successful birth. Also, the demand on energy sets a limit on the number of offspring any female mammal can have at one time.

A main feature of mammals is the female mammary glands, which provide food for the newborn infant. Important immunities are also provided in mother's milk. The ready availability of food increases the child's chance of survival. Although advantageous, nursing also has a price; energy is expended by the mother during this process, and only a limited number of offspring can be taken care of at one time.

Parental Care   The **prenatal** (before birth) and **postnatal** (after birth) patterns of parental care in mammals contrast with those of reptiles, which expend less energy during reproduction and care of offspring. Pregnancy and raising offspring take energy; the more offspring an organism has, the less care a parent can give each of them. Consequently, some animals have many offspring but provide little care to them, whereas other animals have few offspring and provide much more care to each.

Species vary in terms of the balance between number of offspring and degree of parental care. One extreme example is the oyster, which produces

prenatal The period of life from conception until birth.

postnatal The period of life from birth until death.

roughly half a billion eggs a year and provides no parental care. Fish can produce 8,000 eggs a year with a slight amount of parental care. Frogs can lay 200 eggs a year with slightly more parental care.

Compared to other animals, mammals have relatively few offspring but provide much more parental care. The development of the placenta and the mammary glands are biological features that maximize the amount of care given to an offspring. A female lion, for example, has only two offspring per year and provides a great deal of care to them. An extreme example among mammals is the orangutan, an ape that has roughly one offspring every eight years (Galdikas and Wood 1990).

From an evolutionary viewpoint, which strategy is better: having many offspring but providing little care, or having fewer offspring and providing greater care? Each strategy has its advantages and disadvantages. In general, those species that have many offspring tend to be at an advantage in rapidly changing environments, whereas those that provide greater care are at an advantage in more stable environments (Pianka 1983).

Temperature Regulation

Modern mammals are **homeotherms;** they are able to maintain a constant body temperature under most circumstances. Modern reptiles are cold-blooded and cannot keep their body temperature constant; they need to use the heat of the sun's rays to keep them warm and their metabolism active. Mammals maintain a constant body temperature in several ways. Mammals are covered with fur or hair that insulates the body, preventing heat loss in cold weather and reducing overheating in hot weather. Temporary changes in the size of blood vessels also aid in temperature regulation. When blood vessels contract, blood flow is reduced and less heat is lost from the mammal's extremities. When blood vessels dilate, blood flow is increased to the extremities, thus allowing greater heat loss.

Mammals also maintain a constant body temperature by ingesting large quantities of food and converting the food to energy in the form of heat. When you feel hot, your body is not losing the produced heat quickly enough. When you feel cold, you are losing heat too quickly. The ability to convert food energy to heat enables mammals to live comfortably in many environments where reptiles would slow down or even die.

Mammals are thus able to exploit a large number of environments. Heat production and temperature regulation, however, though obviously useful adaptations in certain environments, are not without a price. To obtain energy, mammals need to consume far greater quantities of food than reptiles. In environments where food resources are limited, mammals may be worse off than reptiles. Again, the evolutionary benefit of any trait must be looked at in terms of its cost.

Humans, of course, have gone beyond the basic temperature-regulating abilities of other mammals. We have developed a variety of technologies that help keep us warm or cool. Fire and clothes were the earliest inventions of

homeotherm Organism capable of maintaining a constant body temperature under most circumstances.

FIGURE 8.6

The lower jaws and teeth of a chimpanzee and a modern human.

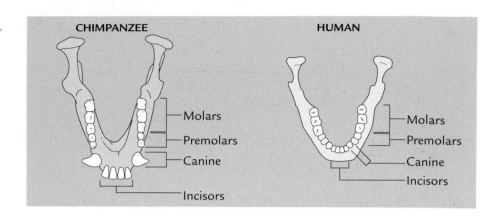

this sort. Today we have all sorts of heating and cooling devices that enable us to live in virtually any environment on the earth, as well as in outer space. Our culture has allowed us to go beyond our biological limits.

Teeth

The saying "You are what you eat" is not usually made literally, but in fact it embodies an important truth of ecology and evolution. The nutritional requirements of organisms dictate, in part, their environmental needs. Also, diet is reflected in the physical structure of organisms, particularly the teeth and jaws. Because mammals maintain a constant body temperature by converting food energy to heat, they require a considerable amount of food. The physical features of mammalian teeth reflect this need.

The teeth of modern reptiles are all the same (**homodontic**); they all have sharp sides and are continually replaced throughout life. A major function of reptilian teeth is to hold and kill prey. The food is then most often eaten whole. Mammals, on the other hand, have different types of teeth in their jaws (**heterodontic**). Mammals usually have two sets of teeth during their lives: a set of deciduous ("baby") teeth and a set of permanent teeth. As a mammal grows and matures, the baby teeth fall out and are replaced with the adult teeth. In modern humans, this replacement normally starts around age 6 and takes the first 18 or 20 years of life to complete.

Types of Teeth   Most mammals have four types of teeth: **incisors, canines, premolars,** and **molars.** These teeth in a chimpanzee and a human are shown in Figure 8.6. The incisor teeth are chisel- or spatula-shaped and located in the front of the jaw. Both the human and the chimpanzee (and other higher primates) have a total of four incisors in each jaw. These teeth are used for cutting and slicing food. You use your incisors when you eat an apple or corn on the cob. Behind the incisors are the canine teeth, which are often long and sharp, resembling fangs or tusks. Apes and humans have two canine teeth in each jaw. In many mammals, the canine teeth are used as weapons or to kill prey. Although the canine teeth of most mammals are rather large and

homodontic All teeth are the same.

heterodontic Having different types of teeth.

incisor The chisel-shaped front teeth used for cutting, slicing, and gnawing food.

canine The teeth located in front of the jaw behind the incisors, which are normally used by mammals for puncturing and defense.

premolar One of the types of back teeth, used for crushing and grinding food.

molar The teeth furthest back in the jaw used for crushing and grinding food.

project beyond the level of the rest of the teeth, human canines are usually small and nonprojecting.

The premolar and molar teeth are also known collectively as the back teeth or cheek teeth. Both of these types of teeth are often large in surface area and are used for grinding and chewing food. When you chew food between your back teeth, you do not simply move your lower jaw up and down. Instead, your upper and lower back teeth grind together in a circular motion as your jaw moves up and down and sideways as well. The structures of the premolar and molar teeth are different, and in some mammals these teeth have different functions as well.

Dental Formulae Mammals can be characterized by the number of each type of tooth they have. The usual method of counting teeth is to consider the number of each type of tooth in one-half of one jaw, upper or lower. Only one-half of the jaw is considered because both right and left sides of the jaw contain the same number of teeth. These numbers are expressed using a **dental formula,** which lists the number of incisors, canines, premolars, and molars in one-half of a jaw. A dental formula looks like this: I-C-PM-M. Here I = number of incisors, C = number of canines, PM = number of premolars, and M = number of molars. For example, the typical dental formula of humans (as well as apes and some monkeys) is 2-1-2-3. This means that in one-half of either jaw there are two incisors, one canine, two premolars, and three molars. Each half of each jaw therefore contains 2 + 1 + 2 + 3 = 8 teeth. The typical number of teeth in humans is therefore 8 × 4 = 32 (two sides of each of two jaws). Some mammals have different numbers of teeth in the top and bottom jaws. In these cases, we use two dental formulae. For example, a dental formula of 2-1-2-3/2-1-2-2 would indicate two fewer molars in the lower jaw.

Diet and Teeth The basic description of the types of teeth is somewhat simplistic. Many mammals have evolved specialized uses of one or more of these tooth types. As noted earlier, human canines are rather different in form and function from those of many other mammals. The general description is useful, however, in showing the importance of differentiated teeth in mammals. By having different types of teeth capable of slicing, cutting, and grinding, mammals are able to eat a wide variety of different foods in an efficient way. In addition, the ability to chew the food rather than swallow it whole allows greater efficiency in eating. By chewing, mammals break down the food into smaller pieces that can be digested more easily and efficiently. Also, saliva released in the mouth during chewing begins the process of digestion.

The nature of mammalian diet and teeth relates to their warm-bloodedness. Mammals need more food than reptiles, and their teeth allow them to utilize a wider range of food and to process it more productively. The benefits of differentiated teeth lie in these abilities. The cost is the fact that the teeth tend to wear out over time. When a mammal's adult teeth are worn down, it may not be able to eat or may develop serious dental problems, which could lead to death. As far as recent humans are concerned, we can circumvent these potential problems to a certain extent with dental technology, hygiene, and

dental formula A shorthand method of describing the number of each type of tooth in one half of one jaw on a mammal.

FIGURE 8.7

The orientation of the limbs to the body in reptiles and in mammals.

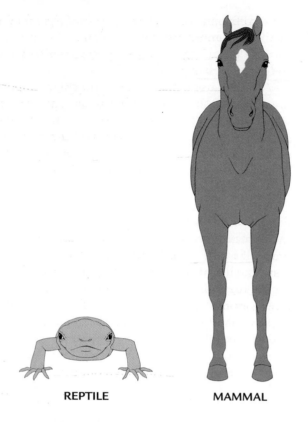

REPTILE   **MAMMAL**

processed foods. Even so, dental problems continue to pose serious difficulties to human health.

Skeletal Structure

Both mammals and reptiles share the basic skeletal structure of all vertebrates, but there are some differences, especially in movement. In reptiles, the four limbs come out from the side of the body for support and movement (Figure 8.7). In four-legged mammals, the limbs slope downward from the shoulders and hips. Having the limbs tucked in under the body allows more efficient and quicker movement. The weight of the body is supported better. Humans differ from the pattern of many mammals by using only two limbs for movement. Even so, the configuration of the legs follows the basic pattern; the legs slope inward from the hips and are not splayed out to the sides.

Behavior

The brains of all vertebrates have similar structures but differ in size, relative proportions, and functions. All vertebrates have a hindbrain, a midbrain, and a forebrain. In most vertebrates, the hindbrain is associated with hearing, balance, reflexive behaviors, and control of the autonomic functions of the body, such as breathing. The midbrain is associated with vision, and the forebrain is associated with chemical sensing, such as smelling ability. Compared to fish, reptiles have a relatively larger midbrain and hindbrain because they rely more extensively on vision and hearing. The midbrain of a reptile is particularly enlarged because it functions to coordinate sensory information and body movements.

The brain of a mammal reveals several important shifts in structure and function. The mammalian brain has a greatly enlarged forebrain that is responsible for processing sensory information and coordination. In particular, the forebrain contains the **cerebrum,** the outermost layer of brain cells, which is associated with learning, memory, and intelligence. The cerebrum becomes increasingly convoluted, which allows huge numbers of interconnections between brain cells. It accounts for the largest proportion of the mammalian brain.

The overall functions of a brain include basic body maintenance, as well as the ability to process information and respond accordingly. Mammals rely more on learning and flexible responses than do reptiles. Behaviors are less instinctual and rigid. Previous experiences (learning) become more important in responding to stimuli. As a consequence, mammals are more capable of developing new responses to different situations and are capable of learning from past mistakes. New behaviors are more likely to develop and can be passed on to offspring through the process of learning. Humans have taken this process even further; our very existence depends on flexible behaviors that must be learned. Although our behavior is to a large extent cultural, our ability to transfer information through learning relies on a biological trait: the mammalian brain.

The behavioral flexibility of mammals ties in with their pattern of reproduction. In general, the more a species relies on parental care, the more intelligent it is and the more it relies on learning rather than instinct. Extensive parental care requires increased intelligence and the ability to learn new behaviors in order to provide maximum care for infants. The increased emphasis on learning requires, in turn, an extended period of growth during which to absorb the information needed for the adult life. Furthermore, the extension of childhood requires more extensive child care so that offspring are protected during the time they need to complete their growth and learning.

The major characteristics of mammals are all interrelated. Reproductive behaviors are associated with learning, intelligence, and social behaviors. The ability to maintain body temperature is related to diet and teeth; warm-bloodedness requires vast amounts of energy that in turn is made available from differentiated teeth and a wide dietary base. Also, the reproductive pattern of placental mammals requires great amounts of energy, which in turn relates to diet. In fact, the major characteristics of any group of animals are not merely a list of independent traits; they represent an integrated complex of traits.

PRIMATE CHARACTERISTICS

There are many different forms of mammals—they are as diverse as mice, whales, giraffes, cats, dogs, and apes. Patterns of biology and behavior vary

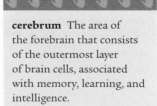

cerebrum The area of the forebrain that consists of the outermost layer of brain cells, associated with memory, learning, and intelligence.

considerably, although all mammals share to some extent the basic characteristics outlined in the last section.

Recall that the mammalian class is broken down into a number of orders. Humans, as noted, are primates, as are the apes, such as the chimpanzee, bonobo, and gorilla, which are our closest living relatives. Monkeys are also primates, as are more biologically primitive forms known as prosimians. The basic characteristics of primates are discussed in this section. The next chapter describes variation in the biology and behavior of primates, including a discussion of different types of primates.

No single characteristic identifies primates; rather, they share a set of features. Many of these features relate to living in the trees. Though it is clear that humans, as well as a few other modern primates, do not live in the trees, they still retain certain features inherited from ancestors who did.

An **arboreal** (tree-living) environment presents different challenges than a **terrestrial** (ground-living) environment. Living in the trees requires an orientation to a three-dimensional environment. Animals that live on the ground generally contend with only two dimensions: length and width. Arboreal animals must also deal with the third dimension, height. Perception of distance and depth is vital to a tree-living form, which moves quickly from one branch to the next and from one level of the forest to another. Agility is also important, as is the ability to anchor oneself in space.

Many forms of animals, such as squirrels and birds, have adapted to living in the trees. Primates, however, are capable of extensive rapid movement through the trees and are able to move to all areas of a tree, including small terminal branches. A squirrel can climb up and down the trunk of a tree and even large branches, but primates are better equipped to move out to feed on even the smallest branches. The two major characteristics of primates that account for their success in the trees are the ability to use hands and feet to grasp branches (rather than digging in with claws) and the ability to perceive distance and depth.

Although many primate characteristics relate to living in the trees, some controversy has arisen over whether the *initial* evolution of these traits was the result of arboreal adaptations. Noting that other mammals, such as squirrels, have adapted to the trees without having grasping hands or depth perception, Cartmill (1974) has suggested an alternative for the origin of primate characteristics. He suggests that grasping hands and depth perception first evolved as adaptations for insect hunting in low branches. Later, these features were adapted for life in the trees. In this section we examine both the arboreal adaptation and insect predation models. The fossil evidence bearing on these models is discussed in Chapter 11.

Not all modern primates have kept the original adaptations of the first primates. For example, humans can still use their hands to grasp objects but cannot do so with their feet. We do not normally use our hands to grasp and hang onto branches. We have taken our inherited ability to grasp and put it to work in another arena: we hold tools, weapons, food, and children. The grasping hands of a human and a tree-living monkey are homologous—that is, they are similar structures because of common descent. The different func-

arboreal Living in trees.
terrestrial Living on the ground.

tions of the hands of humans and tree-living monkeys reflect adaptive changes from the original primate ancestors. Even though humans do things differently, we are still primates and have the basic set of primate characteristics.

The Skeleton

First let us consider some general characteristics in the primate skeletal structure.

Grasping Hands   A characteristic of the earliest known mammals (and reptiles) is five digits on each hand or foot. Certain mammals, such as the horse, have changed from this ancestral condition and only have a single toe on each limb. Other mammals, such as the primates, have kept the ancestral condition.

In the case of primates, the retention of the primitive characteristics of five digits on the hands and feet turned out to be an important adaptation. The hands and feet of primates are **prehensile,** meaning that they are capable of being used to grasp objects. The ability to grasp involves the movement of the fingers to the palm, thus allowing the fingers to wrap around an object. In many primates, the toes can also wrap around an object. This grasping ability is a remarkable adaptation to living in the trees. Primates can grab onto branches to move about, to provide support while eating, and in general to allow for a high degree of flexibility in moving about their environment. More specialized structures, such as the horse's single hoof, would be useless in the trees because there would be no way to grasp branches.

Another feature of primate hands and feet is their expanded tactile pads (such as the ball of your thumb) and nails instead of claws. Nails serve to protect the sensitive skin at the ends of the fingers and the toes. The numerous nerve endings in the tips of fingers and toes of primates provide an enhanced sense of touch that is useful in manipulating objects.

As mentioned earlier, the characteristics possessed by primates are not the only possible solution to the challenge of living in the trees. Squirrels, for example, use their claws to dig into the bark of limbs and branches when they climb in the trees. The grasping ability of primate hands, however, provides much greater flexibility. Food can be reached at the end of small branches by grasping surrounding branches for support, using a free arm to reach out and grab the food, and then bringing it to the mouth. A small branch might not provide enough surface area for a squirrel to dig its claws into, but a primate can use its grasping hands and feet to hold onto it.

Variations on these themes occur even within primates. Humans differ from the general primate conditions. We have lost the ability to use our feet for grasping as a result of anatomical changes relating to our ability to walk on two legs.

Generalized Structure   Biological structures are often classified as specialized or generalized. **Specialized structures** are used in a highly specific way, whereas **generalized structures** can be used in a variety of ways. The hooves

prehensile Capable of grasping.

specialized structure A biological structure adapted to a narrow range of conditions and used in very specific ways.

generalized structure A biological structure adapted to a wide range of conditions and used in very general ways.

of a horse, for example, are a specialization that allows rapid running over land surfaces. The basic skeletal structure of primates is generalized because it allows movement flexibility in a wide variety of circumstances.

The arm and leg bones of primates follow the basic pattern of many vertebrates: each limb consists of an upper bone and two lower bones (refer back to Figure 8.1). This structure allows limbs to bend at the elbows or knees. In climbing or jumping in a tree, you must have this flexibility or you would not be able to move about (imagine trying to jump from one branch to another with your arms and legs made up of one long bone). That the lower part of the limb is made up of two bones provides even greater flexibility. Hold your arm out straight in front of you with your palm down. Now turn your hand so that the palm side is up. This is easy to do, but only because we have two lower arm bones. When turning the hand over, one lower arm bone crosses over the other. Imagine trying to climb in a tree without the ability to move your hand into different positions. This flexibility is obtained by the retention of a generalized skeletal structure.

Although the grasping hands and generalized skeletons of primates can be interpreted as arboreal adaptations, Cartmill (1974) raises the possibility that they first arose as adaptations to insect predation. Grasping hands and feet would be valuable for running along the ground and on small branches in search of insects. Once these traits evolved, they could then have been valuable for further use in arboreal environments.

Vision

The three-dimensional nature of arboreal life requires keen eyesight, particularly depth perception. This feature has evolved from the need to judge distances successfully. (Jumping through the air from branch to branch demands the ability to judge distances. After all, it is not very adaptive to fall short of your target and plunge to the ground!)

Depth perception involves **binocular stereoscopic vision.** *Binocular* refers to overlapping fields of vision. The eyes of many animals are located at the sides of the skull so that each eye receives a different image with no overlap. The eyes of primates are located in the front of the skull so that the fields of vision overlap (Figure 8.8). Primates see objects in front of them with both eyes. The *stereoscopic* nature of primate vision refers to the way in which the brain processes visual signals. In nonstereoscopic animals, the information from one eye is received in only one hemisphere of the brain. In primates, the visual signals from both eyes are received in both hemispheres of the brain. The result is an image that has depth. Moving quickly and safely in three dimensions makes use of depth perception.

Many primates also have the ability to perceive colors. Color vision is extremely useful in detecting objects in moderate-contrast environments. In fact, color vision is found in other animals for this reason, including whales, fish, bumblebees, and certain birds. Color vision is also important in primate species that use color as a visual signal of various emotional states, such as anger or receptivity to sexual relations.

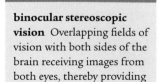

binocular stereoscopic vision Overlapping fields of vision with both sides of the brain receiving images from both eyes, thereby providing depth perception.

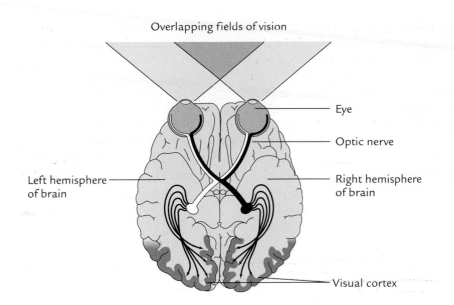

Overlapping fields of vision

Eye

Optic nerve

Left hemisphere of brain

Right hemisphere of brain

Visual cortex

FIGURE 8.8

Binocular stereoscopic vision in primates. The fields of vision for each eye overlap, and the optic nerve from each eye is connected to both hemispheres of the brain. (*From* Human Antiquity: An Introduction to Physical Anthropology and Archaeology, *4th ed., by Kenneth Feder and Michael Park. Fig. 5.1. Copyright © 2001 by Mayfield Publishing Company. Reprinted with permission from The McGraw-Hill Companies*)

Primates are vision-oriented. On average, their sense of smell is less keen. As a result, the areas of the face devoted to smelling are reduced in primates. Compared to other mammals, primates have short snouts.

The Brain and Behavior

Primates have expanded on the basic pattern of mammalian brains. Their brains are even larger relative to body size. Primate brains have larger visual areas and smaller areas for smelling, corresponding to their increased emphasis of vision over smell as the main sense. Also, primate brains are even more complex than those of most other mammals. Primates have larger proportions of the brain associated with learning and intelligence. Areas of the brain associated with body control and coordination are also proportionately larger, as expected from the demands of arboreal life. Hand–eye coordination, for example, is crucial for moving about in the trees.

Learning   The greater size and complexity of primate brains are reflected in their behaviors. Many primates rely extensively on learned behaviors. As a result, it is often difficult to assign specific behaviors to a given species of primate because the increased emphasis on learning allows a great deal of flexibility in behavior patterns.

The increased emphasis on learning means that primates spend a greater proportion of their lives growing up, both biologically and socially, than other animals. The more an animal needs to learn, the longer the period of time needed for learning. An increase in the amount of time spent as an infant or child further means that greater amounts of attention and care are required from parents. Again, we see the intimate relationship among reproduction, care of offspring, learning, and intelligence.

FIGURE 8.9

A macaque washing food in water. (© Steve Gaulin/Anthro-Photo)

The basic pattern of primate learning provides a means by which new behaviors can be passed on from one generation to the next. If we define culture simply as learned behavior, it is obvious that all primates can be said to have culture. Most of the time, however, the distinctive nature of human culture is identified as its reliance on language for transmission. Within this framework, the cultural behaviors and social organization of nonhuman primates are often referred to as *protoculture*. No matter what terms we use, however, or how we define human and nonhuman culture, the fact remains that social learning provides a means by which behaviors are passed on from one generation to the next in all primates (and, indeed, in many other mammals).

An Example of Learned Behavior in Primates   Primate studies have provided many good examples of the introduction of new behaviors to a group by one or more individuals that are then learned by other individuals. Studies of the Japanese macaque monkeys on the island of Koshima during the 1950s revealed a number of cases of cultural transmission of new behaviors. The Koshima troop has been provisioned (provided with food) since the early 1950s to keep all the monkeys out in the open for observation purposes (Figure 8.9).

In 1953, a young female macaque named Imo began washing sweet potatoes in a stream before eating them. Within three years, this behavior had been learned by almost half of the troop. Two years later, only two adults continued this practice. Of the 19 younger monkeys, 15 had adopted this behavior, however, and thereafter almost all newborn infants acquired it by observing their mothers (Bramblett 1976).

Another food-related behavior developed among the troop in 1956 when scientists began feeding the monkeys grains of wheat. The wheat was scattered on a sandy beach to slow down the monkeys' eating so that researchers would have more time to study them. Imo developed a new method of eating the grains of wheat. She took handfuls of sand and wheat down to the water and threw them in. The sand sank while the wheat floated, thus letting her skim the grains off the surface of the water. This new behavior provided a much quicker way of getting the wheat than picking out grains from the sand. The young female's method of wheat washing spread quickly through most of the rest of the troop (Bramblett 1976).

The studies of cultural transmission among the Japanese macaques show the importance of learning in primate societies. Washing sweet potatoes and separating wheat from sand are not innate behaviors in Japanese macaques. These behaviors are transmitted through learning, not genetic inheritance. The studies also show the importance of individual behavior: in both cases, the same monkey introduced the behaviors. If that monkey were not present in that troop, these behaviors might not have developed.

Reproduction and Care of Offspring

As with all mammals, primates are characterized by a small number of offspring and a great deal of parental care. Almost all primates have a reproductive pattern of having one offspring at a time. The next offspring is not born until the previous one is mature enough, biologically and socially, to survive on its own. In some primates, such as the apes, there may be as many as five or more years between offspring. As mentioned earlier, humans are an exception to this rule because we can have overlapping births without sacrificing the quality of parental care.

The Mother–Infant Bond   Primates have a strong and long-lasting bond between mother and infant. Unlike some mammals, infant primates are entirely helpless. They depend on their mothers for food, warmth, protection, affection, and knowledge, and they remain dependent for a long time. Of all the different types of social bonds in primate societies, the mother–infant bond is the strongest. In many primate species, this bond continues well past infancy. Chimpanzees, for example, regularly associate with their mothers throughout their adult lives (Goodall 1986).

The biological importance of the mother-infant bond is easy to see: the infants are dependent on mother's milk for nourishment. Is that all there is to it? Earlier in this century, some researchers suggested that the entire basis of "mother love" seen in primate infants arose from the infant's need for food. Laboratory experiments and field observations soon showed that this is not the case; the social aspects of the mother–infant bond are also crucial for survival.

FIGURE 8.10

Harlow's maternal deprivation experiment on infant rhesus monkeys. These monkeys preferred to spend almost all of their time clinging to the cloth surrogate mother (right), which provided warmth, than to the wire surrogate mother (left), which provided food. Even when hungry, the infants would often remain partially attached to the cloth mother.
(© *Harlow Primate Laboratory, University of Wisconsin*)

One of the most famous of these experiments was performed by psychologist Harry Harlow, who isolated infant rhesus monkeys from their mothers. He raised them in cages in which he placed two "surrogate mothers," the first a wire framework in the approximate shape of an adult monkey and the second the same structure covered with terry cloth. He then attached a bottle of milk to the "wire mother" (Figure 8.10). Harlow reasoned that if the need for food were stronger than the need for warmth and comfort, the infant monkeys would spend most or all of their time clinging to the "wire mother." If the need for warmth and comfort were more important, the infant would spend most or all of the time clinging to the "cloth mother." The monkeys invariably preferred the warmth and security of the "cloth mothers" to the food provided by the "wire mothers." Even when the infants needed to eat, they often kept part of their body in contact with the "cloth mother." Additional experiments showed that under the stimulus of stress or fear, the monkeys would go to the "cloth mothers" for security (Harlow 1959).

These experiments showed that motherhood was not merely important in terms of nutrition; warmth and comfort were also necessary in an infant's development. But do these experiments mean that natural mothers can be replaced by a bottle and a blanket? Definitely not. As Harlow's monkeys grew up, they showed a wide range of abnormal behaviors. They were often incapable of sexual reproduction, they could not interact normally with other monkeys, and they often were extremely aggressive. The motherless females who later had children did not know how to take care of them and often rejected and mistreated them.

These findings have powerful implications. We often speak of "maternal instincts," suggesting that the behaviors associated with successful mothering are somehow innate. Although the basic bond between mother and infant is part of the biological basis of mammals, and maternal feelings are to some extent innate, the specific behaviors that are part of this bond are learned.

What Will Happen to the Primates?

There are approximately 250 different species of primates in the world today, but many are living a precarious existence. More than half of these species are estimated to be in potential danger from a conservation perspective, and 20 percent are currently considered endangered or critically endangered. Although the past decade has seen the discovery of several previously unknown primate species, it has also seen the extinction of one—the red colobus monkey subspecies *Procolobus badius waldroni* (Chapman and Peres 2001). Some estimates suggest that as much as 20 percent of primate species will become extinct at some point during the twenty-first century (Mittermeier and Sterling 1992).

What has caused this danger to living primates? One major factor is the destruction of native habitats. More than 90 percent of all primate species live in tropical forests, which are disappearing at an alarming rate as forest is cleared for human use (Chapman and Peres 2001; Wright 1992). Other species, such as the highly endangered mountain gorilla, have had their habitat reduced through farming to meet the demands for food of growing human populations. Toward the end of the twentieth century, it was estimated that there were fewer than 400 surviving mountain gorillas (Mittermeier and Sterling 1992).

Hunting by humans is another threat to primate survival. In addition to being a food resource, primates are hunted in many parts of the world to use as bait for other animals, for sale of their body parts for ornaments, and because they are considered agricultural pests. Another threat to primates is the capture of live animals for sale, although international efforts have reduced this demand to some extent. Live capture is a particular problem when infants are sought because their mothers are frequently shot during capture of the infant. Logging is another human activity that has endangered many primate species, as the loss of habitat contributes significantly to the endangered status of many primates (Chapman and Peres 2001).

What can be done? There is no single solution; a series of conservation efforts must be applied at an international level. Strier (2000) lists several general strategies, including developing economic incentives for conservation, increasing public awareness of the potential problems, and increasing the role of nongovernmental organizations that have provided an opportunity for interaction and information exchange among conservationists, primate researchers, and policy makers. Other approaches to primate conservation include developing protected parks and preserves, developing less harmful agricultural practices, and breeding endangered primates in captivity (Mittermeier and Sterling 1992; Wright 1992). Chapman and Peres (2001) emphasize the role scientists can play in such conservation efforts. All of these efforts, and more, are needed if we are to save these remarkable relatives of ours.

Mammals, and especially primates, rely extensively on learned behaviors. As a result, variation in behavior is often great and can be influenced by a variety of other factors. Observations of the behavior of primates in their natural environments confirm the fact that maternal behaviors are to a large extent learned. Studies of chimpanzee mothers have shown that young females tend to model their own later parental behaviors after those of their mothers. Similar patterns are seen in humans. For example, the children of abusive parents often tend to be abusive parents themselves. Such research shows us that the study of animal behavior, especially that of other primates, is not an esoteric subject but rather helps us in understanding ourselves.

Paternal Care   Maternal care is found throughout the primate order. The mother–infant bond is the strongest social tie within primate groups. What role does the father play in child care among primates? Paternal care is highly variable among primate species. In general, primates that are **monogamous**

monogamy An exclusive sexual bond between an adult male and an adult female for a long period of time.

223

(characterized by a more or less permanent bond forming between a single male and female) are most likely to show high levels of paternal care. In fact, in some species the fathers do most of the carrying of infants (Jolly 1985). By contrast, species that are polygamous tend, on average, to show less paternal involvement with offspring. In a **polygamous** species, paternal behaviors may be less appropriate from a genetic perspective because a male can never be sure if he is the father.

As with many primate behaviors, there is a great deal of variation from one situation to the next. In one study of baboons (an African monkey), Connie Anderson (1992) found regularity in the degree of paternal behaviors. In cases where females mated with a single male more than 70 percent of the time, that male was much more likely to help by carrying the infant. This finding shows that it is difficult, if not impossible, to ascribe a given behavior to an entire species because there is often a great deal of variation even within single populations. These results also suggest that adult males are aware of the frequency of mating, thus providing them with some idea of the likely paternity of an infant. From an evolutionary perspective, we would expect males to invest time and effort in their own infants, at least infants with a high probability of having been sired by them.

Growing Up   The importance of the extended period of infant and juvenile growth in primates cannot be overstated. The long period of growth is necessary for learning motor skills and social behaviors. The close bond between mother and infant provides the first important means by which an infant primate learns. It is not the only important social contact for a growing primate, however. The process of socialization in most primates depends to a large extent on close contact with peers. Interaction with other individuals of the same age provides the opportunity to learn specific types of social behaviors, as well as how to interact socially in general.

Experiments by Harlow clearly demonstrate the importance of social contact with peers. Monkeys raised by their mothers but kept apart from other infants often grew up showing a range of abnormal behaviors. They would stare at their cages for long periods of time, were often self-destructive, and did not show normal patterns of sexual behavior (Harlow and Harlow 1962). Although some primate species are basically solitary apart from the mother–infant bond, most belong to larger social groups and require contact with peers during their growth.

Growing up and learning as a primate also requires that infants and juveniles play a great deal of the time. Play behaviors have often been ignored in studies of human and nonhuman behavior because they are regarded as nonproductive behavior. In truth, play behaviors are essential to the proper biological and social development of primates.

Play behavior can serve several functions. First, physical play allows an infant to develop and practice necessary motor skills. Second, social play provides the opportunity to learn how to behave with others. Needed social skills are learned through play. The importance of play becomes very obvious when we consider what happened to the monkeys that Harlow had separated from

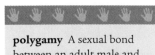

polygamy A sexual bond between an adult male and an adult female in which either individual may have more than one mate at the same time.

their peers. Without normal contact and the opportunity to develop socially, these monkeys became sociopathic.

Social Structure

Primates are essentially social creatures. The close bond between mother and infant, the importance of learning, and the great flexibility in behaviors all point to this fact. Apart from this general need, primates show an amazing amount of variation in the ways in which their societies are structured. The main social group of primates can range in size from two individuals up to several hundred and can have different proportions of males, females, young, and old.

A social group is generally defined as a group within which there is frequent communication or interaction among members. This definition is a bit arbitrary, but it provides us with a starting point for looking at variation in primate societies. **Social structure** consists of the composition of the social group and the way in which it is organized. There are five basic types of primate social structure, with variations on most of these.

Social Groups   The smallest social group is the **solitary group,** which consists of the mother and dependent offspring. Adult males and adult females have infrequent contact, generally for mating. A slightly larger social group is the **monogamous family group,** consisting of an adult male, an adult female, and their immature offspring. The adult male and female form a long-term pair bond and are sexually active only with each other. Although this corresponds to a typical Western notion of "family," it is not that common among primates. The social unit of a few primate species is the **polyandrous group,** a small group of adult males and one or more adult females and their offspring. Although there may be more than one adult female in the group, only one is reproductively active. A **uni-male group** consists of one adult male, several adult females, and their offspring. The most common social structure in nonhuman primate societies is the **multimale/multifemale group,** which consists of more than one adult of each sex and the offspring. Given multiple adult males and adult females, these are complex social groups that are often quite large. Given multiple adults, mating tends to be promiscuous. There is considerable variation in this type of social structure, in terms of size, composition, and distribution (Wolfe 1995).

Social Organization and Dominance   Nonhuman primate societies rank individuals in terms of their relative dominance in the group. A **dominance hierarchy** is the ranking system within the society and reflects which individuals are most and least dominant (Figure 8.11). Dominance hierarchies are found in most nonhuman primate societies, but they vary widely in their overall importance in everyday life. The dominance hierarchy provides stability in social life. All individuals know their place within the society, eliminating to some extent uncertainty about what to do or whom to follow.

The dominance hierarchy in nonhuman primates is usually ruled by those individuals with the greatest access to food or sex or those that control

social structure The composition of a social group and the way it is organized, including size, age structure, and number of each sex in the group.

solitary group The smallest primate social group, consisting of the mother and her dependent offspring.

monogamous family group Social structure in which the primary social group consists of an adult male, an adult female, and their immature offspring.

polyandrous group A rare type of primate social structure, consisting of a small number of adult males, one reproductively active adult female, and their offspring. Other adult females may belong to the group but are not reproductively active.

uni-male group Social structure in which the primary social group consists of a single adult male, several adult females, and their offspring.

multimale/multifemale group A type of social structure in which the primary social group is made up of several adult males, several adult females, and their offspring.

dominance hierarchy The ranking system within a society that indicates which individuals are dominant in social behaviors.

FIGURE 8.11

Two adult male baboons engaged in a dominance dispute. Though physical violence does occur in such encounters, much of the display is bluff. (© M. Peardon/ Photo Researchers, Inc.)

sexual dimorphism The average difference in body size between adult males and adult females.

social behaviors to the greatest extent. Societies with strong male dominance hierarchies are likely to show a moderate to large difference in the sizes of adult males and adult females. The **sexual dimorphism** in body size has often been considered the result of competition among males for breeding females. The males that are larger and stronger are considered more likely to gain access to females and hence pass on their genetic potential for larger size and greater strength.

This pattern does not always hold, however. The adult male most likely to attract mates may not be the male most likely to have access to food. Fedigan (1983) has reviewed the literature on the relationship between dominance rank of males and access to breeding females for a number of primate species and has found that this expected relationship is not always present.

We also see that dominance may reflect additional factors. In the Japanese macaque monkeys, for example, the rank of a male's mother has an influence on the male's dominance rank (Eaton 1976). Males born to high-ranking mothers have a greater chance of achieving high dominance themselves, all other factors being equal.

In a number of primate societies, the dominance hierarchy of females is more stable over time than that of the males. Whereas the position of most dominant males can change quickly, the hierarchy among females remains more constant. Even in cases in which all males are dominant over females, the female dominance hierarchy exerts an effect on social behaviors within the group, as in the case in which mother's rank affects the rank of male offspring.

MODELS OF PRIMATE BEHAVIOR

In terms of both biology and behavior, primates are an extremely variable group of mammals. The exact nature of this variability is explored in the next chapter, which reviews the different subgroups of living primates. For now, however, it is useful to consider the types of evolutionary models that we use to make some sense of this variation. The ultimate objective is to provide explanations of primate behavior from an evolutionary perspective, particularly the complex interaction of nature and nurture.

Behavioral Ecology

Studies of primate behavior have often applied an ecological approach, relating social structure and organization to environmental factors, including habitat, diet, presence of predators, and other aspects of the ecology within which primate groups live. One basic question is this: To what extent are differences in social behaviors related to environmental factors as opposed to genetic ancestry?

Early ecological studies of primates focused on the contrast between species that live in the trees and those that live on the ground (DeVore 1963). This arboreal–terrestrial contrast suggested some basic relationships between habitat and aspects of social organization, territoriality, group size, and **home range** (the size of the geographic area normally occupied by a group). Additional study showed that this simple contrast in habitats did not fully explain variation in primate behavior. Crook and Gartlan (1966) later expanded on this idea by breaking down primate species into five groups defined primarily by habitat and diet. Jolly (1972) later modified this approach and defined six groups: (1) nocturnal insect eaters, (2) arboreal leaf eaters, (3) arboreal omnivores, (4) semiterrestrial leaf eaters, (5) semiterrestrial omnivores, and (6) primates living in arid environments.

Since the middle of the 1980s, the focus has shifted toward the field of **behavioral ecology,** the study of behavior from an ecological and evolutionary perspective. The primary concern of primate behavioral ecology is the evolutionary analysis of behaviors as strategies for adapting to specific conditions, with specific focus on feeding strategies, social strategies, and reproductive strategies (Fedigan and Strum 1999; Strier 2000). This focus relates primate behavior to the basic problems of adaptation from an evolutionary perspective: finding food, getting along with others, and reproducing. Analysis of primate behavior needs to take into account multiple costs and benefits of various behaviors. For example, why live in groups? Some advantages of group living include more successful defense against predators and cooperative defense of valuable food resources (Fedigan and Strum 1999; Wrangham 1987). However, larger groups may be disadvantageous if food resources

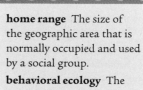

home range The size of the geographic area that is normally occupied and used by a social group.

behavioral ecology The study of behavior from an ecological and evolutionary perspective.

are too limited. To what extent is group size and structure (or any social behavior for that matter) a trade-off between the costs and benefits of different behavioral strategies?

An example of the behavioral ecology approach concerns the relationships between adult females in primate societies (Strier 2000). These relationships often vary even among groups within the same species, and they have a number of environmental correlates. Female kin that live together in groups have an advantage in that they can cooperate with each other against others, but they suffer from the potential disadvantage of having to compete with their own kin for food resources. Likewise, physically remaining in close proximity offers an advantage in terms of defense but increases the likelihood of conflict within the group. If conflict continues, it can be detrimental to both the social group and the individuals within it. In such cases, there is a tendency for an increase in reconciliatory behaviors—that is, making peace after an aggressive conflict. The nature of a social group often leads to conflict, but the actions of reconciliation deter the negative consequences of group living.

The actual data on female relationships are more complex than presented here but provide an example of how a given adaptation (living in groups) can have a cost (conflict) that leads to another adaptation (reconciliation). Other studies of primate behavioral ecology have focused on a wide range of topics, including the relationship between foraging patterns and the distribution of food resources (Oates 1987), the relationship between social structure and predator pressure (Cheney and Wrangham 1987), and the relationship between group cohesiveness and diet (Goldsmith 1999), among *many* others.

Sociobiology

The study of **sociobiology** also deals with evolutionary explanations for behavior but tends to focus more on genetic determinants of behavior, whereas behavioral ecology considers both genetic and environmental factors (Fedigan and Strum 1999). According to one of its main proponents, sociobiology is defined as "the systematic study of the biological basis of all social behavior" (Wilson 1980:322). Most of the work done in sociobiology focuses on natural selection. We assume that a given behavior has at least a partial genetic basis. Given this genetic basis, it is easy to see how certain behaviors could be selected for. If they increase an individual's chance of survival and/or reproduction, then the alleles influencing these behaviors will be passed on to the next generation. Behaviors that seem nonadaptive at first may also be explained by sociobiological hypotheses.

Principles of Sociobiology   Central to much sociobiological theory is the concept of maximizing fitness. This refers to behaviors that increase the probability that an individual's alleles will be passed on to the next generation. If such behaviors are determined even partially by genes, then natural selection will cause those behaviors to increase in frequency. A related concept is the

sociobiology The study of behavior from an evolutionary perspective, particularly the role of natural selection.

FIGURE 8.12

Female chimpanzee and her offspring. The great amount of care and attention given by the mother can be interpreted as maximizing reproductive success by increasing parental investment. (© Gerard Lacz/Peter Arnold, Inc.)

idea of **parental investment,** which refers to parental behaviors that increase the probability that the offspring will survive. According to sociobiological theory, mammalian (and especially primate) females invest a great deal of time and energy in reproduction and care of offspring (Figure 8.12). Even though this investment reduces the number of offspring a female can have, the benefits outweigh the costs.

Mammalian males, however, often contribute only sperm. From the male standpoint of maximizing fitness, it would seem more advantageous to impregnate many females rather than just one. This argument may explain the large number of primate species in which the fathers contribute little to offspring and are not bonded permanently to any one female. However, a number of primate species are monogamous, showing that this relationship is not as simple as it first appears. In certain environments, it may be more adaptive for a primate male to be monogamous and involved in child care, so as to maximize his fitness. Obviously, we should not expect to see a universal pattern but rather one that varies according to environmental circumstances. Thus, an emphasis on sociobiology cannot exclude analysis of environmental factors.

One area of particular interest in sociobiology is the evolution of altruism. At first glance, such behaviors do not appear to make evolutionary sense.

parental investment
Parental behaviors that increase the probability that offspring will survive.

If, for example, you die in an attempt to rescue a child from an oncoming car, then your alleles, including any hypothetical alleles responsible for your altruistic action, will not be passed on. Natural selection would be expected to eliminate any tendencies in future generations.

Is there any evolutionary benefit in sacrificing oneself? Sociobiology has proposed an answer in the form of **kin selection.** Altruistic behaviors may be selected for when they are directed toward one's biological relatives. If you die saving your own child, this act will have two genetic consequences. First, because you die, you will no longer pass alleles on to the next generation. Second, your child will live and have the opportunity to pass on his or her alleles, of which 50 percent came from you. Thus, by saving your child you actually contribute to the survival of some of your own alleles. If your altruistic action was at least partially affected by genetic factors, this behavior also will be passed on through the survival of your child. Sociobiological theory has developed a number of mathematical models that deal with the cost and benefit of altruistic behaviors in terms of the degree of biological relationship between the altruist and the recipient of the action. For example, it is more advantageous to you to save the life of your nephew than your first cousin because you share more alleles with your nephew.

Although the models of sociobiology are often intuitively correct and logical, there remains great difficulty in testing many of their predictions. Perhaps the greatest problem is in demonstrating the genetic predisposition of behaviors. Further, we often lack sufficient information over enough generations to actually demonstrate a direct relationship between fitness and the behavior in question.

An Example of Primate Sociobiology   Some of the most interesting issues in sociobiology focus on behaviors that do not at first seem to be adaptive. One classic example of this problem is from Sarah Hrdy's (1977) study of **infanticide** in a particular group of primates—a species of monkey known as langurs. Langurs typically live in uni-male groups. There is frequently competition between adult males in such groups when a challenger seeks to displace an adult male. When a new male successfully takes over the group, he often then attempts to kill all the infants fathered by the previous male (Figure 8.13). At first, such behavior seems abnormal and contrary to the survival of the group. The sociobiological explanation, however, is that the new male is increasing his own fitness. First, killing the infants from other males can increase the proportion of one's offspring in the next generation. The competition has been eliminated. Second, females who are still nursing infants are not yet able to become pregnant by the new male, and he has to wait. By killing the infants, the new male ensures that the females are more quickly able to have offspring with him. The bottom line is that *if* infanticide has some genetic basis, then this act would be selected for because it maximizes the fitness of the killer.

This interpretation poses a number of problems. First, we do not know how widespread this behavior is and whether it occurs under different envi-

kin selection A concept used in sociobiological explanations of altruism. Sacrificial behaviors, for example, can be selected for if they increase the probability of survival of close relatives.

infanticide The killing of infants.

FIGURE 8.13

Adult female langurs attempting to rescue an infant from an adult male langur. (Sarah Blaffer Hrdy/Anthro-Photo)

ronmental conditions. Second, we do not know the extent to which such behaviors are affected by genetic factors. Finally, the hypothesis that differences in fitness are associated with infanticide needs to be tested. To do this, we need to know something about relative survival and differential reproduction, which requires detailed observations over many groups and generations.

The infanticide hypothesis has been controversial and challenged. One of the critiques focused on problems with both the data and hypothesis (Bartlett et al. 1993; Sussman et al. 1995). First, there have been few direct observations of infanticide by langurs—only 21 (and 27 other cases of infanticide in other primate species). Further, few of these observations involved the expected attack of an incoming male directly on an infant. In many cases, the infant's death was accidental, often the result of clinging to a mother who was being attacked. In terms of the sociobiological hypothesis, Sussman and colleagues (1995) note that there is no evidence for genetic inheritance of this behavior or for increased fitness following the act. Although acknowledging that the data are scanty, Hrdy and her colleagues (1995) argue that there is sufficient evidence to date to make the infanticide hypothesis viable.

Although sociobiological hypotheses can be constructed that are logical and consistent, this does not make them correct. Clearly, more data need to be collected from primate societies to verify or support such hypotheses.

SUMMARY

Taxonomic classification imposes order on the diversity of living creatures. The biological and behavioral nature of human beings is revealed in the different levels of classification to which humans belong. Humans are animals, chordates, and vertebrates. We share certain characteristics, such as a more developed nervous system, with other creatures in these categories.

Humans are mammals, which means we rely a great deal on a reproductive strategy of few births and extensive parental care. This reproductive pattern is associated with higher intelligence and a greater capacity for learned behaviors. Other adaptations of mammals include differentiated teeth, a skeletal structure capable of swift movement, and the ability to maintain a constant body temperature.

Humans belong to a specific order of mammals known as primates. The primates have certain characteristics, such as skeletal flexibility, grasping hands, and keen eyesight, that evolved in order to meet the demands of life in the trees. Though many primate species no longer live in the trees, they have retained these basic characteristics and use them in new ways to adapt to the environment. Most humans no longer use their grasping hands to move about in trees but use them instead for tool manufacture and use.

Primates show a great deal of variation in the size and structure of their social groups, ranging from solitary groups consisting of a female and her offspring to large communities with many adults and offspring. Several different approaches are used to understand the variety of primate social organization. Two approaches seek to place primate behavior in an evolutionary context. The study of sociobiology emphasizes genetic determinants of behavior, whereas the study of primate behavioral ecology has a broader evolutionary approach emphasizing the relationship between ecological factors and social behavior.

SUPPLEMENTAL READINGS

Dolhinow, P., and A. Fuentes, ed. 1999. *The Nonhuman Primates*. Mountain View, Calif.: Mayfield. A textbook on primate behavior with individual chapters written by many leading primatologists. Individual chapters focus on both specific groups of primates and general topics.

Falk, D. 2000. *Primate Diversity*. New York: W. W. Norton. A textbook on primate biology and behavior with most chapters organized by specific types of primates.

Strier, K. B. 2000. *Primate Behavioral Ecology*. Boston: Allyn and Bacon. This text is a comprehensive review of basic principles of primate behavioral ecology.

INTERNET RESOURCES

http://anthro.palomar.edu/animal/default.htm
Classification of Living Things, a tutorial on taxonomic classification.

http://www.ucmp.berkeley.edu/mammal/mammal.html
Hall of Mammals, a discussion of different types of mammals.

http://www.primate.wisc.edu/pin
Primate InfoNet, a comprehensive collection of links to sites on primate taxonomy, biology, and behavior.

CHAPTER 9

The Biology and Behavior of the Living Primates

This chapter looks more closely at the biology and behavior of the living primates, with particular attention to the apes, our closest living relatives.

PRIMATE SUBORDERS

The two major subgroups of the living primates are the suborder **Prosimii** and the suborder **Anthropoidea.** These are the official scientific names (in Latin) for the two suborders, although here we will use the more common terms *prosimians* and *anthropoids.* Each of these suborders is broken down into smaller taxonomic units, such as infraorders, superfamilies, families, and so on. Figure 9.1 shows the traditional primate taxonomy used throughout most of this chapter. Keep in mind that the cladistic approach (Chapter 8) has challenged parts of this classification; some of the controversies are discussed later.

Prosimians

The word *prosimian* means literally "before simians" (monkeys and apes). In biological terms, prosimians are more primitive, or more like early primate ancestors, than are monkeys and apes.

Prosimii (prosimians) The suborder of primates that are biologically primitive compared to anthropoids.

Anthropoidea (anthropoids) The suborder of primates consisting of monkeys, apes, and humans.

◀ *Japanese macaques, one of many species of Old World monkeys, and one of several groups of living primates. (© Steven Kaufman/Peter Arnold, Inc.)*

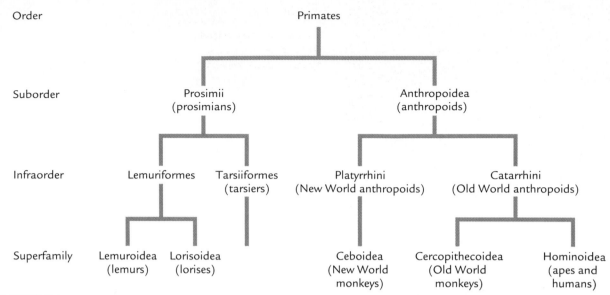

FIGURE 9.1

Summary of traditional primate classification. Names within parentheses are common names. A more detailed classification is provided in Appendix 2.

nocturnal Active during the night.

diurnal Active during the day.

loris Nocturnal prosimian found today in Asia and Africa.

tarsier Nocturnal prosimian found today in Indonesia.

lemur A prosimian found today on the island of Madagascar.

Prosimian Characteristics   The prosimians often lack one or more of the general characteristics of primates. For example, some prosimians lack color vision, and some have a single claw on each hand or foot.

Another primitive characteristic of prosimians is that they rely to a much greater extent on the sense of smell than do the anthropoids. Prosimian brains are also generally smaller relative to body size than are the brains of anthropoids. Prosimians are usually small in size and tend to be solitary, and many are **nocturnal** (active at night). These characteristics and others point to the basic primitive nature of most prosimians. Many prosimians are vertical clingers and leapers. That is, they cling to tree trunks until they are ready to move and then they propel themselves through the air.

Prosimians themselves show considerable variation. Some prosimians have larger body sizes, some have larger social groups, and some are **diurnal** (active in daylight). This variation makes classification difficult, but it does show us both the general trends of the prosimians and specific differences among them.

Types of Prosimians   There are three different groups of prosimians in the world today, each with a number of different species. One group, the **lorises,** are small, solitary, nocturnal prosimians found in Asia and Africa (Figure 9.2). Another group, the **tarsiers,** also small, solitary, and nocturnal, are found in Indonesia. The nocturnal nature of tarsiers is evidenced by their large eyes, the size of which serves to gather available light (Figure 9.3).

The most biologically diverse group of prosimians is the **lemurs,** which are found only on the island of Madagascar off the southeast coast of Africa (Figure 9.4). Some species of lemurs are nocturnal and some are diurnal. The lemurs depart from the typical pattern of prosimians as nocturnal, solitary primates. Their wide range of biological and behavioral characteristics probably reflects their isolation on the island of Madagascar. Because the island

FIGURE 9.2

A loris, a prosimian from Southeast Asia. (© Mark Stouffer/Animals Animals)

FIGURE 9.3

A tarsier, a prosimian from Southeast Asia. Unlike other prosimians, the tarsier does not have a moist nose. (© Zoological Society of San Diego)

FIGURE 9.4

Ring-tailed lemur from the island of Madagascar.
(© Zoological Society of San Diego)

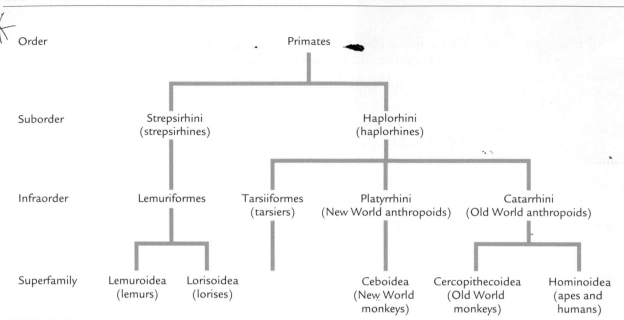

FIGURE 9.5

An alternative primate classification using the suborders Strepsirhini and Haplorhini. Compare this to Figure 9.1, which uses the traditional breakdown into the suborders Prosimii and Anthropoidea. The difference is that the present chart groups tarsiers with monkeys and hominoids in the suborder Haplorhini rather than with lemurs and lorises. According to this view, tarsiers are more closely related to monkeys and hominoids because they lack the moist nose (associated with greater ability to smell) found in lemurs and lorises. There is debate over which approach is the most appropriate.

has no competing monkey or ape species and not many other mammals either, the lemurs have expanded into a variety of ecological niches. Apart from these variations, the lemurs are still definitely prosimians—having, among other primitive features, the characteristic reliance on smell.

Lemurs have some interesting aspects of social structure and behavior compared with other primates. Although some lemur species have the multimale/multifemale social structure, a large proportion (more than 25 percent) live in monogamous family groups, a number much higher than other primates or mammals in general. This high proportion might reflect an adaptation to dietary sources that exist in small patches that are regularly distributed in the environment; in such cases, small groups might be more efficient (Wright 1999).

Another peculiar lemur trait is the predominance of female dominance in lemur species. Among other prosimians, males tend to be dominant. Many lemur species, with clear female dominance, are an exception to this general pattern. Female lemurs typically win aggressive encounters with males and have priority in eating—males generally wait to feed until the females are done. Female dominance in lemurs may reflect a dietary adaptation such that females have priority access to a limited food supply in order to have sufficient food for raising offspring (Wright 1999).

Anthropoids

The anthropoids are the higher primates and consist of monkeys and hominoids (apes and humans). Anthropoids are generally larger in overall body size, have larger and more complex brains, rely more on visual abilities, and show more complex social structures than other primates. Except for one monkey species, all anthropoids are diurnal. The anthropoids include both arboreal and terrestrial species.

All living prosimians are found in the Old World, but anthropoids are found in both the New World and the Old World. (The Old World consists of the continents of Africa, Asia, and Europe; the New World is the Americas.) New World anthropoids are found today in Central and South America. Old World anthropoids are found today in Africa and Asia (and one monkey species in Europe). The only native New World anthropoids are monkeys, whereas native Old World anthropoids include monkeys, apes, and humans.

Alternative Classifications

The traditional division of primates into prosimians and anthropoids is being challenged by a number of scientists. The problem with the traditional classification is that tarsiers, usually classified as prosimians, show several biological characteristics of anthropoids. Lorises and lemurs have moist noses, a trait related to their keen sense of smell. Tarsiers, like anthropoids, lack the moist nose. In addition, recent biochemical investigations have supported the idea that tarsiers are more like anthropoids than prosimians.

Many researchers now advocate placing the lemurs and lorises in one suborder, **Strepsirhini**, characterized by moist noses, and the tarsiers and anthropoids in another suborder, **Haplorhini**, which lacks the moist nose. In this text I will continue to use the traditional division between prosimians and anthropoids because it provides a useful contrast when discussing primate evolution. However, the alternative classification shows that there is considerable debate regarding the taxonomic placement of the tarsiers. The suborders Strepsirhini and Haplorhini are shown in the alternative primate taxonomy in Figure 9.5 and can be contrasted with the traditional scheme of Figure 9.1. The major difference is the placement of the tarsiers. Are they more similar evolutionarily to lemurs and lorises or to monkeys and apes?

What is the relevance of alternative classifications? Once again, this controversy demonstrates the difficulty of taxonomic classification. It is not always possible to place living creatures unambiguously in certain categories. Such problems actually provide us with strong evidence of the evolutionary process. The tarsiers, for example, suggest what a transitional form between prosimians and anthropoids might have looked like.

THE MONKEYS

Anthropoids include monkeys and hominoids (apes and humans). Monkeys and apes are often confused in the popular imagination. In reality, they are easy to tell apart. Most monkeys have tails, whereas apes and humans do not. In general, monkeys also have smaller brains relative to body size than apes or humans. The typical pattern of monkey movement is on all fours (**quadrupedal**), and their arms and legs are generally of similar length so that their spines are parallel to the ground. By contrast, apes have longer arms than legs and humans have longer legs than arms.

Strepsirhini (strepsirhines) One of two suborders of primates suggested to replace the prosimian/anthropoid suborders (the other is the haplorhines). Strepsirhines are primates that have a moist nose (lemurs and lorises).

Haplorhini (haplorhines) One of two suborders of primates suggested to replace the prosimian/anthropoid suborders (the other is the strepsirhines). Haplorhines are primates without a moist nose (tarsiers, monkeys, apes, and humans).

quadrupedal A form of movement in which all four limbs are of equal size and make contact with the ground, and the spine is roughly parallel to the ground.

FIGURE 9.6

A spider monkey, capable of using its tail as a "fifth limb." (© *Zoological Society of San Diego*)

New World Monkeys

The only form of anthropoids found native to the New World are the New World monkeys (there are no New World apes). Although they share many similarities with Old World monkeys, several important differences reflect separate lines of evolution over the past 30 million years or so.

Characteristics   Some of the differences between the New World and Old World monkeys are useful in reconstructing evolutionary relationships. For example, New World monkeys have four more premolar teeth than Old World monkeys. The dental formulae for many New World monkeys is 2-1-3-3, compared to the 2-1-2-3 dental formula of all Old World monkeys. Other differences relate to the way in which the monkeys live; for example, many New World monkeys have prehensile tails.

Because the tail of many New World monkeys is capable of grasping, it is highly useful in moving about and feeding in the trees (Figure 9.6). Typically, the monkey uses this "fifth limb" to anchor itself while feeding on the ends of small branches. Old World monkeys have tails, but none of them have prehensile tails. Those New World monkeys with prehensile tails are thus more proficient in terms of acrobatic agility. This difference probably relates to the fact that all New World monkeys are arboreal, whereas some Old World monkeys are terrestrial. The prehensile tail of many New World monkeys is a derived trait that did not develop in the Old World monkeys.

FIGURE 9.7

A Bolivian red howler monkey, one of the New World monkeys with a prehensile tail.
(© Zoological Society of San Diego)

Case Study: Howler Monkeys One interesting group of New World monkeys are the howler monkeys, consisting of six species in the genus *Alouatta*. Howler monkeys are found in Mexico and in South America (Figure 9.7). Their name reflects their most unusual characteristic—an enlarged hyoid bone (the bone in the throat), which creates a large resonating chamber capable of making loud sounds that can be heard at a considerable distance. Howlers have prehensile tails and are quite at home in the trees, where they eat primarily fruit and leaves. Adult howlers weigh between 6 and 8 kilograms (13–18 pounds), with males larger than females. Males are capable of making deeper and louder howls (Bramblett 1994). Howlers live in multimale/multifemale groups with an average of about 15 members per group (Falk 2000). Some groups have been observed to have only one adult male and could rightly be called uni-male groups (Crockett and Eisenberg 1987). Again, variation is typical of primate social structure.

The loud howling of howler monkeys serves many purposes, including warning and defense. These howls often serve to warn away competitors for food and space, and it has been suggested that these vocalizations are a substitute for active fighting (Carpenter 1965; Crockett and Eisenberg 1987). Because groups are widely separated, fighting may be avoided, and thus the spacing may be a group defense. This spacing has also often been interpreted as evidence that howlers have specific territories, which they defend. A strict

FIGURE 9.8

Japanese macaques, adapted to living in the snow. (© Steven Kaufman/Peter Arnold, Inc.)

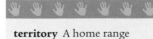

territory A home range that is actively defended.

definition of **territory** is a home range that is actively defended and does not overlap with another group's home range. Actually, few primates are territorial in this sense. Carpenter (1965) noted that howlers do not defend specific and constant boundaries but rather defend wherever they are at a given time. Crockett and Eisenberg (1987) suggest that howlers cannot actually be considered territorial because the overlap in home ranges is often quite large, but they also note that others interpret the data as showing some territoriality. (Perhaps the most telling observation is the variation that howlers [and many primates] show from study to study.) Although much is still unknown about howler monkeys, it is clear that they are not easily pigeonholed into different

FIGURE 9.9

A mandrill, an Old World monkey. (© Zoological Society of San Diego)

categories such as uni-male versus multimale or territorial versus nonterritorial (Crockett and Eisenberg 1987).

Old World Monkeys

Characteristics   Old World monkeys are biochemically and physically more similar to humans than are New World monkeys. For example, Old World monkeys have the same number of teeth as apes and humans (a dental formula of 2-1-2-3). Old World monkeys inhabit a wide range of environments. Many species live in tropical rain forests, but other species have adapted to the **savanna** (open grasslands). One species has even learned to survive in the snowy environment of the Japanese mountains (Figure 9.8).

The Old World monkeys, like the New World monkeys, are quadrupedal, running on the ground and branches on all fours. Though Old World monkeys are agile in the trees, many species have adapted to spending more time on the ground in search of food. Most Old World species eat a mixed diet of fruits and leaves (Figure 9.9), although some show dental and digestive specializations for leaf eating. Some Old World species occasionally supplement their primarily vegetarian diet with insects or small animals that they hunt.

Social structure is highly variable among Old World monkeys. Most known species have been characterized as having either multimale/multifemale or uni-male social groups. However, a large proportion of Old World monkey species has been observed with more than one social structure, depending

savanna An environment consisting of open grasslands in which food resources tend to be spread out over large areas.

FIGURE 9.10

Variation in social structure among Old World monkeys. Numbers represent the percentage of species that have a particular social structure (species for which this information is not known have been excluded). Note that 17 percent of Old World monkey species have been observed with more than one type of social structure. (Source of data: Jolly 1985:129, Table 6.5a)

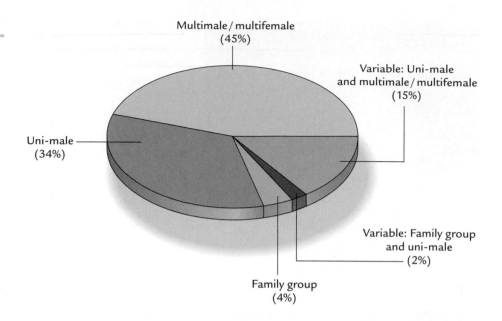

Multimale / multifemale
(45%)

Variable: Uni-male
and multimale / multifemale
(15%)

Uni-male
(34%)

Variable: Family group
and uni-male
(2%)

Family group
(4%)

on the specific group, once again showing behavioral variation (Figure 9.10). One contributing factor to this variation is the availability of food. In species that have less available food, the uni-male structure is more common, perhaps because additional males would consume food without adding much to group survival.

Case Study: Baboons   Baboons are one of the most widely studied and interesting of the Old World monkeys (technically, several different monkeys are given the general label of "baboon"; here we refer to the "savanna baboon"). Baboons live in relatively large (20–200) multimale/multifemale groups on the African savanna (Figure 9.11). The savanna is composed primarily of open grasslands, in which food resources tend to be spread out over large areas. Clusters of trees in the savanna provide additional opportunities for food, as well as for protection. Even though baboons are essentially terrestrial, they still have the basic primate adaptations that allow them to climb effectively, which proves useful in hiding from predators, and for shelter when sleeping. Because food resources are spread out over large areas of the savanna, baboons tend to have rather large home ranges, and they cover this area by foraging as a group. The baboon diet is quite diverse, including grass, leaves, fruit, and occasionally meat that has been obtained from hunting small mammals and birds.

A primary reason baboons are so widely studied is that they live on the savanna. Our analysis of the first humans shows that they too lived in or near a savanna environment (Chapter 12), and thus many scientists have advocated using the baboon as a possible model for the evolution of human behavior. Today we recognize many problems with this simple approach, and "baboon models" are seldom used (Strum and Mitchell 1987). Still, the baboon makes an interesting species to study in its own right, and the more we

FIGURE 9.11

Baboons on the savanna.
(© E. R. Degginger/Animals
Animals)

FIGURE 9.12

An adult male baboon
"yawning"—an expression
that is interpreted by others as
an aggressive display and a
warning. Such threat gestures
are used in disputes over
dominance. (© Irven DeVore,
Anthro-Photo)

find out about their society, the more we again see the variable nature of primate behavior.

Much of the focus in baboon studies has been on social organization. Adult males are dominant over adult females, and there is a constant shift in the relative position of the most dominant males. Aggressive actions play a role in this continual struggle (Figure 9.12). Adult males are considerably larger than adult females, and the largest and strongest males often have a greater chance of being the most dominant.

Size and strength are not, however, the only factors affecting male dominance in baboon society. Coalitions of two or more lower-ranking males have often been observed to displace a more dominant male who was actually larger and stronger than either of the lower-ranking males. The ability to aid others is an important determinant of dominance rank.

Environmental factors also affect the pattern of dominance within baboon society. For example, Rowell (1966) found that forest-living baboons have less rigid dominance hierarchies than groups living on the savanna. In addition, the daily life of the forest baboons was more relaxed, as the level of aggression was lower. In forest environments, food is generally more available and there is less threat from predators. Quite simply, a rigid social organization is not needed in this environment.

In the initial years of baboon research, most of the attention was on the dominance hierarchies of the adult males and less attention was given to the behaviors of adult females. We now realize that the continuity of baboon society revolves around the females and that adult males quite frequently move from one social group to another. The dominance hierarchy of the adult females is generally more stable over time. The importance of female continuity in baboon society must be acknowledged because they are responsible for the care of infants and provide the needed socialization prior to maturity.

THE HOMINOIDS

In addition to the monkeys, the other major group of living anthropoids are the **hominoids,** which is a group composed of apes and humans. The similarity of apes and humans (hence their placement in the same superfamily) has long been a source of interest and fascination. Perhaps one of our most memorable images of this relatedness comes from the classic 1933 movie *King Kong*. The giant gorilla discovered on "Skull Island" is captured and brought to New York City for display as the eighth wonder of the world. Ignoring the fantastic nature of some of the plot elements (gorillas could not be that large and still walk), the film draws close comparisons between Kong's behavior and that of the humans in the film. Kong shows love, curiosity, and anger, among other emotions and behaviors. Kong is a mirror for the humans, and the humans are a mirror for Kong. We see ourselves in the beast and the beast in ourselves.

Hominoid Characteristics

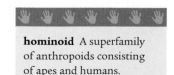

hominoid A superfamily of anthropoids consisting of apes and humans.

Whether we choose to look at apes as humanlike, or humans as apelike, the fact remains that of all living creatures the apes are the most similar to humans in both biology and behavior. Before considering the biology and behavior of living apes (the remainder of this chapter) and humans (next chapter), it is necessary to examine some of the general characteristics of all living hominoids.

Unlike monkeys, hominoids do not have tails. Another hominoid characteristic is size: in general, most hominoid species are larger than monkeys. Hominoid brains as a rule are larger than monkey brains, both in terms of absolute size and in relationship to body size. Their brains are also more complex, which correlates with the hominoid characteristics of greater intelligence and learning abilities. Hominoids also invest the most time and effort in raising their young.

Hominoids share with Old World monkeys the 2-1-2-3 dental formula (two incisors, one canine, two premolars, and three molars in each half of the upper and lower jaws). The structure of the molar teeth, however, is different in monkeys and hominoids. The most noticeable difference is that the lower molar teeth of hominoids tend to have five **cusps** (raised areas) as compared to the four cusps in the lower molars of monkeys. The deeper grooves between these five cusps form the shape of the letter Y. As such, this characteristic shape is called the "Y-5" pattern (Figure 9.13). This difference may seem trivial, but it does help us in identifying fossils because we can often tell whether a form is a monkey or a hominoid on the basis of the molar teeth.

Perhaps one of the most important characteristics of hominoids is their upper body and shoulder anatomy. Hominoids can raise their arms above their heads with little trouble, whereas a monkey would find this difficult. This ability of hominoids to raise their arms above their heads is based on three basic anatomical features. First, hominoids have a larger and stronger collarbone than monkeys. Second, the hominoid shoulder joint is very flexible and capable of a wide angle of movement. Third, hominoid shoulder blades are located more toward the back. By contrast, monkeys' shoulder blades are located more toward the sides of the chest (Figure 9.14). Hominoid shoulder joints face outward, compared to the shoulder joints of monkeys, which are downward-facing.

Most hominoids have longer front limbs than back limbs. Modern humans are an exception to this rule, with longer legs than arms. This trait facilitates upright walking (discussed later). In apes, the longer front limbs represent an adaptation to hanging from tree limbs. In addition, hominoids generally have long fingers that help them hang suspended from branches. The wrist joint of hominoids contains a disc of cartilage (called a meniscus) between the lower arm bones and the wrist bones. This disc cuts down on contact between bones. As a result, the wrist joints of hominoids are more flexible than those of monkeys, allowing greater hanging ability.

Hominoid anatomy allows them a different type of movement from that of monkeys. Hominoids are adept at climbing and hanging from branches. They are **suspensory climbers.** As hominoids, humans have retained this ability, although we seldom use it in our daily lives. One exception is children playing on so-called monkey bars at playgrounds (which should more properly be called "hominoid bars"). The ability to suspend by the arms and then swing from one rung of the bars to the next is a basic hominoid trait.

Living hominoids all share this basic ability but vary quite a bit in terms of their normal patterns of movement. Some apes, for example, are proficient arm swingers, whereas others are expert climbers. Humans have evolved a totally different pattern in which the arms are not used for movement; this

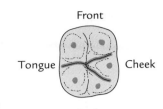

Front

Tongue   Cheek

Back

FIGURE 9.13

The Y-5 lower molar pattern of hominoids. Circles represent cusps. The heavier line resembles the letter Y on its side.

cusp A raised area on the chewing surface of a tooth.

suspensory climbing The ability to raise the arms above the head and hang on branches and to climb in this position.

FIGURE 9.14

Top view of the shoulder complex of a monkey (top) and a human (bottom) drawn to the same scale top to bottom. In hominoids (apes and humans), the clavicle is larger and the scapula is located more toward the rear of the body.

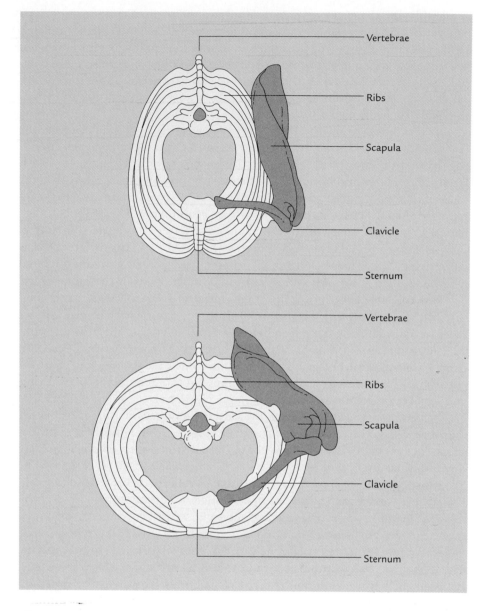

allows us to carry things while walking on two legs. These differences in locomotion are discussed later in the chapter. In spite of these differences in function, the close relationship between apes and humans is seen in their shared characteristics of the upper body and shoulder.

Classification of the Hominoids

Between 20 million and 8 million years ago there were many different types of hominoids. Today we have only the representatives of a few surviving species from this once diverse, widespread group. Living hominoids are divided into three categories: the lesser apes, the great apes, and humans. The

TABLE 9.1   Species of Living Hominoids

	Genus	Species	Common Name
Lesser Apes	Hylobates	agilis	Agile gibbon
	Hylobates	concolor	Crested gibbon
	Hylobates	hoolock	White-browed gibbon
	Hylobates	klossi	Kloss gibbon
	Hylobates	lar	White-handed or common gibbon
	Hylobates	moloch	Silvery gibbon
	Hylobates	muelleri	Gray gibbon
	Hylobates	pilateus	Capped gibbon
	Hylobates	syndactylus	Siamang
Great Apes	Pongo	pygmaeus	Orangutan
	Gorilla	gorilla	Gorilla
	Pan	troglodytes	Chimpanzee
	Pan	paniscus	Bonobo
Humans	Homo	sapiens	Human

Source: Falk (2000)

lesser apes are the gibbons (nine species) and are the least related to humans. The great apes are the Asian orangutan and the African apes, the gorilla, chimpanzee, and bonobo. A list of the scientific and common names of all living hominoids is given in Table 9.1.

That all of these species have certain shared characteristics allows us to classify them as hominoids and to infer that they are related through evolution. The specific evolutionary relationship of the different hominoids is more difficult to establish. To uncover our own origins, we are interested in determining which ape species is the most similar to us. In this way we are able to compare the anatomy of living and fossil hominoids to determine what changed in our line, what changed in the ape line, and what stayed the same.

Methods of Analysis   Two different approaches are used to ascertain evolutionary relationships between different living species. One approach is to focus on the physical anatomy (**morphology**) of living forms. The other approach is to examine the biochemistry and genetics of living species. Similarities and differences between species are revealed by a number of methods that compare proteins and even the genetic code. Constructing taxonomies from biochemical and genetic data has a definite advantage. If we focus on proteins or sections of DNA not affected by natural selection (or at least those we assume not to be affected), then any degree of similarity should reflect relative evolutionary relationships.

One biochemical method consists of looking at immunological reactions. When foreign molecules are introduced into an animal's blood, the animal's immune system provides a defense by producing antibodies to attack the foreign molecules (antigens). If you mix the antibodies from one species with proteins from the blood serum of another species, this reaction

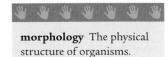

morphology The physical structure of organisms.

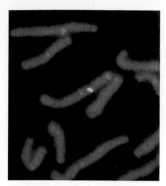

FIGURE 9.15

The genetic structure of apes is very similar to that of humans. In this picture, a small piece of human DNA from a gene called "U2" is fluorescently labeled (greenish-yellow dots) and hybridized to chromosomes from a gorilla (blue). Because of the similarity of base pairs of humans and apes, the human DNA binds to its complementary sequence in the gorilla, revealing the location of the gene in that species. (© Jon Marks. From the Journal of Human Evolution, *March 1993, with permission of* The Academic Press, London)

will not be as strong. The strength of this reaction relates to the degree of similarity between the two species being compared. Stronger reactions indicate closer molecular similarity. Because molecular structure reflects genetic factors, the stronger the reaction, the more similar genetically are the two species being compared.

Comparison of immunological reactions can be used to assess evolutionary relationships and to construct taxonomies. In the case of the hominoids, such research has shown that the orangutan is distinct from the African apes and humans. In other words, the African apes and humans resemble each other more than either resembles the orangutan.

The structure of proteins for two or more species can also be compared. As discussed in Chapter 2, the biochemical structure of proteins can be represented by a sequence of smaller biochemical units called amino acids. The amino acid sequence for a given protein is compared between two or more species to determine the minimum number of genetic differences between one form and another. The smaller the number of differences, the more closely related the two species.

When applied to many proteins, this method produces the same result as that obtained from looking at immunological reactions. Chimpanzees, bonobos, gorillas, and humans form a closely related group; orangutans are set apart from this group. Gibbons are even less similar to African apes and humans. This finding supports the idea that the African apes and humans shared a more recent common ancestor than any of them shared with the orangutan. In terms of a family tree, orangutans split off the main branch earlier than the African apes and humans. Put another way, the African apes are the closest living relatives of humans. The same results have been found for certain physical features, such as soft tissue anatomy (Gibbs et al. 2000).

In recent years, even more sophisticated methods have been developed to make biochemical and genetic comparisons between living species (Figure 9.15). For example, newer methods have allowed the comparison of the individual chemical bases that make up DNA. As even more advanced biotechnological methods continue to be developed, more and more techniques will become available with which we will be able to provide direct comparisons of the genetic codes of different species.

Models of Relationship   What conclusions about hominoid classification can we draw based on these different methods? Anatomical, biochemical, and genetic analyses all support classifications in which the gibbons are distinct from the great apes and humans. In other words, all great apes and humans are more similar to one another than any are to the lesser apes.

The *exact* nature of the relationship among the great apes and humans has long been debated. The oldest of these ideas places all the great apes in a group separate from humans (humans were classified as hominids and all great apes were classified as pongids), implying that all great apes are equally similar to one another and that humans are quite distinct. This model, which had its roots in the then-prevailing concept of human uniqueness, is now rejected. Anatomical and genetic data show that humans and the African

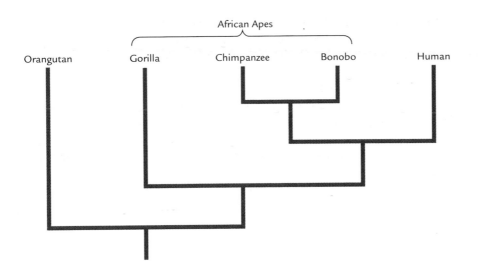

FIGURE 9.16

An evolutionary "tree" showing the relationships among the living great apes and humans. Note that humans, chimpanzees, and bonobos are more closely related to each other than any are to the orangutan. There is still some disagreement regarding the relationship of the gorilla to the other African apes; some suggest that the gorilla, chimpanzee, and bonobo are more closely related to each other than to humans.

apes are more similar to one another than any are to the Asian great ape, the orangutan.

Biochemical and genetic comparisons clearly demonstrate that the African apes and humans are most similar to one another. In a classic study of protein differences and DNA sequences between chimpanzees and humans, King and Wilson (1975) found that the two species are more than 98 percent identical. Subsequent research confirmed this finding and extended it to the bonobo and the gorilla. This finding implies that humans and African apes all split from a common ancestor at roughly the same time.

It is now clear that humans and African apes are more closely related to each other than either is to the Asian great ape, the orangutan. There is also an indication that chimpanzees and bonobos are even more closely related to humans than either is to gorillas (e.g., Gagneux et al. 1999; Horai et al. 1995). If so, then we can reconstruct a family tree of the relationships of the great apes and humans. As shown in Figure 9.16, this tree suggests that the orangutan split off from the common ancestor of African apes and humans. The next split was between the line leading to the gorilla and the line leading to the common ancestor of humans and chimpanzees and bonobos, the latter two of which diverged later in time. Not everyone agrees with the specific order of splitting within the African apes (some suggest that gorillas, chimpanzees, and bonobos diverged *after* the human line diverged), but there is consensus regarding the closer kinship of African apes with humans than with orangutans.

What then is the best way to classify the living hominoids? A traditional classification, shown in Figure 9.17, is based on a phenetic approach that considers overall physical similarity, grouping the great apes together in one family (Pongidae) and placing humans in their own family (Hominidae, or hominids). This classification is problematic. Although separation of the great apes from humans is useful in some discussions of anatomy and behavior, it clearly does not reflect evolutionary relationships. We know from a number of analyses of genetics and anatomy that some of the great apes are

FIGURE 9.17

Traditional taxonomic classification of hominoids. Names in italics refer to common names. To emphasize certain aspects of behavior and physical characteristics, the orangutan, gorilla, chimpanzee, and bonobo are all placed in a separate category from humans. Although useful for some purposes, this classification does not reflect the fact that humans and the African apes are more genetically similar to each other than any are to the orangutan. Compare this classification with Figure 9.18.

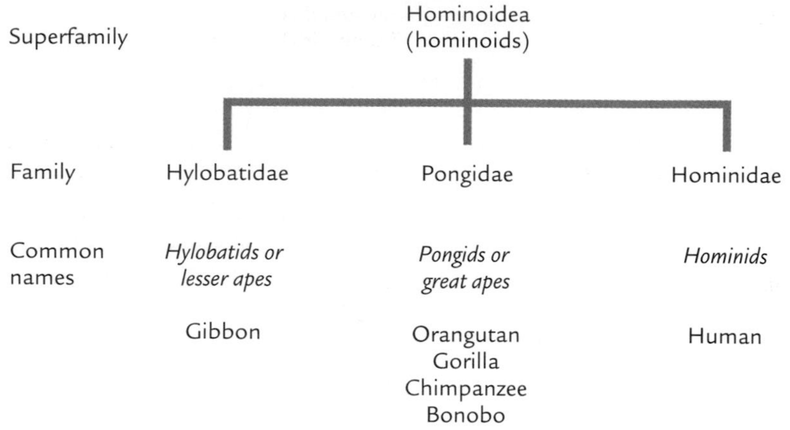

		Hominoidea (hominoids)	
Superfamily			
Family	Hylobatidae	Pongidae	Hominidae
Common names	*Hylobatids or lesser apes*	*Pongids or great apes*	*Hominids*
	Gibbon	Orangutan Gorilla Chimpanzee Bonobo	Human

more closely related to humans than they are to the other great apes. If our focus in classification is cladistic, rather than phenetic, then the classification must place humans and African apes in the same group to the exclusion of the orangutan.

There is considerable controversy at present regarding the best solution to this problem. Some advocate keeping the traditional classification and not being concerned about the lack of correspondence with evolutionary relationships. Others advocate that classification should follow cladistic principles and that the classification should be revised to reflect the greater kinship of African apes and humans. One possible solution is shown in Figure 9.18, which redefines the family Hominidae to consist of humans *and* all of the great apes. Humans, chimpanzees, and bonobos are placed within their own subfamily, and humans are a tribe within this subfamily. This is only one of many proposals that have been suggested to make hominoid classification adhere to cladistic principles. Although many scientists agree that the system needs revising, there is much debate at present on how to go about it. Most agree that grouping all of the great apes under a single family (pongids) makes little sense, but there is little consensus on how to classify humans with respect to the apes (Cela-Conde et al. 2000).

The continuing debate over hominoid classification is apt to seem a bit confusing, particularly because different schemes often wind up using the same name in different ways. Consider, for example, the term **hominid,** traditionally used as a label for humans and humanlike ancestors that have lived since the divergence of the African apes. Under the system proposed in Figure 9.18, the term instead refers to humans *and* the great apes, whereas the term **hominin** is used to describe humans and humanlike ancestors. Because there is no consensus yet, this book will continue to use the term *hominid* to refer to humans and humanlike ancestors. Just keep in mind that you might encounter the term *hominin* as well. In any event, do not read too much into the debate over names. There *is* agreement on the basic facts regarding the evolutionary relationships of hominoids; the debate is over what names to use.

Suggestions on how to fix this

hominid Humans and humanlike ancestors since the time of divergence from the African apes.

hominin Under some taxonomic classifications, this term is used instead of hominid to refer to humans and humanlike ancestors.

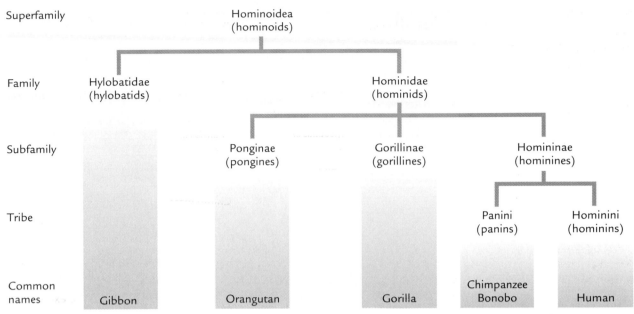

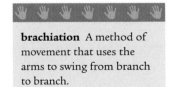

FIGURE 9.18

Revised taxonomic classification of hominoids to emphasize genetic and evolutionary relationships (see Figure 9.16). Humans, chimpanzees, and bonobos form a group separate from the gorilla and orangutan. This classification does not fit our usual informal notion of "ape" and "human" and does not reflect common aspects of behavior or physical appearance. Compare this classification with the one in Figure 9.17. (Wood and Richmond 2000)

THE LIVING APES

To provide a better comparison of the biology and behavior of the apes and humans, it is necessary to consider briefly the physical characteristics, distribution, environment, and social structure of all of the hominoids. Although the living hominoids all share a number of features, they also show a great deal of biological and behavioral variation.

Gibbons

Physical Characteristics   The gibbon is the smallest of the living apes. There are nine recognized species of gibbon.

The physical characteristics of gibbons reflect adaptation to life in the trees. The climbing and hanging adaptations of hominoids have evolved in the gibbon to allow highly agile movement through trees. The gibbon's usual form of movement, known as **brachiation,** consists of hand-over-hand swinging from branch to branch. Many primates are portrayed as arm swingers, but only the gibbon can perform this movement quickly and efficiently (Figure 9.19).

A number of anatomical adaptations allow gibbons efficient arm swinging. Body size ranges from about 5.5 kg (12 lb) to 13.5 kg (30 lb) (Falk 2000; Richard 1985). Their arms are extremely long relative to their trunks and legs. Gibbon fingers are elongated and their thumbs are relatively short. The long fingers enable gibbons to form a hook with their hands while swinging from branch to branch. The thumb is short enough to prevent its getting in the way while swinging but still long enough to allow manipulation.

brachiation A method of movement that uses the arms to swing from branch to branch.

FIGURE 9.19

Gibbons brachiating. Gibbons are the most acrobatic of the apes and can swing by their arms easily. (© Gerard Lacz/ Animals Animals)

On the ground, gibbons walk on two legs, though their arms are so long they look awkward to us. These long arms they use for balance. Gibbons also walk on two legs when they move along a branch, often using their arms to grab onto overhead branches for support.

Gibbons show almost no sexual dimorphism in body size. Males and females are the same body size, and both have large canine teeth, with male canines slightly larger on average than females.

Distribution and Environment   Gibbons are found in the tropical rain forests of Southeast Asia, specifically Thailand, Vietnam, Burma, and the Malay Peninsula. The rain forest environment is characterized by heavy rainfall that is relatively constant throughout the year. Rain forests have incredibly rich and diverse vegetation. The gibbons' diet consists primarily of fruits supplemented by leaves.

Social Structure   Gibbons have long been characterized as having a monogamous family structure—an adult male, an adult female, and their offspring—where the adult male and female form a mating pair for long periods. Fuentes (2000) suggests that this is not always the case, and gibbon groups do not necessarily always form nuclear family units. Instead, he argues that gibbons (like most other primates) originally had a multimale/multifemale social structure but now have a more variable system. Often, the small social groups result in a typical family structure, but not always. Once again, continued research has shown us the variable nature of primate social behavior.

Gibbons actively defend territories. They do this by making loud vocalizations and putting on aggressive displays to warn off other groups. When groups come into contact in overlapping areas, the males often fight to drive the other group away. Females often aid in these fights.

Though it may be interesting to speculate on the nature of gibbon aggression and territorial behavior as it relates to primate behavior, in reality territorial behavior is rather rare among primates, including the hominoids. Territorial behavior is most often a function of the environment. In tropical rain forests, food is abundant and spread throughout the region. Because food resources are not clumped together, neither are the animal populations. Food is spread out over a large area, so family groups come into frequent contact with one another, necessitating territorial boundaries to establish group boundaries (Denham 1971). In environments where food resources are clustered, social groups tend to cluster as well and are spaced apart from one another at the outset.

Orangutans

The orangutan is a large ape found only in certain areas of Southeast Asia. The word *orangutan* translates from Malay as "man of the forest."

Physical Characteristics   One of the orangutan's most obvious physical features is its reddish brown hair (Figure 9.20). Males are roughly twice the size of females; an average adult male weighs between 80 and 90 kg (roughly 175–200 lb), and an average adult female weighs between 33 and 45 kg (roughly 73–99 lb) (Markham and Groves 1990). Males also have large pads of fat on their faces. The high degree of sexual dimorphism in orangutans has often been thought surprising because this trait occurs most often in terrestrial species. More recent evidence, however, suggests that orangutans spend more time on the ground than we had once thought. The orangutan is responsible, with the gorilla and chimpanzee, for many reports by early explorers of "wild men," "monsters," and "subhumans."

Orangutans are agile climbers and hangers. In the trees, they use both arms and legs to climb in a slow, cautious manner. They will use one or more limbs to anchor themselves to branches while using the other limbs to feed (Figure 9.21). Younger orangutans occasionally brachiate, but the larger adults generally move through the trees in a different manner. A large orangutan will not swing from one tree to the next; rather, it will rock the tree it is on slowly in the direction of the next tree and then move over when the two trees are close together. The orangutan's great agility in climbing is due, in part, to its basic hominoid shoulder structure.

Orangutans are largely arboreal. Males, however, frequently come to the ground and travel along the forest floor for long distances. On the ground, orangutans walk on all fours but with their fists partially closed. Unlike monkeys, who rest their weight on their palms, orangutans rest on their fists: a form of movement often called fist walking.

Recent data suggest that orangutans produce offspring more slowly than the other great apes (Galdikas and Wood 1990). The average birth interval (the time between successive births) for orangutans is 7.7 years, compared to birth intervals of 3.8 years for gorillas and 5.6 years for chimpanzees.

FIGURE 9.20

Mother and infant orangutans.
(© Zoological Society of San Diego)

FIGURE 9.21

A young orangutan foraging.
(© Mickey Gibson/Animals Animals)

In some ways, orangutans are very similar to humans. Schwartz (1987) has drawn attention to a number of dental and skeletal traits humans and orangutans share that are not found in the African apes. Humans and orangutans also share certain aspects of their reproductive physiology. For example, both humans and orangutans have the same gestation length (270 days), which is longer than that of the African apes. Also, neither humans nor orangutans have a distinct mating cycle. Most primates have a definite time during the month (**estrus**) when the female is in "heat"—that is, sexually responsive. Neither humans nor orangutans have an estrus cycle. Orangutans are also genetically very similar to humans; the DNA of humans and orangutans differs by slightly more than 2 percent.

Distribution and Environment The orangutan is found today only in Sumatra and Borneo in Southeast Asia. Orangutans are vegetarians, with more than 60 percent of their diet consisting of fruit (Jolly 1985). As does the gibbon, the orangutan lives in tropical rain forests.

The natural range of the orangutan was probably greater in the past, judging from the fact that fossil apes similar to orangutans have been found in Asia dating from 12 million years ago (see Chapter 11). Some of the reduced distribution is the result of climatic change in the past. The limited range of orangutans—and of the other apes—today is also due in part to human intervention. As its natural habitats continue to be destroyed, the orangutan is an endangered species and faces extinction.

Social Structure Orangutans have the solitary social group structure, consisting of a mother and infant. Males are not needed for protection because there is little danger from predators (Horr 1972). Adult males generally live by themselves, interacting only during times of mating. Orangutans are polygamous; they do not form long-term bonds with any one partner. The small group size of orangutans appears to be related to the nature of the environment; when food resources are widely scattered, there is not enough food in any one place for large groups (Denham 1971).

Gorillas

Gorillas, the largest living primates, are found only in equatorial Africa.

Physical Characteristics An adult male gorilla weighs 160 kg (roughly 350 lb) on average. Adult females weigh less but are still very large for primates (70 kg/155 lb) (Leutenegger 1982). Besides a much larger body size, the adult males also have larger canine teeth and often large crests of bone on top of their skulls for anchoring their large jaw muscles. Gorillas usually have blackish hair; fully mature adult males have silvery gray hair on their backs. These adult males are called "silverbacks."

Their large size makes gorillas predominantly terrestrial. Their typical means of movement is called **knuckle walking:** they move about on all fours, resting their weight on the knuckles of their front limbs. This form of

estrus A time during the month when females are sexually receptive.

knuckle walking A form of movement used by chimpanzees and gorillas that is characterized by all four limbs touching the ground, with the weight of the arms resting on the knuckles of the hands.

FIGURE 9.22

An adult male gorilla knuckle walking. Note the angle of the spine relative to the ground because of the longer front limbs. (© Zoological Society of San Diego)

movement is different from the fist walking of orangutans. Gorilla hands have well-developed muscles and strengthened joints to handle the stress of resting on their knuckles. Because their arms are longer than their legs, gorilla spines are at an angle to the ground (Figure 9.22). In contrast, the spine of a typical quadrupedal animal, such as a monkey, is roughly parallel to the ground when walking.

Distribution and Environment   Gorillas are only found in three forested areas in Africa. Their range is disappearing rapidly, primarily as the result of replacement of forests by human farmland and human poaching (Fossey 1983). Three recognized subspecies of gorilla live in different regions in western Africa: the western lowland gorilla, the eastern lowland gorilla, and the mountain gorilla.

Many myths have circulated regarding the gorilla's lust for human and nonhuman flesh, but the truth of the matter is that gorillas eat a diet almost entirely made up of leaves and fruit. Diet varies by location; the lowland gorillas eat more fruit than the mountain gorillas. Differences in diet may affect social organization in the different gorilla subspecies, but it is not yet clear exactly how (Doran and McNeilage 1998).

Social Structure   Gorillas live in small social groups of about a dozen individuals. The social group consists of an adult male (the silverback), several adult females, and their immature offspring (Figure 9.23). Occasionally, one or more younger adult males are part of the group, but they tend not to mate with the females. Though dominance rank varies among the females and subadult males, the adult silverback male is the most dominant individual in the group and is the leader. The silverback sets the pace for the rest of the group, determining when and how far to move in search of food.

FIGURE 9.23

A gorilla social group.
(© Michael K. Nichols/Magnum Photos, Inc.)

A typical day for a gorilla group consists of eating and resting. Given their large body size and the limited nutritional value of leaves, it is not wonder that gorillas spend most of their day eating. Because of their size, gorillas have few problems with predators (except for humans with weapons). The life of a gorilla is for the most part peaceful, a dramatic contrast to their stereotypical image as aggressive, evil creatures.

Because gorillas are rather peaceful and slow-moving, we have a tendency to think they are "slow" in a mental sense as well. This is another myth of gorilla behavior. Laboratory and field studies of gorillas have shown them to be extremely intelligent creatures. As discussed later, they have even learned sign language.

Chimpanzees

The chimpanzee is perhaps the best known of all of the nonhuman primates. Most of our experience with chimpanzees, however, is with captive or trained animals. We like to watch chimpanzees perform "just like humans" and delight in a chimpanzee's smile (which actually signals tension, not pleasure).

From a scientific perspective, chimpanzees are equally fascinating. Genetic studies during the past 20 years have shown that humans and chimpanzees

SPECIAL TOPIC

Social Structure and Testes Size in Primates

Bizarre as it may sound at first, scientists have collected information on the size of the testes, the male reproductive organ that produces sperm, in different primate species and have made some interesting observations. For example, the size of the testes ranges from roughly 1.2 grams (0.04 oz) in one New World monkey species to 119 grams (over 4 oz, or 1/4 lb) in chimpanzees. However, not all hominoids have such large testes. The average testes size is roughly 30 grams (1 oz) in gorillas, 35 grams (1.25 oz) in orangutans, and 41 grams (1.4 oz) in humans.

A quick look at the testes size of all primate species for which we have data shows that part of the reason for so much variation is differences in body size. In general, the larger the body, the larger the testes. The graph shows the overall relationship between average body size and average testes size for 33 primate species, including prosimians, monkeys, apes, and humans. For technical reasons, we plot the logarithms of both body weight and testes weight. The straight line shows the best fit between the logarithm of body weight and the logarithm of testes weight and clearly shows that the larger the body, the larger the testes. (The relationship is actually curved somewhat, which is why we use logarithms. This means that the increase is not linear.)

Nevertheless, when we look at the actual data points on the curve, we can see that, although there is an average relationship between body weight and testes weight, it is not perfect. Some species are above the line, meaning they have larger testes than expected, and some species are below the line, meaning they have smaller testes than expected. For example, humans have testes that are about two-thirds the size expected on the basis of our body weight. Chimpanzees, however, have testes that are 2.5 times that expected! Both orangutans and gorillas have smaller testes than expected on the basis of body weight.

Are these deviations random, or do they reflect that some factor other than body weight may be responsible for testes size? Harcourt and colleagues (1981) investigated this question and came to the conclusion that an important factor was the type of social structure associated with each primate species. The graph shows their results. Species that have a single male (either family structure or uni-male structure) are indicated by the filled-in squares. There is a definite tendency for those species to fall below the predicted line—that is, to have smaller testes than expected. Species with a multimale social structure, indi-

cated by filled-in circles, tend to fall above the predicted line, showing that they have larger testes than expected. The bottom line is that once we control for body size, males in multimale societies have larger testes.

What is the reason for differences according to social structure? Harcourt and colleagues suggest that larger testes are needed in primate societies where mating is frequent and where many males mate with a female during estrus. Chimpanzees are a good example of this. They suggest that natural selection favored males with larger testes, and hence a greater amount of sperm, so they could compete genetically with other males. In primate societies with less frequent mating and where females generally mate with only one male, larger testes would not be selected for. Examples here include orangutans and gorillas.

Of course, testes size is not only a function of body size and social structure. Harcourt and colleagues note other potential influences, such as seasonality of mating. However, the strong relationship observed in their study suggests that there is often a link between biology and behavior that is best interpreted in an evolutionary context.

Source of data: Harcourt et al. (1981)

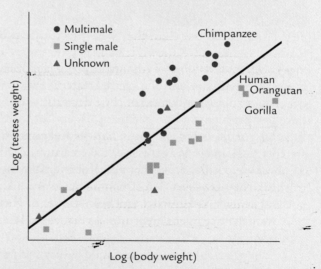

Relationship between body weight (logarithm) and testes weight (logarithm) in 33 primate species. The solid line is the predicted relationship between body weight and testes weight. Individual points correspond to the different species. Species with a uni-male society in breeding are indicated by a filled-in square. Species with multimale societies are indicated by a filled-in circle. Species with an unknown social structure are indicated by a filled-in diamond.

FIGURE 9.24

Variation in chimpanzee faces.
(© Mike Birkhead/Oxford Scientific Films/Animals Animals)

are even more similar than they were previously thought to be. Laboratory and field studies have shown that chimpanzees are capable of behaviors we once thought of as unique to humans, such as toolmaking and language acquisition. Any examination of the human condition must take these remarkable creatures' accomplishments into account.

Physical Characteristics   Chimpanzees are found in Africa. They are smaller than gorillas and show only slight sexual dimorphism. Adult males weigh about 45 kg (99 lb) on average and adult females weigh about 37 kg (82 lb) on average (Leutenegger 1982). Chimpanzees have extremely powerful shoulders and arms. Like humans, chimpanzees show great variation in facial features and overall physical appearance (Figure 9.24).

Chimpanzees, like gorillas, are knuckle walkers, with longer arms than legs. Chimpanzees, however, are more active and agile than gorillas. Chimpanzees are both terrestrial and arboreal. They spend considerable time in the trees, either sleeping or looking for food. They often hang by their arms in the trees. On the ground, they sometimes stand on two legs to carry food or sticks.

Distribution and Environment   Most chimpanzees are found in the African rain forests, although some groups are also found in the mixed forest–savanna environments on the fringe of the rain forests. The chimpanzee diet

FIGURE 9.25

Mother and infant chimpanzees. (© Richard Wrangham/Anthro-Photo)

consists mainly of fruit (almost 70 percent), although they also eat leaves, seeds, nuts, insects, and meat. Chimpanzees have been observed hunting small animals, such as monkeys, and sharing the meat. Though some of the hunting occurs spontaneously when chimpanzees encounter small animals, other hunting behavior appears to be planned and coordinated.

Social Structure   Chimpanzees live in large communities of 50 or more individuals. Their social structure constantly changes, with individuals and groups fragmenting and later rejoining the main group. All chimpanzees recognize and interact with others in the group. Chimpanzee groups are less rigid than other multimale primate societies, such as baboons. Although all members of the group do interact to some extent, it is common for smaller subgroups to form much of the time. The actual composition of these subgroups also changes frequently.

Most social behaviors revolve around the bond between mother and infant (Figure 9.25). Chimpanzees tend to associate with their mothers and other siblings throughout their lives, even after they are fully grown. As with other primates, young females watch and observe their own mothers taking care of children and learn mothering behaviors. There is no close bond between adult males and infants except for associations through the mother. Overall, chimpanzee society can be seen as a collection of smaller groups, defined in terms of mothers and siblings, forming a larger community. Other associations are also common, such as temporary all-male groups. Some chimpanzees are even solitary for periods of time.

Adult males are generally dominant over adult females, although there is much more overlap than found in baboon societies. Some females, for example, are dominant over the lower-ranking males. As with other primates, dominance is influenced by a variety of factors such as size, strength, and the ability to form alliances. Individual intelligence also appears to affect dominance, as was revealed in Jane Goodall's study of the chimpanzees in the Gombe Stream National Park near Lake Tanganyika. In 1964, the community studied by Goodall had 14 adult males. The lowest-ranking male (Mike) replaced the most dominant male (Goliath) after inventing a particularly innovative display of dominance. There were a number of empty kerosene cans lying around Goodall's camp that the chimpanzees generally ignored. Mike would charge other males while hitting the cans in front of him, creating an unusual and very noisy display. This behavior was so intimidating to other males that Mike rose from the lowest to the highest rank at once (Goodall 1986). This study shows not only the changing nature of dominance hierarchy but also the role of individual intelligence and initiative; all the males had access to the cans, but only Mike used them.

Although adult males are generally dominant over adult females, dominance rank among the females also has an influence on the group. Because female dominance is less noticeable, some have suggested that it is of little importance. However, Anne Pusey, Jennifer Williams, and Jane Goodall (1997) found that female dominance rank correlated with reproductive success. Using data from 35 years of observation, they found that the higher-ranking adult female chimpanzees tended to have more offspring. In addition, they found that infants born to the higher-ranking females also tended to have higher rates of survival through infancy.

Studies of the Gombe Stream chimpanzee community have also revealed a number of other interesting features of chimpanzee social behaviors and intelligence. The chimpanzees have been observed making and using tools (discussed at length in Chapter 10), hunting in cooperative groups, and sometimes engaging in widespread aggression against other groups. We examine some of these findings when we consider what behaviors may be considered uniquely human.

Bonobos

The bonobo is the third and least well known of the African apes. The bonobo is closely related to the chimpanzee and is commonly considered a separate species of chimpanzee known as the "pygmy chimpanzee" (compared to what is often termed the "common chimpanzee"). The close similarity of chimpanzees and bonobos is reflected in their assignment to the same genus—*Pan* (the scientific names are *Pan troglodytes* for the chimpanzee and *Pan paniscus* for the bonobo).

Physical Characteristics   At first glance, bonobos seem quite similar to chimpanzees (Figure 9.26). On closer examination, however, we see that the bonobo has relatively longer legs, a higher center of gravity, and a narrower chest. It tends to have a higher forehead and differently shaped face (Savage-Rumbaugh and Lewin 1994). Like gorillas and chimpanzees, bonobos are frequent knuckle walkers. Of particular interest is the fact that bonobos can

FIGURE 9.26

A bonobo mother and infant.
(© Zoological Society of San Diego)

walk upright more easily than other apes (Figure 9.27). This observation, combined with other evidence, suggests that the first hominids may have been quite similar in many ways to bonobos. There is some sexual dimorphism—adult males average 43 kg (95 lb) compared to adult females, which average 33 kg (73 lb) (de Waal 1995).

Distribution and Environment Bonobos are found only in a restricted rain forest region in Zaire in central Africa. It is estimated that there are fewer than 10,000 bonobos alive today. Their diet consists primarily of fruit, supplemented with plants. Unlike chimpanzees, bonobos consume little animal protein and do not hunt monkeys (de Waal 1995).

Social Structure As with chimpanzees, bonobos live in multimale/multi-female groups. However, there are important differences in the social organization of these two species. In chimpanzee society, males are dominant over females, and some of the strongest bonds in the social order are between

FIGURE 9.27

*A bonobo. (© Frans
Lanting/Minden Pictures)*

adult males. In bonobo society, things are quite different. Here the strongest social bonds are between adult females (White 1996), and even though they are physically smaller, it is the females who are most dominant. In addition, the dominance status of a male depends in large part on the dominance of his mother (de Waal 1995).

Some of the most interesting observations of bonobo behavior have to do with the function of sexual activity in their social interactions. In addition to sexual intercourse, bonobos also engage in a variety of sex play, including rubbing of genitals and oral sex. Continued observation of bonobo groups has revealed that such sex play is frequently used to reduce tension and avoid conflict. Researchers have shown repeatedly that bonobos will engage in a brief period of sex play in a tense social situation. In bonobo society, sexual play is a method of peacemaking (de Waal 1995).

SUMMARY

There is a great deal of biological and behavioral variation among the living primates. The order Primates is composed of the more biologically primitive prosimians and the anthropoids, which consist of monkeys (New World and Old World), apes, and humans. Monkeys are quadrupedal (four-footed) and have a tail. Although New World monkeys are exclusively arboreal, some species of Old World monkeys are arboreal and others are terrestrial.

The hominoids (apes and humans) are a group of anthropoids that share certain characteristics, such as the lack of a tail, similar dental features, larger brains, and a shoulder complex suitable for climbing and hanging. Hominoids consist of the "lesser apes" (gibbons) and the "great apes." The great apes consist of an Asian species (orangutan) and three African species (gorilla, chimpanzee, bonobo). The African apes are the most similar to humans, although it is not clear which of these three is the *most* similar.

The living apes show a great deal of environmental and anatomical variation. Some are arm swingers (gibbon), others are knuckle walkers (gorilla, chimpanzee, bonobo), and one is primarily a climber (orangutan). Although the great apes are all similar genetically and have a fairly recent common ancestor (roughly 20 million years ago), they show a great deal of social variation.

SUPPLEMENTAL READINGS

In addition to the primate texts listed in Chapter 8, some other useful sources include:
Ciochon, R. L., and R. A. Nisbett, eds. 1998. *The Primate Anthology: Essays on Primate Behavior, Ecology, and Conservation from Natural History*. A collection of 33 short articles on primate behavior that originally appeared in the magazine *Natural History*.
Fossey, D. 1983. *Gorillas in the Mist*. Boston: Houghton Mifflin. A popular and well-written account of the late Dian Fossey's researches on the behavior of the mountain gorilla. Deals specifically with the problem of human intervention and the likely extinction of the mountain gorilla.
Goodall, J. 1986. *The Chimpanzees of Gombe: Patterns of Behavior*. Cambridge, Mass.: Harvard University Press. A comprehensive review of Jane Goodall's research since the early 1960s, this is a well-written and superbly illustrated description of chimpanzee behavior.

INTERNET RESOURCES

The Web pages listed in Chapter 8 provide many links to information on specific primate species and should be consulted. In addition, here are some other useful links.

http://anthro.palomar.edu/primate
The Primates, a general tutorial that provides information on prosimians, New World monkeys, Old World monkeys, and apes.

http://anthro.palomar.edu/behavior/default.htm
Primate Behavior, a general tutorial on selected aspects of comparative primate behavior.

http://www.janegoodall.org
The Jane Goodall Institute, a comprehensive site containing much information on chimpanzees.

CHAPTER 10

June 3   pg 280-285

The Human Species

What are humans? This question has been a focus of science, art, and literature. Many different fields, from theology to psychology, have addressed its ultimate significance. Our perspective on ourselves is not abstract; the way we define what we are affects the way we treat others and the rest of the world.

One of the earliest written definitions of humanity is found in Psalm 8:4–6 of the Bible, where the question is put to God:

> What is man, that thou art mindful of him? and the son of man, that thou visitest him? For thou hath made him a little lower than the angels, and hast crowned him with glory and honor. Thou hast madest him to have dominion over the works of thy hands; thou hast put all things under his feet.

This brief statement reflects a long-standing belief of Western civilization that humans are inherently superior to all other life forms on the planet, ranking far above animals yet "lower than the angels." The view that humans are the supreme creatures in the natural world is also apparent in the works of many Greek philosophers. Aristotle, for example, constructed an arrangement of all things with inanimate matter at the "bottom" and humans at the "top" (Kennedy 1976).

What is the scientific definition of humans? Many sciences attempt to answer this question—zoology, biochemistry, and even computer science among them. In addition, a wide range of disciplines, such as history, geography,

◀ *Koko the gorilla using sign language to communicate. Koko herself created 10 percent of her 800-word vocabulary. The ability of apes to learn sign language is one of several findings during the late twentieth century that caused us to reassess our own place in nature. To what extent are humans unique? (Photo by Dr. Ron Cohn. Courtesy of The Gorilla Foundation, PO Box 620530, Woodside, CA 94062. http://koko.org)*

economics, political science, sociology, psychology, and anthropology, deal almost exclusively with human beings and their behaviors. From a scientific standpoint, we are interested in a definition of humans that incorporates differences and similarities with other living creatures. This is not always as simple as it sounds. For example, are humans the same as fish? Of course not, but can you explain why? Suppose you answer that humans walk on two legs. Certainly that definition separates fish and humans, but it does not separate humans and kangaroos, which also move about on two legs (albeit quite differently).

This chapter examines modern humans from the same perspective as the previous two chapters, focusing on the biological and behavioral uniqueness assigned to human beings. The final part of this chapter examines the question of how unique we are by comparing certain human behaviors (tool use, culture, language) with similar behaviors seen in some living apes.

CHARACTERISTICS OF LIVING HUMANS

This section focuses on certain key features of modern humans, particularly our brains, upright walking, teeth, reproductive patterns, physical growth, and social structure.

Distribution and Environment

Humans are the most widely distributed living primate species. As later chapters will outline, humans originally evolved in a tropical environment. In fact, much of our present-day biology reflects the fact that we are tropical mammals. During the course of human evolution, however, we have expanded into many different environments. Biological adaptations have aided humans in new environments, such as cold weather and high altitude. The cultural adaptations of humans have allowed even greater expansion. Today there is no place on the planet where we cannot live, given the appropriate technology. Humans can live in the frozen wastes of Antarctica, deep beneath the sea, and in the vacuum of outer space. Our cultural adaptations have enabled us to range far beyond our biological limitations. These adaptations have also permitted incredible population growth. In the past, the planet supported no more than a few million people at a hunting-and-gathering level of existence (Weiss 1984). Today the population of the world is more than 6 billion and continuing to grow. It is easily argued that the quality of life is still low for much of the world's human population, but there is no doubting that our ability to learn and develop technology has led to immense potential for population expansion.

Brain Size and Structure

One very obvious biological characteristic of the human species is the large brain. Our bulging and rounded skulls and flat faces contrast with these fea-

TABLE 10.1 Brain Volume of Selected Living Primates (in Cubic Centimeters)

Primate Species	Range	Average
Macaque monkey		100
Baboon		200
White-handed gibbon	82–125	102
Siamang	100–152	124
Orangutan	276–540	404
Gorilla	340–752	495
Common chimpanzee	282–500	385
Modern human	900–2000	1345

Source: Averages for macaque and baboon from Campbell (1985:233). Hominoid data from Tobias (1971:34–40), where the averages were taken as the means of males and females.

tures in other animals, including the rest of the hominoids. Whereas an ape's skull is characterized by a relatively small brain and large face, modern humans have relatively large brains and small faces.

Table 10.1 lists the brain size (in cubic centimeters) for a number of primate species. There is a clear relationship between taxonomic status and brain size: monkeys have the smallest brains, followed by the lesser apes, great apes, and humans. Absolute brain size is not as useful a measure of intellectual ability because larger animals tend to have larger brains. Elephants and whales, for example, have brains that are four to five times the size of the average human brain.

An alternative way of looking at brain size is to express the weight of the brain as a ratio of body weight. The larger this ratio, the larger the brain is relative to body size. For humans, this ratio is 1/49 = 0.020. However, this ratio is not very useful: many other primates have larger ratios, but we tend not to think of them as more intelligent (for example, the ratio for the squirrel monkey is 1/31 = 0.032) (Passingham 1982).

Among mammals, however, the relationship of brain and body weight is not linear. That is, as the body size increases, the brain size increases—but not at the same rate. Differences in relative size because of disparate growth rates among various parts of the body (known as **allometry**) are common. Parts of the body grow at different rates. Brain size increases at a nonlinear rate with body size. For example, consider two species of primates in which one species is twice the body weight of the other. If the ratio of brain size to body size were linear, we would expect the brain size of the species with the larger body size to be twice that of the smaller species. Actually, the brain size of the larger-bodied species is on average only 1.6 times as large. Because of this relationship, larger species appear to have smaller brain/body size ratios.

This allometric relationship between brain size and body size is quite regular among almost all primates. The most notable exception is humans. We have brains that are three times the size we would expect for a primate of

allometry The study of the change in proportion of various body parts as a consequence of different growth rates.

FIGURE 10.1

Relationship between body weight and brain weight in primates. The line indicates the average relationship among various primate species excluding humans. The two dots show expected and observed brain weight for humans. Our brains are three times the weight expected if we followed the typical primate curve.
(Source: Harvey et al. 1987)

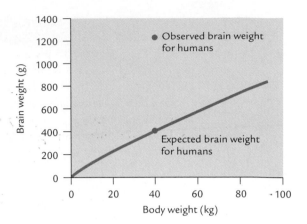

our body size (Figure 10.1). In addition, our brains have proportionately more cerebral cortex than other primate brains. The cerebral cortex is the part of the brain involved in forming complex associations.

These comparisons are across different species. Humans are presumably smarter than other primates because we have a much larger than expected brain size relative to our body. Does this relationship, however, apply to variation *within* our species? That is, do differences in relative brain size among living humans translate to differences in intelligence (at least as assessed using standard IQ tests)?

Most texts state there is no relationship between relative brain size and intelligence within the human species, although only a few studies are without methodological flaws. It is problematic, however, whether the fossil record of human evolution shows an increase in absolute and relative brain size that corresponds to an increase in mental abilities. Could there be a relationship between relative brain size and intelligence between species, but not within species? A study by Willerman and colleagues (1991) helps resolve some of the conflict. They measured the brain size of 40 adults using magnetic resonance imaging (MRI) and compared these values, adjusted for body size, with IQ test scores. Adjusting their results to the general population, they found a correlation of 0.35 between relative brain size and IQ scores (a positive correlation can take on a value from 0 to 1; the higher the value, the closer the correspondence). Several other studies have shown similar results, with an average correlation between relative brain size and IQ of roughly 0.4. In statistical terms, this means that roughly 16 percent of the observed variation in IQ is related to variation in relative brain size. (Without getting into the technical details, this number is derived by squaring the correlation coefficient and multiplying by 100—consult most any introductory statistics book for an explanation.)

If 16 percent of the observed variation in IQ is related to brain size, then 84 percent of the observed variation in IQ is *not* related to brain size. Further, there is now evidence showing that the 16 percent figure is an overestimate of the actual relationship between brain size and IQ. P. Thomas Schoenemann and colleagues (2000) note that the MRI studies are potentially confounded by environmental differences between families. That is, the correlation between brain size and IQ might be affected by environmental factors that vary from one family to the next. To get around this difficulty, they analyzed correlations *within* families and found that the correlation between general IQ and brain size is close to zero. They acknowledge the possibility that correlations between brain size and cognitive tests could be very small and still have an evolutionary impact over long periods of time. But these correlations cannot be used to make any predictions regarding IQ in living humans. That is, differences in brain size between people today are not related to differences in IQ scores.

Studies have also looked at the relationship among brain size, body size, and metabolism. Larger mammals have larger brain sizes and produce greater amounts of metabolic energy. Mammals show a great deal of variation, however, in the amount of energy used by the brain. The brains of many mammals, such as dogs and cats, use from 4 percent to 6 percent of their body metabolism. Primate brains use a considerably greater proportion of energy; the Old World macaque uses 9 percent and modern humans use 20 percent (Armstrong 1983).

What does all this mean? The human brain is not merely large; it also has a different structure than in other primates, with the cortex being disproportionately larger. This difference in structure is also probably related to the higher proportion of metabolic energy used by the human brain. The bottom line is that brain size does not tell the whole story. Thus, the human brain is not only larger than the brain of a chimpanzee; it is also structurally different. The increased convolution of the human cerebral cortex (the folding of brain tissue) means that the brain of a human child with the same volume of that of a chimpanzee has more cerebral cortex.

Discussion of brain size and its relationship to intellectual prowess has historically been part of debates about relative differences in the mental abilities of male and female humans. When *absolute* brain size is used to assess these differences, male brains tend on *average* to be larger. This finding has been used in the past to support ill-conceived beliefs in the mental superiority of males. However, as pointed out by Gould (1981), researchers did not take into account the fact that body size is on average larger in human males and that absolute brain size is closely related to body size. That is, men often have larger brains because they tend to be larger overall. This fact, combined with an understanding of some of the methodological problems of earlier studies, has led Gould to conclude there is no gender difference in relative brain size or overall intellectual ability.

Certain studies, however, do indicate that average gender differences may influence *specific* mental abilities. Falk (1992) has reviewed evidence that females tend on average to score higher on tests of verbal ability and males to score higher on tests of spatial and mathematical abilities. Falk suggests that these findings may be due to gender differences in patterns of brain lateralization. Of course, these tests and measures must be replicated cross-culturally to ensure that various forms of bias are not responsible for such observed differences (such as the fact that females in many cultures are actively discouraged from mathematics). Also, we must never forget that these results focus on *average* test scores and not on total distribution. Both male and female test score distributions overlap each other. For example, some males score higher in verbal skills than some females. As with many comparisons of biology and behavior between the sexes, we do not find exclusively separate distributions, but instead a great deal of overlap.

Bipedalism

Another striking difference between humans and apes is the fact that humans walk on two legs. We are **bipedal** (meaning "two legs"). This does not mean that apes cannot walk on two legs. They can, but not as well and not as often. The physical structure of human beings shows adaptations for upright walking as the normal mode of movement.

Humans are not the only animal that is routinely bipedal. The kangaroo also moves about on two legs but in a totally different manner from humans. Consider walking in slow motion. What happens? First, you stand balanced on two legs. Then you move one leg forward. You shift your body weight so that your weight is transferred to the moving leg. As that leg touches the ground on its heel, all of your body weight has been shifted. Your other leg is then free to swing forward. As it does so, you push off with your other foot.

Human walking is more graceful than a slow-motion description sounds. The act of walking consists of alternating legs from swinging free to standing still. We balance on one leg while the other leg moves forward to continue our striding motion. We tend to take these acts for granted, but they are actually quite complicated, requiring both balance and coordination. For example, when you pick up one leg to move it forward, what keeps your body from falling over?

Human bipedalism is made possible by anatomical changes involving the toes, legs, spine, pelvis, and muscles. In terms of actual anatomy, these changes are not major: after all, no bones are added or deleted; the same bones can be found in humans and in apes. The changes involve shape, positioning, and function. The net effect of these changes, however, is dramatic. Humans can move about effectively on two legs, allowing the other limbs to be free for other activities.

The feet of human beings reflect adaptation to bipedalism. The feet of a human and a chimp are shown in Figure 10.2. The big toe of the chimp sticks out in the same way that the thumb of all hominoids sticks out from the other fingers. The divergent big toe allows chimps to grasp with their feet. The big toe of the human is tucked in next to the other toes. When we walk, we use the nondivergent big toe to push off during our strides.

Our balance while we stand and walk is partly the result of changes in our legs. Figure 10.3 shows a human skeleton from the frontal view. Note that the width of the body at the knees is less than the width of the body at the hips. Humans are literally "knock-kneed." Our upper leg bones (the femurs) slope inward from the hips. When we stand on one leg, the angle of

bipedal Moving about on two legs. Unlike the movement of other bipedal animals such as kangaroos, human bipedalism is further characterized by a striding motion.

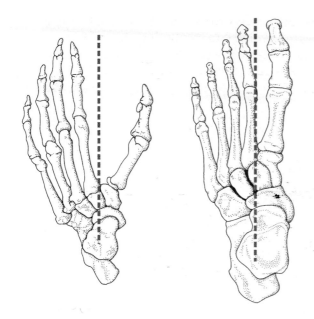

FIGURE 10.2

The skeletal structure of the feet of a chimpanzee (left) and a modern human (right). Note how the big toe of the human lies parallel to the other toes.

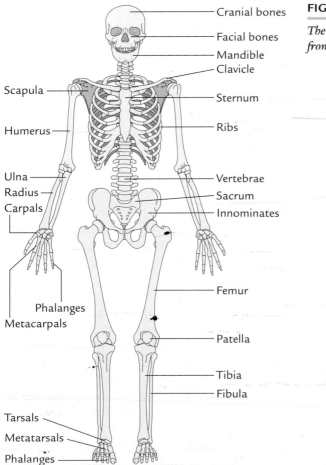

- Cranial bones
- Facial bones
- Mandible
- Clavicle
- Scapula
- Sternum
- Humerus
- Ribs
- Ulna
- Radius
- Carpals
- Vertebrae
- Sacrum
- Innominates
- Phalanges
- Metacarpals
- Femur
- Patella
- Tibia
- Fibula
- Tarsals
- Metatarsals
- Phalanges

FIGURE 10.3

The modern human skeleton from a frontal view.

FIGURE 10.4

Side view of the skeletons of a chimpanzee (left) and a modern human (right), illustrating the shape and orientation of the spine. (Adapted with permission from Bernard Campbell, Human Evolution, 3rd *ed., New York: Aldine de Gruyter, © 1985 Benard Campbell)*

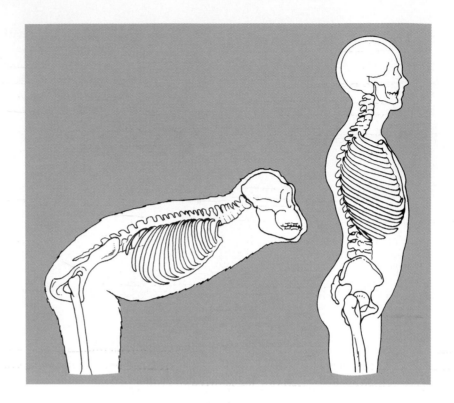

the femur transmits our weight directly underneath us. The result is that we continue to be balanced while one leg is moving. In contrast, the angle of an ape femur is very slight. The legs of an ape are almost parallel from hips to feet. When an ape stands on two legs and moves one of them, the ape is off balance and tends to fall toward one side (more so than humans, because we compensate more quickly). When an ape walks on two legs, it must shift its whole body weight over the supporting leg to stay on balance. This shifting explains the characteristic waddling when apes walk on two legs.

The human spine also allows balance when we walk upright (Figure 10.4). The spinal column of humans is vertical, allowing weight to be transmitted down through the center of the body. In knuckle-walking apes, the spine is bent in an arc so that when the apes stand on two legs, the center of gravity is shifted in front of the body. The ape is off balance and must compensate greatly to stay upright. What is difficult for apes is easy for humans. The human spine is vertical but not straight. It curves in several places, allowing it to absorb the shocks occurring while we walk.

The human pelvis is shaped differently from an ape pelvis (Figure 10.5). It is shorter top to bottom and wider side to side. The sides of the pelvis are broader and flair out more to the sides, providing changes in muscle attachment that permit striding bipedalism. The shortness of the human pelvis allows greater stability when we stand upright.

The changes in the human pelvis also involve changes in the positioning of various muscles. For example, certain leg muscles attach more on the sides of the pelvis. This change allows humans to maintain their balance while

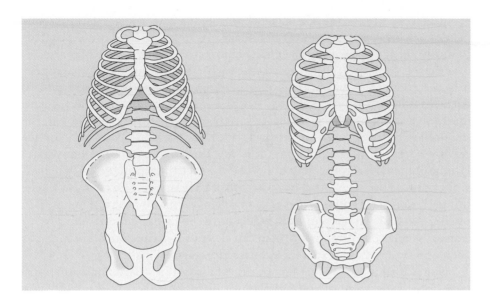

FIGURE 10.5

The trunk skeletons of a chimpanzee (left) and a modern human (right) drawn to the same size. Note the proportionately shorter and wider pelvis of the human being, reflecting adaptations to upright walking (see text). (Adapted with permission from Benard Campbell, Human Evolution, 3rd ed., New York: Aldine de Gruyter, © 1985 Benard Campbell)

standing without having to bend their knees. The gluteus minimus and gluteus medius muscles have also shifted position relative to apes, allowing the pelvis to remain stable when one leg is lifted during walking.

Canine Teeth

As we saw in Chapter 8, human canine teeth are different from canine teeth in many other mammals. Human canines are small and do not project beyond the level of the other teeth. Human canine teeth serve much the same function as the incisor teeth.

That we have small nonprojecting canines has led to much speculation concerning causes and effects of human evolution. Given that canine teeth serve as weapons in many primate species, the lack of large canine teeth in humans seems to imply that we do not need them for weapons anymore. One scenario is that when human ancestors began using tools, they no longer required large canines. As you will see in later chapters, the uniqueness of human canine teeth is a more complex topic than we once thought.

Sex and Reproduction

We humans consider ourselves the sexiest primates. That is, we are more concerned with sex than is any other primate. The fact that humans do not have the estrus cycle has often been cited as a unique aspect of human sexuality. For the most part, temperate-zone domestic animals breed only during certain seasons and mate around the time of ovulation. Human females, in contrast, cycle throughout the year and often mate at any time during the cycle. This distinction between humans and other primates may not be as clear as often suggested. Orangutans, for example, also lack an estrus cycle. Bonobos do have an estrus cycle but have been observed to mate outside of it to some extent.

Sexual positions

Much has been made of the fact that humans have sexual relations while facing each other (the so-called missionary position), whereas other primates typically engage in sex with the male behind the female. One explanation is that there is some social benefit to facing each other during sexual intercourse; it is said to increase emotional bonds between male and female. A problem with this suggestion is that most studies of human sexual behavior have found that humans engage in a wide variety of sexual positions. Though the missionary position has been cited as the most common sexual position for certain societies at certain times, it is not the most common everywhere. Human bipedal anatomy may influence the fact that humans use the missionary position, whereas other primates rarely use it. The changes in the human pelvis have shifted the position of the vagina so that the missionary position is easier to attain. Apes rarely have sex in this manner simply because it is not comfortable for them. An exception is the bonobo, which has been observed to have sexual intercourse face to face.

orgasm

Some authors claim that female orgasm is unique in human beings and have constructed a number of explanations for this fact. There is growing evidence, however, that nonhuman primate females also experience orgasm (de Waal 1995; Jolly 1985).

Breasts

Human females have relatively large breasts, whereas other primate females do not. One hypothesis is that large breasts developed to resemble buttocks. Given that face-to-face sex is desirable in reinforcing emotional bonds and that males prefer the buttocks (both questionable assumptions), large breasts would serve to attract human males to the female's front. Another suggestion is that large breasts in human females is a by-product of the evolution of fat in human females. Fat reserves are important for females in hunting-and-gathering societies because fat is stored energy that can be used for reproduction in times of food shortage. It has been hypothesized that hormonal changes accompanying increased fat reserves led to increased breast size in human females (Mascia-Lees et al. 1986). Pawlowski (1999) has also suggested that permanent breast enlargement in humans was a by-product of increased selection for subcutaneous fat but for a different reason. According to Pawlowski, increased amounts of subcutaneous fat served as insulation against the cool nights that occurred even in tropical Africa. This hypothesis views the increase in subcutaneous fat as a replacement for dense hair that has disappeared during the course of human evolution. Although reasonable, these hypotheses still need to be tested.

penis

Another unique feature of human sexual anatomy is the large relative size of the penis in males. Both penis and testes size varies among apes and humans, with chimpanzees having the largest testes of any hominoid species, as expected given their polygamous mating patterns (see Chapter 9). Humans have the longest erect penises of all hominoids (Diamond 1992b), but no satisfactory evolutionary reason has been proposed. Some have argued that the long penis serves some sort of display function when threatening other males or marks status, but there is no supporting evidence for this.

The human pattern of reproduction is basically the same as that of most primates: single births. Unlike apes, humans have additional infants before the previous offspring have grown up socially or physically. Because of cultural adaptations, humans have increased reproduction without sacrificing parental care. Compared to apes, a greater proportion of the human life cycle is taken up by physical and social growth prior to maturity. Consider, for example, that a chimpanzee is sexually mature at about 10 years and lives roughly 40 years (Jolly 1985). This means that approximately 25 percent of the chimp's life is spent growing up. Further consider that a human matures at about 15 years and that throughout most of history and prehistory, we estimate that humans had an average length of life of roughly 20 to 30 years. Compared to other primates, we mature more slowly and require a greater amount of our life for growing and learning. This logic may seem strange, because the average life expectancy at birth today in the United States is approximately 77 years, not 30. However, keep in mind that our relatively long life is neither universal nor very old. Most of the increase in our average length of life has come only in the past century or so (see Chapter 15).

Social Structure

Human social structure is a topic of almost infinite complexity. One observation is obvious—there is extensive variation. Because variation in social structure is great even among monkeys and apes, it should come as no surprise that humans also show considerable variation.

A common Western assumption is that the "normal" social structure of human beings is the nuclear monogamous family group: mother, father, and children. Actually, the majority of human societies studied have a stated preference for **polygyny**—a pattern in which one husband has several wives (Harris 1987)—and a few cultures practice **polyandry,** in which one woman has several husbands. Because of this, anthropologists have often argued that the basic human pattern is polygyny. However, it must be noted that although many societies state a *preference* for polygyny, it is still much more common for men to have a single wife. In many cases, only the most wealthy or powerful have multiple wives. Helen Fisher (1992) concludes that for all practical purposes monogamy is the predominant *marriage* pattern for humans (although with considerable infidelity in many societies). Clearly it is necessary to consider the difference between stated cultural ideals and actual practices.

Humans show a great deal of variation in other aspects of their culture as well, such as economic systems, political systems, and legal systems. The dramatic changes in such institutions in the past 12,000 years—since the origin of agriculture (see Chapter 14)—shows exactly how variable our species' behavior can be. During this time, humans developed state-level societies, social stratification, formal legal codes, and many other aspects of culture that we take for granted today. Biological needs, such as for food and sex, place some limits on our behavior. One such limitation is the need for a family of some sort to care for dependent children. All humans live in families, although the actual structure can vary considerably depending on circumstances and tradition, including nuclear families, extended families, monogamous and polygamous marriage, single-parent families, and same-sex families.

polygyny A form of marriage in which a husband has several wives.

polyandry A form of marriage in which a wife has several husbands.

THE HUMAN LIFE CYCLE

The major stages of growth and development are prenatal (before birth) and postnatal (after birth). The general nature of these two stages is reviewed briefly, followed by consideration of what is unique about human growth.

Prenatal Growth

Prenatal life is the period from fertilization through childbirth. After fertilization, the fertilized egg (**zygote**) develops into a cluster of identical cells deriving from the initial fertilized egg. During the first week, the fertilized egg multiplies as it travels into the uterus. By this time, there are roughly 150 cells arranged in a hollow ball that implants itself into the wall of the uterus. Cell differentiation begins. During the second week, the outer layer of this ball forms the beginning of the placenta. Some early differentiation of cells can be seen in the remainder of the ball.

The embryonic stage stretches from roughly two to eight weeks after conception. The **embryo** is very small during this time, reaching an average length of 25 mm (1 in.) by the eighth week. During this time, the basic body structure is completed and many of the different organ systems develop; the embryo has a recognizably human appearance, although it is still not complete (Figure 10.6). The fetal stage lasts from this point until birth. Development of body parts and organ systems continues, along with a tremendous amount of body growth and changes in proportions. During the second trimester of pregnancy, the **fetus** shows rapid growth in overall length. Dur-

zygote A fertilized egg.

embryo The stage of human prenatal life lasting from roughly two to eight weeks following conception; characterized by structural development.

fetus The stage of human prenatal growth from roughly eight weeks following conception until birth; characterized by further development and rapid growth.

FIGURE 10.6

A 2-month-old embryo. The fingers have developed and the eye is oval in shape. The total body length at this stage is 3.18 cm (1.25 in.). (© Lennart Nilsson/Albert Bonniers Förlag AB)

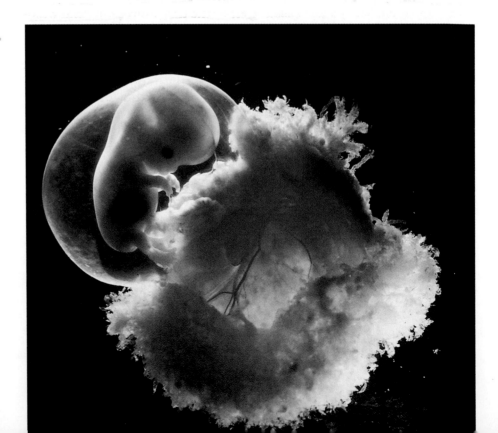

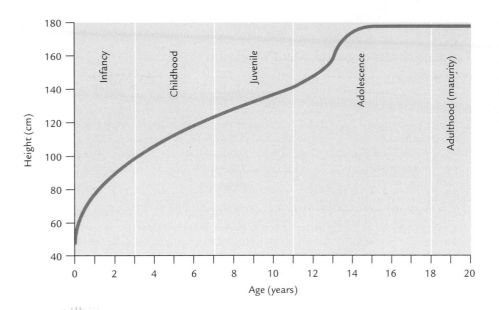

FIGURE 10.7

Typical distance curve for human height. (Adapted from Growth and Development *by Robert M. Malina, © 1975, publisher Burgess Publishing Company, Minneapolis, MN, modified as per Bogin 1995a)*

ing the third trimester, the fetus shows rapid growth in body weight, head size, and brain growth.

The Pattern of Human Postnatal Growth

We can identify five basic stages in growth from birth until adulthood (Bogin 1999, 2001). The first stage, *infancy,* refers to the time from birth until weaning (typically up to 3 years in nonindustrialized societies) and is characterized by rapid growth. The second stage, *childhood,* refers to the time from weaning until the end of growth in brain weight, which takes place at about 7 years (Cabana et al. 1993). The *juvenile* stage is from this point until the beginning of the fourth stage, *adolescence,* which is the time of sexual maturation and a spurt in body growth. Adolescence begins at about age 10 in females and age 12 in males, although there is considerable variation across people and populations. The fifth stage is labeled *adulthood.*

Human growth is usually studied by looking at growth curves. One type of growth curve, the **distance curve,** is a measure of size over time—it shows how big someone is at any given age. Figure 10.7 is a typical distance curve for human height. As we all know, until you reach adulthood, the older you get, the taller you get. However, note that this is not a straight line—you do not grow the same amount each year. This shows that the *rate* of body growth is not the same from year to year. Changes in the rate of growth are best illustrated by a **velocity curve,** which plots the *rate* of change over time. The difference between a distance curve and velocity curve can be illustrated by a simple analogy—driving a car. Imagine driving a car on a highway between two cities. How *far* you have come is your distance, and how *fast* you are going is your velocity.

distance curve A measure of size over time, for example, a person's height at different ages.

velocity curve A measure of the rates of change in growth over time.

Should Infants Sleep with Their Parents? An Evolutionary View

Examination of presumed unique characteristics of humans is complicated by the fact that we often attempt to draw species-wide conclusions based on the behaviors of one or more select groups. This becomes particularly problematic when making species-wide statements based on contemporary Western culture. This approach has two problems. First, it ignores cultural variation among the rest of our species, making it difficult at best to determine if the way we do things is actually characteristic of our species as opposed to being specific to our culture. Second, the world has changed considerably over the past century or so (see Chapter 15); what we find perfectly normal in today's world may not actually characterize the long-term patterns of our species. Failure to acknowledge variation across cultures and time can lead to inaccurate portrayals of humanity.

An example of this problem is how different groups deal with sleeping infants at night. A common pattern in Western cultures is to have infants sleep separately from their parents at night in their own cribs. This contrasts with the sleeping patterns of nonhuman primates, where mothers and infants sleep together. Is the nighttime separation of mothers and infants a unique human characteristic? If so, then one wonders why this behavior evolved in our species, given the importance of the mother–infant bond across the entire primate order.

If we examine human cross-cultural patterns in infant sleeping, it turns out that the Western pattern of separate sleeping is not typical. Some form of cosleeping, either in the same bed or in the same room, is characteristic of the majority of human cultures (Mosko et al. 1997). Separate sleeping is only a century or two old and is *not* characteristic of human behavior in general but is instead a recent change. During the 1960s, American parents were often encouraged to have infants sleep apart from them under the view that infant sleeping practices should accommodate the needs of the parent and not the child (Small 1992).

The reduction of parent–infant cosleeping appears to have some serious implications for the health of the infant. In addition to breaking from a basic primate pattern of close bonding, there is also suggestive evidence that infant sleeping patterns are related to the incidence of Sudden Infant Death Syndrome (SIDS), the leading cause of nonaccidental death in infants under 1 year of age in industrialized nations (McKenna 1996). SIDS (also known as crib death) occurs in otherwise healthy infants during sleep; many cases are related to ceasing to breathe.

By the mid-1990s it was realized that infant sleep patterns could have a dramatic effect on the frequency of SIDS. McKenna (1996) reports that the simple change in having infants sleep on their backs rather than on their stomachs could reduce SIDS rates by as much as 90 percent. McKenna and colleagues suggest that SIDS may also be related to the presence or absence of parent–infant cosleeping. When sleeping together, the breathing of the parent and infant affect one another; when the parent rouses during sleep, the infant tends to do the same. The interaction between parent and infant breathing may prevent situations where the infant is less likely to recover from a disruption of normal breathing, therefore decreasing the probability of SIDS. Observations of mothers and infants sleeping together suggest that sleeping together also minimizes the chances that an infant will lay on its stomach, thus also lowering the likelihood of SIDS. Close proximity of mother and infant also increases low-level exposure of carbon dioxide emitted from the mother, which in turn appears to stimulate infant respiration (Mosko et al. 1997). Another advantage of cosleeping is increased nocturnal breastfeeding, which has also been linked to a decrease in SIDS (McKenna 1996).

These studies show us that human behavior changes quickly, and what is normal or accepted for a given culture may not be characteristic of our entire species. Further, the proposed links between sleeping patterns and SIDS show that recent cultural changes, which may be adaptive from the point of view of parental comfort, may not be healthy for infants.

A typical velocity curve for human height is shown in Figure 10.8. The *rate* of growth is greatest immediately after birth, followed by a rapid deceleration during infancy. Even though the rate of growth decreases, we still continue to grow. Referring again to the car analogy, if you decelerate from 50 miles per hour to 30 miles per hour, you are still going forward, although

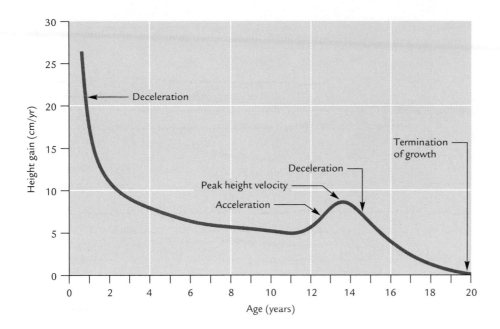

FIGURE 10.8

Typical velocity curve for human height. (Adapted from Growth and Development *by Robert M. Malina, © 1975, publisher Burgess Publishing Company, Minneapolis, MN)*

not as fast. During childhood and the juvenile stage, height velocity decreases slightly, but then it increases rapidly for a short time during adolescence. At adulthood, the rate of growth again decreases until there is no further significant growth.

Comparing distance and velocity curves for human body size with other organisms has revealed two basic differences: humans have an extended childhood and an adolescent period (Bogin 1995a, 2001). In most mammals, the rate of growth decreases from childbirth, and adulthood occurs without any intervening stages. In other mammals, there is a stage of juvenile growth. Only in humans, however, do we see childhood, adolescence, and a long post-reproductive period.

This discussion thus far has centered on body size. To understand the unique aspects of the human growth pattern, it is also necessary to look at changes in growth for other parts of the body, such as the head and brain tissue. Quite simply, not everything grows at the same rate. Figure 10.9 compares human distance curves for body size, brain size, and the reproductive system. All three are drawn to illustrate the percentage of total adult size attained at any given age. Note the differences in these curves—our brains and reproductive systems obviously do not grow at the same rate as our bodies. In particular, our brain grows most rapidly at first, reaching adult weight by roughly 7 years of age (Cabana et al. 1993). The reproductive system grows most slowly, showing hardly any growth until adolescence.

The Evolution of Human Growth

If you think about it for a moment, these differences in timing of growth make sense. Because humans are dependent on learning as a means of survival,

FIGURE 10.9

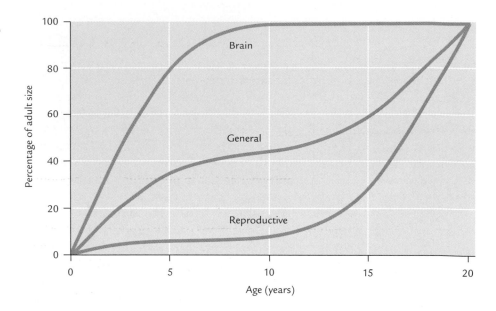

Distance curves for different body tissues, showing the percentage of total adult size reached at different ages. The general curve represents overall body size (height or weight). The brain curve represents brain weight. The reproductive curve represents the weight of sex organs and tissues. From Bogin (1995a), based on Scammon (1930) and updated to include new data on brain growth (Cabana et al. 1993). (Barry Bogin)

it makes sense to have as large a brain in place as soon as possible. The physical limits to the rate of brain growth while in the womb mean that the best time for extended brain growth to occur is during the first few years of life. Likewise, it makes sense to have sexual maturity postponed until later in life so that we have time to develop physically and socially enough to provide adequately for offspring.

The evolutionary advantage to delayed maturation and an extended childhood is clear—a longer childhood allows more time for brain development and learning. In addition, an extended childhood may offer other advantages, such as low-cost feeding, that increase the likelihood of survival (see Bogin 2001 for a more detailed discussion).

Why do humans have an adolescent growth spurt? Traditional explanations see it as a means of "catching up." If our childhood has been extended, then we have proportionately less time in our lives as reproductive adults. Rapid growth during adolescence allows us to reach sexual maturity and adult body size more quickly, thus allowing us to have our extended childhood and an adequate reproductive period. Without this growth spurt, we would reach adulthood later and possibly not have enough time to adequately care for offspring.

Barry Bogin (2001) has questioned this traditional explanation and suggests that an adolescent stage of growth offers advantages in terms of learning social skills before reproduction. Noting that males and females experience their growth spurt at different times relative to their sexual and social maturity, he concludes that "Girls best learn their adult social roles while they are infertile but perceived by adults as mature; whereas boys best learn their adult social roles while they are sexually mature but not yet perceived as such by adults" (p. 140). The evolution of human adolescence is thus seen as having both biological and social dimensions.

Menopause

Menopause is the permanent cessation of menstrual cycles that occurs before the aging of other body systems and before the end of the average life span. Other mammals show a decline in reproductive function with age, but this is not usually considered menopause because it occurs near the end of life or is associated with the decline in other body functions. As defined here, menopause has been found only in humans and in one species of toothed whales (Pavelka and Fedigan 1991; Peccei 2001). Menopause is universal among human societies and generally occurs at about 50 years of age in industrialized populations and somewhat earlier in nonindustrialized populations (Bogin and Smith 1996).

A continuing question concerns the origin of menopause in humans. Is it adaptive (that is, shaped by natural selection) or a by-product of other biological processes? Adaptive explanations generally focus on the presumed benefits of a mother living past her reproductive years. One model, known as the "mother hypothesis," suggests that rather than having additional children, it makes more sense for a woman to invest time and energy in her existing children for the remainder of her life, thus increasing their probability of survival. After a certain point in life, the odds are against a mother living long enough to raise her children. One variant of this model extends the adaptive benefit of menopause to the next generation. This explanation, known as the "grandmother hypothesis," suggests that menopause evolved to provide a period for females to help take care of their slow-growing and big-brained grandchildren. Peccei (2001) argues that the "mother hypothesis" is more likely to be true than the "grandmother hypothesis" but notes that the evidence is inconclusive and testing difficult. Other researchers have argued that menopause is not the result of natural selection but instead represents a by-product of the aging process. Lynnette Leidy (1998), for example, has suggested that menopause is simply the result of humans living beyond their egg supply.

IS HUMAN BEHAVIOR UNIQUE?

Humans and apes show a great many similarities, as well as a great many differences. When we ask whether humans are unique, we do not suggest that we cannot tell an ape and a human apart. Rather, we ask what the extent of these differences is. Are the behaviors of apes and humans completely different, or are differences present only in the expression of specific behaviors? Can we say, for example, that humans make tools and apes do not? Or should we say instead that there are differences in the ways in which these two groups make and use tools?

According to the view that apes and humans show distinct and major differences, humans possess culture and apes do not. Any cultural behaviors found in apes are labeled as fundamentally different from human cultural behaviors. According to the view that ape–human differences are variations on something that is fundamentally similar, both humans and apes possess

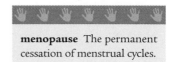

menopause The permanent cessation of menstrual cycles.

culture—the only difference being that humans rely more on culture or that humans have a more developed culture. This debate is semantic to a large extent. A more worthwhile approach is to examine some of the suggested differences between apes and humans in an effort to determine what is truly different.

Tool Use and Manufacture

define tool

Tool use has often been cited as a unique human behavior. As defined here, a tool is an object that is not part of the animal. Human tools include pencils, clothes, eating utensils, books, and houses. All of these are objects that are not part of the biological organism (humans) but are used for a specific purpose. Tool use, however, does not seem to be even a unique primate characteristic. Birds use sticks for nests, and beavers use dirt in their dams. Both sticks and dirt can be considered tools by this definition.

tool manufacture

A more common definition of modern humans focuses on humans as toolmakers (this definition is complicated by the fact that the earliest hominids may not have made tools—see Chapter 12). The key element of this definition is that some object is taken from the environment and modified to meet a new function. Humans take trees to make lumber to build houses. It can be argued that birds modify sticks and beavers modify dirt, but tool manufacture implies something different. Birds, for example, use sticks for building nests, but they do not use these sticks for defensive or offensive weapons. Humans, however, can take sticks and use them to make shelters, defend themselves, hunt, dig up roots, and draw pictures in the sand. When we discuss tool manufacture, we mean the new and different ways to modify an object for a task. Humans can apply the same raw materials to a variety of tasks.

In this sense, tool manufacture has long been considered a unique human activity. But research on apes, particularly Goodall's work on chimpanzees, has since shown that this is not true. Apes make and use tools. Though their tools are extremely simple by modern human standards, it is clear that the difference between apes and humans cannot be reduced to humans making tools and apes not making tools. Differences exist in the method and use of manufactured tools, but not in the presence or absence of toolmaking.

Chimpanzee Termite Fishing   In the early 1960s, Jane Goodall reported a remarkable finding—chimpanzees were making and using tools! Though chimpanzees are predominantly fruit eaters, they also enjoy a variety of other foods, including termites. One group of chimpanzees demonstrated a method for capturing termites. They took a grass stem or a stick, went up to a termite mound, and uncovered one of the entrance holes left by the termites. They inserted the stick into the hole, twirled the stick a bit to attract termites down in the mound, and then withdrew the stick. Termites had attached themselves to the stick, and the chimpanzees ate them directly off the stick (Figure 10.10).

Close analysis of this "termite fishing" behavior shows it to be true tool manufacture along with rather complex tool use. Chimpanzees often spent a

FIGURE 10.10

The chimpanzees have fashioned simple tools to fish for termites. (© Jane Goodall/ National Geographic Society)

great deal of time selecting the appropriate stick. When a suitable stick was not available, they pulled a branch out of the ground or off a bush and stripped away the leaves. This is deliberate manipulation of an object in the environment—toolmaking. The act also reflects a conscious decision-making process.

Termite fishing is not easy. One anthropologist who tried found that it was a difficult process that required a great deal of skill and practice. Even finding the right kind of stick is tricky. If a stick is too flexible or too rigid, it cannot be inserted into the termite tunnel. Taking the stick out without knocking the termites off also calls for careful handling.

Termite fishing is not an innate chimpanzee behavior. It is passed on to others in the group by means of learning. Young chimpanzees watch their elders and imitate them, thus learning the methods and also developing practice. As Goodall has documented, termite fishing has become part of the local group's culture.

Other Examples of Toolmaking   Termite fishing is only one of many types of tool manufacture reported among chimpanzees. Sticks are also used to hunt for ants. A chimpanzee will dig up an underground nest with its hands and then insert a long stick into the nest. The ants begin swarming up the stick, and the chimpanzee withdraws it to eat the ants. Sticks have also been used to probe holes in dead wood and to break into bee nests (Goodall 1986).

In addition, chimpanzees have been observed making sponges out of leaves. After a rainfall, a chimpanzee often drinks out of pools of water that collect in the holes of tree branches. Often the holes are too small for the chimp to fit its head into, so the chimp creates a tool to soak up the water: he takes a leaf, puts it into his mouth, and chews it slightly. (Chewing increases the ability of the leaf to absorb water.) The chimp inserts this "sponge" into the hole in the branch to soak up the water.

Other examples of chimpanzee toolmaking and tool use include using leaves as napkins and toilet paper, using sticks as weapons, using branches and rocks to crack open nuts, and using a bone pick to dig out marrow from a bone, among others (Goodall 1986, McGrew 1992).

An interesting finding is that bonobos do not engage in tool use in their native environments to any great extent. Although a captive bonobo has been taught to make stone tools (Savage-Rumbaugh and Lewin 1994), the only observation of bonobo tool use in the wild has been the use of leafy twigs as shelter from the rain (McGrew 1992). Recent observations in Sumatra show that, although rare, orangutans also use tools (van Schaik and Knott 1998).

Human and Chimpanzee Toolmaking   It is obvious that chimpanzees make and use tools in a systematic manner. It is also clear that they use genuine problem-solving abilities in their toolmaking. They see a problem (e.g., termites in the mound) and create a tool to solve the problem. The implication of these studies is that we can no longer define humans as the only toolmakers.

This does not imply that there are no differences between human and chimpanzee toolmaking. Humans, for example, save their tools and use them again, whereas chimpanzees start over each time (an exception is saving rocks that were used to crack open nuts). Chimpanzees who "fish" for termites do not save the sticks they have made. Humans also have a more elaborate technology, using tools to make other tools.

Regardless of these specific differences, it is clear that we cannot define modern humans solely in terms of the ability to make tools. The observations made by Goodall and others regarding chimpanzee tool manufacture have caused us to redefine human behavior and reconsider our relationship with the apes. We now acknowledge much closer genetic and behavioral similarities than was the case in the middle of the twentieth century.

Do Chimpanzees Have Culture?

Observations of chimpanzee toolmaking have narrowed the perceived gap between humans and apes. Our understanding of the ways in which these behaviors develop and are passed on from one generation to the next through learning (recall the infant chimpanzee watching the adults fish for termites) has led to an interesting question: Is this cultural behavior?

A growing body of evidence suggests that a number of nonhuman species exhibit cultural behavior. That is, certain behaviors are shared among a group and are transmitted from one generation to the next through learning rather than genetically. Certain species of whales and birds, for example, have *culture* characteristic songs that are transmitted culturally (e.g., Noad et al. 2000). In addition, as noted in Chapter 8, one group of Japanese macaques developed the sweet-potato washing behavior. It has been argued, however, that these cases are not conclusive demonstrations of culture because they concern only a single behavior, whereas human culture is characterized by a combination of behavior patterns (de Waal 1999).

In 1999, Andrew Whiten and colleagues published a landmark review of cultural behavior in chimpanzees based on observations made in seven chimpanzee communities. They examined 65 different behaviors in an effort to find behaviors that were specific to some, but not all, communities. Their goal was to identify a set of behaviors in some communities that were not seen species-wide. Of the 65 behaviors, 26 were excluded because they were rare in all communities, could be explained by local ecological conditions (e.g., no termites to fish), or were present in all communities, suggesting species-wide behaviors best explained by genetic rather than cultural transmission. The remaining 39 behaviors were found in high frequencies in some, but not all, communities and were therefore likely to be examples of local culture. For example, ant-fishing using a probe was found in four communities but was absent in the other three. Picking marrow out of bones was found in one community but not the other six.

This study confirmed earlier work (e.g., McGrew 1992) showing that many chimpanzee behaviors are *not* species-wide but are confined to specific communities and passed on to each generation culturally. Further, some behaviors were found to be unique to a single community, whereas others were found in two or more communities. In addition, the cultural profiles of each community were distinct from others, a pattern typical of human cultures and unlike that found in other species.

The answer to the question "Do chimpanzees have culture?" now appears to be "Yes." As noted by primatologist Frans de Waal (1999) in a commentary on the Whiten et al. paper, "The 'culture' label befits any species, such as the chimpanzee, in which one community can readily be distinguished from another by its unique suite of behavioral characteristics. Biologically speaking, humans have never been alone—now the same can be said of culture" (p. 636). Although there are differences between human and chimpanzee culture, such as the use of language in the former, this is a difference of degree and not a difference in kind (McGrew 1998). Of course, these conclusions depend on the definition of culture being used. Some anthropologists prefer to use a more specific definition that could exclude apes.

Language Capabilities

Language has long been considered a unique human property. Language is not merely communication but rather a symbolic form of communication. The nonhuman primates communicate basic emotions in a variety of ways. Chimpanzees, for example, use a large number of vocalizations to convey

emotional states such as anger, fear, or stress (Figure 10.11). Many primates also use their sense of touch to communicate some emotions by **grooming**, the handling and cleaning of another individual's fur (Figure 10.12). Grooming helps keep the animal clean and also acts to soothe and reassure tense or frightened individuals. Grooming is a common form of social communication among primates.

What Is Language?

Primate communication through vocalizations, grooming, or other methods does not constitute language. Language, as a symbolic form of communication, has certain characteristics that distinguish it from simple communication. Language is an *open system;* that is, new ideas can be expressed that have never been expressed before. Chimpanzee vocalizations, on the other hand, form a closed system capable of conveying only a few basic concepts or emotions. Human language can use a finite number of sounds and create an infinite number of words, sentences, and ideas from these sounds.

Another important characteristic of language is *displacement.* Language allows discussion of objects and events that are displaced—that is, not present—in time and/or space. For example, you can say, "Tomorrow I am going to another country." This sentence conveys an idea that is displaced in both time (tomorrow) and space (another country). We can discuss the past, the future, and faraway places. Displacement is very important for our ability to plan future events—imagine the difficulty in planning a hunt several days from now without the ability to speak of future events!

Language is also arbitrary. The actual sounds we use in our languages need not bear any relationship to reality. Our word for "book" could just as easily be "gurmf" or some other sound. The important point is that we un-

grooming The handling and cleaning of another individual's fur or hair. In primates, grooming serves as a form of communication that soothes and provides reassurance.

FIGURE 10.12

Chimpanzees grooming.
(© Gunter Ziesler/Peter Arnold, Inc.)

derstand the relationship of sounds to objects and ideas. This in turn shows yet another important feature of language—it is learned.

Apes and American Sign Language   Early efforts to teach English to apes were failures. One classic experiment was conducted on a young female chimpanzee named Vicki. After years of extensive work, Vicki could speak only four words: "Mama," "Papa," "up," and "cup." Later, researchers noted that the failure of this experiment might mean only that apes cannot speak English; it said nothing about their ability to understand. Looking back at this study, it is no surprise that Vicki could not speak very well, because the vocal anatomy of chimpanzees makes speaking a human language next to impossible.

In the 1960s, two scientists, Allen and Beatrice Gardner, began teaching American Sign Language to a young female chimpanzee named Washoe. Devised for the deaf, American Sign Language (ASL) is a true symbolic language that does not require vocalization but instead uses hand and finger gestures. Because chimpanzees are capable of making such signs, ASL was considered the most suitable medium to determine whether or not they were capable of using language (Figure 10.13). Washoe quickly learned many signs and soon developed an extensive vocabulary.

Washoe also demonstrated the ability to generalize: to take a concept learned in one context and apply it to another. For example, she would use the sign meaning *open* to refer to boxes as well as doors. This suggests that

FIGURE 10.13

A chimpanzee is using American Sign Language.

(© H. S. Terrace/Animals Animals)

Washoe truly understood the general concept of *open* and not just the use of the sign in one specific context. Washoe also invented new signs and "talked" to herself while playing alone, an act human children perform when learning language. Washoe was even observed to swear!

One of the most intriguing findings of the Gardners' research was that Washoe would form simple two- and three-word sentences (for example, "You tickle me"). Early observations suggested that Washoe was not only capable of symbolism but also of grammar and sentence construction.

Washoe was the first ape taught American Sign Language. Since then there have been many experiments into the nature of the language capabilities of apes. Gorillas, as well as chimpanzees, have been taught ASL. Other languages were also invented, including one based on plastic tiles and another using a computer keyboard. Experiments were devised that required two chimpanzees to interact with each other using language. These experiments confirmed the ability to generalize signs and to create new ones. For example, one chimpanzee named Lucy combined the signs *drink* and *fruit* to refer to a watermelon for which she had not been taught a sign. She also invented the phrase "cry hurt food" to refer to radishes, which presumably she found bitter.

As Washoe grew older, it became natural to wonder whether she would some day have an infant that would then learn ASL from her, thus showing cultural transmission of language. During the 1970s, Washoe's adopted infant, Loulis, began using ASL, learning two dozen signs within 18 months. Because care was taken to ensure that Loulis was not exposed to *humans* signing, the results of the study suggest strongly that chimpanzees can learn ASL from each other (Fouts and Mills 1997).

Human and Ape Language Abilities   The purpose of the original research with Washoe was to determine what was unique about the way in which a human child learns language. It was suggested that a comparison of human and chimpanzee language acquisition would reveal at what point human abilities surpassed those of the ape. Washoe's abilities exceeded early expectations, and soon the research focus shifted to the language capabilities of the apes themselves. The ability of Washoe and other apes to learn a symbolic language suggested that language acquisition could no longer be regarded as a unique human feature.

There is considerable debate about the meaning of these studies. Some claim that many of the positive results are the result of unconscious cues given to the apes by humans. Also, there is the problem of interpreting the data and seeing what one wants to see. For example, Washoe signed "water bird" the first time she saw a swan. Some researchers have interpreted this as a true invention. Others have suggested that Washoe simply saw the water and then the bird and responded with the two signs in sequence. Obviously, much of this research is fraught with the danger of speculation and excessive interpretations for the simple reason that we cannot get inside the chimpanzee's mind.

In spite of the debates, however, there is little doubt that apes can learn and understand the meaning of many signs. Chimpanzees, gorillas, and orangutans have all mastered a certain number. Some chimps have learned more than 150 signs by the time they were 7 years old (Snowden 1990). Carefully controlled experiments have shown that the basic vocabulary of apes is not a reflection of unconscious cues given by the scientists. The behavior of signing correctly while playing alone strongly suggests that the apes actually do understand, *in some manner,* the meaning of signs.

Much of the controversy over language acquisition in apes revolves around two different training approaches. Many studies, including the Washoe project, attempted to teach language in an environment similar to that in which human children develop linguistic skills, one offering continued exposure in an unstructured environment with many opportunities for creativity and expression. Other ape studies used controlled, less flexible environments. The controlled experiments were of course designed to minimize cues from humans and to provide more definitive measurements. The problem is that this type of sterile approach is not the most conducive to learning language.

One of the most interesting observations came about by accident during a study conducted by Savage-Rumbaugh, in which researchers were attempting to teach a female bonobo a keyboard-based language. At the time, the bonobo was caring for an infant, Kanzi, who frequently interrupted his mother. Later, when the mother was returned to the breeding colony, Kanzi began to use the keyboard to make requests. Over time, he performed well on a variety of measures (Savage-Rumbaugh and Lewin 1994). Significantly, he learned language by observation, and not through direct training. (After all, the experiment was not designed to teach him; he was simply there to be nursed.) In other words, Kanzi learned elements of language in the same way that human children do.

The suggested ability of apes to understand grammar and to construct sentences is also controversial. Though apes do create correct two- and three-word sentences, the few longer sentences they create are often grammatically incorrect. There has also been evidence that the apes respond to unconscious cues in constructing sentences (as opposed to simple vocabulary identification). Though some see definite evidence of grammar (e.g., Linden 1981), others see little evidence (e.g., Terrace 1979). The debate continues.

Regardless of the outcome, it is clear that the difference between human and ape is not as great as we once thought. We can no longer define modern humans in terms of the capability to learn certain aspects of symbolic language. Apes are certainly capable of symbolic behavior, even if we can debate over exactly how much. Both humans and apes can learn symbols, though humans are clearly better at it. Perhaps one of the major differences is the fact that humans rely on language and apes do not. In their natural habitat, apes do not use sign language. The fact that they are capable of learning language to a certain extent should not detract from the point that they do not use language in their natural environment. As with tool manufacture, we see evidence of capabilities in the apes for behaviors that are optional for them but mandatory for modern humans.

The question of human uniqueness becomes more complicated when we consider possible behaviors of our fossil ancestors. Given a common ancestry with the African apes, at what point did our own patterns of toolmaking and language acquisition begin? Studies of modern apes help answer such questions because we can see the *potential* for such behaviors in the modern apes. Using these potentials as a guide to the behavior of the common ancestor of African apes and humans, we can attempt to determine what changes were necessary to arrive at the modern human condition.

SUMMARY

Humans share many features with the other hominoids but also show a number of differences. The main biological characteristics of humans are a large and complex brain, three times its expected value; bipedalism; and small canine teeth. In addition, humans have a growth pattern that is different from other primates in its extended childhood and adolescent growth spurt. Behaviorally, humans are quite variable.

Past behavioral definitions of humans have often focused on humans as toolmakers. However, studies of apes in their native habitat show that they also make and use simple tools. Accumulated data on chimpanzee behavior in the wild show that they, like humans, possess culture. Another oft-cited human characteristic is the use of symbolic language. Although apes are unable physically to speak a human language, studies of American Sign Language and other symbolic, visually oriented languages show that apes have some language acquisition capabilities. Studies of toolmaking and language acquisition show that the difference between apes and humans may be more a matter of degree than kind. Modern humans remain unique in the specific ways they use tools and language and in their reliance on these behaviors for survival. What is mandatory for humans is optional for apes. Still, the capabilities shown by apes provide us with possible clues regarding human origins.

SUPPLEMENTAL READINGS

Bogin, B. 2001. *The Growth of Humanity.* New York: John Wiley & Sons. This book includes a detailed review of the human life cycle with particular attention to the evolution of human growth.

Fisher, H. 1992. *Anatomy of Love: A Natural History of Mating, Marriage, and Why We Stray.* New York: Ballantine. A well-written and fascinating account of evolutionary explanations of human marriage and mating.

Fouts, R., and S. T. Mills. 1997. *Next of Kin: What Chimpanzees Have Taught Me About Who We Are.* New York: William Morrow.

Savage-Rumbaugh, S., and R. Lewin. 1994. *Kanzi: The Ape at the Brink of the Human Mind.* New York: John Wiley & Sons.

These last two books are excellent popular accounts of the studies of ape language acquisition.

INTERNET RESOURCES

http://www.gwc.maricopa.edu/class/bio201/index.html
Anatomy and Physiology Home Page, containing tutorials on human anatomy and physiology.

http://www.csuchico.edu/anth/Module/skull.html
The Skull Module, a graphic tutorial on the bones of the human skull that has rotation and zoom capabilities.

http://www.emory.edu/LIVING_LINKS
Living Links, a Web site focusing on the comparison of human and ape behavior.

http://chimp.st-and.ac.uk/cultures
Chimpanzee Cultures, featuring an online database describing the cultural behaviors discussed in Whiten et al.'s 1999 paper in *Nature.*

http://www.brown.edu/Departments/Anthropology/apelang.html
Chimpanzee and Great Apes Language Resources on the Internet, a collection of links on all aspects of language acquisition in apes.

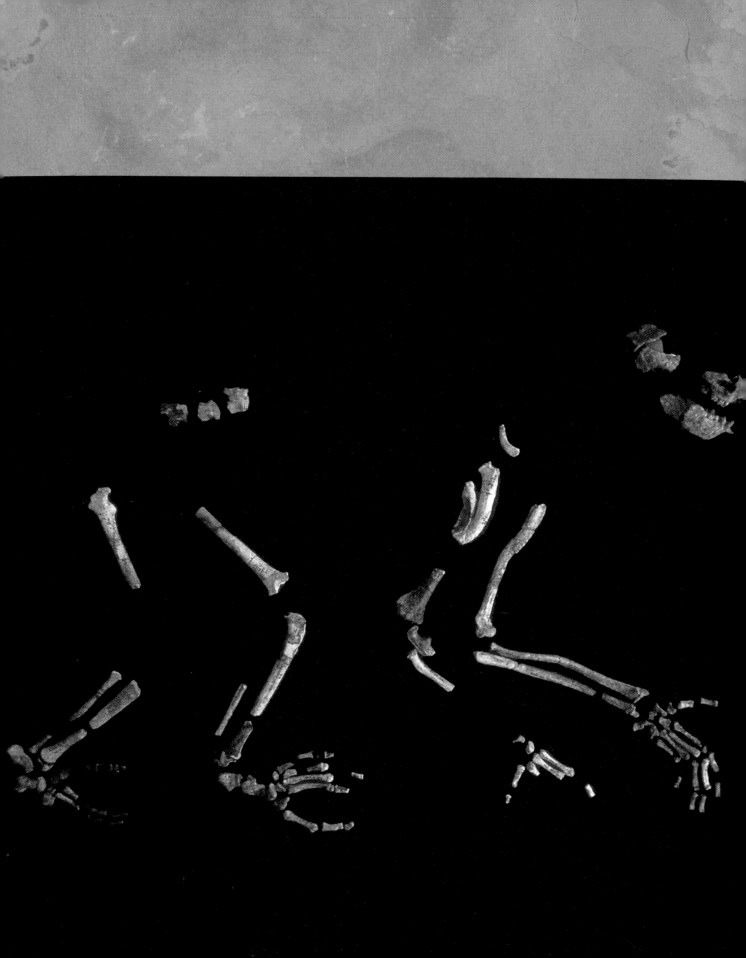

CHAPTER 11

Primate Origins and Evolution

The previous three chapters provided a survey of living primates concluding with the discussion of the human species in Chapter 10. The current chapter places this information in an evolutionary context by examining the major aspects of primate evolution over the past 65 million years.

As discussed in Chapter 4, the dinosaurs became extinct at the end of the Mesozoic Era, 65 million years ago. Their demise opened up numerous opportunities for other animals, particularly the mammals, to expand into new environments. This adaptive radiation of mammals included the ancestors of modern-day primates.

Modern primates did not appear instantaneously 65 million years ago. There were no monkeys, apes, or humans at that time. Rather, a group of mammals began adapting to life in the trees. This change provided a base for further evolution, leading ultimately to modern-day primates. It is important to realize that the definitions of modern forms discussed in Chapters 8 and 9 do not always apply to early fossil forms. Any classification based on *modern* characteristics reflects many millions of years of evolution. The farther back in time we go, the harder it is to distinguish between different forms of primates.

Also, primate and primate-like forms in the past exhibited an amazing diversity. In the past few decades, we have realized it is not a simple matter to draw family trees connecting earlier forms with modern forms. We now know there were many species of prosimians, monkeys, and apes that have no living counterpart.

◄ *The fossil remains of* Proconsul, *one of the earliest known apes, which lived in Africa 20 million years ago.* Proconsul *had a mixture of ape-like and monkey-like traits, showing the origin of the first apes. (© David L. Brill)*

THE STUDY OF THE FOSSIL RECORD

This chapter gives the first glimpse at the fossil record. The origin and evolution of the primates is discussed here, followed by several chapters dealing with the fossil record of human evolution. Before starting these topics, it is necessary to review some basic elements of the analysis of the fossil record.

How do we infer evolutionary patterns from the fossil record? The first step in such an analysis is to determine the age of different fossil specimens (and, in the case of later hominids, archaeological sites). At the very least, we need to know which fossils are older. Because evolution is a process occurring over time, it is essential that we have a way of determining the time sequence of fossils.

Two basic classes of methods are used to date fossil remains. **Relative dating** determines which fossils are older, but not their exact date. **Chronometric dating** determines an "exact" age (subject to statistical fluctuation).

Different nomenclature has been used to refer to geologic and historic dates. The abbreviation **B.P.,** meaning "Before Present," is often used. (The "Present" has been set arbitrarily as the year 1950.) Some people have used the term B.C., meaning "Before Christ," but because not all peoples share a belief in Christ, the term B.P. is preferable and has been agreed upon internationally. A date of 800,000 years B.P. would therefore mean 800,000 years before the year 1950. The term "years ago" is sometimes used instead of "Before Present." Two abbreviations are commonly used in paleontology and throughout this book: ka (thousands of years ago) and Ma (millions of years ago).

Relative Dating Methods

If we have two sites containing fossil material, relative dating methods can tell us which is older, but not by how much. It is preferable to have exact dates, but this is not possible for all sites. Relative dating methods can tell us the basic time sequence of fossil sites.

Stratigraphy   **Stratigraphy** makes use of the geological process of superposition, which refers to the cumulative buildup over time of the earth's surface. When an organism dies or a tool is discarded on the ground, it will ultimately be buried by dirt, sand, mud, and other materials. Winds move sand over the site, and water can deposit mud on it. In most cases, the older a site is, the deeper it is. If you stand on the ground and dig down through the earth, the lower layers are older. If you find one fossil 3 feet deep and another 6 feet deep, the principle of stratification allows you to infer that the latter fossil is older. You still do not know how old the fossil is or the exact amount of time between the two fossils, but you have established which is older in geologic time.

In some situations, stratigraphy is more difficult to use. Where the earth's crust has folded and broken through the surface of the ground, the usual stratigraphic order is disturbed. This does not invalidate the method, however, for careful geological analysis can reconstruct the patterns of disturbance and allow relative dates to be determined.

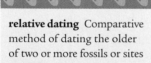

relative dating Comparative method of dating the older of two or more fossils or sites rather than a specific date.

chronometric dating The method of estimating the specific date of fossils or sites.

B.P. Before Present (1950), the internationally accepted form of designating past dates.

stratigraphy A relative dating method based on the fact that older remains are found deeper in the earth because of cumulative buildup of the earth's surface over time.

Other Relative Dating Methods   A number of other methods provide relative dates for fossils. One such method is **biostratigraphy,** which involves comparison of animal remains found at different sites to determine any similarity in time levels. Imagine that you have discovered a site that contains a certain species of fossil pig. Suppose that you know from previous studies that this species of pig has always been found between 2.0 million and 1.5 million years ago. Logically, this suggests that your newly discovered site is also between 2.0 million and 1.5 million years old. The only other possibility would be that patterns of evolution occurred in the same way but at different rates in different areas—an unlikely proposition. Plant pollens sometimes can be used in a similar manner.

Another dating method involves **paleomagnetic reversals.** The magnetic field of the earth runs between the poles, and the polarity of this field changes at irregular intervals over long periods of geological time (Brown 1992). Sedimentary rocks preserve a record of such past changes. By calibrating against known ages derived from other methods (see the next section), we have been able to assign dates to past records of paleomagnetic reversal. When a new site is uncovered that has a good stratigraphic section recording past reversals, we are able to compare it with a known sequence to obtain an approximate date.

Chemical methods also provide relative dates. Fluorine dating, for example, is a method that looks at the accumulation of fluorine in bones. When an organism dies, its bones lose nitrogen and gain fluorine. The rate at which this process occurs varies, so we cannot tell exactly how old a bone is by using the method. The method does, however, allow us to determine if two bones found at the same site are the same age. Other relative dating methods can be applied to human cultural remains. Much like biostratigraphy, these methods assign a range of dates based on a comparison with similar sites with known dates.

Chronometric Dating Methods

Chronometric dating methods provide an "exact" date, subject to statistical variation. Chronometric dating relies on constant physical and chemical processes in the universe. Many of these methods utilize the fact that the average rate of radioactive decay is constant for a given radioactive atom no matter what chemical reaction it might be involved in. If we know that a certain element decays into another at a constant rate, and if we can measure the relative proportions of the original and new elements in some object, then we can mathematically determine the age of the object. Radioactive decay is a probabilistic phenomenon, meaning that we know the average time for decay over many atoms. Such processes allow us to specify an average date within the limits of statistical certainty.

Carbon-14 Dating   Living organisms take in the element carbon throughout their lives. Ordinary carbon, carbon-12 (^{12}C), is absorbed by plants, which take in carbon dioxide gas from the air, and by animals, which eat the plants (or animals that eat the animals that eat the plants). Because of cosmic radiation,

biostratigraphy A relative dating method in which sites can be assigned an approximate age based on the similarity of animal remains with those from other dated sites.

paleomagnetic reversal A method of dating sites based on the fact that the earth's magnetic field has shifted back and forth from the north to the south in the past at irregular intervals.

some of the carbon in the atmosphere is a radioactive isotope known as carbon-14 (^{14}C). An organism takes in both ^{14}C and ^{12}C, and the proportion of ^{12}C to ^{14}C is constant during the organism's life because the proportion is constant in the atmosphere. When an organism dies, no additional ^{14}C is ingested and the accumulated ^{14}C begins to decay. The rate at which ^{14}C decays is constant; it takes 5,730 years for one-half of the ^{14}C to decay into ^{14}N (nitrogen-14). Carbon-14 is therefore said to have a **half-life** of 5,730 years. The half-life is the time it takes for half of a radioactive substance to decay.

Carbon-14 dating uses this constant rate of decay to determine the age of materials containing carbon. The process of the radioactive decay of ^{14}C results in the emission of radioactive particles that can be measured. We look at the rate of radioactive emissions for a sample and compare it to the rate of emissions expected in a living organism (a rate of 15 particles per minute per gram of carbon). For example, suppose a sample is analyzed and is found to emit 3.75 particles per minute per gram of carbon. Compared to a living organism, two half-lives have elapsed (one half-life results in 7.5 particles, and a second half-life results in half of this number = 7.5/2 = 3.75). Because the half-life of ^{14}C is 5,730 years, the age of our sample is $5{,}730 \times 2 = 11{,}460$ years ago. If the sample were analyzed in 2003, its date would be 11,407 years B.P. (or, in abbreviated form, 11.407 ka). Because 53 years have passed since 1950 (the "Present"), the date is $11{,}460 - 53 = 11{,}407$.

In theory, any sample containing carbon can be used. In practice, however, bone tends not to be reliable in all cases because of the chemical changes during fossilization, in which carbon is replaced. In most circumstances, charcoal is the best material to use. If we find that a fire occurred at a certain site, either naturally or human-made, we can use the charcoal for carbon-14 dating. Careful attention must be given to possible contaminants at any given site. Another problem is that there has been a certain amount of variability in the proportions of atmospheric carbon over the last few centuries because of industrial pollution. Techniques exist for partial controlling of this factor.

Carbon-14 dating is only useful for sites dating back over the past 50,000 years at most. Any older samples would contain too little ^{14}C to be detected. Though carbon-14 dating is extremely valuable in studies of recent hominid evolution, it is not useful for dating most of earth's geological history.

Potassium–Argon Dating   Another chronometric dating method that utilizes the process of radioactive decay is **potassium-argon dating.** Here an isotope of potassium (^{40}K) decays into argon gas (^{40}Ar) with a half-life of approximately 1.31 billion years. This rate of radioactive decay means that this method is best used on samples older than 100,000 years (Figure 11.1).

Potassium-argon dating requires rocks that did not possess any argon gas to begin with. The best material for this method is volcanic rock, for the heat generated by volcanic eruptions removes any initial argon gas. Thus, we are sure that any argon gas we find in a sample of volcanic rock is the result of radioactive decay. By looking at the proportions of ^{40}K and ^{40}Ar, we can determine the number of elapsed half-lives and therefore the age of the volcanic rock.

half-life The average length of time it takes for half of a radioactive substance to decay into another form.

carbon-14 dating A chronometric dating method based on the half-life of carbon-14 that can be applied to organic remains, such as charcoal, dating back over the past 50,000 years.

potassium-argon dating A chronometric dating method based on the half-life of radioactive potassium that can be used to date volcanic rock older than 100,000 years.

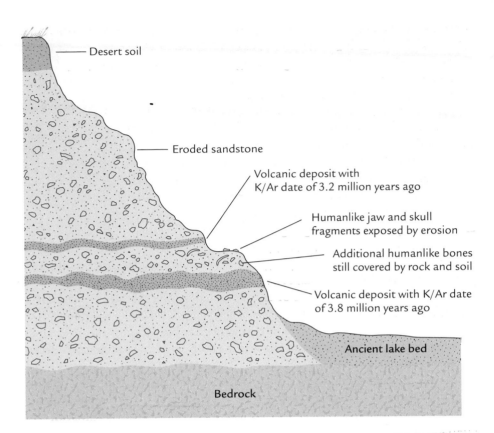

- Desert soil
- Eroded sandstone
- Volcanic deposit with K/Ar date of 3.2 million years ago
- Humanlike jaw and skull fragments exposed by erosion
- Additional humanlike bones still covered by rock and soil
- Volcanic deposit with K/Ar date of 3.8 million years ago

Ancient lake bed

Bedrock

FIGURE 11.1

Hypothetical example of the use of potassium-argon dating. Hominid remains are found between two layers of volcanic ash, one dating to 3.8 million years ago and the other dating to 3.2 million years ago. The hominid can therefore be dated at between 3.8 million and 3.2 million years ago. (From Human Antiquity: An Introduction to Physical Anthropology and Archaeology, 2d ed., by Kenneth Feder and Michael Park, Fig. 7.7. © 1993 by Mayfield Publishing Company. Reprinted with permission from The McGraw-Hill Companies)

Though we cannot date a fossil directly with this method, we can assign a date based on the relationship of a fossil find to different levels of volcanic ash. If we find a fossil halfway between two layers of volcanic rock with dates of 4.6 million and 4.5 million years ago, we can then assign the fossil an age of roughly 4.55 million years ago. Potassium-argon dating is best applied in areas with frequent volcanic eruptions. Fortunately, much of hominid evolution in East Africa took place under such conditions, allowing us to date many fossil sites. A newer and related method, **argon-argon dating,** involves looking at the decay of an argon isotope (^{39}Ar) into argon gas (^{40}Ar). Laser technology allows this method to be applied to very small samples—as small as a single crystal.

Other Chronometric Dating Methods   Many other types of chronometric dating methods can be used in certain circumstances. Some utilize radioactive decay and some use other constant effects for determining age. Archaeologists working on the relatively recent past (within the last 10,000 years) often use a method known as **dendrochronology,** or tree ring counting (Figure 11.2). We know that a tree will accumulate a new ring for every period of growth. The width of each ring depends on available moisture and other factors during that specific period. In dry areas, there is usually only one growth period in a year. By looking at the width of tree rings, archaeologists

argon-argon dating A chronometric dating method based on the half-life of radioactive argon that can be used with very small samples.

dendrochronology A chronometric dating method based on the fact that trees in dry climates tend to accumulate one growth ring per year.

FIGURE 11.2

Tree rings can be dated by the method of dendrochronology.
(Courtesy of The Laboratory of Tree-Research, The University of Arizona)

have constructed a master chart of tree ring changes. Any new sample, such as a log from a prehistoric dwelling, can be compared to this chart to determine its age.

In addition to radioactive decay, other physical constants allow an estimate of age to be assigned to a sample. **Fission-track dating** relies on the fact that when uranium decays into lead in volcanic glass (obsidian), it leaves small "tracks" across the surface of the glass. We can count the number of tracks and determine the age of the obsidian from the fact that these tracks occur at a constant rate.

Thermoluminescence is a dating method that relies on the fact that certain heated objects accumulate trapped electrons over time, thus allowing us to determine, in some cases, when the object was initially heated. This method has been applied to pottery, bronze, and burned flints. Thermoluminescence can be used to date objects as far back as 1 million years.

Electron spin resonance is a fairly new method that provides an estimate of dating from observation of radioactive atoms trapped in the calcite crystals present in a number of materials, such as bones and shells. Although this method can be used for sites over a million years old, it works best for dates under 300,000 years (Grün 1993).

Reconstructing the Past

In addition to dating fossil and archaeological sites, we also need to consider other sources of evidence when putting together a sequence of evolutionary events and interpreting them.

Taphonomy   When describing the behavior of early hominids or other organisms, we rely on a wide variety of data to reconstruct their environment

fission-track dating A chronometric dating method based on the number of tracks made across volcanic rock as uranium decays into lead.

thermoluminescence A chronometric dating method that uses the fact that certain heated objects accumulate trapped electrons over time, which allows the date when the object was initially heated to be determined.

electron spin resonance A chronometric dating method that estimates dates from observation of radioactive atoms trapped in the calcite crystals present in a number of materials such as bones and shells.

and to provide information on population size, diet, presence or absence of predators, and other ecological aspects. Quite often, we rely on what else is found at a given site other than the fossil. For example, the presence of animal bones, particularly those that are fractured, might indicate hunting. The distribution of animal bones might also give us a clue regarding behavior. The types of animal bones found at human hunting sites are different from those found at carnivore sites. A major problem is figuring out how animal bones and other objects got there and what happened to them. Imagine finding the leg bone of a fossil antelope and the leg bone of a fossil hominid at the same site. How did these bones wind up in the same place? Did the hominid hunt and kill the antelope? Did a predator hunt and kill both the antelope and the hominid? Did both bones wash down a river and land at the same place even though they might have originally been separate in time and space?

Some of these questions can be answered by methods developed within the field of **taphonomy,** the study of what happens to plants and animals after they die. This field provides us with valuable information about which bones are more likely to fossilize, which bones are more likely to wash away, the distribution of bones left over by a predator, the likely route of pollen dispersal in the air, and many other similar topics. Taphonomic studies also provide us with ways of finding out whether objects or fossils have been disturbed or whether they have stayed where they were first deposited. Such studies can also help us distinguish between human and natural actions. A fractured leg bone of a deer might result from normal wear and tear on a fossil or reflect the action of a prehistoric hunter. By understanding what happens to fossils in general, we are in a better position to infer what happened to *specific* fossils.

Paleoecology   When reconstructing the past, we need to know more than just what early organisms looked like. We also need to know about the environment in which they lived. What did they eat? Were they predators or prey? What types of vegetation were available? Where were water sources? These questions, and many others, involve **paleoecology,** the study of ancient environments.

One example of the many methods used in reconstructing ancient environments is **palynology,** the study of fossil pollen. By looking at the types of pollen found at a given site, experts can identify the specific types of plants that existed at that time. They can then make inferences about yearly and seasonal changes in temperature and rainfall based on the relative proportion of plant species. Further information on vegetation can be extracted from analysis of fossil teeth. Microscopic analysis of scratch patterns on teeth can tell us whether an organism relied more heavily on leaves, fruits, or meat. Chemical analysis of teeth can also tell us something about diet. For example, the ratio of the element strontium to the element calcium can reveal whether an organism primarily ate plants or meat. Strontium ratios are higher in plant eaters.

Additional examples of the numerous methods for investigating past environments will be given in the following chapters, where applicable.

taphonomy The study of what happens to plants and animals after they die.

paleoecology The study of ancient environments.

palynology The study of fossil pollen.

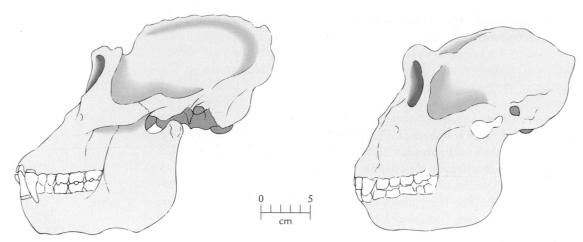

0   5
cm

FIGURE 11.3

Sexual dimorphism in gorilla skulls. The skull of a male gorilla (left) is larger than that of the female gorilla (right) and also shows heavy crests of bones on top of the skull for muscle attachment. Such sexual differences must be taken into account in analyzing fossil remains and assigning such remains to paleospecies.

Identifying Species   Assuming that we have good dates for a sample of fossils and that we know as much as possible about their biology and environment, what do we do next? How do we know which organisms are related to one another? Which species became extinct and which evolved into other species? Some of these issues will be dealt with in later chapters. For now, we concentrate on certain problems in the analysis of fossil remains.

As noted earlier, assignment of fossil specimens into species groups is difficult because we have no direct evidence on which forms were capable of interbreeding. Instead, we have to rely on inferences made from the physical appearance, or morphology, of the fossils. Briefly, we examine physical structure and compare it with other fossils and living organisms, keeping in mind the ranges of variation. When we find two specimens that exceed the normal range of variation for similar organisms, we can make a stronger case for assigning the two specimens into different species.

This approach has problems. Individuals within a species can be mistakenly assigned to different species if care is not taken to consider range of variation. For example, the skulls of adult male and female gorillas are quite different in size and other features (Figure 11.3). When we encounter such differences among fossil specimens, we must rely on a knowledge of variation in similar living organisms to determine whether sexual dimorphism is likely to be the cause.

Species identification is further complicated by philosophical differences among scientists. Some feel that the range of variation within species is often rather large and suggest that it is simpler to assign fossils to species already known and described rather than create new categories. A scientist with this view is often called a "lumper" because of the preference for lumping new fossils into preexisting categories. Others take a different approach, seeing the evolutionary record as one of frequent speciation. In this case, they anticipate numerous species and tend to call any new fossil that is somewhat different a new species. Scientists with this view are often referred to as "splitters." Identification of species is also complicated by scientists' view as to whether species should be used as convenient labels or whether species should represent new evolutionary lines.

EARLY PRIMATE EVOLUTION

Primates evolved during the Cenozoic era, which is the past 65 million years. (The **epochs** of this era are listed in Table 11.1.) Primate evolution should not be thought of as a simple evolutionary "tree" with a few branches. A better analogy would be a series of "bushes" with many different branches at each stage of primate evolution. One or more adaptive radiations of primate forms occurred during each epoch. Many of the new forms became extinct, some evolved to become present-day representatives, and some evolved into the next phase of primate evolution.

Overview of Early Primate Evolution

Before getting into the details of primate origins and evolution, I will summarize some of the major events that took place. An adaptive radiation of primate-like mammals led to the origin of what we would call "true primates." The primate-like mammals showed evidence of an initial adaptation to life in the trees. Most of these species died out, but some evolved into primitive prosimians, which were fully adapted to living in the trees. These early prosimians then underwent another adaptive radiation. Although many of these early prosimian species became extinct, some species survived to ultimately evolve into the different lines of modern prosimians. Some of the early prosimians evolved into early anthropoids. A subsequent adaptive radiation led

TABLE 11.1   Epochs of the Cenozoic Era

Epoch	Millions of Years Ago	Major Events in Primate Evolution
Holocene	0.01–Present	Humans develop agriculture and industry, explore outer space
Pleistocene	1.7–0.01	Evolution of the genus *Homo;* hunting-gathering lifestyle
Pliocene	5–1.7	Adaptive radiation of hominids and origin of the genus *Homo*
Miocene	23–5	Adaptive radiations of hominoids; origins of hominids
Oligocene	34–23	Adaptive radiations of anthropoids
Eocene	54–34	Adaptive radiations of first true primates (primitive prosimians); first anthropoids
Paleocene	65–54	Adaptive radiation of primate-like mammals; origin of primates

Source for dates: Fleagle (1999)

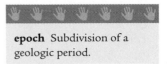

epoch Subdivision of a geologic period.

FIGURE 11.4

A tree shrew, an insectivore similar in certain respects to primates. (© Zoological Society of San Diego)

to separate groups of New World monkeys, Old World monkeys, and the first primitive apes.

Primate Origins

At the end of the Mesozoic era, there existed a number of mammals called **insectivores** that were arboreal and nocturnal and that ate insects. A modern-day representative of this group is the tree shrew (Figure 11.4), which illustrates the probable morphology of the ancestor of primates. Of all living mammals, the insectivores are most similar to the primates, suggesting that they are ancestral to primates. Paleoanthropologists look at the variation in this early group to try to identify forms that show the transition to the order Primates.

Continental Drift and Primate Evolution Most of the fossil evidence on primate origins comes from deposits over 55 million years ago in North America and Europe of a group of insectivores known as the primate-like mammals. This widespread distribution may seem strange given the fact that North America and Europe are now separated by the Atlantic Ocean. This was not, however, the configuration at that time. The continents continually move about on large crusted plates on top of a partially molten layer of the earth's mantle—a process known as **continental drift.** This process continues today: North America is slowly drifting away from Europe, toward Asia. The expansion of the South Atlantic has even been measured from satellites. The placement of the different continents at various times in the past is shown in Figure 11.5.

An understanding of past continental drift is crucial in interpreting the fossil evidence for primate evolution. As continents move, their environments change. When continents separate, populations become isolated; when continents join, there is an opportunity for large-scale migrations of populations. Roughly 230 million years ago, all the continents were joined together as one large land mass. By 180 million years ago, this large mass had split in two: one containing North America, Europe, and Asia and the other containing South America, Africa, Australia, and Antarctica. By the time of the primate-like mammals, South America had split off from Africa, but North America and Europe were still joined. Thus, it is no surprise to find fossils of

insectivore An order of mammals adapted to insect eating.

continental drift The movement of continental land masses on top of a partially molten layer of the earth's mantle that has altered the relative location of the continents over time.

More than 200 million years ago

180 million years ago

65 million years ago

Present

FIGURE 11.5

Continental drift. More than 200 million years ago, all of the continents formed a single land mass (called Pangea). By 180 million years ago, two major land masses had formed (Laurasia and Gondwana). By 65 million years ago (the beginning of primate evolution), South America had split from Africa, but North America and Europe were still joined. (*From* Human Antiquity: An Introduction to Physical Anthropology and Archaeology, *4th ed., by Kenneth Feder and Michael Park. Fig. 3.6. Copyright 2001 by Mayfield Publishing Company. Reprinted with permission from The McGraw-Hill Companies*)

primate-like mammals on both continents—they represent part of the group's range on a single land mass.

The Primate-like Mammals During the **Paleocene epoch** (65–54 million years ago), we find evidence of what are referred to as "primate-like mammals" (technically known as plesiadapiforms), which were small creatures, usually no larger than a cat and often smaller. They were quadrupedal (four-footed) mammals whose arms and legs were well adapted for climbing. Within this general group there was considerable diversity. Fleagle (1999) lists 70 species in 25 different genera. Most of this extensive variation was in body size and dental specializations. Some of the primate-like mammals had large incisors

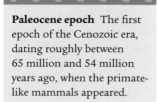

Paleocene epoch The first epoch of the Cenozoic era, dating roughly between 65 million and 54 million years ago, when the primate-like mammals appeared.

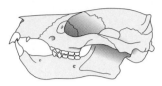

FIGURE 11.6

Side view of a skull of a Paleocene primate-like mammal. (Redrawn from Fleagle, Primate Adaptation and Evolution, *1988, with permission, Academic Press, Inc.)*

for heavy gnawing, others had teeth better adapted for slicing, and still others had teeth adapted for eating nectar and insects. Such variation is expected from an adaptive radiation. These small insectivores had some ability to climb and thus were able to exploit many different types of food.

In spite of their arboreal adaptations, these creatures are not considered true primates. A picture of the skull of one of these creatures (Figure 11.6) shows why. The front teeth are far apart from the rest of the teeth, a feature not found in primates. The eyes are located more toward the sides of the skull, unlike the forward-facing eyes of primates. In addition, the primate-like mammals lack a **postorbital bar,** a bony ring separating the orbit of the eye from the back of the skull. Primates have a postorbital bar. Also, the hands and feet of these animals did not have the grasping ability of primates, and they had claws instead of nails.

Despite these differences, there are some similarities of this group to modern primates, including certain dental traits and some grasping tendency (Gingerich 1986). However, all species found to date tend to be too specialized to be the actual ancestors of later primates (Fleagle 1999); they appear to be a related group that provides us with a general view of the morphology that preceded the origin of primates.

The First Primates   The first "true" primates appeared roughly 50 million to 55 million years ago at the beginning of the **Eocene epoch** (54–34 million years ago). The climate during this time was warm and humid, and the predominant land environment was tropical and subtropical. Initially, the continents of Europe and North America were still joined, resulting in migration and similarity among the fossils we find in this region. Many orders of modern-day mammals first appeared during this time, including aquatic mammals (whales, porpoises, and dolphins), rodents, and horses.

Fossil primates from the Eocene epoch have been found both in North America and in Europe. During the Eocene, there was an adaptive radiation of the first true primates—the early prosimians. This adaptive radiation was part of the general increase in the diversity of mammals associated with the warming of the climate and related environmental changes, and almost 200 different primate species have been discovered (Fleagle 1999).

The Eocene forms possessed stereoscopic vision, grasping hands, and other anatomical features characteristic of primates. A picture of the skull of an Eocene primate (Figure 11.7) shows many of these changes. Compared to the Paleocene primate-like mammals, the snout is reduced and the teeth are closer together. These forms possessed a postorbital bar and had larger brain cases and features of cerebral blood supply similar to that of modern primates. The large size of the eyes of some of the Eocene primates suggests they were still nocturnal.

These early primitive primates were similar, in a *general* sense, to living prosimians. In a rough sense, there are two basic groups of early Eocene primates. One group, primarily diurnal leaf and fruit eaters, is broadly similar to modern lemurs and lorises. The other group, primarily smaller nocturnal fruit and insect eaters, is broadly similar to modern tarsiers.

postorbital bar The bony ring that separates the eye orbit from the back of the skull in primates.

Eocene epoch The second epoch of the Cenozoic era, dating roughly between 54 million and 34 million years ago, when the first true primates, early prosimians, appeared.

What became of these early primates? Many different species ultimately became extinct, leaving no descendants. Others evolved into the present-day prosimians. We lack sufficient data, however, to identify individual species as the ancestors of present-day prosimians. Only in a general sense can we link these two groups of early primates to living prosimians.

Models of Primate Origins   The origin of the first true primates has typically been explained by the **arboreal model,** which focuses on adaptation to life in the trees. In an arboreal environment, natural selection would favor those individuals better able to cope with the demands of life in the trees. As discussed in Chapter 8, living in the trees is quite a different experience from living on the ground. First, a three-dimensional orientation is needed. Leaping from branch to branch requires depth perception, which involves forward rotation of the eyes so that the visual fields overlap. Vision, particularly depth perception, becomes a more important sense than smell. The sense of smell is less important in the trees, where constant breezes and winds act to dissipate any smells.

Second, living in the trees also requires an agile body capable of bending and twisting in midair. The early insectivores retained the early generalized vertebrate skeletal structure, and the first primates made use of this flexibility in the trees. The retention of the primitive trait of five digits was also important because having five digits on hands and feet allows for grasping limbs and branches. Finally, good hand–eye coordination and a brain capable of rapidly processing a large volume of visual information are essential. The early primate-like mammals already had traits on which natural selection could act. They had a generalized skeletal structure and five digits. Individuals possessing certain variations, such as more forward-facing eyes and grasping abilities, would be favored by natural selection.

Primates were not the only animals to adapt to life in the trees. Other mammals, such as squirrels, also adapted to this environment. In considering evolutionary trends, you must remember that there is not necessarily only one set of adaptations to a specific environment. Squirrels use claws to anchor themselves while climbing and do not have the grasping hands and feet of primates. Primates represent only one possible direction, shaped in part by the demands of the environment and the variation present in the original populations. Again, remember that evolution is opportunistic.

Another scenario is the **visual predation model,** developed by Matt Cartmill (1974), who sees the initial changes in grasping ability and vision as adaptations for hunting insects. Other animals besides primates have stereoscopic vision; it is also found in cats, owls, and hawks, among others. These animals are all active hunters, an activity for which the ability to gauge distance is invaluable. Could insect hunting be the reason for the initial origin of several primate characteristics? Cartmill suggests that the early insectivores hunted out their prey on the ground and on low-lying slender branches in the forest. The development of grasping hands allowed more successful hunting of prey along small branches. The development of stereoscopic vision made it easier for the insectivores to locate prey. In particular, stereoscopic vision

FIGURE 11.7

Side view of the skull of an Eocene primate. (Redrawn from Fleagle, Primate Adaptation and Evolution, *1988, with permission, Academic Press, Inc.)*

arboreal model The view of primate origins that hypothesizes that stereoscopic vision and grasping hands first evolved as adaptations for moving around in the trees.

visual predation model The view of primate origins that hypothesizes that stereoscopic vision and grasping hands first evolved as adaptations for hunting insects along branches.

allowed them to judge the distance to potential prey without moving their heads (which could alert the prey). Cartmill notes that a similar development of stereoscopic vision occurred in cats. According to Cartmill's model, primate adaptations first arose as adaptations to more successful insect predation. Once these traits were established, these adaptations later allowed further exploitation of the trees. As is often the case in evolution, preexisting structures can be used for different purposes. The fossil record is not complete enough to fully test Cartmill's model, but the dental evidence does show that many of the early primate-like mammals were insect eaters. This observation is consistent with the insect predation idea, but it is not conclusive.

Yet another alternative has been proposed by Sussman (1991), who suggests that primate origins might be related to eating fruit rather than insects. In Sussman's model, grasping hands are seen as an adaptation for efficiently eating the fruit that grows at the ends of long branches. Other mammals, such as squirrels, take food back to the main trunk of a tree to eat in safety. Grasping hands could have allowed early primates to eat more fruit in less time and to do so more safely. A problem with this model, however, is that it does not explain binocular stereoscopic vision (Cartmill 1992).

Primates became extremely successful in adapting to an arboreal environment because of their biological and behavioral flexibility. This flexibility is even more important when considering the subsequent evolution of the primates.

Anthropoid Origins

What of the anthropoids? Although living anthropoids are more similar to tarsiers than to lemurs or lorises, identification of the first anthropoids and their relationship to other fossil primates is not as clear. Recent fossil discoveries have suggested that anthropoids first evolved during the Eocene epoch, perhaps as much as 50 million years ago. Debate continues over whether anthropoids first evolved in Asia or Africa. Although some fossil evidence supports the view that the first anthropoids evolved in Asia (e.g., Jaeger et al. 1999), some paleontologists argue that the fossil record is still too incomplete to be certain (e.g., Gunnell and Miller 2001).

It is possible that anthropoids developed not from the lemur–loris group or the tarsier group, but from a third, independent line in early primate evolution. It is too soon to determine which of these ideas (if any) is correct. The major lesson we have learned from recent fossil discoveries is that past diversity was much greater than we once thought, and even given our recent accumulation of data, we are unlikely to have sampled more than a fraction of early primate diversity.

Old World Anthropoids   We have evidence of anthropoid fossils from the start of the **Oligocene epoch** (34–23 million years ago) at several locations in the Old World and the New World. The climate cooled during this time, and there was an expansion of grasslands and a reduction in forests. This change in climate seems to have resulted in the southward movement of primate populations, and we find little evidence of further evolution in North America or Europe. Most of the fossil evidence for anthropoid evolution is

Oligocene epoch   The third epoch of the Cenozoic era, dating roughly between 34 million and 23 million years ago, when there was an adaptive radiation of anthropoids.

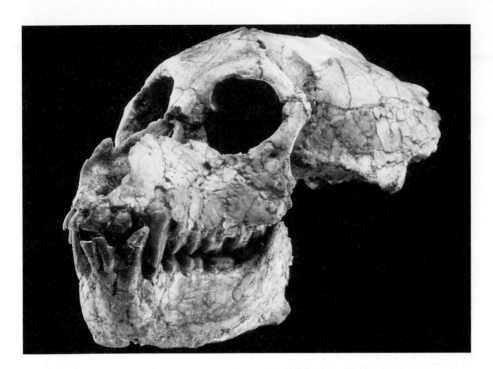

FIGURE 11.8

Three-quarters view of the Oligocene anthropoid Aegyptopithecus, *which lived about 33 million years ago. The smaller eye orbit, relative to the size of the skull, shows that this form was diurnal (nocturnal creatures have bigger eyes).* Aegyptopithecus *was once considered a possible early ape but is now recognized as an anthropoid that lived prior to the split of the Old World monkey and ape lines.*

(© David L. Brill/Brill Atlanta)

found in southern climates in Africa and South America and in parts of eastern Asia (Covert 1997; Fleagle 1995).

The Oligocene primates show the continued radiation of anthropoid forms in both the Old World and the New World. The Oligocene anthropoids show continued reduction of the snout and nasal area, indicating greater reliance on vision than on smell. In addition to the postorbital bar shared with all primates, the Oligocene anthropoids have a fully enclosed eye socket, characteristic of modern anthropoids. All of the Oligocene anthropoids were small and arboreal and were generalized quadrupeds; none show signs of specialized locomotion. Their diet appears to have consisted primarily of fruit supplemented with insects and leaves.

The smaller eye orbits of many early anthropoids suggests that these forms were diurnal (Figure 11.8). The transition from a nocturnal lifestyle to a diurnal lifestyle was extremely important in the later evolution of the anthropoids. Given variation in the daily schedule of living creatures, we can imagine a situation in which some ancestral primates began feeding during daylight hours. As this new environmental niche was exploited, natural selection would act to favor individuals that possessed the abilities needed for such a way of life, such as improved vision. Daylight living also offers increased opportunities for social interactions because animals can see one another at greater distances. As a result, we would expect the development of larger social groups and an increase in social behaviors.

Evolution of the New World Monkeys What about the New World monkeys? The earliest fossil record of New World monkeys dates back roughly 30 million years (Fleagle 1999). Most of this evidence consists of fragmentary dental remains. Many of these fossils resemble living New World monkeys. Other forms have unusual features, such as narrow jaws and protruding incisors, and do not appear to have any living counterparts.

Where did the New World monkeys come from? Decades ago, it was thought that New and Old World monkeys represented a good example of parallel evolution from prosimians. However, current evidence points to enough similarities between the two groups of monkeys to make it more reasonable to assume a single origin for anthropoids somewhere in the Old World. How did the New World monkeys get to the New World? By this time, continental drift had resulted in the separation of the Old and New Worlds.

One explanation is that anthropoids reached South America by "rafting." No, this does not mean that these early primates built rafts and sailed to South America! Ocean storms often rip up clumps of land near the shore, which are then pulled out into the ocean. Sometimes these "floating islands" contain helpless animals. Often they drown, but occasionally they will be washed up on an island or continent. Based on what we know of Atlantic Ocean currents and winds, Houle (1999) has calculated that small populations of monkeys could have survived long enough on these floating islands to complete a trans-Atlantic trip.

Present geological evidence supports this rafting hypothesis, with some researchers advocating that the monkeys rafted from North America to South America and others suggesting they rafted from Africa to South America or from Antarctica. At present, the evidence supports an African origin for three reasons. First, no suitable early anthropoid ancestors have been discovered in North America. Second, there is evidence of other animals (rats) rafting from Africa (Fleagle 1995). Third, New World fossil evidence points to a close similarity with African anthropoids (Flynn et al. 1995).

EVOLUTION OF THE MIOCENE HOMINOIDS

Continued evolution of the Old World anthropoids led to two major branches, one line leading to the modern Old World monkeys and the other line leading to the modern hominoids (apes and humans). The oldest evidence for fossil hominoids is based primarily on dental evidence and comes from Old World sites dating to the **Miocene epoch** (23–5 million years ago). Most Miocene mammals are fairly modern in form, and roughly half of all modern mammals were present during this time. South America and Australia were isolated due to continental drift. The land mass of **Eurasia** (a term given to the combined land masses of Europe and Asia) and Africa joined during part of the Miocene, roughly 16 million to 17 million years ago.

The early and middle Miocene (before 16 million years ago) was a time of heavy tropical forests, particularly in Africa. Subsequently, the climate became cooler and drier and there was an increase in open grasslands and mixed environments consisting of open woodlands, bushlands, and savannas.

Miocene epoch The fourth epoch of the Cenozoic era, dating between 23 million and 5 million years ago, when there was great diversity in hominoids.

Eurasia The combined land masses of Europe and Asia.

The Diversity of Miocene Hominoids

Looking at modern primates, it is apparent that there are more genera and species of monkeys than there are of apes. Monkeys are more diverse than apes. During the Miocene epoch, however, just the reverse was true—apes were incredibly diverse until the past 5 million to 10 million years. Since that time, the number of ape species has been declining. This decline is evident when we consider the diversity of fossil Miocene hominoids now known. Dozens of species are known from Africa, Asia, and Europe (Table 11.2). Compare this to the few apes alive today (see Chapter 9). In addition, remember that the list in Table 11.2 is incomplete—we find new fossils, and often new genera and species, all the time. In fact, this list could be out of date by the time you look at it!

Why have the number of apes declined and monkeys flourished since the Miocene? One possibility is the slow reproduction rate of modern apes. If Miocene apes were as nurturing of their offspring as modern apes are, then they may have reproduced too slowly and died out. This problem would have been exacerbated by environmental changes over time.

For the purpose of reconstructing the evolution of the apes, this past diversity creates a problem. Given that there were more species in the past than are alive today, this means that many fossil species have no living descendants. Decades ago, when the fossil record was less complete, it was tempting to identify any newly discovered fossil ape as the Miocene ancestor of one of the living apes, such as the chimpanzee or gorilla (Fleagle 1995). Today we have evidence of greater diversity in the past, but we now realize that evolution often produces initial diversity followed by later extinction of many branches. It therefore becomes more difficult to find the ancestors of modern apes. We can certainly recognize fossil apes in a general sense and see general evolutionary trends, but it is much more difficult to arrange the known fossils into a definitive evolutionary tree.

The Fossil Evidence

In general, the identification of the Miocene forms listed in Table 11.2 as *hominoid* is based on dental and cranial features. In most cases, much less is known about the **postcranial** skeleton (the skeleton below the skull), and such evidence that does exist shows characteristics different from those of modern apes. Overall, it appears that the postcranial structure of Miocene hominoids was often more generalized than that of modern apes, whose particular adaptations (e.g., knuckle walking) may be more recent. In light of the great diversity of Miocene hominoids, only a few selected forms are discussed here. Keep in mind that many other forms existed.

Proconsul   One early Miocene hominoid that appears to have evolutionary significance is the genus ***Proconsul***, which lived in Africa between 23 million and 17 million years ago. Specimens placed in this genus show considerable variation, particularly in overall size, making assignment to specific species somewhat difficult. The skeletal structure of *Proconsul* shows a mixture of

postcranial Referring to that part of the skeleton below the skull.

Proconsul A genus of fossil hominoid that lived in Africa between 23 million and 17 million years ago and that shows a number of monkey characteristics.

TABLE 11.2   Genera of Miocene Hominoids

		Date		
Region	Genus	Early Miocene	Middle Miocene	Late Miocene
Africa	Dendropithecus	x		
	Kalepithecus	x		
	Limnopithecus	x		
	Micropithecus	x		
	Morotopithecus	x		
	Proconsul	x		
	Rangwapithecus	x		
	Turkanapithecus	x		
	Afropithecus	x?	x	
	Nyanzapithecus	x	x	
	Simiolus	x	x	
	Equatorius		x	
	Mabokopithecus		x	
	Kenyapithecus		x	
	Ardipithecus			x
	Orrorin			x
	Otavipithecus		x	
	Samburupithecus			x
Asia	Griphopithecus		x	
	Ankarapithecus			x
	Gigantopithecus			x
	Lufengpithecus			x
	Sivapithecus			x
Europe	Griphopithecus		x	
	Dryopithecus		x	x
	Pliopithecus		x	x
	Graecopithecus			x
	Oreopithecus			x
	Ouranopithecus			x

This list includes two genera (*Ardipithecus* and *Orrorin*) now known from the Late Miocene that have been classified as hominids (see Chapter 12).

Source: Adapted from Fleagle (1999) with additions from S. Ward et al. (1999), Haile-Selassie (2001), Senut et al. (2001)

monkey and ape features (Figure 11.9). Like modern apes and humans, *Proconsul* did not have a tail (Ward et al. 1991). The limb proportions, however, are more like that of a monkey than an ape, with limbs of roughly the same size. In a modern ape, the front limbs are generally longer than the rear limbs, reflecting knuckle walking. The arms and hands of *Proconsul* are monkey-like, but the shoulders and elbows are more like those of apes. Analyses of the limb structure suggest that *Proconsul* was an unspecialized quadruped that lived in the trees and ate fruit (Pilbeam 1984; Walker and Teaford 1989).

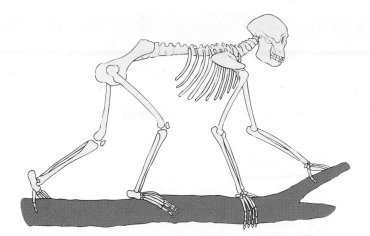

FIGURE 11.9

Reconstructed skeleton of
Proconsul. *(Redrawn from
Fleagle,* Primate Adaptation and
Evolution, *1988, with permission,
Academic Press, Inc.)*

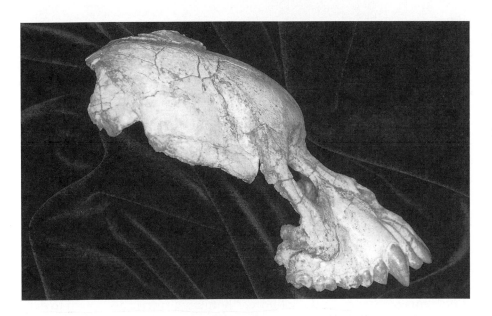

FIGURE 11.10

Side view of the skull of
Proconsul heseloni, *the
smallest of several species of*
Proconsul. *(Courtesy of Milford
Wolpoff, University of Michigan,
Ann Arbor)*

The skull of a typical *Proconsul* specimen (Figure 11.10) is more like that
of an ape in that it is large relative to overall body size. The teeth also demonstrate that these forms were hominoid (Figure 11.11). The shape of the lower
premolar is like that of modern apes, with a single dominant cusp rather than
two more or less equal-sized cusps, as found in humans. In apes, the single
large cusp rubs against, and sharpens, the upper canine tooth. Ape jaws also
have noticeable gaps (called **diastema**) next to the canine teeth, which allow the
jaws to close. Imagine the problem you would have if your canines were long
and protruding and you did not have a gap between the teeth in the opposite
jaw for them to fit into. You would not be able to close your mouth or chew!

Overall, the teeth and jaws of *Proconsul* are similar enough to those of
modern African apes that they were once thought to be direct ancestors of
the chimpanzee and gorilla. Today we realize that the situation is more complex than this. Environmental reconstructions show that *Proconsul* lived in

diastema A gap next to the
canine tooth that allows
space for the canine on the
opposing jaw.

Two upper jaws of Proconsul *specimens. Note the size and shape of the canine teeth.*
(Courtesy of Milford Wolpoff, University of Michigan, Ann Arbor)

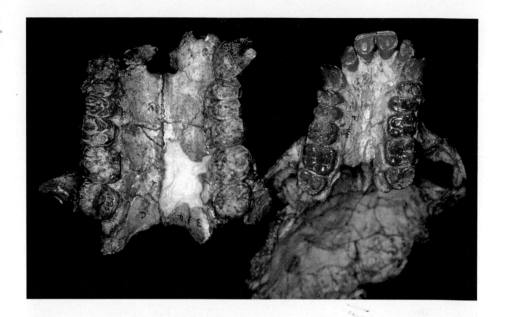

the Miocene forests and ate primarily fruits. The mixture of monkey and ape traits points to them as typical of a transition form from early generalized anthropoid to what we think of as an ape. Though definitely not identical to a modern ape, their overall structure is more like that of an ape than a monkey; hence, we refer to them as an early form of hominoid.

Proconsul was adapted to forest living and was a successful group for millions of years. As the climate cooled and became drier in certain regions during the Miocene, their habitat shrank. As competition for dwindling resources increased, other hominoids developed that were more successful in dealing with the new environments.

Other Miocene Hominoids   As discussed earlier, the sheer diversity of known Miocene hominoids makes constructing specific evolutionary trees difficult. It now appears that most of the Miocene hominoid species discovered to date are not related to the living apes (Larson 1998). Among the Miocene hominoids, some species appear to be too derived to serve as ancestors of any modern-day ape and are therefore representative of extinct side branches. A good example is the genus *Gigantopithecus,* discussed in this chapter's Special Topic.

Some Miocene hominoids show general similarity to living hominoids, but the diversity of the Miocene forms makes it difficult to determine if they are direct ancestors or closely related side branches. An example is the genus *Sivapithecus* (Figure 11.12), which lived in Asia between 14 million and 7 million years ago. The skull and teeth of *Sivapithecus* are very similar to modern-day orangutans (Pilbeam 1982). The overall shape of the skull, particularly when viewed from the side, is different from that of African apes but similar to the orangutan (Figure 11.13). The eye orbit of *Sivapithecus* has an oval shape, and the two eyes are close together, both features found in the orangutan. Arm bones of *Sivapithecus,* however, are different from those of living orangutans

SPECIAL TOPIC

The Giant Ape

One of the most interesting Miocene apes found so far is *Gigantopithecus*, which literally means "giant ape." The remains of *Gigantopithecus* have been found in Asia—China, India, and Vietnam—dating back as far as 9 million years ago (Ciochon et al. 1990). The Chinese specimens may be as recent as 500,000 years ago, meaning that this ape lived at the same time as the species *Homo erectus* (discussed in Chapter 13).

Although it sounds strange, *Gigantopithecus* was first found in a drugstore! Throughout much of Asia, fossil teeth and bones are ground into powder and used in various potions that are said to have healing properties. The teeth are often called "dragon's teeth" and are sold in apothecary shops. In 1935, the anthropologist Ralph von Koenigswald discovered huge teeth in one such store and later named the fossil remains *Gigantopithecus*. Since then, additional teeth and jaws have been recovered from fossil sites.

The major characteristic of *Gigantopithecus* is that it had huge molar and premolar teeth set in a massive jaw. Another interesting feature is that although the canine teeth are large, they are not that large relative to the rest of the teeth. The *relatively* smaller canines and the thick enamel on the molar teeth suggested to some that *Gigan-topithecus* might be related to humans, who have the same characteristics. We now realize that Miocene ape evolution is a lot more complicated than we once thought. *Gigantopithecus* is in some ways similar to *Sivapithecus* and probably represents a side branch in Asian ape evolution.

The large teeth and jaws have always captured people's imaginations. Based on the size of the teeth, some have suggested that *Gigantopithecus* might have stood over 9 feet tall! However, there are wide differences among species in the relationship between tooth size and body size, and it is more likely that *Gigantopithecus* was around 6 feet tall (which is still pretty big!). Until we find more of the body, we will not know for sure.

The large molars, thick molar enamel, small canines, and large jaws all suggest an ape that was well adapted for a diet consisting of items that were very hard to chew. In fact, the tips of the canines are worn down in a manner consistent with heavy chewing.

Some have suggested that *Gigantopithecus* is somehow related to the mythical "Abominable Snowman," presumably because of its geographic location and possible size. There is no support for this idea (nor for the existence of the Snowman). What *Gigantopithecus* really shows us is yet another example of the diversity of Miocene apes.

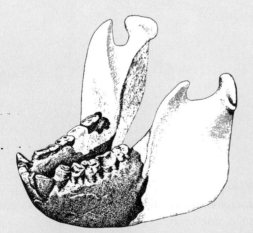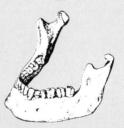

Comparison of the lower jaws of Gigantopithecus *(left), a modern gorilla (middle), and a modern human (right).* Gigantopithecus *has the largest overall size but relatively small canines compared to the gorilla. (Illustrations from* Gigantopithecus, *by E. L. Simons and P. C. Ettel. © 1970 by Scientific American, Inc. All rights reserved. Used with permission of Nelson H. Prentiss)*

FIGURE 11.12

Side view of Sivapithecus *specimen from Pakistan. (From Clark Spencer Larsen, Robert M. Matter, and Daniel L. Gebo,* Human Origins: The Fossil Record, *2nd ed., p. 36. Copyright © 1991, 1985 by Waveland Press, Inc., Prospect Heights, Ill. Reprinted with permission from the publisher)*

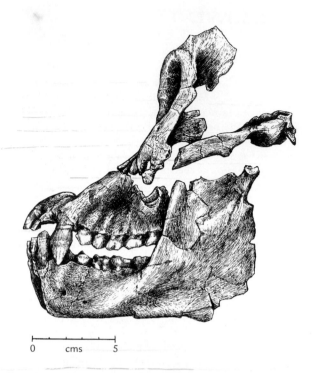

FIGURE 11.13

Comparison of the Sivapithecus *specimen GSP 15000 (*left*) with a modern orangutan (*right*). (Courtesy Dr. Ian Tattersall, American Museum of Natural History)*

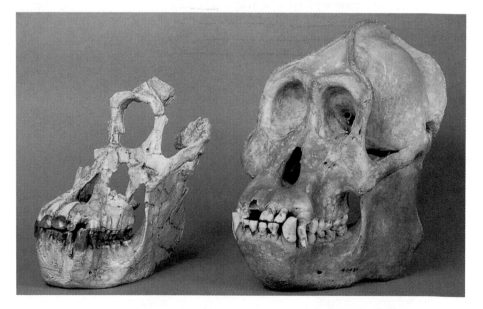

(Pilbeam et al. 1990). Overall, the fossil evidence suggests that *Sivapithecus* was closely related to, but possibly not a direct ancestor of, the orangutan.

Other Miocene hominoids can be placed *roughly* in relationship to living forms, but again we cannot determine if they are direct ancestors or related side branches of hominoid evolution. The African form *Afropithecus,* for example, may be related to a common ancestor of the African and Asian hominoids (Figure 11.14). What of the common ancestor of African apes and hominids?

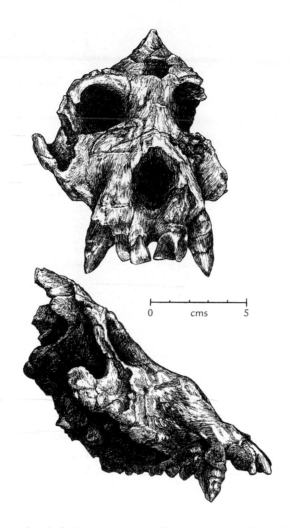

0   cms   5

FIGURE 11.14

Another example of the diversity of Miocene hominoids—the genus Afropithecus. *This specimen dates to roughly 17 million years ago. In some respects, it is similar to both* Proconsul *and to later hominoids such as* Sivapithecus, *but in other details (such as facial profile) it is quite different. It may represent a common ancestor of African and Asian hominoids or may be a side branch in hominoid evolution. (From Clark Spencer Larsen, Robert M. Matter, and Daniel L. Gebo,* Human Origins: The Fossil Record, *2nd ed., p. 27. © 1991, 1985 by Waveland Press, Inc., Prospect Heights, Ill. Reprinted with permission from the publisher)*

Again, we cannot be definite at present. There are a number of potential candidates for this common ancestor, including *Kenyapithecus, Ouranopithecus,* and *Dryopithecus,* but we lack sufficient information to be more specific other than suggesting all of these hominoids belonged to a group that most likely contained the common ancestor.

Genetic Evidence

In addition to fossil evidence, our interpretations of Miocene evolution must also take genetic evidence from the living hominoids into account. Since the 1960s, a comparison of the genetics of living organisms using a set of methods known as **molecular dating** has shed new light on hominoid evolution.

In Chapter 9 you read about how scientists use molecular information to judge the relative relationship between living hominoids. These methods provide some idea of which primates are most closely related. If certain assumptions are made, these methods can be used to provide an estimate of the date at which two species split from a common ancestor. When two species separate, mutations occur and neutral mutations accumulate in each line

molecular dating The application of methods of genetic analysis to estimate the sequence and timing of divergent evolutionary lines.

The diagram shows the genetic relationship between three hypothetical species (A, B, and C). Let us assume that the genetic distances between these species have been measured and are:

   Distance between species A and species B = 2
   Distance between species A and species C = 20
   Distance between species B and species C = 20

Based on these data:

   The distance between A and B is one-tenth the distance
   between A and C (2/20 = 1/10)
   The distance between A and B is one-tenth the distance
   between B and C (2/20 = 1/10)

Therefore, the date that species A and B diverged is one-tenth the date that species C diverged from the common ancestor of A and B. If we know from fossil evidence that species C diverged 40 million years ago, then species A and B diverged 4 million years ago (40 × 1/10 = 4).

independently. If the rate of accumulation is constant in both lines, then a comparison of molecular differences in living forms will provide us with a relative idea of how long the two species have been separated.

Imagine three species, A, B, and C, where molecular evidence indicates that A and B are more closely related to each other than either is to C. We would hypothesize that initially species C split off from a common ancestor of all three, followed by a split of species A and B later on. Suppose we then determine through molecular comparisons that the difference between A and B is one-tenth of the difference between either A or B and species C. This evidence suggests that the date of divergence of A and B was one-tenth that of the date of divergence between their common ancestor and species C. Now suppose that we know from fossil evidence that species C split off 40 million years ago. We can then infer that species A and B split from a common ancestor 4 million years ago because 4 million years is one-tenth of 40 million years. Here we have taken the molecular differences between species and used it as a "molecular clock," with our clock calibrated using the fossil record (Figure 11.15).

Molecular dating rests on two major assumptions. First, we assume that our calibration date is correct. As more fossil evidence accumulates, we might have to change our estimate of the date at which species C first split off. The second, more critical assumption is that neutral mutations do accumulate at the same rate in different lines. There are methods for testing this assumption, and it does appear to hold true for some molecular estimates.

Constancy in rates of mutation might seem inconceivable, given that mutations occur at random. But remember basic probability. If you flip a

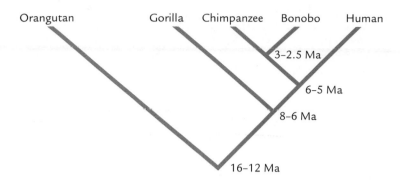

FIGURE 11.16

Suggested evolutionary relationships between humans and the great apes based on genetic analysis. The dates represent the range in estimates from molecular dating. (Horai et al. 1995, Gagneux et al. 1999, Chen and Li 2001)

coin 10 times, you will not expect to get five heads and five tails. If you flip the coin 10 million times, however, you expect to get results closer to the expected 50:50 ratio. Given millions of generations, the random nature of mutations also seems constant.

The first use of molecular dating was by Sarich and Wilson (1967), who looked at differences in albumin protein and found that the difference between humans and the African apes was one-sixth that found between either and the Old World monkeys. Using the then-established estimate of 30 million years for the separation of Old World monkeys, they computed that humans and the African apes had shared a common ancestor 5 million years ago. At that time, most paleoanthropologists thought a date of 15 million to 20 million years ago was more likely and disagreed strongly with Sarich and Wilson's estimate.

Since that time, a great deal of research has been done on molecular dating and its assumptions. Some researchers disputed the idea of constancy in mutation fixation rates and proposed nonlinear models in their place. Other proteins have been analyzed. Additional fossil material was found, and new interpretations of older data were made. Most paleoanthropologists now accept a much more recent split of humans and apes than was the consensus several decades ago.

Different data and different methods lead to some variation in estimates from molecular dating. Still, in general the results are consistent. Figure 11.16 shows these results superimposed on the picture of evolutionary relationships of humans and great apes that was discussed in Chapter 9. The first split was the line leading to orangutans roughly 16 million to 12 million years ago. The other line consisted of the African hominoids (as shown in the next chapter, the first hominids arose in Africa). The gorilla line split off next, at roughly 8 million to 6 million years ago, followed by the split between the hominid and chimpanzee–bonobo lines at roughly 6 million to 5 million years ago. The chimpanzee and bonobo lines then split at roughly 2.5 million years ago.

Conclusions

By the early 1960s, anthropologists thought that they had reconstructed the evolutionary tree of the living hominoids and had suitable fossil species identified as the ancestors of modern species. The preliminary dental evidence suggested a small number of fossil apes dating back 20 million to 15 million

FIGURE 11.17

Alternative models of the evolutionary relationship among the African hominoids. (a) The gorilla splits off first and the chimpanzee–bonobo and human lines have a more recent common ancestor. (b) The gorilla and chimpanzee–bonobo lines have a more recent common ancestor. Genetic and some anatomical evidence favors (a), but some anatomical analysis favors (b).

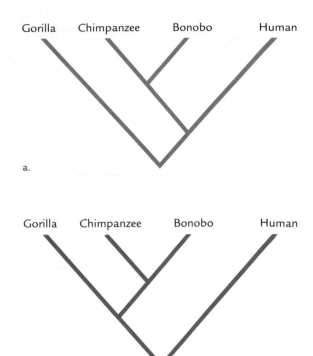

years that resembled, in a general sense, presumed ancestors of gorillas, chimpanzees, and humans. We now realize these conclusions were premature. The Miocene hominoids were much more diverse than once thought. The postcranial remains of the early forms (e.g., *Proconsul*) showed us that the earliest Miocene hominoids were quite primitive in some features and had only recently branched off from the Old World monkeys. This evidence, combined with insights from genetics and molecular dating, led to our current observation of a much later divergence of modern hominoids. Instead of an ape-human split some 20 million to 15 million years ago, we now suggest a more recent date of 8 million to 5 million years ago, with gorillas branching off earlier than the line leading to chimpanzees and bonobos. There is still some debate over the exact branching pattern of the African hominoids. Many accept the earlier divergence of the gorilla line, but others argue that gorillas, chimpanzees, and bonobos all shared a common ancestor after the divergence of hominids (Figure 11.17).

Because there were many more hominoids in the past than live today, the obvious conclusion is that many of the fossils we find belong to species that became extinct side branches. We are able to see, in a general sense, the broad outline of Miocene evolution, but we are not able to draw a detailed and complete "family tree." During the early Miocene, the first hominoids were primitive in many ways, and they represent a link between monkeys and apes. During the rest of the Miocene, several adaptive radiations of Miocene hominoids led to many species in Africa, Europe, and Asia. By 6 million years ago or so, the line leading to later hominids, our own ancestors, had diverged.

As will be discussed in detail in the next chapter, one or two different hominid species evolved by the end of the Miocene.

SUMMARY

Following the extinction of the dinosaurs 65 million years ago, early mammal forms spread out into new environments. Some early insectivores began to adapt more and more to life in the trees, developing grasping hands and binocular stereoscopic vision. These changes may have begun in response to the needs of insect predation and been used later to exploit additional food resources in a three-dimensional environment. The origin of primates began with the primate-like mammals of the Paleocene epoch and the ancient prosimians of the Eocene. Primitive anthropoids evolved from a group of Eocene primates. The early Oligocene anthropoids ultimately gave rise to the separate lines of Old World monkeys and hominoids.

The Miocene epoch is characterized by two major adaptive radiations. In the early Miocene, primitive hominoid forms appeared in Africa. These forms, placed in the genus *Proconsul,* were similar in some ways to later apes but were also monkey-like in a number of features. They had jaws and teeth like those of later apes and lacked a tail. Their postcranial skeleton was generalized and primitive in a number of features.

During the middle Miocene, several new genera of hominoids evolved. These hominoids include the ancestors of present-day great apes and humans, although the specific evolutionary relationships between Miocene species and modern species are not clear at present.

We are not able to identify precisely the common ancestor of the African apes and humans. Evidence from molecular dating supports a fairly recent split, roughly 6 million to 5 million years ago. Although several genera of fossil apes could be a common ancestor (or related to a common ancestor), we cannot be definitive at this time. What is clear, however, is that there was extensive diversity in hominoids during the Miocene.

SUPPLEMENTAL READINGS

Fleagle, J. G. 1999. *Primate Adaptation and Evolution.* San Diego: Academic Press. The most recent and comprehensive text available on primate evolution.

Lewin, R. 1997. *Bones of Contention: Controversies in the Search for Human Origins.* 2d ed. Chicago: University of Chicago Press. A lively summary of historical controversies in primate and human evolution. Chapters 5 and 6 deal with the impact of molecular dating and new fossils on interpretations of Miocene evolution.

INTERNET RESOURCES

http://anthro.palomar.edu/earlyprimates/first_primates.htm
The First Primates, a tutorial covering the broad outline of primate evolution.

http://www.cruzio.com/~cscp/-pics1.htm
Picture Gallery of Fossil Hominoids and Hominids from China.

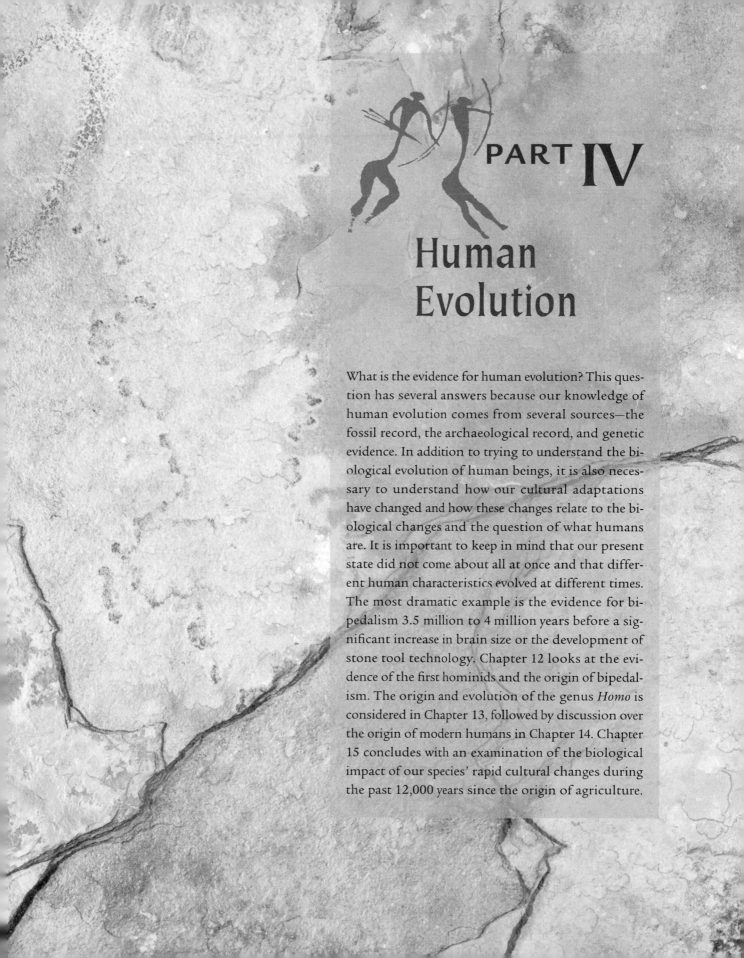

PART IV

Human Evolution

What is the evidence for human evolution? This question has several answers because our knowledge of human evolution comes from several sources—the fossil record, the archaeological record, and genetic evidence. In addition to trying to understand the biological evolution of human beings, it is also necessary to understand how our cultural adaptations have changed and how these changes relate to the biological changes and the question of what humans are. It is important to keep in mind that our present state did not come about all at once and that different human characteristics evolved at different times. The most dramatic example is the evidence for bipedalism 3.5 million to 4 million years before a significant increase in brain size or the development of stone tool technology. Chapter 12 looks at the evidence of the first hominids and the origin of bipedalism. The origin and evolution of the genus *Homo* is considered in Chapter 13, followed by discussion over the origin of modern humans in Chapter 14. Chapter 15 concludes with an examination of the biological impact of our species' rapid cultural changes during the past 12,000 years since the origin of agriculture.

Hominid Origins

How old is the human species? Anthropologists are frequently asked this question, and it seems simple enough. But in fact we have no simple answer. The answer depends on how we define human beings. If we limit our question to humans who are more or less anatomically similar to living humans, the answer is roughly 100,000 years. If we include all large-brained humans, even those with a somewhat different skull shape, the answer might be close to 500,000 years. If we focus on all members of the genus *Homo*, with some significant cranial expansion and a dependence on stone tools, the answer is more than 2 million years. If we include all bipedal hominids, the answer is close to 6 million years.

Past human evolution was not a one-step process. Humans did not emerge instantaneously from an apelike ancestor. What we are, biologically and culturally, is the product of many different evolutionary changes occurring at different times. The fossil record of human evolution is now complete enough to see that the characteristics of *living* humans have evolved over time in a mosaic fashion. New fossil evidence now suggests that bipedalism first arose close to 6 million years ago, around the time of the divergence of hominids and African apes. A number of dental changes took place over the next few million years. The first major increase in brain size, and the first use of stone tool technology, took place between 2.5 million and 2 million

◄ *Fossil footprints at the site of Laetoli, Tanzania. These footprints, dating over 3.7 million years old, were most likely made by the species* Australopithecus afarensis, *an early hominid. The inset shows a reconstruction of what this species might have looked like. (Footprints: © John Reader/Science Photo Library/ Photo Researchers, Inc.; Inset: Neg. #4744(5). Photo by D. Finnin/C. Chesek. Courtesy Department of Library Services, American Museum of Natural History)*

years ago. Brain size roughly equivalent to living humans appeared within the past few hundred thousand years, and modern cranial shape within the past 100,000 years or so. Many of our current cultural patterns appear even more recently. It was only 12,000 years ago that humans began relying on agriculture and only 6,000 years ago that the first civilizations and complex state-level societies appeared. Many of the things we take for granted in our own lives today, such as automobiles, nuclear energy, and computer technology, are even more recent, many developing only in the last generation or two.

This chapter examines the beginning of the story of human evolution, focusing on the earliest hominids prior to the appearance of the genus *Homo*. The fossil species discussed in this chapter all lived in Africa between 6 million and 1 million years ago.

OVERVIEW OF HUMAN EVOLUTION

The study of human evolution is fascinating but often confusing the first time around. To follow the evolutionary history of the first hominids, you must become familiar with a multitude of different names, places, and events. Just as rereading a book often reveals more insight because you now have a framework within which to integrate the information, it is useful to consider the general picture of human evolution before absorbing the details.

A succinct discussion of the *main events* in human evolution goes something like this: "The first hominids appeared in Africa about 6 million years ago. They had apelike teeth and ape-sized brains but walked on two legs. By 2 million years ago, brain size began to increase significantly and stone tools were being used. Hunting added meat to a diet of fruits and vegetable matter obtained from gathering. Some populations expanded out of Africa into Asia and Europe. By half a million years ago, brain size was even larger and technology continued to develop. Ultimately, some of these large-brained forms evolved into us." This summary, while accurate, is of course overly simplistic. For one thing, it implies that there was a steady line of change from the earliest hominids to us. In actuality, the process is quite a bit more complex, and there were several points along the way when more than one hominid line existed at the same time.

The most important concept we learn from this overview is that bipedalism evolved well *before* larger brains. The final section of this chapter looks at the evidence for the origin of bipedalism and examines possible hypotheses for its origin.

Let us look at the story of human evolution now in somewhat more detail (Figure 12.1 provides a graphic representation of this review). As discussed in the previous chapter, our best estimates from molecular dating suggest that the hominid line split from the African apes about 6 million years ago. Our earliest fossil evidence of hominids is at this time, represented by the genus *Ardipithecus* and possibly by another genus, *Orrorin*. These early hominids had very primitive apelike teeth but were bipedal and lived in and around the forested woodlands of eastern Africa. One or more species of

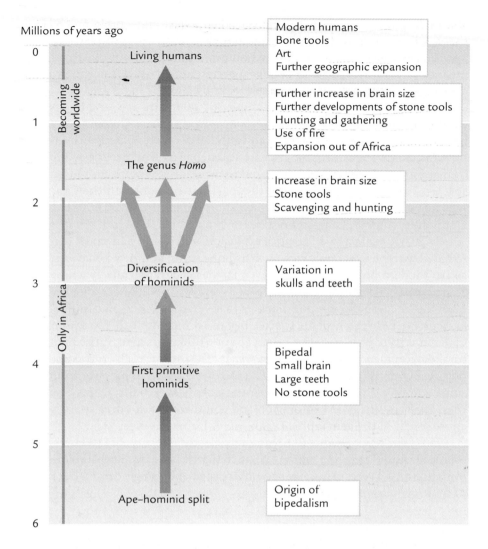

Millions of years ago

Modern humans
Bone tools
Art
Further geographic expansion

Living humans

Further increase in brain size
Further developments of stone tools
Hunting and gathering
Use of fire
Expansion out of Africa

The genus *Homo*

Increase in brain size
Stone tools
Scavenging and hunting

Diversification
of hominids

Variation in
skulls and teeth

First primitive
hominids

Bipedal
Small brain
Large teeth
No stone tools

Ape–hominid split

Origin of
bipedalism

Becoming worldwide

Only in Africa

FIGURE 12.1

*Simplified summary of
hominid evolution emphasizing
major evolutionary events.*

primitive hominids lived in Africa over the next few million years, most classified in the genus *Australopithecus*, and they retained their apelike features in some teeth and had ape-sized brains. These early hominids were bipedal, but they may have spent time climbing in the trees as well as walking on the ground. They foraged for food, primarily fruit, in the woodlands and savanna. By 3 million years ago, a rapid diversification led to at least two distinct lines of hominid evolution. One line led to several species known as the "robusts," named after their large back teeth and powerful chewing muscles. The robusts were well adapted to a diet that was hard to chew, such as seeds, nuts, and hard-skinned fruits. They became extinct by 1 million years ago. The other line of hominid began to rely more and more on learned behavior and perhaps began using the first stone tools.

One species of *Australopithecus* evolved into the first members of the genus *Homo* sometime between 2.5 million and 2 million years ago. The species known as *Homo erectus* appears in Africa by 2 million years ago, having an essentially modern skeleton, full bipedal adaptations, and a brain much larger than earlier hominids (roughly three-fourths the size of a modern human, on average). *Homo erectus* was the first hominid to expand out of Africa, moving into parts of Asia and Europe. *Homo erectus* hunted, used fire, and invented a new form of general purpose stone tool known as the hand axe.

Brain size increased rapidly by about 700,000 years ago, and by 500,000 years ago brain size was roughly the same as ours today. These humans still had a rather large face and a less well-rounded skull compared with modern humans, however. Anthropologists are still debating whether these "archaic" humans are an earlier stage of our own species or represent more than one species. The relationship between these archaic humans and the first more "anatomically modern" humans, which appeared in Africa 130,000 years ago, is still quite controversial (and is discussed in detail in Chapter 14).

By 50,000 years ago, a "creative explosion" of culture had taken place, associated with new technologies, such as bone tools, and new behaviors, such as art. Modern humans dispersed even farther geographically, reaching Australia by 60,000 years ago and the New World by 13,000 years ago. Starting 12,000 years ago, human populations in several different places developed agriculture and the human species began to increase rapidly in number. Cities and state-level societies began about 6,000 years ago. Subsequent cultural developments took place at an ever-increasing pace. The Industrial Revolution began only 250 years ago. The use of electricity as a power source became common only during the twentieth century. Finally, it has been less than 50 years since the exploration and colonization of outer space began, another step in the geographic expansion of human beings.

This brief review shows one thing very clearly—what we are today as modern humans did not come about all at the same time but at different times over millions of years. Thus, we should not speak of a single origin, but rather of multiple origins.

THE FIRST HOMINIDS

When Darwin wrote his first edition of *On the Origin of Species,* very little was known about the fossil record of human evolution. By the beginning of the twentieth century we knew a bit more, but only about species now classified in the genus *Homo.* In 1924, anatomist Raymond Dart discovered an earlier form of hominid that had humanlike teeth and walked upright but still had a small ape-sized brain. Dart (1925) named this new species *Australopithecus africanus* (which translates as the southern ape of Africa, named so because it was found in South Africa). Over the next several decades, additional specimens were discovered and several new species of the genus *Australopithecus* were named.

By the early 1970s, three species of *Australopithecus* were known, with the oldest dating back about 3 million years. By the late 1980s, another two species had been discovered, and the earliest hominid evidence now dated back 4 million years. Since 1990, five new species of early hominid have been discovered. Indeed, two of these species have been discovered since the last edition of this textbook! As you can see, the amount of information we have on these first hominids has increased dramatically in recent years.

We now have evidence for at least 10 species of early hominid from Africa, dating between roughly 6 million and 2 million years ago. This increase has shown us that early hominid evolution was not a simple linear chain with one species evolving into the next; rather, it is a "bush" with many branches. Although there is only one hominid species alive today (us), the situation was different in the past. At several points in time there was more than one hominid species. The challenge for anthropologists is to figure out how these different species were related to each other and our own path of ancestry. Which ones were our direct ancestors, and which ones represent extinct side branches?

The first hominids were bipedal but had small **cranial capacities,** a measure of the interior volume of the brain case, measured in cubic centimeters (cc). In many ways, the early hominids can be considered bipedal apes. They are classified as hominid because they were bipedal and possessed certain derived features of the teeth (although this varies among species). Because they also retained a number of primitive ape characteristics, we generally do not equate them directly with "humans." To do so implies that their biology and behavior were in many ways similar to our own.

The early hominids described in this chapter have been found dating between 6 million and 1 million years ago. This time period includes portions of the Miocene epoch, the **Pliocene epoch** (5–1.7 Ma), and the **Pleistocene epoch** (1.7–0.01 Ma).

The first hominids have all been found only in Africa, which supports Darwin's early idea that Africa was the birthplace of hominids and is consistent with the fact that the closest living relatives of humans are the African apes. It also means that hominids were limited to a specific environment— woodlands and tropical grasslands for the most part. Not until later in the fossil record (see Chapters 13 and 14) do we see evidence for hominids moving outside of Africa. Figure 12.2 shows the location of some of the major sites of the hominids discussed in this chapter, and Table 12.1 lists some of these sites. Note that there have been two major areas of discovery, South Africa and East Africa. The geology of South Africa has made chronometric dating difficult, and for many years we were not sure exactly how old the early South African hominids were. Sites in East Africa are better dated; extensive volcanic activity in East Africa millions of years ago allows us to use potassium-argon and argon-argon dating methods at these sites.

Primitive Hominids (6–3 Ma)

This section focuses on the earliest hominids, dating between 6 million and 3 million years ago. Four species have been discovered within this time range and can be considered as primitive hominids. Remember that "primitive" refers in a biological sense to the possession of traits from earlier ancestors. In this case, the first hominids can be considered primitive in many ways because they retain a number of ape characteristics that are not found in later hominids. From an evolutionary perspective, this makes perfect sense. After

cranial capacity A measurement of the interior volume of the brain case used as an approximate estimate of brain size.

Pliocene epoch The fifth epoch of the Cenozoic era, dating from 5 million to 1.7 million years ago.

Pleistocene epoch The sixth epoch of the Cenozoic era, dating from 1.7 million to 0.01 million years ago.

FIGURE 12.2

Location of some of the major sites in Africa where early hominid specimens have been found.

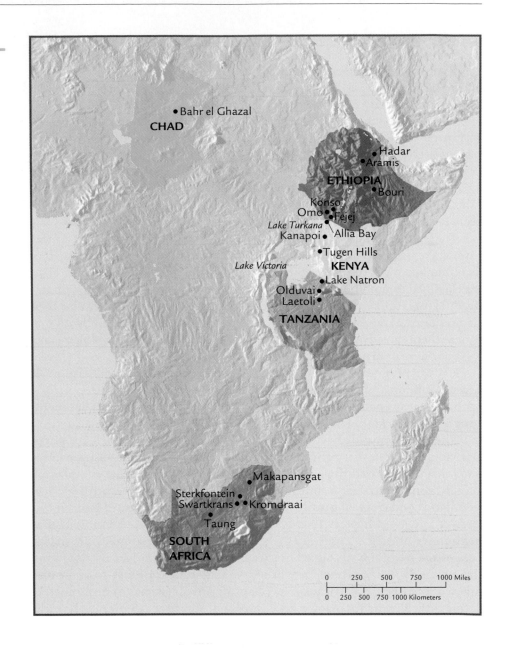

Orrorin tugenensis An early primitive hominid species from Africa dating to the late Miocene (6 Ma).

Ardipithecus ramidus An early primitive hominid species from Africa dating between 5.8 million and 4.4 million years ago.

the African ape and hominid lines split, each line would have retained primitive characteristics of its common ancestor for some time. Among the earliest hominids, such characteristics include large canine teeth, apelike configurations of the skull and teeth, and ape-sized brains. The earliest hominids also had certain derived characteristics, primarily the development of bipedal anatomy. Even here, however, the earliest hominids are somewhat primitive.

Orrorin *and* Ardipithecus—*The First Hominids?* The oldest known species that have been labeled hominid are ***Orrorin tugenesis*** (6 Ma) and ***Ardipithecus ramidus*** (5.8–4.4 Ma). Both are only recently known; *Ardipithecus* was first announced in 1995 and *Orrorin* in 2001. *Orrorin* is known from the frag-

TABLE 12.1 List of Major Fossil Sites for Early Hominids

Species	Country	Locality	Age (Ma)	Figure in Text
Orrorin tugenensis	Kenya	Tugen Hills	6.0	
Ardipithecus ramidus	Ethiopia	Middle Awash	5.8–5.2	
		Aramis	4.4	12.3
Australopithecus anamensis	Kenya	Allia Bay	4.1	12.4
		Kanapoi	4.2–3.9	
Australopithecus afarensis	Kenya	East Turkana	4.0+	
	Tanzania	Laetoli	3.8–3.6	12.8
	Ethiopia	Fejej	3.6+	
		Hadar	3.5–2.9	12.5, 12.6, 12.9
		Maka	3.4	
	Chad*	Bahr el Ghazal	3.4–3.0	
Kenyanthropus platyops	Kenya	Lomekwi	3.5–3.2	12.10
Australopithecus aethiopicus	Kenya	West Turkana	2.5	12.16
Australopithecus robustus	Republic of South Africa	Swartkrans	2.0?–1.5	12.12, 12.14
		Kromdraii	2.0?	
Australopithecus boisei	Ethiopia	Omo	2.0–1.2	
		Konso	1.4	
	Tanzania	Olduvai Gorge	1.8	
	Kenya	Lake Baringo	2.0–1.5	
		Lake Natron	1.5	12.11
		East Turkana	1.5	12.13
Australopithecus africanus	Republic of South Africa	Sterkfontein	3.3–2.3	12.17, 12.18
		Makapansgat	3.0?	
		Taung	2.5?	
Australopithecus garhi	Ethiopia	Bouri	2.5	12.19, 12.20

Note: Some anthropologists consider the robust australopithecines in a separate genus, *Paranthropus,* where they are given the species names *P. aethiopicus, P. robustus,* and *P. boisei.*

*It has been suggested that these specimens comprise another species, *Australopithecus bahrelghazali,* but most authors consider them as *Australopithecus afarensis.*

Sources: Fleagle et al. (1991), Leakey et al. (1995, 2001), Coffing et al. (1994), White (1995), White et al. (1994, 2000), Suwa et al. (1997), Larsen et al. (1998), Asfaw et al. (1999), Clarke (1999), Klein (1999), Haile-Selassie (2001), Senut et al. (2001)

mentary remains of several individuals, including a number of dental remains and some leg and arm bone fragments. According to the discoverers, the leg bone indicates this was a bipedal hominid, although the arm bone indicates that this species still spent a fair amount of time in the trees (Senut et al. 2001).

Ardipithecus was first discovered in the early 1990s at the Aramis site in Ethiopia in remains dated at 4.4 million years ago. In mid-2001, additional specimens of *Ardipithecus* found in the Middle Awash in Ethiopia were dated between 5.8 million and 5.2 million years ago (Haile-Selassie 2001; White 1995; White et al. 1994). The remains of *Ardipithecus* are very fragmentary and not yet fully described, but they do provide strong evidence of an early primitive hominid.

FIGURE 12.3

Fragmentary remains of Ardipithecus ramidus, *an early hominid species (dating back 5.8–4.4 Ma). Although fragmentary, the remains of* Ardipithecus *suggest a species with bipedalism but very apelike teeth. (© 1994 Tim D. White/Brill Atlanta)*

Most of the remains are dental (Figure 12.3), and they have a number of apelike features, such as large canines. Certain features, however, are hominid, such as the canines being more like incisors in structure (as is the case with later hominids and living humans). The cranial remains are also apelike and show many primitive characteristics, although the location of the **foramen magnum** (the large hole in the base of the skull where the spinal cord enters) suggests bipedalism. A toe bone also supports the interpretation that *Ardipithecus* was bipedal.

Both *Orrorin* and *Ardipithecus* are primitive in a number of features. Both species existed around the time molecular dating estimates that the hominid line split off from the African apes. As such, we would expect the earliest fossils to be very primitive and retain a number of apelike traits. This is exactly what the fossils show, although the primitive nature of both species makes evolutionary relationships difficult to interpret. The closer we get to the point of ape–hominid divergence, the more difficult it becomes to tell which line a given species belongs to. This problem is reflected in the ongoing debate over the evolutionary status of these species. At present, most researchers accept *Ardipithecus* as a hominid (although see Senut et al. 2001), but the evolutionary status of *Orrorin* is more in doubt (e.g., Aiello and Collard 2001). Haile-Selassie (2001) argues that *Orrorin* might actually represent the last common ancestor of the hominid and chimpanzee–bonobo lines. Further analysis and data are needed to resolve these questions (at this writing, both *Orrorin* and the oldest *Ardipithecus* specimens had just been announced, and it will take several years for additional comparisons to be made).

Australopithecus Anamensis   A somewhat younger species, ***Australopithecus anamensis,*** is definitely a hominid, although still somewhat primitive. A number of the first hominids have been assigned to the genus ***Australopithecus,*** which literally translates as "southern ape," so named because the

foramen magnum The large opening at the base of the skull where the spinal cord enters, which is located more under the skull in bipeds as compared to four-legged vertebrates.

Australopithecus anamensis A hominid species that lived in East Africa between 4.2 million and 3.9 million years ago. It was a biped but had many primitive apelike features of the skull and teeth.

Australopithecus A genus of fossil hominid that lived between 4.2 million and 1 million years ago and is characterized by bipedal locomotion, small brain size, large face, and large teeth.

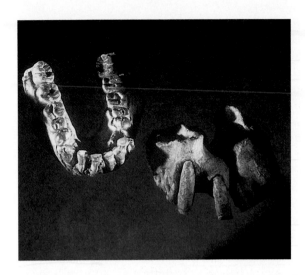

FIGURE 12.4

Some fossil specimens of Australopithecus anamensis: *lower jaw* (left) *and facial* (right). Australopithecus anamensis *was a biped but still had very apelike features in the jaws and teeth.* (© Kenneth Garrett/National Geographic Society Image Collection)

first species discovered in this genus was found in South Africa (Dart 1925). This may sound confusing because *Australopithecus anamensis,* as well as a number of other australopithecine species, are known only from *East* Africa. The reason for this confusion is that scientists have agreed to an international system of naming genera and species in which the first name given takes precedence even if the name is no longer the most appropriate. Although confusing at times, this system is better than having everyone rename things all the time.

The species *A. anamensis* ("*A.*" is an abbreviation of *Australopithecus*) is fairly recently known, having been announced in 1995 (Leakey et al. 1995). Fossils of this species come from two sites along the shores of Lake Turkana (see Figure 12.2). The species name is based on the word for lake (*anam*) in the Turkana language. A total of 52 specimens have been recovered from two sites (Leakey et al. 1995, 1998). The fossil evidence consists primarily of dental remains (Figure 12.4) but also includes skull fragments and pieces of an upper arm bone and lower leg bone. The leg bone is particularly informative because it indicates bipedalism. The teeth, jaw, and skull fragments all show primitive apelike characteristics, such as large canine teeth and a small ear hole. Estimates of weight, based on statistical relationships known to exist between body size and bone measurements, suggest individuals weighed roughly 47 kg to 58 kg (104–128 lb). In summary, *A. anamensis* shows a mix of features that are primitive and derived (such as bipedalism), further evidence that human features did not evolve all at once. It is possible that this species represents a link between the earliest and later hominids (Ward, Leakey, and Walker 1999).

Australopithecus Afarensis   The best known of the primitive hominids is the species ***Australopithecus afarensis,*** which lived in East Africa between 4 million and 2.9 million years ago and may include less well-known hominids found at one site in Chad in central Africa. Much of our data on this

Australopithecus afarensis A primitive hominid found in East Africa dating between 4 million and 3 million years ago.

species comes from Donald Johanson's fieldwork in the 1970s at the site of Hadar, Ethiopia (see Figure 12.2). The fossils collected by Johanson and colleagues date between 3.5 million and 2.9 million years ago. Additional fossils collected by Mary Leakey at the site of Laetoli, Tanzania, date to 3.8 million years ago. Johanson and colleagues (1978) noted the close similarity between the Hadar and Laetoli finds and placed them together in the species *Australopithecus afarensis*. The species name *afarensis* derives from the Afar region where the Hadar site is located. Additional fossils of *A. afarensis* have also been discovered at a number of other sites, mostly in Ethiopia (see Table 12.1). The abundance of data available for *A. afarensis* gives us a more detailed picture of their anatomy than is so far available for the earlier primitive hominids already described.

A. afarensis is less primitive than earlier hominids but still more primitive than later hominids. It is more apelike in certain characteristics, such as cranial features (Figure 12.5), than later hominid species, having a small brain and a lower face that juts out. Nonetheless, it is definitely hominid, for it possessed the human form of bipedalism. The most dramatic find showing bipedalism is the fossil nicknamed "Lucy," a 40 percent complete skeleton of an adult female (Figure 12.6). We know Lucy was an adult because her third molar teeth had fully erupted, an event that occurs in young adulthood in hominids. We also know she was a female because most of her pelvis is intact. Determining the sex of a fossil is best done by examination of the pelvis (Figure 12.7). Females have a wider and more rounded pelvic opening among other features. Such comparisons show that Lucy was a female.

Although an adult, Lucy was small. She was little over a meter tall (about 3 ft 3 in.) and weighed roughly 27 kg (60 lb) (McHenry 1992). Her pelvic bones and femur show bipedal locomotion. In addition to Lucy, other fossils show bipedalism, including a knee joint. In addition, fossil footprints have been found at the Laetoli site dating back almost 3.8 million years (Figure 12.8). These prints show the bipedal characteristics of a nondivergent big toe, heel strike, and a well-developed arch.

All of this evidence indicates that *A. afarensis* was bipedal. Because bipedal locomotion is unique to humans among living primates, we classify *A. afarensis*

FIGURE 12.5

Side view of a cranium of Australopithecus afarensis. *(© Institute of Human Origins, photograph by W. H. Kimbel)*

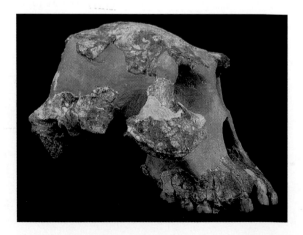

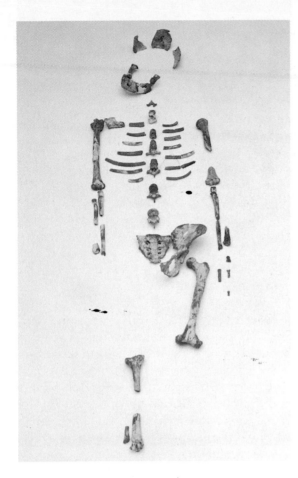

FIGURE 12.6

The skeletal remains of "Lucy," a 40 percent complete specimen of Australopithecus afarensis. *(© John Reader/Science Photo Library/Photo Researchers, Inc.)*

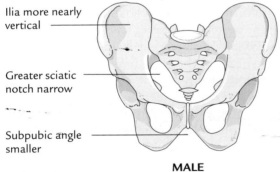

Ilia more nearly vertical

Greater sciatic notch narrow

Subpubic angle smaller

MALE

FIGURE 12.7

Comparison of the pelvic anatomy of modern human males and females. (From Human Antiquity: An Introduction to Physical Anthropology and Archaeology, *2d ed., by Kenneth Feder and Michael Park, Fig. 7.17. Copyright © 1993 by Mayfield Publishing Company. Reprinted with permission of The McGraw-Hill Companies)*

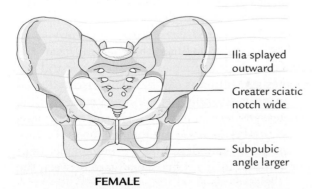

Ilia splayed outward

Greater sciatic notch wide

Subpubic angle larger

FEMALE

FIGURE 12.8

Fossil footprints at the Laetoli site. (© John Reader/Science Photo Library/Photo Researchers, Inc.)

as a hominid, although opinion differs on *how* bipedal it was. Some have noted certain ape tendencies in the postcranial fossils, such as relatively long arms and curved finger and toe bones. These apelike traits have been interpreted in two ways. First, they might simply be retentions from a recent apelike origin. Second, they might indicate that despite its bipedalism *A. afarensis* did not walk exactly the same way we do, had considerable climbing ability, and may have spent a fair amount of time in the trees (Stern and Susman 1983).

Cranial material for *A. afarensis* consists of a number of fragments and a fairly complete skull of an adult male (see Figure 12.5). These remains show a small brain, a large protruding face, and a number of primitive features on the back and bottom of the cranium (Kimbel et al. 1994). The brain size of *A. afarensis* ranges between 400 cc and 500 cc (Aiello and Dunbar 1993). Overall, the skull of *A. afarensis* resembles that of a small ape.

The teeth of *A. afarensis* are less primitive than found in *Orrorin, Ardipithecus,* or *A. anamensis,* but they are still more primitive than in *Homo*. The teeth show a number of characteristics intermediate between apes and humans. The teeth of modern apes and humans can be easily distinguished (Figure 12.9). The canines of apes are generally large and protrude past the surface of the other teeth, whereas modern humans have small, nonprojecting canine teeth. The canine teeth of *A. afarensis* are intermediate; they are larger and more projecting than those of modern humans but smaller than in most modern apes. An ape's upper jaw has a diastema (gap) between the

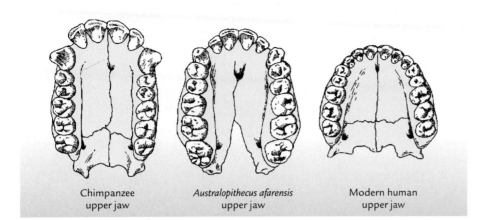

Chimpanzee upper jaw

Australopithecus afarensis upper jaw

Modern human upper jaw

FIGURE 12.9

Comparison of the teeth and upper jaws of a modern chimpanzee, Australopithecus afarensis, *and a modern human. In most features, the teeth and jaws of* Australopithecus afarensis *are intermediate between those of modern apes and modern humans. (From* Lucy: The Beginnings of Humankind, *© 1981 Luba Dmytryk Godz/Brill Atlanta)*

canine and the adjacent incisor. This space is needed for the large lower canine to fit into when an ape closes its jaw. Modern humans do not have a diastema (in fact, we are often lucky to be able to get a piece of dental floss between our front teeth). The jaws of *A. afarensis* show a diastema larger than that of modern humans but smaller than that of modern apes. The lower first premolar of a modern ape is pointed with one cusp, whereas the lower first premolar of a modern human has two cusps ("bicuspid"). The lower premolar teeth of *A. afarensis* have two cusps, but one cusp is more developed than the other—an intermediate condition. Most dental features of *A. afarensis* show a state that is intermediate between apes and humans. As such, *A. afarensis* is a link between the earliest and later hominids.

What can we tell about the behavior of *A. afarensis*? No evidence for stone tool manufacture has been found, but this does not mean they did not use tools made of perishable materials, such as wooden digging sticks. Analyses of anatomical remains show a wide range of variation in size, which suggests extensive sexual dimorphism. If our observations on living primates can be accurately applied, such sexual dimorphism suggests a polygynous social structure (one or several adult males and several adult females).

Kenyanthropus Platyops   Until recently, *A. afarensis* was the only hominid species known for much of the time period between 4 million and 3 million years ago. This situation has now changed. In 2001, Meave Leakey and colleagues proposed a new species of fossil hominid, ***Kenyanthropus platyops*** (which translates as "the flat-faced man from Kenya"). Remains of *Kenyanthropus* were discovered west of Lake Turkana in Kenya in deposits dating between 3.5 million and 3.2 million years ago.

Like *A. afarensis,* this species has a mixture of primitive and derived features, although not the same set as found in *A. afarensis* or other early hominid species. Primitive features include a small brain, a jutting lower face, and a small ear hole (shared with *A. anamensis*). *K. platyops* also has a number of derived features, including small molars, a flat face, and a tall cheek region (Figure 12.10). Apart from the small brain size, this species is similar to one

Kenyanthropus platyops
A species of early hominid in East Africa dating to 3.5 million years ago. This species combines a number of primitive features (small brain, jutting face) and derived features (small molars, flat face). Its evolutionary status is unclear.

FIGURE 12.10

Three-quarters view of the skull of Kenyanthropus platyops, *specimen number KNM-WT 40000. (© National Museums of Kenya)*

of the first species of *Homo* (*Homo rudolfensis,* described in the next chapter). The evolutionary status of *K. platyops* is not yet clear, but it does provide additional evidence of past adaptive radiations of the early hominids (Leakey et al. 2001; Lieberman 2001).

Later Hominids

Starting around 3 million years ago, adaptive radiations of the early hominids were followed by additional diversification within the genus *Australopithecus*. Some of these later species evolved into creatures with immense back teeth, whereas others were less specialized. We suspect that the ancestors of the genus *Homo* belong to this latter group.

Robust Australopithecines   Three species of *Australopithecus* are often referred to collectively as the **robust australopithecines.** The term *robust* comes from the fact that these forms had very large and robust back teeth, jaws, and faces relative to other hominids. These robust species lived in Africa between 2.5 million and 1.2 million years ago, after which time they became extinct. They are not our ancestors but rather our close relatives. Although many anthropologists consider the robusts as part of the genus *Australopithecus,* some have suggested they be given their own genus, *Paranthropus.*

One of the key characteristics of the robust australopithecines is their large back teeth and relatively small front teeth. Apart from size, the overall structure of the teeth is quite human: the canines are nonprojecting, there is no diastema, and the lower premolar has two cusps. In terms of size, however, the robust australopithecines are quite different from modern humans. The front teeth are small, both in absolute size and in relationship to the rest of the teeth. The back teeth (premolars and molars) are huge, more than four times the size of modern humans' in some cases (Figures 12.11 and 12.12). Note how massive the jaws are and how large the back teeth are, especially in

robust australopithecines Species of *Australopithecus* that had very large back teeth, cheekbones, and faces, among other anatomical adaptations to heavy chewing. They lived in Africa between 2.5 million and 1.2 million years ago. Three species are generally recognized: *A. aethiopicus, A. robustus,* and *A. boisei.* Some anthropologists suggest that they be given their own genus name—*Paranthropus.*

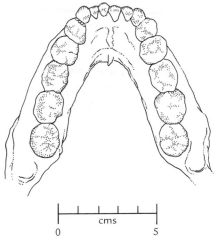

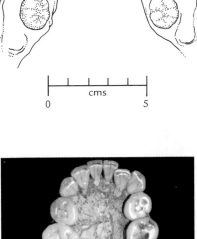

FIGURE 12.11

*Lower jaw of a robust australopithecine (*Australopithecus boisei*) from the Lake Natron site, Tanzania. Note the small front teeth (incisors and canines) and the massive back teeth (premolars and molars). (From Clark Spencer Larsen, Robert M. Matter, and Daniel L. Gebo,* Human Origins: The Fossil Record, *3d ed., p. 72 (bottom). © 1998, 1991, 1985 by Waveland Press, Inc., Prospect Heights, Ill. Reprinted with permission from the publisher)*

FIGURE 12.12

*Lower jaw of a robust australopithecine (*Australopithecus robustus*), specimen SK 23, Swartkrans, Republic of South Africa. Because of distortion, the rows of the jaw are closer than they should be. Note the small front teeth and the large back teeth. (Courtesy Milford Wolpoff, University of Michigan, Ann Arbor)*

relationship to the front teeth. Also, note that the premolars are larger side to side than front to back. These features all show a large surface area for the back teeth, indicating heavy chewing.

The skulls of robust australopithecines also reflect heavy chewing (Figures 12.13 and 12.14). These skulls show massive dished-in faces, large flaring cheekbones, and a bony crest running down the top. All of these features are related to large jaws and back teeth and powerful chewing muscles. As shown in Figure 12.15, two muscles are responsible for closing the mouth during chewing. One, the masseter, runs from the back portion of the jaw to the forward portion of the **zygomatic arch** (the cheekbone, which connects the zygomatic and temporal bones). The zygomatic arch and facial skeleton anchor this muscle. In hominids with large jaws and masseter muscles, the face and zygomatic arch must be massive to withstand the force generated by chewing. The other muscle, the temporalis, runs from the jaw up under the zygomatic arch and attaches to the sides and top of the skull. The larger this

zygomatic arch The cheekbone, formed by the connection of the zygomatic and temporal bones on the side of the skull.

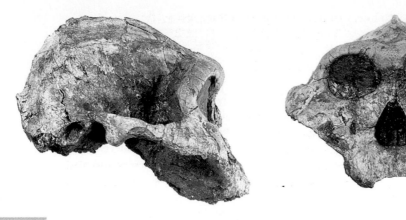

FIGURE 12.13

Side, frontal, and top views of a robust australopithecine (Australopithecus boisei), *skull, specimen KNM-ER 406, from Lake Turkana, Kenya.*
(© *The National Museums of Kenya*)

FIGURE 12.14

Skull of a robust australopithecine (Australopithecus robustus), *specimen SK 48, Swartkrans, Republic of South Africa.* (© *Transvaal Museum*)

sagittal crest A ridge of bone running down the center of the top of the skull that serves to anchor chewing muscles.

muscle is, the more the zygomatic arch must flare out from the side of the skull. To anchor the temporalis muscle on the sides and top of the skull, a ridge of bone sometimes develops down the center of the skull (called a **sagittal crest**). All these cranial and facial features indicate powerful chewing activity.

Despite the name robust, the robust australopithecines were not that large in terms of overall body size, with estimated height ranging from roughly 4 ft to 5 ft. On average, males weighed about 45 kg (roughly 100 lb) and females weighed about 33 kg (73 lb) (McHenry 1992). As with all early hominids, brain size was small, averaging slightly less than 500 cc, with a range of 410 cc to 545 cc (Aiello and Dunbar 1993; Falk et al. 2000; Suwa et al. 1997).

Three species of robust australopithecine are generally recognized. The oldest at 2.5 million years ago is *Australopithecus aethiopicus,* which is very robust but also shows a number of primitive cranial traits that link it to *A. afarensis* (Figure 12.16). The later two species, *Australopithecus robustus* and *Australopithecus boisei,* lived from roughly 2 million to 1 million years ago and differ in terms of geography and size. *A. robustus* is found in South Africa, and *A. boisei* is found in East Africa. Of the two, *A. boisei* is the more robust.

What does the morphology of the robust australopithecines tell us? The massive jaws and back teeth point to powerful chewing ability. Evidence from dental anatomy, including microscopic wear patterns on the teeth, show that all early hominids had a diverse diet that often included food that was hard to chew, such as seeds, nuts, and hard fruits. The robust australopithecines appear to have relied more regularly on such hard to chew food (Teaford and Ungar 2000), which is best exploited with large back teeth and massive chewing muscles.

There is no direct association of stone tool technology and the robust australopithecines. Although stone tools have been found at sites where robust forms were found, fossils of early *Homo* were also found, and most researchers suggest that *Homo* was the toolmaker and not the robusts. There is some evidence for tool use, however, among the robust forms in South Africa. Susman (1988) examined the hand bones of *A. robustus* and concluded that their manual dexterity meant they *could* have made tools. The most direct evidence for tool use comes from the Swartkrans robust australopithecine site

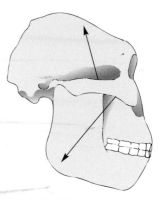

FIGURE 12.15

Skull of a robust australopithecine, with arrows indicating the action of chewing muscles: (top) temporalis, (bottom) masseter.

FIGURE 12.16

Specimen KNM-WT 17000 from Lake Turkana, Kenya, also known as the "Black Skull" because of the color of mineral staining. This skull is dated to 2.5 million years ago. It is a robust australopithecine classified as Australopithecus aethiopicus *by some and as an early example of* Australopithecus boisei *by others. It shows a mixture of specialized robust features (e.g., the sagittal crest) and primitive features (e.g., the forward jutting of the jaw). (© Alan Walker/National Geographic Society Image Collection)*

Australopithecus aethiopicus
The oldest robust australopithecine, dating to 2.5 million years ago in East Africa. It combines derived features seen in other robust australopithecines with primitive features seen in *A. afarensis.*

Australopithecus robustus
A species of robust australopithecine dating between roughly 2 million and 1.5 million years ago and found in South Africa.

Australopithecus boisei A very robust species of robust australopithecine dating between 2 million and 1.2 million years ago and found in East Africa.

FIGURE 12.17

Skull of Australopithecus africanus, *specimen STS 5, Sterkfontein, Republic of South Africa. (© Transvaal Museum)*

in South Africa, where animal bones have been found with scratch patterns indicating their use as digging tools. Based on comparisons with experimentally scratched animal bones, Backwell and d'Errico (2001) conclude that these early hominids were digging for termites.

Australopithecus Africanus   Although debate continues regarding the evolutionary relationships of the robust australopithecines to earlier hominids, there is general agreement that they represent a side branch in human evolution that became extinct 1 million years ago. Who then was our ancestor from the 3-million- to 2-million-year time period separating the earlier primitive hominids and species in the genus *Homo*? There are two major candidates, *Australopithecus africanus* and *Australopithecus garhi*.

A number of australopithecine specimens found in South Africa between roughly 3 million and 2 million years ago have been placed in the species **Australopithecus africanus** (named after Africa). *A. africanus* had reduced canines, large faces, and a small brain, averaging about 460 cc (Aiello and Dunbar 1993; Conroy et al. 1998). A skull of *A. africanus* is shown in Figure 12.17. Like other early hominids, it had a small brain and a large face. The face is not as massive as the robust forms, however, and there is no sagittal crest. A lower jaw of *A. africanus* is shown in Figure 12.18. Compared to the robust forms, the front teeth are not as small relative to the back teeth. In overall size, however, the back teeth are still larger than those of modern humans. *A. africanus* is considered a descendant of *A. afarensis* and may represent an ancestor of the genus *Homo*, although some anthropologists consider it another extinct side branch in hominid evolution.

Australopithecus Garhi   For many years, anthropologists have agreed that the robust australopithecines are not our ancestors. Many have proposed *A. africanus* as the ancestor of *Homo*. Others, however, suggested that *A. africanus* was too specialized to be our ancestor and that the genus *Homo* evolved from *A. afarensis* (Johanson and White 1979). The problem with this idea, how-

Australopithecus africanus A species of australopithecine dating between 3.3 million and 2.3 million years ago and found in South Africa. It is not as massive as the robust forms and may be an ancestor of the genus *Homo*.

Australopithecus garhi A species of australopithecine dating to 2.5 million years ago in East Africa. It differs from other australopithecines in having large front and back teeth, although the back teeth are not specialized to the same extent as found in the robust australopithecines.

ever, was that there was a gap between the last known occurrence of *A. afarensis* and the first evidence of *Homo.* If their idea is correct, a suitable transitional species was needed to fill this gap.

There now appears to be a possible transition. Fossils from Ethiopia dating to 2.5 million years ago have been classified as a new species ***Australopithecus garhi*** (Asfaw et al. 1999). The species name *garhi* means "surprise" in the local Afar language. The major specimen consists of a partial cranium with an upper jaw. The skull (Figure 12.19) has a small brain size (450 cc) and does not have a robust anatomy. Overall, many of its features are similar to *A. afarensis.*

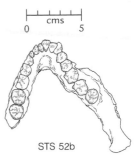

STS 52b

FIGURE 12.18 *(above)*

Lower jaw of Australopithecus africanus, *specimen STS 52b, Sterkfontein, Republic of South Africa. The teeth are larger than in modern humans, but the relative proportions of front and back teeth are more similar to those of modern humans than are those of the robust australopithecines. (From Clark Spencer Larsen, Robert M. Matter, and Daniel L. Gebo,* Human Origins: The Fossil Record, *3d ed., p. 64. © 1998, 1991, 1985 by Waveland Press, Inc., Prospect Heights, Ill. Reprinted with permission from the publisher)*

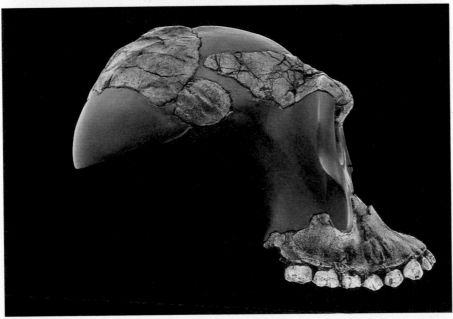

FIGURE 12.19

Top and side views of Australopithecus garhi *skull, specimen BOU-VP-12/130.*
(© David L. Brill)

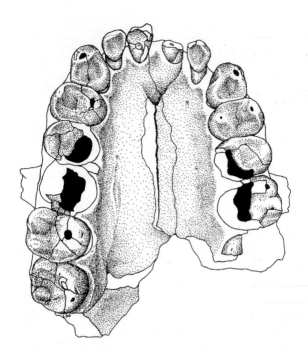

FIGURE 12.20

Upper jaw of Australopithecus garhi, *specimen BOU-VP-12/130. The teeth are large but do not resemble those of robust australopithecines in structure.* (© 1999 Luba Dmytryk Gudz)

Both the front and back teeth of *A. garhi* (Figure 12.20) are large, but they do not show the anatomical specializations of the robust australopithecines.

It is possible that *A. garhi*, and not *A. africanus*, was our ancestor. Because the fossil evidence shows the earliest members of *Homo* appear in East Africa by 2 million years ago, *A. garhi* is "in the right place, at the right time, to be the ancestor of early *Homo*" (Asfaw et al. 1999:634). Its anatomy, compared with other early hominids, does not preclude this possibility.

The discovery of *A. garhi* is even more important when we consider the fact that stone tools were found at the same site (de Heinzelin et al. 1999), suggesting that *A. garhi* was the toolmaker (at 2.5 million year ago, these are among the earliest stone tools known). Analysis of animal bones found at the site show that these hominids used the stone tools to butcher animals and to break open bones for their marrow (a nutritious food high in fats). This evidence shows that by 2.5 million years ago hominids had added meat and marrow to their diet, a pattern continued in the evolution of the genus *Homo*. The similarity of behavior in *A. garhi* with later *Homo* further supports the hypothesis that *A. garhi* was the ancestor of *Homo*. This conclusion is tentative because we still have much to learn about early hominids. Additional species may be awaiting discovery, including others that practiced some type of toolmaking and dietary expansion.

EVOLUTIONARY TRENDS

Given the diversity in early hominids, what conclusions can we reach regarding evolutionary trends and relationships? How were these species related? What were the major evolutionary trends, and what caused them?

Evolutionary Relationships

One of our goals is to use the available information to reconstruct the general patterns of early hominid evolution. The hominids described in this chapter thus far provide a history of evolutionary events that took place from the initial origins of the hominids and the development of bipedalism up to the origin of the genus *Homo*. We are interested, where possible, in trying to link species over time to produce a "family tree."

Historical Overview   The study of the historical development of any scientific discipline is important for a number of reasons. Because science is an ongoing, cumulative process, its current state will partially reflect past ideas and hypotheses. Even after hypotheses have been rejected, they may continue to influence thinking in a field. Scientists do not work in a vacuum but are part of a larger culture, and current intellectual philosophies and trends can have an impact on the formulation of hypotheses and the interpretation of data.

It is also important to remember that our current knowledge is incomplete and not necessarily the final answer. It is not uncommon to read newspaper headlines such as "Fossil Discovery Overturns Previous Ideas about Human Origins" or "Fossil Discovery Uproots Human Family Tree." The impression some people get from such headlines is that anthropologists know little about their subject or else they would not have gotten things wrong. This impression ties in with a common belief that science produces ultimate truth and that mistakes in interpretation are tragic and indicative of serious trouble within a discipline. However, this is not how science works. Ideas are not simply accepted on faith but are tested. If shown to be wrong, they are rejected and alternative hypotheses are constructed. Questioning and skeptical debate form the essence of scientific research.

Many hypotheses in the study of human evolution have been tested and rejected. Others have stood the test of time, some in modified form. Some examples from the study of human evolution show how ideas have been tested as new evidence accumulated and new analyses were conducted. For example, when the first species of early hominid was announced in 1925 (*A. africanus*), it went against then-current thinking that the first stage in human evolution was the origin of a larger brain, followed by the origin of bipedalism. *Australopithecus africanus,* and all the other hominids described in this chapter, shows just the reverse—bipedalism arose millions of years before there was a significant increase in the size of the brain. Although it took time, ultimately the entire scientific community agreed that the "brains first" hypothesis was incorrect.

By the middle of the twentieth century, little was known about early hominid variation. One early debate focused on whether only a single hominid species or two or more hominid species were living at the same time. The single species hypothesis postulated that only one hominid species was living at any one time and that the pattern of human evolution was essentially a straight line, from earliest hominid to the genus *Homo*. As more species were discovered, this view became harder and harder to maintain. There was simply too much variation at any time to lump all specimens under a single species.

The Piltdown Hoax

One of the main points made in this chapter is that characteristics of modern humans did not all appear at the same time. In particular, we know from the fossil record that bipedalism started 3.5 million years before we see any significant increase in brain size or the origin of stone tools. This finding is based on the fossil and archaeological records.

Early ideas about human origins suggested just the reverse—that brain size evolved first. Because there were few fossils to show otherwise at that time, this hypothesis could not then be rejected and was quite popular. The model predicted that the fossil record would ultimately show that, of all modern human characteristics, large brain size would be the oldest. Of course, today we have sufficient information to reject this hypothesis altogether. At the beginning of the twentieth century, however, we did not.

In fact, fossil evidence *was* found to support the antiquity of the large human brain. Between 1911 and 1915, hominid fossils were discovered at Piltdown, England, alongside stone tools and the fossils of prehistoric animals such as mastodons. A primary specimen ("Piltdown Man") consisted of a large skull and an apelike jaw. The teeth, however, were worn flat, more closely resembling the condition of human teeth. The specimen showed a mixture of ape and human traits and had a modern human brain size. It offered clear proof that large brains came first in human origins.

Because of Piltdown, any fossils that had human characteristics but did not have the large brain were rejected, for a time, as possible human ancestors. Indeed, this was part of the reluctance of scientists to accept *Australopithecus* as a hominid. The first australopithecine specimen was discovered by Raymond Dart in 1924. The specimen consisted of the face, teeth, and cranial fragments (including a cast of the brain case) of a young child. Dart named the specimen *Australopithecus africanus.* Based on cranial evidence relating to the angle at which the spinal cord enters the skull, he claimed it was an upright walker. The brain size was apelike, as was the protruding face. The teeth, however, were more like those of humans, particularly in having small canines. Here was another specimen that had a mixture of ape and human traits but that suggested the large brain evolved *after* bipedalism and humanlike teeth. At the time, more people tended to support Piltdown (in fairness, some of their criticisms of *Australopithecus,* including the difficulty in interpreting remains of children, were valid).

Some scientists, however, were more skeptical about Piltdown Man. And, eventually, continuing investigation showed that the find was a fake. In 1953, a fluorine analysis (see Chapter 11) confirmed that the jaw bones and skull bones did not come from the same time period. Closer inspection showed that the skull was that of a modern human and the jaw that of an orangutan. The teeth had been filed down, and all of the bones had been chemically treated to simulate age.

Who was responsible for the Piltdown hoax? Over the years many different suspects have been suggested. One analysis suggests that the guilty party may have been Martin Hinton, then curator of zoology at the London Natural History Museum (Gee 1996), although this is not definite (Feder 2002). The story of Piltdown Man is often offered up as evidence that anthropologists (and other scientists) often do not know what they are talking about. After all, look how easily they were fooled. This criticism misses the point altogether. Science and scientists make mistakes, and sometimes they commit outright fraud. It is ridiculous to expect otherwise. Science does not represent truth per se but rather a means of arriving at the truth. When Piltdown was discovered, scientific investigation did not stop. Instead, scientists kept looking at the evidence, questioning it and various assumptions, and devising new ways of testing. As a result, the hoax was uncovered. This is how science is supposed to work.

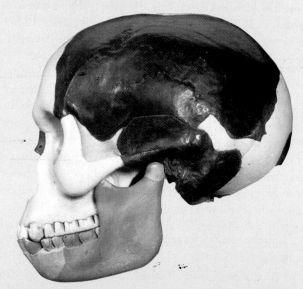

Side view of Piltdown Man. The dark-colored areas and the back part of the lower jaw were found; the rest was reconstructed. This find, which confirmed the then-popular notion that early humans had large brains and apelike jaws, was a hoax; the remains of a modern human and an orangutan were placed together at the Piltdown site.
(© *The Natural History Museum, London*)

Eventually, the single species hypothesis was rejected. Today, anthropologists debate exactly *how many* species lived at any one time, but they are in complete agreement that at certain times there were two or more.

As time went on and new discoveries were made, we realized that the fossil record of early hominids was even more diverse. With four new species announced in the past 10 years, it seems likely that additional species will be found in the near future. The discovery of new species, and integration of these new data with previous data, mean that the *specifics* of our understanding of early hominid evolution continue to change. However, some general findings can be made at this time. First, the earliest evidence of the first hominids goes back 6 million years, a date consistent with genetic evidence on the timing of hominid origins. The earliest hominids were apelike in many ways but were bipedal. Second, there appears to have been considerable diversity throughout the time frame discussed here, with two or more species existing at many points in time. Many of these species are extinct side branches in human evolution. Third, diversity increased even more 3 million years ago, with a variety of robust and nonrobust species living in Africa. It is within the radiation of the nonrobust forms that we see the first beginning of anatomical and behavioral changes that led, in at least one case, to the genus *Homo.*

Family Trees   How might all these early hominids be related? Our first step in trying to answer this question is to reexamine what we know about the dates for these species. Figure 12.21 provides a picture of the dates for each of the 10 species discussed in this chapter and for the genus *Homo.* Keep in mind that these are the dates *as we currently know them.* It is entirely possible that the actual distribution of each species is greater than what we currently know. The diversity of fossil hominids, particularly between 4 million and 2 million years ago, is quite apparent in this figure.

How can these forms be linked? We look for physical similarity and, in particular, forms that share derived characteristics that are not found in other species. Formal cladistic analysis has been done on many of these species, but the results are not always consistent across different traits (e.g., McHenry 1996; Strait et al. 1997). Part of the problem is the frequency of homoplasy, similarity due to independent evolution. For some traits, such as dental size, homoplasy seems more common than we once thought. For example, some argue that the robust australopithecines are all related, but others suggest that the robust anatomy might have developed independently in different species.

Some evolutionary relationships are more definite than others. For example, the robust species *A. aethiopicus* is likely a link between *A. afarensis* and *A. boisei.* Other relationships are less clear. As noted previously, two species, *A. africanus* and *A. garhi,* are possible links of early hominids with the genus *Homo.* The evolutionary relationships of newly discovered species, such as *K. platyops,* are even less clear.

Figure 12.22 represents an attempt to portray some of the current ideas regarding evolutionary relationships as well as possible alternatives. This family tree should be taken as a summary of hypotheses and not the final answer. Regardless of which specific connections are ultimately shown to be

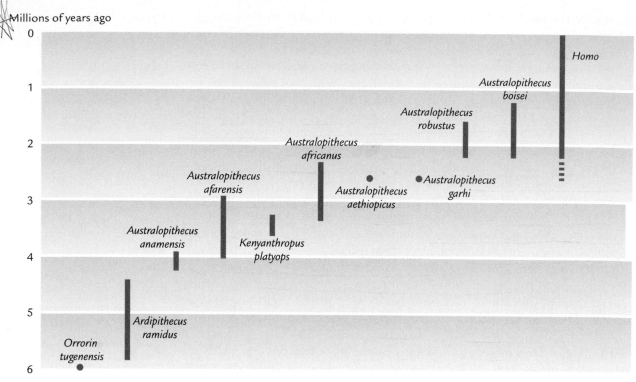

Millions of years ago

FIGURE 12.21

Known dates for hominid species. All species in the genus Homo *are combined in this figure. Keep in mind that these represent currently known dates, and it is likely that the true range in dates is larger for some species. (See Table 12.1 for sources of dates.)*

correct, the tree depicts the basic nature of early hominid evolution—several stages of diversification starting with the earliest primitive hominids, leading to a number of diverse species by 3 million to 2 million years ago, followed by the ultimate extinction of all lines except that leading to the genus *Homo*. Some of the unresolved questions are these:

1. Which early hominid gave rise to later hominids—*Orrorin, Ardipithecus,* both, or neither?

2. Did all of the robust species have a common ancestor (*A. aethiopicus*), or did some evolve independently (e.g., *A. robustus* from *A. africanus* in South Africa)?

3. Which early hominid(s) gave rise to the genus *Homo*? Indeed, did all members of early *Homo* come from the same ancestor, or was an increase in brain size an independent change?

Although the debate over the hominid family tree is fascinating (as well as confusing), it is important not to get bogged down with the specific arguments regarding who is related to whom and miss the general picture and the important points. From a broad perspective, the *general* history of early human evolution is fairly clear (see Figure 12.1). The first hominids walked upright but still had a number of apelike traits. By 3 million to 2 million years ago, there were a number of different species of early hominid resulting from adaptive radiations of these bipedal organisms. From this radiation came hominids with a larger brain and a stone tool culture—the first members of

FIGURE 12.22

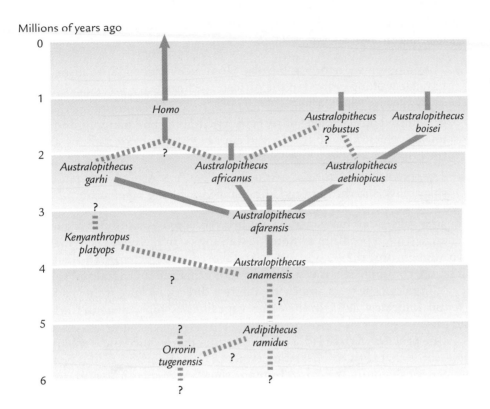

Millions of years ago

A possible family tree of early hominids. All species in the genus Homo *are combined in this figure. Dotted lines and question marks indicate areas of continuing debate.*

the genus *Homo*. Their story will continue in Chapter 13. For the moment, we need to stop and consider the most important question about the first hominids: Why did they become bipedal?

The Origin of Bipedalism

Of all the unique traits used to define hominids, bipedalism is the oldest. Therefore, any model of hominid origins must consider the origin of bipedalism. We are talking here about the specific anatomical changes, outlined in Chapter 10, that define human bipedalism. Chimpanzees can walk upright, and bonobos frequently do so. What makes us different is that we do it all the time, and our anatomy reflects changes that make bipedalism more efficient.

Locomotion in the Hominid–African Ape Ancestor The origin of bipedalism raises an interesting question. How did the common ancestor of African apes and hominids move about on the ground? Because we have not yet precisely identified this common ancestor, we must use reconstruction based on two basic facts. First, among living primates, the African apes are the most closely related to humans. Second, humans are bipedal, and the African apes are all knuckle walkers. (Although the African apes frequently move in other ways, their anatomy shows that knuckle walking is their main means of movement on the ground.) These two observations suggest three possibilities for the common ancestor:

1. The common ancestor was bipedal. Hominids retained bipedalism, and knuckle walking evolved in the African ape lineage.

2. The common ancestor had a different pattern of locomotion, perhaps a generalized form capable of suspensory climbing and hanging, and *both* lineages changed, with the African apes evolving knuckle walking and the hominids evolving bipedalism.

3. The common ancestor was a knuckle walker. The African apes retained this ability, and the hominid line changed, evolving bipedalism.

The first suggestion has generally not been accepted. Anatomists argue that a change from bipedalism to knuckle walking is unlikely. Of the remaining two suggestions, the second has been favored more often than the third. Here, the common ancestor was a hominoid that was a generalized suspensory climber in the trees and evolved in two directions once it moved to the ground, knuckle walking in the African ape line and bipedalism in the hominid line.

One problem with the idea of a climbing common ancestor is that it conflicts somewhat with accumulating evidence that chimpanzees and bonobos are genetically more similar to humans than are gorillas and therefore diverged later than gorillas (recall this discussion from the previous chapter). If the common ancestor of the African apes and hominids was a climber, then knuckle walking would have to evolve twice, once in the line leading to the gorillas and again in the chimpanzee–bonobo line (Figure 12.23). If, however, the African apes as a group diverged only once, then there would be no parallel evolution. But this is not in agreement with the genetic evidence. There has been much debate over the exact pattern of divergence among the African apes (see Figure 11.17 for review), with genetics supporting one view and the anatomy of locomotion supporting the other.

The third idea, that the common ancestor was a knuckle walker, has often been rejected on the ground that there is no indication of a knuckle-walking ancestry in early hominids or modern humans (Johanson and Edey 1981). Although others had argued that a knuckle-walking ancestry *was* compatible with hominid origins, the most convincing evidence to date comes from a comparative analysis of the wrist joint by Brian Richmond and David Strait (2000). They examined four measurements of the wrist bone associated with knuckle walking in African apes and compared living hominoids with data from four fossil hominid species. They found that two early hominids, *A. anamensis* and *A. afarensis*, were very similar to the African apes, whereas the two later hominids, *A. africanus* and *A. robustus*, were more similar to living humans. Their results show that the wrist bones of early hominids retained characteristics indicative of a knuckle-walking ancestry, which then were lost in later hominid evolution. Because African apes are knuckle walkers and because the earliest hominids show some knuckle-walking ancestry, it is rea-

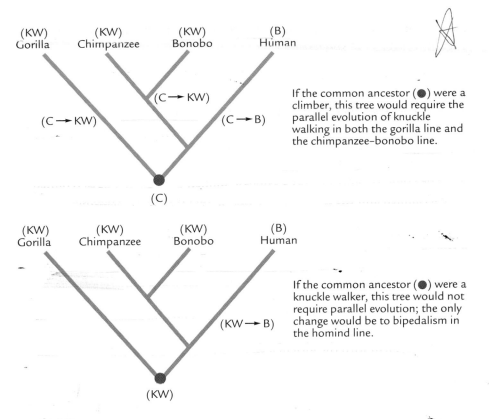

If the common ancestor (●) were a climber, this tree would require the parallel evolution of knuckle walking in both the gorilla line and the chimpanzee–bonobo line.

If the common ancestor (●) were a knuckle walker, this tree would not require parallel evolution; the only change would be to bipedalism in the homind line.

FIGURE 12.23

Possible evolutionary changes in locomotion assuming that humans are more closely related to chimpanzees and bonobos than to gorillas. Locomotion: KW = knuckle walking, B = bipedalism, C = generalized suspensory climber. Two models are shown, one where the common ancestor of African apes and humans was a generalized climber (C) and the other where the common ancestor was a knuckle walker (KW). Note that if the common ancestor was a climber, then knuckle walking would have evolved twice.

sonable to assume that the common ancestor of African apes and hominids was also a knuckle walker. If true, there are no discrepancies between the genetic and anatomic evidence.

The Environmental Context To evaluate hypotheses regarding the origin of bipedalism, it is necessary to consider the environmental context within which bipedalism arose. The earth had been changing during the Late Miocene, resulting in a cooler and drier climate in Africa. Over time, the large forests began to shrink, leading to smaller patches of forest and woodlands surrounded by increasing grassland (savanna).

Traditional explanations for the origin of bipedalism have considered the savanna environment critical in understanding hominid origins. For many years, the oldest known fossil hominids were found in environments that were grasslands or a mix of grasslands and woodlands. Given this association, many explanations for the origin of bipedalism focused on the particular stresses imposed by a savanna existence, including greater difficulty finding food, the need to travel long distances, hotter temperatures, and greater vulnerability to predators, among others. These explanations are now being questioned based on new evidence for the environment of the *earliest* suggested hominids, *Orrorin* and *Ardipithecus*. Before 4.4 million years ago, hominids did not occupy the open grasslands but lived in relatively wet forests and woodlands (Pickford and Senut 2001; WoldeGabriel et al. 2001).

Why Bipedalism?   The early hominids were bipedal. Although there is some anatomical evidence suggesting that they were also active climbers, it is clear from their anatomy that they walked upright on the ground. The critical question is *why* they did so. Ever since Darwin's time, hypotheses have been proposed to account for the origin of bipedalism.

Darwin offered one of the first hypotheses, focusing on the link between bipedalism and tool use. By standing up, early hominids had their hands free to carry tools. This basic model was later expanded by a number of anthropologists such as Washburn (1960) to consider the evolution of a number of human characteristics. The model proposes that as tool use increased and became more important, natural selection led to enhanced learning abilities, intelligence, and larger brains. As larger brains evolved along with longer periods of infant and child dependency, tools would become even more important for survival. Thus, tool use affected brain size increase, which in turn affected tool use. Tool use would benefit from walking upright, such that the model predicts a simultaneous evolution of bipedalism, larger brains, and tool use. Although popular for many years, the tool use model has been rejected because fossil evidence from the past 30 years has shown that bipedalism evolved *before* significant increases in brain size and a stone tool technology. The latest evidence shows that bipedalism may be as old as 6 million years, a full 3.5 million years *before* either the first stone tools or significantly larger brains.

Although the idea of a simultaneous evolution of hominid traits has been rejected, the basic idea that bipedalism offers an evolutionary advantage by freeing the hands to carry things may still have some merit. Wooden tools, such as digging sticks, could be carried. As the early hominids were at least as smart as chimpanzees, which make and use simple tools, it is possible that environmental changes prompted an increase in simple tool use that led to a selective advantage for bipedalism.

Tools are not the only items that can be carried effectively if the hands are free. A hominid could also have carried food and infants, which, under the right conditions, could promote increased survival and reproduction. Owen Lovejoy (1981) has suggested that bipedalism evolved as a strategy to increase the survival of infants and other dependent offspring by having some group members forage for food and then *carry* it back to the group. Consequently, more infants could be cared for, allowing an increase in reproduction and potential population growth. According to Lovejoy, bipedalism is the way in which hominids got around the basic problem faced by apes—a long period of infant dependency leading to slow rates of population growth. Bipedalism might have altered the situation and allowed more infants to be cared for at the same time.

The specifics of Lovejoy's model have been rather controversial, as he proposes that the social structure that evolved along with bipedalism was of monogamous family groups where the male foraged for food and the female stayed with the dependent offspring. The high degree of sexual dimorphism seen in many early hominids does not fit this model because monogamous primates tend to have reduced sexual dimorphism. It is possible that other social structures, such as a group of adult females sharing the care and feeding of offspring, could have produced the same result—bipedalism as an adaptation for carrying food and infants.

Another suggested advantage of bipedalism is predator avoidance. On the savanna, hominids would be in increased danger of being hunted by large carnivores. By standing on two legs, hominids would be able to see farther, particularly above tall grass, giving them the opportunity to spot potential danger. Day (1986) has suggested that this ability, combined with the retention of tree-climbing ability, would be advantageous. Although predator avoidance would be facilitated by bipedalism *on the savanna,* we now know that the earliest hominids were more likely confined to a woodland and forest environment. Thus, predator avoidance may not explain why bipedalism *first* evolved.

The same criticism is true of another hypothesis that links bipedalism with increased ability to tolerate heat stress (Wheeler 1991). Overheating and water loss are considerable threats to organisms exposed to sunlight on the savanna. Based on laboratory experiments, Wheeler found that standing upright reduces the amount of direct solar radiation that strikes the body (less exposed surface area). Further, the greater air movement and lower temperature felt by an animal off the ground would increase the rate of heat dissipation and effective evaporation of sweat. Bipedalism would have been very useful to have in order to venture out onto the savanna, but the evidence suggests that bipedalism had evolved *before* hominids moved into a savanna environment. Therefore, this hypothesis also fails to explain the initial origin of bipedalism.

Bipedalism has also been linked to food acquisition and energy efficiency. Energy efficiency refers to the amount of energy expended relative to the task being performed. Bipedalism is more energy-efficient in traveling long distances in search of food. Increased energy efficiency means using less energy to move about looking for and gathering food.

Though human bipedalism is less efficient than ape locomotion when running, the opposite is true at normal walking speeds. Rodman and McHenry (1980) looked at the energy efficiency of bipedal humans and knuckle-walking chimpanzees at normal walking speeds. The results, shown in Figure 12.24, indicate that bipedalism is more energy-efficient at speeds of both 2.9 km per hour (the normal walking speed of a chimpanzee) and 4.5 km per hour (the normal walking speed of a human). Leonard and Robertson (1995) confirmed these observations and compared the expected daily energy costs for an early hominid (*A. afarensis*) with a knuckle walker of similar size, finding that bipedalism could save more than 50 percent of the expected daily expenditure of calories.

The energy efficiency model is usually discussed in terms of early hominid adaptation to the savanna, which would have necessitated long-distance movement where increased energy efficiency would have been a major advantage. The recent evidence that the earliest hominids lived in the woodlands and forests rather than on the savanna would seem to argue against this model. It may not be that simple, however, because climatic data do show

FIGURE 12.24

The relative energy cost of movement for chimpanzees and humans compared with a quadruped of similar size (set equal to 1.0 in this graph). The knuckle-walking chimpanzee uses more energy for movement (values > 1), and the bipedal human uses less (< 1). These comparisons have been made at two speeds: 2.9 km per hour (the normal speed of a chimpanzee) and 4.5 km per hour (the normal speed of a human). These results show that bipedalism is more energy-efficient at normal walking speeds. (Source of data: Rodman and McHenry 1980)

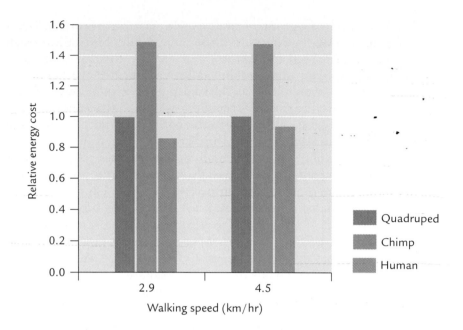

that the forests and woodlands were shrinking. Although the earliest hominids may have spent most of their time in the forests and woodlands, they may have needed to travel *between* shrinking clusters to find enough food. As the forests and woodlands continued to shrink, the advantage of bipedalism may have continued to increase, ultimately leaving a form very well adapted for the savanna.

The hypotheses discussed here (and others) need to be reevaluated in terms of the new environmental evidence. It may be the case that there is no *single* cause for the origin of bipedalism but rather a combination of several, including food sharing, infant care, energy efficiency, and others. It also seems likely that there were additional advantages of bipedalism once it had evolved, such as temperature regulation. In any event, bipedalism ultimately provided the opportunity for other changes in hominid evolution, such as increased brain size, which are discussed in the next chapter.

SUMMARY

The origin of the hominids takes place in Africa. The earliest presumed hominids (*Orrorin* and *Ardipithecus*) date back 6 million years, coinciding with the suggested time for hominid divergence based on genetic studies. These earliest hominids were very primitive, and debate continues as to whether one of them is actually an early ape or the common ancestor of hominids and African apes. Between roughly 4 million and 3 million years ago, two additional species of primitive hominid (*Australopithecus anamensis* and *Australopithecus afarensis*) are definite bipeds but still retain some apelike anatomy, particularly in certain dental features. The evolutionary significance of a newly discovered early hominid, *Kenyanthropus platyops,* is not clear at this time. Starting about 3 million years ago, several lines of hominids, including three species of robust australopithecines, are characterized by large back teeth and huge chewing muscles adapted for a hard to chew diet. Two other hominids, *Australopithecus africanus* and *Australopithecus garhi,* are less robust, and one of them may represent the ancestor of *Homo.* Preliminary analysis suggests that *A. garhi* made stone tools for scavenging animal flesh and bone marrow. All of these early hominids had small brains but were bipedal.

The origin of bipedalism is a major event in hominid evolution for which a number of hypotheses have been proposed. New evidence on ancient environments shows that the first hominids lived in woodlands and forests and may have developed bipedalism as an adaptation because of increased energy efficiency in finding food, having the hands free to carry food and simple tools, or some other reason(s). Once bipedalism evolved, hominids were able to adapt to the open grasslands of Africa.

SUPPLEMENTAL READINGS

Conroy, G. C. 1997. *Reconstructing Human Origins.* New York: W. W. Norton.

Klein, R. G. 1999. *The Human Career: Human Biological and Cultural Origins,* 2d ed. Chicago: University of Chicago Press.

Lewin, R. 1997. *Bones of Contention: Controversies in the Search for Human Origins,* 2d ed. Chicago: University of Chicago Press. A lively summary of historical controversies in primate and human evolution. Chapters 3–4 and 7–12 focus on early controversies in hominid evolution.

Wolpoff, M. H. 1999. *Paleoanthropology,* 2d ed. Boston: McGraw-Hill. Three relatively current and comprehensive advanced texts on human evolution that cover the material in this chapter as well as the following two chapters.

INTERNET RESOURCES

http://anthro.palomar.edu/hominid/australo_2.htm
Analysis of Early Hominids, a tutorial on the anatomy and evolutionary relationships of early hominids.

http://anthro.palomar.edu/hominid/australo_1.htm
Discovery of Early Hominids, a tutorial on hominid origins focusing on the history of discovery.

http://www.asu.edu/clas/iho
Institute of Human Origins, containing updated information on fossil hominid discoveries.

http://www.mnh.si.edu/anthro/humanorigins
The Smithsonian Institution Human Origins Program, containing summaries of fossil hominid species, including excellent photographs of a number of specimens.

CHAPTER 13

The Evolution of the Genus Homo

The history of the australopithecines, discussed in the previous chapter, provides us with some insight into the *beginning* of human evolution and the origin of one of the unique characteristics of humankind—bipedalism. Bipedalism arose close to 6 million years ago, but it was not until roughly 2.5 million years ago that we begin to see the origin of other human characteristics—a substantial increase in brain size and the development of stone tool technology. The genus ***Homo*** is usually defined in terms of an increased brain size, a reduction in the size of the face and teeth, and increased reliance on cultural adaptations. This chapter reviews the major evidence for the origin and evolution of the genus *Homo* up to the origin of modern humans (which is covered in Chapter 14).

THE ORIGIN OF THE GENUS *HOMO*

Hominid fossils are assigned to the genus *Homo* partly, but not exclusively, on the basis of brain size. The range of brain size overlaps slightly between *Australopithecus* and *Homo* (estimates of cranial capacity are not yet available for *Orrorin, Ardipithecus,* or *Kenyanthropus*). The cranial capacity of *Australopithecus* fossils found to date ranges from 400 cc to 545 cc, whereas the capacity

Homo A genus of hominids characterized by large brain size and dependence on culture as a means of adaptation.

◄ *The site of Olduvai Gorge in Tanzania. This site, worked on for many decades by the famous Leakey family, has proven to be a gold mine for hominid fossil studies. The early excavations at Olduvai uncovered many species, including* Homo erectus, *the first hominid species to move outside of Africa. (© E. E. Kingsley/Science Source/Photo Researchers, Inc.)*

FIGURE 13.1

Plot of cranial capacity over time for fossil specimens of **Australopithecus** *and* **Homo** *from 3 million to 10,000 years ago. (Sources of data: Australopithecines and early* Homo *from Aiello and Dunbar 1993; later* Homo *from Ruff et al. 1997; updates and additions from Suwa et al. 1997, Abbate et al. 1998, Conroy et al. 1998, Gabunia et al. 2000, and Falk et al. 2000)*

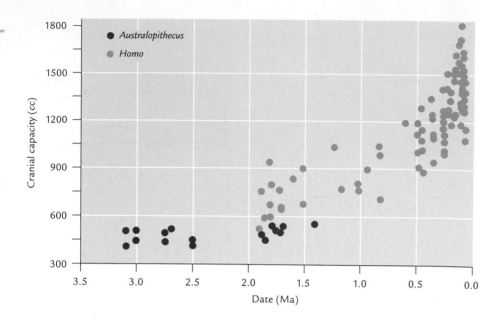

of *Homo* fossils (regardless of species) ranges from 509 cc to 1,880 cc (see Figure 13.1 for bibliographic sources). The point here is that although brain size is an important defining characteristic, it is not the only one. Other characteristics of cranial shape, facial shape, dental size, and postcranial anatomy are also important in identifying fossils.

In addition to having a larger brain size than earlier hominids, the genus *Homo* shows an increase in brain size over time during the past 2 million years. Figure 13.1 plots the cranial capacity of 19 *Australopithecus* and 117 *Homo* crania dating from roughly 10,000 years ago back to slightly more than 3 million years ago. This figure clearly shows changes in hominid brain size over time. Whereas the australopithecines show only a slight change over time, the genus *Homo* shows rapid increase over time, particularly after 700,000 years ago.

Apart from physical appearance, another major characteristic of the genus *Homo* is reliance on cultural behaviors, including increasing sophistication in stone tool technology. Sometime during the course of human evolution, our ancestors became totally dependent on tool making. Keep in mind, however, that the cultural evolution of the genus *Homo* was not simply confined to technological invention and development. As shown in this and the next chapter, *Homo* also used fire, developed hunting-and-gathering strategies, expanded into new and diverse environments, and developed various types of symbolic expression, including intentional burial and art.

The evolution of the genus *Homo* gets confusing at times, in part because of biological and cultural variation over time and space but also because of the different views on how to explain this diversity. A major controversy is over the number and nature of species within *Homo*. How many were there? Who is related to whom? Because we have only one human species today, what happened to the others (assuming there was more than one to begin with)?

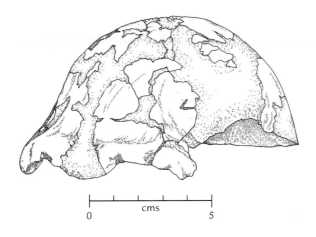

FIGURE 13.2

Skull of Homo habilis, *specimen OH 16, Olduvai Gorge, Tanzania. Although this skull is small compared to that of a modern human, its cranial capacity (638 cc) marks it as much larger than the australopithecine skull.* (From R. E. F. Lackey, J. M. Mungai, and A. C. Walker, 1971, "New Australopithecines from East Rudolf, Kenya," American Journal of Physical Anthropology 35: 175–186. Used with permission)

Early *Homo*

The suggested earliest evidence for the genus *Homo* dates back almost 2.5 million years from sites in Kenya and Ethiopia (Hill et al. 1992; Kimbel et al. 1996). Interestingly, this date also corresponds to some of the oldest known stone tools. Although significant, these fossils are too fragmentary to assign to specific species. However, they do provide us with a glimpse of when the origin of the genus *Homo* happened. Between 2 million and 1.5 million years ago, we see evidence of several species within the genus *Homo*.

Homo Habilis   The species ***Homo habilis*** refers to a number of African hominid fossils that date between 2 million and 1.5 million years ago. *Homo habilis* was first named following research at Olduvai Gorge in Tanzania (see Figures 12.2 and 13.18). Starting in the 1930s, Louis and Mary Leakey conducted fieldwork at this site. Among their early finds were the remains of the then oldest known stone tools. For many years the Leakeys searched Olduvai Gorge looking for the maker of these tools. In 1960, they found a jaw, two cranial fragments, and several postcranial bones dating to 1.75 million years ago. These finds represented a hominid with smaller teeth and a larger brain than that of any of the australopithecines found up to that time (Figures 13.2 and 13.3). Continued work led to the discovery of several more specimens, and in 1964 Louis Leakey and colleagues proposed a new species based on this material: *Homo habilis.* The species, whose name literally translates as "able man," was named for its association with stone tools. Since that time, additional specimens and stone tools have been found elsewhere in East Africa and South Africa.

The most noticeable difference between *H. habilis* and the australopithecines is the larger brain size of *H. habilis*. The average cranial capacity of *H. habilis* is 610 cc (Wood 1996), which is more than 30 percent larger than the average cranial capacity of *Australopithecus africanus* (Aiello and Dunbar 1993; Conroy et al. 1998). The teeth of *H. habilis* are in general smaller than

cms
0   3

FIGURE 13.3

Lower jaw of Homo habilis *specimen OH 7, Olduvai Gorge, Tanzania.* (From R. E. F. Lackey, J. M. Mungai, and A. C. Walker, 1971, "New Australopithecines from East Rudolf, Kenya," American Journal of Physical Anthropology 35: 175–186. Used with permission)

Homo habilis A species of early *Homo* from Africa between 2 million and 1.5 million years ago, with a brain size roughly half that of modern humans and a primitive postcranial skeleton.

FIGURE 13.4

Oldowan tools. (From The Old Stone Age *by F. Bordes, 1968. Reprinted with permission of the publisher, Weildenfeld and Nicolson, Ltd.)*

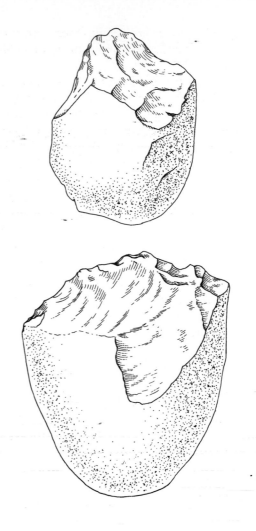

those of most australopithecines but larger than those of modern humans. The postcranial skeleton is particularly interesting. For many years little was known about the postcranial anatomy of *H. habilis* other than a few isolated parts. In 1986, a partial adult skeleton of *H. habilis* was discovered (Johanson et al. 1987). The skeleton is similar to that of many early hominids, being relatively small and having relatively long arms. *H. habilis* may have retained climbing ability (Wood 1996).

Simple stone tools have been found in association with *H. habilis.* These tools, referred to as the **Oldowan tradition,** are relatively simple chopping tools made by striking several flakes off a rounded stone to give it a rough cutting edge (Figure 13.4). They were normally made from materials such as lava and quartz. The stone was held steady and was then struck with another stone at the correct angle to remove a flake of stone. Several strikes would produce a rough edge capable of cutting through animal flesh. This type of tool manufacture may sound easy, but it actually involves considerable skill, as anthropologists attempting to duplicate these tools have found (Schick and

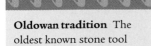

Oldowan tradition The oldest known stone tool culture.

Toth 1993). Proper tool manufacture requires skill in finding the right materials and using the right amount of force. Mistakes could ruin a tool and injure a hominid's hand.

These tools could have been used for a variety of purposes. For many years the emphasis in archaeological investigations has been on the stone cores produced by flaking. The small flakes, often found in great abundance, were felt to be nothing more than waste material. Analysis of the scratch marks on these flakes, however, shows that they were often used for a variety of tasks, including scraping wood, cutting meat, and cutting grass stems (Ambrose 2001).

Stone tools are often associated with butchered animal bones. At Olduvai Gorge, both stone tools and animal bones appear to have been brought there from farther away. There is also extensive evidence of carnivore activity at these sites. The evidence suggests that *H. habilis* was not a hunter but instead scavenged the remains of carnivore kills. More than half the cut marks left by stone tools are found on bones with little meat, such as the lower legs. This suggests that *H. habilis* was taking what was left over from carnivores. Also, there is no evidence of complete carcasses of larger animals brought to the Olduvai sites, only portions—and these are most often the bones left over by carnivores (Potts 1984).

Homo Rudolfensis For many years there was the tendency to lump any specimen of *Homo* dating to around 2 million years ago into the species *H. habilis.* This became problematic after the discovery of fossils with even larger cranial capacities and different measurements of the face and teeth. Several analyses support the idea of two separate species (Kramer et al. 1995; Wood 1996; but see Miller 2000). This second species of early *Homo,* dating to 2 million years ago, has been named ***Homo rudolfensis,*** after the site of Lake Turkana in Kenya, which had, at one time, been named Lake Rudolf (as mentioned in the previous chapter, the history behind species names is often quite convoluted and confusing).

Figure 13.5 shows the most famous *H. rudolfensis* fossil—a cranium with a cranial capacity of 752 cc. In addition to being larger, there is also evidence that the brain of *H. rudolfensis* was structurally different. Falk (1983) investigated an **endocast** (a cast of the interior brain case) of this specimen and found fissures in the frontal lobes similar to those of modern humans but different from other early hominid species. Although these features are more similar to those of later humans, many dental and facial measurements of *H. rudolfensis* are more similar to those of the australopithecines.

Evolutionary Relationships

Both *H. habilis* and *H. rudolfensis* date back to 2 million years ago. Which of these species is ancestral to later humans? This is not an easy question to answer. First, each species has some features in common with later humans and some that are different. *H. habilis,* for example, has a more primitive postcranial skeleton. Although *H. rudolfensis* has a larger and more complex brain, it also has a number of primitive cranial and dental characteristics (Wood

Homo rudolfensis A species of early *Homo* from Africa approximately 2 million years ago, with a brain size somewhat larger than *H. habilis.*

endocast A cast of the interior of the brain case used in analyzing brain size and structure.

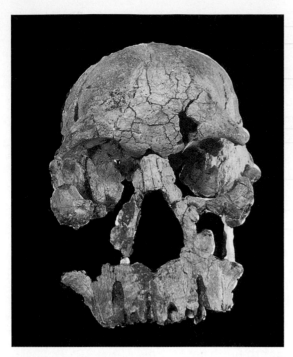 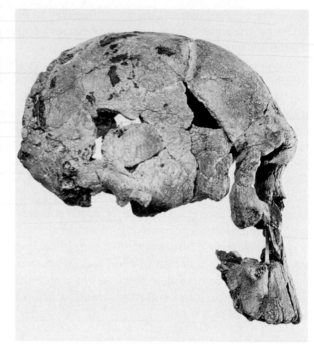

FIGURE 13.5

Frontal and side views of Homo rudolfensis, *specimen KNM-ER 1470, Lake Turkana, Kenya. (© The National Museums of Kenya)*

1996). Based on these primitive features, some anthropologists have proposed reassigning both of these species to the genus *Australopithecus* (Wolpoff 1999; Wood and Collard 1999).

Given the dates of both species, it is possible that *neither* one is directly ancestral to later humans. There is also evidence of a third species arising in Africa almost 2 million years ago—***Homo erectus***—which is the best candidate for an ancestor to later humans. Given our present knowledge, we see a pattern whereby one species of *Homo* arises roughly 2.5 million years ago and by 2 million years ago splits into three different species: *H. habilis, H. rudolfensis,* and *H. erectus.* It is possible that the earliest remains of *Homo* may represent an early appearance of either *H. habilis* or *H. rudolfensis.* At this point in time, however, this early evidence is too fragmentary to assign definitively to one species or the other.

HOMO ERECTUS

The species name *Homo erectus* literally means "upright walking human." This may sound odd, given the fact that earlier species also walked upright. When the first specimens of *H. erectus* were found in the late nineteenth century, they were thought to represent the oldest evidence of bipedalism. Originally, the species was called "*Pithecanthropus erectus*" (upright walking ape-man). Later the genus name *Homo* was assigned because of the similar adaptations of this early hominid species to those of our species: larger brains and a reliance on culture. This section reviews the currently known biological and behavioral evidence for *Homo erectus.*

Homo erectus A species of genus *Homo* that arose 2 million years ago, first appearing in Africa and then spreading to parts of Asia and Europe.

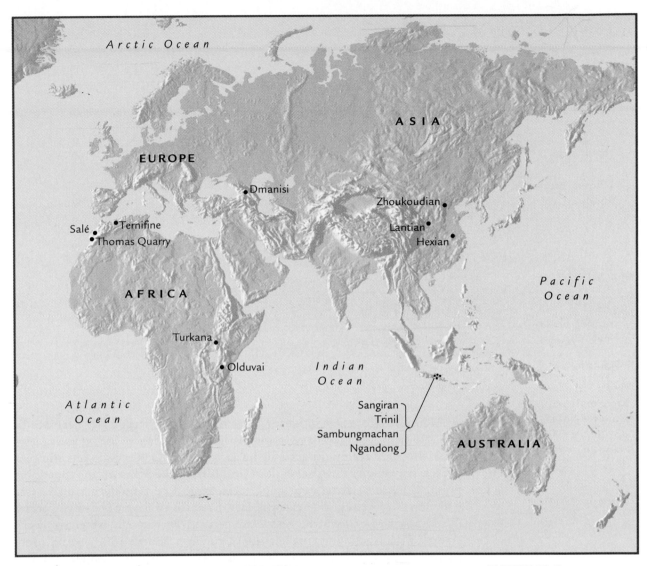

FIGURE 13.6

Location of major Homo erectus *sites.*

Distribution in Time and Space

The distribution of *H. erectus* sites is shown in Figure 13.6, and a list of the major fossil sites is given in Table 13.1. The most important feature of the spatial distribution of *H. erectus* is that it is the first species to move out of Africa. Current evidence points to an African origin for *H. erectus,* followed by movement of some populations into Asia and Europe. For many years the status of *H. erectus* in Europe was not clear. Fossil finds often consisted of teeth and jaws, and it is not clear whether these are from *H. erectus* or *Homo sapiens.* The question was resolved in 2000, when two *H. erectus* crania were discovered in the Republic of Georgia dating to 1.7 million years ago (Gabunia et al. 2000). We now know that populations of *H. erectus* moved into parts of Eastern Europe, although the situation in Western and Central Europe is still not clear.

TABLE 13.1   Some Major Fossil Sites for *Homo erectus*

Geographic Region	Country	Site/Specimen	Age (Ma)	Figure in Text
East Africa*	Kenya	East Turkana	2.0–1.3	13.9
		West Turkana	1.6	13.15
	Tanzania	Olduvai Gorge	1.2–0.7	
South Africa	Republic of South Africa	Swartkrans	1.7–0.9	
North Africa	Algeria	Ternifine	0.7	13.14
	Morocco	Sale	0.2	
Eastern Europe	Republic of Georgia	Dmanisi	1.7	
Southeast Asia	Indonesia	Sangiran	1.8–1.6	13.11
		Trinil	0.9?	
		Sambungmachan	0.4	
		Ngandong**	0.2/0.05–0.03	
East Asia	China	Lantian	0.8	
		Zhoukoudian	0.55–0.30	13.10
		Hexian	0.25	

*Some anthropologists classify the early East Africa specimens as *Homo ergaster*.

**The Ngandong site has often been estimated at roughly 200,000 years old. More recent work suggests it might be as young as 53,000 to 27,000 years old. There is also debate over whether the Ngandong hominids should be considered *H. erectus* or archaic *H. sapiens*.

Sources: Swisher et al. (1994, 1996), Larsen et al. (1998), Klein (1999), Wolpoff (1999), Gabunia et al. (2000)

The dates for the youngest *H. erectus* fossils have typically been about 200,000 years ago. Recent redating of the Ngandong site in Indonesia suggests that this site might actually be as young as 53,000 years old and perhaps even younger (Swisher et al. 1996). If true, then this means that some populations of *H. erectus* were living at the same time as modern humans (see Chapter 14 for dates). If this is the case, then the overlap of the two species (*H. erectus* and *H. sapiens*) suggests cladogenesis. There are, however, some critiques of the Ngandong redating (e.g., Grün and Thorne 1997). In addition, some suggest the Ngandong remains are actually archaic humans and not *H. erectus* at all (the problem is compounded by the fact that none of the Ngandong remains have faces—they are all the upper portions of the brain case, and some feel they are difficult to classify).

For many years, researchers believed Asian *H. erectus* was much younger than African *H. erectus* and suggested the oldest Asian populations (in Indonesia) were roughly 1 million years old. Given these dates, it appeared that *H. erectus* had remained in Africa for almost 1 million years before some groups moved out to Asia. However, evidence based on argon-argon dating caused a reassessment of this scenario. The new evidence dates *H. erectus* to 1.8 million to 1.6 million years ago in Indonesia (Swisher et al. 1994). This new date suggests that some *H. erectus* populations moved out of Africa into Asia soon after their initial African origin. The same is now true for Eastern Europe.

The movement of *H. erectus* into Indonesia might seem puzzling given the fact that today the islands of Indonesia are separated from the Asian mainland by water. In the past, however, the sea level was lower and there was a direct land connection between mainland Asia and Indonesia. Anthropologists have long suggested that *H. erectus* simply walked to Indonesia. Work on the Indonesian island of Flores has challenged this view. Because of differences in ocean depth, this island could have been reached only across water even during times of lowered sea level. Stone tools similar to those used elsewhere by *H. erectus* have been found on the island of Flores and dated to 840,000 years ago (O'Sullivan et al. 2001). This evidence suggests that *H. erectus* may have been capable of using simple rafts to cross water. Of course, the lack of fossil evidence means that we can only presume that the toolmakers were *H. erectus* and not another species. Either way, the evidence does show that some hominid was crossing water in very ancient times.

General Physical Characteristics

The following section focuses on the physical characteristics of *Homo erectus,* specifically those of the skull, teeth, and postcranial skeleton. Some biological differences have been found between African and Asian populations of *H. erectus.* Given the large geographical distance between the two populations, such differences are not surprising. Some anthropologists (e.g., Tattersall 1995) have interpreted these differences as indicating two separate species, *Homo ergaster* in Africa and *Homo erectus* in Asia, but most evidence to date points to a single species (e.g., Kramer 1993; Rightmire 1990).

contested 2 species

Brain Size   The most obvious characteristic of *H. erectus,* compared to earlier hominids, is its larger brain size (Figure 13.7). The average cranial capacity of *H. erectus* is 970 cc, which is approximately 72 percent of the average of modern

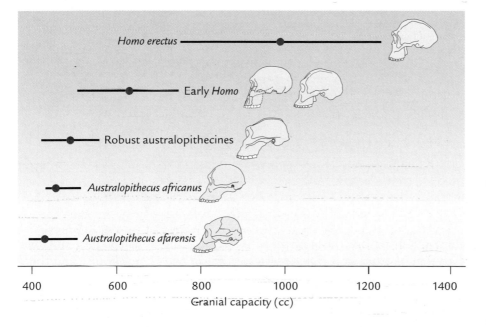

FIGURE 13.7

Comparison of the cranial capacity of Australopithecus, *early* Homo *(*H. habilis *and* H. rudolfensis*), and* Homo erectus. *The dots indicate the average cranial capacity (in cubic centimeters) for each group. The lines indicate the range of cranial capacity from minimum to maximum. The data for* H. erectus *includes the Ngandong hominids; if excluded, the average is slightly lower. (Sources of data: Australopithecines and early* Homo *from Aiello and Dunbar 1993;* H. erectus *from Ruff et al. 1997; updates and additions from Suwa et al. 1997, Conroy et al. 1998, Gabunia et al. 2000, and Falk et al. 2000)*

FIGURE 13.8

Plot of cranial capacity over time for fossil specimens of early Homo *(H. habilis and* H. rudolfensis*) and* Homo erectus. *The data for* H. erectus *includes the Ngandong hominids. (Sources of data: Early* Homo *from Aiello and Dunbar 1993; H. erectus from Ruff et al. 1997, Gabunia et al. 2000)*

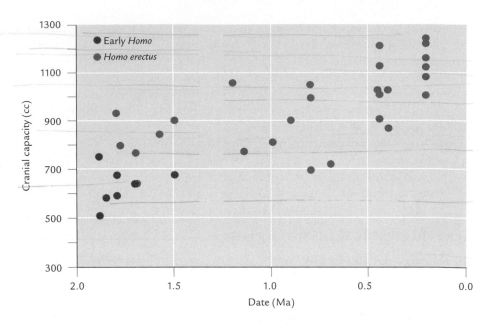

FIGURE 13.9

Homo erectus *skull, specimen KNM-ER 3733, Lake Turkana, Kenya. Dated at 1.8 million years ago, this is one of the oldest known specimens of* Homo erectus *(some anthropologists consider this specimen a different species,* Homo ergaster*). (© The National Museums of Kenya)*

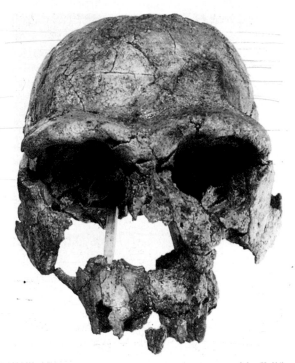

humans. On average, the brain size of *H. erectus* is more than 50 percent larger than that of other early *Homo* species (*H. habilis* and *H. rudolfensis*), and there is an increase in the cranial capacity of *H. erectus* over time (Figure 13.8).

Cranial and Dental Characteristics   One of the earliest *H. erectus* skulls, from Lake Turkana, Africa, is shown in Figure 13.9. Examples of Asian *H. erectus*

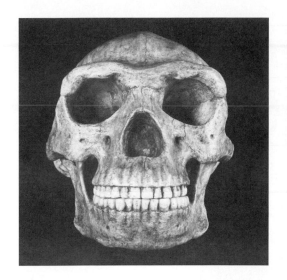

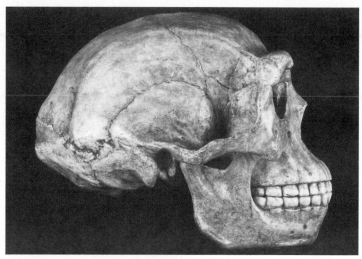

FIGURE 13.10 *(above)*

Frontal and side views of Homo erectus *from the site of Zhoukoudian, China. The specimens from this site are sometimes referred to as "Peking Man" in older literature. (Negs. No. 315446 [left], and 315447 [right]. Courtesy Department of Library Services, American Museum of Natural History)*

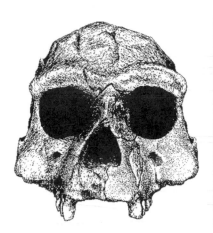

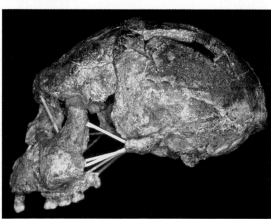

FIGURE 13.11 *(left)*

Frontal and side views of Homo erectus *skull, specimen Sangiran 17, from Sangiran, Indonesia. (Courtesy Milford Wolpoff, University of Michigan, Ann Arbor)*

are shown in Figure 13.10 (China) and Figure 13.11 (Indonesia). Overall, the brain case of *H. erectus* is larger than that of earlier hominids, but it is still smaller than that of modern *H. sapiens*. The skull is lower, and the face still protrudes more than in modern humans. Neck muscles are attached to a ridge of bone along the back side of the skull. The development of this bony ridge shows that *H. erectus* had powerful neck muscles.

Figure 13.12 shows a *H. erectus* skull and a *H. sapiens* skull from a top view. The frontal region of the *H. erectus* skull is still rather narrow (**postorbital constriction**), suggesting lesser development in the frontal and temporal lobes of the brain relative to modern humans. This implies that the intellectual abilities of *H. erectus* were not as great as in modern humans. The best evidence for the mental aptitude of *H. erectus,* however, comes from the archaeological record, discussed later. Figure 13.13 shows a *H. erectus* skull and a *H. sapiens* skull from the rear view. Note that the brain case of *H. erectus* is much broader toward the bottom of the skull.

postorbital constriction
The narrowness of the skull behind the eye orbits, a characteristic of early hominids.

FIGURE 13.12

Top views of the skulls of Homo erectus *(left) and* modern Homo sapiens *(right). Note the greater constriction behind the eyes in* Homo erectus.

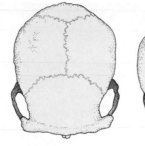
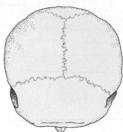

FIGURE 13.13

Rear views of the skulls of Homo erectus *(left) and* modern Homo sapiens *(right). Note the broader brain case of* Homo sapiens.

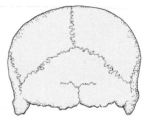

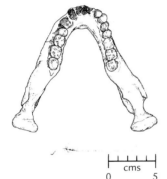

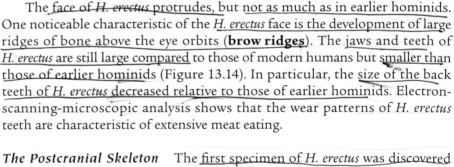

FIGURE 13.14

Lower jaw of Homo erectus, *specimen, Ternifine 3, Ternifine, Algeria, 700,000 years ago. (From Clark Spencer Larsen, Robert M. Matter, and Daniel L. Gebo,* Human Origins: The Fossil Record, *3d ed., p. 101. © 1998, 1991, 1985 by Waveland Press, Inc., Prospect Heights, Ill. Reprinted with permission from the publisher)*

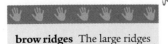

brow ridges The large ridges of bone above the eye orbits, most noticeable in *Homo erectus* and archaic humans.

The face of *H. erectus* protrudes, but not as much as in earlier hominids. One noticeable characteristic of the *H. erectus* face is the development of large ridges of bone above the eye orbits (**brow ridges**). The jaws and teeth of *H. erectus* are still large compared to those of modern humans but smaller than those of earlier hominids (Figure 13.14). In particular, the size of the back teeth of *H. erectus* decreased relative to those of earlier hominids. Electron-scanning-microscopic analysis shows that the wear patterns of *H. erectus* teeth are characteristic of extensive meat eating.

The Postcranial Skeleton   The first specimen of *H. erectus* was discovered by Eugene Dubois in Java in 1891. This find consisted of the upper portion of a skull and a femur. Most scientists in the late nineteenth century would have been hesitant to include the skullcap in our genus, for the then-current view was that all human ancestors had modern-sized brains. Any fossil with a smaller brain was excluded from our ancestry. The femur that Dubois found, however, was virtually the same as that of a modern human. Because the two bones were found together, Dubois reasoned that upright walking had developed before the completion of a modern human skull. Though this statement now seems perfectly reasonable, it was controversial at the time.

For many years, the postcranial evidence for *H. erectus* was limited to portions of individuals—a femur here or a pelvic bone there. In 1984, this situation changed with the discovery of a nearly complete *H. erectus* skeleton at Lake Turkana dating 1.6 million years ago (Brown et al. 1985). This skeleton (Figure 13.15) is that of a young male. The pattern of dental eruption suggests he was about 12 years old when he died. This age estimate depends on the extent to which his growth patterns were similar to those of modern humans; some have suggested he might have been younger. One of the most striking features of this extremely complete skeleton is that he was tall; had

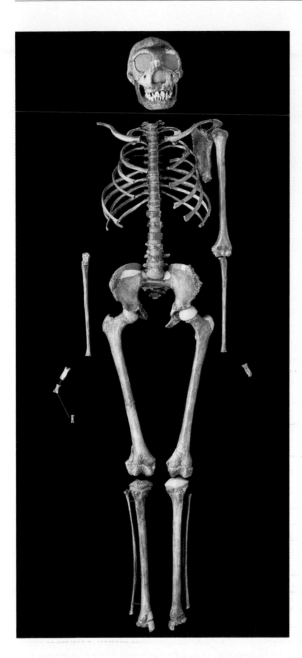

he lived to adulthood, he might have been 6 feet tall, well above the average for many modern human populations (although this estimate is not accepted by all—see Bogin and Smith 1996). Also, note that the body proportions are very similar to those of modern humans and different from those of earlier hominids, which had slightly longer arms.

This *H. erectus* find also provides us with valuable information about the evolution of brain size in early human evolution. Portions of the pelvis are narrow relative to those of modern humans. Because little sexual dimorphism is apparent in certain pelvic dimensions, Brown and colleagues (1985) feel

FIGURE 13.16

Making an Acheulian tool. Nicholas Toth uses a piece of antler to remove small flakes from both sides of the flint, producing a symmetric hand axe. Shown are flint hand axes and a cleaver. (Courtesy of Nicholas Toth, Indiana University)

that some measurements taken from this specimen can apply to both males and females. Their analysis leads to the suggestion that *H. erectus* females could not have given birth to very large-brained babies. To reach the relatively large brain sizes shown by *H. erectus*, the rate of brain growth must have continued to increase after birth. Had *H. erectus* shown the typical primate pattern of the brain size simply doubling after birth, their brains would not have been as large as they were. It seems that the modern human pattern of extensive postnatal brain growth had begun.

Cultural Behavior

Given the increase in brain size in *H. erectus,* it is no surprise that corresponding changes took place in cultural adaptations. The stone tool technology of *H. erectus* was more sophisticated and specialized than that of *H. habilis* and *H. rudolfensis*. Although not all agree, most anthropologists suggest that *H. erectus* was a skilled cooperative hunter. Some populations of *H. erectus* used caves for shelter, and others, perhaps, made their own temporary shelters when caves were not available. *H. erectus* also used fire for cooking and warmth, although it is not clear whether they made fire or relied instead on natural fire.

Stone Tool Technology   In general, the stone tool technology of *H. erectus* was more diverse and sophisticated than the simple Oldowan tool technology

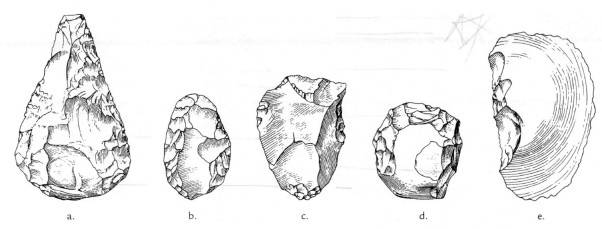

a.   b.   c.   d.   e.

FIGURE 13.17

Examples of tools made by Homo erectus: *(a) hand axe, (b) side scraper, (c) small chopping tool, (d) chopper, (e) cleaverlike tool. (From* The Old Stone Age *by F. Bordes, 1968. Reprinted with permission of the publisher, Wiedenfeld and Nicolson, Ltd.)*

used by *H. habilis* and *H. rudolfensis.* This cultural change did not, however, take place immediately with the origin of *H. erectus;* that is, these biological and cultural changes did not occur simultaneously. Initially, early *H. erectus* in Africa made tools similar to but somewhat more sophisticated than Oldowan tools (often called "Evolved Oldowan"). Starting 1.5 million years ago, however, *H. erectus* developed a new type of stone tool technology referred to as the **Acheulian tradition.**

The Acheulian tool kit includes **bifaces,** stone tools that are worked on both sides. These tools are flatter and have straighter, sharper sides than Oldowan tools. The change in manufacture produced a more efficient tool. To produce a bifacial tool, smaller flakes must be removed than is necessary to produce an Oldowan chopping tool, a process that requires greater skill. One method of flake removal involves the use of some softer material, such as wood or antler, instead of another stone. Softer materials absorb much of the shock in flake removal, allowing more precise control over flaking.

The basic Acheulian tool is the hand axe (Figure 13.16), which could be used for a variety of purposes, including meat preparation. Other tools were made for different purposes. Scrapers were used for cleaning animal flesh, and cleavers were used for breaking animal bones during butchery (Figure 13.17).

The use of individual tools for different purposes marks an important step in the cultural evolution of hominids. Increased specialization allows more efficient tool use and also requires greater mental sophistication in tool design and manufacture.

For many years, anthropologists were puzzled by striking geographic variation in the stone tools of *H. erectus.* Whereas Acheulian hand axes were found in Africa and Europe, they appeared to be absent in Asia, where a large number of less sophisticated chopping tools were found (see Figure 13.17d and 13.17e). One explanation for this difference was cultural or perhaps biological differences in *H. erectus* populations. Others suggested that this difference might reflect differences in available natural resources. For example, Pope (1989) suggested that Asian *H. erectus* may have been using bamboo for making sharp cutting implements. Others noted some Asian sites that did have similar levels of stone tool technology, but the dating on many of these

Acheulian tradition
The stone tool culture that appears first with *Homo erectus* and is characterized by the development of hand axes and other bifacial tools.

biface Stone tool with both sides worked, producing greater symmetry and efficiency.

FIGURE 13.18

Olduvai Gorge, Tanzania.
Homo erectus *fossils and*
Acheulian *hand axes have been*
found at this site, as well as
other hominid fossils and tools.
(© Bildarchiv Okapia/Science
Source/Photo Researchers, Inc.)

sites is unclear. Recently, stone tools made using Acheulianlike technology have been found in China dating to the time of *H. erectus,* 803,000 years ago (Hou et al. 2000).

Hunting and Gathering   The fossil and archaeological records show that *H. erectus* was definitely a hunter of small and large game. The earliest evidence of hunting dates from Olduvai Gorge (Figure 13.18) 1.5 million years ago. All of the bones from larger animals are found, suggesting a single butchering site rather than fragmentary scavenging. The bones are also more fragmented, showing greater use of the animal carcass (Wolpoff 1999). The complete use of animal carcasses matches the pattern found with modern hunting-and-gathering groups and is different from that expected with scavenging. The increased variety of stone tools for butchering also supports the idea that *H. erectus* was a hunter, as does dental evidence, which shows a significant amount of meat in the diet.

One of the best-known *H. erectus* sites showing evidence of hunting is Zhoukoudian, China. Here *H. erectus* populations lived intermittently in caves between approximately 550,000 and 300,000 years ago (Larsen et al. 1998). The caves were used as living sites and are littered with animal bones, tools and tool scraps, and fossilized hominid feces. In addition, parts of the remains of more than 40 *H. erectus* individuals have been found at the Zhoukoudian caves. This site has long been known as the place of "Peking Man," named after the nearby city of Beijing (Peking), China.

The bones and stones at different sites show that hunting was an important source of food. Was it the only source? Gathering vegetables, fruits, nuts, and other foods was surely just as important to the survival of *H. erectus*. In modern hunting-and-gathering societies, up to 75 percent of the total caloric intake of a group comes from gathering. In the past, anthropologists have tended to focus more on hunting than on gathering. This focus was in part a consequence of the nature of the archaeological record (bones and stones preserve more easily than do vegetables or wooden containers).

Another factor behind this emphasis on hunting was male bias, unfortunately common in many scientific fields. Modern hunting-and-gathering societies show a clear division of labor by sex—men are generally the hunters and women the gatherers. The early interpretation of (mostly male) anthropologists focused on what was considered the more "important" and "difficult" task of male hunting. This interpretation influenced other hypotheses on prehistoric human behavior. Males were assumed to be the hunters because they had the necessary strength. However, although males are generally stronger than females, this slight difference would not have mattered in hunting. Not even the strongest male today can knock down an elephant by himself! Hunting requires skill and stealth more than strength. The important distinction between hunting and gathering is that the former activity requires greater mobility, and moving around may not be conducive to successful human pregnancy or nursing. Gathering can be performed in a local area, whereas hunting requires traveling long distances over many days. Also, the crying of infants would make hunting difficult.

Because gathering accounts for the majority of calories, we could also argue for a female-centered view: instead of "man the hunter" we could have "woman the gatherer." Both of these ideas, however, miss the main feature of hunting-and-gathering society—food sharing. Hunting and gathering were equally important activities, and the survival and geographic expansion of *H. erectus* depended on both. The division of labor and food sharing of hunter-gatherers show close and cooperative social structures. We cannot observe *H. erectus* society firsthand, of course. Using what we know from the archaeological record and from modern hunting-and-gathering societies, however, we can safely infer the existence of small social groups banded together for mutual benefit.

Fire   The movement of *H. erectus* into East Asia shows the importance of cultural adaptations. Hominids are tropical primates, and expansion into colder climates required an appropriate level of technology. Fire was an important source of warmth and light and made cooking possible so that food was easier to chew and digest. In addition, fire can be used for tool manufacture. The tip of a wooden spear can be placed in a fire for a short period to harden the point. We can also speculate that fire allowed social interactions and teaching after dark.

Evidence for controlled fire comes from the cave hearths at Zhoukoudian and other *H. erectus* sites. The oldest possible use of fire by *H. erectus* was in Africa roughly 1.6 million years ago (Wolpoff 1999), although these early

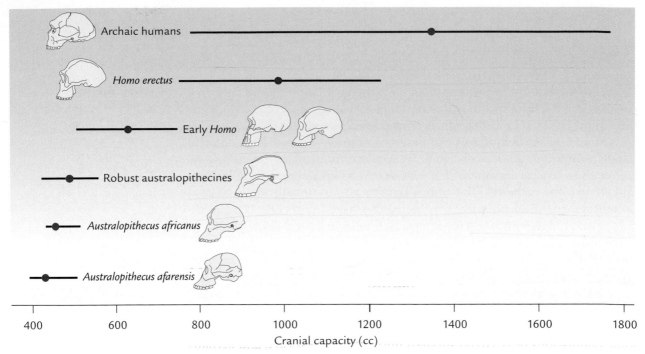

FIGURE 13.19

Comparison of the cranial capacity of Australopithecus, *early* Homo *(*H. habilis *and* H. rudolfensis*),* Homo erectus, *and archaic humans. The dots indicate the average cranial capacity (in cubic centimeters) for each group. The lines indicate the range of cranial capacity from minimum to maximum. The data for* H. erectus *includes the Ngandong hominids; if excluded, the average is slightly lower.* (Sources of data: Australopithecines and early Homo from Aiello and Dunbar 1993; H. erectus and archaic humans from Ruff et al. 1997; updates and additions from Suwa et al. 1997, Abbate et al. 1998, Conroy et al. 1998, Gabunia et al. 2000, and Falk et al. 2000)

dates are still controversial. The evidence at Zhoukoudian has recently been questioned; new analyses could not detect any ash or charcoal in the same layer as stone tools. There is, however, indirect evidence in the form of burned animal bones in association with stone tools (Weiner et al. 1998). Thus, the evidence at Zhoukoudian, although suggestive, is not as conclusive as once thought.

Although we suspect that members of *H. erectus* used fire, we do not know if they made it. The earliest evidence of fire starters, only 15,000 years old, consists of a ball of iron pyrites with deep grooves left by repeated striking. Even if members of *H. erectus* could not make fire, however, and had to rely on nature, they could, nevertheless, keep fires smoldering for long periods of time at campsites.

Regardless of how *H. erectus* obtained fire, its use marks an important step in human cultural evolution. Making and using fire represent the controlled exploitation of an energy source. Because we rely on many other sources of controlled energy today, we tend to overlook the vital importance of fire as an energy source.

ARCHAIC HUMANS

At the simplest level, the fossil record shows the evolution of *Homo erectus* into *Homo sapiens*. Closer examination, however, shows this statement to be a bit too simplistic, masking variation across time and space. As we have seen,

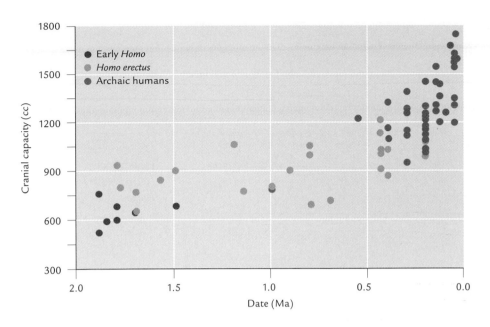

FIGURE 13.20

Plot of cranial capacity over time for fossil specimens of early Homo *(H. habilis and H. rudolfensis), Homo erectus, and archaic humans. The data for* H. erectus *includes the Ngandong hominids. (Sources of data: Early* Homo *from Aiello and Dunbar 1993;* H. erectus *and archaic humans from Ruff et al. 1997, Abbate et al. 1998, Gabunia et al. 2000)*

some populations of *H. erectus* survived until 200,000 years ago and perhaps even longer. Elsewhere in the Old World, however, we see fossils different from *H. erectus* appear roughly 500,000 years ago (and perhaps earlier). Many anthropologists classify these non-*erectus* fossils as early *H. sapiens,* in large part because they are clearly not *H. erectus* and they had larger brains. However, they are not the same as modern *H. sapiens,* thus creating a problem in naming and classification. What do we call them? Some anthropologists suggest lumping all of these fossils together as early examples of *Homo sapiens,* whereas other anthropologists argue that these fossils represent two or more species. For the purpose of discussion here, we will refer to these large-brained (but not modern) specimens as **archaic humans.**

The most noticeable characteristic of the archaic humans is the further increase in brain size (Figures 13.19 and 13.20). The average brain size of the archaic specimens plotted in these figures is virtually identical to the average for modern humans of 1350 cc. These values mask some important variation. The earliest archaics generally have smaller cranial capacities. Also, there has been a slight reduction in average brain size over the past 35,000 years or so, probably reflecting a reduction in overall body size (Henneberg 1988; Ruff et al. 1997).

Anagenesis or Cladogenesis?

Some paleoanthropologists view the transition from *H. erectus* to archaic humans to modern humans as evolution within a single evolutionary line; that is, anagenesis, as described in Chapter 4. Proponents of this model view *all* of these forms as different stages within a single species over time and have suggested that they all be considered *Homo sapiens.* Under this model, *H. erectus*

archaic humans Specimens of *Homo* with brain size close to that of modern humans but with differently shaped skulls. There is considerable controversy over whether they are an earlier form of *Homo sapiens* or represent different species.

TABLE 13.2   Examples of How Paleoanthropologists Name Fossils in the Genus _Homo_

Labels Used in This Text	Number of Species	
	Minimum Number	Current Maximum Number
Homo erectus	Early _Homo sapiens_	_Homo erectus_
		Homo ergaster
Archaic humans	Archaic _Homo sapiens_	_Homo antecessor_
		Homo heidelbergensis
		Homo neanderthalensis
Modern humans	Recent _Homo sapiens_	_Homo sapiens_

Sources: Based on information from Tattersall (1995), Bermúdez de Castro et al. (1997), and Wolpoff (1999)

should be renamed "early _Homo sapiens_" (Wolpoff 1999). Not everyone agrees with this view. Others suggest that _H. erectus_ was a separate biological species and that the origin of later species was through cladogenesis (e.g., Rightmire 1992, 1996). Some go further and suggest that _H. erectus_ fossils actually represent two different species (Tattersall 1995).

Disagreement also exists when considering the archaic humans. Some view them simply as "archaic _Homo sapiens_," whereas others see evidence of two or more separate species. We will deal with these debates in more detail throughout the remainder of this chapter and the next. A summary of several views is shown in Table 13.2.

Distribution in Time and Space

Archaic humans have been found at a number of sites in Africa, Europe, and Asia (Figure 13.21) dating, for the most part, between approximately 500,000 and 28,000 years ago. This time range is conservative—discoveries from the Atapuerca site in Spain suggest that members of the genus _Homo_ might date back as far as 650,000 years ago (Bermúdez de Castro et al. 1997). Although these remains are not those of _H. erectus,_ it is not clear whether they are an early group of archaic _H. sapiens_ or a different species altogether (the authors suggested a new species, "_Homo antecessor,_" but few anthropologists have yet accepted this suggestion). Another example is the discovery of a cranium, roughly 1 million years old, from the Ethiopian site of Danakil (Abbate et al. 1998). This specimen has a mix of features found in both _H. erectus_ and in _H. sapiens._ Future debate will focus on whether this specimen can be assigned to a given species, requires a new species name, or simply represents a transition between _H. erectus_ and _H. sapiens._

Given the large number of sites and specimens, it is useful to look more closely at patterns of regional variation. Some of the better known regions include sub-Saharan Africa, North Asia, South Asia, and Southeast Asia and

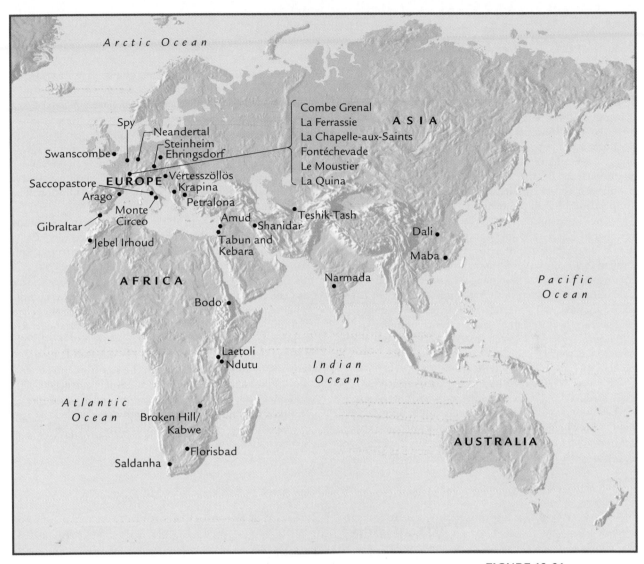

FIGURE 13.21

Map of some archaic human sites.

Australia (often lumped together as "Australasia"). Table 13.3 lists a number of the major sites of archaic humans. Note the heavy concentration of sites in Europe. In the past, scientists tended to focus most of their efforts on these sites. Now it is generally recognized that human evolution needs to be studied on a *global* level.

Because of this interest in European fossils, particular emphasis in the past was placed on a regional population known as the **Neandertals.** The word *Neandertal* is German for simply "Neander Valley," the site where one of the first specimens was discovered. The Neandertals lived in the regions surrounding the Mediterranean, including Western Europe, Central and Eastern Europe, and the Middle East. Neandertal remains have been found dating between roughly 150,000 and 28,000 years ago.

Neandertals

Neandertals A population of archaic humans that lived in Europe and the Middle East, dating between 150,000 and 28,000 years ago.

Neandertals: Names and Images

The name *Neandertal* comes from the site in the Neander Valley in Germany where Neandertals were first found. In German, *tal* means "valley." Hence, *Neandertal* means "Neander Valley." You may be more familiar with an alternative spelling ("Neanderthal") and an alternative pronunciation (emphasizing the "THAL" sound). However, the *h* is silent in German so that *thal* is actually pronounced "tal." Because of this characteristic of German pronunciation, many (although not all) anthropologists simply drop the *h* in the spelling as well.

The very mention of Neandertals usually invokes a number of images and preconceptions. You may, for example, conjure up one of many images of the Neandertals as crude and simple subhumans with limited intelligence that walk bent over. These images have become such a part of our popular culture that a typical dictionary definition includes "Neandertal" as an adjective meaning "suggesting primitive man in appearance or behavior (*Neandertal* ferocity)" and "extremely old-fashioned or out-of-date," as well as a noun meaning "a rugged or uncouth person" (*Webster's Third International Dictionary*).

Why do Neandertals have such a bad reputation? As discussed in this chapter, Neandertals are viewed by most anthropologists as a regional population of archaic humans. The distinctive appearance of Neandertals is often acknowledged by scientists who refer to them as a different subspecies of humans—that is, *Homo sapiens neander-thalensis,* as opposed to modern humans, who are classified in the subspecies *Homo sapiens sapiens.* Some anthropologists argue that Neandertals are sufficiently different to be placed in a different species altogether—*Homo neanderthalensis* (note that the *h* remains in the species and subspecies names, as per international agreement). Regardless of classification, however, we know that Neandertals had large brains, walked upright, and possessed a sophisticated culture including stone tools, hunting, use of fire, and cave burial.

Part of the image problem comes from an inaccurate reconstruction of a Neandertal skeleton in the early 1900s. Because of certain physical features, such as curved thigh bones, scientists of the time believed that Neandertals did not walk completely upright, moving about bent over instead. It was discovered later that the curved bones and other features were simply a reflection of the poor health, including severe arthritis, of that particular Neandertal. Other features once taken to indicate mental inferiority, such as large brow ridges, are now recognized as biomechanical in nature. Even though the scientific interpretation has changed, the popular images of Neandertals remain to this day. More information on the history of Neandertals, including further discussion of their image, can be found in Trinkaus and Shipman (1992) and Stringer and Gamble (1993).

Early Archaics

Early archaic humans are found throughout much of the Old World between about 500,000 and 150,000 years ago.

Physical Characteristics Both archaic and anatomically modern humans have large brains, and brain size cannot be used to distinguish between the two groups. The cranial shape of these two groups, however, is on average different. Archaic humans had low skulls with sloping foreheads, whereas modern humans have high skulls and vertical foreheads. Also, the face and teeth of archaic humans are larger than those in modern humans. Specimens of archaic humans rarely have a chin, something found in modern humans. The postcranial skeleton of many archaic human specimens is very similar to modern forms. In general, the bones of archaic humans are thicker and show markings for greater musculature.

An example of an early archaic human is shown in Figure 13.22. This skull, from Petralona, Greece, is roughly 200,000 years old. Its cranial capacity (1,230 cc) places it at the upper range of later *H. erectus* and slightly lower

TABLE 13.3	Some Archaic Human Sites			
Geographic Region	*Country*	*Site/Specimen*	*Age (ka)*	*Figure in Text*
Africa	Tanzania	Lake Ndutu	400	
	Tanzania	Laetoli	130	
	Zambia	Kabwe	300	13.23
North Africa	Morocco	Jebel Irhoud	150	
Asia	China	Dali	300	13.24
		Maba	140	
	India	Narmada	300	
	Indonesia	Ngandong*	200/50–27?	
Europe	Croatia	Krapina (N)	130	
		Vindija (N)	28	
	England	Swanscombe	400	
	France	Arago	400	
		La Chapelle (N)	52	13.27
		La Quina (N)	50	
		La Ferrassie (N)	72	13.26
		Le Moustier (N)	40	
		St. Césaire (N)	36	
	Germany	Steinheim	300	
		Neandertal (N)	50	
	Gibraltar	Forbe's Quarry (N)	50	
	Greece	Petralona	200	13.22
	Italy	Saccapastore (N)	100	
		Mt. Circeo (N)	57	
	Spain	Atapuerca	300	
Middle East	Iraq	Shanidar (N)	50	13.29
	Israel	Amud (N)	45	
		Kebara (N)	60	
		Tabun (N)	150	13.28

This table is not meant to be complete; many other specimens of archaic humans have been found. A number of these dates are uncertain.

N = Neandertal

*The age of the Ngandong site has often been estimated at roughly 200,000 years. More recent work suggests it might be as recent as 53,000 to 27,000 years ago. There is also disagreement whether the Ngandong hominids should be considered *H. erectus* or archaic *H. sapiens*.

Sources: Swisher et al. (1996); Ruff et al. (1997), Smith et al. (1999); Wolpoff (1999)

than the average for *H. sapiens*. Another example of an archaic specimen is the skull shown in Figure 13.23, which was discovered in Zambia, Africa, and dates to approximately 300,000 years ago. The large brain size (1,280 cc) is readily apparent. The face is rather large and so are the brow ridges. The shape of the skull shows typical archaic features: a sloping forehead and a low skull.

Another example of an archaic human skull (Figure 13.24) is from the site at Dali, China, and dates to approximately 300,000 years ago. The cranial capacity is on the low end of the range for *H. sapiens* (1,120 cc), and the

FIGURE 13.22

The Petralona skull, Greece. An example of an early archaic human from Europe. (From Clark Spencer Larsen, Robert M. Matter, and Daniel L. Gebo, Human Origins: The Fossil Record, *3d ed., p. 117. © 1998, 1991, 1985 by Waveland Press, Inc., Prospect Heights, Ill. Reprinted with permission from the publisher)*

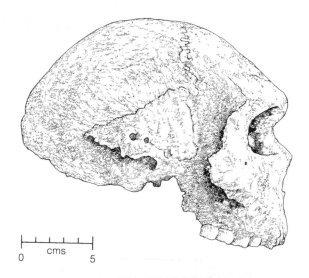

FIGURE 13.23

The Broken Hill skull, Kabwe, Zambia. An example of early archaic Homo sapiens *from Africa. (© The Natural History Museum, London)*

FIGURE 13.24

The Dali skull, Dali County, People's Republic of China. An example of archaic Homo sapiens *from Asia. (From Clark Spencer Larsen, Robert M. Matter, and Daniel L. Gebo,* Human Origins: The Fossil Record, *3d ed., p. 128. © 1998, 1991, 1985 by Waveland Press, Inc., Prospect Heights, Ill. Reprinted with permission from the publisher)*

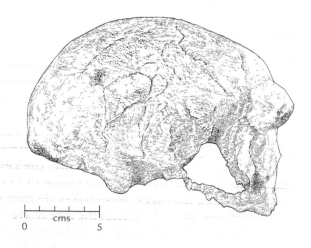

Side Views   Top Views

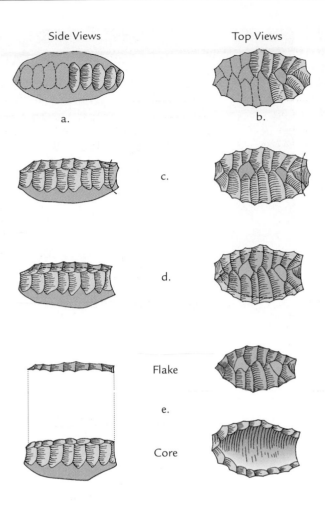

a.   b.

c.

d.

Flake

e.

Core

FIGURE 13.25

Manufacture of a stone tool, using the prepared-core method. First, the core is shaped by removing small flakes from the sides and top (a–d). Then the finished tool is removed from the core (e). (From Archaeology: Discovering Our Past, *2d ed., by Robert Sharer and Wendy Ashmore, Fig. 10.3. © 1993 by Mayfield Publishing Company. Reprinted with permission from The McGraw-Hill Companies)*

brow ridges are large. The skull is low and has a sloping forehead, both typical archaic features. The Dali skull also illustrates regional variation. As in many archaic North Asian specimens, the face is smaller and flatter than in other regions of the world. These traits, among others, are also found in earlier and later North Asian specimens (Thorne and Wolpoff 1992).

Cultural Behavior   Like *H. erectus,* archaic humans were hunters and gatherers, exploiting a wide variety of natural resources. Remains of animal bones at their sites show that they hunted both small game and large, including bears, mammoths, and rhinoceroses. In some areas it appears that archaic humans hunted year round; in others they apparently migrated along with animal herds.

The early archaic humans continued using Acheulian tools such as hand-axes but often showed improvement in technique. Archaic humans also developed a new method of manufacture, the Levallois, or **prepared-core, method** (Schick and Toth 1993). As Figure 13.25 shows, a flint nodule is first chipped around the edges. Small flakes are then removed from the top surface of the core. In the final step, the core is struck precisely at one end. This type of method allows maximum utilization of stone cores.

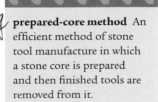

prepared-core method An efficient method of stone tool manufacture in which a stone core is prepared and then finished tools are removed from it.

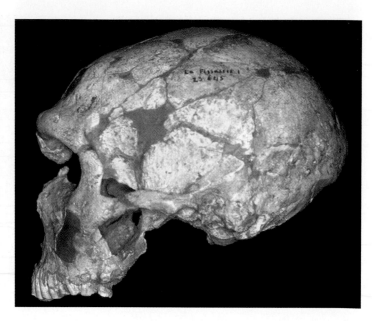
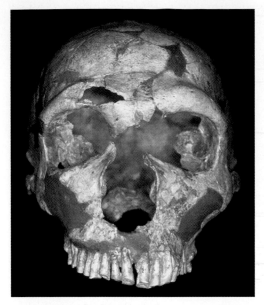

FIGURE 13.26

Frontal and side views of La Ferrassie skull, a Neandertal from France. (Courtesy Milford Wolpoff, University of Michigan, Ann Arbor)

The use of the prepared-core technique, which produces sharp and symmetric tools, tells us two important things about archaic humans. First, they were capable of precise toolmaking, which implies an excellent knowledge of flaking methods and the structural characteristics of stone. Second, they were able to visualize the final tool early in production. Not until the last step does the shape of the finished tool become apparent. Such manufacture is a process quite different from simply chipping away at a stone until a tool is finished.

The Neandertals

Of all the regional populations of archaic humans, the best known (and the most puzzling) are the Neandertals. Many of the Neandertals lived during glacial times. The Pleistocene epoch witnessed alternating periods of glaciation and interglacials as the earth's climate changed. In the Northern Hemisphere, large sections of land were covered with advancing ice sheets during glaciations, which receded during interglacial periods. The climate changed frequently, perhaps as many as 17 times, in this period. Even during times typically characterized as "ice ages," the temperature and southern advancement of ice varied considerably. In any case, the Neandertals lived during times when the climate was cooler in their habitat. They did not live right on the ice, but the reduction in average temperature surely had an effect on their environments, especially in Western Europe. The ability of the Neandertals to survive in these conditions is proof of their cultural adaptations, which included hunting, shelter, and use of fire.

Physical Characteristics   Neandertals had the typical archaic features of sloping forehead, low skull, lack of chin, and large brow ridges. They also

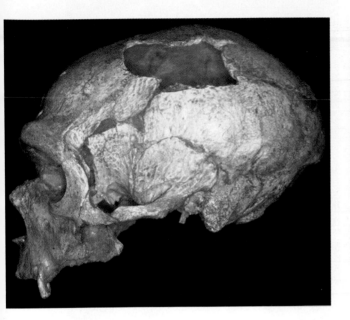
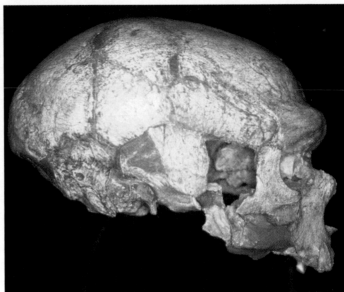

FIGURE 13.27

Two side views of La Chapelle skull, a Neandertal from France. (Courtesy Milford Wolpoff, University of Michigan, Ann Arbor)

possessed several unique characteristics that tend not to be found in other regions (or to be found at a much lower frequency). The Neandertals had very large brains, averaging close to 1,500 cc. Although this was larger in overall size than those of living humans, the Neandertals also had larger body mass. Relative to body size, Neandertal cranial capacity is slightly lower than living humans (Ruff et al. 1997). According to Holloway (1985), the structural organization of Neandertal brains, as assessed from endocasts, is no different from that of modern humans.

Neandertals differ from other archaic human populations in several features. Figures 13.26 and 13.27 show two skulls of Western European Neandertals, both from sites in France between 75,000 and 50,000 years ago. Neandertal faces are generally long and protrude more than in other archaic populations. The nasal region is large, suggesting large noses, and the sinus cavities to the side of the nose expand outward. The large nasal and midfacial areas on Neandertal skulls have often been interpreted as some type of adaptation to a cold climate. However, Rak (1986) interprets the large faces of Neandertals in terms of the biomechanics of the skull. He suggests that the Neandertal face acted to withstand stresses brought about by the use of relatively large front teeth. The front teeth of Neandertals are large in relation to their back teeth and often show considerable wear, suggesting that they were used as tools. Spencer and Demes (1993) also suggest that Neandertal morphology was to a large extent shaped by the use of the front teeth. Many Neandertal specimens have a large crest of bone running from behind the ear toward the back of the skull. The back of the skull is rather puffed out (a feature called an **occipital bun**). Though this feature is most common in Neandertals, it is also found in other archaic and modern human populations. Cranial differences between Neandertals and humans that are more modern appear to be present early in life, a finding that

occipital bun The protruding rear region of the skull, a feature commonly found in Neandertals.

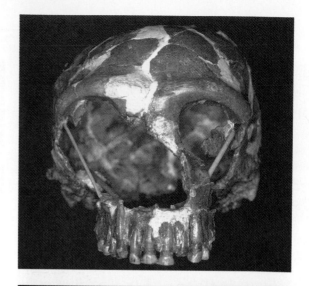

FIGURE 13.28

Frontal and side views of Neandertal skull from Tabun, Israel. (Courtesy Milford Wolpoff, University of Michigan, Ann Arbor)

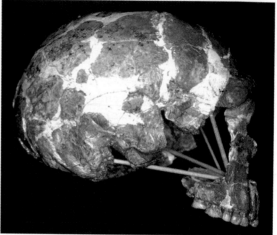

suggests to some that they were a separate species (Ponce de León and Zollikofer 2001).

There is also variation within Neandertals. Figures 13.28 and 13.29 show the skulls of two Middle Eastern Neandertals. Though they possess the general characteristics of Neandertals, they are not as morphologically extreme. The skulls are a bit more well rounded than most Western European Neandertal skulls.

Neandertal postcranial remains show essentially modern bipedalism but also a few differences compared with other archaic populations. Neandertals were relatively short and stocky. The limb bone segments farthest from the body (lower arm and lower leg) are relatively short, most likely reflecting cold adaptation (Trinkaus 1981). The limb and shoulder bones are more rugged than those of modern humans. The areas of muscle attachment show that the Neandertals were very strong. It has been suggested that Neandertal hands were not as capable of fine manipulation as modern human hands nor had at least different patterns of manipulation (Stoner and Trinkaus 1981).

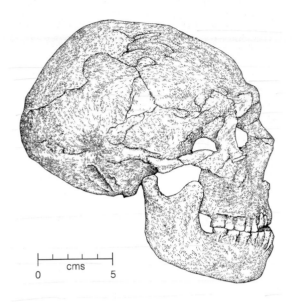

FIGURE 13.29

*Shanidar 1 skull, Iraq. (From
Clark Spencer Larsen, Robert M.
Matter, and Daniel L. Gebo,*
Human Origins: The Fossil
Record, *3d ed., p. 136. © 1998,
1991, 1985 by Waveland Press, Inc.,
Prospect Heights, Ill. Reprinted with
permission from the publisher)*

The pelvic bones are also rather robust compared with those of modern humans, with the exception of the upper portion of the pubis (at the front of the pelvis), which is actually thinner and longer than in modern humans. The uniqueness of the Neandertal pelvis seems to reflect a biomechanical function (Rak and Arensburg 1987).

Neandertal DNA   In the summer of 1997, an article in the journal *Cell* announced to the world an amazing technological breakthrough—the extraction of a DNA sequence from a Neandertal fossil at the Feldhofer site in Germany (Krings et al. 1997). This marked the first time human DNA had been successfully extracted from such an old specimen (the date is not precise but is usually estimated to lie between 70,000 and 35,000 years ago). The extracted sequence consisted of 378 mitochondrial DNA bases. Mitochondrial DNA (discussed in Chapter 5) preserves better than nuclear DNA and is increasingly used in studies of ancient DNA. Since that time, mitochondrial DNA has been extracted from two additional Neandertal specimens, one from Mezmaiskaya Cave in the northern Caucasus dating to 29,000 years ago (Ovchinnikov et al. 2000) and one from Vindija Cave in Croatia dating to 42,000 years ago (Krings et al. 2000).

These DNA sequences are quite different from those of living humans. For example, in the first analysis comparing 378 DNA positions, there were 27 differences between Neandertal mitochondrial DNA and living human DNA, compared to an average of 8 differences between pairs of living humans. The other two Neandertal specimens also show this high genetic difference relative to living humans. Overall, the Neandertal DNA analyses have been taken by many as evidence that the Neandertals were not among our ancestors and were likely a separate species that became extinct in Europe 28,000 years ago.

The situation is perhaps not that simple. Three observations have been made based on Neandertal DNA to argue for a separate species, and each of these has alternative explanations that do not require Neandertals to be a separate species (Relethford 2001c). First, their mitochondrial DNA is different from that of living humans. The question is *how* different? Is it different because they were a separate species, or because they lived many thousands of years ago? There has likely been genetic change in mitochondrial DNA during that time, and we need to consider the possibility of genetic change *within a species over time*. Comparative DNA analysis of living primates offers some clues. The difference between Neandertals and living humans is actually *less* than that found in two out of three comparisons of chimpanzee subspecies (Krings et al. 1999). This suggests that Neandertals might be a different *subspecies* but still be among our ancestors (Relethford 2001c).

A second observation is that we do not find any mitochondrial DNA as divergent as Neandertal DNA among living humans. One possible reason they left no mitochondrial DNA is that they were a separate species that became extinct. Another possibility is that their mitochondrial DNA was lost due to genetic drift (much in the same way that a person's surname might be lost among their descendants, even though they contribute other genetic traits). This possibility has received support by the extraction of another mitochondrial DNA sequence, this time from a modern human fossil 60,000 years old from Australia. This specimen is acknowledged as being anatomically human and characteristic of some of our known ancestors, but it has a DNA sequence quite different from that of living humans in Australia or elsewhere (Adcock et al. 2001), suggesting that its DNA sequence was lost because of genetic drift. If a mitochondrial DNA sequence present in a known modern human has become extinct over tens of thousands of years, then the same thing *might* have happened to the Neandertal DNA sequences. Although this does not show that the Neandertals are among our ancestors, it raises doubt that the observed Neandertal DNA sequences prove they were a separate species (Relethford 2001b).

The third observation offered to support a view that Neandertals were a separate species is absence of any particular affinity of Neandertal DNA with living Europeans. If the European Neandertals were partially ancestral to living Europeans, some have suggested that the Neandertal DNA should be more similar to DNA from living Europeans than to living Africans or living Asians. In fact, Neandertal DNA is roughly equidistant to DNA from living humans across the world, which is the pattern expected if the Neandertals were an extinct species. However, this pattern is also predicted under models of gene flow where Neandertals are part of our ancestry (Relethford 2001c). Given sufficient time, all living human DNA would be equidistant from Neandertal DNA due to gene flow. In sum, although the Neandertal DNA is consistent with a model where Neandertals were a separate species, it is also consistent with a model where they were part of a widespread single species and form *part* of our ancestry. The question of the "fate" of the Neandertals will be revisited in the next chapter.

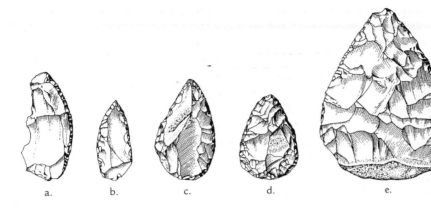

FIGURE 13.30

Examples of Mousterian tools: (a) scraper, (b) point, (c) scraper, (d) point, (e) hand axe. (From The Old Stone Age *by F. Bordes, 1968. Reprinted with permission of the publisher, Weidenfeld and Nicolson, Ltd.)*

Cultural Behavior   The stone tool technology of the Neandertals is known as the **Mousterian tradition.** It is not exclusively Neandertal, however, and is often found with other archaic populations. The Mousterian culture continued using the prepared-core method, producing a wide variety of different types of tools, including a preponderance of scrapers (Figure 13.30). There is also evidence that Neandertals thinned many of the tools so that they could be attached to handles or spears (Schick and Toth 1993).

Archaeological evidence suggests that Neandertals may have been capable of symbolic thought, perhaps even holding beliefs in the supernatural. Neandertals were the first hominids to bury their dead deliberately. Evidence of burial comes from a number of European and Middle Eastern sites, where dead persons' bones have been arranged carefully in graves, often in association with tools, food, and flowers.

The intentional burial of the dead has suggested a ritualistic purpose to some researchers. At a site in Belgium, fires had been lit above two buried bodies. One interpretation of this is that they believed the fires would counteract the "coldness" of death. At the Shanidar Cave site in Iraq, flowers had been placed all over the bodies, an event that was reconstructed based on the presence of fossil pollen in the graves.

Such evidence suggests the evolution of symbolic expressions and the possibility of supernatural beliefs. This standard interpretation, however, is changing. The flexed positions of many of the dead might not reflect intentional posing but rather be a consequence of digging the smallest possible graves. In addition, although the Shanidar burial is still considered one of the best examples of symbolic behavior, it is possible the pollen was introduced by rodents burrowing into the grave *after* burial.

The physical condition of fossil remains offers another window on the behavior of Neandertals. By looking at bone fractures, condition of teeth, and other features, we can get a good idea of the age and health status of early humans. Many Neandertal remains are of elderly individuals with numerous medical problems. Some of the elderly had lost all of their teeth, many had arthritis, and one had lost part of his arm. By looking for signs of healing or

Mousterian tradition
The prepared-core stone tool technology of the Neandertals.

infection, we can tell that many of these elderly individuals did not die from these afflictions. How, then, did they survive, particularly if they had lost all of their teeth? Survival of many of the elderly and impaired Neandertals suggests that others cared for them. This implies not only compassion as a social value but also the existence of a social system that allowed for the sharing of food and resources.

This perspective may be based more on our interpretive biases, however, than on reality. Dettwyler (1991) questions the traditional view of the elderly and disabled as nonproductive members of a group who must be cared for. Drawing on cross-cultural studies, she notes that physically disabled individuals in many societies still frequently make important contributions.

Language Capability   Did the Neandertals have language? Lieberman and Crelin (1971), who reconstructed the vocal anatomy of Neandertals, concluded they were incapable of vocalizing certain vowel sounds. The implication was that Neandertals did not possess as wide a range of sounds as modern humans and perhaps had limited language abilities. This hypothesis was criticized, however, because of differences of opinion on vocal anatomy reconstruction. The lack of direct fossil evidence at the heart of the debate was ultimately furnished with the discovery of the first Neandertal hyoid bone, a bone lying in the neck that can be used to provide information on the structure of the respiratory tract. That this specimen is almost identical in size and shape to the hyoid bone of modern humans indicates that there were no differences in vocal ability between archaics and moderns (Arensberg et al. 1990). Indeed, no evidence exists from brain anatomy to show that Neandertals lacked speech centers (Holloway 1985).

SUMMARY

The earliest evidence for the genus *Homo* dates back 2.5 million years ago. These early fossils are too fragmentary to place into any specific species. By 2 million years ago, there is evidence of at least three species of *Homo: Homo habilis, Homo rudolfensis,* and *Homo erectus,* the latter of which is ancestral to later hominids. *Homo erectus* appears in Africa 2 million years ago and is the first hominid to leave Africa, with some populations appearing in Asia 1.8 million to 1.6 million years ago and in Europe 1.7 million years ago. *H. erectus* shows signs of cranial expansion (the average brain size was roughly three-fourths that of modern humans) and human body proportions. The cultural adaptations of *H. erectus* include development of more sophisticated stone tools (including hand axes), hunting and gathering, and use of fire.

Fossils with close to modern brain size begin to appear in the fossil record roughly 400,000 years ago, although their skulls were somewhat differently shaped than modern humans'. The stone tool technology of archaic humans included tools made by the prepared-core method, a technique that allows greater sophistication and diversity in tools. Later archaic humans, the Neandertals, are found in Europe and the Middle East between 150,000 and 28,000 years ago. The Neandertals are somewhat physically different from other archaics, and there is continued debate over whether they represent a separate species. The culture of Neandertals includes burial of the dead.

There is considerable controversy over the relationship of all archaic humans to earlier and later hominid populations. Some argue that the evolution from *H. erectus* to archaic human to modern human took place within a single, evolving species over time. Others argue that "archaic humans" actually represent several different species, only one of which is ancestral to living humans.

SUPPLEMENTAL READINGS

Stringer, C., and C. Gamble. 1993. *In Search of the Neanderthals: Solving the Puzzle of Human Origins*. New York: Thames and Hudson. An excellent review of Neandertal (and other archaics) biology and culture, as well as the history of debates over modern human origins.

Trinkaus, E., and P. Shipman. 1992. *The Neandertals: Changing the Image of Mankind*. New York: Knopf. An excellent review of the history of Neandertal discoveries and interpretations.

Walker, A., and P. Shipman. 1996. *The Wisdom of the Bones: In Search of Human Origins*. New York: Alfred A. Knopf. A very readable summary of human evolution focusing on *Homo erectus*.

INTERNET RESOURCES

In addition to the Web sites listed in Chapter 12, the following are of particular relevance to the current chapter:

http://anthro.palomar.edu/homo/homo_1.htm
Early Transitional Humans, a tutorial focusing on *Homo habilis* and *Homo rudolfensis*.

http://anthro.palomar.edu/homo/homo_2%20.htm
Homo erectus, a tutorial.

http://anthro.palomar.edu/homo/homo_3.htm
Early Human Culture, a tutorial focusing on Oldowan and Acheulian stone tool technology.

http://anthro.palomar.edu/homo2/archaic.htm
Early Archaic *Homo sapiens* and their Contemporaries, a tutorial on early archaic humans.

http://anthro.palomar.edu/homo2/neandertal.htm
Neandertals, a tutorial.

http://thunder.indstate.edu/~ramanank/index.html
Neandertals: A Cyber Perspective, another Web page devoted to Neandertals.

CHAPTER 14

The Origin of Modern Humans

Beginning roughly 130,000 years ago, populations of archaic humans started evolving into what we refer to as **anatomically modern *Homo sapiens.*** This is the name by which we refer to ourselves today, as well as the name by which we classify our early ancestors, who possessed certain physical characteristics unlike those of archaic humans: a more well-rounded skull and a noticeable chin. The evolution of archaic to modern humans is a subject of considerable debate today among anthropologists.

At the heart of this debate is a series of basic questions. What is the nature of this change? When and where did it occur? Did the change occur in only one place, or was it widespread? Why did it occur? What cultural changes took place, and how are they related to the biological changes? In short, our questions concern the recent (130,000+ years) history of the human species.

ANATOMICALLY MODERN
HOMO SAPIENS

Human evolution did not end with archaic humans. All fossil humans since 28,000 years ago are anatomically modern in form. Though it is clear that archaic humans evolved into anatomically modern humans, the exact nature of this evolution is less certain. This section deals with the biological and cultural characteristics of anatomically modern humans, followed by consideration of the nature of their evolution.

anatomically modern *Homo sapiens* The modern form of the human species, which dates back 130,000 years or more.

◀ *A prehistoric cave painting of two bison from the Altamira Caves in Spain. Cave art is one of several behaviors that either originated with or became much more common with the advent of modern humans. (© Scala/Art Resource, NY)*

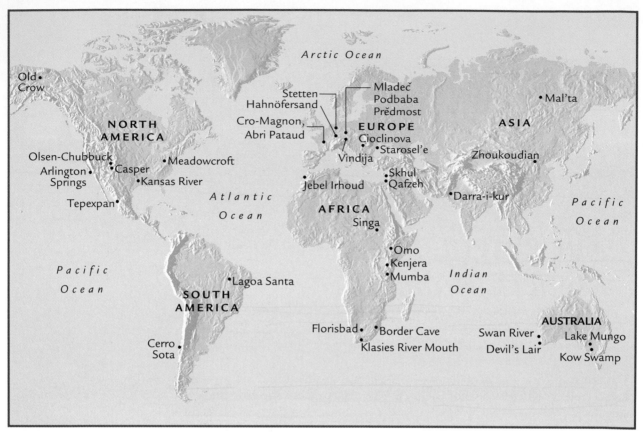

FIGURE 14.1

Location of some anatomically modern H. sapiens *sites.*

Distribution in Time and Space

Anatomically modern *H. sapiens* are found in many sites across both the Old World and the New World (Figure 14.1). Although only modern *H. sapiens* have been found dating within the past 28,000 years, we now have growing evidence that this form is actually much older than once thought. Cranial remains from the Border Cave site in southeast Africa are fragmentary but show typical anatomically modern features (Figure 14.2). The dating for this site is not definite but could range between 115,000 and 90,000 years ago. Modern humans may have occupied the Klasies River Mouth, South Africa, at least as early as 90,000 years ago (Grün et al. 1990). Other African sites also provide evidence of an early appearance of anatomically modern *H. sapiens*: Omo, Ethiopia (roughly 130,000 years ago), and Laetoli (perhaps 120,000 years ago). There is also evidence of an early occurrence of anatomically modern *H. sapiens* in the Middle East, with both the Qafzeh and Skhul sites in Israel dating to 92,000 years ago (Grün et al. 1991). Although some argument about these dates continues, it is certain that modern *H. sapiens* existed *before* the youngest known archaic forms.

Physical Characteristics

Figure 14.3 shows a skull from one of the more famous anatomically modern sites—Cro-Magnon, France, dating between 27,000 and 23,000 years ago. This skull shows many of the characteristics of anatomically modern *H. sapiens*. It

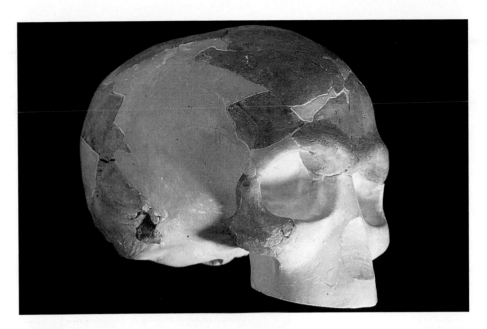

FIGURE 14.2

The Border Cave skull, South Africa. The fragmentary remains are clearly those of anatomically modern Homo sapiens *(note the vertical forehead). Dating is not precise, but current estimates suggest an age of more than 100,000 years ago. (Courtesy Milford Wolpoff, University of Michigan, Ann Arbor)*

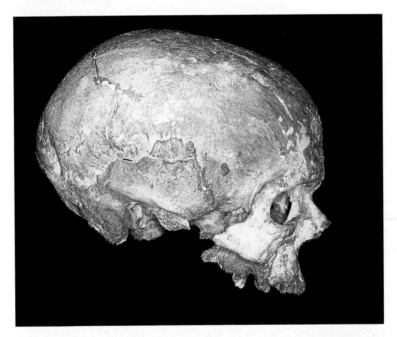

FIGURE 14.3

Side and frontal views of Cro-Magnon skull, France. This specimen is one of the best-known examples of anatomically modern Homo sapiens. *(Courtesy Milford Wolpoff, University of Michigan, Ann Arbor [left] Musée de l'Homme [right])*

is high and well rounded. There is no occipital bun; the back of the skull is rounded instead. The forehead rises vertically above the eye orbits and does not slope, as in archaic humans. The brow ridges are small, the face does not protrude very much, and a strong chin is evident.

Another example of anatomically modern *H. sapiens* is shown in Figure 14.4, a skull from the Skhul site at Mt. Carmel, Israel. This skull also has a high, well-rounded shape without an occipital bun and with a small chin. Compared to the Cro-Magnon skull, the brow ridges are larger and the face

FIGURE 14.4

An early anatomically modern Homo sapiens *skull from Skhul, Israel. (© David L. Brill)*

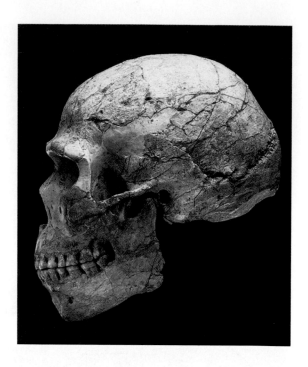

protrudes slightly. The differences between the Skhul and Cro-Magnon skulls are typical of variation within a species, particularly when we consider that they existed at different times in separate places. Other specimens also show similarities and differences when compared to one another. The skull in Figure 14.5 (Combe Capelle, France, 35,000 to 30,000 years ago) is high and well rounded, but the face protrudes slightly, and the chin is rather weak. The recent skull from Five Knolls, England (3,500 to 1,500 years ago), is high and well rounded, has small brow ridges and face, and a small chin (Figure 14.6). There is clearly variation within both archaic and anatomically modern forms of *H. sapiens.* This variation makes evolutionary relationships difficult to assess.

Cultural Behavior

Discussing the cultural adaptations of anatomically modern *H. sapiens* is difficult because they include prehistoric technologies as well as more recent developments, such as agriculture, generation of electricity, the internal combustion engine, and nuclear energy. So that we may provide a comparison with the culture of the archaic forms, this section is limited to prehistory before the development of agriculture (roughly 12,000 years ago).

Tool Technologies   There is so much variation in the stone tool technologies of anatomically modern *H. sapiens* that it is impossible to define a single tradition. For the sake of discussion, the types of stone tool industries are often lumped together under the term **Upper Paleolithic** (which means "Upper Old Stone Age"). **Lower Paleolithic** consists of the stone tool tradi-

Upper Paleolithic The Upper Old Stone Age, a general term used to collectively refer to the stone tool technologies of anatomically modern *Homo sapiens.*

Lower Paleolithic The Lower Old Stone Age, a general term used to collectively refer to the stone tool technologies of *Homo habilis/Homo rudolfensis* and *Homo erectus.*

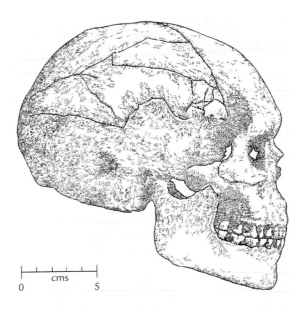

FIGURE 14.5

The Combe Capelle skull, anatomically modern Homo sapiens, *France. (From Clark Spencer Larsen, Robert M. Matter, and Daniel L. Gebo,* Human Origins: The Fossil Record, *3d ed., p. 169. © 1998, 1991, 1985 by Waveland Press, Inc., Prospect Heights, Ill. Reprinted with permission from the publisher)*

cms
0   5

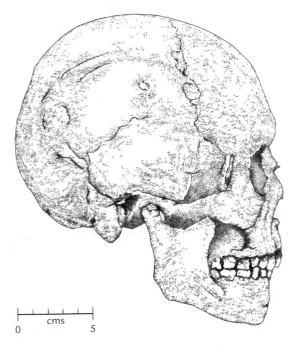

FIGURE 14.6

Skull of anatomically modern Homo sapiens, *specimen 18, from the Five Knolls site, England, 3,500–1,500 years ago. (From Clark Spencer Larsen, Robert M. Matter, and Daniel L. Gebo,* Human Origins: The Fossil Record, *3d ed., p. 174. © 1998, 1991, 1985 by Waveland Press, Inc., Prospect Heights, Ill. Reprinted with permission from the publisher)*

cms
0   5

tions of *H. habilis/H. rudolfensis* and *H. erectus*, and **Middle Paleolithic** includes the stone tool traditions of archaic humans. Even though we use a single label to describe common features of Upper Paleolithic tool industries, do not be misled into thinking that all traditions were the same. Variation, both within and among sites, is even greater in the Upper Paleolithic than in earlier cultures. This variation demonstrates the increasing sophistication and specialization of stone tools.

Middle Paleolithic The Middle Old Stone Age, a general term used to collectively refer to the stone tool technologies of archaic humans.

Examples of Upper Paleolithic stone tools: (a) knife, (b) scraper, (c) point, (d) scraper, (e) point. Tools a, b, and c are from the Perigordian culture; tool d is from the Aurignacian culture; tool e is from the Solutrean culture. (From The Old Stone Age *by F. Bordes, 1968. Reprinted with permission of the publisher, Weidenfield and Nicolson, Ltd.)*

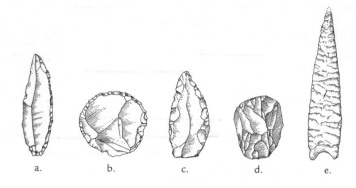

a.   b.   c.   d.   e.

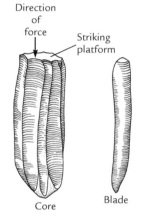

Direction of force

Striking platform

Core   Blade

FIGURE 14.9 *(above)*

Method of blade tool manufacture. A striking platform is formed, and a blade tool can then be made by flaking off a long vertical piece from the side. (From Discovering Anthropology *by Daniel R. Gross, Fig. 7.10. © 1993 by Mayfield Publishing Company. Reprinted with permission of The McGraw-Hill Companies)*

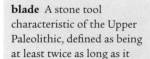

blade A stone tool characteristic of the Upper Paleolithic, defined as being at least twice as long as it is wide.

burin A stone tool with a sharp edge that is used to cut and engrave bone.

FIGURE 14.8 *(right)*

Example of a flint blade tool. (From Human Antiquity: An Introduction to Physical Anthropology and Archaeology, *4th ed., by Kenneth Feder and Michael Park, Fig. 13.3. © 2001 by Mayfield Publishing Company. Reprinted with permission of The McGraw-Hill Companies)*

Figure 14.7 shows some examples of Upper Paleolithic stone tools. These tools are much more precisely made than the stone tools of earlier hominids and are also quite a bit more diverse in function and styles. One notable characteristic of the Upper Paleolithic is the development of **blades,** stone tools defined as being at least twice as long as wide (Figure 14.8). Blade tools are made by removing long, narrow flakes off a prepared core. The core is struck by a piece of antler or bone, which in turn is struck by a stone. That is, the core is not hit directly by the hammerstone; rather, the force of the blow is applied through the antler. This method allows very thin and sharp blade tools to be made (Figure 14.9).

Upper Paleolithic tools were also used to make tools out of other resources, such as bone. A small stone tool called a **burin** has an extremely sharp edge

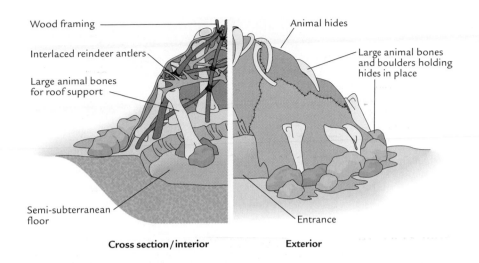

Wood framing

Animal hides

Interlaced reindeer antlers

Large animal bones
and boulders holding
hides in place

Large animal bones
for roof support

Semi-subterranean
floor

Entrance

Cross section/interior **Exterior**

FIGURE 14.10

*Reconstruction of a hut at
the Mal'ta site in Russia. This
site dates to 18,000 years ago.*
(From Human Antiquity: An
Introduction to Physical
Anthropology and Archaeology,
4th ed., by Kenneth Feder and
Michael Park, Fig. 13.5. © 2001 by
Mayfield Publishing Company.
Reprinted with permission from The
McGraw-Hill Companies)

that is used to cut, whittle, and engrave bone. Bone was used to make needles, awls, points, knives, and harpoons, as well as art objects. Bone tools and elaborate art objects first appear with modern *H. sapiens;* they are not found in the culture of earlier hominids (although there are suggestions of art objects associated with archaic humans, these finds are controversial). For years, it appeared that bone tools were fairly recent, dating back roughly 40,000 years. Research in Zaire, however, has produced a much earlier age of 90,000 years (Brooks et al. 1995; Yellen et al. 1995).

Shelter As with archaic *H. sapiens,* modern *H. sapiens* lived in caves and rock shelters where available. The archaeological evidence also shows definite evidence of manufactured shelter—huts made of wood, animal bone, and animal hides. Although much of this material decomposes, we can still find evidence of support structures. One example of hut building comes from the 18,000-year-old site of Mal'ta in south-central Russia (Figure 14.10). This hut is particularly interesting because people used mammoth ribs and leg bones for structural support. Other sites, such as the 15,000-year-old site of Mezhirich in the Ukraine, contain evidence of shelters built almost entirely from mammoth bones.

Art Another form of symbolic behavior appears with modern *H. sapiens*—cave art. Cave art dates back more than 30,000 years (although most is not this old) and has been found in Europe, Africa, and Australia. Some of the best-known cave art, primarily paintings of large game animals and hunting, comes from sites in Europe (Figures 14.11 and 14.12). These paintings are anatomically correct and are well executed. Painting is a human activity that is spiritually rewarding but has no apparent function in day-to-day existence. Why, then, did early humans paint images on the walls of caves? Several interpretations have been offered, including sympathetic magic (capturing the image of an animal may have been felt to improve hunters' chances of actually killing it). Other interpretations focus on cultural symbolism

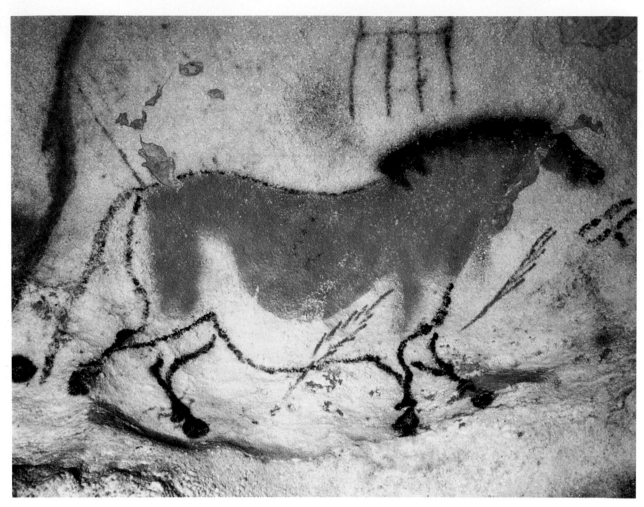

FIGURE 14.11

Cave painting of a running horse from Lascaux Cave, France. (Musée de l'Homme, Paris, photo by F. Windels)

(e.g., male–female images) or a means of communicating ideas and images. We will never know exactly *why* early humans made these paintings. What is clear, however, is that they did something that serves a symbolic purpose. Although we cannot know the reason for these behaviors, the art shows us that humans by this time had developed a need to express themselves symbolically. To these early moderns, life was not just eating and surviving—something else was important to them as well.

Cave paintings are not the only form of art associated with early modern *H. sapiens*. We also find evidence of engravings, beads and pendants, and ceramic sculpture. One of the best-known examples is the "Venus" figurines found throughout parts of Europe. These figures are pregnant females with exaggerated breasts and buttocks (Figure 14.13). Although these figurines are often interpreted as fertility symbols (fertility would have been a critical factor to survival), we are not sure of their exact meaning or function. However, as with cave paintings, the Venus figurines show us that symbolism was fully a part of the life of early modern *H. sapiens*.

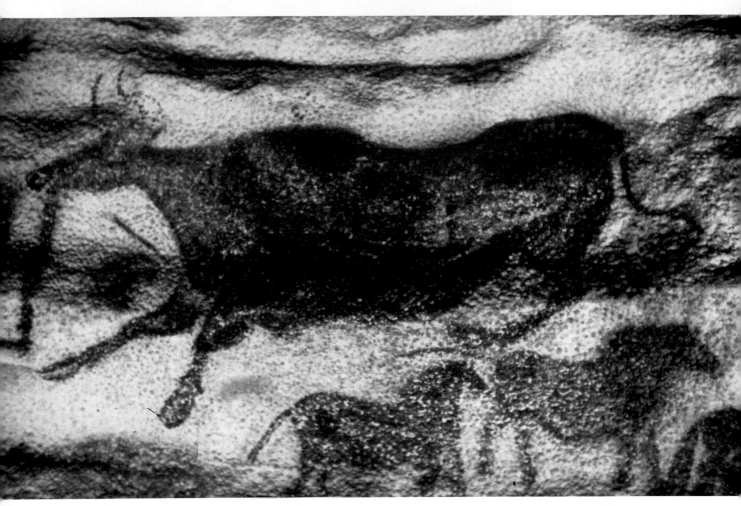

FIGURE 14.12

Cave painting of a cow from Lascaux cave, France. (© 2002 Artists Rights Society (ARS), New York/DACS, London)

Geographic Expansion The archaeological evidence shows that humans become more and more successful in adapting to their environments, and consequently populations grew and expanded.

By 60,000 years ago, populations of anatomically modern *H. sapiens* had reached Australia. During times of glaciation, the sea levels drop, extending the land mass of the continents. The drop in sea level had allowed earlier populations of hominids to reach Southeast Asia, but Australia was not then connected to the Asian continent. For humans to reach Australia, they had to cross many kilometers of sea. The only way they could do this was by some sort of raft or boat.

Anatomically modern *H. sapiens* also moved into the New World. The number of such movements and their dates are a continuing source of controversy. All agree, however, that humans were living in the New World by 15,000 years ago. Some argue that these dates are the earliest, whereas others cite newer evidence and reanalysis of previous finds indicating a much earlier initial occupation—perhaps 30,000 to 20,000 years ago.

FIGURE 14.13

A Venus figurine.
(© Naturhistorisches Museum Wien,
Photo by Alice Schumacher)

Genetic evidence shows a close relationship between modern Native Americans and modern northeast Asians. Archaeological evidence also demonstrates an Asian origin for the first migrants to the New World. The most commonly suggested route is across the Bering Land Bridge. During periods of glaciation, the sea levels fell, exposing a stretch of land connecting Asia and North America. This "land bridge" was almost 2,100 kilometers (roughly 1,300 miles) wide (Figure 14.14). It did not appear or disappear suddenly but instead developed over thousands of years as the sea levels dropped. Groups of humans following game herds moved across this region and eventually moved down into North, Central, and South America. Debate continues over the routes of migration (inland or coastal) as well as the number of different migrations: some argue for a single wave of migrants, and others argue for three different migrations (Crawford 1998).

First Appearance of the Culture of Early Modern H. sapiens There is debate over the speed of the emergence of the culture of early modern humans, with some favoring a model of rapid development and others a more gradual accumulation of these behaviors over time. For many years, the archaeological record of early modern humans often has been interpreted as sup-

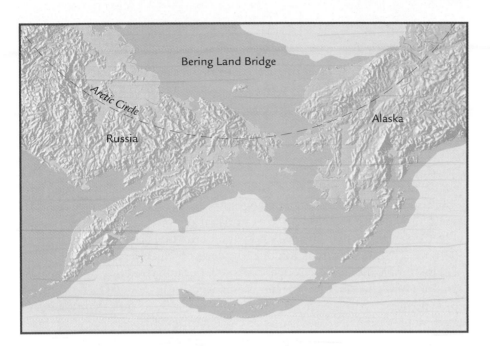

FIGURE 14.14

The Bering Land Bridge. Today the former Soviet Union and Alaska are separated by water. During the "Ice Ages," water was trapped in glaciers, producing a drop in the sea level that exposed the land area known as the Bering Land Bridge. This "bridge" connecting North America and Asia was actually 2,100 km wide!

porting a rapid "creative explosion" of new technologies and behaviors that first appeared about 40,000 to 50,000 years ago. This interpretation was based in part on the first appearance of modern behaviors in the European archaeological record and did not take into account changes happening elsewhere. In recent decades, archaeological research from Africa suggests that many of these behaviors actually appeared tens of thousands of years earlier, and the emergence of modern human culture did not take place all at once but instead cumulatively over time in Africa (McBrearty and Brooks 2000).

THE ORIGIN OF ANATOMICALLY MODERN HUMANS

When, where, and how did anatomically modern *H. sapiens* evolve from archaic humans? The general trend indicated by the fossil record is clear; some archaic populations evolved into the more modern forms. The specific questions are harder to answer. Did *all* populations of archaics evolve into modern forms? If so, did this occur at the same time in different places? Or did only a few archaic populations evolve into modern forms and then expand out to replace, or interbreed with, the remaining archaic forms? If so, where and when did the transition to anatomically modern *H. sapiens* first take place? Finally, does our use of such terms as *archaic* and *modern* obscure variation over time and space? We use these categories as a useful sorting device, but we may be in danger of obscuring reality by pigeonholing all human fossil remains into two groups.

Early Models

Many models have been proposed to answer these questions. Past analyses have been complicated by the fact that the best-known samples of archaic humans were the western European Neandertals, which in many ways are the most unique of all the archaic populations. The distinctiveness of the Neandertals had given rise to various interpretations of the origin of anatomically modern *H. sapiens*. In the early part of this century, it was common to view Neandertals as a side branch of human evolution, perhaps even a different species. At that time the fossil record suggested a 5,000-year "gap" between the last Neandertals and the first modern humans. Such a gap was felt to be too short in duration for the evolutionary changes needed for a transition from Neandertals into modern humans. Another explanation was that the modern forms evolved elsewhere, then invaded and wiped out the Neandertals (see Brace [1964] for a thorough discussion of early views on Neandertal evolution).

This simple model is no longer accepted. For one thing, we now have evidence of overlap in dates for archaic and anatomically modern *H. sapiens*. The major problem with the invasion hypothesis is that it was strongly influenced by previous interpretations of the extent of differences between archaic and modern forms. This early idea emphasized the differences between these forms and tended to ignore their similarities.

Current Models and Debates

There are two basic models for the evolution of modern humans—the African replacement model and the multiregional evolution model (which in turn has several variants). The debate over modern human origins is a "hot" topic in anthropology today, with new data and analyses appearing all the time. Don't be surprised in class to learn of newer developments.

As pointed out in the previous chapter, debates over the evolution of *Homo* center on differences in opinion regarding the number of species and the mode of evolution—anagenesis or cladogenesis. Some see the fossil record in terms of a single evolving lineage where what we call *Homo erectus* changes over time to become what we call archaic, and then modern, humans. The difference between these forms is considered arbitrary, and they all represent stages along a continuum. Others advocate cladogenesis and see the fossil record quite differently. Instead of a single evolving species, they see numerous species within the genus *Homo*, of which only one (*Homo sapiens*) still survives—the others became extinct. Further, proponents of cladogenesis argue that *H. sapiens* emerged as a separate species fairly recent in time.

The African Replacement Model   According to the **African replacement model,** modern humans emerged as a new species in Africa between 150,000 and 200,000 years ago. Some populations left Africa roughly 100,000 years ago and spread throughout the Old World, replacing preexisting archaic human populations outside of Africa (Cann et al. 1987; Stringer and Andrews 1988). The model proposes that the transition from archaic to modern humans took place *only* in one region (Africa), that the transition was a specia-

African replacement model The hypothesis that modern humans evolved as a new species in Africa between 150,000 and 200,000 years ago and then spread throughout the Old World, replacing preexisting archaic human populations.

cladogenesis

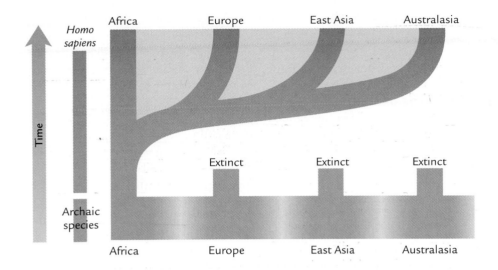

FIGURE 14.15

A simplified diagram of the relationships expected between archaic humans and modern humans under the African replacement model. A new species, Homo sapiens, *arises in Africa between 200,000 and 150,000 years ago and then spreads out to other geographic regions in the Old World. The archaic human populations outside of Africa are considered to go extinct, contributing few, if any, genes to modern humans.*

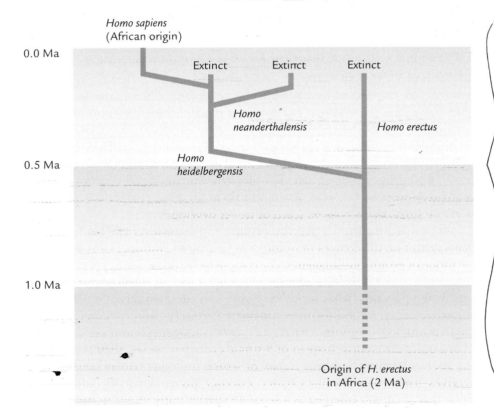

FIGURE 14.16

The African replacement model considered in a broader perspective by those who view human evolution over the past 2 million years as a series of speciations. Here, the species name Homo sapiens *refers only to modern humans that arose in Africa roughly 200,000 to 150,000 years ago. "Archaic" humans are considered to represent a number of distinctly different species, including* Homo heidelbergensis *and* Homo neanderthalensis. Homo erectus *is considered a separate species as well. Some researchers further suggest that* Homo erectus *actually includes two separate species.*

tion, and that the transition occurred recently (150,000 to 200,000 years ago). Under this model, any archaic populations outside of Africa (such as the Neandertals) became extinct and are not part of our ancestry (Figure 14.15). Some anthropologists (e.g., Tattersall 1997) suggest that this recent speciation is only the last of a series of speciations extending back over the past 2 million years (Figure 14.16).

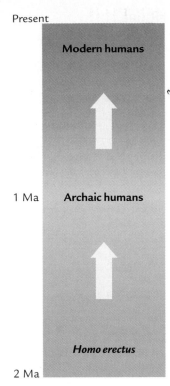

Present

Modern humans

Archaic humans

1 Ma

Homo erectus

2 Ma

FIGURE 14.17

A simplified diagram of the multiregional evolution model. The fossils typically assigned to Homo erectus, *archaic humans, and modern humans are all considered part of a single evolving lineage throughout the Old World.*

multiregional evolution model The hypothesis that modern humans evolved throughout the Old World as a single species after the first dispersal of *Homo erectus* out of Africa.

Multiregional Evolution   The **multiregional evolution model** proposes that human evolution over the past 2 million years has taken place within a single evolving lineage from *H. erectus* to archaic humans to modern humans. According to the general model, the start of our species began with *H. erectus* in Africa 2 million years ago. Some populations later spread into Asia and Europe. The species continued to evolve over time, with further increases in brain size and reductions in cranial and dental size, ultimately leading to what we call modern humans. As such, what we call early humans (*H. erectus*), archaic humans, and modern humans are merely convenient labels for different stages of evolution over time (Figure 14.17). Multiregional evolution has often been incorrectly portrayed as the independent and simultaneous evolution of humans in different regions, which is not the case (Wolpoff et al. 2000).

Another way to contrast the difference between these models is to consider the question of where our ancestors might have lived 200,000 years ago. Under the African replacement model, *all* of our ancestors lived in Africa at that time. Under multiregional models, *some* lived in Africa, but some also lived outside of Africa.

There are several different versions of the general multiregional evolution model (see Wolpoff et al. 1994), and Relethford (2001c) has suggested two main variants: the regional coalescence model and the primary African origin model. The **regional coalescence model** suggests that the transition from archaic to modern humans took place piecemeal across the Old World, with some changes occurring in different places and at different times. According to this model, modern humans arose through the coalescence, or mixing, of these changes as gene flow spread them across the Old World. The **primary African origin model** is a variant of the multiregional evolution model that proposes that most of the transition from archaic to modern humans did take place within Africa and then spread throughout the rest of the Old World via gene flow.

Figure 14.18 summarizes the African replacement and multiregional models for the origin of modern humans. There are two issues of concern regarding the transition from archaic to modern humans. The first is *how* this transition took place. Was it evolution within a lineage (anagenesis) or the formation of a new species (cladogenesis)? The African replacement model suggests cladogenesis, whereas the multiregional model proposes anagenesis. The second issue is *where* the initial transition took place. Did it occur primarily in Africa or across the Old World? Note that the primary African origin multiregional model and the African replacement model both suggest that the transition took place within Africa; the difference is what happens to the archaic populations outside of Africa. Under the African replacement model, they become extinct; under the primary African origin model, they eventually became modern as the result of gene flow between populations within a single species.

The Fossil Evidence

Which model does the fossil evidence support? It is important to realize that each model makes certain predictions that in theory can be tested using the

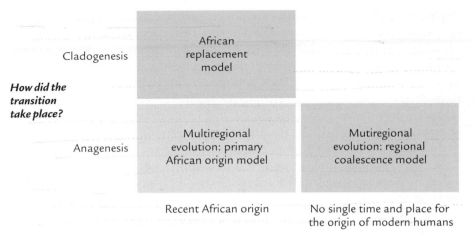

FIGURE 14.18

Classification of different models of modern human origins and the transition from archaic to modern humans focusing on how *the transition took place (cladogenesis or anagenesis) and* where *the initial transition took place (only in Africa or worldwide).* (Adapted from Relethford 2001c)

fossil evidence of archaic and modern humans. Predictions are made regarding the biological relationships between archaic and modern forms within each region and the relationship between regions.

The First Modern Humans   The African replacement model predicts that anatomically modern humans will appear first in Africa and then later outside of Africa. A first step is to examine the earliest known dates for modern humans in each region. This is not always as easy as it sounds because there are differing definitions of what it means to be "modern" (Wolpoff and Caspari 1997) and disagreements about which physical features are primitive or derived. In addition, we must deal with the incomplete nature of the fossil record and the possibility that we have not yet found the earliest moderns in any given region. In spite of these problems, the evidence to date presents a pattern that is compatible with the predictions of the African replacement model. In Africa, modern-looking fossils date to between 130,000 and 100,000 years ago. Modern anatomy, to some extent, is present among *some* Middle Eastern fossils by roughly 90,000 years ago. Modern human anatomy is at least 60,000 years old in Australia and appears in different parts of Europe between 40,000 and 30,000 years ago. The fossil record for Asia is less clear but suggests a date of perhaps 60,000 years ago (Stringer and McKie 1996). It is clear that modern humans were present in some parts of the Old World at the same time as some archaics, such as the Neandertals in Europe.

Does the earlier appearance of modern humans support the African replacement model? Yes, but it does not necessarily reject all multiregional models. The primary African origin model also suggests that modern anatomy appears first in Africa and then later spread out across the Old World. Quite simply, it takes time for genes to flow from one part of the world to another, and differences in timing are expected. Thus, the earlier appearance of modern humans in Africa does not distinguish between these models. Instead, we need to focus on the nature of the contact between moderns and archaics outside of Africa—was there an exchange of genes (multiregional evolution) or replacement of the archaics?

regional coalescence model A variant of the multiregional evolution model of the origin of modern humans that suggests the transition from archaic to modern humans resulted from the coalescence of genetic and anatomic changes that took place in different places at different times, all mixing together to produce modern humans.

primary African origin model A variant of the multiregional evolution model of the origin of modern humans that suggests most of the transition from archaic to modern humans took place first in Africa and then spread throughout the rest of the species across the Old World by gene flow.

Regional Continuity   A number of anthropologists have supported a multiregional evolution model based on the observed pattern of **regional continuity** in the fossil record—the appearance of similar traits within the same geographic region over time. For example, some humans, past and present, have a particular dental trait known as shovel-shaped incisors, which have a ridge on the outer margins of the incisor teeth. Although this trait is found across the world today, it is found most frequently in both living and ancient populations in East Asia. The fact that this trait is most common throughout time in the same geographic region suggests genetic continuity over time; that is, early and archaic humans in Asia contributed some of their genes to living Asian populations. Another example is the high angle of the nose, found most frequently in both European Neandertals and in living Europeans.

Regional traits form as the result of evolutionary forces (namely, genetic drift and selection) that make a given region somewhat different genetically from others. At first glance, this seems to pose a problem. If regional populations became different from one another, then how could they remain part of a single species? Gene flow is needed to maintain populations in a single species, but shouldn't gene flow eradicate regional differences? The answer is actually quite simple: evolution results from the *balance* of the evolutionary forces. Under continued gene flow, many regional traits will be lost over time, but some will persist because of genetic drift and selection (Relethford 2001c). This balance means that the transition from archaic to modern humans could have taken place across the Old World due to shared gene flow while populations still retained some regional traits (Thorne and Wolpoff 1992; Wolpoff et al. 1994; Wolpoff and Caspari 1997).

For our purposes, the important point is that regional continuity of many traits is best explained by the genetic continuity over time predicted by multiregional evolution. It is more difficult to explain regional traits under the African replacement model because such traits would be eliminated by replacement and would then have to reappear independently. Although there is debate over which traits show continuity and in which regions, many anthropologists agree that the evidence for continuity is strong for the fossil record in Asia and Australasia (e.g., Kramer 1991; Hawks et al. 2000; Thorne and Wolpoff 1992; Wolpoff et al. 2001).

The situation is less clear in Europe, where the coexistence of both Neandertal and modern populations, followed by the disappearance of the Neandertals, is often considered evidence of replacement. It is this pattern, combined with the distinct morphology of Neandertals and the findings of divergent ancient DNA (discussed in the previous chapter), that has led a number of anthropologists to support the idea that Neandertals were a separate species—*Homo neanderthalensis*—that became extinct.

Not everyone agrees, and there is fossil evidence for regional continuity in Europe. One example is the skeleton of a 4-year-old child from 25,000 years ago that was found in Portugal. The cranium shows a mixture of features usually associated with Neandertals and early modern humans, but the postcranial skeleton shows Neandertal characteristics (Duarte et al. 1999). This find possibly represents an example of admixture between Neandertals and

regional continuity The appearance of similar traits within a geographic region that remain over a long period of time.

SPECIAL TOPIC

The Iceman

Our understanding of ancient times comes from reconstructions based on the fossil and archaeological records, supplemented by evidence from past environments. Although new methods and techniques for analysis have aided our ability to reconstruct the past, we are nevertheless dealing with only bits and pieces of what actually once existed.

Occasionally, though, we come across more detailed evidence. On September 19, 1991, hikers in the glacial mountains between Austria and Italy stumbled upon the body of a man. This is not unusual—bodies are often found in this region, the result of accidents while climbing or hiking in the mountains. Initial investigation, however, showed that this was a naturally occurring mummy (mummification occurs when a corpse is cut off from oxygen). How did the corpse remain so well preserved? The man died in a shallow depression in the ground, and the advancing glacier moved over him, preserving him in a mummified state without carrying his body downhill. In 1991, the ice had receded and the body was exposed. Because of his discovery in the glacier, he is known today as "The Iceman."

The body became of greater interest because of several items found with it, including a flint knife and an axe. The axe consisted of a wooden shaft attached to what appeared to be a bronze axe head. The bronze implied that the axe and the body dated to the European Bronze Age, roughly 4,000 years ago. Closer analysis of the axe head showed, however, that it was not bronze (which is a mixture of copper and tin) but almost entirely pure copper. Use of copper is known to be even older than 4,000 years ago. The greater age was confirmed by carbon-14 dating of the body, which placed it at 5,250 years ago.

Research continues on the Iceman, but preliminary study has revealed much about his life and death. Marks have been found on the body that might possibly be tattoos. In addition to the knife and the axe, he had a bow, arrows, and a leather quiver. Remains of his clothes show that they were made of fur, and boots have also been found. He also had two lumps of fungus connected by a leather strap. At first, it was thought that the fungus might have been used as tinder for starting fires. The fungus has now been identified as a species that is known to have antibiotic properties, so we might be seeing some evidence of ancient medicine.

How did the Iceman die? Initial analysis suggested the possibility of exhaustion and dehydration, although this was based on circumstantial evidence. More recently, a detailed examination of the body revealed that he had been shot in the shoulder with an arrow, most likely leading to paralysis of the right arm and a painful death (BBC News 2001).

moderns as the two populations came into contact with each other in western Europe, although others argue that this is simply a stocky early modern human child (Tattersall and Schwartz 1999). Several other studies have also shown evidence for regional continuity in Europe. Milford Wolpoff and colleagues (2001) compared features in early modern human skulls to Neandertals and early moderns from Africa and the Middle East and concluded that the evidence is consistent with some genetic continuity in Europe.

Another clue comes from changes in the frequency of Neandertal features in Europe over time. Wolpoff (1999) lists 18 anatomical traits considered unique to Neandertals and examines their occurrence in the earliest post-Neandertal European moderns and in living Europeans. Under a replacement model, these traits should be absent in the modern populations, but instead there is a pattern of reduction over time. For example, one unique Neandertal dental trait is found in 53 percent of Neandertals, 18 percent of post-Neandertal early moderns, and 1 percent of living Europeans. Instead of the pattern of complete elimination predicted from replacement, this trait shows a decline over time consistent with Neandertals experiencing gene flow from outside Europe. If verified, this means that Neandertals "disappeared" due to the cumulative effects of gene flow—they were absorbed into a larger gene pool.

The Genetic Evidence

In addition to the fossil evidence, many researchers have examined questions of modern human origins using information on genetic variation in living people. We can observe patterns of genetic variation in the present day and ask what evolutionary model could have given rise to these observed patterns. Whereas with fossils we work from the past to the present, genetic studies start with the present in an effort to reconstruct the past. We view the patterns of contemporary genetic variation as reflections of the past. Although much of the genetic evidence is compatible with the African replacement model, it is also compatible with multiregional evolution (Relethford 2001c).

Gene Trees   One way of reconstructing the past is to compare DNA sequences from pairs of living people and use them to build a "tree" showing the history of a particular gene. Many of these studies have focused on mitochondrial DNA because it is inherited maternally and does not recombine, making genealogical reconstruction easier. Studies of mitochondrial DNA show that the human species today forms two basic clusters. One cluster consists of people with African ancestry, and the other cluster contains people of different ancestries, both African and non-African. Further analysis shows that the original female ancestor was African. These findings have been interpreted as reflecting population history; an initial origin of modern humans in Africa followed by a subsequent split of non-African populations. Further, these studies estimate that the common mitochondrial DNA ancestor of all living humans lived roughly 200,000 years ago, which is felt by many to be definite proof of the African replacement model (e.g., Cann et al. 1987; Penny et al. 1995; Vigilant et al. 1991). Although these studies are compatible with the African replacement model, they do not necessarily disprove a multiregional evolution hypothesis. Alan Templeton (1998) notes that an African origin for mitochondrial DNA is also possible under a multiregional interpretation. The common female ancestor had to live somewhere, and the fact that she lived in Africa does not rule out *either* a replacement or a multiregional model. Others note that the date for the common ancestor does not directly inform us about the origin of our species (Relethford 2001c; Rogers and Jorde 1995). The history of a particular gene or DNA sequence is not necessarily the history of our species.

Gene tree analysis has also been applied to a number of different genes, including Y chromosome data and nuclear DNA. Although some show the same patterns of mitochondrial DNA, others show more ancient "roots" (e.g., Harris and Hey 1999) and still others show non-African origins (e.g., Harding et al. 1997). Although the bulk of gene tree analysis suggests a recent African origin of modern humans, it does not unequivocally support a replacement out of Africa. It may be the case, as argued next, that our species' origin is mostly, but not exclusively, out of Africa.

mitochondrial Eve

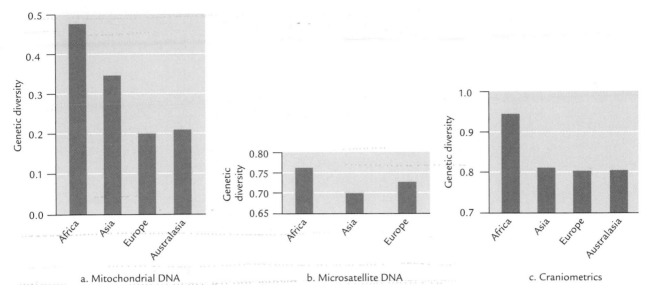

a. Mitochondrial DNA   b. Microsatellite DNA   c. Craniometrics

FIGURE 14.19

Comparison of genetic diversity among different geographic regions of living humans based on (a) mitochondrial DNA variation, (b) microsatellite DNA variation, and (c) craniometric variation. In each case, different measures of "diversity" are used so that the scales (vertical axes) cannot be compared directly. Instead, simply note that in each case Africa is the most diverse region genetically. (Source of data: Cann et al. 1987; Relethford and Harpending 1994; Jorde et al. 1997)

Genetic Diversity   Another avenue of research is to compare patterns of genetic diversity in living humans. Here we use a variety of data from human populations, including DNA sequences, blood types and other genetic markers, and measures of the face and skull.

One way to look at genetic diversity is to compare the level of genetic variation within different populations. Studies using a variety of different traits have shown that Africa tends to be more genetically diverse than other geographic regions, such as Europe or Asia (Figure 14.19). The greater diversity of African populations has been used to argue for the African replacement model under the assumption that the oldest population will accumulate the most mutations over a long period of time and therefore be more genetically diverse. If modern humans arose as a new species in Africa and then later spread to other regions, the African populations would be the oldest and therefore show the highest amount of variation.

This is not the only possible interpretation because factors other than age can influence a population's genetic diversity. One such factor is population size. Recall from Chapter 3 the relationship between genetic drift and population size. Smaller populations lose more alleles because of genetic drift than do larger populations and consequently show lower levels of diversity. Larger populations experience less genetic drift and will show higher levels of diversity. It is possible that the finding of higher African diversity simply reflects a larger African population in our species' past.

Using mathematical models relating diversity and population size, Relethford and Harpending (1994) and Relethford and Jorde (1999) found that genetic diversity in living humans is consistent with a model where most of our ancestors (50–70 percent) several hundred thousand years ago lived in Africa. Today, of course, the majority of the human species does not live in Africa, but in Asia. The distribution of humans today is influenced strongly

FIGURE 14.20

Genetic distance between living humans in different geographic regions. (Based on genetic distances obtained from 120 alleles reported by Cavalli-Sforza et al. 1994)

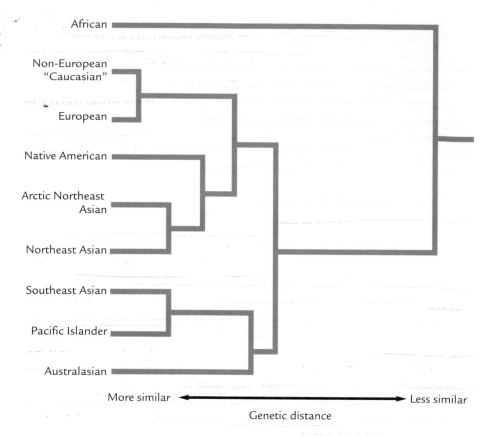

by relatively recent events, particularly those occurring after the origin of agriculture within the past 12,000 years. Throughout most of the past, however, it is quite likely that the majority of human ancestors lived in Africa because it has the largest usable land mass and best ecological conditions for large populations (Wolpoff and Caspari 1997). The data on genetic diversity may therefore simply be a reflection of regional differences in population size and tell us nothing about whether modern humans arose through cladogenesis or anagenesis.

Genetic Distance Analysis   Another way of looking at genetic variation in living humans is to examine variation between different geographic regions. Here we take data on various regions and compute the genetic distances between them. These studies usually reveal a pattern in which African populations are the most genetically distinct; in other words, European, Asian, and other regional populations tend to be more similar to each other. An example is shown in Figure 14.20, based on 120 different alleles. Populations in Southeast Asia, Australasia, and the Pacific Islands tend to cluster together, as do populations in northern Asia, Europe, and the Americas. Africa is somewhat more distinct.

   This pattern has often been interpreted as support for an African replacement model. If modern humans began as a new species in Africa and later spread out, splitting into groups that colonized different regions, then these *— to support African replacement* non-African populations should be more closely related to each other than to African populations. Once again, however, this is not the only alternative. The same pattern of genetic distances can be replicated if there were differences in gene flow between regions, perhaps affected by geographic distance and other factors. The pattern of genetic distances we see in the world today can be explained by slightly less gene flow *into* Africa than *out* of Africa over time (Relethford 2001c). Thus, genetic distance analysis may provide information on ancient migration, but it does not help us distinguish between replacement and multiregional evolution hypotheses.

Population Size and Modern Human Origins   One of the most interesting findings in the past decade is that patterns of genetic variation in living humans contain a signature of past population size. By comparing observed variation in DNA sequences and other data with different mathematical models, we can tell that the human species increased rapidly in size roughly 50,000 years ago (e.g., Sherry et al. 1994). Furthermore, the genetic evidence suggests that there were only a few thousand ancestors living before this population growth (Rogers 1995). Various analyses of genetic data suggest that our ancestors 200,000 years ago numbered no more than 10,000 adults. If true, this figure argues strongly against a multiregional evolution model, because this is too small a number of people to have been spread out over three continents (Harpending et al. 1998). The small size instead suggests that all of our ancestors 200,000 years ago were located in one area—a portion of Africa. This pattern is expected under the African replacement model, where a new species would initially have a small number of people.

As with other genetic analyses, however, the answer is not definite. The main problem with the population size studies is that these methods provide an estimate of population size under a set of idealized assumptions. The *actual* number of ancestors under real-world conditions may be quite a bit larger than the *genetic* estimates suggest. Depending on demographic and ecological conditions, the genetic estimate of 10,000 adults could be equivalent to as many as several hundred thousand, a number close to that predicted from archaeological analysis (Relethford 2001c; Templeton 1997). Thus, although the genetic data show us that the human species increased rapidly in size, we have no clear indication of the actual number of ancestors.

Consensus—Mostly Out of Africa?

The debate over modern human origins is not over. Both African replacement and multiregional evolution models have some support from the fossil record and genetic data, but in many cases the results can be interpreted in more than one way. The question of modern human origins is not likely to be solved by any single study but rather by a consensus based on the accumulated evidence using a variety of approaches and methods.

Given the evidence to date, what is the bottom line? Keeping in mind that new data and analyses continue to come in all the time, and could conceivably

Summary

change any current conclusions, we can still summarize some main points. Based on the fossil evidence to date, there is some consensus that modern human anatomy appeared first in Africa, although the issue of genetic involvement from other geographic regions is not settled. The genetic evidence has frequently been taken as supporting the African replacement model because these observations are compatible with that model. Unfortunately, genetic observations are also compatible with some versions of the multiregional evolution model, making it difficult to distinguish between them. The fossil evidence for regional continuity outside of Africa is also accepted by many (although not all) anthropologists. This evidence, combined with some genetic data of non-African ancestry before 200,000 years ago, suggests that modern humans arising in Africa did not totally replace archaic humans outside of Africa.

Elsewhere, I have suggested that a variant of the primary African origin model best fits the available data (Relethford 2001c). In this view, our recent origins can be considered *mostly, but not exclusively, out of Africa*, with most of our ancestors 200,000 years ago living in Africa (perhaps because there were likely to be more people there than elsewhere). Many modern human traits appeared first in Africa but then spread throughout the rest of the Old World via gene flow. The contribution of non-African populations may have varied from place to place; for example, it may be the case that there was more continuity in Australasia than in Europe.

This model combines two basic lines of evidence—the central evolutionary importance of Africa and regional continuity outside of Africa. Further, the genetic evidence for a larger African population size may have had a major impact on the recent evolution of our species. Quite simply, if more of our ancestors lived in Africa than elsewhere, then Africa would have a greater evolutionary impact than other regions. Although this model does suggest a recent African origin for our species, it is multiregional—more than one region was involved. If true, then modern humans do not represent a new species but the continuation of a more ancient evolutionary line. Further research is needed to determine if this hypothesis is correct.

Why Did Modern Humans Evolve?

The alternative models for the origin of modern humans are fascinating to debate, but we don't want to lose track of a basic fact that all agree on: only modern human fossils have been found within the past 28,000 years or so. In addition to explaining the timing and nature of the transition from archaics to moderns, we must also ask ourselves why this transition occurred in the first place. The available evidence suggests that anatomically modern humans had some evolutionary advantage over archaic humans. But what was this advantage?

Modern humans differ from the archaics in several features, including a more well-rounded skull, smaller brow ridges, and a prominent chin. Daniel Lieberman (1998) suggests that these and other changes are all related to reduction in the length of the sphenoid, a bone in the cranial base. Because the

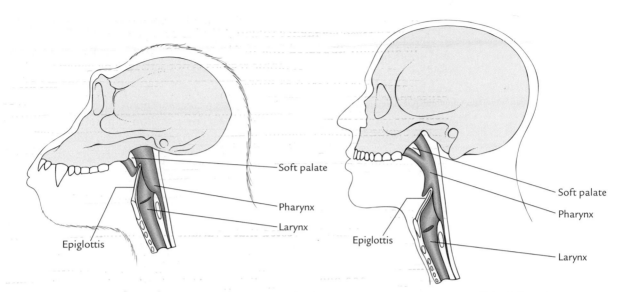

FIGURE 14.21

The vocal anatomy of a chimpanzee (left) and a modern human (right). In apes, the larynx is higher in the throat. In humans, it is lower, allowing a greater number of sounds but increasing the possibility of choking on food. (From Roger Lewin, In the Age of Mankind: A Smithsonian Book of Human Evolution, *1989: 181, Smithsonian Institution Press)*

anatomical development of a skull consists of interrelated components, a change in one part can influence changes throughout. His analysis suggests that most of the changes from archaic to modern are related to this relatively simple change. However, a problem remains—what caused this change?

Language and Modern Human Origins   It has often been suggested that the development of human language capabilities marks the origin of modern *H. sapiens*. Cranial changes are seen to relate to changes in language ability, with a claim that modern *H. sapiens* was linguistically superior to the archaics. This view is tempting when evidence for the increased symbolic and technological achievements of modern *H. sapiens* is also considered. Can cranial changes and these cultural achievements be related? It is possible—but the basic problem remains that these cultural changes took place well after the initial *biological* changes associated with modern *H. sapiens*. Of course, cave art, bone tools, and other achievements may actually be older than we think, an idea supported to some extent by the new dating of bone tools in Africa. However, basing a model on what has *not* been found is not a good idea. We must always deal with the known fossil and archaeological records and be willing to make appropriate revisions when we make new discoveries.

How can we date the origin of language? This question is central to any discussion of differences in language ability between archaics and moderns. One approach is to examine the fossil evidence of vocal anatomy. Striking differences exist between the vocal tract of a modern human and an ape. The **larynx** is part of the respiratory system that contains the vocal chords for speech. Apes, like other mammals, have their larynx high in the throat. In humans, however, the larynx is farther down in the throat, a position that allows the throat to serve as a resonating chamber capable of a greater number of sounds (Figure 14.21). Humans can make a wider number of sounds, and do it faster, than apes. We pay a price for this adaptation, though—unlike apes,

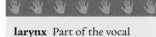

larynx Part of the vocal anatomy in the throat.

we cannot breathe and eat at the same time, and we are in far greater danger of choking to death. Human infants still have the larynx high in the throat and *can* breathe and swallow at the same time. By early childhood, however, the larynx has descended into the throat, making this phenomenon no longer feasible (Lewin 1998).

The position of the larynx represents a clear-cut anatomical difference between humans and apes, and, as such, larynx position can help in assessing the language abilities of any fossil hominid. Unfortunately, the throat, like all soft tissue, decomposes and we cannot recover it. We can get clues about the positioning of the larynx, however, by looking at the base of a cranium. Note that in Figure 14.21 the lower profile of the ape skull is fairly straight, whereas in the modern human it is flexed. The degree of this flexion is directly related to the position of the larynx. Given this relationship, what do the fossils tell us? Laitman and colleagues (1979) investigated the crania of a number of fossil hominids and concluded that whereas *Australopithecus* had the ape pattern, the crania of many archaic humans are more similar to modern-day humans. The Neandertals had a pattern that was between those of a modern subadult and modern adult human, suggesting that their language abilities may have been somewhat different. Other reconstructions and interpretations are possible (Houghton 1993; Schepartz 1993); some suggest there was little difference in language ability between any of the archaics and modern humans. Schepartz (1993) argues instead that complex language began with the initial origin of the genus *Homo*.

Another source of information on language origins is the archaeological record. Some argue that complex language is of recent origin, coinciding with a rapid spread of new behaviors roughly 50,000 years ago (e.g., Klein 1999). Others argue that modern human behaviors actually developed over a longer period of time (e.g., McBrearty and Brooks 2000; Schepartz 1993). This latter group feels that by focusing on the more recent cultural innovations, such as bone tools and cave art, we are ignoring significant earlier innovations, such as complex stone tool manufacture and burial of the dead. Could such things be possible without some language abilities? Although it seems unlikely, the possibility exists nevertheless that some enhancement of language ability coincided with the origin of modern *H. sapiens*. We have too few data at present to answer these questions.

Technology and Biological Change   If changes in language abilities are not the reason for the origin of modern *H. sapiens,* what else might have been involved? Technological changes have also been suggested as mechanisms for the change from archaic to modern forms. This view holds that many of the structural characteristics of archaic humans were the result of stresses generated by the use of their front teeth as tools. The large size and wear patterns of the incisor teeth of archaics (especially Neandertals) support the notion that these teeth were used for a variety of purposes. The stresses generated by heavy use of the front teeth can also be used to explain the large face, large neck muscles, and other features of archaic skulls. Once technological adaptations had developed sufficiently, these physical adaptations were no longer necessary and would not be selected for. Smaller teeth and faces might then be advantageous because smaller structures require correspondingly less energy for growth and maintenance (Smith et al. 1989). Similar arguments can be made to explain the reduction in body size and musculature (e.g., Frayer 1984). Once cultural behaviors took the place of larger teeth, faces, and bones, smaller structures actually became more adaptive.

Calcagno and Gibson (1988) present evidence that larger teeth can be nonadaptive. They cite clinical evidence from contemporary human populations that show that large teeth can have many disadvantages. Larger teeth are more susceptible to dental decay due to crowding of teeth and periodontal disease. In earlier prehistoric times, the advantages of larger teeth as tools may have outweighed the disadvantages. When cultural change led to more efficient tools, however, these advantages diminished, and selection would then have been *against* large teeth.

Once again, evolution is best seen in terms of the overall balance between costs and benefits. Human evolution is particularly interesting because human behaviors frequently affect this balance. In the past, as new technologies and behaviors arose, they changed the balance between cost and benefit. At some point in the past, for example, the less rugged and less muscular modern morphology may have shifted from being a disadvantage to being an advantage. The origin of modern *H. sapiens* may itself reflect this type of process. If so, we would expect the kind of "lag" between cultural and biological change that we see in the fossil record. Biological changes allow further cultural changes, which in turn allow further biological changes. Each change shifts the balance.

RECENT BIOLOGICAL AND CULTURAL EVOLUTION IN *HOMO SAPIENS*

Human evolution did not end with the origin of modern *H. sapiens*. Biologically, we have continued to change in subtle ways even over the past 10,000 to 20,000 years or so. Cranial capacity has declined somewhat (Henneberg 1988), probably a reflection of a general decrease in size and ruggedness, as discussed in the last section. Teeth have also become somewhat smaller (Brace et al. 1987), most likely reflecting the changing costs and benefits of larger teeth.

Within the very recent past (10,000–15,000 years), the major changes in human evolution have been cultural. One major change in human existence—the invention of agriculture—began roughly 12,000 years ago. Up to this point, humans had been exclusively hunters and gatherers. Agriculture changed the entire ecological equation for human beings. Humans began manipulating the environment to increase the availability of food through the domestication of plants and animals. Many explanations are offered as to why agriculture developed, including that it was a solution to the increased

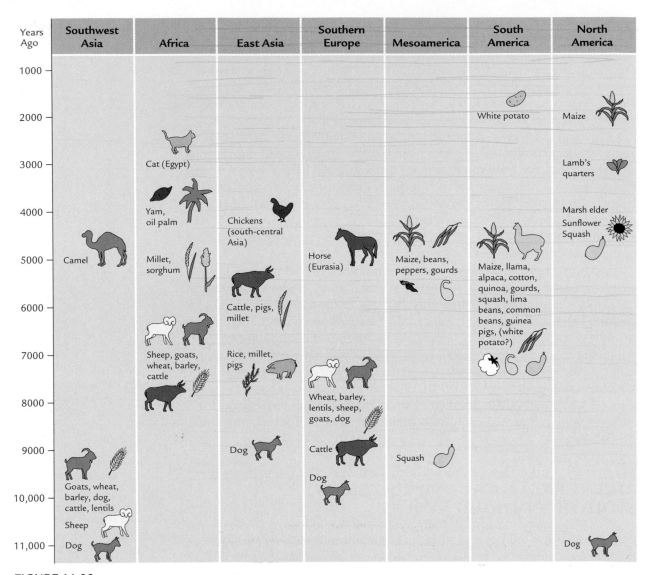

FIGURE 14.22

Chronological outline of the origins of domestication and agriculture. (From Human Antiquity: An Introduction to Physical Anthropology and Archaeology, *3d ed., by Kenneth Feder and Michael Park, Fig. 14.1. Copyright © 1997 by Mayfield Publishing Company. Reprinted with permission from The McGraw-Hill Companies)*

population size that had resulted from more efficient hunting and gathering. In any case, the effects of agriculture were and continue to be quite dramatic—the human population grew and continues to do so today (see Chapter 15).

Agriculture did not have a single origin but rather developed independently in many parts of both the Old World and the New World. Over the next several thousand years, the use of agriculture became increasingly dominant around the world (Figure 14.22). Today there are very few hunters and gatherers left. Our current focus on agriculture often blinds us to the reality that we have changed so much culturally in so short a time. Biologically, we are still hunters and gatherers.

FIGURE 14.23

The space shuttle is one feature of our species' continuing exploration and utilization of new environments. (Courtesy NASA)

Cultural change continued at an even faster rate following the origin of agriculture and rapid population growth. Cities and state-level societies developed. Exploration brought the inhabitants of the Old World and the New World back into contact, and industrialization spread rapidly. Today, only 12,000 years after the time our ancestors survived by hunting and gathering, we are able to explore and live in every environment on earth and beyond (Figure 14.23). However one feels about the rapid cultural changes of *H. sapiens*, these changes can be viewed as a continuation of the basic adaptations of culture and learning that have been apparent for at least the past 2.5 million years of human evolution. The final chapter focuses on the biological impact of our species' rapid cultural change, particularly in the past 12,000 years.

SUMMARY

Among other features, anatomically modern *Homo sapiens* is characterized by a higher, more well-rounded skull and a smaller face than most archaics and by the presence of a noticeable chin. Modern *H. sapiens* is best known from fossil records dating over the past 30,000 years. There is considerable evidence, however, that these humans appeared first more than 100,000 years ago in Africa and by 100,000 to 90,000 years ago in the Middle East. By 50,000 years ago, the culture of *H. sapiens* had begun to change rapidly; the use of more sophisticated stone tools (especially blade tools) and bone tools spread, burials of the dead became more elaborate, and art appeared. Modern humans had colonized Australia by 60,000 years ago and the New World by at least 15,000 years ago.

There is continuing controversy regarding the origin of anatomically modern humans. The multiregional evolution model hypothesizes that the transition from *H. erectus* to archaic humans to modern *H. sapiens* occurred throughout the Old World. According to this model, the evolution of modern humans took place within a widespread species across several continents. Gene flow is considered here to be sufficient to have maintained a single species of human after the initial dispersal of *H. erectus* from Africa. Conversely, the African replacement model hypothesizes that the evolution of modern humans occurred in one place—Africa, between 200,000 and 100,000 years ago—and that modern humans then spread outward across the world, replacing preexisting archaic populations. There are variants of each model, including the possibility of a primary African origin combined with mixture with archaic populations. Fossil and genetic data have been used to examine these hypotheses. There is still considerable debate about *why* modern humans first evolved.

Human evolution did not end after the initial appearance of modern humans. Although there have been some biological changes during our recent past, most of our species' evolution during the past 10,000 years has been cultural. Perhaps the single most important event was the development of agriculture, which changed our entire way of life. Predicting the specifics of future human evolution is problematic, but it does appear clear that our future will involve more and more cultural change, which occurs at a far greater rate than biological evolution. This does not mean that biological evolution has stopped but rather that our fate is becoming increasingly affected by cultural change.

SUPPLEMENTAL READINGS

Relethford, J. H. 2001. *Genetics and the Search for Modern Human Origins.* New York: Wiley-Liss. A review of different models for the origin of modern humans and the genetic evidence that has been used to test them.

Stringer, C., and R. McKie. 1996. *African Exodus: The Origins of Modern Humanity.* New York: Henry Holt.

Wolpoff, M. H., and R. Caspari. 1997. *Race and Human Evolution.* New York: Simon and Schuster.

These two books are excellent and interesting summaries of the modern human origins debate, coauthored by the leading proponents of the African replacement model (Stringer) and multiregional evolution model (Wolpoff).

INTERNET RESOURCES

http://anthro.palomar.edu/homo2/modern_humans.htm
Early Modern *Homo sapiens,* a tutorial including discussion of models of modern human origins.

http://www.mnh.si.edu/anthro/humanorigins/ha/sap.htm
Homo sapiens, a similar Web page.

http://anthro.palomar.edu/homo2/sapiens_culture.htm
Early Modern Human Culture, a tutorial focusing on stone tool technology and cave art.

CHAPTER 15

June 5

Human Biology and Culture Change

Human evolution has been increasingly driven by cultural changes in our species' recent history. Although we continue to evolve biologically, these changes are much slower than changes in human cultural adaptation. During the past 12,000 years, we have changed from being hunters and gatherers to being agriculturalists; an increasing portion of humanity lives in or near large urban centers; and our population has exploded from 5 million to 10 million people to more than 6 billion. In many ways, we live in a world very unlike that of our ancestors.

These cultural changes have happened much faster than biological change. As a result, biologically we are still hunters and gatherers to some extent but live in conditions that are often quite different from those under which our ancestors evolved. We live in larger groups, eat different foods, and structure our societies in different ways. The disparity between rates of cultural change and biological evolution has had serious consequences for our biology. An example of this type of change was described briefly in the section on nutritional adaptation in Chapter 7, which noted the biomedical impact of a changing diet and lifestyle on Samoan populations. This example is only one of many that show how rapid cultural changes have affected our biology—not always to our benefit. This chapter considers the impact of culture change on human biology by focusing on some major cultural changes in human evolution over the past 12,000 years.

◀ *Chinese farmers working in rice paddies. The transition to agriculture began in the human species 12,000 years ago. This major cultural event has led to many changes in human biology, including shifts in disease, death, and fertility.*
(© *Michael S. Yamashita/Corbis*)

THE BIOLOGICAL IMPACT OF AGRICULTURE

A major shift in human adaptation was the transition from hunting and gathering to agriculture. Human populations began relying increasingly on agriculture starting 12,000 years ago. Although a small proportion of human populations today still rely on hunting and gathering, most are agricultural. The reasons for this change are still widely debated, and there was probably no single cause responsible for this shift. Feder (2000) notes that there is a general pattern in the archaeological record that shows that human populations became more **sedentary** (settled in one place) *before* agriculture developed. Human populations might have been able to settle down because of increased efficiency at hunting and gathering and/or changes in the environment resulting from the warming climate near the end of the Pleistocene. Some archaeologists suggest that the shift to a sedentary life led to population growth, which in turn led to the need for more food resources. Under such conditions, sedentary populations would shift their methods of acquiring food and adopt a variety of agricultural strategies that increased the food supply, such as weeding, protecting plant resources, and clearing forests. Over time, human populations became more reliant on such methods, and the domestication of plants and animals became their primary means of feeding themselves.

The study of the biological impact of the transition to agriculture relies extensively on the field of **paleopathology,** the study of disease in prehistoric populations. The primary evidence is from skeletal remains, which can provide a variety of information on health and disease, including age at death, cause of death, nutritional status, growth patterns, and trauma (Cohen 1989; Larsen 2000). Diseases such as osteoarthritis may affect bones directly (Figure 15.1). Other diseases, such as syphilis and tuberculosis, may leave indications of their effects on the skeletal system (Figure 15.2). Physical trauma due to injury or violence often leaves detectable fractures. Signs of healing or infection tell us the long-term effects of such trauma (Figure 15.3). X-ray and chemical analysis can provide us with information about nutrition and growth patterns. Collectively, these methods and others provide us with a view of the health of prehistoric populations.

Population Growth

The shift to agriculture led to many changes in human populations. A major change was the increase in population size, which in turn led to a greater reliance on agriculture, and ultimately to further population growth. The relationship between population size and agriculture is clear when considering the maximum size, or **carrying capacity,** of human populations. Hunting and gathering populations tend to be small, usually no more than a couple of dozen people, because there would not be enough food for more. Agriculture can support much larger populations.

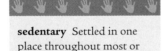

sedentary Settled in one place throughout most or all of the year.

paleopathology The study of disease in prehistoric populations based on analysis of skeletal remains and archaeological evidence.

carrying capacity The maximum population size capable of being supported in a given environment.

FIGURE 15.1

Osteoarthritis in a prehistoric Peruvian. The head of the femur is deformed. (© The Field Museum, Chicago: Neg. #74749B)

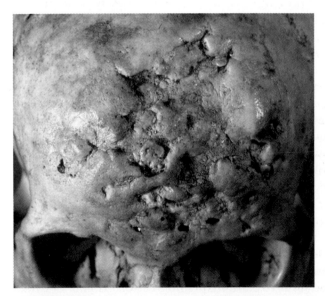

FIGURE 15.2

The skull of a prehistoric Eskimo who suffered from treponemal infection. The marks on the top of the skull are typical of a long-term syphilitic infection. (© Hrdlicka Paleopathology Collection, Courtesy San Diego Museum of Man)

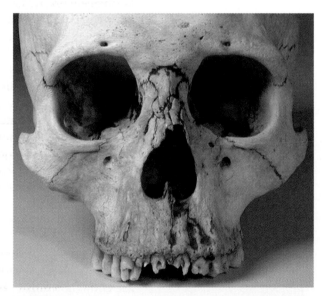

FIGURE 15.3

Nasal fracture in a prehistoric Peruvian. The affected area shows signs of healing, indicating that this individual survived the initial trauma. (© Hrdlicka Paleopathology Collection, Courtesy San Diego Museum of Man)

Why did agricultural populations become larger? Population growth results from the net effects of fertility, mortality, and migration. Births increase the population size, and deaths decrease the population size. Migration can either increase or decrease the population size, depending on whether more people move into a population or leave it. Ignoring migration for the moment, the change in population size because of **natural increase** is the number of births minus the number of deaths. If the number of births exceeds the number of deaths, then the population grows. If the number of births is less than the number of deaths, then the population declines.

The fact that the human species grew in numbers following the rise of agriculture suggests that this growth was due to an increase in fertility (more births per year), a decrease in mortality (fewer deaths per year), or both. There does not appear to have been a reduction in overall mortality, as assessed by estimates of the **life expectancy at birth,** a measure of the average length of life for a newborn child. Life expectancy at birth is derived by looking at a population's **life table,** which is the age distribution of members of a population that is used to compute the probability that someone will die by a certain age based on the current distribution of the age at death. Life tables are routinely used in demographic research, and by the insurance industry, and can be compiled for prehistoric populations by estimating from skeletal remains the age at death.

Hunting and gathering populations typically have a low life expectancy at birth—roughly 20 to 40 years (Cohen 1989). Keep in mind that the life expectancy at birth is an *average* length of life. The value of 20 to 40 years does *not* mean that everyone only lives 20 to 40 years total. Some live much longer, and others do not live this long. This average provides a crude index of overall health in a population. Skeletal evidence suggests that, in general, agricultural populations did not improve on this figure; in fact, in some cases mortality rates actually increased and life expectancy at birth declined somewhat following the transition to agriculture. For example, analysis of skeletal remains from Dickson Mound, a prehistoric Native American site in Illinois, shows that life expectancy at birth was 26 years at a time when they were exclusively hunters and gatherers but decreased to 19 years following the transition to agriculture (Cohen 1989).

If lowered mortality rates are not responsible for increase in population size following the adoption of agriculture, then it seems logical that the answer must lie in increased fertility rates. A traditional explanation is that the shift to a sedentary life and diet resulted in improved ovarian function and shorter intervals of breast-feeding. Studies of living hunters and gatherers have shown that breast-feeding has a contraceptive effect. When a women nurses her child, hormonal changes take place that reduce the probability of ovulation (Wood 1994). Among some contemporary hunting-gathering populations, the women breast-feed for several years, contributing to a long interval between births—44 months on average among the !Kung of the Kalahari Desert in Africa (Potts 1988). The shift to agriculture resulted in foods available to infants that allowed earlier weaning, and hence shorter intervals between children, leading to an increase in population size. In addition, there

natural increase Number of births minus the number of deaths.

life expectancy at birth A measure of the average length of life for a newborn child.

life table A compilation of the age distribution of a population that provides an estimate of the probability that an individual will die by a certain age, used to compute life expectancy.

would be less need to carry dependent children. In nomadic populations, the need to carry children limits the number of dependent children; it is not easy to have another child until the earlier children can walk on their own. The sedentary nature of agricultural populations may have allowed short birth intervals (Livi-Bacci 1997).

Not everyone accepts the traditional hypothesis of fertility increase. Renee Pennington (1996) notes that several studies have shown no significant difference between fertility levels in contemporary hunter-gatherers and agriculturalists. She argues that age-related variation in mortality is a more likely cause of population growth in agricultural populations. There is evidence that agriculture lowers the mortality rate of *children* and that "this decrease is so critical that levels of mortality can increase drastically at later ages and still produce an increasing population" (p. 271). Measures of total mortality in a population, such as the life expectancy at birth, obscure the important nature of age-specific mortality. Daniel Sellen (2001) came to a similar conclusion, noting in his cross-cultural analysis that a reduction in childhood mortality is associated with dependence on agriculture. However, he argues that agriculture also increases fertility and that the combination of increased fertility and decreased childhood mortality (although not adult mortality) is related to agriculture.

Disease

A popular myth is that life improved across the board when humans developed agriculture. Clearly this is not the case. The transition to agriculture resulted in major shifts in the leading causes of disease and death, including an increase in epidemics of infectious disease and nutritional diseases, leading Jared Diamond (1992b) to consider agriculture a "mixed blessing."

Disease in Hunting–Gathering Populations   Before considering the effect of the transition to agriculture on disease, it is necessary to review briefly general patterns of health and disease in hunting-gathering populations. Information on health and disease in hunting-gathering populations has been obtained by studying the few remaining hunting-gathering societies and from the study of prehistoric hunter-gatherers using the methods of paleopathology.

The two most common types of infectious disease in hunting-gathering populations are those due to parasites and those due to **zoonoses,** diseases that are transmitted from other animals to humans. Parasitic diseases may reflect the long-term evolutionary adaptation of different parasites to human beings. Among hunting-gathering societies, these parasites include lice and pinworms. The zoonoses are introduced through insect bites, animal wounds, and ingestion of contaminated meat. These diseases include sleeping sickness, tetanus, and schistosomiasis, among others (Armelagos and Dewey 1970). The prevalence of various parasitic and zoonotic diseases varies among different hunting-gathering environments. The disease microorganisms found in arctic or temperate environments are generally not found in tropical environments.

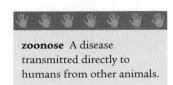

zoonose A disease transmitted directly to humans from other animals.

FIGURE 15.4

!Kung women gathering vegetables. The small size and nomadic nature of hunting-gathering populations mean that infectious disease is endemic, not epidemic.

(© Irven DeVore)

epidemic A pattern of disease rate when new cases of a disease spread rapidly through a population.

endemic A pattern of disease rate when new cases of a disease occur at a relatively constant but low rate over time.

The spread of infectious diseases is often classified as being either epidemic or endemic. An **epidemic** pattern is one in which new cases of a disease spread quickly. A typical epidemic starts with a few new cases of a disease, increases geometrically in a short period of time as more people are infected, and then declines rapidly as the number of susceptible individuals declines. An **endemic** pattern shows a low but constant rate; a few cases are always present but no major spread occurs. In general, hunting-gathering populations do not experience epidemics. This is because of two ecological factors associated with a hunting-gathering way of life: small population size and a nomadic lifestyle (Figure 15.4). Hunters and gatherers live in small groups of roughly 25 to 50 people that interact occasionally with other small groups in their region. Under such conditions, infectious diseases tend not to spread rapidly. There are not enough people to become infected to keep the disease going at high rates. Without enough people to infect, the disease microorganisms die off. This does not apply to chronic infectious diseases, whose microorganisms can stay alive long enough to infect people coming into the group. Certain diseases caused by parasitic worms fall into this category. In such cases, the prevalence of infectious diseases does not increase rapidly. Although infectious diseases are the leading cause of death in some hunting-gathering populations (Howell 2000), the rate is *endemic,* not epidemic. The difference has to do with whether the deaths are concentrated in a short interval of time (epidemic) or not (endemic).

The noninfectious diseases common in industrial societies, such as heart disease, cancer, diabetes, and high blood pressure, are rare in hunting-gathering societies. Part of the reason for these low rates may be the diet and lifestyle of hunters and gatherers, but it is also because fewer individuals are likely to live long enough to develop these diseases. The nutrition of hunting-gathering populations is varied and provides a well-balanced diet low in fat and high in

FIGURE 15.5

Chinese farmers planting rice. The larger size and sedentary nature of agricultural populations contribute to epidemics of infectious disease.
(© *Michael S. Yamashita/Corbis*)

fiber. In fact, some researchers have suggested people in Western society should emulate this diet to improve their health (Eaton et al. 1988). A major nutritional problem in hunting-gathering societies is the scarcity of food during hard times, such as droughts. The rate of malnutrition and starvation in most hunting-gathering groups is usually very low (Dunn 1968).

Apart from endemic infectious disease, what else accounts for the major causes of death in hunting-gathering societies? Injury deaths are one factor. In most environments, death could result from hunting injuries and burns. Depending on the specific environment, death can result from drowning, cold exposure, or heat stress. In some hunting-gathering populations, injuries are the leading cause of death (Dunn 1968). For females, an additional factor is death during childbirth.

Infectious Disease in Agricultural Populations   The pattern of disease is different in agricultural populations. Agriculture allows larger population size and requires a sedentary life. The increased size and lack of mobility has certain implications for the spread of disease (Figure 15.5). Large populations with many susceptible individuals allow for rapid spread of short-lived microorganisms. Such conditions exist in agricultural populations because of increased population size and the increased probability of coming into contact with someone who has the disease. As a result, agricultural populations have often shown epidemics of diseases such as smallpox, measles, and mumps. The size of a population needed to sustain an epidemic varies according to disease. Some infectious diseases, such as measles, require very large populations for rapid spread.

Sedentary life increases the spread of infectious disease in other ways. Large populations living continuously in the same area accumulate sewage. Poor sanitation and contamination of the water supply increase the chance for disease epidemics.

Agricultural practices also cause ecological changes, making certain infectious diseases more likely. The introduction of domesticated animals adds to waste accumulation and provides the opportunity for further exposure to diseases carried by animals. Cultivation of the land can also increase the probability of contact with insects carrying disease microorganisms. For example, standing pools of water are created when forests are cleared for agriculture, creating an opportunity for an increase in the mosquito population that transmits malaria.

The use of feces for fertilization can also have an impact on rates of infectious disease. In addition to contamination from handling these waste products, the food grown in these fertilizers can become contaminated. This problem was so acute in South Korea that steps had to be taken to reduce the use of feces as fertilizer (Cockburn 1971). In addition, irrigation can lead to an increase in the spread of infectious disease. One of the major problems in tropical agricultural societies is the increased snail population that lives in irrigation canals and carries schistosomiasis. Irrigation can pass infectious microorganisms from one population to the next.

Nutritional Disease in Agricultural Populations   Although agriculture provides populations with the ability to feed more people, this way of life does not guarantee an improvement in nutritional quality. Extensive investment in a single food crop, such as rice or corn, may provide too limited a diet for many people, and certain nutritional deficiency diseases can result. For example, populations relying extensively on corn as a major food source may show an increase in pellagra (a disease caused by a deficiency in niacin) as well as protein deficiency. Dependency on highly polished rice is often associated with protein and vitamin deficiencies (McElroy and Townsend 1989).

Perhaps the greatest problem of reliance on a single crop is that if that crop fails, starvation can result. The population has become so dependent on a major crop that if a drought or plague wipes it out, not enough food is left for the people. An example of this is the Great Famine in Ireland between 1846 and 1951. The population of Ireland had grown rapidly since the introduction of the potato in the early 1700s, which provided a nutritious food that could be grown easily. Marriage in Ireland was linked to land inheritance; owning land was often a prerequisite for marriage, and only one son tended to inherit. However, the introduction of the potato provided more efficient use of the land, which allowed families to subdivide their property and give more sons the opportunity to start a family. The population of Ireland

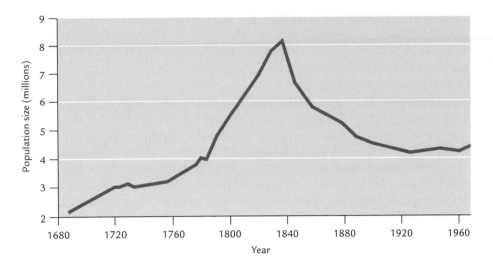

FIGURE 15.6

Population growth in Ireland from 1687 to 1971. Data from the two currently separate nations, the Republic of Ireland and Northern Ireland, have been pooled. (Source of data: Vaughan and Fitzpatrick 1978)

grew rapidly, but this resulted in a precarious ecology. The potato crop was often destroyed by blight, and during the Great Famine there were five continuous years of blight with no relief (Connell 1950). Roughly 1.5 million people died and 1 million left the country (Woodham-Smith 1962), starting a pattern of population decline that continued into the twentieth century (Figure 15.6).

An agricultural diet can also lead to dental problems. The increased amount of starches in an agriculturalist's diet, combined with an increase in dirt and grit in the food, can lead to an increase in dental wear and cavities. Such changes are readily apparent in many studies of paleopathology (Cohen 1989; Larsen 2000).

THE BIOLOGICAL IMPACT OF CIVILIZATION

Following the origin and spread of agriculture in different parts of the world, a number of human populations began to develop urban centers and civilization as much as 6,000 years ago. As defined by archaeologists, a civilization is a large state-level society that has a number of specific characteristics including large population size, high population density, cities, social stratification, food and labor surpluses, monumental architecture, and a system of record keeping (Feder 2000).

Urbanization and Disease

Preindustrial cities date back several thousand years. Such cities often develop as market or administrative centers for a region, and their increased population size and density provide many opportunities for epidemics of infectious disease. In addition, a number of early cities had inadequate sewage disposal and contaminated water, both major factors increasing the spread of epidemics. To feed large numbers of people, food had to be brought in from the surrounding countryside and stored inside the city. In Europe during the Middle Ages, grain was often stored inside the house. Rats and other vermin had easy access to these foods and their populations increased, furthering the spread of disease. In preindustrial cities located in dry parts of the world, grain was stored in ceramic containers, which limited the access of vermin.

Perhaps the best-known example of an epidemic disease in preindustrial cities is the bubonic plague in Europe during the fourteenth century. Bubonic plague, also known as the Black Death, is caused by a bacterium spread by fleas among field rodents. With the development of large urban areas and the corresponding large indoor rat populations, the disease spread to rats in the cities. As the rats died, the fleas jumped off them to find a new host, which was frequently a human being. The spread of bubonic plague during this time was **pandemic,** a widespread epidemic affecting large continental areas. It is estimated that up to 20 million Europeans died from bubonic plague between 1346 and 1352 (McEvedy 1988). A major factor in the spread of plague was trade; rats would board ships sailing across the Mediterranean Sea and disembark at distant ports, infecting more rats and ultimately the human population. The ecological changes accompanying the development of urbanization in Europe provided an opportunity for the rapid spread of fleas, rats, and the disease. Bubonic plague is still around today, including in the American Southwest, although treatment with antibiotics has kept the incidence of death close to zero.

Industrialization, which began more than 250 years ago, accelerated population growth in urban areas. Technological changes provided more efficient methods of agriculture and the means to support more people than in previous eras. The increased growth of urban areas was accompanied initially by further spread of infectious diseases, compounded by problems in waste disposal. By the end of the nineteenth century, however, some populations began a transition wherein the rate of infectious disease declined and the rate of noninfectious disease increased. This shift in disease patterns was accompanied by a reduction in mortality, especially infant mortality, and an increase in life expectancy. In evolutionary terms, all of these changes are very recent.

Culture Contact

One consequence of expanding civilizations is the increase in long-distance contact with other societies through exploration, colonization, trade, and conquest. With the rise of European exploration in the 1500s, many previously separate human populations met one another. In addition to the vast cultural, economic, and political problems resulting from such contact, infectious diseases could now spread into populations that had no prior immune experience. The results were generally devastating.

The epidemiologic effects of culture contact have been documented for a number of populations, particularly Native Americans and Pacific Islanders.

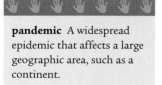

pandemic A widespread epidemic that affects a large geographic area, such as a continent.

Many infectious diseases, such as smallpox, measles, and mumps, were introduced into the New World at this time, leading to massive loss of life in many populations (Cohen 1989; McNeill 1977). The actual impact of infectious disease varied across populations—some were hit much harder than were others, and at different times (Larsen 1994). The overall impact was a severe reduction in population size across the Americas (Crawford 1998).

The flow of disease seems to have been primarily in one direction, from the Old World to the New World. The reason for this might have to do with fewer domesticated animals in the New World. These animals are often the initial source of diseases that infect humans (Diamond 1992a). One possible exception to this one-way flow of human disease is treponemal diseases, including venereal syphilis. Venereal syphilis (spread by sexual contact) increased rapidly in Europe after 1500, a date that coincides with the contact between New World and Old World populations. Following European settlement in the Americas, it was also noted that many Native Americans had syphilis. Did the disease evolve in Europe and then spread to the Americas? Or did it first appear in the New World and then spread to Europe? Or did it evolve independently in both the New World and the Old World? Evidence from paleopathology suggests that cases of treponemal disease occurred in the New World before European contact, suggesting that venereal syphilis evolved in the New World (Baker and Armelagos 1988). This remains a controversial topic, and some have suggested that treponemal disease was present in Europe before contact, which would support the idea of the independent evolution of syphilis.

RECENT CHANGES

The last hundred years has seen dramatic shifts in our species. Industrialization and economic development have spread throughout much (but not all) of the world, resulting in major biological impacts on disease, mortality, fertility, and population growth. The exact changes experienced by a society are in part a reflection of its economic status. Demographers routinely classify nations into two groups: more developed countries and less developed countries. Over much of the last century, the more developed countries have seen a reduction in death rates and birth rates, a shift from infectious disease to noninfectious disease as the leading causes of death, a slowing (and in some cases a reversal) of population growth, and an aging population. Less developed countries have seen some reduction in mortality and fertility, although infectious disease still dominates and birth rates remain high in parts of the world. Population growth continues at a high rate in many less developed countries.

The Epidemiologic Transition

In the more developed countries, life expectancy at birth has increased more than 50 percent, and the leading causes of death have shifted from infectious

FIGURE 15.7

Life expectancy at birth in the United States from 1900 to 1999. Life expectancy at birth increased during the twentieth century, with the major exception of 1918, the year of an influenza pandemic. (Source of data: 1900–1996 data from Anderson 1998; 1997 data from Centers for Disease Control and Prevention Web page: <http://www.cdc.gov/nchs/data/lewk3_97.pdf>; 1998 data from Kochanek et al. 2001)

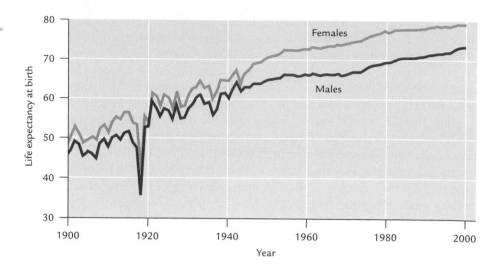

to noninfectious diseases. The increase in life expectancy and the shift from infectious to noninfectious diseases as the primary cause of death is a feature of the **epidemiologic transition** that has been observed in the more developed countries and that is under way, to varying degrees, in the less developed countries.

The Nature of the Epidemiologic Transition   According to the model developed by Omran (1977), a pretransition population has high death rates, particularly because of epidemics of childhood infectious disease. As public health, sanitation, and medical technologies improve, epidemics become less frequent and less intense. The overall death rate declines, and life expectancy at birth increases. Following the transition, the leading causes of death are primarily noninfectious rather than infectious diseases.

A major characteristic of the epidemiologic transition is the increase in life expectancy at birth. In the United States in 1900, life expectancy was 49 years, but by 1999 life expectancy had risen to 77 years (Kochanek et al. 2001). Figure 15.7 shows the life expectancy at birth for males and females in the United States from 1900 through 1999. Females tend to live longer, as reflected in their higher life expectancies; in 1999, the life expectancy of a newborn girl was 79.4 years, compared with 73.9 for newborn boys. Excepting a noticeable dip in 1918 (the year of a major worldwide influenza pandemic), life expectancy at birth rose during the twentieth century.

The increase in life expectancy is not limited to the more developed societies. Other groups undergoing modernization and the epidemiologic transition have also shown an increase, such as the residents of the modernizing population of American Samoa. From 1950 to 1980, life expectancy at birth increased 10 years for males and 18 years for females (Crews 1989).

A controversial topic today is the extent to which life expectancy can be expected to increase in developed societies. Based on statistical analysis of death rates, Olshansky and colleagues (1990, 2001) argue that even with major reductions in chronic disease, life expectancy at birth will not increase past

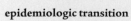

epidemiologic transition
The increase in life expectancy and the shift from infectious to noninfectious disease as the primary cause of death.

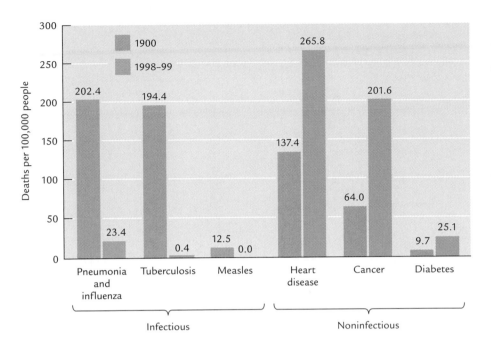

FIGURE 15.8

Death rates (per 100,000 people) for selected infectious and noninfectious diseases in the United States in 1900 and 1998–1999. Note the decrease in infectious disease and the increase in noninfectious disease. (Source of data: 1900 rates from Centers for Disease Control and Prevention Web page: <http:// www.cdc.gov/nchs/data/lead0078. pdf >, and Molnar 1998 for measles and diabetes; 1999 rates from Kochanek et al. 2001 except for tuberculosis rates, taken for 1998 from CDC Web page: <http://www. cdc.gov/nchs/data/gm250_98.pdf >, and measles, taken for 1998 from CDC Web page: <http://www.cdc. gov/nchs/data/98gm3_01.pdf >)

85 years of age because the decline in mortality rates will slow down. Others, however, suggest that mortality rates will continue to decline and that life expectancy at birth could reach as high as 90 years of age in some developed nations by the year 2050 (Tuljapurkar et al. 2000).

The increase in life expectancy is related to a dramatic decline in deaths due to infectious diseases. Infants and young children are at greater risk for such diseases, and a large number of deaths in this age group lowers the average length of life in a population. As infectious disease death rates decline, the average length of life increases. A consequence of people living longer is that the death rate from degenerative noninfectious diseases, such as cancer and heart disease, begins to rise. Thus, there was a shift from infectious to noninfectious diseases as the primary causes of death. In the United States in 1900, the top three causes of death were all infectious diseases: pneumonia/ influenza, tuberculosis, and diarrheal diseases. In 1999, the top three causes of death were all degenerative diseases: heart disease, cancer, and stroke (Kochanek et al. 2001).

Figure 15.8 illustrates this dramatic shift by comparing the mortality rate (deaths per 100,000 people) for selected diseases in the United States in 1900 and in 1998–1999. Note the tremendous decline in infectious disease mortality and the increase in noninfectious diseases. As we continue to live longer lives, we are more likely to die from a degenerative noninfectious disease. The major health problems today are quite different than they were only several generations in the past when infectious diseases were the primary cause of death. Figure 15.9 shows the 10 leading causes of death in the United States in 1999. Heart disease and cancer are the two major causes of death, accounting for 53 percent of all deaths. Only two of the top 10 causes of death are due to infectious disease, pneumonia/influenza and septicemia

FIGURE 15.9

Leading causes of death in the United States in 1999. The death rate is the number of deaths per 100,000 people. The abbreviation COPD = chronic obstructive pulmonary diseases. (Source of data: Kochanek et al. 2001)

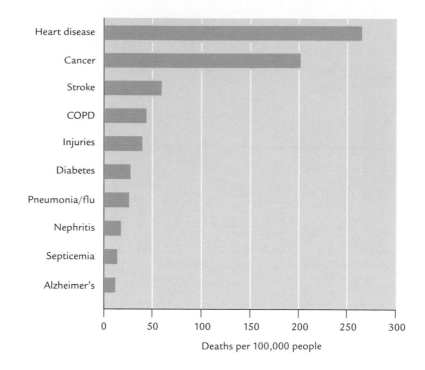

Deaths per 100,000 people

(blood poisoning). Heart disease, cancer, and stroke are likely to remain as the major causes of death in the near future, but the other leading causes often change rapidly, primarily because of new technologies and aggressive public health measures. Since the previous edition of this text, HIV infection (the viral agent responsible for AIDS), suicide, and liver disease have dropped below tenth place, and Alzheimer's disease, nephritis, and septicemia have all moved into the leading causes of death.

It is important to remember that these figures refer to the United States, and although typical of other nations that have undergone the epidemiologic transition, they do not represent the entire world. Infectious disease remains a leading cause of death in many human populations, particularly among the less developed countries. Figure 15.10 shows the leading causes of death worldwide, illustrating that infectious disease is still a leading cause of death in the human species. HIV infection, which has dropped significantly in the United States, remains high elsewhere in the world and is the fourth leading cause of death in our species. The magnitude of infectious disease is even more apparent when considering the leading causes of death in Africa (Figure 15.11), where HIV infection is the leading cause of death and malaria is second. Measles, which has disappeared as a cause of death in the more developed countries, is the sixth leading cause of death in Africa. Populational differences in disease and death are due to differences in the level of economic development and public health measures, and different populations are at different points in the epidemiologic transition.

Causes of the Epidemiologic Transition   What has caused these rapid changes in disease rates and life expectancy? Cultural changes in industrial so-

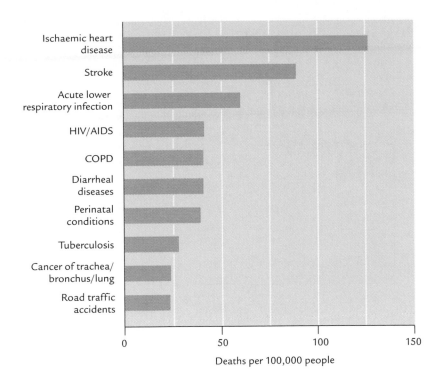

FIGURE 15.10

Leading causes of death in the world in 1998. The death rate is the number of deaths per 100,000 people. The abbreviation COPD = chronic obstructive pulmonary diseases. (Source of data: World Health Organization 1999)

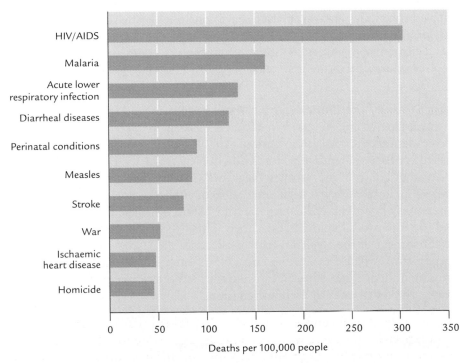

FIGURE 15.11

Leading causes of death in Africa in 1998. The death rate is the number of deaths per 100,000 people. (Source of data: World Health Organization 1999)

cieties have often resulted in major improvements in health care, public sanitation, and water quality. These factors aid in reducing the spread and effect of infectious diseases, particularly in infancy. Advances in medical technology,

FIGURE 15.12

Changes in the death rate in New York City during the nineteenth and twentieth centuries. (Source: Omran [1977:12]. Courtesy Population Reference Bureau, Inc., Washington, D.C.)

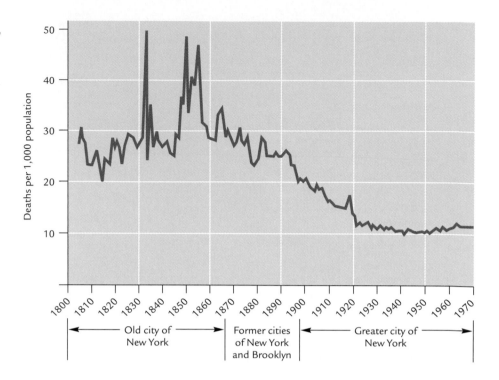

such as antibiotics and vaccination, have continued to help reduce the death rate due to infectious diseases, but the major reason for the initial decline was a cleaner environment brought about by civil engineering—particularly sewers and water treatment systems.

Case Study of the Epidemiologic Transition   The relationship between cultural change and disease rates emerges clearly in specific case studies of the epidemiologic transition. Omran (1977) looked at overall death rates in his study of the epidemiologic transition in New York City. Figure 15.12 shows the changes in total mortality in New York City over time. Before the 1860s, the overall death rate was high and had frequent spikes, primarily because of epidemics of cholera. Following the mid-1860s, both the overall death rate and the intensity of epidemics declined. This decrease corresponds with the establishment of the Health Department. After the 1920s, the continued incorporation of better sanitation and a clean water supply, along with an improvement in drugs and health care and the introduction of pasteurized milk, caused the death rates to decline even more.

Secular Changes in Human Growth

The epidemiologic transition affects more than disease and death rates; its effects have also been observed in studies of child growth. During the past century, many industrialized nations have shown several secular changes in

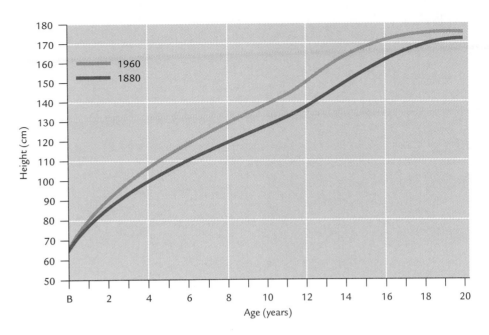

FIGURE 15.13

Secular change in European American males in North America. At all ages the males living in 1960 have greater height than those who lived in 1880. (Adapted from Growth and Development *by Robert M. Malina, © 1975, publisher Burgess Publishing Company, Minneapolis, Minn. With permission from the publisher)*

child growth. A **secular change** is simply a change in the pattern of growth across generations.

Types of Secular Change   Three basic secular changes have been observed over the past century: an increase in height, an increase in weight, and a decrease in the age of sexual maturation. Children in many industrialized nations are taller and heavier today than children the same age a century or so ago. Figure 15.13 shows the average distance curve for height of North American males of European ancestry in 1880 and 1960. There is no noticeable difference in body length at birth. Note, however, that at all postnatal ages the 1960 males are consistently taller than the 1880 males. This difference is most noticeable during adolescence. Comparison of distance curves for weight shows the same pattern.

Another secular change is a decrease in the age of maturation. This is most apparent in a specific measure of human development—the **age at menarche,** the age at which a female experiences her first menstrual period. Figure 15.14 plots the average age at menarche for the United States and several European industrial nations over time. The general trend is one of earlier biological maturation.

Causes of Secular Change   The basic secular changes observed in industrialized nations during the past century reflect environmental change. These changes came too fast and were too pervasive to be due to genetic change; rather, environmental changes have enabled more people to reach their genetic potential for growth. These trends, however, should not be projected indefinitely into the future. Some data suggest that the secular changes in

secular change A change in the average pattern of growth or development in a population over several generations.

age at menarche The age at which a female experiences her first menstrual period.

FIGURE 15.14

Secular change in age at menarche (the age of a female's first menstrual period) in the United States and several European countries. (Adapted from Growth and Development *by Robert M. Malina, © 1975, publisher Burgess Publishing Company, Minneapolis, Minn. With permission from the publisher)*

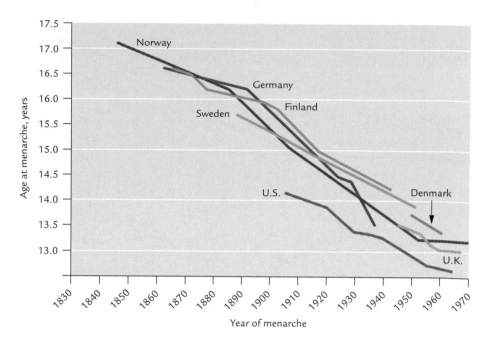

height, weight, and age at menarche have slowed down or stopped in some countries (Eveleth and Tanner 1990). Future environmental improvements could enable more and more children to reach their genetic potential for growth, but we should not expect average heights of 8 feet or more in another hundred years!

Many environmental factors have been suggested as being responsible for these secular changes, including improved nutrition, reduction of childhood infectious disease, improved availability of health care, improved standard of living, and reduction of family size. Many of these factors are interrelated, making precise identification of causes difficult. Malina (1979) notes that improved nutrition has often been cited as a primary cause of the observed secular changes. Though availability of nutritional intake has improved for many people, especially during infancy, Malina does not think it is solely responsible for secular changes and argues that one of the most important factors was an improvement in health conditions resulting in the reduction in childhood infectious diseases. Thus, the epidemiologic transition appears to be related to secular changes in human growth as well.

Pollution and Human Biology

The spread of industrialization has led to a dramatic increase in levels of air and water pollution on our planet. Exposure to such toxins was probably rare for our species before widespread industrialization (Schell 1991). A glance at any newspaper reveals the number of potential pollution-related problems that now plague humanity, including global warming, acid rain, and others. The biological impact of increased pollution is often discussed in terms of health problems such as cancer and asthma, but these are only some of the observed impacts. This section discusses two other effects of increased pollution.

Pollution and Human Growth   Many potential health problems are detected by studying patterns of human growth because the pattern of human growth and development is very sensitive to environmental changes. Schell (1991) has reviewed a number of studies showing a link between environmental pollution and human growth. Detrimental effects on human growth have been demonstrated or suggested for air pollution, lead poisoning, and exposure to toxic chemicals.

One of the most dramatic examples of pollution is the infamous case of Love Canal, a community in New York State named after a canal that was used in the 1940s and early 1950s as a dumping site for 19,000 tons of industrial chemicals. Several studies have shown a definite impact of living near Love Canal on human growth. Some studies have focused on low birth weight (less than 2.5 kg), a useful measure of environmental stress and a risk factor for a number of medical and behavioral problems. Vianna and Polan (1984) found that the rate of babies born with low birth weight was much higher in the neighborhood closest to the dumping; 12 percent of all births had low birth weight as compared with 7 percent for the remainder of upstate New York. The growth deficit continued through later years (Paigen et al. 1987). Children who had lived at least 75 percent of their lives in Love Canal were significantly shorter than a control group. The Love Canal studies are just one of many examples showing the negative impact of environmental pollution on human growth (Schell 1991).

The Environmental Endocrine Hypothesis   Industrialization has introduced many chemicals into our environment. Although much of the concern focuses on biomedical problems such as cancer and deficits in human growth, there is also growing concern about the potential effects of such chemicals on our endocrine system (the organs and tissues of the body involved in hormone secretion). The environmental endocrine hypothesis proposes that industrial and agricultural chemicals act to mimic or obstruct hormone function. According to this view, these chemicals are not simply foreign material in our bodies but act to provide new instructions to our endocrine system, causing disruption of normal hormone function. There is vigorous debate over this hypothesis, which has suggested links with declining sperm quality, cognitive impairment (including Attention Deficit Disorder), and breast cancer, among others (Krimsky 2000). As with many other environmental issues, such as global warming, there is continued debate over the magnitude of effects, but it is also clear that the potential harm dictates continued study. The environmental endocrine hypothesis may provide another example of the potential biological costs of rapid cultural change.

The Reemergence of Infectious Disease

The success in reducing infectious disease in developed nations during the first half of the twentieth century gave rise to an overly optimistic view that *all* infectious diseases would be eliminated by the year 2000. Smallpox, once a killer of millions, had been eliminated by 1977, and polio and tuberculosis were close behind. This view is now known to be incorrect; despite our efforts, new infectious diseases are emerging, and old ones are coming back in new forms (Garrett 1994). A dramatic example occurred in May 1995 with the outbreak of a frequently fatal disease, Ebola, in the Democratic Republic of the Congo (then known as Zaire) in Africa. Although the Ebola virus was discovered only in 1976, previous epidemics had killed hundreds of people in Zaire and Uganda (Cowley et al. 1995).

Emergent Infectious Disease   This outbreak was not an isolated event. There are many other examples of **emergent infectious diseases,** newly evolved diseases that have only appeared in the past few decades, including Legionnaire's Disease, Korean hemorraghic fever, *E. coli,* Hantavirus, and HIV (Armelagos et al. 1996).

The emergence of new diseases shows the evolution of microorganisms, a process often exacerbated by environmental changes brought about by human populations. New environments are created by rapid deforestation and conversion of land for agriculture and industrialization. Conversion of remote and isolated habitats provides the opportunity for previously rare microorganisms to encounter the human species. Continued pollution can increase the mutation rate of microorganisms in addition to interfering with ecosystems. New forms of quick travel, such as jet planes, and international commerce increase the amount of contact between human groups, enabling diseases to spread quickly and to new populations, many of which have no prior immune experience. New technologies often lend themselves to the emergence of infectious diseases by creating new microenvironments conducive to bacterial spread. Air conditioning, for example, has been implicated in the origin and spread of Legionnaire's Disease. Cultural and environmental changes have provided new opportunities for the evolution of microorganisms (Garrett 1994; Levins et al. 1994).

Reemergent Infectious Disease   An additional problem is **reemergent infectious diseases,** which are infectious diseases that have evolved resistance to antibiotics. Tuberculosis, for example, is a respiratory disease that had been treated very successfully with antibiotics in the last half of the twentieth century, but tuberculosis rates began to increase in the 1980s and 1990s. Figure 15.15 shows tuberculosis rates in New York, a state hard hit by the increase in tuberculosis from 1984 through 1997. Tuberculosis rates increased into the mid-1990s due to a number of factors, including the outbreak of antibiotic-resistant strains of the bacterium. Aggressive public health mea-

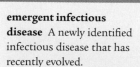

emergent infectious disease A newly identified infectious disease that has recently evolved.

reemergent infectious disease Infectious disease that had previously been reduced but that increases in frequency when microorganisms evolve resistance to antibiotics.

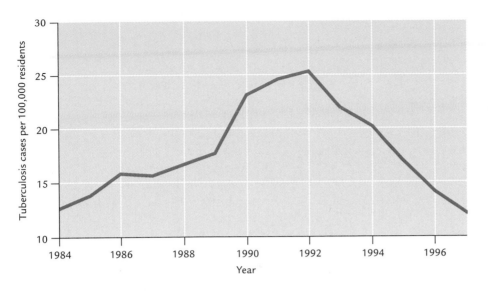

FIGURE 15.15

Tuberculosis rates (number of cases per 100,000 residents) in New York State from 1984 to 1997. (Source of data: 1984–1993 from New York State Department of Health Web page: <http://www.health. state.ny.us/nysdoh/epi/93/tb.pdf>; 1994 rates from NYSDOH Web page: <http://www.health.state.ny.us/ nysdoh/cdc/1994/section2.pdf>; 1995 rates from NYSDOH Web page: <http://www.health.state.ny. us/nysdoh/cdc/1995/rates95.pdf>; 1996 rates from NYSDOH Web page: <http://www.health.state.ny. us/nysdoh/cdc/1996/rates96.pdf>; 1997 rates from NYSDOH Web page: <http://www.health.state.ny.us/ nysdoh/cdc/1997/rates1.pdf>)

sures have reversed this trend, but it remains a problem for many residents and illustrates the danger of bacteria evolving resistance to antibiotics.

Antibiotic resistance illustrates the principle of natural selection applied to disease-causing microorganisms. Sometimes a mutant form of bacteria exists that has resistance to a specific antibiotic. Although most bacteria are killed, the mutant form will multiply and become more common in successive generations of bacteria. Because bacteria have short life spans, an antibiotic-resistant form of bacteria can spread very quickly. The problem of reemergence of infectious diseases is linked to indiscriminate use of antibiotics for treating illness in humans and the increasing use of antibiotics in animal feed (Armelagos et al. 1996). As these practices have increased, so have antibiotic-resistant forms of bacteria. This problem has required development of new antibiotics, which in turn lead to new forms of antibiotic resistance.

The problems of emergent and reemergent infectious diseases show us that infectious disease is not gone, and is unlikely ever to be gone. We will always have to deal with infectious disease, but the nature of this threat will change over time as the microorganisms continue to evolve and as we continue to change our environment. The continued struggle against infectious disease will require increased funding, global coordination, and a holistic approach to cultural, environmental, and technological factors affecting the spread of infectious disease (Binder et al. 1999).

Demographic Change

The reduction in death rates and the increase in life expectancy throughout much of the world have an obvious implication in terms of population growth. The natural increase of our species reflects the difference between the rate of births and deaths. If death rates drop but birth rates remain the same, then

FIGURE 15.16

World population growth over the past 2,000 years. Rapid growth began after the eighteenth century. If you look closely, you will see a slight dip in world population size during the fourteenth century corresponding to the Black Death pandemic. (Source of data: Livi-Bacci 1997)

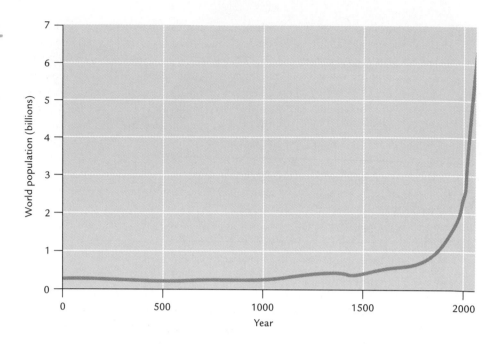

a population will grow in size. This is what happened to our species during the twentieth century, when the world population tripled in size from roughly 2 billion to 6 billion (Figure 15.16).

The Demographic Transition   What led to such high rates of population growth in our species and the variation in growth rates among nations today? As death rates dropped, there was a lag before birth rates also declined, resulting in a time of significant population growth. Observations on these demographic patterns in a number of European countries led to the development of **demographic transition theory.** The utility of this model to explain and predict demographic shifts in all human populations has been questioned (e.g., Cohen 1995), but it does provide a convenient summary of some basic demographic trends.

Demographic transition theory states that as a population becomes more economically developed, a reduction in death rates will take place first, followed by a reduction in fertility rates. Three stages are usually identified in this model (Swedlund and Armelagos 1976). Stage 1 populations are those of undeveloped areas with high mortality and high fertility rates. Because the high number of births is balanced by the high number of deaths, the overall population size remains more or less stable. In Stage 2, the transitional stage, demographic and economic factors are changing rapidly and there is high fertility but lowered mortality. The transition to lowered mortality, especially in childhood, is a consequence of improvements in public health and medical technology. Because fertility rates remain high, there are more births than deaths and the population grows quickly in size. Stage 3 populations have completed the transition with a reduction in fertility rates. Because of technological, social, economic, and education changes, people in the more

demographic transition theory A model of demographic change that states that as a population becomes economically developed, a reduction in death rates (leading to population growth) will take place, followed by a reduction in birth rates.

developed countries have more of a desire and opportunity to control family size and the birth rate declines. Because the rates of both births and deaths are low, such populations tend to show little growth (ignoring migration).

The demographic transition model does describe the experience seen in some of the more developed countries today, but it has a number of problems. Although it serves as a rough description of the types of changes that tend to take place as populations become more economically developed, there is considerable variation in the timing of these events, with some populations having less of a lag between falling death rates and falling birth rates than others. The model is less accurate in predicting the timing of fertility declines, and the assumption that economic development must occur before a decline in mortality rate does not fit all cases (Cohen 1995). There are also cases of the basic trends reversing, such as in the United States in the twentieth century, when fertility rates declined at first and then increased rapidly for a short time following World War II before falling again.

World Population Growth   Today there is a wide range of variation in the rate of population growth. In 2001, the world numbered more than 6.1 billion people and had a rate of natural increase of 1.3 percent per year. At this rate, the world's population would double in slightly more than 50 years. The more developed countries make up roughly 19 percent of the world's population and have low birth and death rates. Estimates made in mid-2001 show a very low annual rate of natural increase (births minus deaths) of 0.1 percent and total growth is expected to be only 4 percent by the year 2050. The less developed countries, which currently make up 81 percent of the world's population, have a rate of natural increase of 1.6 percent per year and are expected to increase in total by 58 percent by the year 2050. There is variation within the less developed countries. For example, sub-Saharan Africa has a rate of natural increase of 2.5 percent per year, whereas China has a rate of 0.9 percent per year (Population Reference Bureau 2001). Some countries in Europe are actually declining in size (Bouvier and Bertrand 1999).

There are two critical and interrelated questions regarding the growth of the human species: (1) What will global population size be in the immediate future? and (2) How many people can the planet support? Estimates of future population size are difficult to make because the factors underlying population growth continue to change. If rates were constant, prediction of future numbers would be a simple mathematical exercise. For example, given a world population of 6.1 billion and assuming that the rate of growth observed in mid-2001 remains the same (1.3 percent per year), the expected size of the human species would be 11.5 billion in the year 2050 and 21.9 billion in the year 2100. This estimate would be inaccurate, however, because it assumes that the rate of growth will remain constant and that rates of the underlying components of growth (mortality and fertility) will remain constant. This is not the case; analysis of recent global demographic trends shows that the global rate of population growth is slowing (Lutz et al. 1997). Indeed, the lesson from studies of the epidemiologic and demographic transitions is that such rates have *not* stayed the same in recent times.

The Baby Boom

A classic example of how changing social and economic factors affect population growth is the "Baby Boom" in the history of the United States. At the beginning of the twentieth century, fertility rates in the United States had begun to decline, as expected under a demographic transition. In 1909, the fertility rate (the number of births per 1,000 women of reproductive age, 15–44 years) was 127. By the end of World War II, this number had declined to 85 per 1,000. As shown in the figure, the fertility rate *increased* dramatically after World War II, peaking at 123 in 1957, after which there was a subsequent decline.

This temporary increase in fertility is labeled the Baby Boom, a term for the generation of children born between 1946 and 1964, a period of high fertility relative to prewar years. Several social and economic factors account for the Baby Boom. It was not simply that men returning from the war made up for lost time with their wives. Such an effect often accompanies the end of a war, but the Baby Boom lasted much longer. The economic growth of the United States continued to increase rapidly following World War II. As economic growth increases, so does the demand for labor. This demand is often met by new immigrants in a population. In the United States, however, restrictive laws had reduced the number of immigrants. The pool of available labor was also reduced by the fact that there had been fewer births during the 1920s and 1930s, perhaps in part due to the Great Depression.

Thus, fewer men were available to meet the increased demand. Women tended to be locked out of many occupations because of sex bias. Though it is true that women took the place of men in the workforce during the war, afterward the preference for women to remain at home raising children prevailed.

The relative lack of available labor meant that young men returning from the war often had excellent opportunities for employment. A good income meant that men could afford to marry and raise families earlier than they could under poorer conditions. The economic conditions prevailing after World War II meant that a couple could have several children without lowering their standard of living (Weeks 1981). People married earlier and the spacing between births was shorter than in previous times, both of which contributed to an increase in the birth rate. Of course, not everyone married or had larger families or even shared in economic growth. On average, however, these changes were sufficient to affect the birth rate, and therefore the rate of population growth.

After 1958, the fertility rate in the United States began to decline. By the mid-1960s, the Baby Boom was over. From this point on, changing economic conditions and greater educational and economic opportunities contributed to delayed marriage and childbirth, as well as the desire for smaller families. By the mid-1980s, the fertility rate had dropped to 65 per 1,000 and the average number

Most models of demographic projection attempt to model likely changes in mortality and fertility rates, usually under a range of scenarios that assume the eventual drop of fertility rates to replacement level, but at different rates. The United Nations, for example, projects between 8 billion and 11 billion people by the year 2050, with a midrange estimate of 9.4 billion (Bouvier and Bertrand 1999). To deal with the rapidity and complexity of demographic change, demographers refine these estimates as new data accumulate. Several major changes have occurred just in the past decade, including a noticeable reduction in the fertility rate of China and an increase in mortality due to AIDS in sub-Saharan Africa (Bouvier and Bertrand 1999; U.S. Bureau of the Census 1999).

There seems to be some consensus that world population growth will eventually stabilize, but there is less agreement about when this will occur. Demographers have shifted from giving exact estimates to developing probability-based estimates. Wolfgang Lutz and colleagues (2001) estimate that there is

Changes in fertility rate in the United States from 1909 to 1997. Fertility rate is the number of births per 1,000 women of reproductive age (15–44 years). From the start of the twentieth century, the fertility rate declined until the end of World War II, at which point it increased rapidly to give rise to the Baby Boom. (Source of data: 1909–1959 data from the Centers for Disease Control and Protection Web page: http://www. cdc.gov/nchs/data/t1x0197.pdf; 1960–1997 data from Ventura et al. 1999)

of children per couple was less than replacement (that is, fewer than 2 children per couple). Of course, the United States continues to grow in part because so many women were born during the Baby Boom (and in part due to immigration). Even if the average number of children born per woman is less than 2, the sheer number of women will continue to lead to population growth in the short term. In fact, the total number of births in the United States rose starting in 1977 and peaked in 1990 (Gabriel 1995). This short burst of births is often referred to as the "Baby Boomlet," brought about by the fact that so many of the original Baby Boomers were now in their childbearing years. Thus, the Baby Boom continues to affect fertility levels and population growth a generation later.

an 85 percent chance that the population of the world will stop growing before the end of this century.

The question of global carrying capacity, the number of people that the earth can support, is also complex. An answer must include a number of variables that are difficult at best to estimate, including future economic, political, and technological changes. In addition, we also need to consider these factors in relationship to a desired standard of living; the actual number would be higher if we assume a level of bare subsistence, which is not desirable, as compared with a higher standard of living (Bouvier and Bertrand 1999). Joel Cohen (1995) reviewed the history of answers to the question of global carrying capacity and found a wide range. Most estimates range from 4 billion to 16 billion, although some were as low as 1 billion. Cohen concludes that the range of likely values is dependent primarily on food and water supply. A more recent paper by J. Kenneth Smail (1997) argues that the earth's carrying capacity at an adequate to comfortable standard of living for all is in the

FIGURE 15.17

The age-sex structure of Chad, Africa, in 2000. (Source of data: U.S. Census Bureau International Database Web page: <http://www.census.gov/ipc/www/idbpyr.html>)

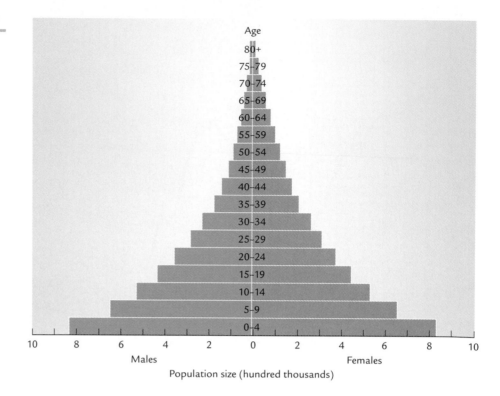

range of 2 billion to 3 billion. The lower estimates cited by Cohen and Smail are particularly troublesome because we have already exceeded them with more than 6 billion humans alive at present. Smail (1997) also notes that this is an issue of primary importance: "Population stabilization and subsequent reduction is the primary issue facing humanity; all other matters are subordinate" (p. 190). World population is a critical variable for humanity's future, and one that requires a coordinated effort across all societies.

Implications of Changing Age Structure   The demographic transition of decreasing mortality and fertility rates affects not only the size of human populations but also their composition. A major effect of a transition is on the age structure of a population. Most demographic studies look at the number of males and females in different age groups in a population—the **age-sex structure** of a population. A device known as a **population pyramid** is the best way to describe a population's age-sex structure at a particular point in time. The population pyramid is a graph showing the actual numbers of both sexes at different age groups, normally at five-year intervals (e.g., 0–4 years of age, 5–9 years of age, and so forth).

The population pyramid looks different for the less developed and more developed countries. Figure 15.17 shows the population pyramid of Chad, a less developed country in Africa. The bottom axis represents the number of males on the left and the number of females on the right. The vertical axis rep-

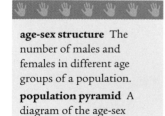

age-sex structure The number of males and females in different age groups of a population.

population pyramid A diagram of the age-sex structure of a population.

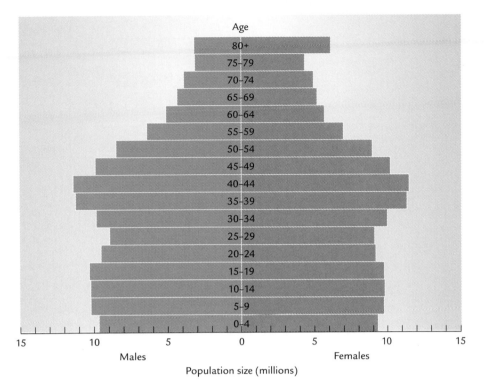

Age

FIGURE 15.18

The age-sex structure of the United States in 2000. (Source of data: U.S. Census Bureau International Database Web page: <http://www.census.gov/ipc/www/idbpyr.html>)

Males   Females

Population size (millions)

resents different age groups, from 0–4 years of age at the bottom to 80+ years of age at the top. The population pyramid has a true pyramid shape, broad on the bottom and tapering to a small point at the top. This picture shows graphically the age structure of the population. The largest segment of the society is infants and young children. The older the age group, the fewer the number of people, trailing to a relative handful after 80 years of age. This shape is characteristic of populations with relatively high birth and death rates. The broad base, corresponding to infants and young children, is a product of high fertility. The other age groups are less numerous because of high death rates, which limits the number of children living to increasingly older ages.

By contrast, Figure 15.18 shows the age-sex structure of the United States, one of the more developed countries. Excepting the oldest age groups, the shape of the graph looks more like a rectangle than a pyramid. This shape is consistent with low birth and death rates. Fewer births mean a decreasing base, and fewer deaths mean less of a decline in numbers with age. Note that there are more females than males among the elderly, reflecting the greater longevity of women. This figure also reflects the demographic history of the United States. There is a noticeable bulge in the graph corresponding to people in their mid-30s to late 40s. This is the Baby Boom generation discussed earlier; children born during the Baby Boom of 1946 to 1964 were between 36 and 54 years of age in the year 2000. As this generation continues to age, this bulge will move upward on the population pyramid.

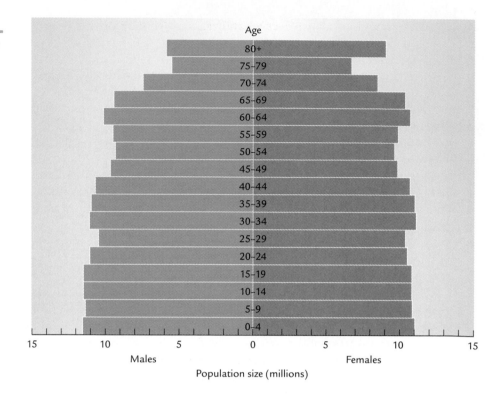

The age structure of a population will change over time depending on birth and death rates of different age groups. By examining current birth and death rates and estimating likely changes in both over the short term, we can estimate the population pyramid for the near future. Figure 15.19 shows the projected population pyramid for the United States in 2025. The shape has become even more rectangular, and most of the Baby Boom generation will be in their 70s.

By comparing Figures 15.17 and 15.18, we can see the impact of different rates of mortality and fertility on the age structure of a population. A decline in both birth and death rates results in an aging population. As fewer people are born and as people live longer, the population pyramid of the more developed nations will continue to resemble a rectangle. The median age of Chad is 16 years, meaning that half of the population is less than this age, and only 3 percent of the population is 65 years or older. By comparison, the median age of the United States is 36 years, and 13 percent of the population is 65 or older. By the year 2025, this figure is expected to increase to 19 percent.

We can expect many cultural changes to accompany such a shift to an older population. Many of these shifts are apparent today in the United States. For example, if we assume current average ages for retirement, it is clear that there will be fewer people of working age in the future. Such a shift might be seen as having both advantages and disadvantages. A smaller labor pool might mean better economic opportunities for working-age people. On the other hand, we may also expect greater taxation to help provide for the well-being of the retired portion of the population.

Many questions are being asked by those concerned with social and economic shifts. For example, how well will our Social Security system function when more people are drawing from it? What changes need to be made in the insurance industries? How can we provide adequate health and other care to an aging population?

Economic shifts can also be examined. Perhaps one of the best examples of the effects of changing age structure is in our system of higher education. During the 1960s and early 1970s, as more and more Baby Boom children reached college age, the demand for colleges and universities increased. This demand was accompanied by an increased desire for a college education, in part because of a changing economy and the value of a college degree in earning potential. As college enrollments increased, more schools were built, and more faculty and staff were hired. By the mid-1970s, the effects of the Baby Boom were over and enrollments began to diminish at many institutions. How, then, can we afford to maintain our colleges? Increases in tuition and taxes are remedies, but they are generally not very popular. Should schools be closed? If so, what happens to the local economies, which are often highly dependent on these schools? What about the future? If we cut back on programs now, will we need to start them up again in a few years?

These questions have no easy answers. Awareness of the problems and their connections to a variety of economic, social, and political factors is a start in the right direction. Today's world is marked by an unusually high level of rapid change. A society's successful integration of demographic change requires analysis of current trends and, above all, a basic acknowledgment that, for good or ill, these changes are indeed taking place.

SUMMARY

The evolution of the human species continues through the present day. Although biological change continues in human populations, the rate of such change is most often exceeded by the rapid rate of cultural change. During the past 12,000 years, the human species has changed from hunting and gathering to agriculture to feed itself, and the total size of the human species has increased roughly a thousandfold. These rapid cultural changes have affected aspects of human biology by affecting our patterns of health, physical growth, nutrition, mortality, and fertility, among other factors. The transition to agriculture was a major change in human adaptation, and the domestication of plants and animals provided the opportunity to maintain much larger populations, which in turn allowed the development of complex state-level societies. Larger sedentary populations led to many epidemics of infectious disease. Although more food could be produced, many people in early agricultural societies suffered from nutritional stress. Overall, life expectancy did not increase with the origins of agriculture.

The subsequent rise of state-level societies with large urban populations was accompanied by further epidemics and nutritional problems. Exploration, trade, and conquest resulted in contact between cultures that had been isolated previously, resulting in catastrophic epidemics and social upheaval. By the end of the nineteenth century, modernization had begun the epidemiologic transition, where improvements in public health and civil engineering, later supplemented by improvements in medical science, led to a reduction in deaths from infectious diseases and a dramatic increase in life expectancy at birth.

As people lived longer on average, the death rate due to noninfectious degenerative diseases increased. In the more developed countries, children mature faster and grow larger because of changes in disease and diet. In recent decades, evidence has shown a resurgence in infectious diseases, in part due to the evolution of new diseases and in part due to the reemergence of diseases as microorganisms evolve resistance to antibiotics. The world's population tripled in size during the twentieth century as death rates declined. Many populations have since seen a reduction in fertility rates, such that the rate of population growth has declined somewhat. Even given this trend, most projections suggest a global population of roughly 9 billion by the middle of the twenty-first century. Another consequence of recent demographic change is the changing age structure of the more developed countries. As birth rates decline and people live longer, populations become older on average. All of these demographic changes are interrelated with many contemporary social, economic, and political problems.

SUPPLEMENTAL READINGS

Bouvier, L. F., and J. T. Bertrand. 1999. *World Population: Challenges for the 21st Century*. Santa Ana, Calif.: Seven Locks Press. A thorough discussion of contemporary demographic trends focusing on social, political, and economic responses to world population growth.

Cohen, J. E. 1995. *How Many People Can the Earth Support?* New York: W. W. Norton. A comprehensive and fascinating discussion of the demographic history of the human species, population projection, and the question of global carrying capacity.

Howell, N. 2000. *Demography of the Dobe !Kung*, 2d ed. New York: Aldine de Gruyter. An extensive description of the demography of a hunting-gathering society focusing on mortality and fertility.

Larsen, C. S. 2000. *Skeletons in Our Closet: Revealing our Past through Bioarchaeology*. Princeton: Princeton University Press. A detailed survey of the field of paleopathology and what it can tell us about disease and life in prehistoric times, focusing on the transition to agriculture and culture contact among prehistoric Native Americans.

INTERNET RESOURCES

http://www.cdc.gov
Centers for Disease Control and Prevention (CDC), the main Web page of this government organization, which includes a wide range of statistical data and other information on health and disease in the United States.

http://www.who.int/disease-outbreak-news
Disease Outbreak News, containing up-to-date news about recent outbreaks of infectious diseases around the world.

http://www.who.int/home-page
World Health Organization, the main Web page of this international organization, which includes a wide range of statistical data and other information on health and disease worldwide.

http://www.census.gov
U.S. Census Bureau, the official Web page of the United State Bureau of the Census, containing a wealth of demographic data on the United States. This site also includes links to an international database.

http://www.prb.org
Population Reference Bureau, containing comparative data from around the world on health, disease, and demography.

The Future of Our Species

This book has focused on human biological variation and evolution, past and present. What about the future? Can biological anthropology, or indeed any science, make predictions about the future of our species? What possible directions will our biological and cultural evolution take?

One thing is certain—we continue to evolve both biologically and culturally and will do so in the future. Human evolution is increasingly complex because of our biocultural nature. Much of our adaptive nature is culturally based. We can adapt to a situation more quickly through cultural evolution than through biological evolution. Theoretically, we can also direct our cultural evolution. We can focus our efforts on solutions to specific problems, such as finding a vaccine for AIDS or developing ways to further reduce dental decay. Biological evolution, however, has no inherent direction. Natural selection works on existing variation, not on what we might desire or need.

Our success with cultural adaptations should not lead us to conclude that we do not continue to evolve biologically. Regardless of our triumphs in the field of medicine, many incurable diseases still carry on the process of natural selection. Biological variation still takes place in potential and realized fertility. Perhaps as many as a third to half of all human conceptions fail to produce live births. We still live in a world in which up to 50 percent of the children have an inadequate diet. Even if all inhabitants of the world were raised to an adequate standard of living tomorrow, we would still be subject to natural selection and biological evolution. The fact that we are cultural organisms does not detract from the fact that we are also biological organisms. Scholars in various fields throughout history have argued about whether humans and human behavior should be studied biologically, as products of nature, or culturally, as products of nurture. Both sides were wrong. Humans must be studied as *both* biological and cultural organisms.

Given that we will continue to evolve, *how* will we evolve? This question cannot be answered. Evolution has many random elements that cannot be predicted. Also, the biocultural nature of humans makes prediction even harder. The incredible rate of cultural and technological change in the past century was not predicted. What kinds of cultural evolution are possible in the next hundred years? We may be able to forecast some short-term changes, but we know nothing about the cultural capabilities of our species hundreds or thousands of years in the future.

Another problem is that our own viewpoint can influence our predictions. An optimistic view might focus on the success of past cultural adaptations and the rate of acquisition of knowledge and then develop a scenario including increased standard of living for all, cheap energy sources, and an elevated life expectancy. A pessimistic view might consider all the horrors of the past and present and project a grim future. A pessimist might envisage widespread famine, overcrowding, pollution, disease, and warfare. Most likely, any possible future will be neither pie-in-the-sky nor doom but a combination of positive and negative changes. If the study of evolution tells us one thing, it is that every change has potential costs and benefits. We need to temper our optimism and pessimism with a sense of balance.

In any consideration of the future, we must acknowledge change as basic to life. Many people find it tempting to suggest we would be better off living a "simpler" life. Others argue that we should stop trying to deal with our problems and let nature take its course or that we should trust in the acts of God. This is unacceptable—indeed our understanding of human evolution argues for the reverse. Our adaptive pattern has been one of learning and problem solving. More than that, this is our primate heritage. Our biology has allowed us to develop the basic mammalian patterns of learned behavior to a high degree. We have the capability for rational thought, for reason, and for learning. Even if many of our cultural inventions have led to suffering and pain, our *potential* for good is immense. In any case, we must continue along the path of learning and intelligence; it is our very nature. Good or bad, the capabilities of the human mind and spirit may be infinite.

APPENDIX 1

Mathematical Population Genetics

Population genetics was discussed in Chapter 3 with a minimum of mathematical formulae. This appendix is intended for those wishing to obtain an elementary understanding of the mathematical basis of population genetics. Additional sources, such as Hartl and Clark (1997), are recommended for further information.

The formulae presented here are limited to a simple genetic case—a single locus with two possible alleles, *A* and *a*. Following convention, the symbol *p* is used to denote the frequency of the *A* allele, and the symbol *q* is used to denote the frequency of the *a* allele. Because there are only two alleles, $p + q = 1$. For this simple case, there are three genotypes: *AA*, *Aa*, and *aa*.

HARDY-WEINBERG EQUILIBRIUM

The Hardy-Weinberg equilibrium model, discussed briefly in Chapter 3, states that: (1) under random mating, the expected genotype frequencies are $AA = p^2$, $Aa = 2pq$, and $aa = q^2$, and (2) under certain conditions, the allele frequencies *p* and *q* will remain constant from one generation to the next.

There are a number of ways to demonstrate the first conclusion of the Hardy-Weinberg model. Perhaps the simplest proof rests on the fact that *p* and *q* represent probabilities. If the frequency of the *A* allele is *p*, then the probability of drawing an *A* allele from the entire gene pool is equal to *p*. To obtain the *AA* genotype in the next generation, it is necessary to have an *A* allele from both parents. Assuming that the allele frequencies are the same in both sexes, the probability of getting an *A* allele from one parent is *p* and the probability of getting an *A* allele from the other parent is also *p*. The probability of *both* these events happening is the product of these probabilities, or $p \times p = p^2$. The same method can be used to determine the probability of getting the *aa* genotype ($q \times q = q^2$).

Getting an *Aa* genotype in the next generation requires one parent contributing the *A* allele (probability = p) and the other parent contributing the *a* allele (probability = q). The joint probability is $p \times q = pq$. It is also possible, however, that the order may be reversed. The first parent could contribute the *a* allele, and the second parent could contribute the *A* allele. The joint probability of this happening is also equal to pq. The overall probability of having the *Aa* genotype is therefore $pq + pq = 2pq$.

The reasoning behind the Hardy-Weinberg model is summarized as follows:

	Allele from Parent		
Genotype of Child	*1*	*2*	*Probability*
AA	*A*	*A*	$p \times p = p^2$
Aa	*A*	*a*	$p \times q = pq$
	or		
	a	*A*	$q \times p = pq$
aa	*a*	*a*	$q \times q = q^2$

$$pq + pq = 2pq$$

Also note that the sum of genotype frequencies ($p^2 + 2pq + q^2$) is equal to 1.

The second part of the Hardy-Weinberg model states that in the absence of evolutionary forces the allele frequencies will remain the same from one generation to the next. This may be easily demonstrated by using the genotype frequencies in a given generation to predict the allele frequencies in the next generations. Allele frequencies are easily derived from genotype frequencies. In the present example, the frequency of allele *A* is computed as the frequency of genotype *AA* plus *half* the frequency of genotype *Aa* (we only wish to count the *A* alleles that make up half the total number of alleles in heterozygotes). The frequency of the *A* allele in the next generation, designated p', is therefore equal to

$$p' = \text{frequency of } AA + (\text{frequency of } Aa/2)$$

which is equal to

$$p' = p^2 + \frac{2pq}{2}$$

The 2s cancel out, giving

$$p' = p^2 + pq$$

Factoring p from the equation gives

$$p' = p(p + q)$$

Now, because the quantity ($p + q$) is equal to 1 by definition, the equation becomes

$$p' = p$$

The fact that the allele frequency in the next generation (p') is equal to the initial allele frequency (p) shows that given certain assumptions there will be no change in the allele frequency over time. Therefore, when we *do* see a change in allele frequency over time, we know that one of the assumptions of the Hardy-Weinberg model has been violated. Because the model assumes no evolution has taken place, the fact that the model does not fit means this assumption is incorrect and, therefore, that a change in allele frequency (evolution) has taken place.

INBREEDING

Inbreeding does not change allele frequencies, but it does change genotype frequencies. The genotype frequencies predicted by Hardy-Weinberg require the assumption that mating is random and that there is no inbreeding. The inbreeding coefficient, F, is a measure of the probability that a homozygous genotype is the result of common ancestry of the parents. For example, the inbreeding coefficient for offspring born to first cousins is $F = 0.0625$. This value indicates the *additional* probability of the child having a homozygous genotype because the parents were first cousins. Inbreeding coefficients are most often computed from genealogical data, although with certain assumptions they may also be estimated from frequencies of last names and from allele frequencies (in certain cases).

At the populational level, there is also a probability of having a homozygous genotype due to random mating (p^2 or q^2, depending on the genotype). Inbreeding increases this probability. Under inbreeding, the genotype frequencies are

AA: $p^2 + pqF$
Aa: $2pq (1 - F)$
aa: $q^2 + pqF$

Thus, inbreeding increases the frequency of homozygotes (*AA* and *aa*) and decreases the frequency of heterozygotes. As an example, consider a population where $p = 0.5$ and $q = 0.5$. Under random mating ($F = 0$), the genotype frequencies are $AA = 0.25$, $Aa = 0.50$, and $aa = 0.25$. If the population had an inbreeding coefficient of $F = 0.05$, these frequencies would be $AA = 0.2625$, $Aa = 0.4750$, and $aa = 0.2625$.

It is easy to see why inbreeding does not change allele frequencies. Given the genotype frequencies expected under inbreeding, we can compute the frequency of the *A* allele in the next generation as

$$p' = \text{frequency of } AA + \left(\text{frequency of } \frac{Aa}{2} \right)$$

Substituting the formulae for *AA* and *Aa* given earlier, this equation becomes

$$p' = p^2 + pqF + \frac{2pq(1 - F)}{2}$$

The 2s in the equation cancel out. When the remaining terms are multiplied out, the equation becomes

$$p' = p^2 + pqF + pq - pqF$$

After subtracting pqF from pqF, the equation then becomes

$$p' = p^2 + pq$$

Factoring the p in the equation gives

$$p' + p(p + q)$$

Because $p + q = 1$, the allele frequency in the next generation is

$$p' = p$$

Thus, the allele frequency does not change from one generation to the next under inbreeding.

MUTATION

Mutation involves the change from one allele into another. For the simple case given here, let us assume that allele a is the mutant form. The mutation rate, usually denoted as u, is the proportion of A alleles that mutates into a alleles in a single generation. The value u therefore represents the probability of any A allele mutating into the a allele. Models also exist to deal with backward mutation (a into A), but these are not presented here because the rate of back mutations is usually very low.

How can mutation change the allele frequency in a population over time? To answer that, assume that mutation is the only force acting to change allele frequencies. The frequency of allele a in the next generation (q') depends on the current frequency of a alleles (q), the frequency of A alleles that have not mutated ($p = 1 - q$), and the rate of mutation (u). The frequency of the a allele in the next generation, q', is therefore equal to

$$q' = q + u(1 - q)$$

The first part of this equation represents the initial frequency of a alleles (q), and the second part represents the expected increase in a alleles due to mutation of A alleles.

As an example, assume that the initial allele frequencies are $p = 1.0$ and $q = 0.0$ and that the mutation rate is $u = 0.0001$. The allele frequencies in the next generation are

$$q' = 0 + 0.0001(1 - 0)$$
$$= 0.0001$$
$$p' = 1 - q' = 0.9999$$

If we carry this to an additional generation, the allele frequencies in the second generation (q' and p') are

$$q'' = 0.0001 + 0.0001(1 - 0.0001)$$
$$= 0.0001 + 0.00009999$$
$$= 0.00019999$$
$$p'' = 1 - q'' = 0.9980001$$

Continued mutation, in the absence of any other evolutionary forces, will lead to an increase in q and a decrease in p. For example, after 50 generations of mutation the allele frequencies in the example here are $p = 0.99501223$ and $q = 0.00498777$.

The mutation model presented here is simplified and does not take into consideration back mutation, changes in mutation rates over time, or any of the other evolutionary forces. It does, however, illustrate how mutation will lead to a cumulative increase in the frequency of the mutant allele. These examples also show that such increases are relatively low, even over many generations. Of course, evolution is not caused only by mutation. Other evolutionary forces act to increase, or decrease, the allele frequencies.

NATURAL SELECTION

Natural selection is modeled mathematically by assigning a fitness value to each genotype. Fitness is defined as the probability that an individual will survive to reproductive age. The actual proportion of individuals surviving is known as *absolute fitness*. Mathematically, the effects of natural selection are easier to model if relative fitness is used; here the absolute fitness values are converted such that the largest relative fitness equals 1.

As an example, consider absolute fitness values of $AA = 0.8$, $Aa = 0.8$, and $aa = 0.4$. These numbers mean that 80 percent of those with the AA genotype survived, 80 percent of those with the Aa genotype survived, and 40 percent of those with the aa genotype survived. Because the largest absolute fitness is 0.8, relative fitness values are obtained by dividing each fitness by 0.8. Thus, the relative fitness values are $AA = 1.0$, $Aa = 1.0$, and $aa = 0.5$. The genotype aa has a fitness value of 0.5 relative to the most fit genotypes (AA and Aa). As another example, consider the following absolute fitness values: $AA = 0.7$, $Aa = 0.9$, and $aa = 0.3$. The relative fitness values are $AA = 0.7/0.9 = 0.778$, $Aa = 0.9/0.9 = 1.0$, and $aa = 0.3/0.9 = 0.333$.

The symbol w is used to designate relative fitness. Here w_{AA} is the relative fitness of genotype AA, w_{Aa} is the relative fitness of genotype Aa, and w_{aa} is the relative fitness of genotype aa. The effect of natural selection can now be determined by looking at the genotype frequencies before and after selection. The genotype frequencies before selection are obtained from the Hardy-Weinberg model: $AA = p^2$, $Aa = 2pq$, and $aa = q^2$. The genotype frequencies after selection are obtained by multiplying the genotype frequencies before selection by the respective relative fitness values. After selection, the genotype frequencies are therefore

$$AA = w_{AA}p^2$$
$$Aa = 2w_{Aa}pq$$
$$aa = w_{aa}q^2$$

The frequency of the A allele after selection is then computed by adding the frequency of genotype AA to half the frequency of genotype Aa and dividing this figure by the sum of all genotype frequencies after selection. That is,

$$p' = (w_{AA}p^2 + (2w_{Aa}pq/2)) / (w_{AA}p^2 + 2w_{Aa}pq + w_{aa}q^2)$$
$$= (w_{AA}p^2 + w_{Aa}pq) / (w_{AA}p^2 + 2w_{Aa}pq + w_{aa}q^2)$$

As an example, consider a population with initial allele frequencies of $p = 0.8$ and $q = 0.2$. Assume relative fitness values for each genotype as $AA = 1.0$, $Aa = 1.0$, and $aa = 0.5$. In this example, there is partial selection against the homozygous genotype aa. Logically, we expect that such selection will lead to a reduction in the frequency of the a allele and an increase in the frequency of the A allele.

Using Hardy-Weinberg, the expected genotype frequencies before selection are

$$AA: p^2 = (0.8)^2 = 0.64$$
$$Aa: 2pq = 2(0.8)(0.2) = 0.32$$
$$aa: q^2 = (0.2)^2 = 0.04$$

Using the relative fitness values, the relative proportion of each genotype after selection is

$$AA: w_{AA}p^2 = (1)(0.8)^2 = 0.64$$
$$Aa: 2w_{Aa}pq = 2(1)(0.8)(0.2) = 0.32$$
$$aa: w_{aa}q^2 = (0.5)(0.2)^2 = 0.02$$

The frequency of the A allele after selection is computed as

$$p' = (0.64 + (0.32/2)) / (0.64 + 0.32 + 0.02)$$
$$= (0.64 + 0.16) / (0.64 + 0.32 + 0.02)$$
$$= 0.8 / 0.98$$
$$= 0.8163$$

Also, the frequency of the a allele after selection is

$$q' = 1 - p' = 0.1837$$

The entire process can be repeated for additional generations. To extend the analysis another generation, use the new values of $p = 0.8163$ and $q = 0.1837$. After an additional generation of selection, the allele frequencies will be $p =$

0.8303 and $q = 0.1697$. If you continue this process, the frequency of A keeps increasing and the frequency of a keeps decreasing.

Some forms of natural selection can be represented using simplified formulae. For example, complete selection against recessive homozygotes involves relative fitness values of $AA = 1.0$, $Aa = 1.0$, and $aa = 0.0$. Given these values, the frequency of the A allele after one generation of selection is

$$
\begin{aligned}
p' &= (w_{AA}p^2 + w_{Aa}pq) / (w_{AA}p^2 + 2w_{Aa}pq + w_{aa}q^2) \\
&= ((1)p^2 + (1)pq) / ((1)p^2 + 2(1)pq + (0)q^2) \\
&= (p^2 + pq) / (p^2 + 2pq) \\
&= (p(p + q)) / (p(p + q + q)) \\
&= (p + q) / (p + q + q) \\
&= 1 / (1 + q) \\
&= 1 / (1 + (1 - p)) \\
&= 1 / (2 - p)
\end{aligned}
$$

which is a much easier formula to work with. Other forms of natural selection also have simplified formulae and are listed in the references given at the beginning of this appendix.

As an example, assume initial frequencies of $p = 0.5$ and $q = 0.5$. The frequency of the A allele in the next five generations of natural selection would be 0.6667, 0.7500, 0.8000, 0.8333, and 0.8571.

GENETIC DRIFT

The process of genetic drift is random. As a result, we cannot predict the exact allele frequencies resulting from a generation of genetic drift. We can, however, describe the probability of obtaining a given allele frequency caused by genetic drift. For example, assume a population of six people (and hence 12 alleles at each locus) with initial allele frequencies of $p = 0.5$ and $q = 0.5$. A generation of genetic drift could result in the frequency of the A allele ranging from $0/12 = 0.0$ to $12/12 = 1.0$. Other possible allele frequency values are $1/12 = 0.083$, $2/12 = 0.167$, $3/12 = 0.250$, $4/12 = 0.333$, $5/12 = 0.417$, $6/12 = 0.500$, $7/12 = 0.583$, $8/12 = 0.667$, $9/12 = 0.750$, $10/12 = 0.833$, $11/12 = 0.917$.

The frequency of the A allele depends on how many A alleles are represented in the next generation (which can range from 0 to 12). Because genetic drift is a random process, we cannot tell how many A alleles will be represented in the next generation. We can, however, compute the probability of each of these events occurring. We would expect, for example, that getting 6 A alleles is more likely than getting 12 A alleles (just as we would expect it to be more likely that we get 6 heads rather than 12 heads or 1 if we flipped a coin 12 times). The exact formula used is a bit complex and is not presented here (see Hartl 1988:70). Using this formula, the probability of getting 6 A alleles in the next generation (and an allele frequency of $6/12 = 0.5$) is 0.223. Therefore, the probability of getting *some* change in the allele frequency (some number *other* than 6 *A* alleles) is $1 - 0.223 = 0.777$. Mathematical investigation also shows that smaller populations are more likely to experience genetic drift than larger populations.

GENE FLOW

The process of gene flow is best described mathematically by considering allele frequencies in two populations, 1 and 2. The allele frequencies of population 1 are denoted p_1 and q_1, and the allele frequencies of population 2 are denoted p_2 and q_2. What happens when gene flow takes place between these two populations? Assume that populations 1 and 2 mix together at rate m. The term m is a measure of the proportion of migrants moving from one population into the other. For simplicity, further assume that the rate of migration from population 1 into population 2 is the same as the rate of migration from population 2 into population 1.

The frequency of the *A* allele in population 1 after one generation of gene flow is then expressed as

$$(1 - m)p_1 + mp_2$$

The first part of the right-hand side of the equation shows the contribution to allele frequency from the proportion of individuals who stayed in population 1 $(1 - m)$. The second part of the right-hand side of the equation shows the contribution to allele frequency caused by the proportion of individuals migrating from population 2 (m). Likewise, the frequency of allele *A* in population 2 after one generation of gene flow is

$$mp_1 + (1 - m)p_2$$

As an example, assume initial allele frequencies in population 1 are $p_1 = 0.7$ and $q_1 = 0.3$ and that initial allele frequencies in population 2 are $p_2 = 0.2$ and $q_2 = 0.8$. Further assume a rate of gene flow of $m = 0.3$. After one generation of gene flow, the frequencies of the *A* allele are

$$(1 - 0.3)(0.7) + (0.3)(0.2) = 0.49 + 0.06 = 0.55$$

for population 1, and

$$(0.3)(0.7) + (1 - 0.3)(0.2) = 0.21 + 0.14 = 0.35$$

for population 2. Thus, the frequency of the *A* allele has made populations 1 and 2 more similar as a result of gene flow. An additional generation of gene flow at the same rate would result in allele frequencies of

$$(1 - 0.3)(0.55) + (0.3)(0.35) = 0.385 + 0.105 = 0.49$$

for population 1, and

$$(0.3)(0.55) + (1 - 0.3)(0.35) = 0.165 + 0.245 = 0.41$$

for population 2. The two populations continue to become more similar genetically. Another generation of gene flow would result in allele frequencies of 0.466 for population 1 and 0.434 for population 2. After only a few more generations of gene flow, the allele frequencies of the two populations would be essentially equal.

Summary

The formulae presented here represent a simplified view of mathematical population genetics. Each model ignores the effects of other evolutionary forces, although they can easily be extended to consider simultaneous effects. These models also deal only with a simple situation of one locus with two alleles. More complicated analyses require more sophisticated mathematical methods that are best performed on a computer. Nonetheless, these formulae do demonstrate the basic nuts and bolts of population genetic theory.

Classification of
Living Primates

The chart that begins on the next page lists representatives of all living primate groups. This classification is fairly "traditional" and was taken from Ciochon and Nisbett (1998), with additional examples of common names from Fleagle (1999). As discussed in Chapter 8, there are alternative classifications, most notably the strepsirhine-haplorhine subdivision (rather than prosimian-anthropoid). There are also alternative classifications of the hominoids that reflect the greater genetic and evolutionary similarity of African apes with humans rather than with the orangutan.

Order: Primates
Suborder: Prosimii

Infraorder	Superfamily	Family	Subfamily	Number of Genera	Number of Species	Common Name(s)
Lemuriformes	Lemuroidea	Daubentoniidae		1	1	Aye-aye
		Indriidae		3	4	Indriid
						Sifaka
		Lemuridae		3	10	Lemur
		Lepilemuridae		1	1	Sportive lemur
	Lorisoidea	Cheirogaleidae		5	7	Dwarf lemur
						Mouse lemur
		Galagidae		4	11	Bush baby
		Lorisidae		4	5	Potto
						Slender loris
						Slow loris
Tarsiiformes	Tarsioidea	Tarsiidae		1	4	Tarsier

Order: Primates
Suborder: Anthropoidea

Infraorder	Superfamily	Family	Subfamily	Number of Genera	Number of Species	Common Name(s)
Platyrrhini	Ceboidea	Atelidae	Atelinae	4	13	Howler monkey
						Spider monkey
			Pitheciinae	3	9	Saki
						Uakari
		Callitrichidae	Callitrichinae	5	22	Marmoset
						Tamarin
		Cebidae	Aotinae	2	4	Owl monkey
						Titi
			Cebinae	2	5	Capuchin
						Squirrel monkey

				Order: Primates		
				Suborder: Anthropoidea		
Infraorder	Superfamily	Family	Subfamily	Number of Genera	Number of Species	Common Name(s)
Catarrhini	Cercopithecoidea	Cercopithecidae	Cercopithecinae	9	53	Baboon Gelada baboon Guenon Macaque Mandrill Mangabey Patas
			Colobinae	9	28	Colobus Langur
	Hominoidea	Hylobatidae		1	9	Gibbon
		Pongidae		3	4	Bonobo Chimpanzee Gorilla Orangutan
		Hominidae		1	1	Human

Conversion Factors

Conversion Factors for Common Measures Used in the Text

To Convert	Into	Multiply By
Centimeters	Inches	0.3937
Cubic centimeters	Cubic inches	0.06102
Cubic inches	Cubic centimeters	16.39
Feet	Meters	0.3048
Grams	Ounces	0.03527
Inches	Centimeters	2.54
Inches	Millimeters	25.4
Kilograms	Pounds	2.205
Kilometers	Miles	0.6214
Kilometers	Yards	1,094
Meters	Feet	3.281
Meters	Yards	1.094
Miles	Kilometers	1.609
Millimeters	Inches	0.03937
Ounces	Grams	28.349527
Pounds	Kilograms	0.4536
Yards	Kilometers	9.144×10^{-4}
Yards	Meters	0.9144

Temperature conversion:
From Celsius to Fahrenheit: $(C° \times 1.8) + 32$
From Fahrenheit to Celsius: $(F° - 32) / 1.8$
Source: Frisancho (1993)

Comparative Primate Skeletal Anatomy

This appendix provides a general background in comparative primate anatomy by showing the skeletons of three primates—a modern human, an ape (gorilla), and an Old World monkey (baboon). In addition to noting the differences between these species, you should also note the similarities, particularly in terms of the homology of the skeletons (see Chapter 8 for a review of the principle of homology).

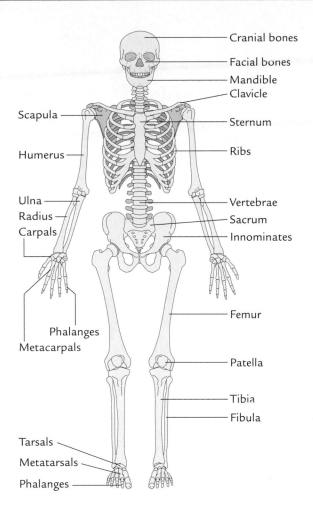

- Cranial bones
- Facial bones
- Mandible
- Clavicle
- Scapula
- Sternum
- Humerus
- Ribs
- Ulna
- Radius
- Carpals
- Vertebrae
- Sacrum
- Innominates
- Phalanges
- Metacarpals
- Femur
- Patella
- Tibia
- Fibula
- Tarsals
- Metatarsals
- Phalanges

FIGURE 1

The human skeleton is made up of 206 bones on average (not all of which are shown here). Of these, 29 bones are found in the crania, 27 are found in each hand, and 26 are found in each foot. Note the homology between the human skeleton and the skeleton of the gorilla (Figure 2) and the baboon (Figure 3). Also note differences in certain anatomical structures, such as the pelvis, that reflect human bipedalism (discussed in Chapter 10).

FIGURE 2

Skeleton of a gorilla, one of the African apes (discussed in Chapter 9) shown in the typical knuckle-walking mode of locomotion. Note the longer arms and shorter legs when compared with the human (Figure 1) and the baboon (Figure 3).

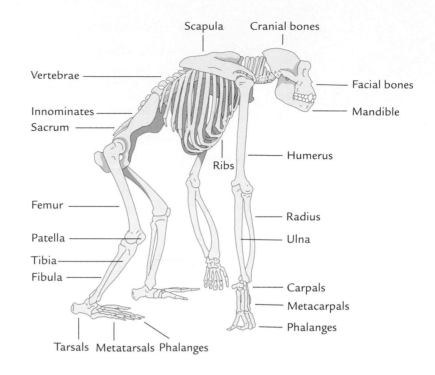

FIGURE 3

Skeleton of a baboon, an Old World monkey, shown in the typical quadrupedal mode of locomotion. Note the similar length of the arms and legs, particularly when compared with the human (Figure 1) and the gorilla (Figure 2).

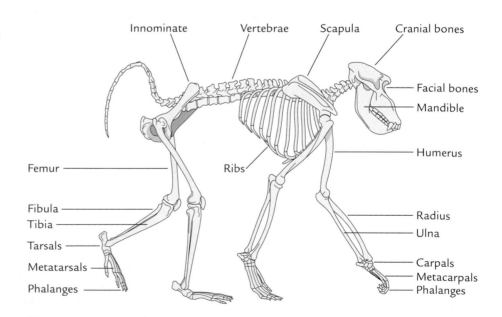

acclimation   Short-term physiologic responses to a stress, usually occurring within minutes or hours.

acclimatization   Long-term physiologic responses to a stress, usually taking from days to months.

Acheulian tradition   A stone tool technology that appears first with *Homo erectus* and is characterized by the development of hand axes and other bifacial tools.

adaptation   The process of successful interaction between a population and an environment. Cultural or biological traits that offer an advantage in a given environment are adaptations.

adaptive radiation   The formation of many new species following the availability of new environments or the development of a new adaptation.

African replacement model   The hypothesis that modern humans evolved as a new species in Africa between 150,000 and 200,000 years ago and then spread throughout the Old World, replacing preexisting archaic human populations.

age at menarche   The age at which a human female experiences her first menstrual period.

age-sex structure   The number of males and females in different age groups of a population.

allele   The alternative form of a gene or DNA sequence that occurs at a given locus. Some loci have only one allele, some have two, and some have many alternative forms. Alleles occur in pairs, one on each chromosome.

Allen's rule   States that mammals in cold climates tend to have shorter and bulkier limbs, allowing less loss of body heat, whereas mammals in hot climates tend to have long, slender limbs, allowing greater loss of body heat.

allometry   The study of the change in proportion of various body parts as a consequence of their growth at different rates.

Alu **insertions**   A sequence of DNA repeated at different locations on different chromosomes.

anagenesis   The transformation of a single species over time.

anatomically modern *Homo sapiens*   The modern form of the human species, which dates back 130,000 years or more.

Anthropoidea (anthropoids)   The suborder of primates consisting of monkeys, apes, and humans.

anthropology   The science that investigates human biological and cultural variation and evolution.

anthropometrics   Measurements of the human body, skull, and face.

antibody   A substance that reacts to other substances invading the body (antigens).

antigen   A substance invading the body that stimulates the production of antibodies.

arboreal   Living in trees.

arboreal model   The view of primate origins that hypothesizes that stereoscopic vision and grasping hands first evolved as adaptations for moving around in the trees.

archaeology   The subfield of anthropology that focuses on cultural variation in prehistoric (and some historic) populations by analyzing the culture's remains.

archaic humans   Specimens of *Homo* with brain size close to that of modern humans but with differently shaped skulls. There is considerable controversy over whether they are an earlier form of *Homo sapiens* or represent different species.

Ardipithecus ramidus   An early primitive hominid species from Africa dating between 5.8 million and 4.4 million years ago.

argon-argon dating   A chronometric dating method based on the half-life of radioactive argon that can be used with very small samples.

assortative mating   Mating between phenotypically similar or dissimilar individuals, for example, between two people with the same hair color.

Australopithecus   A genus of fossil hominid that lived between 4.2 million and 1 million years ago and is characterized by bipedal locomotion, small brain size, large face, and large teeth.

Australopithecus aethiopicus   The oldest robust australopithecine, dating to 2.5 million years ago in East Africa. It combines derived features seen in other robust australopithecines with primitive features seen in *A. afarensis*.

Australopithecus afarensis   A primitive hominid found in East Africa dating between 4 million and 2.9 million years ago. The teeth and postcranial skeleton show a number of primitive and apelike features.

Australopithecus africanus   A species of australopithecine dating between 3.3 million and 2.3 million years ago and found in South Africa. It is not as massive as the robust forms and may be an ancestor of the genus *Homo*.

Australopithecus anamensis   A hominid species that lived in East Africa between 4.2 million and 3.9 million years ago. It was a biped but had many primitive apelike features of the skull and teeth.

Australopithecus boisei   A very robust species of robust australopithecine dating between 2 million and 1.2 million years ago and found in East Africa.

Australopithecus garhi   A species of australopithecine dating to 2.5 million years ago in East Africa. It differs from other australopithecines in having large front and back teeth, although the back teeth are not specialized to the same extent as found in the robust australopithecines.

Australopithecus robustus   A species of robust australopithecine dating between roughly 2 million and 1.5 million years ago and found in South Africa.

balancing selection   Selection for the heterozygote and against the homozygotes (the heterozygote is most fit). Allele frequencies move toward an equilibrium defined by the fitness values of the two homozygotes.

base   Chemical units (adenine, thymine, guanine, cytosine) that make up part of the DNA molecule and specify genetic instructions.

behavioral ecology   The study of behavior from an ecological and evolutionary perspective.

Bergmann's rule   States that (1) among mammals of similar shape, the larger mammal loses heat less rapidly than the smaller mammal and that (2) among mammals of similar size, the mammal with a linear shape will lose heat more rapidly than the mammal with a nonlinear shape.

biface   Stone tool with both sides worked, producing greater symmetry and efficiency.

bilateral symmetry   Symmetry in which the right and left sides of the body are approximately mirror images, a characteristic of vertebrates.

binocular stereoscopic vision   Overlapping fields of vision (binocular), with both sides of the brain receiving images from both eyes (stereoscopic), thereby providing depth perception.

biocultural approach   A method of studying humans that looks at the interaction between biology and culture in evolutionary adaptation.

biological anthropology   The subfield of anthropology that focuses on the biological evolution of humans and human ancestors, the relationship of humans to other organisms, and patterns of biological variation within and among human populations. Also referred to as physical anthropology.

biological species concept   A definition of species that focuses on reproductive capabilities, where organisms from different populations are considered to be in the same species if they naturally interbreed and produce fertile offspring.

biostratigraphy   A relative dating method in which sites can be assigned an approximate age based on the similarity of animal remains with other dated sites.

bipedal   Moving about on two legs. Unlike the movement of other bipedal animals such as kangaroos, human bipedalism is further characterized by a striding motion.

blade   A stone tool characteristic of the Upper Paleolithic, defined as being at least twice as long as it is wide. Blade tools were made using an efficient and precise method.

B.P.   Before Present (1950), the internationally accepted form of designating past dates.

brachiation   A method of movement that uses the arms to swing from branch to branch. Gibbons are brachiators.

breeding population   A group of organisms that tend to choose mates from within the group.

brow ridges   The large ridges of bone above the eye orbits, most noticeable in *Homo erectus* and archaic humans.

burin   A stone tool with a sharp edge that is used to cut and engrave bone.

canine   One of four types of teeth found in mammals. The canine teeth are located in the front of the jaw behind the incisors. Mammals normally use these teeth for puncturing and defense. Unlike most mammals, humans have small canine teeth that function like incisors.

carbon-14 dating   A chronometric dating method based on the half-life of carbon-14 that can be applied to organic remains such as charcoal dating back over the past 50,000 years or so.

carrying capacity   The maximum population size capable of being supported in a given environment.

Cenozoic era   The third and most recent geologic era of the Phanerozoic eon, dating roughly to the past 65 million years. The first primates appeared during the Cenozoic era.

cephalic index   A measure of cranial shape defined as the total length of a skull divided by the maximum width of the skull.

cerebrum   The area of the forebrain that consists of the outermost layer of brain cells. The cerebrum is associated with memory, learning, and intelligence.

Chordata   A vertebrate phylum consisting of organisms that possess a notochord at some period during their life.

chromosome   A long strand of DNA sequences.

chronometric dating   Method of dating fossils or sites that provides an estimate of the specific date (subject to probabilistic limits).

cladistics   A school of thought that stresses evolutionary relationships between organisms in forming biological classifications. Organisms are grouped together on the basis of the number of derived traits they share.

cladogenesis   The formation of one or more new species from another over time.

codominant   Both alleles affect the phenotype of a heterozygous genotype, and neither is dominant over the other.

comparative approach   Comparing human populations to determine common and unique behaviors or biological traits.

continental drift   The movement of continental land masses on top of a partially molten layer of the earth's mantle. Because of continental drift, the relative location of the continents has changed over time.

convergent evolution   Independent evolution of a trait in rather distinct evolutionary lines. The development of flight in birds and certain insects is an example of convergent evolution.

cranial capacity   A measurement of the interior volume of the brain case measured in cubic centimeters (cc) and used as an approximate estimate of brain size.

crossing over   The exchange of DNA between chromosomes during meiosis.

cultural anthropology   The subfield of anthropology that focuses on variations in cultural behaviors among human populations.

culture   Behavior that is shared, learned, and socially transmitted.

cusp   A raised area on the chewing surface of a tooth.

demographic transition theory   A model of demographic change that states that as a population becomes economically developed, a reduction in death rates (leading to population growth) will take place, followed by a reduction in birth rates.

dendrochronology   A chronometric dating method based on the fact that trees in dry climates tend to accumulate one growth ring per year. The width of the rings varies according to climate, and a sample can be compared with a master chart of tree rings over the past 10,000 years.

dental formula   A shorthand method of describing the number of each type of tooth in half of one jaw of a mammal. The dental formula consists of four numbers: I-C-PM-M, where I is the number of incisors, C is the number of canines, PM is the number of premolars, and M is the number of molars. When a mammal has a different number of teeth in the upper and lower jaws, two dental formulae are used.

derived trait   A trait that has changed from an ancestral state. The large human brain is a derived trait relative to the common ancestor of humans and apes.

dermatoglyphics   Measurements of finger and palm prints, including type classification and ridge counts.

developmental acclimatization   Changes in organ or body structure that occur during the physical growth of any organism.

diastema   A gap next to the canine teeth that allows space for the canine on the opposing jaw.

directional selection   Selection against one extreme in a continuous trait and/or selection for the other extreme.

distance curve   A measure of size over time, for example, a person's height at different ages.

diurnal   Active during the day.

DNA (Deoxyribonucleic acid)   The molecule that provides the genetic code for biological structures and the means to translate this code.

dominance hierarchy   The ranking system within a society that indicates which individuals are dominant in social behaviors.

dominant allele   An allele that masks the effect of the other allele (which is recessive) in a heterozygous genotype.

electron spin resonance   A chronometric dating method that estimates dates from observation of radioactive atoms trapped in the calcite crystals present in a number of materials, such as bones and shells. This method is useful for dating sites back to roughly 1 million years.

electrophoresis   A laboratory method that uses electric current to separate proteins, allowing genotypes to be determined.

embryo   The stage of human prenatal life lasting from roughly two to eight weeks following conception, characterized by structural development.

emergent infectious disease   A newly identified infectious disease that has recently evolved.

endemic   A pattern of disease rate when new cases of a disease occur at a relatively constant but low rate over time.

endocast   A cast of the interior of the brain case used in the analysis of brain size and structure.

Eocene epoch   The second epoch of the Cenozoic era, dating roughly between 54 million and 34 million years ago. The first true primates, early prosimians, appeared during this epoch as well as the first anthropoid.

eon   The major subdivision of geologic time.

epidemic   A pattern of disease rate when new cases of a disease spread rapidly through a population.

epidemiologic transition   The increase in life expectancy and the shift from infectious to noninfectious disease as the primary cause of death.

epoch   Subdivision of a geological period.

era   Subdivision of a geological eon.

estrus   A time during the month when females are sexually receptive (also known as "heat"). Among primates, human and orangutan females lack an estrus period.

Eurasia   The combined land masses of Europe and Asia.

evolution   The transformation of species of organic life over long periods of time. Anthropologists study both the cultural and biological evolution of the human species.

evolutionary forces   Four mechanisms that can cause changes in allele frequencies from one generation to the next: mutation, natural selection, genetic drift, and gene flow.

exogamy   The tendency to choose mates from outside the local population.

exon   A section of DNA that codes for the amino acids that make up proteins. It is contrasted with an intron.

fetus   The stage of human prenatal growth from roughly eight weeks following conception until birth, characterized by further development and rapid growth.

fission-track dating   A chronometric dating method based on the number of tracks made across volcanic rock as uranium decays into lead.

fitness   An organism's probability of survival and reproduction. Fitness is generally measured in terms of the different genotypes for a given locus.

foramen magnum   The large opening at the base of the skull where the spinal cord enters, which is located more under the skull in bipeds as compared to four-legged vertebrates.

founder effect   A type of genetic drift caused by the formation of a new population by a small number of individuals. The small size of the sample can cause marked deviations in allele frequencies from the original population.

gene   A DNA sequence that codes for a functional polypeptide or RNA product.

gene flow   A mechanism for evolutionary change resulting from the movement of genes from one population to another. Gene flow introduces new genes into a population and also acts to make populations more similar genetically to one another.

generalized structure   A biological structure adapted to a wide range of conditions and used in very general ways. For example, the grasping hands of humans are generalized structures allowing climbing, food gathering, toolmaking, and a variety of other functions.

genetic distance   An average measure of relatedness between populations based on a number of traits. Genetic distances are used for understanding effects of genetic drift and gene flow, which should affect all loci to the same extent.

genetic distance map   A picture that shows the genetic relationships between populations, based on genetic distance measures.

genetic drift   A mechanism for evolutionary change resulting from the random fluctuations of gene frequencies from one generation to the next, or from any form of random sampling of a larger gene pool.

genome   The total DNA sequence of an organism.

genotype   The genetic endowment of an individual from the two alleles present at a given locus.

genus   Groups of species with similar adaptations.

gradualism   A model of macroevolutionary change whereby evolutionary changes occur at a slow, steady rate over time.

grooming   The handling and cleaning of another individual's fur or hair. In primates, grooming serves as a form of communication that soothes and provides reassurance.

half-life   The average length of time it takes for half of a radioactive substance to decay into another form.

Haplorhini (haplorhines)   One of two suborders of primates suggested to replace the prosimian/anthropoid suborders (the other is the strepsirhines). Haplorhines are primates without a moist nose (tarsiers, monkeys, apes, and humans).

Hardy-Weinberg equilibrium   In the absence of nonrandom mating and evolutionary forces, genotype and allele frequencies will remain the same from one generation to the next.

hemoglobin   The molecule in blood cells that transports oxygen.

heritability   The proportion of total variance in a trait due to genetic variation. This measure is not always the same; the actual value depends on the degree of environmental variation in any population.

heterodontic   Having different types of teeth. Mammals have four different types of teeth: incisors, canines, premolars, and molars.

heterozygous   The two alleles at a given locus are different.

holistic   Refers to the viewpoint that all aspects of existence are interrelated and important in understanding human variation and evolution.

homeobox gene   A group of regulatory genes that encode a sequence of 60 amino acids that regulate embryonic development. Homeobox genes subdivide from head to tail a developing embryo into different regions, which then form limbs and other structures. These genes are similar in many organisms, such as insects, mice, and humans.

homeostasis   In a physiologic sense, the maintenance of normal limits of body functioning.

homeotherm   Organism capable of maintaining a constant body temperature under most circumstances. Mammals are homeotherms.

home range   The size of the geographic area that is normally occupied and used by a social group.

hominid   Humans and humanlike ancestors since the time of divergence from the African apes. Some researchers advocate a somewhat different definition, including the African apes, and use the term "hominin" to refer to humans and their bipedal ancestors.

hominin   Under some taxonomic classifications, this term is used instead of "hominid" to refer to humans and humanlike ancestors.

hominoid   A superfamily of anthropoids consisting of apes and humans. Hominoids have a shoulder structure adapted for climbing and hanging, lack a tail, are generally larger than monkeys, and have the largest brain to body size ratio among primates.

Homo   A genus of hominids characterized by large brain size and dependence on culture as a means of adaptation.

homodontic   All teeth are the same.

Homo erectus   A species of genus *Homo* that arose 2 million years ago, first appearing in Africa and then spreading to parts of Asia and Europe.

Homo habilis   A species of early *Homo* from Africa between 2 million and 1.5 million years ago with a brain size roughly half that of modern humans and a primitive postcranial skeleton.

homology   Similarity due to descent from a common ancestor.

homoplasy   Similarity due to independent evolution.

Homo rudolfensis   A species of early *Homo* from Africa roughly 2 million years ago with a brain size somewhat larger than *H. habilis*.

homozygous   Both alleles at a given locus are identical.

horticulture   A form of farming in which only simple hand tools are used.

hypothesis   An explanation of observed facts. To be scientific, a hypothesis must be testable.

hypoxia   Oxygen starvation, which occurs frequently at high altitudes.

inbreeding   Mating between biologically related individuals.

incisor   One of four types of teeth found in mammals. The incisors are the chisel-shaped front teeth used for cutting, slicing, and gnawing food.

infanticide   The killing of infants.

infectious disease   A disease caused by the introduction of an organic foreign substance into the body. Such substances include viruses and parasites.

insectivore   An order of mammals adapted to insect eating.

intelligent design creationism   The idea that the biological world was created by an intelligent entity and did not arise from natural processes.

intron   A section of DNA that does not code for the amino acids that make up proteins. It is contrasted with an exon.

Kenyanthropus platyops   A species of early hominid in East Africa dating to 3.5 million years ago. This species combines a number of primitive features (small brain, jutting face) and derived features (small molars, flat face). Its evolutionary status is unclear.

kin selection   A concept used in sociobiological explanations of altruism. Sacrificial behaviors, for example, can be selected for if they increase the probability of survival of close relatives.

knuckle walking   A form of movement used by chimpanzees and gorillas that is characterized by all four limbs touching the ground, with the weight of the arms resting on the knuckles of the hands.

kwashiorkor   An extreme form of protein-calorie malnutrition resulting from a severe deficiency in proteins but not calories.

lactase persistence   The ability to produce the enzyme lactase after 5 years of age.

lactose intolerance   A condition characterized by diarrhea, cramps, and other intestinal problems resulting from the ingestion of milk.

larynx   Part of the vocal anatomy in the throat.

lemur   A prosimian found today on the island of Madagascar. Lemurs include both nocturnal and diurnal species.

life expectancy at birth   A measure of the average length of life for a newborn child.

life table   A compilation of the age distribution of a population that provides an estimate of the probability that an individual will die by a certain age, used to compute life expectancy.

linguistic anthropology   The subfield of anthropology that focuses on the nature of human language, the relationship of language to culture, and the languages of nonliterate peoples.

linkage   Alleles on the same chromosome are inherited together.

locus   The specific location of a gene or DNA sequence on a chromosome.

loris   Nocturnal prosimian found today in Asia and Africa.

Lower Paleolithic   The Lower Old Stone Age, a general term used to refer collectively to the stone tool technologies of *Homo habilis/Homo rudolfensis* and *Homo erectus*.

macroevolution   Long-term evolutionary change. The study of macroevolution focuses on biological evolution over many generations and on the origin of higher taxonomic categories, such as species.

major genes   Genes that have the primary effect on the phenotypic distribution of a complex trait. Additional variation can be due to smaller effects from other loci and/or environmental influences.

malnutrition   Poor nutrition, either from two much or too little food or the improper balance of nutrients.

marasmus   An extreme form of protein-calorie malnutrition resulting from severe deficiencies in both proteins and calories.

mass extinction   Many species becoming extinct at about the same time.

meiosis   The creation of sex cells by replication of chromosomes followed by cell division. Each sex cell contains 50 percent of an individual's chromosomes (one from each pair).

Mendelian genetics   The branch of genetics concerned with patterns and processes of inheritance. This field was named after Gregor Mendel, the first scientist to work out many of these principles.

Mendel's Law of Independent Assortment   The segregation of any pair of chromosomes does not affect the probability of segregation for other pairs of chromosomes.

Mendel's Law of Segregation   Sex cells contain one of each pair of alleles.

menopause   The permanent cessation of menstrual cycles.

Mesozoic era   The second geologic era of the Phanerozoic eon, dating roughly between 245 million and 65 million years ago, when the first mammals and birds appeared.

messenger RNA   The form of RNA that transports the genetic instructions from the DNA molecule to the site of protein synthesis.

microevolution   Short-term evolutionary change. The study of microevolution focuses on changes in allele frequencies from one generation to the next.

microsatellite DNA   Repeated short sequences of DNA; the number of repeats is highly variable.

Middle Paleolithic   The Middle Old Stone Age, a general term used to refer collectively to the stone tool technologies of archaic humans.

Miocene epoch The fourth epoch of the Cenozoic era, dating between 23 million and 5 million years ago. The first apes evolved during the Miocene. The first hominids are dated to the Late Miocene.

mitochondrial DNA A small amount of DNA that is located in the mitochondria of cells. Mitochondrial DNA is inherited only through the mother.

mitosis The process of replication of chromosomes in body cells. Each cell produces two identical copies.

molar One of four types of teeth found in mammals. The molars are back teeth used for crushing and grinding food.

molecular dating The application of methods of genetic analysis to estimate the sequence and timing of divergent evolutionary lines.

monogamous family group Social structure in which the primary social group consists of an adult male, an adult female, and their immature offspring.

monogamy An exclusive sexual bond between an adult male and an adult female for a long period of time.

monosomy A condition in which one chromosome rather than a pair is present in body cells.

morphology The physical structure of organisms.

Mousterian tradition The prepared-core stone tool technology of the Neandertals.

multimale/multifemale group A type of social structure in which the primary social group is made up of several adult males, several adult females, and their offspring.

multiregional evolution model The hypothesis that modern humans evolved throughout the Old World as a single species after the first dispersion of *Homo erectus* out of Africa. According to this view, the transition from *Homo erectus* to archaic humans to modern *Homo sapiens* occurred within a single evolutionary line throughout the Old World.

multivariate analysis The analysis of human biological variation that considers the interrelationships of several traits at a time.

mutation A mechanism for evolutionary change resulting from a random change in the genetic code; the ultimate source of all genetic variation. Mutations must occur in sex cells to cause evolutionary change.

nasal index A measure of the shape of the nasal opening, defined as the width of the nasal opening divided by the height.

natural increase Number of births minus the number of deaths.

natural selection A mechanism for evolutionary change favoring the survival and reproduction of some organisms over others because of their biological characteristics.

Neandertals A population of archaic humans that lived in Europe and the Middle East dating between 150,000 and 28,000 years ago.

nocturnal Active during the night.

noninfectious disease A disease caused by factors other than the introduction of an organic foreign substance into the body.

nonrandom mating Patterns of mate choice that influence the distributions of genotype and phenotype frequencies. Nonrandom mating does not lead to changes in allele frequencies.

notochord A flexible internal rod that runs along the back of an animal. Animals possessing a notochord at some period in their life are known as chordates.

occipital bun The protruding rear region of the skull, a feature commonly found in Neandertals.

odontometrics Measurements of the size of teeth.

Oldowan tradition The oldest known stone tool culture.

Oligocene epoch The third epoch of the Cenozoic era, dating roughly between 34 million and 23 million years ago, when there was an adaptive radiation of anthropoids.

Orrorin tugenensis An early primitive, possibly hominid, species from Africa dating to the late Miocene (6 Ma).

orthogenesis A discredited idea that evolution would continue in a given direction because of some vaguely defined "force."

outgroup A group used for comparison in cladistic analyses to determine whether the ancestral state of a trait is primitive or derived.

Paleocene epoch The first epoch of the Cenozoic era, dating roughly between 65 million and 54 million years ago. The primate-like mammals lived during the Paleocene.

paleoecology The study of ancient environments.

paleomagnetic reversal A method of dating sites based on the fact that the earth's magnetic field has shifted back and forth from the north to the south in the past at irregular intervals.

paleopathology The study of disease in prehistoric populations based on analysis of skeletal remains and archaeological evidence.

paleospecies   Species identified from fossil remains based on their physical similarities and differences relative to other species.

Paleozoic era   The first geologic era of the Phanerozoic eon, dating roughly between 545 million and 245 million years ago, when the first vertebrates appeared.

palynology   The study of fossil pollen. Palynology allows prehistoric plant species to be identified.

pandemic   A widespread epidemic that affects a large geographic area, such as a continent.

parallel evolution   Independent evolution of a trait in closely related species. One example might be the parallel development of large back teeth in several hominid species.

parental investment   A concept used in sociobiological models that describes parental behaviors that increase the probability that offspring will survive.

period   Subdivision of a geologic era.

Phanerozoic eon   The past 545 million years.

phenetics   A school of thought that stresses the overall physical similarities among organisms in forming biological classifications.

phenotype   The observable appearance of a given genotype in the organism. The phenotype is determined by the relationship of the two alleles at a given locus, the number of loci, and often environmental influences as well.

placenta   An organ that develops inside a pregnant placental mammal that provides the fetus with oxygen and food and helps filter out harmful substances.

plasticity   The ability of an organism to respond physiologically or developmentally to environmental stress.

pleiotropy   A single allele that has multiple effects on an organism.

Pleistocene epoch   The sixth epoch of the Cenozoic era, dating from 1.7 million to 0.01 million years ago.

Pliocene epoch   The fifth epoch of the Cenozoic era, dating from 5 million to 1.7 million years ago.

polyandrous group   A rare type of primate social structure, consisting of a small number of adult males, one reproductively active adult female, and their offspring. Other adult females may belong to the group but are not reproductively active.

polyandry   In humans, a form of marriage in which a wife has several husbands. In more general terms, it refers to an adult female having several mates.

polygamy   A sexual bond between an adult male and an adult female in which either individual may have more than one mate at the same time.

polygenic   A complex genetic trait affected by two or more loci.

polygyny   In humans, a form of marriage in which a husband has several wives. In more general terms, it refers to an adult male having several mates.

polymorphism   A discrete genetic trait in which there are at least two alleles at a locus having frequencies greater than 0.01.

population pyramid   A diagram of the age-sex structure of a population.

postcranial   Referring to that part of the skeleton below the skull.

postnatal   The period of life from birth until death.

postorbital bar   The bony ring that separates the eye orbit from the back of the skull. The postorbital bar is a primate characteristic.

postorbital constriction   The narrowness of the skull behind the eye orbits, a characteristic of early hominids.

potassium-argon dating   A chronometric dating method based on the half-life of radioactive potassium (which decays into argon gas) that can be used to date volcanic rock older than 100,000 years.

Precambrian eon   The eon from the earth's beginning (4.6 billion years ago) until 545 million years ago. During this eon, single-celled and simple multicelled organisms first evolved.

prehensile   Capable of grasping. Primates have prehensile hands and feet, and some primates (certain New World monkeys) have prehensile tails.

premolar   One of four types of teeth found in mammals. The premolars are back teeth used for crushing and grinding food.

prenatal   The period of life from conception until birth.

prepared-core method   An efficient method of stone tool manufacture in which a stone core is prepared and then finished tools are removed from it.

primary African origin model   A variant of the multiregional evolution model of the origin of modern humans that suggests most of the transition from archaic to modern humans took place first in Africa and then spread by gene flow throughout the rest of the species across the Old World.

primates   The order of mammals that has a complex of characteristics related to an initial adaptation to life in the trees, including binocular stereoscopic vision and grasping hands. The primates include prosimians, monkeys, apes, and humans.

primitive trait   In biological terms, a trait that has not changed from an ancestral state. The five digits of the human hand and foot are primitive traits inherited from earlier vertebrate ancestors.

Proconsul A genus of fossil hominoid that lived in Africa between 23 million and 17 million years ago. Though classified as apes, this genus also shows a number of monkey characteristics. It most probably represents one of the first forms to evolve following the divergence of the monkey and ape lines.

Prosimii (prosimians) The suborder of primates that are biologically primitive compared to anthropoids.

protein-calorie malnutrition A group of nutritional diseases resulting from inadequate amounts of protein and/or calories. Protein-calorie malnutrition is a severe problem in less developed countries today.

punctuated equilibrium A model of macroevolutionary change in which long periods of little evolutionary change (stasis) are followed by relatively short periods of rapid evolutionary change.

quadrupedal A form of movement in which all four limbs are of equal size and make contact with the ground, and the spine is roughly parallel to the ground. Monkeys are typical quadrupedal primates.

race A group of populations sharing certain biological traits that make them distinct from other groups of populations. In practice, the concept of race is very difficult to apply to patterns of human variation.

recessive allele An allele whose effect is masked by the other allele (which is dominant) in a heterozygous genotype.

recombination The production of new combinations of DNA sequences caused by exchanges of DNA during meiosis.

regional coalescence model A variant of the multiregional evolution model of the origin of modern humans that suggests the transition from archaic to modern humans resulted from the coalescence of genetic and anatomic changes that took place in different places at different times, all mixing together to produce modern humans.

regional continuity The appearance of similar traits within a geographic region that remain over a long period of time.

regulatory gene Gene that codes for the regulation of biological processes such as growth and development.

relative dating Comparative method of dating fossils and sites that provides an estimate of the older find but not a specific date.

remergent infectious disease Infectious disease that had previously been reduced but that increases in frequency when microorganisms evolve resistance to antibiotics.

reproductive isolation The genetic isolation of populations that may render them incapable of producing fertile offspring.

restriction fragment length polymorphism (RFLP) A genetic trait defined in terms of the length of DNA fragments produced when certain enzymes cut the DNA sequence.

Rhesus incompatibility A condition in which a pregnant woman and her fetus have incompatible Rhesus blood group phenotypes.

RNA (Ribonucleic acid) The molecule that functions to carry out the instructions for protein synthesis specified by the DNA molecule.

robust australopithecines Species of *Australopithecus* that had very large back teeth, cheekbones, and faces, among other anatomical adaptations to heavy chewing. They lived in Africa between 2.5 million and 1.2 million years ago. Three species are generally recognized: *A. aethiopicus, A. robustus,* and *A. boisei.* Some anthropologists suggest that they be given their own genus name—*Paranthropus.*

sagittal crest A ridge of bone running down the center of the top of the skull that serves to anchor chewing muscles.

savanna An environment consisting of open grasslands in which food resources tend to be spread out over large areas.

secular change A change in the average pattern of growth or development in a population over several generations.

sedentary Settled in one place throughout most or all of the year.

sexual dimorphism The average difference in body size between adult males and adult females. Primate species with sexual dimorphism in body size are characterized by adult males being, on average, larger than adult females.

sickle cell allele An allele of the hemoglobin locus. Individuals homozygous for this allele have sickle cell anemia.

sickle cell anemia A genetic disease that occurs in a person homozygous for the sickle cell allele, which alters the structure of red blood cells.

single-nucleotide polymorphisms (SNPs) Specific positions in a DNA sequence that differ at one base. For example, the DNA sequences CCTGAA and CCCGAA differ in the third position—one sequence has the base T and the other the base C.

social structure   The composition of a social group and the way it is organized, including size, age structure, and number of each sex in the group.

sociobiology   The study of behavior from an evolutionary perspective, particularly the role of natural selection.

solitary group   The smallest primate social group, consisting of the mother and her dependent offspring.

specialized structure   A biological structure adapted to a narrow range of conditions and used in very specific ways. For example, the hooves of horses are specialized structures allowing movement over flat terrain.

speciation   The origin of a new species.

species   A group of populations whose members can interbreed naturally and produce fertile offspring.

stabilizing selection   Selection against extreme values, large or small, in a continuous trait.

stratigraphy   A relative dating method based on the fact that older remains are found deeper in the earth (under the right conditions). This method makes use of the fact that a cumulative buildup of the earth's surface takes place over time.

Strepsirhini (strepsirhines)   One of two suborders of primates suggested to replace the prosimian/anthropoid suborders (the other is the haplorhines). Strepsirhines are primates that have a moist nose (lemurs and lorises).

stress   Any factor that interferes with the normal limits of operation of an organism.

suspensory climbing   The ability to raise the arms above the head and hang on branches and to climb in this position. Hominoids are suspensory climbers.

taphonomy   The study of what happens to plants and animals after they die. Taphonomy helps in determining reasons for the distribution and condition of fossils.

tarsier   Nocturnal prosimian found today in Indonesia. Unlike other prosimians, tarsiers lack a moist nose.

taxonomy   The science of describing and classifying organisms.

terrestrial   Living on the ground.

territory   A home range that is actively defended.

theistic evolution   The belief that God operates through the natural process of evolution.

theory   A set of hypotheses that have been tested repeatedly and that have not been rejected. This term is sometimes used in a different sense in social science literature.

therapsid   An early group of mammal-like reptiles; therapsids were the ancestors of later mammals.

thermoluminescence   A chronometric dating method that uses the fact that certain heated objects accumulate trapped electrons over time, which allows the date when the object was initially heated to be determined.

transfer RNA   A free-floating molecule that is attracted to a strand of messenger RNA, resulting in the synthesis of a protein chain.

trephination   Surgery involving the removal of a section of bone from the skull.

trisomy   A condition in which three chromosomes rather than a pair occur. Down syndrome is caused by trisomy by the addition of an extra chromosome to the 21st chromosome pair.

uni-male group   Social structure in which the primary social group consists of a single adult male, several adult females, and their offspring.

univariate analysis   The analysis of human biological variation focusing on a single trait at a time.

Upper Paleolithic   The Upper Old Stone Age, a general term used to collectively refer to the stone tool technologies of anatomically modern *Homo sapiens*.

variation   The differences that exist among individuals or populations. Anthropologists study both cultural and biological variation.

vasoconstriction   The narrowing of blood vessels, which reduces blood flow and heat loss.

vasodilation   The opening of the blood vessels, which increases blood flow and heat loss.

velocity curve   A measure of the rates of change in growth over time.

Vertebrata   A subphylum of the phylum Chordata, defined by the presence of an internal, segmented spinal column and bilateral symmetry.

visual predation model   The view of primate origins that hypothesizes that stereoscopic vision and grasping hands first evolved as adaptations for hunting insects along branches.

zoonose   A disease transmitted directly to humans from other animals.

zygomatic arch   The cheekbone, formed by the connection of the zygomatic and temporal bones on the side of the skull.

zygote   A fertilized egg.

Abbate, E., A. Albianelli, A. Azzaroli, M. Benvenuti, B. Tesfa-mariam, P. Bruni, N. Cipriani, R. J. Clarke, G. Ficcarelli, R. Macchiarelli, G. Napoleone, M. Papini, L. Rook, M. Sagri, T. M. Tecle, D. Torre, and I. Villa. 1998. A one-million-year old *Homo* cranium from the Danakil (Afar) depression of Eritrea. *Nature* 393:458–60.

Adcock, G. J., E. S. Dennis, S. Easteal, G. A. Huttley, L. S. Jermiin, W. J. Peacock, and A. Thorne. 2001. Mitochondrial DNA sequences in ancient Australians: Implications for modern human origins. *Proceedings of the National Academy of Sciences, USA* 98:537–42.

Aiello, L. C., and M. Collard. 2001. Our newest oldest ancestor? *Nature* 410:526–27.

Aiello, L. L., and R. Dunbar. 1993. Neocortex size, group size, and the evolution of language. *Current Anthropology* 34:184–93.

Allen, J. S., and S. M. Cheer. 1996. The non-thrifty genotype. *Current Anthropology* 37:831–42.

Ambrose, S. H. 2001. Paleolithic technology and human evolution. *Science* 291:1748–53.

Anderson, C. M. 1992. Male investment under changing conditions among Chacma baboons at Suikerbosrand. *American Journal of Physical Anthropology* 87:479–96.

Anderson, R. N. 1998. United States abridged life tables, 1996. *National Vital Statistics Reports,* vol. 47, no. 13. National Center for Health Statistics, Centers for Disease Control and Prevention.

Arensberg, B., L. A. Schepartz, A. M. Tillier, B. Vandermeersch, and Y. Rak. 1990. A reappraisal of the anatomical basis for speech in Middle Paleolithic hominids. *American Journal of Physical Anthropology* 83:137–46.

Armelagos, G. J., K. C. Barnes, and J. Lin. 1996. Disease in human evolution: The re-emergence of infectious disease in the third epidemiologic transition. *AnthroNotes, National Museum of Natural History Bulletin for Teachers,* vol. 18, no. 3 (Fall 1996). Washington: Smithsonian Institution.

Armelagos, G. J., and J. R. Dewey. 1970. Evolutionary response to human infectious diseases. *BioScience* 157:638–44.

Armstrong, E. 1983. Relative brain size and metabolism in mammals. *Science* 220:1302–4.

Asfaw, B., T. White, O. Lovejoy, B. Latimer, S. Simpson, and G. Suwa. 1999. *Australopithecus garhi:* A new species of early hominid from Ethiopia. *Science* 284:629–35.

Backwell, L. R., and F. d'Errico. 2001. Evidence of termite foraging by Swartkrans early hominids. *Proceedings of the National Academy of Sciences, USA* 98:1358–63.

Baker, B. J., and G. J. Armelagos. 1988. The origin and antiquity of syphilis: Paleopathological diagnosis and interpretation. *Current Anthropology* 29:703–37.

Barbujani, G., A. Magagni, E. Minch, and L. L. Cavalli-Sforza. 1997. An apportionment of human DNA diversity. *Proceedings of the National Academy of Sciences, USA* 94:4516–19.

Bartlett, T. Q., R. W. Sussman, and J. M. Cheverud. 1993. Infant killing in primates: A review of observed cases with specific reference to the sexual selection hypothesis. *American Anthropologist* 95:958–90.

BBC News. 2001. Scientists solve Iceman mystery. Sci/Tech (July 26). Available on the Internet at: http://news.bbc.co.uk/hi/english/sci/tech/newsid_1458000/1458198.stm.

Beall, C. M., J. Blangero, S. Williams-Blangero, and M. C. Goldstein. 1994. Major gene for percent of oxygen saturation of arterial hemoglobin in Tibetan highlanders. *American Journal of Physical Anthropology* 95:271–76.

Beall, C. M., and A. T. Steegmann Jr. 2000. Human adaptation to climate: Temperature, ultraviolet radiation, and altitude. In *Human Biology: An Evolutionary and Biocultural Perspective,* ed. S. Stinson, B. Bogin, R. Huss-Ashmore, and D. O'Rourke, pp. 163–224. New York: John Wiley.

Beals, K. L. 1972. Head form and climatic stress. *American Journal of Physical Anthropology* 37:85–92.

Beals, K. L., C. L. Smith, and S. M. Dodd. 1983. Climate and the evolution of brachycephalization. *American Journal of Physical Anthropology* 62:425–37.

Becker, L., R. J. Poreda, A. G. Hunt, T. E. Bunch, and M. Rampino. 2001. Impact event at the Permian-Triassic boundary: Evidence from extraterrestrial noble gases in fullerenes. *Science* 291:1530–33.

Bermúdez de Castro, J. M., J. L. Arsuaga, E. Carbonell, A. Rosas, I. Martínez, and M. Mosquera. 1997. A hominid from the

Lower Pleistocene of Atapuerca, Spain: Possible ancestor to Neandertals and modern humans. *Science* 276:1392–95.

Binder, S., A. M. Levitt, J. J. Sacks, and J. M. Hughes. 1999. Emerging infectious diseases: Public health issues for the 21st century. *Science* 284:1311–13.

Bindon, J. R., and P. T. Baker. 1985. Modernization, migration and obesity among Samoan adults. *Annals of Human Biology* 12:67–76.

Bittles, A. H., W. M. Mason, J. Greene, and N. A. Rao. 1991. Reproductive behavior and health in consanguineous marriages. *Science* 252:789–94.

Blum, H. F. 1961. Does the melanin pigment of human skin have adaptive value? *Quarterly Review of Biology* 36:50–63.

Bodmer, W. F., and L. L. Cavalli-Sforza. 1976. *Genetics, Evolution, and Man.* San Francisco: W. H. Freeman.

Bogin, B. A. 1995a. Growth and development: Recent evolutionary and biocultural research. In *Biological Anthropology: The State of the Science,* ed. N. T. Boaz and L. D. Wolfe, pp. 49–70. Bend, Ore.: International Institute for Human Evolutionary Research.

———. 1995b. Plasticity in the growth of Mayan refugee children living in the United States. In *Human Variability and Plasticity,* ed. C. G. N. Mascie-Taylor and B. Bogin, pp. 46–74. Cambridge: Cambridge University Press.

———. 1999. *Patterns of Human Growth,* 2d ed. Cambridge: Cambridge University Press.

———. 2001. *The Growth of Humanity.* New York: John Wiley & Sons.

Bogin, B. A., and B. H. Smith. 1996. The evolution of the human life cycle. *American Journal of Human Biology* 8:703–16.

Bottini, N., G. F. Meloni, A. Finocchi, G. Ruggiu, A. Amante, T. Meloni, and E. Bottini. 2001. Maternal-fetal interaction in the ABO system: A comparative analysis of healthy mothers and couples with recurrent spontaneous abortion suggests a protective effect of B incompatibility. *Human Biology* 73:167–74.

Bouchard, T. J., D. T. Lykken, M. McGue, N. L. Segal, and A. Tellegen. 1990. Sources of human psychological differences: The Minnesota study of twins reared apart. *Science* 250:223–28.

Bouvier, L. F., and J. T. Bertrand. 1999. *World Population: Challenges for the 21st Century.* Santa Ana, Calif.: Seven Locks Press.

Brace, C. L. 1964. The fate of the "classic" Neandertals: A consideration of hominid catastrophism. *Current Anthropology* 5:3–43.

Brace, C. L., K. R. Rosenberg, and K. D. Hunt. 1987. Gradual change in human tooth size in the Late Pleistocene and Post-Pleistocene. *Evolution* 41:705–20.

Brace, C. L., D. P. Tracer, L. A. Yaroch, J. Robb, K. Brandt, and R. Nelson. 1993. Clines and clusters versus "race": A test in ancient Egypt and the case of a death on the Nile. *Yearbook of Physical Anthropology* 36:1–31.

Bramblett, C. A. 1976. *Patterns of Primate Behavior.* Palo Alto, Calif.: Mayfield.

———. 1994. Patterns of Primate Behavior, 2d ed. Prospect Heights, Ill.: Waveland.

Brooks, A. S., D. M. Helgren, J. S. Cramer, A. Franklin, W. Hornyak, J. M. Keating, R. G. Klein, W. J. Rink, H. Schwarcz, J. N. L. Smith, K. Stewart, N. E. Todd, J. Verniers, and J. E. Yellen. 1995. Dating and context of three Middle Stone Age sites with bone points in the Upper Semliki Valley, Zaire. *Science* 268:548–53.

Brown, F. H. 1992. Methods of dating. In *The Cambridge Encyclopedia of Human Evolution,* ed. S. Jones, R. Martin, and D. Pilbeam, pp. 179–86. Cambridge: Cambridge University Press.

Brown, F., J. Harris, R. Leakey, and A. Walker. 1985. Early *Homo erectus* skeleton from west Lake Turkana, Kenya. *Nature* 316:788–92.

Brown, R. A., and G. J. Armelagos. 2001. Apportionment of racial diversity: A review. *Evolutionary Anthropology* 10:34–40.

Brues, A. M. 1977. *People and Races.* New York: Macmillan.

Buss, D. M. 1985. Human mate selection. *American Scientist* 73:47–51.

Cabana, T., P. Jolicoeur, and J. Michaud. 1993. Prenatal and postnatal growth and allometry of stature, head circumference, and brain weight in Québec children. *American Journal of Human Biology* 5:93–99.

Calcagno, J. M., and K. R. Gibson. 1988. Human dental reduction: Natural selection or the probable mutation effect. *American Journal of Physical Anthropology* 77:505–17.

Campbell, B. G. 1985. *Human Evolution,* 3d ed. New York: Aldine.

Cann, R. L., M. Stoneking, and A. C. Wilson. 1987. Mitochondrial DNA and human evolution. *Nature* 325:31–36.

Carpenter, C. R. 1965. The howlers of Barro Colorado Island. In *Primate Behavior: Field Studies of Monkeys and Apes,* ed. I. DeVore, pp. 250–91. New York: Holt, Rinehart, and Winston.

Carroll, S. B., S. D. Weatherbee, and J. A. Langeland. 1995. Homeotic genes and the regulation and evolution of insect wing number. *Nature* 375:58–61.

Cartmill, M. 1974. Rethinking primate origins. *Science* 184:436–43.

———. 1992. New views on primate origins. *Evolutionary Anthropology* 1:105–11.

Cavalli-Sforza, L. L., and W. F. Bodmer. 1971. *The Genetics of Human Populations.* San Francisco: W. H. Freeman.

Cavalli-Sforza, L. L., P. Menozzi, and A. Piazza. 1994. *The History and Geography of Human Genes.* Princeton: Princeton University Press.

Cela-Conde, C. J., E. Aguirre, F. J. Ayala, P. V. Tobias, D. Turbón, L. C. Aiello, M. Collard, M. Goodman, C. P. Groves, F. C. Howell, J. H. Schwartz, D. S. Strait, F. Szalay, I. Tattersall, M. H. Wolpoff, and B. Wood. 2000. Systematics of humankind. Palma 2000: A working group on systematics in human paleontology. *Ludus Vitalis* 12:127–30.

Chapman, C. A., and C. A. Peres. 2001. Primate conservation in the new millennium: The role of scientists. *Evolutionary Anthropology* 10:16–33.

Chen, F-C., and W-H. Li. 2001. Genomic divergences between humans and other hominoids and the effective population size of the common ancestor of humans and chimpanzees. *American Journal of Human Genetics* 68:444–56.

Cheney, D. L., and R. W. Wrangham. 1987. Predation. In *Primate Societies,* ed. B. B. Smuts, D. L. Cheney, R. M. Seyfarth, R. W. Wrangham, and T. T. Struhsaker, pp. 227–39. Chicago: University of Chicago Press.

Ciochon, R. L., and R. A. Nisbett. 1998. *The Primate Anthology: Essays on Primate Behavior, Ecology, and Conservation from Natural History.* Upper Saddle River, N.J.: Prentice Hall.

Ciochon, R., J. Olsen, and J. James. 1990. *Other Origins: The Search for the Giant Ape in Human Prehistory.* New York: Bantam Books.

Clarke, R. J. 1999. Discovery of complete arm and hand of the 3.3-million-year-old *Australopithecus* skeleton from Sterkfontein. *South African Journal of Science* 95:477–80.

Cockburn, T. A. 1971. Infectious diseases in ancient populations. *Current Anthropology* 12:45–62.

Coffing, K., C. Feibel, M. Leakey, and A. Walker. 1994. Four-million-year-old hominids from East Lake Turkana, Kenya. *American Journal of Physical Anthropology* 93:55–65.

Cohen, J. E. 1995. *How Many People Can the Earth Support?* New York: W. W. Norton.

Cohen, M. N. 1989. *Health and the Rise of Civilization.* New Haven: Yale University Press.

Comuzzie, A. G., J. E. Hixson, L. Almasy, B. D. Mitchell, M. C. Mahaney, T. D. Dyer, M. P. Stern, J. W. MacCluer, and J. Blangero. 1997. A major quantitative trait locus determining serum leptin levels and fat mass is located on human chromosome 2. *Nature Genetics* 15:273–76.

Connell, K. H. 1950. *The Population of Ireland 1750–1845.* Oxford: Clarendon Press.

Conroy, G. C., G. W. Weber, H. Seidler, P. V. Tobias, A. Kane, and B. Brunsden. 1998. Endocranial capacity in an early hominid cranium from Sterkfontein, South Africa. *Science* 280:1730–31.

Covert, H. H. 1997. The early primate adaptive radiations and new evidence about anthropoid origins. In *Biological Anthropology: The State of the Science,* 2d ed., ed. N. T. Boaz and L. D. Wolfe, pp. 1–23. Bend, Ore.: International Institute for Human Evolutionary Research.

Cowen, R. 1995. *History of Life,* 2d ed. Boston: Blackwell.

Cowley, G., J. Contreras, A. Rogers, J. Lach, C. Dickey, and S. Raghavan. 1995. Outbreak of fear. *Newsweek,* May 22, 1995.

Coyne, J. A. 1992. Genetics and speciation. *Nature* 355:511–15.

Crawford, M. H. 1998. *The Origins of Native Americans: Evidence from Anthropological Genetics.* Cambridge: Cambridge University Press.

Crews, D. E. 1989. Cause-specific mortality, life expectancy, and debilitation in aging Polynesians. *American Journal of Human Biology* 1:347–53.

Crockett, C. M., and J. F. Eisenberg. 1987. Howlers: Variations in group size and demography. In *Primate Societies,* ed. B. B.

Smuts, D. L. Cheney, R. M. Seyfarth, R. W. Wrangham, and T. T. Struhsaker, pp. 54–68. Chicago: University of Chicago Press.

Crook, J. H., and J. S. Gartlan. 1996. Evolution of primate societies. *Nature* 210:1200–3.

Crow, J. F. 1958. Some possibilities for measuring selection intensities in man. *Human Biology* 30:1–13.

Damon, A. 1977. *Human Biology and Ecology.* New York: W. W. Norton.

Dart, R. A. 1925. *Australopithecus africanus:* The man-ape of South Africa. *Nature* 115:195–99.

Dawkins, R. 1987. *The Blind Watchmaker: Why the Evidence of Evolution Reveals a Universe without Design.* New York: W. W. Norton.

Day, M. H. 1986. Bipedalism: Pressures, origins and modes. In *Major Topics in Primate and Human Evolution,* ed. B. Wood, L. Martin, and P. Andrews, pp. 188–202. Cambridge: Cambridge University Press.

de Heinzelin, J., D. Clark, T. White, W. Hart, P. Renne, G. WoldeGabriel, Y. Beyene, and E. Vrba. 1999. Environment and behavior of 2.5-million-year-old Bouri hominids. *Science* 284:625–29.

Denham, W. W. 1971. Energy relations and some basic properties of primate social organization. *American Anthropologist* 73:77–95.

De Robertis, E. M., G. Oliver, and C. V. E. Wright. 1990. Homeobox genes and the vertebrate body plan. *Scientific American* 263(1): 46–52.

Dettwyler, K. A. 1991. Can paleopathology provide evidence for "compassion"? *American Journal of Physical Anthropology* 84:375–84.

———. 1994. *Dancing Skeletons: Life and Death in West Africa.* Prospect Heights, Ill.: Waveland.

Devlin, B., M. Daniels, and K. Roeder. 1997. The heritability of IQ. *Nature* 388:468–71.

DeVore, I. 1963. A comparison of the ecology and behavior of monkeys and apes. In *Classification and Human Evolution,* ed. S. L. Washburn, pp. 301–9. Chicago: Aldine.

de Waal, F. B. M. 1995. Bonobo sex and society. *Scientific American* 272(3):82–88.

———. 1999. Cultural primatology comes of age. *Nature* 399:635–36.

Diamond, J. 1992a. The arrow of disease. *Discover* 13 (October): 64–73.

———. 1992b. *The Third Chimpanzee: The Evolution and Future of the Human Animal.* New York: HarperCollins.

Doran, D. M., and A. McNeilage. 1998. Gorilla ecology and behavior. *Evolutionary Anthropology* 6:120–31.

Duarte, C., J. Maurício, P. B. Pettitt, P. Souto, E. Trinkaus, H. van der Plicht, and J. Zilhão. 1999. The early Upper Paleolithic human skeleton from the Abrigo do Lagar Velho (Portugal) and modern human emergence in Iberia. *Proceedings of the National Academy of Sciences, USA* 96: 7604–9.

Dunn, F. L. 1968. Epidemiological factors: Health and disease among hunter-gatherers. In *Man the Hunter,* ed. R. B. Lee and I. DeVore, pp. 221–28. Chicago: Aldine.

Eaton, G. G. 1976. The social order of Japanese macaques. *Scientific American* 235(4): 96–106.

Eaton, S. B., M. Shostak, and M. Konner. 1988. Stone agers in the fast lane: Chronic degenerative diseases in evolutionary perspective. *American Journal of Medicine* 84:739–49.

Eldredge, N., and S. J. Gould. 1972. Punctuated equilibria: An alternative to phyletic gradualism. In *Models in Paleobiology,* ed. T. J. M. Schopf, pp. 82–115. San Francisco: Freeman, Cooper.

Ereshefsky, M., ed. 1992. *The Units of Evolution: Essays on the Nature of Species.* Cambridge: MIT Press.

Erlich, H. A., D. Gelfand, and J. J. Sninsky. 1991. Recent advances in the polymerase chain reaction. *Science* 252:1643–51.

Eveleth, P. B., and J. M. Tanner. 1990. *Worldwide Variation in Human Growth,* 2d ed. Cambridge: Cambridge University Press.

Falk, D. 1983. Cerebral cortices of East African early hominids. *Science* 221:1072–74.

———. 1992. *Braindance.* New York: Henry Holt.

———. 2000. *Primate Diversity.* New York: W. W. Norton.

Falk, D., J. C. Redmond Jr., J. Guyer, G. C. Conroy, W. Recheis, G. W. Weber, and H. Seidler. 2000. Early hominid brain evolution: A new look at old endocases. *Journal of Human Evolution* 38:695–717.

Feder, K. L. 2000. *The Past in Perspective: An Introduction to Human Prehistory.* Mountain View, Calif.: Mayfield.

———. 2002. *Frauds, Myths, and Mysteries: Science and Pseudoscience in Archaeology,* 4th ed. New York: McGraw-Hill.

Fedigan, L. M. 1983. Dominance and reproductive success in primates. *Yearbook of Physical Anthropology* 26:91–129.

Fedigan, L. M., and S. C. Strum. 1999. A brief history of primate studies: National traditions, disciplinary origins, and stages in North American field research. In *The Nonhuman Primates,* ed. P. Dolhinow and A. Fuentes, pp. 258–69. Mountain View, Calif.: Mayfield.

Fisher, H. 1992. *Anatomy of Love: A Natural History of Mating, Marriage, and Why We Stray.* New York: Ballantine.

Fleagle, J. G. 1995. The origin and radiation of anthropoid primates. In *Biological Anthropology: The State of the Science,* ed. N. T. Boaz and L. D. Wolfe, pp. 1–21. Bend, Ore.: International Institute for Human Evolutionary Research.

———. 1999. *Primate Adaptation and Evolution,* 2d ed. San Diego: Academic Press.

Fleagle, J. G., D. T. Rasmussen, S. Yirga, T. M. Brown, and F. E. Grine. 1991. New hominid fossils from Fejej, Southern Ethiopia. *Journal of Human Evolution* 21:145–52.

Flynn, J. J., A. R. Wyss, R. Charrier, and C. C. Swisher. 1995. An early Miocene anthropoid skull from the Chilean Andes. *Nature* 373:603–7.

Fossey, D. 1983. *Gorillas in the Mist.* Boston: Houghton Mifflin.

Fouts, R., and S. T. Mills. 1997. *Next of Kin: What Chimpanzees Have Taught Me About Who We Are.* New York: William Morrow.

Franciscus, R. G., and J. C. Long. 1991. Variation in human nasal height and breadth. *American Journal of Physical Anthropology* 85:419–27.

Frayer, D. W. 1984. Biological and cultural change in the European Late Pleistocene and Early Holocene. In *The Origins of Modern Humans: A World Survey of the Fossil Evidence,* ed. F. H. Smith and F. Spencer, pp. 211–50. New York: Alan R. Liss.

Friedlaender, J. S. 1975. *Patterns of Human Variation.* Cambridge: Harvard University Press.

Frisancho, A. R. 1990. Introduction: Comparative high-altitude adaptation. *American Journal of Human Biology* 2:599–601.

———. 1993. *Human Adaptation and Accommodation.* Ann Arbor: University of Michigan Press.

Frisancho, A. R., and P. T. Baker. 1970. Altitude and growth: A study of the patterns of physical growth of a high altitude Peruvian Quechua population. *American Journal of Physical Anthropology* 32:279–92.

Fuentes, A. 2000. Hylobatid communities: Changing views on pair bonding and social organization in hominoids. *Yearbook of Physical Anthropology* 43:33–60.

Futuyma, D. J. 1983. *Science on Trial: The Case for Evolution.* New York: Pantheon Books.

———. 1986. *Evolutionary Biology,* 2d ed. Sunderland, Mass.: Sinauer.

Gabriel, T. 1995. A generation's heritage: After the boom, a boomlet. *New York Times,* February 12, 1995.

Gabunia, L., A. Vekua, D. Lordkipanidze, C. C. Swisher III, R. Ferring, A. Justus, M. Nioradze, M. Tvalchrelidze, S. C. Antón, G. Bosinski, O. Jöris, M. A. de Lumley, G. Majsuradze, and A. Mouskhelishvili. 2000. Earliest Pleistocene hominid cranial remains from Dmanisi, Republic of Georgia: Taxonomy, geological setting, and age. *Science* 288: 1019–25.

Gagneux, P., C. Wills, U. Gerloff, D. Tautz, P. A. Morin, C. Boesch, B. Fruth, G. Hohmann, O. A. Ryder, and D. S. Woodruff. 1999. Mitochondrial sequences show diverse evolutionary histories of African hominoids. *Proceedings of the National Academy of Science, USA* 96:5077–82.

Galdikas, B. M. F., and J. W. Wood. 1990. Birth spacing patterns in humans and apes. *American Journal of Physical Anthropology* 83:185–91.

Garn, S. M. 1965. *Human Races,* 2d ed. Springfield, Ill.: Charles C. Thomas.

Garrett, L. 1994. *The Coming Plague: Newly Emerging Diseases in a World Out of Balance.* New York: Farrar, Straus, and Giroux.

Gee, H. 1996. Box of bones "clinches" identity of Piltdown palaeontology hoaxer. *Nature* 381:261–2.

Gibbs, S., M. Collard, and B. Wood. 2000. Soft-tissue characters in higher primate phylogenetics. *Proceedings of the National Academy of Sciences, USA* 97:11130–32.

Gingerich, P. D. 1986. *Plesiadapis* and the delineation of the order Primates. In *Major Topics in Primate and Human Evolution,* ed. B. Wood, L. Martin, and P. Andrews, pp. 32–46. Cambridge: Cambridge University Press.

Gingerich, P. D., B. H. Smith, and E. L. Simons. 1990. Hind limbs of Eocene *Basilosaurus:* Evidence of feet in whales. *Science* 249:154–57.

Glass, H. B. 1953. The genetics of the Dunkers. *Scientific American* 189(2): 76–81.

Goldsmith, M. 1999. Gorilla socioecology. In *The Nonhuman Primates,* ed. P. Dolhinow and A. Fuentes, pp. 58–63. Mountain View, Calif.: Mayfield.

Goodall, J. 1986. *The Chimpanzees of Gombe: Patterns of Behavior.* Cambridge: Harvard University Press.

Goodman, A. H., and T. L. Leatherman, eds. 1998. *Building a New Biocultural Synthesis: Political-Economic Perspectives on Human Biology.* Ann Arbor: University of Michigan Press.

Gould, S. J. 1981. *The Mismeasure of Man.* New York: W. W. Norton.

———. 1983. *Hen's Teeth and Horse's Toes.* New York: W. W. Norton.

———. 1991. *Bully for Brontosaurus.* New York: W. W. Norton.

———. 1999. Non-overlapping magisterial. *Skeptical Inquirer* 23(4):55–61.

Gould, S. J., and N. Eldredge. 1977. Punctuated equilibria: The tempo and mode of evolution reconsidered. *Paleobiology* 3:115–51.

Gould, S. J., and R. C. Lewontin. 1979. The spandrels of San Marco and the Panglossian paradigm: A critique of the adaptationist programme. *Proceedings of the Royal Society of London* (Series B), 205:581–98.

Grant, P. R. 1991. Natural selection and Darwin's finches. *Scientific American* 265(4): 82–87.

Grant, V. 1985. *The Evolutionary Process: A Critical Review of Evolutionary Theory.* New York: Columbia University Press.

Greksa, L. P. 1990. Developmental responses to high-altitude hypoxia in Bolivian children of European ancestry: A test of the developmental adaptation hypothesis. *American Journal of Human Biology* 2:603–12.

———. 1996. Evidence for a genetic basis to the enhanced total lung capacity of Andean highlanders. *Human Biology* 68:119–29.

Grün, R. 1993. Electron spin resonance dating in paleoanthropology. *Evolutionary Anthropology* 2:172–81.

Grün, R., N. J. Shackleton, and H. J. Deacon. 1990. Electron-Spin-Resonance dating of tooth enamel from Klasies River Mouth. *Current Anthropology* 31:427–32.

Grün, R., C. B. Stringer, and H. P. Schwartz. 1991. ESR dating of teeth from Garrod's Tabun cave collection. *Journal of Human Evolution* 20:231–48.

Grün, R., and A. Thorne. 1997. Dating the Ngandong humans. *Science* 276:1575.

Gunnell, G. F., and E. R. Miller. 2001. Origin of anthropoidea: Dental evidence and recognition of early anthropoids in the fossil record, with comments on the Asian anthropoid radiation. *American Journal of Physical Anthropology* 114:177–91.

Hagelberg, E. 1994. Ancient DNA studies. *Evolutionary Anthropology* 2:199–207.

Haile-Selassie, Y. 2001. Late Miocene hominids from the Middle Awash, Ethiopia. *Nature* 412:178–81.

Hamer, D. H., S. Hu, V. L. Magnuson, N. Hu, and A. M. L. Pattatucci. 1993. A linkage between DNA markers on the X chromosome and male sexual orientation. *Science* 261: 321–27.

Hammer, M. F., and S. L. Zegura. 1996. The role of the Y chromosome in human evolutionary studies. *Evolutionary Anthropology* 5:116–34.

Harcourt, A. H., P. H. Harvey, S. G. Larson, and R. V. Short. 1981. Testis weight, body weight, and breeding system in primates. *Nature* 293:55–57.

Harding, R. M., S. M. Fullerton, R. C. Griffiths, J. Bond, M. J. Cox, J. A. Schneider, D. S. Moulin, and J. B. Clegg. 1997. Archaic African *and* Asian lineages in the genetic ancestry of modern humans. *American Journal of Human Genetics* 60:772–89.

Hardy, G. H. 1908. Mendelian proportions in a mixed population. *Science* 28:49–50.

Harlow, H. F. 1959. Love in infant monkeys. *Scientific American* 200(6): 68–74.

Harlow, H. F., and M. K. Harlow. 1962. Social deprivation in monkeys. *Scientific American* 207(5):136–46.

Harpending, H. C., M. A. Batzer, M. Gurven, L. B. Jorde, A. R. Rogers, and S. T. Sherry. 1998. Genetic traces of ancient demography. *Proceedings of the National Academy of Science, USA* 95:1961–67.

Harpending, H. C., and T. Jenkins. 1973. Genetic distance among southern African populations. In *Methods and Theories of Anthropological Genetics,* ed. M. H. Crawford and P. L. Workman, pp. 177–99. Albuquerque: University of New Mexico Press.

Harris, E. E., and J. Hey. 1999. X chromosome evidence for ancient human histories. *Proceedings of the National Academy of Sciences, USA* 96:3320–24.

Harris, M. 1987. *Cultural Anthropology,* 2d ed. New York: Harper & Row.

Harrison, G. A., J. M. Tanner, D. R. Pilbeam, and P. T. Baker. 1988. *Human Biology: An Introduction to Human Evolution, Variation, Growth, and Adaptability,* 3d ed. Oxford: Oxford University Press.

Hartl, D. L. 1988. *A Primer of Population Genetics,* 2d ed. Sunderland, Mass.: Sinauer.

Hartl, D. L., and A. G. Clark. 1997. *Principles of Population Genetics,* 3d ed. Sunderland, Mass.: Sinauer.

Harvey, P. H., R. D. Martin, and T. H. Clutton-Brock. 1987. Life histories in comparative perspective. In *Primate Societies,* ed. B. B. Smuts, D. L. Cheney, R. M. Seyfarth, R. W. Wrangham, and T. T. Struhsaker, pp. 181–96. Chicago: University of Chicago Press.

Harvey, P. H., and M. D. Pagel. 1991. *The Comparative Method in Evolutionary Biology.* Oxford: Oxford University Press.

Hawks, J., S. Oh, K. Hunley, S. Dobson, G. Cabana, P. Dayalu, and M. H. Wolpoff. 2000. An Australasian test of the recent African origin model using the WLH-50 calvarium. *Journal of Human Evolution* 39:1–22.

Henneberg, M. 1988. Decrease of human skull size in the Holocene. *Human Biology* 60:395–405.

Herrnstein, R. J., and C. Murray. 1994. *The Bell Curve: Intelligence and Class Structure in American Life*. New York: The Free Press.

Hill, A., S. Ward, A. Deino, G. Curtis, and R. Drake. 1992. Earliest *Homo*. *Nature* 355:719–22.

Hoff, H., I. Thorneycroft, F. Wilson, and M. Williams-Murphy. 2001. Protection afforded by sickle-cell trait (Hb AS): What happens when malarial selection pressures are alleviated? *Human Biology* 73:583–86.

Holden, C., and R. Mace. 1997. Phylogenetic analysis of the evolution of lactose digestion in adults. *Human Biology* 69:605–28.

Holick, M. F., J. A. MacLaughlin, and S. H. Doppelt. 1981. Regulation of cutaneous previtamin D_3 photosynthesis in man: Skin pigment is not an essential regulator. *Science* 211:590–93.

Holloway, R. L. 1985. The poor brain of *Homo sapiens neanderthalensis*: See what you please. In *Ancestors: The Hard Evidence*, ed. E. Delson, pp. 319–24. New York: Alan R. Liss.

Hooton, E. A. 1946. *Up from the Ape*. New York: Macmillan.

Horai, S., K. Hayasaka, R. Kondo, K. Tsugane, and N. Takahata. 1995. Recent African origin of modern humans revealed by complete sequences of hominoid mitochondrial DNAs. *Proceedings of the National Academy of Sciences, USA* 92:532–36.

Horr, D. A. 1972. The Borneo orangutan. *Borneo Research Bulletin* 4(2):46–50.

Hou, Y., R. Potts, B. Yuan, Z. Gou, A. Deino, W. Wang, J. Clark, G. Xie, and W. Huang. 2000. Mid-Pleistocence Acheulian-like stone technology of the Bose Basin, South China. *Science* 287:1622–26.

Houghton, P. 1993. Neandertal supralaryngeal vocal tract. *American Journal of Physical Anthropology* 90:139–46.

Houle, A. 1999. The origin of the Platyrrhines: An evaluation of the Antarctic scenario and the floating island model. *American Journal of Physical Anthropology* 109:541–59.

Howell, N. 2000. *Demography of the Dobe !Kung*, 2d ed. New York: Aldine de Gruyter.

Howells, W. W. 1989. *Skull Shapes and the Map: Craniometric Analyses in the Dispersion of Modern* Homo. Papers of the Peabody Museum, vol. 79. Cambridge: Harvard University.

Hrdy, S. B. 1977. *The Langurs of Abu*. Cambridge: Harvard University Press.

Hrdy, S. B., C. Janson, and C. van Schaik. 1995. Infanticide: Let's not throw the baby out with the bath water. *Evolutionary Anthropology* 3:151–54.

Hu, S., A. M. L. Pattatucci, C. Patterson, L. Li, D. W. Fulker, S. S. Cherny, L. Kruglyak, and D. H. Hamer. 1995. Linkage between sexual orientation and chromosome Xq28 in males but not in females. *Nature Genetics* 11:248–56.

Hunt, E. 1995. The role of intelligence in modern society. *American Scientist* 83:356–68.

International Human Genome Sequencing Consortium. 2001. Initial sequencing and analysis of the human genome. *Nature* 409:860–921.

Jablonski, N. G., and G. Chaplin. 2000. The evolution of human skin coloration. *Journal of Human Evolution* 39:57–106.

Jaeger, J-J., T. Thein, M. Benammi, Y. Chaimanee, A. N. Soe, T. Lwin, S. Wai, and S. Ducrocq. 1999. A new primate from the Middle Eocene of Myanmar and the Asian early origin of anthropoids. *Science* 286:528–30.

Johanson, D. C., and M. A. Edey. 1981. *Lucy: The Beginnings of Humankind*. New York: Simon & Schuster.

Johanson, D. C., F. T. Masau, G. G. Eck, T. D. White, R. C. Walter, W. H. Kimbel, B. Asfaw, P. Manega, P. Ndessokia, and G. Suwa. 1987. New partial skeleton of *Homo habilis* from Olduvai Gorge, Tanzania. *Nature* 327:205–9.

Johanson, D. C., and T. D. White. 1979. A systematic assessment of early African hominids. *Science* 203:321–30.

Johanson, D. C., T. D. White, and Y. Coppens. 1978. A new species of the genus *Australopithecus* (Primates: Hominidae) from the Pliocene of Eastern Africa. *Kirtlandia* 28:1–14.

Jolly, A. 1972. *The Evolution of Primate Behavior*. New York: Macmillan.

———. 1985. *The Evolution of Primate Behavior*, 2d ed. New York: Macmillan.

Jorde, L. B., A. R. Rogers, M. Bamshad, W. S. Watkins, P. Krakowiak, S. Sung, J. Kere, and H. C. Harpending. 1997. Microsatellite diversity and the demographic history of modern humans. *Proceedings of the National Academy of Sciences, USA* 94:3100–3.

Karn, M. N., and L. S. Penrose. 1951. Birth weight and gestation time in relation to maternal age, parity, and infant survival. *Annals of Eugenics* 15:206–33.

Katzmarzyk, P. T., and W. R. Leonard. 1998. Climatic influences on human body size and proportions: Ecological adaptations and secular trends. *American Journal of Physical Anthropology* 106:483–503.

Kennedy, K. A. R. 1976. *Human Variation in Space and Time*. Dubuque, Iowa: Wm. C. Brown.

Kimbel, W. H., D. C. Johanson, and Y. Rak. 1994. The first skull and other new discoveries of *Australopithecus afarensis* at Hadar, Ethiopia. *Nature* 368:449–51.

Kimbel, W. H., R. C. Walter, D. C. Johanson, K. E. Reed, J. L. Aronson, Z. Assefa, C. W. Marean, G. G. Eck, R. Bobe, E. Hovers, Y. Rak, C. Vondra, T. Yemane, D. York, Y. Chen, N. M. Evenson, and P. E. Smith. 1996. Late Pliocene *Homo* and Oldowan tools from the Hadar formation (Kada Hadar Member), Ethiopia. *Journal of Human Evolution* 31: 549–61.

King, M. C., and A. C. Wilson. 1975. Evolution at two levels: Molecular similarities and biological differences between humans and chimpanzees. *Science* 188:107–16.

Kitcher, P. 1982. *Abusing Science: The Case Against Creationism*. Cambridge: MIT Press.

Klein, R. G. 1999. *The Human Career: Human Biological and Cultural Origins*, 2d. ed. Chicago: University of Chicago Press.

Kochanek, K. D., B. L. Smith, and R. N. Anderson. 2001. Deaths: Preliminary data for 1999. *National Vital Statistics Reports*, vol. 49, no. 3. National Center for Health Statistics, Centers for Disease Control and Prevention.

Kollar, E. J., and C. Fisher. 1980. Tooth induction in chick epithelium: Expression of quiescent genes for enamel synthesis. *Science* 207:993–95.

Kramer, A. 1991. Modern human origins in Australasia: Replacement or evolution? *American Journal of Physical Anthropology* 86:455–73.

———. 1993. Human taxonomic diversity in the Pleistocene: Does *Homo erectus* represent multiple hominid species? *American Journal of Physical Anthropology* 91:161–71.

Kramer, A., S. M. Donnelly, J. H. Kidder, S. D. Ousley, and S. M. Olah. 1995. Craniometric variation in large-bodied hominoids: Testing the single-species hypothesis for *Homo habilis*. *Journal of Human Evolution* 29:443–62.

Krimsky, S. 2000. *Hormonal Chaos: The Scientific and Social Origins of the Environmental Endocrine Hypothesis*. Baltimore: Johns Hopkins University Press.

Krings, M., C. Capelli, F. Tschentscher, H. Geisert, S. Meyer, A. von Haeseler, K. Grossschmidt, G. Possnert, M. Paunovic, and S. Pääbo. 2000. A view of Neandertal genetic diversity. *Nature Genetics* 26:144–46.

Krings, M., H. Geisert, R. W. Schmitz, H. Krainitzki, and S. Pääbo. 1999. DNA sequence of the mitochondrial hypervariable region II from the Neandertal type specimen. *Proceedings of the National Academy of Sciences, USA* 96:5581–85.

Krings, M., A. Stone, R. W. Schmitz, H. Krainitzki, M. Stoneking, and S. Pääbo. 1997. Neandertal DNA sequences and the origin of modern humans. *Cell* 90:19–30.

Laitman, J. T., R. C. Heimbuch, and E. S. Crelin. 1979. The basicranium of fossil hominids as an indicator of their upper respiratory systems. *American Journal of Physical Anthropology* 51:15–34.

Larsen, C. S. 1994. In the wake of Columbus: Native population biology in the postcontact Americas. *Yearbook of Physical Anthropology* 37:109–54.

———. 2000. *Skeletons in Our Closet: Revealing Our Past through Bioarchaeology*. Princeton: Princeton University Press.

Larsen, C. S., R. M. Matter, and D. L. Gebo. 1998. *Human Origins: The Fossil Record*, 3d ed. Prospect Heights, Ill.: Waveland.

Larson, E. J. 1997. *Summer for the Gods: The Scopes Trial and America's Continuing Debate Over Science and Religion*. Cambridge, Mass.: Harvard University Press.

Larson, S. G. 1998. Parallel evolution in the hominoid trunk and forelimb. *Evolutionary Anthropology* 6:87–99.

Leakey, L. S. B., P. V. Tobias, and J. R. Napier. 1964. A new species of the genus *Homo* from Olduvai Gorge. *Nature* 202:7–10.

Leakey, M. G., C. S. Feibel, I. McDougall, and A. Walker. 1995. New four-million-year-old hominid species from Kanapoi and Allia Bay, Kenya. *Nature* 376:565–71.

Leakey, M. G., C. S. Feibel, I. McDougall, C. Ward, and A. Walker. 1998. New specimens and confirmation of an early age for *Australopithecus anamensis*. *Nature* 393:62–66.

Leakey, M. G., F. Spoor, P. N. Gathogo, C. Kiarie, L. N. Leakey, and I. McDougall. 2001. New hominin genus from eastern Africa shows diverse middle Pliocene lineages. *Nature* 410:433–40.

Lee, R. B. 1968. What hunters do for a living, or, how to make out on scarce resources. In *Man the Hunter*, ed. R. B. Lee and I. DeVore, pp. 30–48. Chicago: Aldine.

Leidy, L. E. 1998. Accessory eggs, follicular atresia, and the evolution of human menopause. *American Journal of Physical Anthropology*, Supp. 26:148–49 (abstract).

Leonard, W. H., T. L. Leatherman, J. W. Carey, and R. B. Thomas. 1990. Contributions of nutrition versus hypoxia to growth in rural Andean populations. *American Journal of Human Biology* 2:613–26.

Leonard, W. R. 2000. Human nutritional evolution. In *Human Biology: An Evolutionary and Biocultural Perspective*, ed. S. Stinson, B. Bogin, R. Huss-Ashmore, and D. O'Rourke, pp. 295–343. New York: John Wiley & Sons.

Leonard, W. R., and M. L. Robertson. 1995. Energetic efficiency of human bipedality. *American Journal of Physical Anthropology* 97:335–38.

Lerner, I. M., and W. J. Libby. 1976. *Heredity, Evolution, and Society*. San Francisco: W. H. Freeman.

Lerner, L. S. 2000. *Good Science, Bad Science: Teaching Evolution in the States*. Thomas B. Fordham Foundation. Available on the Internet at: http://www.edexcellence.net/library/lerner/gsbsteits.html.

Leutenegger, W. 1982. Sexual dimorphism in nonhuman primates. In *Sexual Dimorphism in* Homo sapiens: *A Question of Size*, ed. R. L. Hall, pp. 11–36. New York: Praeger.

Levins, R., T. Awerbuch, U. Brinkman, I. Eckardt, P. Epstein, N. Makhoul, C. A. de Possas, C. Puccia, A. Spielman, and M. E. Wilson. 1994. The emergence of new diseases. *American Scientist* 82:52–60.

Lewin, R. 1998. *Principles of Human Evolution: A Core Textbook*. Malden, Mass.: Blackwell Science.

Lewis, D. E., Jr. 1990. Stress, migration, and blood pressure in Kiribati. *American Journal of Human Biology* 2:139–51.

Lieberman, D. E. 1998. Sphenoid shortening and the evolution of modern cranial shape. *Nature* 393:158–62.

———. 2001. Another face in our family tree. *Nature* 410:419–20.

Lieberman, P., and E. S. Crelin. 1971. On the speech of Neanderthal. *Linguistic Inquiry* 2:203–22.

Linden, E. 1981. *Apes, Men, and Language*, rev. ed. Middlesex, England: Penguin Books.

Little, M. A., and P. T. Baker. 1988. Migration and adaptation. In *Biological Aspects of Human Migration*, ed. C. G. N.

Mascie-Taylor and G. W. Lasker, pp. 167–215. Cambridge: Cambridge University Press.

Livi-Bacci, M. 1997. *A Concise History of World Population,* 2d ed. Oxford: Blackwell.

Livingstone, F. B. 1958. Anthropological implications of sickle cell gene distribution in West Africa. *American Anthropologist* 60:533–62.

———. 1964. On the nonexistence of human races. In *The Concept of Race,* ed. A. Montagu, pp. 46–60. New York: Collier.

———. 1984. The Duffy blood groups, vivax malaria, and malaria selection in human populations: A review. *Human Biology* 56:413–25.

Loehlin, J. C., G. Lindzey, and J. N. Spuhler. 1975. *Race Differences in Intelligence.* San Francisco: W. H. Freeman.

Loomis, W. F. 1967. Skin-pigment regulation of vitamin-D biosynthesis in man. *Science* 157:501–6.

Lovejoy, C. O. 1981. The origin of man. *Science* 211:341–50.

Lutz, W., W. Sanderson, and S. Scherbov. 1997. Doubling of world population unlikely. *Nature* 387:803–5.

———. 2001. The end of world population growth. *Nature* 412:543–45.

Mackintosh, N. J. 1998. *IQ and Human Intelligence.* Oxford: Oxford University Press.

Madrigal, L. 1989. Hemoglobin genotype, fertility, and the malaria hypothesis. *Human Biology* 61:311–25.

Malina, R. M. 1975. *Growth and Development: The First Twenty Years in Man.* Minneapolis, Minn.: Burgess.

———. 1979. Secular changes in size and maturity: Causes and effects. *Monograph for the Society of Research in Child Development* 44:59–102.

Markham, R., and C. P. Groves. 1990. Brief communication: Weights of wild orangutans. *American Journal of Physical Anthropology* 81:1–3.

Marks, J. 1995. *Human Biodiversity: Genes, Races, and History.* New York: Aldine de Gruyter.

Mascia-Lees, F. E., J. H. Relethford, and T. Sorger. 1986. Evolutionary perspectives on permanent breast enlargement in human females. *American Anthropologist* 88:423–28.

Mayr, E. 1982. *The Growth of Biological Thought.* Cambridge: Harvard University Press.

McBrearty, S., and A. S. Brooks. 2000. The revolution that wasn't: A new interpretation of the origin of modern human behavior. *Journal of Human Evolution* 39:453–563.

McElroy, A., and P. K. Townsend. 1989. *Medical Anthropology in Ecological Perspective,* 2d ed. Boulder, Colo.: Westview Press.

McEvedy, C. 1988. The bubonic plague. *Scientific American* 258(2): 118–23.

McGrew, W. C. 1992. *Chimpanzee Material Culture.* Cambridge: Cambridge University Press.

———. 1998. Culture in nonhuman primates? *Annual Review of Anthropology* 27:301–28.

McHenry, H. M. 1992. How big were the early hominids? *Evolutionary Anthropology* 1:15–20.

———. 1996. Homoplasy, clades, and hominid phylogeny. In *Contemporary Issues in Human Evolution,* ed. W. E. Meikle, F. C. Howell, and N. G. Jablonski, pp. 77–92. San Francisco: California Academy of Sciences.

McKenna, J. J. 1996. Sudden Infant Death Syndrome in cross-cultural perspective: Is infant–parent cosleeping protective? *Annual Review of Anthropology* 25:201–16.

McKenzie, R. L., and J. M. Elwood. 1990. Intensity of solar ultraviolet radiation and its implications for skin cancer. *New Zealand Medical Journal* 103:152–54.

McNeill, W. H. 1977. *Plagues and Peoples.* New York: Doubleday.

Meindl, R. S., and A. C. Swedlund. 1977. Secular trends in mortality in the Connecticut River Valley, 1700–1850. *Human Biology* 49:389–414.

Miller, J. M. A. 2000. Cranifacial variation in *Homo habilis:* An analysis of the evidence for multiple species. *American Journal of Physical Anthropology* 112:103–28.

Mittermeier, R. A., and E. J. Sterling. 1992. Conservation of primates. In *The Cambridge Encyclopedia of Human Evolution,* ed. S. Jones, R. Martin, and D. Pilbeam, pp. 33–36. Cambridge: Cambridge University Press.

Molnar, S. 1998. *Human Variation: Races, Types and Ethnic Groups,* 4th ed. Englewood Cliffs, N.J.: Prentice-Hall.

Molnar, S., and I. M. Molnar. 2000. *Environmental Change and Human Survival: Some Dimensions of Human Ecology.* Upper Saddle River, N.J.: Prentice Hall.

Montagu, A., ed. 1984. *Science and Creationism.* Oxford: Oxford University Press.

Moran, E. F. 1982. *Human Adaptability: An Introduction to Ecological Anthropology.* Boulder, Colo.: Westview Press.

Mosko, S., C. Richard, J. McKenna, S. Drummond, and D. Mukai. 1997. Maternal proximity and infant CO2 environment during bedsharing and possible implications for SIDS research. *American Journal of Physical Anthropology* 103:315–28.

National Academy of Sciences. 1989. *Recommended Dietary Allowances,* 10th ed. Washington: National Academy Press.

Noad, M. J., D. H. Cato, M. M. Bryden, M-N. Jenner, and K. C. S. Jenner. 2000. Cultural revolution in whale songs. *Nature* 408:537.

North, K. E., L. J. Martin, and M. H. Crawford. 2000. The origins of the Irish travelers and the genetic structure of Ireland. *Annals of Human Biology* 27:453–65.

Oates, J. F. 1987. Food distribution and foraging behavior. In *Primate Societies,* ed. B. B. Smuts, D. L. Cheney, R. M. Seyfarth, R. W. Wrangham, and T. T. Struhsaker, pp. 197–209. Chicago: University of Chicago Press.

Olshansky, S. J., B. A. Carnes, and C. Cassel. 1990. In search of Methuselah: Estimating the upper limit to human longevity. *Science* 250:634–40.

Olshansky, S. J., B. A. Carnes, and A. Désesquelles. 2001. Prospects for human longevity. *Science* 291:1491–92.

Omran, A. R. 1977. Epidemiologic transition in the United States: The health factor in population change. *Population Bulletin* 32:3–42.

O'Sullivan, P. B., M. Morwood, D. Hobbs, F. A. Suminto, M. Situmorang, A. Raza, and R. Maas. 2001. Archaeological implications of the geology and chronology of the Soa Basin, Flores, Indonesia. *Geology* 29:607–10.

Ovchinnikov, I., A. Götherstrom, G. P. Romanova, V. M. Kharitonov, K. Lidén, and W. Goodwin. 2000. Molecular analysis of Neanderthal DNA from the northern Caucasus. *Nature* 404:490–93.

Paigen, B., L. R. Goldman, M. M. Magnant, J. H. Highland, and A. T. Steegmann Jr. 1987. Growth of children living near the hazardous waste site, Love Canal. *Human Biology* 59:489–508.

Pasachoff, J. M. 1979. *Astronomy: From the Earth to the Universe.* Philadelphia: W. B. Saunders.

Passingham, R. 1982. *The Human Primate.* San Francisco: W. H. Freeman.

Pattatucci, A. M. 1998. Molecular investigations into complex behavior: Lessons from sexual orientation studies. *Human Biology* 70:367–86.

Pavelka, M. S. M., and L. M. Fedigan. 1991. Menopause: A comparative life history perspective. *Yearbook of Physical Anthropology* 34:13–38.

Pawlowski, B. 1999. Permanent breasts as a side effect of subcutaneous fat tissue increase in human evolution. *Homo* 50:149–62.

Peccei, J. S. 2001. Menopause: Adaptation or epiphenomenon? *Evolutionary Anthropology* 10:43–57.

Pennington, R. L. 1996. Causes of early human population growth. *American Journal of Physical Anthropology* 99:259–74.

Pennisi, E. 2001. The human genome. *Science* 291:1177–80.

Pennock, R. T. 1999. *Tower of Babel: The Evidence against the New Creationism.* Cambridge, Mass.: MIT Press.

Penny, D., M. Steel, P. J. Waddell, and M. D. Hendy. 1995. Improved analyses of human mtDNA sequences support a recent African origin for *Homo sapiens. Molecular Biology and Evolution* 12:863–82.

Pianka, E. R. 1983. *Evolutionary Ecology,* 3d ed. New York: Harper & Row.

Pickford, M., and B. Senut. 2001. The geological and faunal context of Late Miocene hominid remains from Lukeino, Ethiopia. *Comptes Rendus de l'Académie des Sciences, Paris* 332:145–52.

Pier, G. B., M. Grout, T. Zaidi, G. Meluleni, S. S. Mueschenborn, G. Banting, R. Ratcliff, M. J. Evans, and W. H. Colledge. 1998. *Salmonella typhi* uses CFTR to enter intestinal epithelial cells. *Nature* 393:79–82.

Pilbeam, D. 1982. New hominoid skull material from the Miocene of Pakistan. *Nature* 295:232–34.

———. 1984. The descent of hominoids and hominids. *Scientific American* 250(3): 84–96.

Pilbeam, D., M. D. Rose, J. C. Barry, and S. M. Ibrahim Shah. 1990. New *Sivapithecus* humeri from Pakistan and the relationship of *Sivapithecus* and *Pongo. Nature* 348:237–39.

Pillard, R. C., and M. Bailey. 1998. Human sexual orientation has a heritable component. *Human Biology* 70:347–65.

Plomin, R., M. J. Owen, and P. McGuffin. 1994. The genetic basis of complex human behaviors. *Science* 264:1733–39.

Ponce de León, M., and C. P. E. Zollikofer. 2001. Neanderthal cranial ontogeny and its implications for late hominid diversity. *Nature* 412:534–38.

Pope, G. G. 1989. Bamboo and human evolution. *Natural History,* October:49–56.

Population Reference Bureau. 2001. *2001 World Population Data Sheet.* Washington, D.C. Available on the Internet at: http://www.prb.org/pubs/wpds2001/.

Post, P. W., F. Daniels Jr., and R. T. Binford Jr. 1975. Cold injury and the evolution of "white" skin. *Human Biology* 47:65–80.

Potts, M. 1988. Birth control. In *The New Encyclopaedia Britannica,* vol. 15, pp. 113–20. Chicago: Encyclopaedia Britannica.

Potts, R. 1984. Home bases and early hominids. *American Scientist* 72:338–47.

Pusey, A., J. Williams, and J. Goodall. 1997. The influence of dominance rank on the reproductive success of female chimpanzees. *Science* 277:828–31.

Rak, Y. 1986. The Neanderthal: A new look at an old face. *Journal of Human Evolution* 15:151–64.

Rak, Y., and B. Arensburg. 1987. Kebara 2 Neanderthal pelvis: First look at a complete inlet. *American Journal of Physical Anthropology* 73:227–31.

Relethford, J. H. 1992. Cross-cultural analysis of migration rates: Effects of geographic distance and population size. *American Journal of Physical Anthropology* 89:459–66.

———. 1994. Craniometric variation among human populations. *American Journal of Physical Anthropology* 95:53–62.

———. 1997. Hemispheric difference in human skin color. *American Journal of Physical Anthropology* 104:449–57.

———. 2001a. Absence of regional affinities of Neandertal DNA with living humans does not reject multiregional evolution. *American Journal of Physical Anthropology* 115:95–98.

———. 2001b. Ancient DNA and the origin of modern humans. *Proceedings of the National Academy of Sciences, USA* 98:390–91.

———. 2001c. *Genetics and the Search for Modern Human Origins.* New York: John Wiley & Sons.

Relethford, J. H., and J. Blangero. 1990. Detection of differential gene flow from patterns of quantitative variation. *Human Biology* 62:5–25.

Relethford, J. H., and M. H. Crawford. 1995. Anthropometric variation and the population history of Ireland. *American Journal of Physical Anthropology* 96:25–38.

Relethford, J. H., and H. C. Harpending. 1994. Craniometric variation, genetic theory, and modern human origins. *American Journal of Physical Anthropology* 95:249–70.

Relethford, J. H., and L. B. Jorde. 1999. Genetic evidence for larger African population size during recent human evolution. *American Journal of Physical Anthropology* 108:251–60.

Richard, A. F. 1985. *Primates in Nature.* New York: W. H. Freeman.

Richmond, B. G., and D. S. Strait. 2000. Evidence that humans evolved from a knuckle-walking ancestor. *Nature* 404: 382–85.

Rightmire, G. P. 1990. *The Evolution of* Homo erectus: *Comparative Anatomical Studies of an Extinct Human Species.* Cambridge: Cambridge University Press.

———. 1992. *Homo erectus:* Ancestor or evolutionary side branch? *Evolutionary Anthropology* 1:43–49.

———. 1996. The human cranium from Bodo, Ethiopia: Evidence for speciation in the Middle Pleistocene? *Journal of Human Evolution* 31:21–39.

Roberts, D. F. 1968. Genetic effects of population size reduction. *Nature* 220:1084–88.

———. 1978. *Climate and Human Variability,* 2d ed. Menlo Park, Calif.: Benjamin Cummings.

Robins, A. H. 1991. *Biological Perspectives on Human Pigmentation.* Cambridge: Cambridge University Press.

Rodman, D. M., and S. Zamudio. 1991. The cystic fibrosis heterozygote—advantage in surviving cholera? *Medical Hypotheses* 36:253–58.

Rodman, P. S., and H. M. McHenry. 1980. Bioenergetics and the origin of human bipedalism. *American Journal of Physical Anthropology* 52:103–6.

Rogers, A. R. 1995. Genetic evidence for a Pleistocene population explosion. *Evolution* 49:608–15.

Rogers, A. R., and L. B. Jorde. 1995. Genetic evidence on modern human orgins. *Human Biology* 67:1–36.

Rowell, T. E. 1966. Forest-living baboons in Uganda. *Journal of Zoology, London* 149:344–64.

Roychoudhury, A. K., and M. Nei. 1988. *Human Polymorphic Genes: World Distribution.* Oxford: Oxford University Press.

Ruff, C. B. 1994. Morphological adaptations to climate in modern and fossil hominids. *Yearbook of Physical Anthropology* 37:65–107.

Ruff, C. B., E. Trinkaus, and T. W. Holliday. 1997. Body mass and encephalization in Pleistocene *Homo. Nature* 387: 173–76.

Sagan, C. 1977. *The Dragons of Eden: Speculations on the Evolution of Human Intelligence.* New York: Ballantine Books.

Sarich, V. M., and A. C. Wilson. 1967. Immunological time scale for hominoid evolution. *Science* 158:1200–3.

Savage-Rumbaugh, S., and R. Lewin. 1994. *Kanzi: The Ape at the Brink of the Human Mind.* New York: John Wiley & Sons.

Scammon, R. E. 1930. The measurement of the body in childhood. In *The Measurement of Man,* ed. J. A. Harris, C. M. Jackson, D. G. Paterson, and R. E. Scammon, pp. 171–215. Minneapolis: University of Minnesota Press.

Scarr, S., and A. Weinberg. 1978. Attitudes, interests, and IQ. *Human Nature* 1(4):29–36.

Schell, L. M. 1991. Effects of pollutants on human prenatal and postnatal growth: Noise, lead, polychlorobiphenyl compounds, and toxic wastes. *Yearbook of Physical Anthropology* 34:157–88.

Schepartz, L. A. 1993. Language and modern human origins. *Yearbook of Physical Anthropology* 36:91–126.

Schick, K. D., and N. Toth. 1993. *Making Silent Stones Speak: Human Evolution and the Dawn of Technology.* New York: Simon and Schuster.

Schoenemann, P. T., T. F. Budinger, V. M. Sarich, and W. S-Y. Wang. 2000. Brain size does not predict general cognitive ability within families. *Proceedings of the National Academy of Sciences, USA* 97:4932–37.

Schopf, J. W., ed. 1992. *Major Events in the History of Life.* Boston: Jones and Bartlett.

———. 1999. *Cradle of Life: The Discovery of Earth's Earliest Fossils.* Princeton: Princeton University Press.

Schow, D. J., and J. Frentzen. 1986. *The Outer Limits: The Official Companion.* New York: Ace.

Schwartz, J. H. 1987. *The Red Ape: Orangutan-utans and Human Origins.* Boston: Houghton Mifflin.

Seckler, D. 1980. Malnutrition: An intellectual odyssey. *Western Journal of Agricultural Economics* 5:219–27.

Sellen, D. W. 2001. Relationships between fertility, mortality, and subsistence: Results of recent phylogenetic analyses. In *Humanity from African Naissance to Coming Millennia,* ed. P. V. Tobias, M. A. Raath, J. Moggi-Cecchi, and G. A. Doyle, pp. 51–64. Firenze, Italy: Firenze University Press.

Senut, B., M. Pickford, D. Gommery, P. Mein, K. Cheboi, and Y. Coppens. 2001. First hominid from the Miocene (Lukeino formation, Kenya). *Comptes Rendus de l'Académie des Sciences, Paris* 332:137–44.

Shea, B. T., and A. M. Gomez. 1988. Tooth scaling and evolutionary dwarfism: An investigation of allometry in human pygmies. *American Journal of Physical Anthropology* 77: 117–32.

Sheehan, P. M., D. E. Fastovsky, R. G. Hoffman, C. B. Berghaus, and D. L. Gabriel. 1991. Sudden extinction of the dinosaurs: Latest Cretaceous, Upper Great Plains, U.S.A. *Science* 254:835–39.

Sherry, S. T., A. R. Rogers, H. Harpending, H. Soodyall, T. Jenkins, and M. Stoneking. 1994. Mismatch distributions of mtDNA reveal recent human populations expansions. *Human Biology* 66:761–75.

Smail, J. K. 1997. Beyond population stabilization: The case for dramatically reducing global human numbers. *Politics and the Life Sciences* 16:182–236.

Small, M. 1992. A reasonable sleep. *Discover,* April 1992.

Smith, F. H., A. B. Falsetti, and S. M. Donnelly. 1989. Modern human origins. *Yearbook of Physical Anthropology* 32:35–68.

Smith, F. H., E. Trinkaus, P. B. Pettitt, I. Karavanić, and M. Paunović. 1999. Direct radiocarbon dates for Vindija G_1 and Velika Pećina Late Pleistocene hominid remains. *Proceedings of the National Academy of Sciences, USA* 96:12281–86.

Smouse, P. E. 1982. Genetic architecture of swidden agricultural tribes from the lowland rain forests of South America. In *Current Developments in Anthropological Genetics. vol. 2,*

Ecology and Population Structure, ed. M. H. Crawford and J. H. Mielke, pp. 139-78. New York: Plenum Press.

Snowden, C. T. 1990. Language capacities of nonhuman animals. *Yearbook of Physical Anthropology* 33:215-43.

Spencer, M. A., and B. Demes. 1993. Biomechanical analysis of masticatory system configuration in Neandertals and Inuits. *American Journal of Physical Anthropology* 91:1-20.

Stern, J. T., Jr., and R. L. Susman. 1983. The locomotor anatomy of *Australopithecus afarensis. American Journal of Physical Anthropology* 60:279-317.

Stone, A. C., and M. Stoneking. 1993. Ancient DNA from a Pre-Columbian Amerindian population. *American Journal of Physical Anthropology* 92:463-71.

Stoneking, M. 1993. DNA and recent human evolution. *Evolutionary Anthropology* 2:60-73.

Stoneking, M., J. J. Fontius, S. L. Clifford, H. Soodyall, S. S. Arcot, N. Sasha, T. Jenkins, M. A. Tahir, P. L. Deininger, and M. A. Batzer. 1997. *Alu* insertion polymorphisms and human evolution: Evidence for a larger population size in Africa. *Genome Research* 7:1061-71.

Stoner, B. P., and E. Trinkaus. 1981. Getting a grip on the Neandertals: Were they all thumbs? *American Journal of Physical Anthropology* 54:281-82.

Strachan, T., and A. P. Read. 1996. *Human Molecular Genetics.* New York: John Wiley & Sons.

Strait, D. S., F. E. Grine, and M. A. Moniz. 1997. A reappraisal of early hominid phylogeny. *Journal of Human Evolution* 32:17-82.

Strier, K. B. 2000. *Primate Behavioral Ecology.* Boston: Allyn and Bacon.

Stringer, C., and C. Gamble. 1993. *In Search of the Neanderthals: Solving the Puzzle of Human Origins.* New York: Thames and Hudson.

Stringer, C., and R. McKie. 1996. *African Exodus: The Origins of Modern Humanity.* New York: Henry Holt.

Stringer, C. B., and P. Andrews. 1988. Genetic and fossil evidence for the origin of modern humans. *Science* 239:1263-68.

Strum, S. C., and W. Mitchell. 1987. Baboon models and muddles. In *The Evolution of Human Behavior: Primate Models,* ed. W. G. Kinzey, pp. 87-104. Albany, N.Y.: State University of New York Press.

Sturm, R. A., N. F. Box, and M. Ramsay. 1998. Human pigmentation genetics: The difference is only skin deep. *BioEssays* 20:712-21.

Susman, R. L. 1988. Hand of *Paranthropus robustus* from Member I, Swartkrans: Fossil evidence for tool behavior. *Science* 240:781-84.

Sussman, R. W. 1991. Primate origins and the evolution of angiosperms. *American Journal of Primatology* 23:209-23.

Sussman, R. W., J. M. Cheverud, and T. Q. Bartlett. 1995. Infant killing as an evolutionary strategy: Reality or myth? *Evolutionary Anthropology* 3:149-51.

Sutton, H. E., and R. P. Wagner. 1985. *Genetics: A Human Concern.* New York: Macmillan.

Suwa, G., B. Asfaw, Y. Beyene, T. D. White, S. Katoh, S. Nagaoka, H. Nakaya, K. Uzawa, P. Renne, and G. WoldeGabriel. 1997. The first skull of *Australopithecus boisei. Nature* 389: 489-92.

Swedlund, A. C., and G. J. Armelagos. 1976. *Demographic Anthropology.* Dubuque, Iowa: Wm. C. Brown.

Swisher, C. C., G. H. Curtis, T. Jacob, A. G. Getty, A. Suprijo, and Widiasmoro. 1994. Age of the earliest known hominids in Java, Indonesia. *Science* 263:1118-21.

Swisher, C. C., W. J. Rink, S. C. Antón, H. P. Schwarcz, G. H. Curtis, A. Suprijo, and Widiasmoro. 1996. Latest *Homo erectus* of Java: Potential contemporaneity with *Homo sapiens* in southeast Asia. *Science* 274:1870-4.

Tattersall, I. 1995. *The Fossil Trail: How We Know What We Think We Know About Human Evolution.* New York: Oxford University Press.

———. 1997. Out of Africa again . . . and again? *Scientific American* 276(4):60-7.

Tattersall, I., and J. H. Schwartz. 1999. Hominids and hybrids: The place of Neanderthals in human evolution. *Proceedings of the National Academy of Sciences, USA* 96:7117-19.

Tchernov, E., O. Rieppel, H. Zaher, M. J. Polcyn, and L. L. Jacobs. 2000. A fossil snake with limbs. *Science* 287:2010-12.

Teaford, M. F., and P. S. Ungar. 2000. Diet and the evolution of the earliest human ancestors. *Proceedings of the National Academy of Sciences, USA* 97:13506-11.

Templeton, A. R. 1997. Testing the Out of Africa replacement hypothesis with mitochondrial DNA data. In *Conceptual Issues in Modern Human Origins Research,* ed. G. A. Clark and C. M. Willermet, pp. 329-60. New York: Aldine de Gruyter.

———. 1998. Human races: A genetic and evolutionary perspective. *American Anthropologist* 100:632-50.

Terrace, H. S. 1979. *Nim: A Chimpanzee Who Learned Sign Language.* New York: Knopf.

Thorne, A. G., and M. H. Wolpoff. 1992. The multi-regional evolution of humans. *Scientific American* 266(4): 76-83.

Tills, D., P. Teesdale, and A. E. Mourant. 1977. Blood groups of the Irish. *Annals of Human Biology* 4:23-34.

Tobias, P. V. 1971. *The Brain in Hominid Evolution.* New York: Columbia University Press.

Trinkaus, E. 1981. Neanderthal limb proportions and cold adaptation. In *Aspects of Human Evolution,* ed. C. B. Stringer, pp. 187-224. London: Taylor and Francis.

Trinkaus, E., and P. Shipman. 1992. *The Neandertals: Changing the Image of Mankind.* New York: Knopf.

Tuljapurkar, S., N. Li, and C. Boe. 2000. A universal pattern of mortality decline in the G7 countries. *Nature* 405:789-92.

Underwood, J. H. 1979. *Human Variation and Human Microevolution.* Englewood Cliffs, N.J.: Prentice-Hall.

UNICEF. 1998. *The State of the World's Children 1998.* Oxford: Oxford University Press.

U.S. Bureau of the Census. 1999. *World Population Profile 1998.* Washington, D.C.: U.S. Government Printing Office.

van Schaik, C. P., and C. Knott. 1998. Orangutan culture? *American Journal of Physical Anthropology*, Supp. 26:233 (abstract).

Vaughan, W. E., and A. J. Fitzpatrick. 1978. *Irish Historical Statistics: Population, 1821–1971*. Dublin: Royal Irish Academy.

Venter, J. C., et al. 2001. The sequence of the human genome. *Science* 291:1304–51.

Ventura, S. J., J. A. Martin, S. C. Curtin, and T. J. Mathews. 1999. Births: Final data for 1997. *National Vital Statistics Reports*, vol. 47, no. 18. National Center for Health Statistics, Centers for Disease Control and Prevention.

Vianna, N. J., and A. K. Polan. 1984. Incidence of low birth weight among Love Canal residents. *Science* 226:1217–19.

Vigilant, L., M. Stoneking, H. Harpending, K. Hawkes, and A. C. Wilson. 1991. African populations and the evolution of human mitochondrial DNA. *Science* 253:1503–7.

Vogel, G. 2001. Objection #2: Why sequence the junk? *Science* 291:1184.

Walker, A., and M. Teaford. 1989. The hunt for *Proconsul*. *Scientific American* 260(1): 76–82.

Ward, C., M. Leakey, and A. Walker. 1999. The new hominid species *Australopithecus anamensis*. *Evolutionary Anthropology* 7:197–205.

Ward, C. V., A. Walker, and M. F. Teaford. 1991. *Proconsul* did not have a tail. *Journal of Human Evolution* 21:215–20.

Ward, S., B. Brown, A. Hill, J. Kelley, and W. Downs. 1999. *Equatorius*: A new hominoid genus from the Middle Miocene of Kenya. *Science* 285:1382–86.

Washburn, S. L. 1960. Tools and human evolution. *Scientific American* 203:62–75.

Weeks, J. R. 1981. *Population: An Introduction to Concepts and Issues*, 2d ed. Belmont, Calif.: Wadsworth.

Weiner, J. 1994. *The Beak of the Finch*. New York: Vintage Books.

Weiner, S., Q. Xu, P. Goldberg, J. Liu, and O. Bar-Yosef. 1998. Evidence for the use of fire at Zhoukoudian, China. *Science* 281:251–53.

Weiss, K. M. 1984. On the number of members of the genus *Homo* who have ever lived, and some evolutionary implications. *Human Biology* 56:637–49.

Weitz, C. A., R. M. Garruto, C-T Chin, J-C Liu, R-L Liu, and X. He. 2000. Morphological growth of Han boys and girls born and raised near sea level and at high altitude in western China. *American Journal of Human Biology* 12:665–81.

Wheeler, P. E. 1991. The thermoregulatory advantage of hominid bipedalism in open equatorial environments: The contribution of increased convective heat loss and cutaneous evaporative cooling. *Journal of Human Evolution* 21:107–15.

White, F. 1996. *Pan paniscus* 173 to 1996: Twenty-three years of field research. *Evolutionary Anthropology* 5:11–17.

White, R., and J. M. Lalouel. 1988. Chromosome mapping with DNA markers. *Scientific American* 258:40–48.

White, T. D. 1995. Corrigendum: *Australopithecus ramidus*, a new species of early hominid from Aramis, Ethiopia. *Nature* 375:88.

White, T. D., G. Suwa, and B. Asfaw. 1994. *Australopithecus ramidus*, a new species of early hominid from Aramis, Ethiopia. *Nature* 371:306–12.

White, T. D., G. Suwa, S. Simpson, and B. Asfaw. 2000. Jaws and teeth of *Australopithecus afarensis* from Maka, Middle Awash, Ethiopia. *American Journal of Physical Anthropology* 111:45–68.

Whiten, A., J. Goodall, W. C. McGrew, T. Nishida, V. Reynolds, Y. Sugiyama, C. E. G. Tutin, R. W. Wrangham, and C. Boesch. 1999. Culture in chimpanzees. *Nature* 399:682–85.

Wilford, J. N. 1985. *The Riddle of the Dinosaur*. New York: Knopf.

Willerman, L., R. Schultz, J. N. Rutledge, and E. D. Bigler. 1991. In vivo brain size and intelligence. *Intelligence* 15:223–28.

Williams-Blangero, S., and J. Blangero. 1992. Quantitative genetic analysis of skin reflectance: A multivariate approach. *Human Biology* 64:35–49.

Wilson, E. O. 1980. *Sociobiology: The Abridged Edition*. Cambridge: Harvard University Press.

WoldeGabriel, G., Y. Haile-Selassie, P. R. Renne, W. K. Hart, S. H. Ambrose, B. Asfaw, G. Heiken, and T. White. 2001. Geology and palaeontology of the Late Miocene Middle Awash valley, Afar rift, Ethiopia. *Nature* 412:175–78.

Wolfe, L. D. 1995. Current research in field primatology. In *Biological Anthropology: The State of the Science*, ed. N. T. Boaz and L. D. Wolfe, pp. 149–68. Bend, Ore.: International Institute for Human Evolutionary Research.

Wolpoff, M. H. 1999. *Paleoanthropology*, 2d ed. Boston: McGraw-Hill.

Wolpoff, M. H., and R. Caspari. 1997. *Race and Human Evolution*. New York: Simon and Schuster.

Wolpoff, M. H., J. Hawks, and R. Caspari. 2000. Multiregional, not multiple origins. *American Journal of Physical Anthropology* 112:129–36.

Wolpoff, M. H., J. Hawks, D. W. Frayer, and K. Hunley. 2001. Modern human ancestry at the peripheries: A test of the replacement theory. *Science* 291:293–97.

Wolpoff, M. H., A. G. Thorne, F. H. Smith, D. W. Frayer, and G. G. Pope. 1994. Multiregional evolution: A world-wide source for modern human populations. In *Origins of Anatomically Modern Humans*, ed. M. H. Nitecki and D. V. Nitecki, pp. 175–200. New York: Plenum Press.

Wood, B. 1996. Origin and evolution of the genus *Homo*. In *Contemporary Issues in Human Evolution*, ed. W. E. Meikle, F. C. Howell, and N. G. Jablonski, pp. 105–14. San Francisco: California Academy of Sciences.

Wood, B., and M. Collard. 1999. The changing face of the genus *Homo*. *Evolutionary Anthropology* 8:195–207.

Wood, B., and B. G. Richmond. 2000. Human evolution: Taxonomy and paleobiology. *Journal of Anatomy* 196:19–60.

Wood, J. W. 1994. *Dynamics of Human Reproduction: Biology, Biometry, Demography*. New York: Aldine de Gruyter.

Woodham-Smith, C. 1962. *The Great Hunger: Ireland 1845–1849*. New York: Harper & Row.

Workman, P. L., B. S. Blumberg, and A. J. Cooper. 1963. Selection, gene migration and polymorphic stability in a U.S. White and Negro population. *American Journal of Human Genetics* 15:71–84.

World Health Organization. 1997. *Weekly Epidemiological Record* 72:269–76.

———. 1999. *The World Health Report 1999: Making a Difference.* Geneva: Office of Publications, World Health Organization.

Wrangham, R. W. 1987. Evolution of social structure. In *Primate Societies,* ed. B. B. Smuts, D. L. Cheney, R. M. Seyfarth, R. W. Wrangham, and T. T. Struhsaker, pp. 282–96. Chicago: University of Chicago Press.

Wright, F. A., W. J. Lemon, W. D. Zhao, R. Sears, D. Zhuo, J-P. Wang, H-Y. Yang, T. Baer, D. Stredney, J. Spitzner, A. Stutz, R. Krahe, and B. Yuan. 2001. A draft annotation and overview of the human genome. *Genome Biology* 2(7): research0025.1–0025.17. Available on the Internet at: http://genomebiology.com/2001/2/7/research/0025.

Wright, P. C. 1992. Primate ecology, rainforest conservation, and economic development: Building a national park in Madagascar. *Evolutionary Anthropology* 1:25–33.

———. 1999. Lemur traits and Madagascar ecology: Coping with an island environment. *Yearbook of Physical Anthropology* 42:31–72.

Yellen, J. E., A. S. Brooks, E. Cornelissen, M. J. Mahlman, and K. Stewart. 1995. A Middle Stone Age worked bone industry from Katanda, Upper Semliki Valley, Zaire. *Science* 268: 553–56.

Allen & Beatrice Gardner
Fouts and Mills 1997
Snowden 1990
        – language acquisition

Savage – Rumbaugh
Linden, 1981
Terrace 1979
look up KOKO